SAINSBURY

— *The* —
COOK'S
COMPANION

SAINSBURY

The

COOK'S
COMPANION

Josceline Dimbleby

Consultant Home Economist
Roz Denny

Published in the UK exclusively for J Sainsbury plc,
Stamford House, Stamford Street, London SE1 9LL
by Webster's Wine Price Guide Ltd, Axe & Bottle Court,
70 Newcomen Street, London SE1 1YT

First published 1991

ISBN 1 870604 08 3

Colour separations by Scantrans (PTE) Ltd, Singapore
Printed and bound in Italy by Arnoldo Mondadori, Verona

Conceived, edited and designed by
Websters International Publishers

NOTES ON RECIPES

All spoon measures are level
1 tablespoon = 15ml
1 teaspoon = 5ml

Eggs are size 3 unless otherwise stated.
Pepper is freshly ground black pepper unless otherwise stated.
Milk is full-fat unless otherwise stated.

Ovens should be preheated to the specified temperature.
For all recipes, quantities are given in both metric and imperial
measures. Follow either metric or imperial measures but not a
mixture of both.

Contents

$\mathcal{I}$NTRODUCTION

Cooking is the great passion of my life. I have always enjoyed my food but it is more than that; cooking, with its changing tastes, textures, smells and colours, and its infinite scope for variety, satisfies a deep creative urge. As a young child, moving from country to country with my diplomat parents, the kitchens of our temporary foreign homes became my haven. They were warm busy places full of exciting and unfamiliar foods; I watched, I smelled, I tasted, and my interest in food developed. Every three years as we moved to another part of the world the cuisine changed dramatically. Because of this I have always had an adventurous palate. But it was not until years later, in a tiny mildewed basement shared with a girl-friend, that I began to cook. I learnt by experiment, and because I knew no rules I was able to cook in the way I still enjoy most: using straightforward methods to combine unusual tastes or to create real fantasies of my own. I soon realized that each basic cooking technique which I mastered opened up a host of new possibilities. My hope in writing this book is that it will do the same for you.

I have always searched for methods which are the least time consuming, and do not require a great deal of practice or skill. The step-by-step recipes on these pages are those which I have found the most useful. Each chapter offers a framework for a different aspect of cooking designed to help you build up your repertoire. In the tinted boxes are ideas and suggestions which should give you the confidence to do this. If you are a reluctant cook I hope you will discover that by making small changes to your old standbys, what you think of as a chore can become something to enjoy and take pride in. If you are already an enthusiast I hope that I can lead you to new ways of cooking, to dishes or ideas you may not have tried before. In cooking and eating there are always more pleasures to discover. At the end of each chapter there are original recipes in which I have used variations of methods covered in that chapter and often unusual combinations of ingredients. These reinforce the techniques explained in the chapter and show how you can progress from them to produce something both personal and exciting.

When I started the book I thought that I would enjoy working on some of the chapters more than others. I knew that I would love the puddings chapter because I have always had a childish passion for puddings and have enjoyed the fun of making them. As I expected I could have written far more than there was space for about vegetables – their beauty and flavour and the increasing varieties available make them an inspiring subject. Fish is also something I like to write about because, although it is such an exquisite and healthy food, it is often ruined by careless cooking. It is important to learn quick and simple ways to bring out its delicate taste and succulence. However, in the end, there was not a single chapter which did not fire me with renewed enthusiasm for the subject as I cooked and wrote. I worked on jams, jellies and pickles just before Christmas, so solving the problem of several presents. I have always made bread and cakes from time to time, but when I was working on these chapters I wondered why I did not make them every day. Even days of experiments with eggs, which might have become tedious, revealed what a magical ingredient they are.

I knew that this book should contain practical, comprehensive, reliable information. But I did not want it to be like a text book or manual. Instead I hope it becomes a friend. A friend you can trust, a friend you can turn to for advice and inspiration whenever you like. I would be happy if it made you feel that you are not alone in your kitchen, and that cooking is a more rewarding experience as a result.

Josceline Dimbleby

THE STORE CUPBOARD

A well-stocked store cupboard should give you a satisfying sense of security; you will always be able to produce a last minute meal, impromptu guests will be impressed at your ingenuity, and you will be able to find something to vary or revive an ordinary dish. If you keep bottles of fruits in alcohol on your shelves, you can even be sure that you can produce a real treat as well, when the occasion demands.

A store cupboard can be anything from a standard, small cupboard in your kitchen to a cold, north-facing, walk-in larder. If you are lucky enough to have a really cold larder, you can keep boxes of fruit such as apples and citrus fruits when in season, strings of fresh garlic and bunches of drying herbs – which look so attractive if you can hang them up on hooks. But most people have to make do with less space and warmer conditions, so we must rely on non-perishable items: cans, bottles, jars, vacuum-sealed packages and a variety of dried ingredients.

If you have enough shelves and keep your stores neatly arranged, you can fit a lot into a very small space. It is also necessary to be ordered so that little containers do not get lost and totally forgotten: put similar ingredients together and always keep certain spaces for particular items so that you get to know what is there and when it has run out. Always put something newly bought to the back of an existing container of the same ingredient so that you use them up in order of age.

The skills of stocking a practical store cupboard come from learning which non-perishable ingredients work best to produce unplanned meals or quick dishes. All too often, store cupboards contain packets and jars which are never used and become dusty with age at the back of the shelf. However, the possibilities available nowadays for long-lasting ingredients which will really ease and enhance impromptu meals are endless.

The following are things which I like to have in my store cupboard, and a few ideas of what I use them for. I try to keep a similar hoard in our holiday cottage in Devon so that if we arrive late with no time to shop, we can be sure of a good meal on the first night in next to no time.

Bottles and jars
• Bottles and jars of cockles and mussels in brine can be used in salads or stirred into a tomato or cream sauce for rice or pasta.
• Italian-style tomato sauce in jars is an excellent standby, and tastes even better if you add some butter and chopped herbs.
• Capers are useful for sauces to go with fish, and for adding to salads.
• A good bottled mayonnaise is an invaluable standby; you can add ingredients such as fresh herbs, curry paste, crushed green peppercorns, chopped anchovies, tomato purée, crushed garlic, to suggest a few, to it, and then use it to coat cold chicken. Once opened keep in the refrigerator.
• Jars of pesto are excellent if you like pasta, but pesto is also delicious as a filling for baked potatoes. Red pesto, which contains tomatoes too, is excellent.
• Chutneys, relishes and pickles, particularly lime pickle, as well as for eating with hot and cold meat, can be added to an ordinary stew to make it into a kind of curry.
• Jars (or cans) of olives are useful not only to nibble with drinks, but to add to stews, stuffings and sauces.
• With vine leaves in brine you can make a quick dish with alternate layers of mince and vine leaves baked in the oven and topped with cheese sauce.
• Fruit jellies are an excellent accompaniment to pork, game or lamb.
• I love really special honeys; it is worth using the most fragrant kind for making ice cream, but for baking and other cooking I keep a large jar of ordinary honey. Clear honey is useful for sweetening dressings.
• Mustard has countless uses; it can be added to stews and casseroles, soups, sauces or bread doughs, or used as part of a marinade. I like mild wholegrain and French Dijon mustard in sauces and salad dressings.
• Soy sauce is an invaluable flavour enhancer, and is by no means only for Chinese dishes. As well as using in stir-fried vegetables, soy sauce enormously enlivens a simple dish of green vegetables, and is very good on plain cold chicken, veal or pork.
• Various essences, such as anchovy, are good flavour enhancers for casseroles, stews, sauces and gravies. It is worth keeping a jar of Marmite or Bovril for this purpose, too.
• Flower waters, either orange, rose or violet, give an authentic and romantic touch to exotic or old-fashioned puddings.
• Many different flavoured oils are available. Keep extra virgin olive oil for salad dressings and pasta sauces, and less expensive olive oil for shallow frying. Walnut and hazelnut oils are lovely for leafy salads which include bitter leaves, but these oils must not be kept too long as they go rancid quickly once opened. Keep in the refrigerator after opening. Sunflower, grapeseed and groundnut oils are lighter alternatives to fruity olive oil in salad dressings and mayonnaise.
• The choice of vinegars is enormous. Sherry and balsamic vinegars are my favourites for adding to sauces and stews as well as salad dressings, but red and white wine and herb vinegars are excellent, too. Cider is the lightest vinegar and is useful for pickling. Raspberry and other fruit vinegars are lovely for more delicate salad dressings.
• Sun-dried tomato paste in a jar is good for enriching sauces, and really mouthwatering spread on to hot toast with crushed garlic.

Cans
• I often use chopped canned tomatoes for quick pasta sauces and for putting into casseroles, soups and countless other dishes.
• When you have no time, cans of pulses, such as green flageolets, white cannellini, kidney beans and chick peas, are a boon for salads and for making into a quick bean stew with added vegetables or bacon.
• Smoked oysters and mussels are delicious in salads, and also in stuffings for meat and chicken, imparting their smoky flavour.
• Soft cod or herring roe makes a quick, nutritious snack, sautéed briefly in butter and served on toast.
• Tuna is universally popular and can be used in many dishes, including dips, quiches, pasta, stuffings, and, of course, salads.
• Boneless skinned sardines in olive oil are perfect for making sardine pâté in seconds.
• I find anchovies the most useful canned fish and a wonderful flavour enhancer. They can be used on pizzas, with pasta, or chopped and added to meat stews, stuffings or spiked into meat, particularly lamb, before roasting. They can also be emptied into a heatproof bowl with their oil and stirred over hot water until they form a cream to use as a base for sauces or with pasta.

Dried and dry ingredients
• A key dried ingredient for the store cupboard must be pasta. If you have pasta, olive oil and seasonings in the house, you will always have a complete meal at the ready. Pasta comes, of course, in all shapes and sizes. Don't forget also oriental noodles which are useful for stir-fries.
• Rice is another invaluable standby, and wonderful varieties which have real flavour are available; arborio is a marvellous type of rice used for risotto, a useful dish if you have only leftovers or store cupboard ingredients in the house. Then there is my favourite – basmati, the delicate, long grain rice prized above all others in India. Wholegrain basmati rice is to me much the nicest of the wholegrain rices, because it is lighter in texture and takes less time to cook.
• Flour becomes stale sooner than most people think, so always keep an eye on the best before date. I always keep a stock of strong bread flour, including wholemeal,

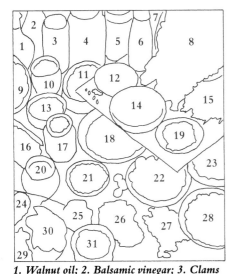

1. Walnut oil; 2. Balsamic vinegar; 3. Clams in shells; 4. Vine leaves in brine; 5. Sunflower oil; 6. Extra virgin olive oil; 7. Red wine vinegar; 8. Dried pasta twists and bows; 9. Ready-to-eat dried apricots; 10. Cockles; 11. Dried green lentils; 12. Pine kernels; 13. Wholemeal flour; 14. Dried flageolet beans; 15. Dried spaghetti; 16. White flour; 17. Wholegrain mustard; 18. Risotto rice; 19. Sea salt; 20. Apricot conserve; 21. Demerara sugar; 22. Green and black olives; 23. Shelled walnut and pecan halves; 24. Dried black mushrooms; 25. Sun-dried tomatoes; 26. Basmati rice; 27. Dried chick peas; 28. Dried haricot beans; 29. Dried wild mushrooms; 30. Dried cèpes; 31. Tomato purée.

unbleached white, and malted wheat grain flours. You can also keep a little rye flour to vary your loaves by mixing with wheat flour.
• I keep sunflower and pumpkin seeds, bulgar and sesame seeds to add to bread doughs and to use as a general topping.
• I always keep a good store of dried fruits; these get eaten up very quickly as I used to try and to make my children eat dried fruit instead of sweets, and they have become as addicted as I am. Dried fruit is useful to nibble after a meal when you have no pudding and have run out of fresh fruit.
• Dried mushrooms seem expensive, but the wonderfully pungent flavour of wild mushrooms which they give to dishes makes it worth the cost, and since their flavour is strong, you do not have to use a large quantity. Try adding a few dried mushrooms to the creamy sauce of a lasagne.
• Sun-dried tomatoes are fairly new to our shelves; they have a rather addictive, intense flavour and you can buy them preserved in oil, or simply dried. The ones in oil are softer in texture and can be sliced and used as they are in pasta and salads, while the dried ones should be cooked in juicy casseroles.
• Nuts should not be stored for too long unless they are vacuum packed, but they are useful for adding to cakes, puddings, salads, stuffings and so on. You can buy ready

shelled pistachio nuts which are marvellous for pâtés, stuffings and in ice cream – and I always keep ground almonds for baking.
• Pine kernels are a great favourite of mine; they are good toasted and scattered into salads, into spicy mince dishes, in stuffed vine leaves, aubergines and peppers, or simply on top of a dish of green vegetables.
• Green and red lentils, unlike most dried pulses, need no soaking before cooking; delicious green lentils can simply be boiled for 30–45 minutes until just soft, and used in salads, stews or as a vegetable on their own with plenty of butter and seasoning. Red lentils cook even more quickly and are useful for thickening stews, or can quickly transform stock into a sustaining soup.
• Spices of all kinds (page 12) are obvious candidates for the store cupboard, but buy whole spices if possible and grind them yourself in a coffee grinder just before using.
• Most herbs are better fresh (page 10), but oregano is, in fact, best dried, so this is an extremely versatile herb which you can always keep. The other herbs which dry successfully are thyme, tarragon, dill (surprisingly) and bay leaves.
• Coconut milk powder comes in packets; it is the quickest and easiest way of making

coconut milk or cream, which can be used in many spicy dishes and puddings.
• Aromatic tea, such as Earl Grey, makes an excellent poaching liquid for skinless chicken breasts or white fish.

Miscellaneous
• Long-life cream and milk can be used for sauces and soups when you have run out of fresh; refrigerate after opening.
• Tubes of olive, garlic and tomato purées are perfect for flavouring mince mixtures, dips and pâtés, and for stirring into casseroles.
• I always keep plenty of the darkest cooking chocolate but I have a special hiding place or it gets eaten by members of my family. Stirred in before serving, a little dark chocolate enriches the juices of a game casserole and is also useful for quickly made sauces for ice cream or poached fruit.
• A few chicken, meat, fish and vegetable stock cubes should be kept for when you have no homemade stock, and they can also be used for intensifying the flavour of a sauce.
• Vacuum-packed French-style crêpes save time and skill. As they are slightly sweet, they are better for quick puddings, stuffed with fruit or jam, or simply rolled up, soaked in a fruit syrup, and served with cream.

HERBS

I realized what a miraculous effect the use of herbs can have in cookery when I first went to the Lubéron hills in the south of France. The dry hillsides are covered with wild thyme and rosemary, and these dusty little plants give off a wonderful smell as you walk through them. It was the exquisite combination of this aromatic thyme and pink, succulent baby lamb which fired my enthusiasm for using herbs in my own cooking.

Herbs really transform food, and some combinations seem to have been designed for each other: basil with tomato, tarragon with chicken, both thyme and rosemary with lamb and oregano with cheese and eggs. Yet there should be no compulsory combinations; what is exciting is that there is always more scope for experiment and the possibility of a new and successful mixture of tastes. I never tire of trying new fusions.

Herbs should be used fresh whenever possible, oregano being the one exception, as for some reason it has an even better aroma when dried. Most herbs are easy to grow, too. Thyme can be as good dried as fresh, but only if it has recently been dried. Now that it is so easy to obtain fresh herbs all the year round, it is strange to think that not so long ago you could only buy little drums of a narrow selection of dried herbs. In any case many of the tender herbs such as basil and parsley lose their character completely the moment they are dried; if you have a glut and want to preserve herbs you can either freeze small quantities in ice cubes (page 312) or, best of all, keep them covered in oil in sealed jars. Then, when you have used the herbs, the aromatic oil can be used in salad dressings (page 204).

Nothing matches the fragrance of fresh herbs in salads or scattered on to cooked vegetables, and those with pretty shaped leaves make an effective garnish or stunning border to a dish. As long as you have some fresh herbs in the house you needn't worry if the dish you have made turns out a rather colourless mess – if the basic taste of the food is good, you can swiftly glamorize the appearance with a scattering of herbs. Even perfectly executed casseroles, stews and soups look more appetizing and attractive if you throw in a handful of roughly chopped herbs at the last moment, and they make all the difference to gravies and sauces, too.

Angelica Dried or fresh, this is a useful herb for flavouring fish and salads. In candied form, the stalks can be chopped and used in fruit cakes or softened under warm water and then cut into decorations for the top of puddings, cakes and biscuits. Angelica's flavour is often compared with juniper.

Aniseed Cultivated since the days of the Pharoahs, aniseed's most popular use today is in Mediterranean drinks like ouzo. You can also scatter a few seeds into fish soups, stews and cooked vegetables or into biscuit doughs, cakes and even egg custards.

Balm or lemon balm These fresh leaves have a flavour and scent resembling lemon. Use whole leaves in punches and fruit drinks and chopped leaves in soups and salads.

Basil One of the most versatile herbs to grow at home, basil is also one of my favourites. The green leaves have a tantalizingly heady aroma and pungent flavour. If you are cooking with it rather than using raw, add it at the end of cooking to preserve the flavour. Basil is used a great deal in Italian and French cooking to flavour tomatoes, with which it has an extraordinary affinity, and also in mixed salads and various sauces – the most popular being Italian pesto (page 207). Except when making pesto, basil leaves should not be chopped, which discolours them, but instead torn across with your fingers into pieces.

Bay Aromatic bay leaves are used fresh or dried for flavouring soups and stews and as an essential part of bouquet garni. They go particularly well with fish and also with game and pulses. If you remove the spine of the fresh leaves and chop them very finely they have a wonderful effect in cream and egg sauces. In sweet custards the whole leaves are infused in the hot milk before baking. Add to the water when boiling potatoes.

Borage This is a very easily grown herb with a pretty blue flower which is traditionally used in summer drinks like Pimms. The flower is decorative but the leaves taste of cucumber and, when very young, can be added to salads. The flowers can also be crystallized (page 275) and used to decorate cakes or frozen in ice cubes for drinks (page 312).

Bouquet garni This is a parcel of fresh thyme, parsley stalks and bay leaves used to flavour soups, stews and sauces. Make up your own version of bouquet garni with any herbs – and spices – of your choice.

Chervil This is a pretty feathery leaved plant with the delicate aroma of aniseed. Use quickly because once picked the leaves wilt. Chervil is used a lot in French cooking for flavouring omelettes and fish dishes, but can also be used in salads.

Chives The bright green stems of this herb have an oniony taste, making them an ideal garnish for tomato salads, soups, baked potato fillings and egg dishes.

Coriander The leaf, root, stem and seeds of this strongly aromatic herb all taste slightly different. The fresh leaves are pretty and add an instant exotic taste to any dish if added just before serving, but they are also excellent in salads and as a garnish. Cook the roots and stems in casseroles and soups but remove before serving.

Dill Available either fresh or dried, dill is mainly used for flavouring soups, sauces, pickles and pickled salmon or gravad lax (page 135). Fresh dill has a lovely flavour and enhances salads, fish stews, potatoes and other vegetables when added at the last moment. A mixture of prawns, soured cream and fresh dill is a delicious, quick first course.

Elder Both the flowers and berries of this rampant weed can be used in the kitchen but in the early summer the flowers have a short, wonderful season as they won't freeze or dry.

Their musky smell gives no hint of the exquisite flavour (similar to muscatel grapes) which they add to syrups, sorbets, jellies, jams and cordials and to stewed gooseberries and apricots. In the autumn the berries can be used in jams, jellies and chutneys.

Fennel The stalks and leaves of this aromatic herb have a delicate liquorice flavour. Fennel's feathery leaves are an ideal garnish for vegetables and for fish dishes. The dried stalks are very effective as a bed to lay fish on when grilling.

Fenugreek leaves This is a soft green, clover-like herb, and the seed is often used in Indian cooking as its bitter aromatic flavour blends well with other spices. The leaves taste like a curry-flavoured walnut.

Fines herbes A French term used to describe a blend of fresh herbs – usually parsley, tarragon, chives, chervil – which are finely chopped and often used to flavour omelettes.

Garlic Although really a member of the onion family, garlic is as much of a flavouring ingredient as any fresh herb. To me, the smell of garlic cooking is more appetizing than any other, and I would hate to live without it. It enhances all but the most delicate ingredients if used in the right way. When raw or briefly cooked, the taste is robust and strong, but cooked long and gently garlic becomes mild and sweet. Thus some dishes or sauces need the smallest addition of garlic while long-cooked dishes benefit from several cloves. Even people who claim not to like garlic are surprised at the flavour change.

Lemon grass Most frequently used in Thai and Vietnamese dishes, lemon grass is available both fresh and dried. It has a lemony flavour which goes well with fish. The dried variety should be soaked for a few hours before use.

Lovage The seeds, leaves and stems of this

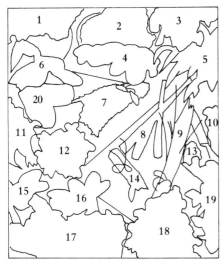

1. *Flat-leaved parsley; 2. Thyme; 3. Coriander;*
4. Rocket; 5. Sage; 6. Bay leaves; 7. Rosemary;
8. Lemon grass; 9. Chives; 10. Curly parsley;
11. Tarragon; 12. Marjoram; 13. Chopped
chives; 14. Bouquet garni; 15. Mint; 16. Basil;
17. Dill; 18. Chervil; 19. Oregano; 20. Sorrel.

herb have a slight celery flavour but also a very definite pungent flavour of their own. The decorative leaves make a beautiful garnish round the side of a dish and they are also excellent roughly chopped and thrown into soups and casseroles just before serving. Lovage is particularly good with tomato dishes. It is a handsome, easily grown herb which is extremely useful.

Marjoram This is a sweet herb similar to oregano, only far less assertive. The delicate flavour is destroyed by prolonged cooking, so it is best added shortly before serving. It is good stirred in to chicken casseroles or vegetable soups.

Mint Among the most important of culinary herbs, mint has a wide range of flavours – such as spearmint, apple mint or eau-de-cologne. As a change from mint sauce, mint is excellent chopped and spiked into a lamb roast or cooked in a lamb casserole or meatballs. It is also an interesting flavour to add to chutneys and to stewed blackcurrants, damsons and other summer fruits, and is excellent in fruit salads. Chopped mint is also good sprinkled on cooked vegetables.

Oregano Closely related to marjoram but stronger and more aromatic, oregano is very useful as it is the only herb which is arguably better dried than fresh. It goes well with meat and chicken and with cheese and eggs. This herb is best known for its uses in Italian and Greek cooking.

Parsley Although traditionally used as a garnish only, fresh parsley also adds a wonderful flavour to soups and sauces. Curly or flat-leaved varieties are available; the flat-leaved being more decorative, as well as having a stronger flavour. Lots of chopped flat-leaved parsley, a little crushed garlic and seasoned extra virgin olive oil is an excellent finishing touch to grilled meat and fish.

Parsley can also be fried and added to fish, or puréed with a little butter to make a quick sauce to serve with chicken or veal. In moments of glut, parsley makes a good salad leaf or can be used to make a green sauce in the same way as pesto (page 207).

Rocket Rocket, or *arugula* as it is called in Italy where it is very popular, is a salad herb, used as whole, young leaves. It has a strong but delicious watercress-type taste which is much enhanced by a good vinaigrette dressing (page 204). Rocket is also excellent stirred into cooked pasta with butter and crushed garlic.

Rosemary Often used with lamb, rosemary is also excellent with pork, rabbit, chicken and sausages. It has a strong flavour, so is best used sparingly and finely chopped. Whole sprigs make a good bed on which to grill meat or poultry. Try it infused in sweet dishes, too, such as creams, custards, syrups and vanilla ice cream.

Sage An excellent herb to combine with tomatoes, garlic and olive oil, sage is best used with fatty meats such as pork or duck, or with liver. It also goes surprisingly well in beef casseroles which contain tomatoes as well and in hot cheese dishes. Sage has a powerful flavour, so use sparingly. It is an

excellent herb to include in stuffings.

Savory The winter and summer varieties of this herb taste vaguely like thyme but are more bitter. Winter savory is slightly milder. Use (with discretion) in bean and pasta soups and in stews and meat casseroles.

Sorrel Specially popular in France, and with me, this sour, lemon-flavoured herb makes the most delicious soups and sauces, stirred in at the end to cook only briefly. Sorrel leaves dissolve quickly and lose their bright green colour when heated; often spinach is used with sorrel to add depth of colour. A few raw leaves can also be added to salads.

Tarragon A pretty fine-leaved herb with a strong but subtle flavour. If you grow any make sure you plant the French variety as the Russian type grows prolifically but has none of the flavour. Tarragon is famous for its uses with chicken, butters, sauces, eggs and fish but can also be used with meat and game and in salad dressings.

Thyme Best suited to long, slow-cooking dishes and casseroles. Unlike most herbs, except oregano, thyme is as good dried or fresh. It is wonderful with young roast lamb but also good with pork, chicken, fish and eggs. Use sparingly, as it can easily overpower other flavourings.

SPICES

My passion for spices began at an age when most children scorn them. This was when my family went to live in Syria, and memories of the exciting smells and sights of the Street of Spices in the Damascus *souk*, or market, are still with me. In fact, spicy food does not mean food which burns the tongue; it means a complex variety of aromatics which can bring out unknown aspects of ingredients – only a few spices such as chillies, peppers and ginger actually add heat.

In Damascus, I learnt to love the typically Middle Eastern mixtures of cumin, coriander, cinnamon and so on; years later when I began travelling in India, I came across the same spices and many more, but combined and used in quite different ways. This was what led me to begin using spices in my own recipes, sometimes a mixture and sometimes just one spice sparingly added to a mild dish, which can often be extremely effective. A single spice can also be a miraculous last-minute seasoning to so many things, both savoury and sweet; for example, grating nutmeg on to vegetables, milk puddings and cheese dishes, or adding caraway seeds to sweet potatoes and pumpkin.

Cardamom is one of the spices I feel almost addicted to; it is wonderful, not only with meat, poultry and fish – a crushed pod or two will transform a fish stew – but also to add a scented magic to milky puddings and ice creams. For savoury dishes of all kinds, the mixture of cardamom with garlic and fresh ginger is – to me – one of the most mouthwatering combinations there

can be. Cinnamon is another spice which enhances both savoury and sweet dishes; it is particularly good in chicken, using whole sticks to flavour a stew. Cinnamon toast, bread fried in butter and spread with ground cinnamon, is irresistible.

Just as it is best to use fresh herbs, so the pungency of spices is far more pronounced if you buy them whole and grind them as you need them. When using either whole or ground spices you should heat them briefly in a dry frying pan first to bring out their full aromas. I keep an extra electric coffee grinder just to grind spices but if you use them only rarely you can wipe out your coffee grinder and use it, or pound them in a pestle and mortar, though this is more difficult with harder spices like cinnamon, cloves and star anise. In North Africa and the Middle East, coffee is often made with a pod of cardamom infused in it, and my husband often grinds the beans with a few cardamom seeds included.

You can experiment with different spices in the same way as you can with herbs but in my experience people are even more intrigued by the hard-to-define taste of a certain spice in a dish. You can also concoct your own mixture of spices to use in curries as housewives do in India. Careful spicing of food seems to excite people, and spiced food at a party is nearly always more remarked on and remembered. It is often difficult to know what drink to have with very spice food; beer usually goes well and, when you want to celebrate, serve champagne or another sparkling wine.

Allspice This spice looks like large peppercorns but the taste resembles a mix of nutmeg, mace, cinnamon and especially cloves. Use it in fruit cakes, mince pies and Christmas puddings, and it is an important ingredient for spicing salt beef. Ground allspice is a single spice, not a combination of spices as the name can imply.

Caraway A spice with brown, sickle-shaped seeds used for flavouring cakes, biscuits, bread, cheese and pickles. Caraway seeds are also very effective scattered on to cooked vegetables, particularly root vegetables, and are a classic with hot cabbage.

Cardamom This spice tastes vaguely like eucalyptus but, to me, sweeter and richer. I find it irresistible. The pods are naturally green but are sometimes bleached white; larger black cardamoms are much coarser and inferior in taste. Cardamom comes from an Indian plant and is much used in Indian dishes, both savoury and sweet. It is wonderful in milky puddings (page 216). Use whole pods for a subtle flavour but break them open for a stronger one. Ground cardamom loses its best oils so use fresh seeds and grind them as required.

Cayenne pepper A very hot pungent spice, cayenne is derived from the dried pods of a red chilli pepper native to Central America. Use this for giving heat to curries, and seasoning cheese and fish dishes.

Chilli This member of the vast capsicum family comes in all shapes, sizes and colours. Chillies are the ingredient which give heat and flavour to curries but individual ones

vary in strength. Fresh green chillies are picked unripe, whereas red ones are ripe but not necessarily more pungent. On the whole, the fleshier, fatter chillies are milder than the small thin ones. The seeds are the hottest part of all and best discarded. Always prepare chillies under water (page 49) and don't touch your eyes or mouth afterwards.

Chinese five-spice powder This is a subtle blend of spices consisting of equal parts of finely ground Sichuan pepper, star anise, cinnamon, cloves and fennel seeds, widely used in oriental cooking.

Cinnamon Made from the bark of an evergreen native of Sri Lanka, cinnamon is sold either as sticks or as a ground spice, and has good keeping qualities. Cassia is similar to cinnamon but has a coarser texture and less delicate taste. Use cinnamon sticks for spicy chicken, lamb or vegetable casseroles, and ground cinnamon for baking and puddings. The flavour is especially good with apples, pears and chocolate.

Clove A familiar spice, clove is highly aromatic. It is traditionally married with apple dishes and also used with cinnamon in hot spiced wines and punches and in pickles. A few cloves are good in rich beef or oxtail casseroles and in curries.

Coriander The spicy dried seeds of this aromatic herb have a totally different taste to the fresh stems and leaves. Coriander seeds are good in pickles and curry spice and are excellent for flavouring pork, leafy green and root vegetables and any casserole.

Cumin Cumin seeds have a pungent,

medium-hot and slightly bitter taste. They can be used whole or ground, and are useful for flavouring cheese, breads, sauces and curries. An excellent spice, particularly when combined with mint, for roast or stewed lamb, and also for mince dishes.

Dill Similar but milder in taste to caraway or fennel seeds, these seeds go well with mashed potatoes and boiled cabbage and with casseroled or minced pork.

Fennel These delicate liquorice-flavoured seeds are used in curries, and are good with vegetable and dried bean casseroles.

Garam masala This name literally means 'hot mixture' and garam masala is a combination of roasted spices such as coriander seed, cumin, cardamom, cloves and cinnamon. Every Indian housewife makes up her own version and grinds the whole spices freshly for it.

Ginger Available fresh, ground, preserved in syrup and crystallized, ginger is a hot, spicy ingredient widely used in Indian and oriental dishes and British baking. Fresh ginger is a revelation when you first try it as it has a clean flavour and wonderful lemony smell, quite different to dried or preserved ginger. It combines well with garlic and is excellent with shellfish, fish and chicken dishes. I like the flavour so much that I use it in an enormous range of dishes.

Juniper Famous as the flavour for gin, these small purply black, pine-scented berries are also useful in marinades, casseroles and terrines – in particular pork and game – and for making spiced beef.

1. Star anise; 2. Dried red chillies; 3. Fresh red and green chillies; 4. Caraway seeds; 5. Juniper berries; 6. Green cardamom pods; 7. Cayenne pepper; 8. Whole and sliced fresh ginger; 9. Mace; 10. Saffron; 11. Ground turmeric; 12. Cumin seeds; 13. Tamarind; 14. Vanilla pods; 15. Pink, white and black dried peppercorns; 16. Cassia bark; 17. Black and white mustard seeds; 18. Whole and grated nutmeg; 19. Fennel seeds; 20. Cloves; 21. Dill seeds; 22. Green dried peppercorns; 23. Cinnamon sticks.

Mace A 'cage' surrounding the nutmeg seed, mace is bright red when fresh but changes to creamy brown when dried. It tastes only slightly like nutmeg, and whole blades can be used to improve the flavour of soups and stews. Ground mace is useful when baking cakes and biscuits. I use it in creamy sauces for poultry, fish and game.

Mixed spice This is a blend of ground mace, coriander, caraway, cassia, cloves, ginger, cinnamon and pimento and is used to flavour biscuits, puddings and cakes. Use as fresh as possible as it stales very quickly.

Mustard This is available in powdered and prepared forms. English, French, German and American prepared mustards are popular. Seeds may be white, black or brown – the last two contain the most piquant oils, and are often used in Indian dishes but can be effective in everyday poultry, game or pork casseroles, too. Wholegrain mustard in jars is useful to stir into creamy sauces.

Nutmeg This is a versatile spice with a pungent nutty flavour. It is traditionally sprinkled to great effect on to milk puddings, such as rice pudding or junket, but is also a perfect accompaniment to pumpkin, spinach and pasta dishes, and is wonderful combined with cheese and in all root vegetable purées. Grate fresh nutmeg just before use as its essential oils and flavour are quickly lost.

Pepper As well as hot, spicy cayenne pepper made from chillies, this spice group also includes black, green and white peppercorns. These are the berries of vine peppers. You can buy ground pepper but it is far better to keep dried peppercorns in a pepper mill and grind it freshly as needed. Make up your own mixture for a grinder. Whole green peppercorns in brine are wonderful in sauces for chicken, beef and steaks. Although not a true pepper, pink peppercorns are milder, very aromatic and look pretty.

Saffron These dried stigmas of a special crocus are the most expensive spice in the world as they are harvested by hand. Saffron imparts a strong yellow colour and has a unique, penetrating taste – only a pinch is needed to flavour and colour any dish. To capture the most flavour, put a few filaments in to boiling liquid to infuse for at least 15 minutes and then add the golden liquid with the saffron to the main ingredients. It is best used with rice and fish – for example, Spanish paella, Italian risottos and Indian pilaffs. It is good with fish dishes which have creamy sauces, and saffron-flavoured cream is excellent in mashed potato. It is also used traditionally in cakes and biscuits.

Star anise A pretty star-shaped pod used in classic Chinese dishes, star anise has an overall flavour of liquorice and aniseed but is spicier. Use in fish stews and root vegetable purées and with cabbage, leeks or pumpkin.

Tamarind Mainly used in curries, tamarind is a brown, slightly sticky substance which comes from the seed pods of the tamarind tree. It has a sour fruity taste which adds something more complex than just lemon juice to curries and other spicy casseroles and soups. Usually sold in a compacted or dried form, it is a vital ingredient in chutneys and many Indian and Far Eastern dishes.

Turmeric Usually sold as a ground orange/yellow powder, turmeric is often used instead of saffron to colour food yellow but the taste – warm and spicy – is quite different. It is most often used in curries and pickles but is also good used sparingly in chicken and fish stews.

Vanilla This wonderful flavouring is derived from the pods of a Mexican orchid. The best vanilla is grown in Madagascar and it is the white crystals of vanillin which cling to the pod that provide the flavour and marvellous aroma. The pods are expensive but they can be used several times and can be stored in a jar of sugar which they will also flavour for use in puddings (page 235). Synthetic vanilla flavouring does not compare with the flavour you get from a real vanilla pod but you can buy natural vanilla essence. Vanilla can also be used to flavour fish stews and sauces for fish.

BASIC KITCHEN EQUIPMENT

Cooking can be a pleasure, and it can be a chore. To prevent the day-to-day preparing of meals becoming drudgery, it helps immensely to have good, well-made kitchen equipment. That is not to say that you need indulge in expensive professional pans and tools, but you should buy the finest equipment you can afford, adding to your collection as your budget allows and when you have a better idea of what you will actually use.

Good equipment lasts for ever, so the investment is worth it, paying you back time and time again with reliability and service. Poorly made kitchen equipment that is flimsy and liable to break, buckle or burn, will cause you great frustration, and will make cooking an onerous task that you will want to avoid.

Efficiency in the kitchen depends as much on the quality of the equipment being used as it does on your skills and organization, and together these can make cooking a very satisfying and pleasurable experience as well as making you less tired.

Bottle opener This works by levering off the cap of a bottle and sometimes forms the top of a corkscrew. It should be sturdy and comfortable to grip.

Can opener The most widely available is a butterfly-handled opener with a gear-driven cutting wheel, and it is easier to use than a simple ratchet opener or one with a blade and cog wheel. A wall-mounted version of the gear-driven opener is convenient although more expensive. Buy one that is easy to clean frequently. Electric can openers take up space on the work surface and are more difficult to clean but require no strength to use.

Colander This rigid bowl-shaped strainer can be metal, enamel, rigid plastic or earthenware and should have holes all over the bottom and partly up the sides to ensure speedy draining. For everyday washing and draining jobs a 2-handled colander with a broad pedestal base is suitable (on legs it is less sturdy). If you plan to use your colander as a steamer over a saucepan as well, choose one with a flat bottom, one long handle and, ideally, a hook on the side opposite the handle so it can rest securely on the pan's rim, as well as on bowls.

Corkscrew Many types are available so choose one according to the strength of your hands. One of the easiest to use, a Screwpull, has a comfortable handle and large, open spiral screw for a better grip on the cork, and it works by pushing against the rim of the bottle as leverage to draw out the cork. A cork puller, with thin, flexible metal prongs that are eased down between cork and bottle, is good for fragile corks and can also be used to re-cork bottles.

Fish slice and lifter Fish slices or broad metal turners should have thin, flexible yet sturdy blades that will slide easily under food, and then be strong enough to lift or turn the food. Some turners are squarish or rectangular, and may have slots or holes to let excess fat or other liquid drain away; others are rounded or triangular, to fit against the walls of a saucepan.

Fork Sturdy forks with 2–4 straight or curved, sharply pointed metal (usually stainless steel) tines or prongs are used to lift food out of deep pans so as to taste it or test texture, to manipulate food that is being roasted or grilled, and to hold joints of meat or birds steady while they are carved (page 166). As with a good knife (page 16), a metal kitchen fork should be riveted at the handle, and the metal should extend through to the end of the heat-resistant wooden or plastic handle for added strength.

Large strong, wooden forks, with 3–4 tines, have many uses, including swirling and separating spaghetti and vegetables, such as shredded cabbage, in their cooking water.

Metal spoon and ladle Large, long-handled metal spoons are used for stirring, folding, lifting and basting. They must be strongly made as the foods they stir and lift will often be stiff or heavy. The bowl of the spoon should also be shallow so that food is not caught in it. Ideally, choose spoons with heat-resistant handles.

Slotted or perforated metal spoons enable you to easily remove solid foods from liquid or fat, for tasting or serving. They may also be used for skimming fat or scum from the surface of a simmering liquid, although a circular perforated skimmer does this job more easily and thoroughly (the most thorough is a wire mesh skimmer). Wire skimmers, which are really shallow wire baskets, are best to use for removing items from deep hot fat.

Ladles used in the kitchen, for pouring a batter into a hot pan or for serving a soup or stew, should have a long handle, to keep your hand away from the hot food, and a deep bowl. Special basting ladles for skimming gravy have an oval bowl and should have a lip at one side to make pouring easy.

Nutcracker A cracker with a ratchet action is the easiest to use and is sturdy enough to crack the legs and claws of shellfish such as crabs and lobster, too. A wooden cracker with a screw is not as strong but is easy to use. The traditional nutcracker that employs a simple squeezing action requires the most effort and does not give as much control over pressure so the nut inside the shell may be crushed as well.

Palette knife This knife has a long, narrow blade that is thin and flexible yet sturdy; the tip is rounded, and one side of the blade may be serrated. Use this as a turner for thin flat items, such as small fish fillets or steak or pancakes, as well as for folding and mixing and lifting delicate biscuits off a baking sheet. It can also be used to loosen a baked cake or cheesecake from its tin, spread soft mixtures such as icing or buttercream on a cake, or for making a decorative effect on a vegetable purée. A large palette knife with a serrated edge is used to cut a cake into layers.

FOR A WELL-STOCKED BASIC KITCHEN

Anyone setting up home for the first time can use this as a guideline for stocking a kitchen. There will be very few cooking preparations that you won't be able to accomplish with these pieces of equipment. More expensive specialist equipment (page 24) can be bought gradually as you become more experienced and accomplished.

- set of metric measuring spoons
- measuring jug
- kitchen scales
- can opener
- bottle opener
- pair of strong kitchen scissors
- set of mixing bowls in varying sizes
- swivel-bladed vegetable peeler
- large, medium and small cook's knives
- flat, sturdy chopping board
- box grater
- medium-sized wire whisk
- wooden spoons of various sizes
- large plain metal spoon
- large 2-pronged metal fork
- slotted metal fish slice
- rubber spatulas

- colander
- slotted spoon
- medium-sized sieve
- pestle and mortar
- rolling pin
- set of heavy-based saucepans in at least 4 sizes
- heavy-based frying pan
- omelette pan
- roasting tin with rack
- pie dish
- medium-sized flameproof casserole
- 2 flan rings
- at least 2 baking sheets
- deep cake tins in various sizes, from 18–25cm (7–10in)
- 2–4 sandwich tins, 18–20cm (7–8in)

1. *Tapered pasta rolling pin*
2. *Rolling pin*
3. *Spindle rolling pin*
4. *Large deep ladle*
5. *Mini-ladle*
6. *Basting ladle*
7. *Shallow ladle*
8. *Nutcracker with ratchet action*

9. *Selection of wooden spoons*
10. *Scissor-style tongs*
11. *Two-handled colander with base*
12. *Wire skimmer*
13. *Flat perforated skimmer*
14. *Fine wire mesh skimmer*
15. *Wooden fork*

16. *Spaghetti tongs*
17. *Metal fork*
18. *Single-handled colander*
19. *Can opener*
20. *Palette knife*
21. *Fish slice*
22. *Traditional fish slice*
23. *Rubber spatula*

24. *Large metal spoon*
25. *Perforated spoon*
26. *Pastry brush*
27. *Pastry brush*
28. *Slotted wooden spatula*
29. *Bottle opener*
30. *Screwpull corkscrew*

Pastry brush These are handy for a multitude of uses, from greasing a pan or mould, to brushing an egg glaze over a pie before baking or moistening the edges of pastry to seal, to basting kebabs during grilling and so on. Choose brushes with natural bristles that will not melt like plastic ones. The brushes that look like paint brushes are the most versatile. It is best to have several, one for greasing, one for glazing and so on. Wash frequently in hot soapy water.

Rolling pin For general use, choose a long, heavy hardwood rolling pin without handles for closest contact with pastry. The smooth, silky finish will hold a dusting of flour, which ceramic and glass pins will not, and its weight and length will enable a smooth sheet of pastry to be rolled out almost effortlessly. Spindle wooden rolling pins with handles that remain stationary as you roll are easy to use, but be sure the handles are not painted

because in time the paint will flake off into the pastry. An extra-long tapered rolling pin (at least 60cm/24in long) is worth having if you often make pasta dough by hand; it can be used for rolling out very thin, large pieces of pastry. Do not soak wooden ones in water or they may warp.

Spatula Pliable yet firm rubber spatulas are excellent for folding and blending light mixtures, such as whisked egg whites, and for scraping every bit of a mixture out of a bowl. Rubber spatulas should not be used in very hot mixtures or in hot pans, as the rubber will degrade. Wooden spatulas, on the other hand, don't have this drawback and are suitable for mixing and folding all kinds of mixtures, as well as for doubling as a turner. Wooden spatulas come in a variety of shapes, both flat and curved, and may also be slotted.

Tongs Very hot or very cold food is best handled with metal or wooden tongs rather

than with your fingers. Tongs that use a scissor-action are more sturdy and accurate to use than simpler 2-sided tongs, unless you are proficient. Scissor-style tongs are also usually able to open wide enough for large items.

Wooden spoon Use these for beating, mixing and stirring, both during preparation and cooking. General-purpose spoons, in the traditional shape, are available in varying sizes. There are also a variety of flat spoons without bowls for creaming mixtures, and spoons that have an angled point or flat bottom to get into corners of pans or dishes. Wood does not conduct heat, so spoons stay cool while you are stirring a hot mixture; the long handle also helps to keep your hand and arm away from the source of the heat so you do not burn yourself. Do not keep wooden spoons in a pan during cooking – they can burn and even catch fire! Wooden spoons with holes need careful washing.

CUTTING *and* CHOPPING

Cooking is a matter of control – making your tools do exactly what you want. And nowhere is control more important than in the use of particular knives for specific jobs. I would rather have sharp knives in the kitchen than any other good equipment – an inefficient knife is unbearably frustrating and a really sharp knife is much safer than a blunt one as it is less likely to slip.

Kitchen knives must be sturdily made. The tang – the part of the blade that extends into the handle – should be 'full', that is it should extend all the way to the end of the handle and be visible all round. Ideally, the blade of the knife should be riveted to the handle, not glued, and the riveting should be flush to the handle. Finally, the handle should be heat-resistant and non-slip.

The metal of the blade may be carbon steel or high-carbon stainless steel alloy. Carbon steel will take a very sharp edge, sharper than the alloy will, but it will rust and stain unless meticulously cared for and dried after washing. High-carbon stainless steel resists discoloration, but is much more expensive than carbon steel. Most ordinary stainless steel knives cannot be sharpened as well as either of the carbon knives.

SHARPENING KNIVES

The difference between using a well-sharpened knife and a dull one is the difference between easy, accurate food preparation and hard labour. A sharpening steel, ideally with coarse rather than fine grooves, is the tool to use in the kitchen – any knife, whether carbon or steel alloy, needs a quick run over the steel from time to time, or even before every use. When you find a blade losing efficiency, wash it in soapy water, dry it thoroughly and then run it over the steel several times, holding it at a shallow angle (30–45°). This procedure will not really sharpen a knife; it just restores the edge on it temporarily. If you use your knives every day, they should be sharpened 3 or 4 times a year by a specialist. Only use your knives for cutting or chopping food and cut only on wooden or polyethylene boards.

Apple corer This hollow cylindrical blade has sharp edges to cut into fruit skin, and is long enough to go all the way through an apple or pear.

Boning knife Use this for removing bones from raw meat and poultry. The strong, rigid blade, 12–15cm (5–6in) long, has a fine, razor-sharp point to cut as close to the bone as possible. Choose a boning knife with a moulded handle to prevent your hand slipping on to the blade.

Bread knife Most of these are serrated, to cut deftly through the crust without squashing the crumb, but they may also be scalloped or fluted.

Butcher's knife This is a large, fairly long knife with a firm blade shaped like a scimitar. Use to cut joints, steaks and chops. The handle has a deep notch or 'shoulder' where it meets the blade to guard fingers and to give the hand maximum leverage when cutting.

Carving knife and fork Buy knives at least 25cm (10in) long of medium to thin width for carving hot meats. The blade does not need to be as sturdy as that of a cook's knife but should be quite firm with some flexibility towards the point. Poultry carvers have shorter blades (about 20cm/8in), and sometimes curve upwards towards the point; some have a gently fluted edge. Carving forks should have a guard to protect your hand if the knife accidentally slips.

Chinese cleaver Available in several sizes and shapes, this versatile implement is used in as many ways as cook's knives: it can mince, slice, bone and flatten; the widest blade is an effective chopper, and is heavy enough to cut through chicken bones and to joint meat. For Chinese cooks it is their only knife and when very sharp it can do almost anything.

Cook's knife Also called chef's knives, cook's knives have a rigid triangular blade with a sharp point and gently curved edge; the curve allows you to hold the point and rock the knife up and down, for fine chopping. The most versatile and frequently used one for chopping and slicing has a 15–20cm (6–8in) long blade. The smallest cook's knife, sometimes called paring knife, is a useful all-purpose knife. With a 7–10cm (3–4in) long blade, it is used for peeling, chopping and removing 'eyes' from potatoes and pineapple. The longer cook's knife, with a blade up to 35cm (14in) long, is used for cutting and slicing large foods.

Cutting board The best wooden boards are heavy and thick, to act as good shock absorbers, and ideally made from one piece of densely grained wood (strips of wood glued together can eventually come apart); wooden surfaces are better for cutting and chopping because they will not blunt the knife. However, disadvantages of wood are many: it is porous and so absorbs moisture which can cause warping and cracking, and it can retain stains, odours and bacteria. It is important to wash wooden boards well, scrubbing in the direction of the grain. Rinse and dry well. Polyethylene cutting boards, available in many sizes, are more hygienic than wood because they can be thoroughly cleaned, even in a dishwasher, and are soft enough to avoid blunting a knife.

Personally, I much prefer the look and feel of wood and keep several boards of varying sizes for different ingredients. Using the same small board for crushing garlic only means other delicately flavoured foods do not end up tasting of garlic.

Filleting knife Ideal for boning and skinning fresh fish without damaging the flesh, this knife has a slender and flexible blade, 18–23cm (7–9in) long. The sharp point is good for piercing fish skin and flesh, and the blade is ideal for skinning fish fillets. Because this knife is continuously wet during use, high-carbon stainless steel is best.

Grapefruit knife This has a curved, serrated flexible blade that cuts neatly round citrus fruit segments removing peel and membranes.

Grater Simple box graters, with 4 surfaces offering a choice of cutting holes, are more stable in use than flat graters. Metal ones are

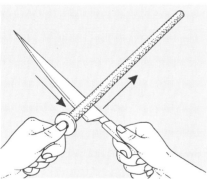

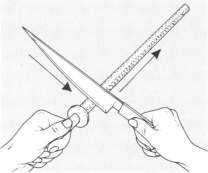

To sharpen a knife: **1** *Hold the steel level in front of you, pointing 45° away from your body. Place the wide end or heel of the knife under the steel at the handle end of the steel. Pull the knife along the steel away from you in one swift movement, at the same time working from the knife heel to the point.*

2 *Repeat on the other side of the knife on the top of the steel, again starting with the knife heel at the handle end of the steel, and working along the steel in a single swift movement. Repeat both these steps several times until the blade is sharp, and again before using the knife next time.*

1. Slicer
2. Boning knife
3. Meat chopper
4. Chinese cleaver
5. Mezzaluna
6. Wooden chopping board
7. Box grater
8. Butcher's knife
9. Coarse sharpening steel

10. Bread knife
11. Bread board
12. Rotary grater
13. Serrated vegetable knife
14. Paring knife
15. Grapefruit knife
16. Poultry shears
17. Small and large polyethylene
    chopping boards

18. Pine knife block
19. Kitchen scissors
20. Magnetic knife rack
21. Cook's knife
22. Cook's knife
23. Cook's knife
24. Oyster knife
25. Cheese knife
26. Filleting knife

27. Paring knife
28. Poultry carver
29. Carving knife
30. Carving fork
31. Serrated cook's knife
32. Nutmeg grater
33. Nutmeg grater
34. Swivel-bladed vegetable peeler
35. Apple corer

best and have sharper cutting holes. Safer is a rotary grater, with selection of fine and coarse drums turned by crank, although this can only be used for small food items. A nutmeg grater enables the cook to enjoy this spice at its freshest and most aromatic.

Japanese knife Similar in shape to a samurai sword, these traditional knives have flat backs and very sharp-angled edges so the cook can cut and slice very accurately. I find these beautiful knives are wonderfully satisfying to use; they make an excellent, if expensive, gift.

Knife rack If knives are stored in a drawer they bang together and the blades become dull, so protect your investment in knives with a wall-mounted magnetic rack or a slotted block. Don't hang heavy knives on a magnetic rack or they might fall.

Meat chopper This has a heavy, rectangular blade and will go through most joints or

bones. It is a useful general chopper and comes in varying sizes.

Mezzaluna This double-handled knife with a thick curving blade uses a satisfying rocking motion for fine chopping and mincing of herbs, vegetables and meat.

Oyster knife The short, pointed blade is used for prising open the oyster shells (page 123), and the horizontal guard protects your fingers from the shell's sharp edges.

Scissors and shears Kitchen scissors should be strong and sharp, and made from stainless steel so they can be thoroughly cleaned after use. One serrated blade gives more grip to cut, especially when working with fish or other slippery items. Shears must be even more robust so they can cut through poultry bones; the best have a coiled spring between handles as well as a little notch in one blade to grasp chicken bones.

Slicer Use slicers to cut cold meats into even, thin slices. They are long and fairly narrow with a flexible blade and a straight, fluted or scalloped edge. A smoked salmon slicer is similar in shape but has a very narrow straight-edged blade.

Vegetable or salad knife This is used for cutting and slicing smooth-skinned fruits and vegetables and citrus fruits. The blade is long and narrow with a finely serrated edge so it can cut cleanly through the skin without bruising or crushing the flesh. The blade is usually made of stainless steel as the acid in fruits and vegetables could cause a carbon steel knife to corrode.

Vegetable peeler A swivel-action blade peels all vegetables and fruits easily and thinly, as the blade follows contours better than a stationary blade or knife; the pointed tip is used to dig out blemishes.

TOP OF THE STOVE

To cook efficiently and with pleasure, it is essential to fit out your kitchen with the best equipment you can afford. Nowhere is this more important than in choosing pans and dishes for cooking on top of the stove.

Saucepans, frying pans, flameproof casseroles and so on receive heat only through their bases. For this reason, they should have thick or heavy bases; if they are too thin, the food being cooked in them is apt to burn and the pans themselves may buckle. In addition, the material used to make the pan must be able to conduct, or diffuse, the heat evenly from the base up the sides. Metal is the best conductor of direct heat which is why it is the material most frequently used. But, as you can see in the box below, a range of metals are used to make pots and pans. Pans should be well made so that they will last: lids should fit snugly and knobs and handles should be sturdy and securely fixed to the pan or lid. Also, be sure to lift up any stovetop equipment before buying. Many pieces, especially those made of cast iron, can be very heavy, and there isn't any point in spending the money on something you will find difficult to use.

It is also worth considering whether the chosen pans are easy to keep clean. Copper pans, for example, are beautiful, and they heat up and cool down rapidly, but they require regular maintenance because if stains are left on them too long the stains become almost impossible to remove. However, their incomparable way of diffusing the heat makes them a real joy to cook with, particularly for sautéing.

Crêpe pan Look for a pan made of good heat-conducting metal, such as cast iron, but lightweight enough and with a long handle so crêpes can be flipped easily. It has low, very sloping sides and comes in various sizes.

Deep-fat fryer Choose a deep pan with 2 short, sturdy handles and a long-handled basket; some have a charcoal filter in the lid, which prevents the unpleasant smell of fat escaping. Electric fryers are not worth the expense unless you do a lot of deep-frying.

Double boiler or double saucepan The lower pan holds simmering water, while the upper pan sits securely on it so delicate mixtures, such as custards or sauces, can be cooked or kept warm over gentle, indirect heat. The lower pan may be made of tin-lined copper, enamelled steel or aluminium, and the upper pan is usually a thinner gauge metal or can be a ceramic bowl. A metal upper pan will cool more quickly than a ceramic bowl when removed from over simmering water. A double boiler can also serve as a bain-marie to make delicate sauces such as hollandaise without fear of curdling.

Fish kettle Long and narrow in shape to accommodate whole fish such as salmon, this has a perforated platform with handles so the fish can be lifted in and out of the poaching liquid without breaking up. Choose one made of tinned steel or tin-lined copper as other metals such as unlined copper could discolour acidulated poaching liquids. Squarer fish kettles are also available.

Flameproof casserole Sometimes made of cast iron but most often enamel-coated cast iron, these are heavy, fairly deep and straight-sided pots. They may be round or oval. After initial browning or other brisk cooking, food is left to cook more gently on top of the stove or in the oven. The lid should fit tightly to trap in moisture, and the handles should be strong. These casseroles are supremely practical for all-in-one dishes.

Frying pan These shallow, wide, flat-bottomed pans have gently sloping straight or curved sides so the food can be fried and turned easily. The base must be thick and the pan must be made of good heat-conducting metal. For prolonged frying over high heat, cast iron is best but very heavy. The handle should be long, strong and ideally of wood which is heat-resistant.

Griddle This wide flat pan has very low sides or none at all so as not to impede the turning of flat foods such as drop scones. Even, high heat is required for cooking, so choose one made of cast iron or enamelled cast iron.

Grill pan This is a very heavy, flat, cast iron pan that is rectangular- or frying pan- shaped, with parallel ridges over the base and a spout on the side for pouring off fat. The ridges keep steaks, chops and so on away from fat, which could make them soggy, and creates a seared exterior while retaining a moist interior, just like grilling and barbecuing.

Milk pan These stainless steel pans with non-stick linings have slightly sloping sides with a lipped rim, giving room for milk to rise and bubble up.

Omelette pan The sloping sides should be slightly curved so omelettes can be rolled over and turned out; do not choose a big pan or the omelette will be difficult to turn; a 23cm (9in) pan is ideal to serve 2–3.

A GUIDE TO MATERIALS

Aluminium Good heavy-gauge aluminium pans are sturdy, conduct and hold heat well, will not dent easily or warp, are hard to scratch, and are relatively easy to clean. However, big pans are heavy, and the aluminium may affect the taste and colour of some acidic or egg dishes cooked slowly in them, as well as being stained by the food. Some aluminium pans have non-stick linings, but this reduces heat conduction.

Cast iron This is an excellent material for frying pans in particular because it distributes the heat slowly and evenly, and finally with great intensity for good browning. It also cools slowly. Cast iron needs to be seasoned before first use, and carefully cleaned (without soap) and thoroughly dried after each use to prevent rusting. Wiping with oiled paper helps.

Copper Beautiful – and expensive – copper pans conduct heat perfectly, heating and cooling more quickly than any other metal. Yet, unless they are lined with tin or stainless steel, copper pans can not be used to make chutneys or pickles because the high vinegar content of these preserves can react with the metal to cause a poisonous reaction; a tin lining cannot be scoured or it will deteriorate, but a stainless-steel lining can be cleaned easily and will last for ever, so is much the best buy. If, however, you do have a pan that needs re-lining, large kitchen equipment shops can usually arrange for this to be done. If you buy stainless steel-lined copper you will have the best pan possible as it will last forever. For copper pans to retain their beauty the outside must be polished regularly. Clean by rubbing with a cut lemon dipped in salt.

Enamelled cast iron Pans made from this are sturdy and distribute heat well but they are heavy and slow to heat or cool, so are not suitable for quick sautéing and preparing delicate sauces. The enamel may crack or chip if the pan is dropped, and the interior can be scratched if metal tools are used. Some enamelled pans need treating before first use so follow the manufacturer's instructions. After use, if any food sticks to the lining, soak in warm water then use a plastic pad, not a scouring pad, to loosen.

Glass and porcelain These are suitable only for gentle cooking because they are used over a very low flame or heat-retarding mat. Glass 'pans' have average heat conduction but are easy to clean.

Stainless steel This excellent hard-wearing material is easy to clean, and does not scratch easily when scoured. On its own it is not a good heat conductor so most stainless steel pans have a layer of aluminium or copper, or both, in the base to retain and distribute heat better. Good stainless steel pans will last a lifetime.

1. Stainless steel sauté pan with domed lid
2. Cast iron frying pan
3. Enamelled cast iron milk pan with pouring spouts
4. Expandable steaming basket
5. Two-handled stainless steel stockpot
6. Deep-frying wire basket
7. Stainless steel fish kettle
8. Small tin-lined copper saucepan
9. Stainless steel steamer and pan
10. Enamelled cast iron flameproof casserole
11. Enamelled steel double boiler
12. Cast iron griddle
13. Cast iron omelette pan
14. Crêpe pan
15. Chinese bamboo steaming basket
16. Cast iron grill pan
17. Small stainless steel saucepan

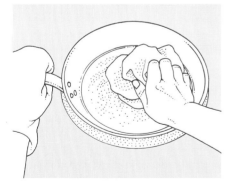

To season an omelette or crêpe pan before using the first time, thinly cover the base with oil and a thick sprinkling of sea salt then heat until the oil is very hot. Wipe clean with a very thick wad of kitchen paper, taking care not to burn your fingers. After this, the pan shouldn't be washed without seasoning again, and it shouldn't need seasoning unless some food burns on and you have to soak and lightly scour the base.

Saucepan For general cooking, choose straight-sided pans that are reasonably deep (to contain heat). For sauce-making, a slope-sided pan will allow more rapid reduction and easier stirring and whisking. Pans come in a range of sizes – ideally a set of 4 pans, from 1 litre (1¾ pints) up to 3.5 litres (6 pints) – will meet most needs. Handles should be long enough to give a safe grip away from the heat, and if they are not heat-resistant, you will need to protect your hand with an oven glove when lifting the pan. Suitable materials are heavy-gauge aluminium, stainless steel with copper or aluminium in the base and steel-lined copper.

Sauté pan Heavy and deep with a wide, flat base and straight sides, this pan is used for brisk sautéing. It needs to be made of a good heat-conductor such as, best of all, tin or stainless steel-lined copper, or stainless steel with a copper cladding on the bottom. Choose a sturdy pan with a handle that allows for a firm and relatively cool grip, so you can agitate the pan to move food around quickly. This pan is more versatile than a frying pan, doubling as a flameproof casserole when covered.

Steamer Steamers come in many shapes and sizes – round with a basket; tall and narrow with an inner perforated 'sleeve' for long vegetables such as asparagus; a double saucepan with holes in the base of the upper pan; and round stacking baskets made of bamboo. There are also expandable steaming baskets on legs that can be used in any size of pan, but these tend not to last all that long. Any large stacking steamers with 2 or more layers, such as the decorative Chinese bamboo baskets, are extremely useful as you can steam different ingredients at the same time, removing a layer when cooked.

Stockpot This large, tall pot is relatively narrow to reduce evaporation of the liquid and to encourage flavours to be extracted from the ingredients. It is usually made of stainless steel. It needs 2 sturdy handles as the pot is heavy to lift when full.

IN THE OVEN

The heat conductor in baking and roasting is, primarily, the air of the oven. This means tins and moulds used in the oven don't have to conduct heat especially well, and those made of aluminium, copper, steel, cast iron and glass are equally efficient. Yet, there are factors other than just heat conduction to consider in choosing equipment for baking and roasting.

The size of a tin for roasting can be crucial – if it is too large, the juices from the bird or joint could evaporate and even burn; too small and it is difficult to spoon the juices over the bird or joint to keep it moist. If a tin or mould is flimsy, it could buckle and warp, spilling its contents. Foods cooked in the oven are often large and heavy, and the tin or mould used will be very hot all over, so handles, a lip or a ridged side are needed to ensure a firm grip. Cooks who are not especially strong will prefer tins and moulds made from a lighter material, such as stainless steel or aluminium rather than cast iron.

Finally, bear in mind that many ovenproof dishes can be used for serving – copper, china, decorated oven-to-tableware, enamelled cast iron, glass and earthenware can all be very attractive – and this saves on washing up, too.

Baking dish Available in many shapes and sizes, baking dishes are relatively shallow and ideally have a handle or lipped rim to facilitate lifting. They should be ovenproof, and glass, earthenware and stoneware absorb heat best.

Baking sheet and tray These should be flat, rigid, not too thin (or they can warp and buckle, causing uneven cooking) and fit into your oven leaving enough space all round for heat circulation. The sides, if any, should be no higher than 1cm (½in). Those made of dark-surfaced materials will quickly absorb heat and produce crisp, well-browned pastry, biscuits and so on; those made of shiny, light materials tend to deflect heat and so are preferable for delicate pastries and meringues.

Brioche mould Usually made from shiny tinned steel that deflects some of the oven heat from the rich yeast dough being baked, these moulds are round with a distinctive flaring, fluted side. They are available in several sizes, including small ones for individual brioches. They can also do double duty as a decorative mould for puddings set with gelatine.

Bun tin These usually come as a sheet with 12 round holes or cups, which may be deep or shallow and sometimes with a decorative pattern. Use for making individual cakes, tarts, buns and American-style muffins. A similar sheet with 4 large cups is used for Yorkshire puddings. Most bun tins are made of sturdy tinned steel, and some have a non-stick finish for easy removal.

Casserole These are large, heavy pots with lids, made of good heat-absorbing and -retaining material, such as enamelled cast iron, earthenware (unglazed ones absorb heat more easily) and ovenproof porcelain (with unglazed base). The lids should fit snugly, to keep in moisture, and the pots should have sturdy handles.

Deep cake tin Rich fruit cakes that require a long baking time are best baked in these tins made of heavy tinned steel rather than lighter aluminium. (If you do have an aluminium tin, however, you can insulate the tin by wrapping it on the outside in thick brown paper.) The base may be fixed or loose, and on some loose-bottomed tins it is made from a double thickness of metal with air space in between. This helps insulate the base of rich cakes, preventing them from burning before the centre is baked.

Flan dish Also called a quiche dish, these are made of ovenproof porcelain, usually plain white, but many decorative ones are also available. The bottom of the base is unglazed so the heat is efficiently absorbed to bake the bottom of the pastry case; to intensify heat from the bottom and ensure a crisper baked base, place the dish on a preheated dark, heavy baking sheet. The classic shape is round with fluted, slightly sloping sides.

Flan ring Place this on a flat baking sheet to form a 'tin' for baking a pastry case. After baking, the ring, usually made of tinned steel with a rolled edge, is just lifted off. Only buy ones which are rigid and sturdy. Available in many sizes, these can be rectangular or round, with or without fluting inside.

Flan tin A removable base sits in a fluted or plain rim, and after baking, the flan or tart can be easily pushed up and out of the rim and then slid off the base (see below).

Gratin dish This is an extremely versatile shallow, oval or round dish, with gently sloping sides and 2 flat handles or lips; it should be flameproof as the food cooked in it is often put under the grill for browning.

Loaf tin Heavy, strong steel loaf tins keep their shape better than aluminium or non-stick finished tins. The standard sizes are 500g (1lb) or 1kg (2lb), and those with a dark finish encourage a crisp crust all round.

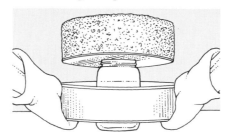

To remove a baked cake from a loose-bottomed deep cake tin, cool the cake in its tin on a wire rack according to the time specified in the recipe, until it comes away from the sides slightly. Stand the tin on a jam jar and gently push down the outer ring. Remove the cake carefully from the base and transfer to a plate. Use this method also for a flan tin with a removable base.

Pastry and biscuit cutter These are available in many shapes and sizes, either plastic or, preferably, metal. Buy ones that are sturdy with a sharp cutting edge.

Pie dish A traditional pie dish, made of earthenware or stoneware, is oval but it may also be square, round or rectangular. The best are at least 5cm (2in) deep, with a flat rim.

Pie plate This is a shallow round tin, usually made of heat-deflecting material such as stainless steel, with smooth, sloping sides and a wide rim.

Roasting tin Look for a tin about 5cm (2in) deep (higher sides discourage browning and produce a moister result), and which will fit into your oven, with at least 5cm (2in) all round so that heat can circulate evenly. The tin must be strongly made, with rigid handles or a large lip for a good grip as a roasted joint or bird can be heavy. They may be made of stainless steel, aluminium or enamelled cast iron. Some very deep tins have lids, in which food is more steamed or pot-roasted than roasted; for a crisp finish, the lid must be removed towards the end of cooking.

Sandwich cake tin Use these round, square or decoratively shaped shallow tins for baking sponge cakes; the shiny stainless steel or aluminium deflects heat so the sponge cooks evenly. Some tins have a lever for easy removal of the baked cake.

Skewers and needles Thin stainless steel skewers, 10–15 cm (4–6in) long, are used to hold boned joints of meat in shape and secure poultry openings during cooking, while longer, flatter skewers are used for kebabs. Both kinds of skewers should have sharp points. Use a trussing needle, 20–25cm (8–10in) long for chicken and 35cm (14in) long for turkey, with kitchen string to truss birds.

Soufflé dish These round, deep dishes have straight, smooth insides so the soufflé mixture rises evenly. The outside of the dish usually has a traditional 'pleated' appearance, and the base should be unglazed to encourage oven heat to penetrate and cook the bottom of the soufflé. Available in many sizes, the 1.2 litre (2 pint) dish is the most useful.

Sponge flan tin This large round tin has slightly sloping, fluted sides and a raised centre which creates a hollow for filling with fruit and cream when the baked sponge is turned out upside-down (page 266).

1. **Roasting tin**
2. **V-shaped roasting rack**
3. **Earthenware casserole**
4. **Fluted tube tin**
5. **Earthenware pie dish**
6. **Bun tin**
7. **Ramekin dishes**

8. **Baking sheet**
9. **Wire rack**
10. **Star cutter**
11. **Trussing needle and string**
12. **Fluted flan dish**
13. **Soufflé dish**
14. **Sandwich tin with lever**

15. **Baking dish**
16. **Gratin dish**
17. **Individual brioche mould**
18. **Loaf tin**
19. **Sponge flan tin**
20. **Swiss roll tin**
21. **Springform loose-bottomed tin**

22. **Loose-bottomed deep cake tin**
23. **Selection of metal skewers of various sizes**
24. **Flan rings**
25. **Individual tartlet tin with removable base**

To remove a rich cake or cheesecake from a springform tin, let the cake cool if it has been baked according to the time specified in the recipe. Run a thin palette knife between the tin and the cake, then undo the spring-clip so that the ring gently pulls away from the sides of the cake. Run the palette knife between the base of the tin and the cake, remove the base and slide the cake carefully on to a serving plate.

Springform tin Used for making delicate cakes, such as cheesecakes which can't be turned out, this tin has a loose, flat round base that fits into a deep, straight-sided ring; when the spring-clip is opened, the ring gently pulls away from the sides of cake.

Swiss roll tin This is a large, rectangular tin with sides only 2–2.5cm (¾–1in) high. As the cake traditionally made in this tin is thin and the baking time is short, the tin should be made of good heat-conducting metal such as aluminium or black steel. Only buy tins that are sturdy so they do not warp or buckle. A 35 x 27cm (14 x 10½in) tin will make a Swiss roll or savoury roulade to serve 4–6. Lining the tin with greased greaseproof paper is usually recommended so the base of the cake remains soft enough to roll (page 262).

Tube tin This is a deep, round tin with a hollow tube in the centre to conduct heat to the middle of thick cakes for even cooking; often used for baking dry cakes that will be saturated with syrup or liqueur, or sweet, rich yeast-risen cakes. They may be shallow with a curved base (for baking savarins) or with a fluted base, or deep with a decoratively etched base and sides (for baking kugelhopfs). An even deeper tube tin with a flat plain base is used for baking feather-light, American-style angel cakes.

Wire racks and grids Wire cake racks are essential for cooling cakes, biscuits and other baked goods, so buy the biggest rack you can accommodate, and check that it stands level and is sturdy enough to support a heavy cake. Wire racks for roasting meat are not essential but they hold the joint or bird above the fat in the tin. The most useful rack is V-shaped, and adjustable to hold different-sized joints.

Grilling racks, or grids, consist of 2 layers of thin wire which hold food in between. These enable delicate foods, such as whole fish, to be turned for even cooking without breaking up and are ideal for using on a barbecue.

MIXING, MASHING *and* MEASURING

Despite the advances of modern appliance technology, many tasks in the kitchen are still done by traditional means. This is particularly true in the way foods are mixed, minced and mashed. Electrical appliances such as blenders, food processors, mixers and beaters can take the hard work out of many everyday jobs, but they cannot entirely replace whisks, sieves, mashers and even the old-fashioned pestle and mortar. The traditional wire whisk, ideally in tandem with a copper bowl, incorporates more air into egg whites than an electric mixer.

All this is not to say that electrical appliances are unnecessary – the dough hook attachment on a tabletop electric mixer will knead dough perfectly, and with far less effort than doing it by hand; a blender whizzes softly cooked vegetables and stock into a cream soup in seconds; a food processor can mix biscuits, cakes, pâtés, dips and sauces in no time at all and it can uniformly chop, shred, slice and grate vegetables even faster than a professional chef. However, with a food processor, people are apt to use the slicing blade too much; most salads look and taste better if the ingredients are prepared slightly unevenly by hand. For certain things such as finely slicing cucumber a food processor is invaluable. For accurately measuring ingredients use either traditional or modern electronic scales.

Citrus juicer and squeezer Many juicers and squeezers are available. The simple, cheap and efficient juicer, usually made of glass or plastic, has a ridged dome in the centre of the dish on to which halved fruit is pressed and twisted. 'Teeth' round the dome will not always hold back pips, so it is better to choose a juicer with a strainer that fits on to the base dish.

Copper bowl Ideal for whisking egg whites because a chemical reaction between the egg and copper makes the volume of the egg white foam greater and more stable. Look for a rounded bottom and rolled edge.

Electric mixer Both small and hand-held and large tabletop versions are available. A hand-held mixer is ideal for beating mixtures over the heat on top of the stove, as well as for light mixtures such as whipping cream. Choose a mixer with several speeds for maximum control. Tabletop mixers, although more bulky, efficiently cream large quantities of cake or pudding mixtures and knead bread dough if they have a bread hook. These mixers also have many attachments available for mincing, shredding, extracting juice, and so on.

Food mill This hand-cranked rotary food mill comes with a selection of discs for producing coarse to fine purées allowing you to control the texture more than with a food processor. Pips, fibres and other unwanted material are sieved out. Hooks on the rim hold it securely over a pan or bowl.

Food processor Most models come with a very sharp double-bladed knife for chopping, puréeing and mincing, with extra discs for slicing, grating and shredding. An optional plastic blade kneads dough, and there are optional juice extractors and coffee grinders. Ideally it should have rubber footpads to keep it in place while running.

Garlic press A sturdy press crushes garlic cloves and forces the flesh and juice of garlic through the holes. If the holes are too small the press can be fiddly to clean.

Kitchen scale These may be the traditional balance scales, uncomplicated and precise but space-consuming; spring-balance scales, more suited to lighter loads but not good at weighing less than 25g (1oz); or beam scales, which are very accurate but again can be space-consuming. Be sure the scales show both metric and imperial calibrations.

Masher The simplest and cheapest masher for potatoes and other root vegetables has a sturdy, meshed metal disc on the end of a long handle. For a smoother result, use a ricer that forces the vegetable through the mesh or cutting grid.

Measuring jug Clear toughened glass such as Pyrex is best because the level of the ingredient being measured is easily seen, and the glass is not affected by boiling liquid. Be sure both metric and imperial calibrations are given on the side.

Measuring spoon Metric spoons give accurate measures of small quantities of dry and liquid ingredients; they are available in inexpensive sets comprising 1.25ml (¼tsp), 2.5ml (½tsp), 5ml (1tsp) and 15ml (1tbsp).

Meat mallet Usually made of wood, most meat mallets have both smooth and spiked sides; the smooth surface is used to flatten pieces of meat, such as veal escalopes or pure tenderloin, for quick cooking; the spiked side breaks down fibres and thus tenderizes tough cuts of meat. It can also be used to crush whole spices such as cinnamon and star anise roughly for use in marinades.

Mincer An old-fashioned manually operated mincer with screw clamps to hold it securely on the worktop is always useful, especially if it has a selection of discs – coarse, medium and fine. Be sure it can be dismantled for thorough cleaning.

Mixing bowl Traditional bowls are heavy glazed porcelain, earthenware or stoneware, but more modern bowls are made of heatproof glass or stainless steel. Stainless steel is easy to clean, will not interact with any food like aluminium does, won't chip, shatter or melt, and cools and heats more quickly than ceramic, glass or plastic. Whatever kind of bowls you prefer, however, choose ones with rounded rather than straight sides so that a whisk or spoon will work efficiently, be sure they have flat bases so that they sit securely on the worktop. Several bowls in graduated sizes will prove invaluable, and if they stack, they'll store easily.

Pastry scraper Shaped like a decorator's scraper or a rectangle and sometimes with a handle along one side, this should be made of thin, stainless or carbon steel or plastic. Use for mixing and cutting pastry and bread doughs, for turning and lifting rolled-out pastry, for handling hot mixtures when making sweets, for scraping the worktop clean, and for folding in light mixtures.

Pestle and mortar A deep, curved bowl on a sturdy base and compatibly shaped pestle are used for grinding tiny, hard seeds, such as cumin and fennel, as well as garlic, anchovies and nuts. They can be made of white vitrified porcelain, heavyweight ceramic, tough unglazed porcelain, stone, wood, glass or marble. The end of the pestle and the inside bottom surface of the bowl should both be slightly rough for maximum friction.

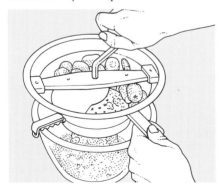

To use a food mill fit the appropriate disc for the desired texture and place the mill securely over a pan or bowl. A hand-operated crank forces food through the sieving disc into the bowl.

Use a sturdy pestle and mortar to grind whole spices, or for the traditional method of making mayonnaise or pesto sauce. Work the pestle round and round against the sides and base of the mortar.

1. Nylon sieve
2. Kitchen scales
3. Glass mixing bowl
4. Citrus juicer
5. Wooden citrus juicer
6. Stainless steel mixing bowl
7. Food processor
8. Copper bowl
9. Pestle and mortar
10. Conical metal sieve
11. Hand-held electric mixer
12. Masher
13. Meat mallet
14. Wooden vegetable masher
15. Utensil container
16. Mixing bowl
17. Glazed porcelain pudding
    basin
18. Pastry scraper
19. Tea strainer or mini-sieve
20. Fine conical strainer
21. Wire strainer
22. Mincer
23. Measuring jug
24. Food mill
25. Pudding basin
26. Measuring cups
27. Roasting thermometer
28. Oven thermometer
29. Small whisk for sauces
30. Flat whisk for batters
31. Balloon whisk
32. Adjustable balloon whisk
33. Garlic press

Pudding basin Used primarily for cooking boiled and steamed puddings, these distinctive thick basins with sloping sides are made from earthenware or glazed porcelain. They must have a sturdy, flat base and a lip under the rim for securing a tied-on cover. A basin is also useful as a mixing bowl, as a top of a double boiler, as a cold pudding mould and so on. I find that pudding basins have so many uses that I never seem to have enough of them.

Sieve These can be bowl-shaped, conical or flat-bottomed, with a fine to coarse mesh or holes, according to use. Fine bowl-shaped and very pointed conical sieves (also called chinois) made from tinned wire, stainless steel or nylon (best for fruit and other foods that could be discoloured by metal) are used for sifting, straining and gentle puréeing. For puréeing coarser mixtures, use a heavy conical stainless steel sieve with a less pointed bottom

or strongly woven fine-mesh chinois and press food through with a narrow conical pestle. Chinois sieves are also used for straining fine sauces, custards, stocks and gravy. A sturdy wooden drum-shaped sieve or tamis has a fine nylon mesh for puréeing fibrous or seed-filled fruits. Wash all sieves by soaking in hot water first to dislodge particles of food and then rub with a washing-up brush on both sides.

Thermometer These are essential for safe storage and preparation of food. Appliance thermometers for use in freezers, refrigerators and ovens check that correct temperatures are achieved and maintained; sugar and deep-frying thermometers measure the temperature of sugar syrup, a preserve or oil to be sure the required stage is reached and maintained; a meat thermometer, inserted into a large roasting joint or bird, registers the internal temperature so you can tell when the food has

been cooked through (page 159); a rapid-response thermometer gives instant reading of the temperature of food cooked in a microwave oven (page 311), and is a good investment if you do a lot of microwaving.

Whisk These come in many different sizes and shapes for different functions: a large, springy balloon-shaped whisk with 10–12 thin wires looping over each other, is used for whisking egg whites and is ideal for use with a copper bowl; a smaller, longer and relatively stiff whisk with only about 8 thicker wires is used for mixing and stirring a roux-based sauce; a flat whisk with only a few wires is used for beating batters. Wires may be made of tinned steel or stainless steel, and the handles of metal or wood. Choose whisks that won't rust and ones with wires soldered into handles because they will not pop out and are easier to clean.

SPECIALIST EQUIPMENT

Once you have assembled the foundation of your kitchen equipment – good-quality pans, knives and so on – it may then be time to consider speciality tools that could make your style of cooking more efficient and at the same time artistic.

The utensils and appliances here are not essential in everyone's kitchen, but they may be useful in yours. It all depends on what you like to cook – if you make pasta often, for example, it may be worth investing in a pasta machine; if you like to serve moulded puddings and savoury jellies, you might want to have some pretty moulds; pastry makers will value a marble board and lots of individual tins in different shapes; a Chinese wok is indispensable for anyone who likes the quick cooking style of stir-frying.

Many of the tools here do not involve spending a lot of money. A cheap salad spinner, for example, efficiently and quickly dries salad leaves and other leafy vegetables. The cost of a zester, a canelle knife or a ball cutter is almost negligible, but they add a flair to food presentation.

Canelle knife This is a rounded stainless steel blade with a little V-shaped tooth in a horizontal hole on the side. Use it to peel single decorative strips about 5mm (¼in) wide from citrus fruits and to cut grooves in fruit and vegetables such as cucumbers . When the vegetables are then cut across, the slices have notched edges like flower petals.

Charlotte mould This plain, slope-sided mould has 2 small handles to facilitate unmoulding, and may be made of copper, aluminium or tin-lined steel. Puddings prepared in this mould are called charlottes (charlotte russe, for example, consists of Bavarian cream surrounded by sponge fingers and apple charlotte has an apple filling in a bread case) but the mould is also useful for savoury mousses, jellies and so on.

Cheese slicer In my experience a simple cheese wire is useful for cutting close-textured cheeses like Gruyère or Emmental into really thin slices. The other option is a hand-held cheese slicer with either a rolling-action cutting wire or a slot in the blade.

Chinese wok Designed for stir-frying, woks are shallow, curved and often with a long handle. Long-handled woks are better to use, as you can then give the food a good toss without the fat spitting too much. The distribution of heat is important, so choose a wok made of rolled steel or iron rather than thin stainless steel or aluminium.

Citrus zester This is a stainless steel blade with 5 little holes in a line along the downward-curving end. Use to peel fine wisps of citrus skin or rind without taking off any of the bitter white pith.

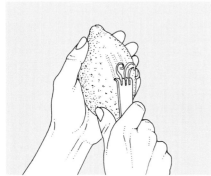

Use a citrus zester to remove thin, delicate strips of rind that are ideal for flavouring or garnishing foods. Draw the sharp side down the skin.

Couscoussière Used to cook couscous (page 110), the North African grain dish, this is a covered pot with perforations on the base that sits snugly on top of a round, deep pot. The semolina grains or couscous are steamed in the upper pot over an aromatic stock or a meat and vegetable stew in the lower pot. It may be made of earthenware, copper or aluminium, and is also useful for steaming rice, vegetables and fish.

Decorative moulds These can transform even the most basic pudding or jellied dish into an ornamental centrepiece. Moulds come in all shapes and designs and are made of many materials: expensive tin-lined copper (handsome enough to be displayed in the kitchen), porcelain, durable stainless steel (suitable for both hot and chilled preparations), earthenware, aluminium (may discolour), tin (may rust), glass (can be fragile), tinned steel and hard plastic. Moulds for cooked dishes must be ovenproof; for chilled dishes, the moulds are best made of thin metal which gets cold quickly and then warms again quickly to unmould easily. Be sure moulds are seamless or they might leak, and that the design has shallow indentations or the food will be difficult to turn out without some sticking to the mould.

Ice cream scoop A sturdy cast aluminium scoop is best for solidly frozen ice cream because of a chemical sealed inside the handle that absorbs hand heat, softening the ice cream as you scrape.

Individual moulds and tins Many moulds for individual portions are available, such as the heart-shaped porcelain *coeur à la crème* mould with draining holes in the base to make a sweetened cream cheese pudding; ramekins, like very small soufflé dishes, sometimes oval, used for baked eggs, crème brûlée and so on; little porcelain or ceramic pots with lids for baked custard; metal timbale, dariole or castle pudding moulds with tall and sloped sides for crème caramel, small sponge puddings, vegetable purées and so on; shallow, oval metal moulds for eggs in aspic; metal rings for rum babas; and small loaf tins. Tins for individual pastries may be round and shallow (for tartlets or flans), round and deep (for pies), boat-shaped (plain or fluted) or conical (for cream horns). Small cake tins come in many shapes and sizes from tiny hearts, ovals and diamonds, to scallop-shaped madeleines.

Jelly bag A strongly made flannel or felt bag with hanging loops or tapes will strain clear juice from the pulp of cooked or raw fruit, which is then used to make jelly (page 301) or wine; the finer the weave of the cloth, the clearer the juices will be. The loops or tapes are used to attach the bag to either a special plastic stand, a broom handle between two chairs or the legs of an upturned chair or stool, so the bag can be suspended over a bowl which catches the juice as it drips through the bag.

Melon baller Also called a parisienne cutter or melon scoop, this has small bowl-shaped cutters at each end, one larger than the other. Use to cut balls of fruit such as melons and vegetables such as carrots and potatoes, using a rotating movement.

Paella pan This large round pan is usually less than 5cm (2in) deep with sloping sides and a handle on each side. It may be made of steel, aluminium or, more traditionally, cast iron. Designed for cooking and serving the Spanish dish of the same name that consists of saffron rice with a variety of vegetables, meat and seafood. I also use mine for making large flat omelettes to feed crowds (page 73).

Pasta machine Adjustable rollers (ideally made of rust-resistant stainless steel) knead and roll dough, and cutters produce the desired width of noodles. Some are operated with a hand-turned crank, while others are electrically powered. Be sure hand-operated machines can be fixed securely to the worktop, for example with a clamp.

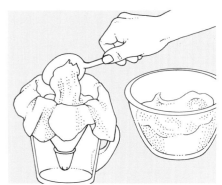

A clean and easy way to fill a piping bag is by putting it, with a nozzle already inserted, point down in a tall jug or jar and rolling the end of the bag over the rim. Then spoon in the mixture. It can be messy filling the bag holding it in your hand.

1. *Single-handled wok*
2. *Collapsible wire salad spinner*
3. *Pressure cooker*
4. *Couscoussière*
5. *Copper preserving pan*
6. *Jelly bag*
7. *Hand-operated pasta maker*
8. *Cast iron paella pan*
9. *Aluminium charlotte mould*
10. *Decorative copper mould*
11. *Individual bread tin*
12. *Dariole mould*
13. *Melon baller*
14. *Canelle knife*
15. *Citrus zester*
16. *Boat-shaped pastry mould*
17. *Ice cream scoop*
18. *Cheese slice*
19. *Individual tartlet tin*
20. *Earthenware terrine*
21. *Raised game pie mould*
22. *Ceramic heart-shaped mould*
23. *Piping nozzles*
24. *Piping bag*

Piping bag and nozzles Available in varying sizes, these cone-shaped bags should be sturdily made with double-stitched seams and hemmed ends. A flexible, tightly woven cotton or nylon bag will last longer than a plastic one. A set of nozzles, or tubes, with openings in several sizes and shapes, gives great scope for decorating cakes and puddings, piping fillings on to canapés and into pastries. A coupler enables you to change the nozzle without having to empty the bag first.

Preserving pan Buy a deep one so hot mixtures do not bubble over, and one wide enough to allow maximum evaporation. A heavy base prevents the mixture from burning and sticking, and 2 strong handles or a bucket-type handle are essential. They are usually made of heavy-gauge aluminium or lined copper.

Pressure cooker This is a heavy pan with a tightly fitting lid that has a pressure valve that works by trapping steam from boiling water,

raising the pressure and temperature. Food cooks much faster than with conventional steaming, stewing or boiling while using up relatively little energy. A pressure cooker is particularly useful for cooking dried pulses quickly without the need for presoaking, and for steamed puddings.

Raised pie mould This is a large oval or rectangular tinned steel mould used for baking game pies and pâtés encased in pastry. The sides of the patterned or plain mould are held together over the base by small clips; the clips and sides are removed after baking. This is expensive but pies baked in one of these moulds do look attractive.

Rice boiler This is a perforated aluminium ball that is suspended in boiling water, making boiled rice easy to drain. I like to line mine with foil and use it for steaming my round Christmas pudding (page 219).

Salad spinner This may be a simple wire basket that is shaken (outdoors) to remove excess water from salad leaves, or a plastic

basket inside a covered bowl that spins like a top, using centrifugal force to expel the water. Plastic spinners are bulky, whereas wire baskets can usually be collapsed flat for more convenient storage, but plastic spinners require much less effort to use.

Terrine This is a heavy ovenproof dish, traditionally with a long rectangular shape but it may also be oval, round or square and is used for cooking pâtés, hence the name 'terrine' for baked pâtés. The slightly domed lid should have a tiny steam hole to prevent the pâté from becoming soggy. As well as ovenproof porcelain or earthenware, this dish may also be made of enamelled cast iron.

Waffle iron The hand-held version with long handles can be used on gas or an electric hob, and may produce traditionally heart-shaped waffles. Easier and more foolproof to use is the electric waffle iron, with non-stick grill plates. Some electric waffle irons have reversible plates so they can double as sandwich toasters.

STOCKS and SOUPS

Stocks are the basis of much good cooking – thus the French word for stock, *fond*, which means foundation, is very apt. Soups, sauces, gravies and stews are all greatly enhanced if they are made with a good homemade stock. Still, I would never discourage someone from making a soup if they only had a stock cube as there are all sorts of additions such as lemon juice, wine and sherry which can transform the flavour. Nor do I feel, as we are told by chefs, that stocks must always be made with fresh main ingredients not previously cooked – these stocks may be supreme but a stock is the obvious thing to make from carcases and leftover trimmings, and a very good flavour can still be extracted from cooked bones and meat if they have not been overcooked.

Nevertheless, it is worth getting into the habit of making a stock from fresh ingredients. There is something very satisfying about it, rather like bread-making, and it is a simple procedure. The best stocks are made from gelatinous parts of the animal such as pigs' feet, oxtails and general bones and carcases. Sweet root vegetables give flavour to a stock and onion is almost compulsory.

If you make a large amount of stock you can freeze it to use as needed (page 312). Stocks can also be reduced to an intensely flavoured glaze which you can freeze in small pots, and then use in sauces or stews to give depth of flavour. If you plan to make a clear soup or aspic, it is nice to colour the stock with ingredients such as beetroot, tomatoes, spinach or even carrots, which will give a warm glow. In fact, I find reduction the most useful way of keeping stocks, as they take up much less room in the freezer and so often it is the concentrated flavour, not a lot of extra liquid that you really need. If

possible do not use an aluminium pan when making stock as the pan can affect the taste and colour.

Soup has been a basic food almost all over the world for as long as what we eat has been recorded. Every culture has a long tradition of soups, and in some countries, such as Portugal, it is still unusual not to have soup every day. The homely French *potage* is a major part of everyday meals in rural France, and thin, aromatic soups are also part of everyday meals in China and the Far East. Britain, however, does not have such a good soup history: the uninspired Brown Windsor is an example of this.

Soups range from the most delicate, clean variety to the thick main course soups which are almost like a stew. They can be smooth and creamy, thin and clear, thick with vegetable purées or full of chopped ingredients – the unifying factor is that soups are eaten with a spoon.

Homemade soup has no parallel and people tend to forget how simple it is to make, and how nutritious it is, too: a robust soup full of gently cooked vegetables and served with wholemeal bread can be a complete, healthy, balanced meal. I find this kind of soup invaluable for holiday lunches.

A good soup is always welcome; it is one of the ultimate comfort foods – when you are cold, hungry or simply depressed, or when you have eaten too much at the previous meal or are feeling tired or simply want a bowl of homely, soothing nourishment. Quite another thing is the first course soup; chilled or hot, with the purpose of being a tantalizing appetizer; this can be a fine vegetable purée with cream, or a crystal clear soup made from clarified stock with a few crisp ingredients or chopped fresh herbs.

Clockwise from top: Fish Bisque (page 39) a modern version of this traditional creamy soup, flavoured with kipper fillets and spices, contains large prawns and red pepper rings; Shallot and Mustard Soup with Tarragon (page 38) is a puréed cream soup that makes an unusual start to any meal; Chicken Soup with Smoked Oysters (page 38) is a hearty mixture with mushrooms, red pepper and chopped chives for extra flavour; Clear Vegetable Soup with Quails' Eggs (page 39) has an aromatic stock with delicate eggs and fine lettuce shreds added at the last moment; Indian Summer Soup (page 38) combines aubergine and tomatoes in a spiced stock flavoured with creamy coconut.

MEAT, POULTRY *and* GAME STOCKS

There are two basic kinds of meat stock – white and brown. Although raw meat and poultry make the best stock of all, you can, of course, use leftover carcases and bones. In a white stock, like poultry stock, the ingredients are simply brought to the boil and then simmered slowly, but in a brown stock, like beef stock, the bones are first browned in a hot oven. It is important in all meat stocks to include bones for real depth of flavour, and a stock can be made very well with only raw meatless bones.

Boiling tends to make the stock cloudy so lower the heat to a very gentle simmer after it has boiled once. Skimming the stock from time to time while it cooks will also help to reduce cloudiness. If you have little time you can make stock quickly, in about 20 minutes, in a pressure cooker but the result will be cloudy and it cannot be used for clear soups, though it is fine for thick soups.

Richly flavoured homemade stocks are also the essential ingredient of sparkling consommés (page 32). These soups are simply stocks that have been clarified with egg shells and whites, then strained through muslin.

BONES FOR STOCK-MAKING
Bones contain collagen which dissolves during cooking to form gelatine. The best bones to use for stocks are the most gelatinous – beef shin, oxtail, veal and ham bones, knuckle bones and poultry and game carcases. You should always break up carcases or saw bones so all the collagen is extracted during cooking.

MAKING MEAT STOCK

White meat stocks are not really white but, in fact, paler in colour and with a different character to brown stocks. Veal is the best meat to use for white stock, though it is possible to use pork as such lean pigs are bred today.

1 *Put cut-up bones and other flavouring ingredients into a large stockpot or saucepan with water to cover. Season lightly with salt, especially if using uncooked bones.*

2 *Bring to the boil. Skim off the scum that rises to the surface with a large spoon. Simmer, covered, adding a little water from time to time, if necessary.*

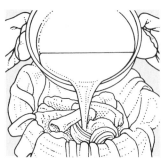

3 *Continue to add cold water and skim the stock until no more scum rises, then simmer gently for 2–3 hours. Strain the stock through a colander lined with damp muslin. Check the seasoning unless you are going to reduce down (opposite).*

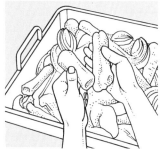

To make brown stock, *brown the bones and onion skins in a pan in a hot oven, 220°C, 425°F, Gas Mark 7, then boil to produce a rich, dark-coloured stock. Unpeeled onions add extra colour. Beef bones are particularly good.*

STOCK VARIATIONS

• Classic flavourings for meat, poultry and game stocks are onions (unskinned for brown stock), carrots and celery. I also use many other root vegetables such as parsnips, turnips and celeriac. Do not use potatoes if you want a clear stock. If making a very pale stock remember that carrots contribute quite a lot of colour.

• Bulb fennel which is past cooking as a vegetable still adds an excellent flavour to stock.

• I add peeled and sliced garlic at the beginning of cooking for a mild sweet flavour, or just before the end for a strong garlicky taste.

• For a richly coloured and flavoured stock add slightly overripe tomatoes or some tomato purée. I sometimes add sweet red peppers, too, for extra flavour.

• Herbs should be as fresh as possible and tied into a bunch or added as a bouquet garni in a muslin bag (page 10).

• Sage, which grows profusely and for which it can be difficult to find enough uses, is surprisingly good in beef stock if used sparingly.

• Spices are not a standard addition to stocks but peppercorns, whole cloves, blades of mace, cinnamon sticks, slices of fresh root ginger, star anise and caraway, coriander and cumin seeds can be used to add extra character.

• Cinnamon sticks, tarragon leaves and sliced but unpeeled fresh root ginger perk up a chicken stock.

• Sliced fresh root ginger is also a good addition to beef stock.

• Try adding crushed juniper berries, whole allspice and bay leaves when you are making game stock.

• Salt should only be used sparingly at the beginning of cooking to draw out the flavours of the ingredients. Rather than salting stock at the end of cooking wait until you have incorporated it with the other ingredients in the final dish. Any stock that is going to be reduced as a sauce should not be salted until after reducing because reduction intensifies the flavours and the stock can end up tasting salty.

• Use whole peppercorns in stocks: ground pepper cooked for a long time can give an acrid taste.

• Since you may often want to serve just the boned breasts of pigeon, use the carcases to produce a wonderful game stock with good flavour.

• It is also possible to make stocks in the microwave (page 311): put all the ingredients in a deep bowl, cover loosely and cook on High (100%) until boiling, then cook on Defrost (30%) for 45–60 minutes. (Check your user's manual for specific instructions.)

REDUCING STOCK

Stock that has been reduced by gentle boiling adds a rich flavour to soups and sauces. You can reduce the stock to varying intensities of flavour, and finally all the way down to a rich meat glaze which will set as a solid jelly. Keep reduced stock in the refrigerator for up to one week, after which it should be boiled again to prevent spoiling. Add a little meat glaze to sauces when they finish cooking for a really rich taste and shiny finish.

1 *Put the strained stock in a saucepan and boil gently, skimming the surface as necessary, until reduced by half.*

2 *To make a rich, glossy meat glaze continue reducing the stock until it is thick enough to coat a spoon. Chill until set.*

DEGREASING STOCK

Stock is degreased so it does not add fat to other ingredients, and to make the pure clear liquid essential for making consommé (page 32). For best results stock should be completely cold before degreasing but you can still remove excessive fat from warm stock.

Allow the strained stock *to become completely cold, then chill it until the fat sets in a hard layer on the surface. Use a large metal spoon or palette knife to lift off the solidified fat carefully and discard it.*

If the stock is still warm *spoon off as much grease as possible from the surface using a shallow ladle or large tablespoon, then use several thicknesses of kitchen paper to mop up the remaining grease on the surface.*

POULTRY OR GAME STOCK

Ideally use raw bones, with or without meat and giblets, excluding the liver. Alternatively, use leftover carcases. You can use bones from fattier types of poultry such as duck but avoid using the skin and any fat.

Break up the bones or carcases and put them in a large pan with chopped onions – unpeeled for a richer-coloured stock – carrots, celery and leeks. Game carcases also make a dark stock. Add a bunch of fresh herbs – rosemary and tarragon are very good in poultry and game stocks – and some whole peppercorns. Pour on water to cover, then bring slowly to the boil, skimming until there is no more scum.

Reduce the heat and continue simmering, covered, for about 3 hours, skimming occasionally, if necessary. Strain and cool, then refrigerate the stock until the fat sets in a solid layer, then degrease (above).

Bubbling poultry stock ingredients – bones, leeks, carrots, onions, onion skins, black peppercorns and fresh herbs in a bouquet garni. Adding salt at the start of cooking draws out the flavours.

FISH *and* VEGETABLE STOCKS

Fish and vegetable stocks are more delicate than meat, poultry and game stocks. Fish stock, in particular, should not be cooked for more than 25 minutes – simmering for even a little too long can make it unacceptably bitter, and if allowed to reduce too much the gelatinous fish bones will turn the stock into an inedible glue. If you want to reduce the cooked stock slightly you must strain the liquid before boiling down further.

Gelatinous white fish, especially flat fish, make the best stock – plaice, sole, turbot, brill, cod, John Dory, whiting, hake and haddock are all suitable. Include as many thoroughly cleaned heads, tails and bones of filleted white fish as you can get from the fishmonger. For a smoky flavoured stock use some smoked haddock. Salmon heads and tails are also good. Do not, however, use trimmings from oily fish such as mackerel, sardines or herring because you will just be adding excess oiliness and too strong a flavour. Prawn and lobster heads and shells and crab shells are wonderful as they contribute a delicious sweet flavour and a pretty colour, too.

As fish stock tends to be rather grey looking you can add colour by using onion skins as well as chopped onions and shallots to add flavour. Use carrots for colour along with a little sweetness which I think is necessary in a good fish stock – you can even add a teaspoon or two of sugar. I often add tomatoes for flavour and colour, and occasionally a dash of fresh orange juice. White wine or dry cider is something I also often include – as much of it as I can spare – and either a couple of tablespoons of lemon juice or a tablespoon of white wine vinegar. A little spice can be good, too: try coriander seed, one or two crushed cardamom pods or a blade of mace. Use whole black peppercorns, not ground pepper, and include a generous bundle of fresh herbs, with some dill and fennel, if you like. Do not use dried herbs.

COURT BOUILLON AND FUMET

A court bouillon is used for poaching delicate ingredients such as fish, shellfish and chicken. Usually prepared and cooled before using for poaching, court bouillon is made by boiling vegetables with water and wine or wine vinegar – normally white wine though red may be used – or lemon juice. A reduced fish stock is also known by its French name, *fumet*, and makes a richer poaching liquid.

VEGETABLE STOCKS

Now that more people are vegetarian vegetable stocks are gaining in popularity, and they can be useful for all sorts of vegetable soups and sauces. Almost any fresh vegetables can be used: cabbage, leeks and spinach produce a green-coloured stock; parsnips, carrots and celeriac all add a rounded taste; tomatoes, red pepper, onions and garlic make a rosy Mediterranean-flavoured stock, and chopped raw beetroot cooked with onions results in a beautiful scarlet stock which can be used as a clear broth or to make pink soups and sauces.

I nearly always add a little lemon juice or a tablespoon or two of sherry or cider vinegar to vegetable stocks, and caraway seed is an excellent spice for stocks made from root vegetables. The vegetables must be boiled until nearly mushy, then thrown away as all their goodness will have seeped into the water during the cooking.

VEGETABLE STOCK

Chop but don't peel about 750g (1½lb) mixed washed vegetables. Put the vegetables in a pan with 10 black peppercorns, 4 tablespoons lemon juice, 1.2 litres (2 pints) water and a little salt. Bring to the boil, skimming the surface with a large metal spoon, if necessary. Reduce the heat and simmer gently, covered, for 30–45 minutes. Strain through a fine sieve and discard the vegetables. Makes about 900ml (1½ pints) stock. This can be stored for up to 2 days in the refrigerator.

A selection of vegetables and flavourings for vegetable stock.

FISH STOCK

For every 1kg (2lb) of fish trimmings use about 1 litre (1¾ pints) water and 300ml (½ pint) white wine and include a carrot and an onion, both chopped roughly, a generous bundle of fresh herbs (parsley and bay leaf, and fennel is particularly good, too), 2–3 tablespoons of lemon juice, 2 teaspoons caster sugar and 10–12 black peppercorns. Do not use any trimmings from oily fish. Makes about 1.2 litres (2 pints).

1 *Place all the fish trimmings in a large stockpot or saucepan with the chopped carrot, onion, bundle of herbs, lemon juice, sugar and black peppercorns.*

2 *Add the water and wine to the pan, bring to the boil, then simmer gently for 20–25 minutes, skimming the surface as necessary with a large spoon.*

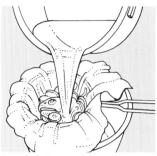

3 *Strain the stock through a sieve lined with damp muslin. Use the stock at once or cool and then chill. Keep for up to 2 days in the refrigerator in a covered container.*

USING FISH AND VEGETABLE STOCKS

• Fish stock is used primarily as the base for fish soups. Use it either in the Mediterranean style as a thin liquid in which a variety of fish and shellfish are briefly cooked before serving, or thicken the stock with a little flour and plenty of cream to make a rich, smooth bisque.

• It is best to use clear, well-coloured fish stock for clear soups. For a really clear broth I like to strain the stock a second time through a clean piece of fine muslin.

• To turn fish stock into a soup, add breadcrumbs, rice or puréed cooked vegetables – try potatoes, sweet potatoes, peppers and courgettes.

• Add reduced fish stock to double cream and bubble for a minute or two to make a delicious almost instant sauce to serve with poached or steamed fish (page 130).

• Strained fish stock can be made into aspic (page 33) in which to set prawns, other pieces of fish and fresh herbs. I serve this in the summer as a pretty first course.

• I make wonderful quick stews by briefly simmering slivers of vegetables and filleted fish or shellfish in well-flavoured thickened fish stock. Cook lightly for 5–8 minutes before adding a handful of fresh herbs such as dill or coriander leaves.

• Use thin or thick vegetable stock to make a variety of soups and sauces. It is also the perfect liquid in which to cook either vegetables, chicken or light meat for stews and casseroles.

• All sorts of puréed vegetables (page 53) and pulses (page 113) can be used to thicken vegetable stock – for example, puréed cauliflower is creamy and light, while a purée of cooked, dried haricot beans is a more substantial thickener. For extra smoothness I rub the purée through a sieve using a wooden spoon.

• Unthickened vegetable stock is ideal for minestrone-type soups with thickly sliced vegetables and pasta shapes lightly cooked in the liquid.

• Little pasta shapes and thin noodles can also transform a good vegetable stock into a hearty soup. Sprinkle over some freshly grated Parmesan cheese just before serving, if you like.

• To make simple and flavourful sauces, reduce the stock to intensify the flavour, then thicken with cream, a little cornflour (page 199) or a fine vegetable purée (page 53).

• Arrowroot is the thickener which produces the most glossy, translucent effect (page 199).

• Strained vegetable stocks, especially ones with a good colour, can be used to make an aspic (page 33) in which to set eggs, herbs and vegetables. Clear beetroot stock makes the most stunning aspic of all – a ruby-red mould in which you can set a feathery pattern of fresh green herbs.

Saffron, paprika and fresh herbs add colours and flavours to Mussel, Salmon and Scallop Soup (page 39), a luxurious soup for occasions when you want to really impress.

CLEAR SOUPS *and* ASPICS

Clear soups are both beautiful and appetizing. They are also versatile as many different ingredients can be added to poach gently in the liquid– for example, thinly sliced vegetables, slivers of fish, prawns or baby scallops .

Clear soups are made like stocks but with a lower proportion of water to other ingredients. They can be made from any kind of meat or vegetables except for starchy vegetables which cause cloudiness. Many Chinese soups, like the recipe opposite, are good examples of well-flavoured clear soups made with a variety of ingredients. Straining the stock through a sieve lined with muslin or a clean tea towel usually clears it enough but if you want a really shiny clear soup you can clarify it as for consommé by using egg shells and whites (below).

CONSOMMÉ
Real consommé is a rich clear veal, beef or chicken stock made by cooking flavouring ingredients in a thoroughly degreased stock. The consommé will sparkle even more served chilled and jellied: if the original stock has not been made with plenty of gelatinous bones you can add a little gelatine – about 1 sachet for 1.2 litres (2 pints) liquid – during the clarification process to make sure it will turn to a good jelly. Chilled consommé is good either plain, sprinkled with herbs or with a dribble of soured cream.

ASPIC
Homemade aspic, made from concentrated, rich stock, is something of a labour of love but in terms of flavour it is well worth the effort for a special buffet or party dish. Coat cold cooked chicken, salmon or lamb chops by placing them on a wire rack and slowly spooning over a layer of aspic. Allow to set and arrange a garnish on top. Give it a second coat if required. Moulded savoury dishes for turning out look pretty if you arrange fresh herbs between two thin layers of aspic in the base of the mould.

BEEF CONSOMMÉ

To make crystal-clear consommé the stock should be clarified with egg whites and shells: these trap in a scum particles which might otherwise cloud the stock. Egg whites also remove flavour so more must be added in the form of fresh meat and vegetables – use 1 small onion, 1 carrot and 1 stick of celery, all chopped finely, plus 250g (8oz) very lean minced beef to every 1.8 litres (3 pints) cold beef stock.

1 *Put the thoroughly degreased stock (page 28) in a very clean saucepan with the meat, vegetables and some salt and black peppercorns.*

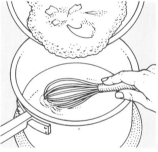

2 *Add the lightly whisked whites and crushed shells of 2 eggs to the pan, then slowly bring to the boil, whisking constantly. A scummy froth will form.*

3 *Stop whisking when the froth is quite firm and covers the top of the pan. Allow the soup to boil through the crust on a medium boil for 20 minutes.*

A well-chilled jellied beef consommé finely chopped for serving.

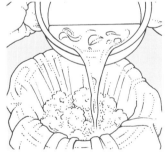

4 *Line a colander with a double layer of clean wet muslin and set it over a large bowl. You can also use a jelly bag. Lift the crust into the centre of the colander using a large perforated skimming spoon, then slowly pour the soup through it into the bowl.*

5 *If the consommé is not absolutely clear, you can pour it through the crust again in to a clean bowl. Stir in 1 or 2 spoonfuls of sherry or Madeira and some finely chopped herbs. Serve hot or chilled. If chilled, lightly chop the consommé.*

CHINESE-STYLE CLEAR SOUP

The Chinese are great soup drinkers. Their soups are light and clear but always full of flavour and visually very attractive. The variations are endless, as almost any fresh, good-quality vegetables can be used, along with meat, noodles or a combination of both. An essential start, however, is a good stock made with fresh chicken.

To make soup for 8 you will need a 1.5kg (3lb) chicken (if the giblets are provided do not use the liver) and 375g (12oz) pork sparerib bones.

Before cooking assemble 6 sliced spring onions, 1 sliced carrot, 2 tablespoons chopped fresh root ginger and 1 stick celery, chopped.

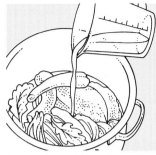

1 *Begin by making a simple flavourful chicken stock. Put the chicken and giblets, if using, into a large stockpot or saucepan with the pork sparerib bones, half the spring onions, the carrot, ginger, celery and a few crushed fresh parsley or coriander stalks. Stir in 2 tablespoons light soy sauce, 150ml (¼ pint) white wine and 2.4 litres (4 pints) cold water. Season to taste.*

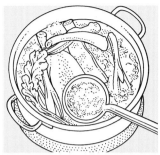

2 *Bring to the boil slowly, skimming the surface as necessary. Reduce the heat, cover and simmer for 1 hour. Strain the flavourings out of the stock, then chill and remove any fat from the surface (page 29). Using a knife or cleaver, shred the chicken breast meat finely and reserve; use the remaining chicken meat in salads or sandwiches. Return the stock to a clean pan.*

3 *Boil the stock, uncovered, for 10 minutes, add remaining spring onions, shredded chicken, 125g (4oz) sliced oyster or shiitake mushrooms, 125g (4oz) broccoli florets and 2 tablespoons dry sherry. Simmer for 5 minutes, then add 25g (1oz) cooked or instant rice noodles, 1 teaspoon sesame oil, 1 teaspoon sugar and 2 tablespoons light soy sauce. Cook for 1 minute more.*

MAKING ASPIC

To make aspic from meat stock follow the instructions for consommé (opposite) but use minced veal or chicken instead of beef as a light-coloured aspic is more useful. For fish aspic, make a good fish stock (page 31) and clarify with egg shells and whites (opposite). Gelatine is needed to make aspic – 1 sachet should be enough to set 1.2 litres (2 pints) consommé, but you may need to use a little more, particularly in hot weather. If making aspic from ordinary meat stock, not consommé, or vegetable or fish stock you will need about twice as much gelatine (1 sachet will set 600ml/1pint.)

Sprinkle the gelatine over a few tablespoons of cold water in a small pan. Leave until spongy, then dissolve over a very gentle heat; do not boil.

Meanwhile, heat the consommé to boiling. When the gelatine liquid is clear stir it gently into the consommé. Cool, then chill until just on the point of setting when it is ready to use.

A flavoursome chicken stock is the basis of this Chinese-style clear soup with a selection of lightly cooked vegetables and noodles. Light soy sauce also adds an authentic oriental taste.

FLAVOURING CLEAR SOUPS

• There are endless possibilities for additions to clear soup – try rice, eggs (either cooked in the soup or added hard-boiled and sliced), little pasta shapes, slivers of fresh vegetables, shellfish and pieces of fish, small slices of cooked meats, chicken and ham, chopped spring onions and so on.

• One of my favourite fresh clear soups is made by cooking roughly chopped ripe tomatoes in water with a squeeze of lemon juice and a teaspoon or two of sugar until tender. Then strain the mixture through clean, wet muslin and reheat with little cubes of skinned fresh tomato and shredded strips of basil leaves added as a garnish.

• Drop quails' eggs into a hot clear soup and lightly poach the eggs before serving.

• If you are serving consommé hot only add garnishes at the last moment so the consommé loses none of its clarity. You can add tiny slivers of ham or cold meats, fresh herbs or little bits of cooked vegetables or simply a hint of sherry.

THICKENED *and* PURÉED SOUPS

Soups can be thickened in various ways. The most usual way is with flour which you add to melted butter and the uncooked ingredients in the saucepan before stirring in the stock. You can also mix the flour with a little liquid until smooth, then stir it in at the end of cooking, stirring until the soup thickens. (Flour must always be cooked thoroughly or the soup will taste starchy.) Adding fresh breadcrumbs is another way I like to thicken more homely, filling soups.

Cream and/or egg yolks added at the last minute make a richer flavoured and thicker soup. To thicken thin soups slightly, add cream and egg yolks, lightly whisked together, but only heat gently as boiling causes the eggs to scramble and single cream to curdle. I think a little flour

thickening at the beginning followed by a cream and egg addition at the end is the most successful method. Most cream soups, whether vegetable, chicken or fish, are thickened this way to achieve their smooth consistency.

Puréed cooked vegetables also make excellent thickeners for soups but will, of course, add distinctive flavours (page 53). Some people like the texture obtained by passing the vegetables through a food mill, but since I have had a food processor with which I can control the texture quite well, I have abandoned my food mill.

Using thoroughly cooked and puréed pulses as a thickener makes a more substantial soup (page 113). Red lentils, which cook more quickly than dried beans, are specially good for this, and add colour as well.

THICKENING SOUPS WITH EGGS AND CREAM

Whisked egg yolks and cream thicken a soup slightly but mainly add a rich creamy finish. Do not let the soup boil after you have added eggs or single cream as the eggs will scramble and single cream will curdle. As the egg yolks cook they will thicken the soup. If the soup has been previously thickened with a little flour it will be less vulnerable to curdling but it should still not be boiled.

Allow 75ml (3fl oz) double cream and 2 egg yolks for every 1.2 litres (2 pints) soup already thickened with flour; increase the number of yolks to 4 if the soup has not been previously thickened.

1 *Although soups can be made well in advance, only thicken them just before serving. To make the thickening mixture put the egg yolks and cream in a medium-sized mixing bowl. Using a fork or whisk, whisk them together lightly until well combined. It is best to use double cream because it will not curdle if the soup is boiled accidentally.*

2 *Meanwhile, reheat but do not boil the soup. Add a ladleful of hot soup to the eggs and cream mixture. Use a wooden spoon to stir them together.*

3 *Stir the eggs, cream and soup mixture into the pan of hot soup. Continue to stir the soup over a gentle heat until it has thickened slightly but do not allow it to boil. Serve immediately.*

CREAM OF VEGETABLE SOUP

This is a most versatile kind of soup as almost any vegetable can be used depending on what is in season. For ultimate smoothness I find it best to purée the cooked vegetables and stock in a food processor first, then rub the purée through a fine sieve. The amount of stock and exact cooking time depends on how thick or thin you like your soup and how much liquid there is in the vegetables used. Obviously, tomatoes will make a thinner soup than sweet peppers. These quantities serve 4.

1 *Melt about 25g (1oz) butter in a large saucepan, then stir in about 750g (1½lb) prepared chopped vegetables.*

2 *Add about 1.2 litres (2 pints) stock or milk, or a mixture of both, then cover and simmer until the vegetables are tender.*

3 *Purée in a food processor or through a food mill. For a very smooth soup rub the purée through a sieve with the back of a wooden spoon.*

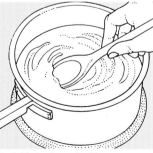

4 *Add single or double cream or fromage frais and reheat gently without boiling, stirring. Serve with your choice of garnishes (see box opposite for ideas).*

SIMPLE THICKENED SOUP

Whenever I want to make a soup quickly this is the method I choose. It is the easiest way of binding ingredients into a stock and, because the flour is added at the beginning it cooks long enough so there is no danger of a raw, starchy taste.

You can, of course, use leftovers as well as freshly prepared ingredients. To add depth of colour brown the ingredients in the butter before adding the flour and stock. If you want to enrich the soup stir in some cream at the end of cooking just before serving.

All sorts of ingredients are suitable – just choose ones that all take about the same amount of time to cook; cut pieces to the same size for even cooking. Delicious combinations include smoked haddock and prawns; cooked pulses and bacon, and cooked chicken and leeks. These quantities serve 4–6.

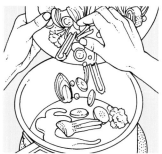 

1 *Melt about 50g (2oz) butter in a saucepan and add about 500g (1lb) prepared chopped ingredients. Stir to coat the ingredients well with the butter.*

2 *Mix in about 4 tablespoons flour, then gradually stir in 1.2 litres (2 pints) stock. Bring to the boil, then simmer, covered, until the ingredients are tender. Season.*

MAKING CROÛTONS

Croûtons are a very traditional garnish for soups. To make your own, remove the crusts from slices of stale bread and cut the bread into even-sized cubes. Heat plenty of oil or fat – olive oil, duck or goose fat or garlic butter with some oil are specially good – in a large frying pan, then add the bread cubes in a single layer. Fry gently, tossing the cubes often, so they become crisp and evenly browned, then drain well on crumpled kitchen paper.

You can make fat-free croûtons from slices of toast or day-old bread dried out in a warm oven.

Add flavour by rubbing the surfaces with a peeled garlic clove. For variety, cut into shapes using small cutters.

FINISHING TOUCHES

• I think garnishes of all kinds look most attractive if you add them after the soup has been ladled into individual bowls.
• I use fresh herbs more than anything else. Flat-leaved parsley, dill, fennel, strips of basil, sorrel and lovage, chives and summer savory all look extremely pretty as garnishes and add delicate flavours too.
• Coriander is an especially suitable garnish for lightly spiced soups.
• Be cautious with tarragon as a garnish as it can be too strong for some soups. The same applies to rosemary, as well, which is too fibrous and tends to stick in the teeth.
• Swirl cream, creamed smetana, fromage frais or natural yogurt on to non-creamy soups or stir in a herb-flavoured butter or soft cheese just before serving.
• Toasted flaked almonds are delicious sprinkled on top of cream soups.
• Finely grated Gruyère cheese sprinkled on top of hot soup melts in attractive, long strings.
• I add thin slivers of raw courgette, red or green pepper, cucumber or carrot for a decorative crunchiness in smooth soups.
• Add a spoonful or two of pesto (page 307) to tomato soup.
• Crisp fried bacon crumbled over soup adds lots of flavour as well as texture.

Simple ways to add body
• Well-flavoured, country-style vegetable soups can be thickened with bread. Use dry bread which dissolves and binds the broth, or stir in some fresh breadcrumbs.
• Lay a slice of toasted or baked French bread in a soup bowl and ladle over the hot soup. The bread will swell up and thicken the soup most effectively.
• Top French onion soup with a slice of French bread sprinkled with finely grated cheese, then brown under a hot grill: be sure to use a flameproof bowl.
• Small pieces of peeled starchy potatoes cooked in a good broth will eventually disintegrate and thicken the soup when stirred in.

Carrot and Cranberry Soup (page 38) has a refreshing taste as well as a vibrant colour which makes a striking presentation. Ideal for Christmas, this can be made all year with frozen cranberries.

CHILLED SOUPS

With such a variety of vegetables now available to us, together with a wide range of yogurts and other milk products, there have never been so many possibilities for making chilled soups from both cooked and uncooked ingredients. Chilled soups are most welcome in the summer when you can make the best of tender young vegetables and flavour-packed soft fruit.

The variations of chilled soups are endless, and the techniques are simple. Easiest to make are uncooked blended soups, with puréed raw vegetables mixed with thick Greek yogurt or creamed smetana. A bit more time consuming are soups like tomato and red pepper soup (below), made from puréed cooked vegetables. Raspberry and mint soup (opposite) is made by a simple technique you can adapt for any fruit. Simply vary the amount of liquid in these soups depending how much moisture or juice there is in the vegetable or fruit.

Many soups which are normally served hot can also be served chilled but flour-based soups tend to taste more starchy when cold, and, on the whole, starchy vegetables are not good in chilled soups. Creamy vichyssoise, made from potatoes and leeks, is a notable exception. I prefer to make chilled soups without butter or egg yolks as both of these ingredients can become too solid and rather cloying.

UNCOOKED BLENDED SOUPS

Quick delicious soups can be made in a food processor or blender using fresh vegetables such as cucumbers, tomatoes or avocados and creamy textured dairy products.

To make 6 servings you will need 300–600ml (½–1 pint) fresh vegetable purée, depending on how watery the vegetable is, about 600ml (1 pint) yogurt and about 300ml (½ pint) smetana.

Fresh herbs are a must for flavouring uncooked soups. Spiced oil garnish (right) is also a favourite of mine for garnishing chilled soups.

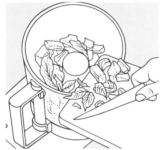

1 *Prepare the vegetable of your choice for the purée and put it in a food processor or electric blender with a generous handful of chopped fresh herbs and a little salt. (If you are using an avocado also add plenty of lemon juice to prevent discoloration.)*

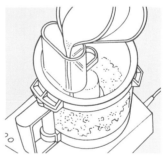

2 *Whizz the vegetables and herbs to a purée. Gradually whizz in the yogurt, then the smetana. Pour into a bowl and chill thoroughly. Check the seasoning, then ladle the soup into individual bowls and garnish with fresh herbs or a swirl of the spiced oil.*

Spiced oil garnish *Toss 1–2 teaspoons cumin seeds in a small pan over a medium heat for 30 seconds. Add 3 tablespoons olive oil and 2 teaspoons paprika, then stir for about 2 minutes without the oil bubbling. Tip out of the pan and set aside to cool.*

TOMATO AND RED PEPPER SOUP

This is an example of a chilled soup in which the vegetables are cooked first until tender, then puréed, flavoured with herbs and seasonings. Chilled borsch and vichyssoise are two classic soups made by this simple method.

Cooking times depend on the vegetable used. Courgettes, for example, soften in about 5 minutes, while the red peppers in this recipe take about 20 minutes to become tender enough.

You will find it easy to adapt this recipe to use with all sorts of vegetables. The quantities suggested here will serve 4.

1 *Put 1 very large deseeded and chopped red pepper in a pan with 1 large garlic clove, 2 tablespoons tomato purée and 450ml (¾ pint) water. Season. Bring to the boil, then reduce the heat, cover and simmer gently for 15–20 minutes until the pepper and garlic are tender.*

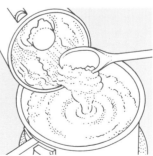

2 *Purée the pepper, garlic and a little of the water. Stir back into the remaining liquid. Add 750g (1½lb) skinned, seeded and chopped tomatoes, juice of 1 lemon and 1 teaspoon sugar. Bring to the boil, cover and simmer for 8–10 minutes until cooked but not mushy.*

3 *Check the seasoning. Cool the soup, then chill it thoroughly. To serve, ladle the soup into individual bowls, dribble a little olive oil over each bowl and sprinkle with chopped fresh herbs, if you like. I often add torn fresh basil leaves to this full-flavoured soup just before serving.*

A selection of quick-and-easy chilled soups: tomato and red pepper soup (left), raspberry and mint soup (top right) and a quick uncooked blended soup of cucumber and yogurt topped with spiced oil.

RASPBERRY AND MINT SOUP

Especially in summer I think this style of chilled soup is most refreshing, and it makes an ideal first course.

The best fruits to choose are those which are full flavoured and rather sharp – raspberries and cherries are excellent, as are tangy apples. Adjust the flavour with lemon juice and sugar to taste. Instead of wine or cider you can use light stock, and, of course, a mixture of fruits. The quantities here serve 4.

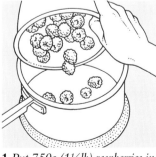

1 *Put 750g (1½lb) raspberries in a saucepan over a gentle heat with 4 tablespoons lemon juice and 1–2 tablespoons sugar and stir well with a wooden spoon.*

2 *When the sugar dissolves and the juices just begin to run, purée with about 150ml (¼ pint) white wine or sweet cider. Press through a fine nylon sieve with a ladle.*

3 *Add another 300ml (½ pint) wine or cider and the strained juice of 1 orange and a handful of chopped fresh mint. Chill. Ladle into bowls and swirl with cream.*

CARROT AND CRANBERRY SOUP (35)

The vibrant combination of orange carrots and scarlet cranberries gives this soup a spectacular colour. Because this is a smooth soup with a flavour which is slightly sweet and sharp, people find it hard to define the exact ingredients – but they always enjoy it. Use either fresh or frozen cranberries.   *SERVES 6*

500g (1lb) carrots, chopped roughly
6 large cloves garlic
1.2 litres (2 pints) water
300ml (½ pint) freshly squeezed
 orange juice
2 teaspoons caster sugar
175g (6oz) cranberries, thawed if frozen
Good handful of fresh dill or fennel leaves,
 chopped roughly
300ml (½ pint) creamed smetana or
 soured cream
Sea salt and black pepper

Put the carrots, garlic cloves, water, orange juice, caster sugar and a sprinkling of sea salt and black pepper in a large pan. Cover and bring to the boil, then reduce the heat and simmer gently for 30–40 minutes until the carrots are very soft.

Add the cranberries, cover and simmer for about 10 minutes. Pour into a food processor – you will probably have to do this in two or three goes depending on the size of your machine – and whizz until smooth. Strain the soup through a sieve into a clean saucepan. Taste and adjust the seasoning.

Reheat the soup and serve in individual bowls, sprinkled with some chopped dill or fennel. Spoon a dollop of creamed smetana on to each serving.

SHALLOT AND MUSTARD SOUP WITH TARRAGON (26)

Shallots are far sweeter than larger onions. My family love this soup's mild mustardy flavour.   *SERVES 4*

25g (1oz) butter
4 cauliflower florets, chopped roughly
1 large onion, sliced roughly
750ml (1¼ pints) chicken stock (page 29)
2 teaspoons Dijon mustard
1 tablespoon caster sugar
250g (8oz) shallots, halved lengthwise
2 tablespoons chopped fresh tarragon
150ml (¼ pint) double or single cream
Salt and black pepper

Melt the butter in a large pan, add the cauliflower and onion and stir over a gentle heat for 10 minutes or until the onion is translucent and the cauliflower is tender. Whizz in a food processor with 300ml (½ pint) stock, the mustard and sugar until smooth. Return to the pan and stir in the remaining stock. Season.

Bring to a rolling boil, then add the shallots. Cover and simmer 25–30 minutes. Stir in the tarragon and the cream, check the seasoning and serve.

CHICKEN SOUP WITH SMOKED OYSTERS (26)

An ideal soup to make ahead and reheat to serve. It also makes a good supper dish served with lots of French bread.   *SERVES 4*

3 tablespoons olive oil
1 large red pepper, cored, deseeded and
 sliced very thinly (page 49)
2 teaspoons paprika
8 tablespoons lemon juice
2 large skinless boned chicken breasts,
 sliced into very thin strips
300ml (½ pint) double cream
125g (4oz) chestnut mushrooms, stalks
 left on, sliced very thinly
300ml (½ pint) single cream
105g (3½oz) can smoked oysters, drained
Generous bunch chives, chopped
Sea salt and black pepper

Heat the olive oil in a large pan over a fairly low heat. Add the pepper and paprika, cover and cook gently for about 10 minutes until the pepper slices are soft. Stir in the lemon juice and chicken then

cover the pan and cook for 5 minutes.

Remove from the heat and stir in the double cream and the mushrooms. Bring to the boil over a medium heat, stirring. Still stirring, let the mixture bubble for 2–3 minutes, then add the single cream and heat through but do not boil.

Stir in the oysters, remove from the heat and season to taste with sea salt and black pepper. Just before serving add the chopped chives.

INDIAN SUMMER SOUP (26)

This deliciously aromatic soup is Indian in character and can be served either hot or cold according to the weather.   *SERVES 6*

2 aubergines, cut into 1cm (½in) cubes
3 tablespoons groundnut oil
25g (1oz) butter
2 teaspoons garam masala
2.5–5cm (1–2in) piece fresh root ginger,
 peeled and chopped finely
3 large cloves garlic, peeled and
 chopped finely
1kg (2lb) tomatoes, chopped
2 tablespoons tomato purée
1.2 litres (2 pints) vegetable stock
 (page 30) or water
4 tablespoons lemon juice
2 teaspoons caster sugar
50g (2oz) creamed coconut, chopped
2–5 pinches cayenne pepper
6 tablespoons natural yogurt
Salt and cayenne pepper

Rub the cubed aubergine all over with salt. Leave the cubes in a colander in the sink for about 30 minutes to drain off any bitter juices, then rinse off all the salt, drain and pat dry with kitchen paper.

Heat the oil in a large, heavy-based saucepan over a fairly high heat. Add the aubergine cubes and brown them all over. Reduce the heat and stir in the butter, garam masala, chopped ginger and garlic. Stir around for a minute or so, then add the tomatoes and tomato purée. Gradually stir in the stock or water, lemon juice and caster sugar. Bring to the boil, cover and simmer gently for about 45 minutes, stirring occasionally.

Remove from the heat and add the creamed coconut, stirring until melted and smoothly mixed. Season with the cayenne pepper and salt to taste. Just before serving top each bowl of soup with a tablespoon of yogurt.

CLEAR VEGETABLE SOUP WITH QUAILS' EGGS (26)

The broth in this soup, which has a slightly Eastern flavour, can be made ahead and then reheated with the quails' eggs and thin ribbons of lettuce dropped in to poach at the very last moment. *SERVES 4–6*

2 onions, unpeeled
250g (8oz) carrots, chopped roughly
8 tomatoes, chopped roughly
2 sticks celery, chopped roughly
5cm (2in) piece fresh root ginger, peeled and chopped roughly
1.8 litres (3 pints) water
1 rounded teaspoon whole coriander seeds, crushed
4 cardamom pods, crushed
1 egg white, lightly whisked
4 tablespoons lemon juice
12 quails' eggs
2 Little Gem lettuces or 1 dense-hearted lettuce, sliced very thinly crosswise
3 tablespoons roughly chopped fresh coriander leaves
Salt and black pepper

Put the onions, carrots, tomatoes, celery, ginger and water in a saucepan with some salt and pepper. Add the crushed coriander seeds, cardamom pods and egg white and stir thoroughly. Bring to the boil, then reduce the heat, cover and simmer very gently for 1½ hours without stirring. Remove from the heat, skim off as much scum from the surface as you can with a large metal spoon, then stir in the lemon juice.

Put a double layer of clean, wet muslin or a clean tea towel into a colander or sieve over a large bowl. Strain the liquid through the colander and discard the vegetables.

Put a clean piece of muslin or a tea towel into the sieve and strain the liquid back into the rinsed-out saucepan. Season to taste with salt and freshly ground black pepper.

Shortly before serving bring the soup to a rolling boil, then break in the quails' eggs one by one, carefully but fairly quickly. Add the shredded lettuce and stir in very gently. The eggs will be softly poached after about 1 minute.

Remove the saucepan from the heat, throw in the chopped fresh coriander leaves and serve immediately in warmed soup plates, distributing the quails' eggs evenly among each portion.

FISH BISQUE (26)

This is a delicate soup that is easy to make and has a wonderful flavour. The kipper fillets cooked in the stock add a faint smokiness, while fresh ginger contributes to the soup's sharp flavour. *SERVES 6*

750g–1kg (1½–2lb) fish scraps
1kg (2lb) kipper fillets, chopped roughly
1 small celeriac, peeled and chopped roughly
1 onion, halved
2 carrots, left unpeeled and chopped roughly
5cm (2in) piece fresh root ginger, unpeeled and chopped roughly
4 large cloves garlic, peeled and chopped roughly
1.8 litres (3 pints) water
3–4 pinches cayenne pepper
1 teaspoon turmeric
1 small red pepper, deseeded and sliced into very thin rings (page 49)
4 tablespoons lemon juice
6 tablespoons double cream
250g (8oz) large peeled cooked prawns
Handful of lovage, coriander or mint leaves, chopped roughly
Salt

To make the stock, put the fish scraps, kipper fillets, celeriac, onion, carrots, ginger, garlic and water in a large saucepan or stockpot. Add a little salt, the cayenne pepper and turmeric, cover and bring to the boil, then reduce the heat and simmer very gently for 1 hour.

Strain the liquid through a fine sieve into a clean saucepan. If possible, refrigerate the soup overnight to make it easier to remove the fat before reheating the soup. Otherwise, remove the liquid fat with a large spoon or pieces of kitchen paper (page 29).

Return the soup to the heat. Add the pepper rings and bring slowly to the boil, then cover, reduce the heat and simmer for 10 minutes. Uncover and continue simmering another 5 minutes to reduce the soup and intensify the flavours. Stir in the lemon juice and remove the saucepan from the heat.

Just before serving stir the double cream into the soup and taste, adjusting the seasoning, if necessary. Return the soup to the heat and bring to just below boiling point, then remove from the heat, stir in the prawns and chopped fresh herbs and serve immediately.

MUSSEL, SALMON AND SCALLOP SOUP (31)

This is a rich but delicately flavoured fish soup. If you like, keep a few of the cooked mussels in their shells to garnish the soup. *SERVES 4–6*

300ml (½ pint) white wine
1kg (2lb) fresh mussels, scrubbed and debearded (discard any open ones)
600ml (1 pint) fish stock (page 31)
12–14 strands saffron
1 teaspoon paprika
300ml (½ pint) double cream
50g (2oz) butter
25g (1oz) plain flour
625g (1¼lb) tail piece of salmon, skinned, filleted and sliced thinly
4 scallops, sliced and corals cut in half
Handful of fresh dill, chopped roughly
Handful of fresh parsley, chopped roughly
2 tablespoons lemon juice, strained
Salt and black pepper

Boil the wine in a large pan. Add the mussels, cover and boil for about 2 minutes until the shells have opened. Transfer to a bowl, then remove them from their shells, discarding any that haven't opened. Tip the juices through a fine sieve into a clean pan and add the stock, saffron and paprika. Bring to the boil, remove from the heat, cover and leave for 30 minutes. Stir in the cream.

Melt the butter in a large heavy pan, then remove from the heat and stir in the flour. Add the stock and cream mixture, gradually at first, stirring until combined. Bring to the boil, then simmer gently, still stirring, for 4–5 minutes and remove from the heat. Season and cover.

To serve, bring to a rolling boil, stirring. Drop in the salmon and simmer for 2 minutes, then add the scallops and simmer for 2–3 minutes. Add the mussels, dill, parsley and lemon juice. Heat through for 30 seconds and serve.

VEGETABLES

Although I could never become a total vegetarian, vegetables are definitely the last food I would want to give up. They offer a vast scope of tastes, shapes, textures, colours and characters and, as a result they provide one of the most inspiring areas of cookery. Yet, vegetables are often not given much thought at all – carelessly prepared, overlooked and plonked on the table as if they were simply obligatory but unimportant accompaniments. These indifferent vegetables are nearly always boiled as if that was the only thing you could do with them. In fact, it is vegetables above all ingredients which adapt well to every kind of cooking method.

Vegetable cookery is chameleon-like to suit the seasons and your moods. There are cold-weather, comforting dishes such as all kinds of vegetable gratins, stuffed and baked vegetables, root vegetable purées, fritters, toppings, vegetable stews and even vegetable pies. Then there is the thrill of summer vegetables eaten in season at their prime; delicately cooked, crisp and bright green, served with simple accompaniments such as butter, extra virgin olive oil, fresh herbs, soured cream, hollandaise sauce, fresh tomato sauce, or a simple vinaigrette. There can also be ethereal results with vegetable cookery in the form of featherlight soufflés, Japanese tempura, and vegetable mousses and terrines.

But with all their qualities, one exceptional bonus of vegetables is their beauty: their rhapsody of colours, their sculptural shapes, their tactile textures. I particularly like combining vegetables so that contrasting colours and textures will complement each other. I find shopping for vegetables, with all its variety, the most pleasurable kind of food shopping there is – as much a feast for the eye as the palate.

Knowing when a vegetable is cooked for the right amount of time is partly a matter of experience, and also, of course, of personal taste. However, it does seem to me a terrible waste if you overcook tender vegetables such as mange tout and sugar snap peas, young asparagus and spring greens. These, and other green vegetables, when they are young and fresh, should only be boiled or steamed briefly. Yet, some green vegetables, such as cabbage and leeks, can either be cooked briefly to retain crispness, or long and gently to a melting softness – both results are delicious, but very different.

My oldest daughter has been a vegetarian for several years, though luckily for me, she will eat fish. I don't believe in planning a meal entirely to suit one vegetarian in the family or party, and I don't really like the idea of one guest sitting eating something completely different which doesn't fit in with the rest of the meal. I do think, however, that a vegetarian in your midst inspires you to do more interesting things with the vegetable part of the meal, and as a result makes you appreciate vegetables as a main ingredient. Since my daughter stopped eating meat, I have grown to realize that combinations of vegetables can be made into really satisfying main courses which are welcomed by even the most voraciously carnivorous from time to time.

Vegetable main courses and side dishes, clockwise from top left: semolina gnocchi and Parmesan cheese top a Leek and Celeriac Cobbler (page 65); Carrot Salad with Oranges and Spring Onions (page 64) adds a fresh taste to any meal; a golden puff pastry crust tops sliced vegetables and softly poached eggs in Egg, Fennel and Tomato Pie (page 64); Grilled Courgettes and Goat Cheese with Walnuts (page 62) makes an interesting first course; Sautéed Potatoes with Chopped Ginger and Spices (page 65) also contains cumin, caraway seeds and fresh parsley; Spinach and Pea Purée with Cabbage and Parmesan (page 64) can be made year round with frozen peas; Hot and Cold Salad (page 62) combines dwarf green beans, mushrooms, pine kernels, radicchio and Little Gem lettuce.

ROOTS *and* TUBERS

Root and tuberous vegetables, including potatoes, sweet potatoes, yams, eddoes, carrots, parsnips, turnips, beetroots, salsifys, radishes, swedes, celeriacs and jerusalem artichokes, are great favourites with me. They are extremely versatile and can form the base of marvellous soups, fritters, purées, soufflés and so on, while for vegetarians they can provide the sustaining body and sweetness which most green vegetables lack.

Celeriac, despite its unprepossessing, knobbly appearance, has a wonderful flavour, combining the freshness of celery and the sweet taste of a root. I also like the pepperiness of swede, but it suffers from a rather watery consistency so it is best puréed and enriched with butter or cream, and sometimes combined with a finer, smoother root such as potatoes. The pleasurable qualities of carrots made into a purée or soup are by now well known, and their brilliant colour and sweetness enhances many creations, both savoury and sweet, cooked or raw. Parsnip is definitely one of the roots I eat most, perhaps because I so often use spices in my cooking, and all roots, but parsnips in particular, have a great affinity with spices.

But my favourite root of all must be the potato.

Potatoes are so varied in type, taste and texture, making them suitable for quite different ways of serving, from a delicate dish of silky smooth new potatoes tossed in butter and fresh dill, to a crusty baked potato with its comfortingly soft and fluffy centre. Potatoes must be the most versatile of all vegetables as they combine so well with all manner of flavourings and accompaniments, and can be cooked by every method, though unlike most other vegetables they are not good raw.

BUYING AND STORING

Ideally, store root and tuberous vegetables in a well-ventilated bag in a cool, dry and dark place, preferably not the refrigerator unless there really is nowhere else. In these conditions they should keep for a good two weeks. Exposure to daylight can cause potatoes to sprout and turn green in which case they should be discarded. Most potatoes are now sold ready washed but still benefit from a light scrubbing if they are to be cooked in their skins. Very earthy potatoes can be soaked first in cold water to loosen the soil, then scrubbed in cold water or peeled before cooking, depending if you like the peel or not.

PREPARING ROOT VEGETABLES

For maximum vitamin retention, scrub or peel thinly and don't soak vegetables in cold water as the water-soluble vitamins B and C will leach out. Certain vegetables like celeriac, jerusalem artichokes and salsify discolour when peeled so these must be prepared just before cooking or dropped into acidulated water, simply cold water with some added lemon juice or white vinegar. Beetroot is different – it needs to be cooked first, then peeled to maintain its vibrant colour.

To peel long, smooth *vegetables, such as carrots and parsnips, with a swivel-bladed peeler, hold the vegetable root end pointing downwards in one hand. Use your other hand to run the blade away from you, scraping off the skin in thin strips. Hold rounder vegetables, such as potatoes and kohl rabi, in your hand and peel towards you.*

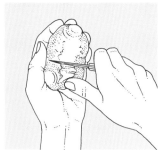

Use a paring knife *to peel knobbly vegetables like jerusalem artichokes and celeriac. Hold the knife in one hand and the vegetable in the other hand. For smaller vegetables place the thumb of your knife hand on the bottom of the vegetable to hold it still. Slice downwards to cut off the skin in thin strips or chop roughly for soups or purées.*

HOW TO CHOP VEGETABLES

A large cook's knife, about 20cm (8in) long, with a sharp blade is best for cutting up vegetables. With practice you should be able to do this with the lightning quick precision of a chef. When chopping it is vital to keep your fingers on the hand holding the vegetable firmly at right angles to the knife for safety's sake. This prevents you from cutting your fingertips. You can chop vegetables either into dice or slices. Use small dice for the classic mirepoix vegetables mixture for stuffings and larger dice for chunky casseroles and stews. Make sure that chopped or sliced vegetables are cut evenly so they all cook within the same amount of time.

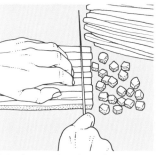

To dice, *peel and cut the vegetable lengthwise into thick or thin slices depending on the size dice required. Pile slices on top of each other and cut downwards into strips, then gather the strips together and cut across into square dice ready for cooking.*

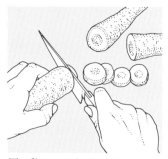

To slice *parsnips, carrots or potatoes peel or not as you choose, then, holding the vegetable firmly, cut straight down crosswise or diagonally in thin or thick slices, depending on the end use. Wafer-thin slices can be cut in a food processor using a slicing disc.*

POTATO VARIETIES

Some potato varieties are more suitable than others for specific purposes. Most packaged potatoes contain information on the bag about what they should be used for but use the guide below if you are buying loose ones.

Baking   Cara, Estima, Kerr's Pink, King Edward, Marfona, Pentland Squire, Record

Boiling   Alcmaria, Cara, Cleopatra, Desirée, Elvira, Estima, Home Guard, Jersey Royal, King Edward, Kingston, Maris Peer, Maris Piper, Pentland Squire, Pentland Javelin, Pink Fir Apple, Romano, Royal Kidney, Wilja

Chipping   Kerr's Pink, King Edward, Maris Piper, Pentland Squire, Romano

Mashing   King Edward, Maris Piper, Pentland Squire, Wilja

Roasting   Cara, King Edward, Maris Piper, Romano

Salads   Belle de Fontenay, Carlingford, Charlotte, Jersey Royal, Pink Fir Apple, Ratte

Steaming   Almost all varieties are suitable for steaming.

HANDLING VEGETABLES

• Only buy vegetables in peak condition – they should be hard and firm, crisp and brightly coloured with no yellowing leaves or bruised, soft patches.
• All vegetables are best eaten as fresh as possible. From the moment vegetables are picked, the enzymes that cause decay start discoloration and destroying flavours. The vegetables then start to dehydrate and become limp. Two processes slow down this deterioration – cool temperatures and loosely covering food with plastic or polythene to cut down on dehydration. This makes the refrigerator the ideal place to store most vegetables. But bags or containers should not be tightly closed or they will become too wet and the by-products of deterioration will cause mould.
• Remove packaged vegetables from any tight wrapping as soon as you get them home and store them loosely in food bags or plastic boxes.
• Ideally, all vegetables should be prepared just before cooking to help maintain the maximum nutritive value and freshness. If you need to prepare them in advance, however, store them in a loosely closed polythene food bag in the refrigerator.
• Root vegetables go limp when they begin to deteriorate and are difficult to peel, but they are fine for the stockpot.

PREPARING HOMEMADE POTATO CHIPS

For chips it is important to choose a potato variety that holds its shape well and yet cooks to a light fluffiness inside (above). Chips can be made either using a sharp cook's knife for straight chips or in a food processor for game chips. After cutting into sticks, it is important to soak for about 30 minutes in water to remove excess starch. This prevents the chips from sticking together.

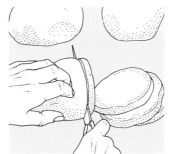

1 *Large potatoes are best for chips. Peel them thinly, then cut into 5mm–1cm (¼–½in) slices, depending on desired thickness.*

2 *Stack up several slices and cut downwards into 5mm–1cm (¼–½in) sticks. Soak the chips in water for 30 minutes.*

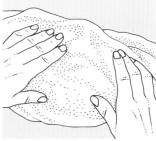

3 *Drain well, then place on a clean tea towel and pat dry. If not properly dried, the chips will spatter in the hot fat (page 54).*

If making your own chips, you can cut them to the thickness you like.

To make game chips, *fit a slicing disc to a food processor and twist on the lid. Cut the potatoes to fit the feed tube, then push them down with the plunger. The less you push the thinner the chips will be. Fry as for chips (page 54) but only with 1 frying (190°C, 375°F for 1½–2 minutes). Thin game chips are a traditional accompaniment to roast game.*

GREENS, PEAS *and* BEANS

This large group of vegetables provides great variety and pleasure. Peas and beans should be exceptionally fresh so that short and simple cooking will reveal their delicate flavour at its best. If you have ever picked peas and beans straight from the garden you will know that it is almost as difficult not to eat them immediately as it is when picking soft fruits at the height of summer.

Ordinary cabbages are one of the most underrated vegetables; they are delicious if they are cooked briefly, remaining crisp and fresh, or equally good stewed long and gently in a little buttery stock until really soft and mellow flavoured. Neither of these cooking methods will produce the terrible smell which put off many of us during schooldays or while in hospital; now I love a plate of vibrant green and tender kale leaves or sliced spring greens briefly cooked and sprinkled with dark soy sauce.

Cauliflower tastes good cooked fairly briefly, or alternatively for much longer with added flavourings, or raw in salads and for dips. I love it as a purée or as the base of a creamy soup. Look for ivory white, tightly clustered and unblemished florets surrounded by small leaves which are also good to eat. It is important to remember that broccoli and calabrese, which are such excellent and useful vegetables when still bright green and slightly crunchy, can become quite bitter when overcooked.

Spinach, to me as well as Popeye, is the wonder vegetable. It is tender, has a unique flavour, and retains its bright dark green colour even when slightly overcooked. The small leaves of young spinach make a lovely raw salad.

BUYING AND STORING

It is best to use greens, peas and beans on the day of purchase but if buying ahead store loosely wrapped in the salad drawer. Do not buy any with yellow or limp leaves or tips. Fresh pods pop open easily, leafy vegetables should be firm and green and fresh beans snap easily if bent in half.

PREPARATION

Most vegetables today require only the minimum of preparation, either because they are harvested when young and tender, or because they are offered for sale ready trimmed. Also, fashions have changed and over trimming is no longer thought necessary with some vegetables, like green beans. The tails of beans, for example, are quite edible, and look more natural left on. Also, many more people like crisp vegetables so it is not vital to prepare them for more thorough cooking. All these vegetables need only brief cooking in rapidly boiling water or by steaming (page 52) until bordering on what is now called tender-crisp – soft enough but still with a bite, and bright green.

When possible, prepare vegetables just before cooking, rather than hours in advance and leaving them to soak in a bowl of water. Soaking destroys the B-complex vitamins and vitamin C, which are water soluble and leach out into the water.

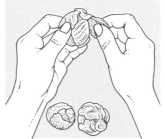

Brussels sprouts *Peel off the outer leaves, trim and discard the stems. If the sprouts are large and older, cut a cross on each stem base for even cooking.*

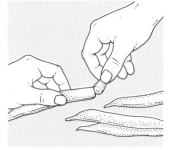

French beans *need their tops snapped or cut. Cut off the tails, too, if liked, bunching several beans together at a time so they are all the same size.*

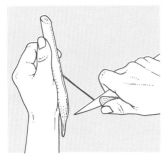

Older runner beans *need their tough string removed. Cut almost through the top, then pull it downwards on the inside curve, pulling away the string. Cut through the tail end and pull away the string on the outside. Cut into long diagonal slices.*

Broad beans and peas *pop open easily when the tail end is pressed firmly if they are fresh. Run your thumb along the curved side and scoop out the beans or peas. Purists will then pop broad beans out of their inner skins, too, after cooking – a treat if you have time.*

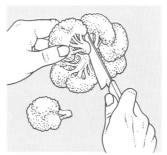

Cauliflower and broccoli *Turn the heads over and trim away the outside leaves, leaving on any thin light green ones. Cut off the florets, including a little of the thick stem. Large florets should be sliced in half. Slice off and discard the lower stalk.*

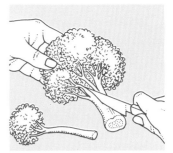

Broccoli spears *Trim the base stem from the head of florets down through the stalk to make spears. Or trim off the florets, then cut the thick stem into slices. Cook these first, adding the florets a few minutes later so they cook evenly.*

PREPARING SPINACH

Depending on the time of year, spinach is sold in differing sizes of leaves and stalks. Only large thick and dark green leaves need to be trimmed of their stalks; younger stalks can be left on. Only buy leaves that are not damaged or yellow and without extra-hard stalks or any flowering shoots. Most fresh spinach contains some dirt, so a good washing in several changes of water really is necessary. Drain the leaves well, then cook with only the water left clinging to the leaves.

This colourful coleslaw is bursting with the flavours of shredded red and white cabbage, sliced green peppers, chopped spring onions, raisins and caraway seeds.

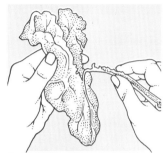

1 *Carefully pick over and throw away any wilted and decayed leaves. Tear the stalks from large leaves and discard.*

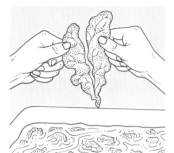

2 *Tear the leaves into 2 or 3 pieces. Wash in at least 2 changes of fresh clean water, then drain well, shaking off most of the water.*

PREPARING CABBAGE

A really fresh cabbage, simply shredded and cooked in the smallest amount of water for the least possible time, must surely rate as one of the world's tastiest vegetables. It needs little adornment save adding a small knob of butter and no complicated preparation. Although it is a green leafy vegetable, cabbage retains its crispness for longer than lettuce or cress. It is also a good source of vitamins B and C, but these deteriorate on long storage and leach out if soaked too long in water. There is no need to soak or cook cabbage with bicarbonate of soda as was the fashion a decade or two ago. Although this preserves colour it destroys vitamins and gives a strange taste.

COLESLAW

This is perhaps one of the world's most popular salads, but if badly made it can be the most dreary. Coleslaw, essentially a shredded raw cabbage salad, can be as simple or elaborate as you please, with the addition of grated carrot, chopped celery, thinly sliced green pepper, grated apple, raisins, finely chopped spring onions and cucumber. Instead of dressing simply with homemade mayonnaise (page 202) and single or soured cream (below) coleslaw can also be dressed first with a little French mustard, wine vinegar, sea salt, caster sugar and caraway seeds and then left to stand for 30 minutes before tossing with a thick mayonnaise mixed with single or soured cream. For added interest use half white and half red cabbage. Leafy green vegetables, however, are not sufficiently firm to use in coleslaw.

Leafy cabbage *Cut the head in half vertically, then cut out the woody core in a 'V' shape. Pull off the large outer leaves and cut out the thick stalks. Roll the leaves together and shred finely. Halve the remaining cabbage and place each piece flat side down on a chopping board. Slice downwards into fine shreds.*

Round cabbage *Cut the cabbage into quarters. Stand each quarter upright and cut out the hard core. Lay on its side and shred, finely for salads and coleslaw, more thickly for cooking. If you need whole leaves for stuffing (page 60), peel these off the cabbage before quartering and cut out the stalks, then blanch and stuff.*

1 *Finely grate 3 carrots into a large bowl, then add any other crisp vegetable you like (above), either grated or very finely chopped. Mix together with 300ml (½ pint) homemade mayonnaise and a little single or soured cream.*

2 *Finely shred about 500g (1lb) cabbage in a food processor or by hand (left). Add to the grated carrots and mayonnaise mixture and stir until well coated. Season well with sea salt and freshly ground black pepper, then set aside for 30 minutes.*

ONIONS, STALKS *and* SHOOTS

My favourite of these vegetables is fennel; this has a totally different character and flavour when raw as opposed to cooked, but both are invaluable for producing interesting dishes. Cooking it produces a rounded, mellow flavour. Sliced thinly and eaten raw in salads, the aniseed flavour is much more pungent and refreshes the whole mouth.

Onions and shallots can hardly be overcooked; long and gentle frying or stewing brings out the best in them, a sweet and mild softness and the most enticing smell. If you cry when peeling and cutting onions the tears stop miraculously when you rinse your hands under running water.

Asparagus is a vegetable with a unique and fascinating flavour. It can be plump or thin, almost white, bright green or a dark purply green, which is the kind I prefer.

The globe artichoke is a member of the thistle family which belies its ferocious uncooked appearance. The base of the spiky leaves tastes divine, and last to be revealed, but best of all, is the artichoke heart.

Corn on the cob must be eaten as fresh as possible; immediately after picking, the corn is wonderfully sweet, tender and juicy, but as soon as corn is picked the sugar starts converting to starch so the longer the cob is stored before cooking, the more starchy it will become.

BUYING AND STORING

As with most vegetables, keep them cool and crisp in the bottom of the refrigerator, wrapped loosely in polythene. Onions, however, need cool, dry and dark storage.

CHOPPING AN ONION

Chopping an onion correctly is deemed the art of a true professional cook! If you ever get the chance to watch a chef, you'll be amazed at his lightning speed. Once you have mastered the technique, regular practice will speed things up. The secrets are to make sure your cook's knife is good and sharp and to keep the onion root intact to act as an anchor. Chop just before using the onion so the juice will not dry up.

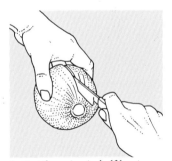

1 *Cut the onion in half leaving some of the root on each half. Peel each half and work with one at a time. Place the cut side down on a board.*

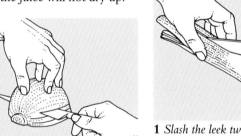

2 *With the knife held horizontally, make cuts almost right through to the root end at 5mm (¼in) intervals. Do not cut through the root.*

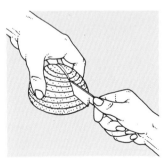

3 *Make vertical cuts downwards, at 5mm (¼in) intervals, again leaving the onion root attached and holding the onion firmly with your free hand.*

4 *Holding the onion with your fingers at a 90° angle, keep the knife tip on the board and rock the blade up and down, slicing as you go. Discard the root.*

PREPARING LEEKS

Ready-trimmed leeks need little extra washing, but older loose ones sold with long dark green tops may well have a lot of dirt trapped inside. Wash off any obvious mud on the outside and cut off and discard the root and tough tops.

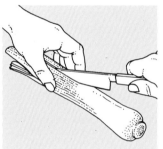

1 *Slash the leek twice lengthwise from the green tip down to the start of the white stalk. Wash well in at least 2 changes of cold water until all the dirt is removed.*

2 *Cut into 3 or 4 shorter lengths, then slice into thin strips. Alternatively, slice whole leeks across in rounds at 5mm (¼in) or 1cm (½in) intervals.*

PREPARING FENNEL

Fennel, also known as Florence fennel, is sold in tight, flattish or round, oblong bulbs with small fronds which can be reserved and used as an attractive garnish. Look for pale green to white bulbs and do not buy any which are dark green or they will be too bitter tasting.

Fennel can be halved or quartered and cored and then braised, steamed or baked, or sliced thinly to use in salads, or in stir-fries and casseroles.

Pluck off the fronds *and reserve. Trim off the top stalks and halve the bulb. Cut out the root core in a 'V' shape, then lay cut side down and slice thinly crosswise.*

PREPARING GLOBE ARTICHOKES

Globe artichokes make one of the most attractive starters, and – once you've mastered the initial technique – are easy to prepare and cook. Look for ones with firm green leaves and avoid any with brown tips or a dried-up appearance. Once cooked, the artichoke can be served hot or cold. Pull off the leaves and dip the leaf base in dressing or melted butter. Then scrape off the soft flesh with your front teeth. Eat the heart separately with a knife and fork. Discard the hairy choke in the centre.

Tenderly cooked hot asparagus spears with melted butter, and Artichokes with Yellow Mystery Sauce (page 65).

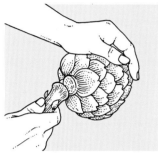

1 *Score round the stem base with a sharp knife, then pull down sharply to remove. Use a sharp knife to cut off the top for presentation if you like.*

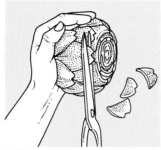

2 *Trim the tips of the leaves with scissors. Cook by simmering in water with some fresh lemon juice until the base leaves separate easily, about 40 minutes.*

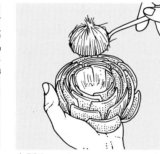

3 *Drain and cool upside down in a colander. Pull the top leaves apart to reveal the inner purple ones. Grasp these firmly and pull up hard, revealing the hairy choke.*

4 *Using a teaspoon, scrape out the choke in one piece as much as possible and discard, exposing the heart. Replace the purple leaves, reshape and serve.*

PREPARING FRESH SWEETCORN

For the freshest flavour, sweetness and juiciness, sweetcorn should be bought with the husks still intact, as the kernels become stale quickly when exposed to air. To capture the fresh flavour, eat sweetcorn on the day of purchase. Best of all is if you can pick your own and then go straight home to cook it. Kernels also taste wonderful eaten raw as long as the corn is absolutely fresh.

PREPARING ASPARAGUS

Once only available for several weeks in each spring, imports now mean we can enjoy asparagus all year round.

The stalks of thick asparagus, whether white or green, need peeling. After peeling, break off the woody base and discard. Sprue, which are young, thin, long asparagus stems, need little preparation, except trimming at the base. Prepare asparagus just before cooking (page 52) to prevent the stalks drying out.

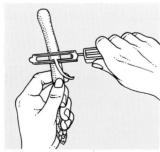

To peel thick asparagus, *use a swivel-bladed vegetable peeler or sharp paring knife and peel gently away from you from about half the way up the stalk to the base.*

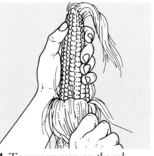

1 *To prepare corn on the cob, hold the cob firmly in one hand, and pull off the green leafy husks. Trim the stalk, then peel away the silky brown threads. There is no need to wash before cooking.*

2 *To remove the kernels, hold the prepared cob upright, stalk end down on a board. Using a sharp cook's knife, cut straight down. The kernels may scatter a bit, so allow plenty of space.*

VEGETABLE FRUITS *and* SQUASHES

Vegetable fruits, which include tomatoes, peppers, aubergines, cucumbers and okra, are a delicious group which are botanically classified as fruits, but eaten as vegetables. In fact, they all contain an element of sweetness, as does the squash family. They combine well with each other in dishes such as ratatouille (page 59) or vegetable curries (page 58).

The joy of aubergines lies in their creamy, almost dissolving consistency. So, whether they are baked, grilled, fried or stewed, they must become completely soft before eating. Some people are wary of okra but if you buy them small and an unblemished green, they are excellent. The versatile squash family, including courgettes, marrow and pumpkin, all differ slightly in flavour and texture, but can be combined with all sorts of complementary ingredients.

BUYING AND STORING
Store most of these vegetables in the refrigerator, wrapped loosely in polythene and use within a couple of days. Peppers and aubergines start to wrinkle when ageing but are still usable. Avocados are best kept at room temperature until ripened, then stored in the refrigerator to prevent overripening. Marrows keep well in a cool, dry place.

STONING AVOCADOS

Avocados are ripe if they feel slightly soft when pressed gently cupped in your hand. Although available all year round, there are different varieties and colours of avocado, but they are all prepared in the same way. Once you have cut one open, brush the flesh with lemon juice to prevent discoloration if you do not plan to eat it once.

1 *Cut the avocado in half lengthwise right through to and around the stone. Holding in both hands, twist the halves in opposite directions and pull apart gently but still firmly.*

2 *Hold one half cupped in your hand and hit the stone firmly in the centre with a cook's knife. Lift up the stone, which will stay on the knife. Serve in the skin or peel and slice for salads.*

DEGORGING AUBERGINES

Look for firm full aubergines with smooth skins. Cooked whole, the flesh can then be scooped out for a smooth pâté (page 97), but normally aubergines are prepared in slices or dice. Classically, aubergines are degorged, meaning sprinkled with salt so the bitter juices drain out and the flesh firms slightly. This is especially useful when frying slices so they don't absorb quite as much oil, and helps keep the texture soft. Degorging is not necessary for chopped aubergines being put straight into a stew.

1 *Cut off the stalk and cut the flesh in slices 1cm (½in) thick, then layer in a colander, sprinkling each layer with salt.*

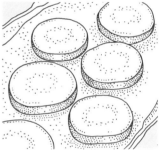

2 *Leave to drain for 30 minutes over a sink, then rinse well. Place the slices on several layers of kitchen paper and pat dry.*

PREPARING TOMATOES

It really is worth the small effort to skin fresh tomatoes for making stews, sauces, soups and coulis.

Choose firm, just ripe fruit. Single tomatoes can be skinned by spearing on a fork and holding over a gas flame until the skin blackens and pops, but for batches of tomatoes a brief dunk in boiling water to loosen the skins is easiest. For cooking, the plum variety, really ripe, are the best tomatoes to use.

1 *Remove any stalks then cut a small cross on the opposite sides. Place the tomatoes in a deep heatproof bowl and pour over fresh boiling water.*

2 *Leave for 1 minute or until the skins split. Drain and pour over plenty of cold water so the tomatoes do not cook. Using a paring knife, remove the skins.*

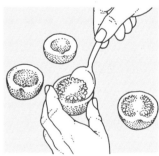

To deseed tomatoes, *remove the stalk core, then cut the tomato in half and scoop out the seeds. Chop if using in sauces or light casseroles, or slice.*

PREPARING PEPPERS

Versatile sweet peppers, also called capsicums, can be eaten either raw with a creamy dip, or even better, grilled (page 55) and sliced in salads, or cooked long and gently in stews and sauces. Hollowed out, they are an ideal container for stuffing and baking (page 61), or for holding a dip for other crudités. Peppers also make a wonderful purée.

Apart from the familiar red, green and yellow ones, look for orange or black-skinned peppers.

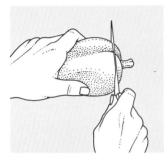

To hollow out, *cut off the top of the pepper with a sharp knife and reserve it as a lid if you plan to stuff the pepper. Use a spoon to scrape out the whole core and seeds. For rings, slice across thinly.*

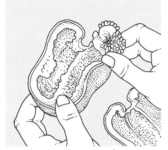

To slice or chop, *cut the peppers in half lengthwise, then remove the cores and seeds. Slice lengthwise or crosswise for half rings. For kebabs, quarter the peppers, then cut into square chunks.*

DESEEDING CHILLIES

These require care when handling if you are not to cause yourself great discomfort. The juice stings intensely so avoid rubbing your eyes or nose after cutting or handling a chilli. I find preparing chillies under cold running water helps, but care is still the best course of action. If you have sensitive skin, wear a pair of rubber gloves.

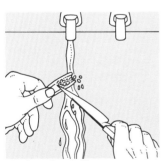

To deseed a chilli, *use a paring knife to slice it open, then use the tip of the knife to scrape out the seeds under running cold water. Chop or slice the chilli as finely as required.*

TRIMMING OKRA

Also known as ladies' fingers, okra are a favourite vegetable ingredient of Indian and Creole cuisines. Buy bright green firm pods without dark blemishes. Okra are often cooked whole because inside the pod is a sticky substance that acts as a thickening agent. Trim just before cooking to avoid the sticky juice oozing out unless they are intended to be used as a thickener.

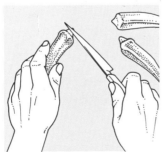

To prepare whole okra, *trim the very tip of the stalk, then peel the sides of the stalk working around it. Try not to cut the tip completely off.*

STUFFING MARROWS

Autumnal marrows are delicious prepared either as a side vegetable chopped up with onions and tomatoes, sliced in rings or stuffed and baked as a main course. Unlike those of younger courgettes, marrow skins are too tough to be eaten. Biggest isn't necessarily best when buying marrows; if they are too large they will have coarse, dry flesh with lots of seeds. Instead, look for marrows 22–30cm (9–12in) long. Larger marrows can be chopped and used to make jam or chutney. Marrow flesh benefits from plenty of coarsely ground pepper, and can be stuffed with spicy mince or vegetable mixtures.

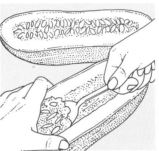

For stuffing, *cut the marrow in half lengthwise and scoop out the seeds, using a sharp tablespoon or paring knife. Make up a stuffing (page 61) and spoon it into the shell. Put the 2 halves back together again and wrap the marrow in foil for baking.*

For rings, *cut a whole marrow in thick slices. Using a teaspoon, scoop out the seeds from the centres, then place the rings in a buttered ovenproof dish for cooking. Or, chop the rings in coarse dice and cook in a ratatouille-style stew (page 59).*

Warm, spicy Middle Eastern flavours permeate Aubergine and Okra Stew with Mint and Pine Kernels (page 62).

SALADS *and* RAW VEGETABLES

Lettuce, the most basic salad ingredient, varies very much in type; there is the normal round lettuce loosely packed with floppy leaves, which has a mild, pleasant flavour, and is ideal on its own with chopped fresh herbs and a good vinaigrette. There is Iceberg lettuce or crisp lettuce, very tightly packed with hardly any taste but a refreshing crunchiness, and there is my favourite, the Cos lettuce, with its long, dark green, crisp leaves, which has the best flavour of all. Very popular, too, are the tightly packed Little Gem lettuces which have both crispness and flavour, and can be stored in the refrigerator far longer than other salad leaves. There are also very decorative lettuces which make leaf salads so pretty. Watercress and cress both have a peppery bite which is nice combined with creamy flavoured, rich slices of avocado. Raw mushrooms are wonderful in salads, and absorb a flavourful vinaigrette made with extra virgin olive oil.

BUYING AND STORING

Salad leaves should be kept loosely wrapped in polythene in the bottom of the refrigerator and eaten as soon as possible, particularly the softer leaves.

THE PERFECT TOSSED SALAD

Aim to use at least 2 types of leaves, one sweet, like a Cos, and one frilly and bitter, such as frisée, or a different colour, such as red radicchio. Optional extras include watercress or rocket, and lots of fresh chopped parsley, chives and other tender herbs. Crunchy vegetables like spring onion, cucumber, and green peppers are best left for mixed salads. A well-flavoured dressing (page 204) is essential but don't drench the salad. Use just enough to coat the leaves.

1 *Separate the lettuce leaves and tear into bite-size pieces, placing in a colander. Discard any damaged outer ones. Wash well with other smaller leaves such as watercress and drain in a colander, shaking off any excess water.*

2 *Place the leaves on a clean tea towel, top with another towel and pat lightly to dry, or dry by spinning in a salad spinner. (If preparing ahead, store in the refrigerator in a polythene food bag to keep it crisp.)*

3 *Pour just enough vinaigrette to coat the leaves into the bottom of a large mixing bowl. Add the leaves and toss well with your hands or with salad servers. Transfer to a serving bowl immediately.*

IDEAS FOR SALADS

• Ordinary round lettuce leaves are really best as a salad on their own, dressed with a good mustard vinaigrette, but the most decorative lettuces are good in mixed-leaf salads.
• All the chicories, with their slight bitterness, take well to a vinaigrette which has been sweetened with honey (page 204), or mixed with other sweet ingredients such as slices of orange, fresh apricots or watermelon. The colours also help make a pretty salad.
• Frisée tastes delicious with orange slices and a walnut-oil or hazelnut-oil vinaigrette.
• To make crudités to serve with taramasalata (page 137) cut carefully cleaned and prepared carrots, fennel, peppers and celery into neat, thin pieces.

• An excellent salad is finely sliced bulb fennel with thin slices of blood orange, simply dribbled with a little white wine vinegar and either olive or walnut oil, and sprinkled with crushed sea salt, pink peppercorns and a pinch or two of cayenne pepper.
• Another salad I really enjoy is watercress and rocket mixed with halved yellow cherry tomatoes and a hot bacon dressing, which also goes well with a spinach leaf salad. Make the dressing by frying little pieces of Tendersweet bacon and then heating a vinaigrette mixture (page 204) with the bacon and its fat before mixing it into the salad.
• Cucumber is best peeled and cubed, and mixed with seasoned yogurt and fresh mint.

MAKING A MIXED SALAD

I think a mixed salad is much more interesting if some of the ingredients are raw and some are lightly blanched vegetables such as mange tout, thin french beans or asparagus tips. Peeled and parboiled root vegetables can also enhance mixed salads; slices of parsnip, turnip, celeriac and swede, steamed or boiled until just beginning to soften but still with a bite, are delicious. Strips of grilled peppers (page 55), with their mellow, smoky taste, are wonderful. Bulb fennel, sliced across, are excellent if grilled briefly before adding to salads. You can also pour boiling water on to fresh broad beans and then pop the beans out of their skins into the salad. A little finely shredded red cabbage adds crunch and colour to a green salad.

I never use tomatoes, except whole or halved cherry tomatoes, in mixed salads as I think they are far better on their own with a generous sprinkling of fresh herbs and olive oil.

Prepare all the ingredients for a salad and assemble in a large bowl, adding chopped herbs if liked. Dress with a garlicky dressing, including wholegrain mustard (page 204). Any root vegetables should be put into a separate bowl and tossed with some dressing while still hot so that they absorb the flavour of the dressing as they cool.

SALADE NIÇOISE

This classic Provençal salad is a glorious jumble of the ingredients that Mediterranean France excels in – tomatoes, black olives, crunchy green french beans and capers, topped with sliced anchovy fillets. Serve it as a starter or a light main course; to make it more of a main meal, add quartered hard-boiled egg and cold potato slices. A mustard-flavoured vinaigrette (page 204) is particularly good with salade niçoise.

1 *Put 250g (8oz) each of cooked and still warm green beans and sliced waxy potatoes into a large bowl with 2 large roughly chopped tomatoes.*

The flavours of the south of France are captured in salade niçoise, ideal as a light meal just with chunks of French bread.

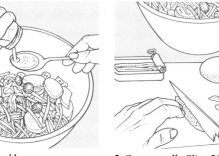

2 *Mix in 2 tablespoons capers, 198g (7oz) can tuna, drained and flaked, 1 handful small black olives, 1 tablespoon chopped flat-leaved parsley and 4–6 tablespoons vinaigrette.*

3 *Season well. Slice 50g (2oz) drained canned anchovy fillets, in half lengthwise. Quarter 1 or 2 hard-boiled eggs. Arrange the salad on a platter and garnish with the anchovies and eggs.*

POTATO SALAD

The most important thing about a potato salad is that regardless of how the potatoes are ultimately going to be dressed, either with a garlicky mustard vinaigrette (page 204) with plenty of chopped dill, a yogurt dressing (page 205) or homemade mayonnaise flavoured with dill (page 202), they should first be tossed in a bowl while still hot with extra virgin olive oil, a little vinegar and seasoning, then left to absorb the flavours. Serves 4.

1 *Scrub well or rub the skins off 500–750g (1–1½lb) new potatoes, and either leave whole or cut up, depending on size. Steam or boil (page 52) until just soft.*

2 *Put the hot potatoes in a bowl, toss with a vinaigrette (page 204) and leave until cold. Transfer to a serving bowl and then coat with your chosen dressing.*

TOMATO SALAD

A simple tomato salad dressed with a drizzle of extra virgin olive oil, a sprinkle of crushed sea salt and garnished with chopped fresh basil is so good.

Slice the tomatoes and arrange on a serving dish. Vinaigrette dressing is often used on tomato salad but I prefer just oil as the tomato juices balance the oil; if they lack flavour add some lemon juice. After dressing, cover and leave for 1 hour.

Drizzle over *enough olive oil to lightly coat. Sprinkle with crushed sea salt, black pepper and chopped fresh basil.*

PREPARING MUSHROOMS

Cultivated mushrooms, including oysters and shiitakes, are grown in sterilized compost so they don't need washing or peeling. A wipe with a clean damp cloth is more than sufficient. Baby-sized buttons can be used whole, while open caps can be sliced, quartered or skewered whole for kebabs. Flat mushrooms, however, are best brushed with oil, stuffed and grilled (page 60).

Wipe mushrooms *with a clean, damp cloth. Trim the base of the stems, then slice thickly or thinly as required.*

STEAMING *and* BOILING

I nearly always steam vegetables in preference to boiling, except for very quick-cooking vegetables like mange tout, which should be cooked for only a minute or two in a large pan of salted, rapidly boiling water, and leaves for blanching such as spinach and lettuce where boiling is more successful. I find that steaming keeps in more flavour, particularly with root vegetables, and produces less waterlogged results. A wide range of steamers is available (page 19) and if you steam regularly and in large quantities buy a two-tiered steamer.

Traditionally, green vegetables were put directly into boiling water while roots and tubers went into cold water to be brought up to the boil. But if you start all vegetables off in a small amount of boiling water it helps preserve the vitamins. Boiled vegetables are usually cooked in salted water, while steamed vegetables are not salted. They need more seasoning before serving, but they do have more flavour in themselves. With both steaming and boiling, test frequently for doneness, because it is impossible to predict exactly when they will reach the right point.

BOILING CABBAGE

Cabbage is one of the most underrated vegetables; it can be supremely delicious if it is cooked carefully.

Either cook cabbage briefly, leaving it bright green and still slightly crunchy, or long and very gently so it becomes meltingly soft and almost sweet tasting. If you boil cabbage, it should be done in a minimum amount of water, really just enough to steam it – the thinner-leaved cabbages like green and savoy cabbages respond well to quick cooking, with the crisper, fresh-tasting results.

Shred the cabbage *finely (page 45) and rinse well. Bring about 1cm (½in) salted water to a vigorous boil in a heavy-based saucepan, then add the cabbage, cover and boil for 5–8 minutes until softened, but still with a slight crunch to it.*

USING BOILED AND STEAMED VEGETABLES

• Celeriac mashed with potato and lots of butter is a lovely topping for either shepherd's or fish pie or can be used for making fish cakes (page 129).
• Roughly chopped sweet peppers, boiled with whole cloves of unpeeled garlic until soft, and then puréed together – first popping the soft garlic easily out of its skin – make an excellent purée. You can whizz in butter to serve as a hot purée, or olive oil for a cold one. Or sieve the purée with cream or vegetable stock to make it into a sauce.
• Peppers can also be boiled with other vegetables and puréed together. Try carrots with red peppers, and courgettes or bulb fennel with green peppers.
• To enhance a dish of boiled

or steamed vegetables, the easiest and most effective thing to do is to sprinkle them with soy sauce just before serving. This is also useful if you are on a low-fat diet and don't want to use butter.
• Fresh herbs such as mint, parsley and fennel leaves are good on all vegetables, with or without other flavourings.
• A sprinkling of hickory-flavoured smoked salt is very good on green vegetables.
• Grated nutmeg seems to enhance all vegetables, and is marvellous included in a grated cheese topping.
• Freshly boiled, hot beetroot is nice with a white sauce (page 196) to which you have added soured cream or Greek yogurt and chopped, fresh herbs at the end of the cooking.

STEAMING BROCCOLI

Broccoli should retain a bright-green colour and a slight firmness, so it is very important not to cook it for too long. It can be too crunchy, however, so it is also vital to test it at least once or twice during the cooking. It is best to cut the broccoli into equal-sized florets (page 44), using only the part of the stem which looks green and tender. With calabrese broccoli – the bright green variety which has large, tightly flowering heads – the stems are almost always tender, except at the thickest part which should be cut away.

Place the broccoli *florets in the top half of a steamer over boiling water. Cover and steam for 5–10 minutes until just tender but still bright green. Season with salt and pepper and serve at once with plenty of melted butter or with hollandaise sauce (page 200).*

COOKING ASPARAGUS

Because asparagus tips are more tender, care must be taken to ensure they do not overcook before the stems are ready. They are best cooked either upright in a tall pan so the tips steam while the stems simmer or flat in a shallow pan or frying pan.

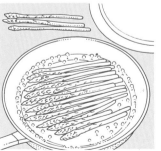

1 *Prepare the asparagus (page 47). Bring salted water to the boil in a shallow pan, then add the asparagus spears in a single layer without overcrowding. Reduce to a simmer and cover.*

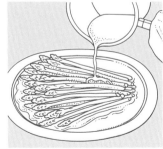

2 *Cook for 5 minutes or until the stems are just tender. Remove with a fish slice and drain well. Arrange on a hot serving dish and pour over melted butter or serve with hollandaise sauce (page 200).*

PURÉEING VEGETABLES

Many vegetables make delicious purées to serve with roasts and comforting casseroles. The purées, however, should not be tasteless overcooked vegetable slurries but, instead, light creams retaining flavour and body. Suitable vegetables for puréeing include cauliflower, carrots, swedes, brussels sprouts, parsnips, celeriac, peas and spinach but root purées are best of all.

Often it is nice to combine two vegetables, one of which can be a vegetable that is too watery to purée on its own, but adds good flavour, such as leeks. The mixture of celeriac and potato is a well-known combination but celeriac is also delicious if combined with carrots, parsnips and swedes. Bulb fennel combines well with root vegetables in a purée, or is delicious as a purée on its own or blended with Greek yogurt.

Enrich vegetable purées with butter, cream, fromage frais, yogurt or olive oil. Serve purées topped with toasted nuts, spiced oil (page 36), fried breadcrumbs, chopped herbs or simply swirled attractively with a fork.

Spinach and Peppers in a Sweet Potato and Parsnip Bowl (page 63) uses two puréed root vegetables to make an unusual case for the spinach and red peppers.

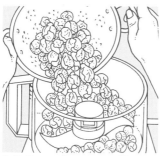

1 *Boil your chosen vegetable in a small amount of water until just tender but not overcooked. Drain, reserving the cooking liquid, and place in a food processor. Whizz until smooth, adding a little of the cooking liquid to moisten and make blending easier.*

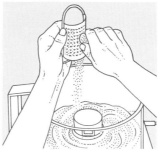

2 *Add butter to taste or a couple tablespoons of fromage frais or other soft white cheese. Freshly ground spices or chopped herbs such as nutmeg, cinnamon, thyme or coriander can be added at this point. Taste again and season with salt and pepper.*

Purées can also be made *with a food mill (page 22), resulting in a thicker texture. Process the vegetable in batches. Return the puréed vegetable to the saucepan on low heat until any excess moisture is evaporated, stirring, and then beat in any flavourings.*

PERFECT MASHED POTATOES

There is something so comforting about good mashed potatoes – light, fluffy and creamy all at the same time. These are potatoes to go with sausages, chops, veal escalopes or roasts, as well as homely stews, appealing to the young and old alike.

The secret to excellent mashed potato lies in choosing the right variety of potato that boils to a soft texture without disintegrating (page 43). Luxury mashed potatoes can be made by mixing in saffron-infused milk or cream.

1 *Cut peeled potatoes into equal-sized pieces for even boiling. Cook in lightly salted boiling water until tender but not too soft. Drain well. Return the potatoes to the saucepan over a gentle heat to dry out slightly.*

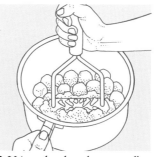

2 *Using a hand masher, or small electric beater, mash the potatoes to a smooth purée. Do not mash potatoes in a food processor, as it turns the potatoes gluey. If you want saffron potatoes infuse several threads in hot milk or cream.*

3 *Beat in butter to taste and trickle in milk, ideally hot for extra fluffy mash. Season well, adding freshly grated nutmeg or ground mace. Mound up the potatoes on a hot serving dish and top with knobs of butter.*

FRYING *and* GRILLING

Fried vegetables can be irresistible, but it is important to cook them carefully as they can burn easily. The oil or fat they are cooked in is important as it will become very much part of their flavour; a mixture of olive oil and butter can be brought to a higher temperature than just butter without burning, but for quickly fried vegetables, I think extra virgin olive oil is the best. For Chinese-style stir-fries the vegetables should be cut to the same size and, to add an authentic flavour, you can mix in some nutty-tasting toasted sesame oil with groundnut or sunflower oil, but use it sparingly, as it is very dominating.

Some people never think of grilling any vegetables other than tomatoes and mushrooms, but all the squash family, and other sliced vegetables which have a softish consistency, grill very well, and in the process lose much of their excess water. With grilling, it is best to keep the heat very high so the vegetables actually burn black in places, giving them a lovely smoky taste.

SHALLOW FRYING

Shallow frying vegetables adds a lovely flavour. As with all shallow frying, vegetables are best cooked quickly in hot oil for a light crisp texture on the outside, leaving the inside just tender but still with a good bite. Fry in a wide, heavy-based frying pan and use a good quality oil, such as olive, groundnut or sunflower. Vegetables should be thinly sliced or grated. Mixing them with, or dipping them in, egg batters or breadcrumbs before frying helps protect the flesh from the heat. Grated potatoes can be pressed together and fried for traditional Jewish latkes or Swiss rösti.

To make courgette fritters, mix 375g (12oz) grated courgettes and 1 small grated onion into a batter made with 125g (4oz) flour, 1 egg, 1 teaspoon each salt and garam masala and 150ml (¼ pint) milk. Drop tablespoons into hot shallow oil and fry for 5 minutes, turning once. Drain on kitchen paper.

To make potato latkes, grate 1kg (2lb) peeled potatoes and soak for 1 hour in cold water. Drain for 15 minutes. Beat 2 tablespoons self-raising flour with 2 eggs, 1 tablespoon grated onion, salt and pepper. Mix in the potatoes. Fry in tablespoonfuls in shallow hot oil for 3 minutes on each side until browned.

To make rösti, boil 750g (1½lb) unpeeled potatoes for 10 minutes. Drain, cool, peel and grate coarsely. Season. Heat 1 tablespoon oil and 25g (1oz) butter in a 23cm (9in) frying pan. Spoon in the potatoes, levelling the top. Fry 10 minutes, then invert on to a plate. Slide back to cook the other side. Serve in wedges.

DEEP FRYING

Deep-fried potatoes and coated vegetables are crispest if eaten freshly cooked. For best results use groundnut or sunflower oil as these can be heated to high temperatures. All vegetables, except roots, need protection in the form of batters or flour coatings, which add delicious flavours of their own.

Homemade chips are one of the most popular deep-fried vegetables. These are cooked in two stages, the first to cook the potato properly and the second to crisp. After frying, keep the chips warm in a low oven, sitting on several layers of crumpled kitchen paper.

1 Prepare the chips (page 43). Soak for 30 minutes, then drain and pat dry. Fill a deep, heavy-based saucepan one-third full with oil. Heat to 160°C, 325°F or until a cube of bread browns in 1 minute. Cover the base of the chip basket with raw chips and fry for about 5 minutes until they are pale golden brown.

2 Remove the chips from the pan and drain well on kitchen paper. Cook the remaining chips. Raise the temperature to 190°C, 375°F or until a cube of bread browns in 30 seconds. Re-fry the chips for just 1 minute until crisp. Reheat the oil between batches. Drain the chips well on kitchen paper and sprinkle with salt.

For simple vegetable fritters, toss sliced onions, broccoli florets, parsnip sticks and button mushrooms in flour seasoned with mild curry spices. Heat oil to 185°C, 360°F, or until a cube of bread browns in 40 seconds. Fry the vegetables in batches for about 2 minutes. Drain well on kitchen paper.

GRILLING PEPPERS

Grilled peppers are one of my favourite vegetables. The grilling transforms the slightly watery texture and taste to something smooth, mellow and sweet.

To remove pepper skins the peppers have to be grilled until charred and black. The slightly smoky taste grilling leaves once the peppers are skinned is an added bonus. Grilled and skinned peppers are excellent in salads, pasta and fish dishes.

To prepare peppers for grilling, cut in half lengthwise, and discard the core and seeds (page 49).

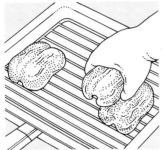 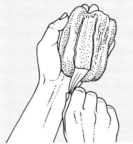

1 *Put the peppers, skin side upwards, under the highest possible preheated grill. Leave until charred black nearly all over. Remove from the grill and wrap in a tea towel or place in a paper bag until cool enough to handle.*

2 *Using just your fingers, peel off the skin, bit by bit, and discard. Then slice the peppers as liked. Either add the peppers while still hot to cooked pasta or use later when cool to make Peppers in Oil (page 307) or add to a salad.*

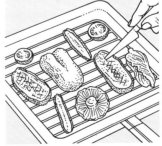

A selection of charcoal-grilled vegetables – aubergines, yellow peppers, radicchio, tomatoes, courgettes and mushrooms.

MIXED VEGETABLE GRILL

Grilled vegetables can be absolutely wonderful. Courgettes, mushrooms, tomatoes, peppers, aubergines, slices of bulb fennel and clusters of radicchio leaves are particularly delicious grilled and can be served either on their own or as an accompaniment to roast meat or poultry. The grill should be very, very hot as the vegetables must become charred on the outside to give them their irresistible smoky flavour. If you are lucky enough to have a ribbed griddle pan or a char-grill on your stove, the vegetables will be attractively striped with black lines, but an overhead grill can also produce good results. In the summer, a charcoal or fruitwood barbecue, especially with a few rosemary, thyme or fennel sprigs on it, can be fantastic, but it is more difficult to get the cooking exactly right.

Prepare the vegetables as follows: Halve tomatoes and peppers or leave them whole; trim mushroom stalks so that they stay level on the grill; leave courgettes and aubergines unpeeled and slice thinly lengthwise, but score the cut surfaces of large aubergines in a criss-cross pattern so that the heat penetrates fully; radicchio simply needs halving lengthwise so the root end holds together the layers of leaves. Smear the vegetables all over with plenty of olive oil and a little salt, and also Mediterranean herbs such as oregano, rosemary or thyme.

IDEAS FOR GRILLING AND FRYING

• Oyster mushrooms are a most successful ingredient in a mixed vegetable grill (right).

• Sweetcorn can also be grilled as long as the cobs are very fresh and therefore juicy – they are best grilled still protected by their outside husk.

• A little beer added to a batter instead of some of the milk or water makes it lighter. You can also add herbs, grated lemon rind and ground or whole spices to batters for frying.

• Very thin slices of peeled root vegetables such as parsnip, celeriac or swede are lovely fried briefly in olive oil with crushed garlic and chopped flat-leaved parsley added at the end of frying. They can be eaten as an appetizer or as a hot first course.

• A true revelation are the thinnest slices of pumpkin swiftly fried in olive oil with a little crushed garlic over a fairly high heat so that the edges begin to blacken slightly, but the pumpkin is still fairly firm. Chopped fresh mint perfects this dish, adding freshness to the sweet pumpkin.

• Courgette flowers are a real delicacy served as the Italians do, sautéed in olive oil or stuffed with cheese, dipped in batter and deep-fried.

• The skin is arguably the best bit of the potato; I love deep-fried pieces of skin. Choose long, narrow potatoes and cut them into fairly large slices which contain quite a lot of the flesh as well as the skin, parboil them very briefly in salted water just to soften a little and pat dry with kitchen paper before deep-frying in hot oil until crispy.

• Whole, medium-sized courgettes can be smeared with olive oil and salt and grilled until blackened all over with the inside soft and white; cut into long strips, sprinkle with oregano and black pepper and dribble with olive oil.

• Thinly shredded spring greens are irresistible deep fried and served in a crispy mass as the Chinese do.

1 *Lay out the prepared vegetables on or under the hottest possible grill – when they are charred on one side, turn them over.*

2 *The vegetables are cooked when there is little resistance to a small pointed knife inserted in the centre. Serve at once.*

ROASTING *and* BAKING

The most familiar roast vegetables are, of course, potatoes, but other root vegetables can all be roasted if you parboil them first. Vegetables which contain a lot of sugar such as sweet potatoes and parsnips burn very quickly and should not be roasted at too high a heat. Roast vegetables should have a really crisp exterior and softish centre, and are best roasted in quite a lot of hot fat or oil. One of the great treats are whole cloves of garlic, roasted in their skins with a slowly cooked joint of meat. They become brown and caramelized, with a sweet mellowness within the skin.

There are many possibilities for baking vegetables, again baked potatoes being the best known. Sweet potatoes also bake well and can be filled as ordinary potatoes. Vegetables can also be baked in shallow dishes in a béchamel sauce (page 196), or with crunchy toppings. Alternatively, you can arrange mixed layers of prepared vegetables with butter or olive oil and other flavourings in a covered terrine to be baked gently in the oven.

Baking is done at a moderate heat if you have not parboiled the vegetables first, whereas roast vegetables, for the best crispness, should be parboiled and then roasted at a high heat which is then reduced to moderate after 20–30 minutes. For perfect roasting, vegetables need to be watched carefully as ovens often vary.

BAKED POTATOES

There are times when I feel I would like to eat a baked potato more than anything else; they are a most reassuring food, either eaten simply (and to me best of all) with melted butter, or with all manner of fillings (below) to suit your mood.

Although it is extremely convenient to 'bake' potatoes quickly in a microwave, it is only by proper baking for at least an hour in a conventional oven, that you achieve a really crusty skin which contrasts irresistibly with the smoothly soft centre. The chart on page 43 lists the varieties most suitable for baking.

If you have any leftover duck fat after roasting a duck (page 179), you can use it to smear over the potatoes, otherwise use butter or olive oil – and sprinkle with crushed sea salt for its flavour, too. If you want the skin to be extra crunchy, cook the potatoes for a bit longer. Piercing the potatoes through with metal skewers (right) conducts the heat and speeds up the cooking, but it is not essential.

Remember that you can bake sweet potatoes in the same way as ordinary ones, and they will soften slightly more quickly.

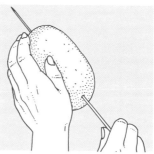

1 *Scrub the potatoes and cut out any blemishes. Either push a metal skewer through the centre of each potato or cut a line in the potato skin, so it has no chance of bursting while cooking. Smear the potatoes generously all over with duck fat, butter or olive oil.*

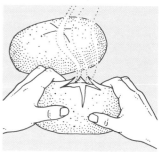

2 *Sprinkle with crushed sea salt and lay on a baking sheet in the centre of a preheated oven at 200°C, 400°F, Gas Mark 6 and bake for 1–1½ hours until soft. Remove the skewers. Cut a deep cross in each top and squeeze open for filling.*

IDEAS FOR ROASTING AND BAKING

• If you want to roast potatoes without parboiling, peel medium-sized potatoes and cut thinly almost right through so that they look a bit like a folded fan, then spread crushed garlic or pesto sauce (page 207) between the slices with a knife, sprinkle all over with sea salt, black pepper and olive oil and roast in a fairly hot oven.
• To make roast parsnips, peel them and cut into thick strips, then boil for 5 minutes. Drain well and roast as for potatoes (opposite) but at a slightly lower heat and for a shorter time.
• I love vegetables baked in the oven in a shallow gratin dish and topped with grated cheese or scattered with a mixture of

grated Parmesan, fresh breadcrumbs, crushed garlic and olive oil. The vegetables should be boiled until just tender first, then drained very well before putting into the dish and adding the topping. A crunchy topping can also be achieved by mixing chopped nuts – hazelnuts or almonds especially – with the grated cheese.
• Pumpkin is spectacular baked whole with a filling (page 60) but large peeled pieces can also be smeared with oil and seasoning and roasted in an oven at 180°C, 350°F, Gas Mark 4 until brown outside and just tender in the centre.
• You can also bake whole turnips with the stems cut off

and smeared with olive oil and salt. Serve with a sauce made by beating honey with a little finely chopped garlic and balsamic vinegar, seasoned with salt and freshly ground black pepper.
• Baked dishes include vegetable soufflés and terrines – coarsely grated courgettes or pumpkin are excellent in a cheese soufflé mixture (page 76).
• Aubergine can be baked whole, or cut in half lengthwise while still raw then filled with a sautéed stuffing and baked.
• Good fillings for baked potatoes include crumbled crispy bacon on top of a little puréed spinach mixed with cream; soured cream topped with lumpfish or salmon roe (or real

caviar if you can afford it); chopped smoked salmon mixed with fromage frais and lots of chopped fresh dill; chopped pickled herring mixed with soured cream, ground coriander and chopped chives – and the simplest but one of the best, a dollop of pesto sauce (page 207).
• A most wonderful vegetable to bake is beetroot. It needs slow, long cooking and should be left unpeeled but wrapped in foil. Eat with soured cream or yogurt and plenty of black pepper.
• Soured cream or Greek yogurt whizzed in the food processor with plenty of chives and/or mint make a marvellous green sauce for baked potatoes or baked beetroot.

BAKED SPAGHETTI SQUASH

Spaghetti squash, or vegetable spaghetti, has one of the best flavours of the squash family, a lovely yellow colour, and an intriguing consistency after cooking. It looks like a tangled mass of spaghetti – hence its name.

This is most delicious served with a strong, cheesy sauce, flavoured with grated nutmeg and put briefly under the grill or in a high oven before serving, so that the top browns a little. If you don't want to make a cheese sauce (page 196), simply mix the baked flesh with plenty of butter, salt and black pepper and sprinkle with grated Parmesan cheese on top.

Spaghetti squash seeds are usually tender and good to eat, so do not bother to remove.

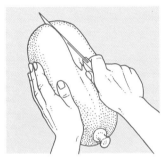 

1 *Cut the spaghetti squash in half lengthwise and wrap the cut sides in foil. Put, foil sides down, on a baking sheet and bake at 180°C, 350°F, Gas Mark 4 for 40–50 minutes, until the flesh is soft when tested with the tip of a small knife.*

2 *Using a fork, scrape out the insides into a colander and transfer to a serving bowl. Top with a strong cheese sauce (page 196) flavoured with a grated quarter of nutmeg and plenty of pepper. Sprinkle with Parmesan and grill to brown slightly.*

FENNEL GRATIN

Vegetables topped with cheese are very appetizing, but I don't think any more so than fennel, especially when combined with Parmesan cheese, olive oil and garlic. The dish can be served hot or cold as an accompaniment or a first course. Serves 4.

 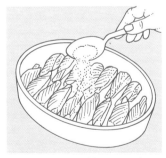

1 *Cut the base and stalks off 4 large bulbs of fennel, then slice lengthwise into quarters, or sixths if very large. Steam or boil the fennel until soft, and drain, then arrange the pieces in a single layer in a shallow, lightly greased gratin dish, with their rounded sides facing upwards.*

2 *Dribble 5–6 tablespoons olive oil over the fennel, sprinkle with 2 large finely chopped garlic cloves, 40–50g (1½–2oz) grated Parmesan cheese, crushed sea salt and plenty of black pepper. Bake at 200°C, 400°F, Gas Mark 6 for 20–30 minutes, until the surface is well browned.*

ROAST POTATOES

It was my mother who made me realize how good roast potatoes can be; richly golden and crunchy-crisp all over with a meltingly soft inside. She cuts her potatoes smaller than usual and boils them until just cooked, but not breaking up. A generous amount of very hot fat or oil is needed and it must have a good flavour, as this is absorbed by potatoes. Goose fat is best but duck fat and olive oil are also excellent. If you have other dishes in the oven, you can adjust the temperature but an initial high heat for at least 20 minutes is important.

1 *Peel potatoes and cut up into 2.5–5cm (1–2in) pieces. Boil in salted water for about 15 minutes until just tender, then drain. Put enough fat or oil in a roasting tin to come at least 1cm (½in) up the side and place in the oven at 230°C, 450°F, Gas Mark 8. When the fat is very hot, add the potatoes and turn them over.*

2 *Roast for about 20–30 minutes, turning them over once, then turn down the oven to 180°C, 350°F, Gas Mark 4 for 45–75 minutes until very crisp and golden brown. Check from time to time. Drain well on kitchen paper and sprinkle with crushed sea salt, then transfer to a serving dish. Serve hot.*

Potatoes and Fennel Cooked with Cheese and Cream (page 63) makes a wonderful vegetarian main course or an ideal accompaniment to roast meats.

BRAISING *and* STEWING

Gentle braising or stewing of vegetables gives very different results. Vegetables are usually braised by cooking slowly in a covered dish in the oven with the addition only of a little butter, olive oil or liquid, and seasonings such as herbs or spices, including garlic, fresh ginger or chillies. Use robust herbs such as bay leaves, rosemary, thyme and tarragon to braise with vegetables, but only stir in tender herbs such as leaf fennel, dill, basil, fresh coriander and parsley at the end of cooking.

Vegetables can also be stewed in a saucepan or casserole on top of the stove, or in the oven, with more liquid, like a normal stew – this can be done more quickly than braising, but doesn't achieve quite the same melting consistency and intensity of flavours which mingle together irresistibly. Apart from the delicious results, it is useful to have a braised vegetable sitting happily in the oven, and needing less attention before you serve the meal.

Certain vegetables are particularly suited to gentle braising or stewing, especially those which are slightly fibrous such as celery, bulb fennel, cabbage and leeks and also, above all, onions. It is only with slow cooking and absorption of seasoning and juices that the full and wonderful flavours of these vegetables really emerge. When you are braising or stewing several different vegetables together they should be added at different moments, depending on the time they are going to take to cook, so none are overcooked. Garlic is almost always a welcome addition to braised or stewed vegetables; plenty can be used because with the long cooking it becomes beautifully sweet. Whole spices such as cinnamon also enhance a vegetable stew.

VEGETABLE CURRY

An easy vegetable curry can be made from all sorts of vegetables, according to what you have. This is a good way to use up vegetables which may be past their prime. All root vegetables are good with spices because of their sweetness, while the addition of pulses such as chick peas, will make the dish more substantial for a main course. Halved hard-boiled eggs are also a harmonious addition. This is a good lunch or supper dish, especially if you have a vegetarian in the family.

Remember that some vegetables take much longer to cook than others, and they should be added at different times. This is why I always make a vegetable curry in a flameproof casserole on top of the stove. Serves 4.

25g (1oz) butter
3 tablespoons groundnut oil
2 onions, peeled and sliced
2.5cm (1in) piece fresh ginger, finely chopped
3–4 cloves garlic, finely chopped
2 teaspoons ground coriander
1 teaspoon ground cumin
1 teaspoon ground cinnamon
½ teaspoon ground turmeric
½ teaspoon cayenne pepper
4 parsnips, peeled and diced
1 cauliflower, divided into florets
1 large red pepper, deseeded and sliced (page 49)
500g (1lb) ripe tomatoes, skinned and chopped
2 tablespoons lemon juice
2 teaspoons caster sugar
250g (8oz) spinach, washed, drained and chopped roughly
Salt

1 *Melt the butter and oil in a large flameproof casserole. Add the onions and stir until beginning to soften. Add the ginger and garlic with the spices and cayenne pepper.*

IDEAS FOR BRAISING AND STEWING

• Chestnut mushrooms retain their body and are less watery even when cooked over a longish period than other mushrooms, so they are the best to use for braising and stewing. Mushrooms marry beautifully with Indian spices – try braising them in a covered dish with butter and a mixture of Indian spices or mild curry paste and some chopped fresh ginger or green chilli. Stir in chopped fresh coriander or mint leaves just before serving.
• Black onion seeds, available from Indian shops, are effective and look interesting in all braises and stews.
• Braised whole or halved chicory or fennel are mouthwatering if they are cooked gently in a covered dish with a little chicken stock, browned butter, brown sugar and seasoning – they are the most perfect accompaniment to pork, poultry and game.
• I also like to braise a little dish of whole peeled garlic cloves and shallots mixed with butter, olive oil, a dash of balsamic vinegar, 1–2 teaspoons of honey, salt and plenty of ground black pepper to be served as a side dish with roast or grilled poultry, meat or game.
• Coconut milk made up either from creamed or instant coconut powder is good stirred into spicy vegetable stews at the end of the cooking time.

2 *Stir for 1 minute. Add the parsnips, cauliflower and red pepper and stir around. Add the tomatoes, lemon juice and caster sugar. Cover the casserole tightly and cook over the lowest possible heat, stirring around once or twice with a wooden spoon, for 30–40 minutes until all the vegetables are very tender and the tomatoes reduced to a pulp.*

3 *Add the chopped spinach and stir in, cover the casserole and cook gently for another 8–10 minutes until the spinach is soft. Season with salt and more cayenne if you like a spicy taste. Boiled basmati rice (page 108) is an ideal accompaniment, or serve with Saffron and Chilli Rice Cooked in Coconut Milk (page 115) or with Indian bread (page 293).*

SIMPLE VEGETABLE BRAISING

Certain vegetables which benefit from longer cooking like celery or roots are wonderful simply left in the oven to braise slowly, covered with stock or tomatoes and whatever herbs take your fancy. Cook at 180°C, 350°F, Gas Mark 4 for 40–50 minutes or until tender when pierced with a sharp knife.

To make braised celery, pull the tough outer ribs off a whole head of celery stalks. Trim the leaves and slice.

Place the celery slices in a casserole with 1 sliced red onion, 2 sliced carrots and 600ml (1 pint) stock. Season and add herbs to taste. Cook as left.

RATATOUILLE

Ratatouille, a traditional Provençal vegetable stew, is a wonderfully versatile dish; it tastes as good hot or cold, and it can be eaten on its own or as an accompanying vegetable to meat, chicken and fish dishes. It is important to cook ratatouille gently so any wateriness evaporates and the vegetables become soft, sweet and mellow. Use only the best-quality ingredients, and really ripe tomatoes (the plum variety if available). Proportions and ingredients can be varied. It looks prettiest if you use different-coloured peppers.

Prepare 1 large unpeeled aubergine by cutting across in thick slices and then in half, sprinkle with salt and leave in a colander for 30 minutes (page 48). Wash and drain thoroughly. You will also need 5–6 tablespoons extra virgin olive oil, 2–3 sliced onions, 2–3 peppers, cut into strips (page 49), 500g (1lb) skinned and chopped ripe tomatoes (page 48), 250g (8oz) sliced courgettes, 4 large cloves chopped garlic, 2 tablespoons lemon juice, 2 teaspoons caster sugar, 1 handful roughly chopped flat-leaved parsley and salt and black pepper. Serves 4.

1 Heat the olive oil in a large flameproof casserole over a medium heat. Add the onion slices and cook, stirring occasionally. When the onions have softened, after about 20 minutes, stir in the pieces of aubergine and pepper strips. Reduce the heat, cover the casserole and cook gently for 15 minutes.

2 Add the tomatoes, courgettes, garlic, lemon juice and sugar. Cook, uncovered, over a low heat, stirring often, for 35–45 minutes until the tomatoes are a thick, mushy sauce and the vegetables very soft but still retaining their shape. Season with salt and plenty of black pepper and stir in the chopped parsley. Serve at once.

Fennel or dill seeds add extra flavour to Braised Leeks with Tomatoes and Balsamic Vinegar (page 64). The slow, gentle braising brings out the leeks' sweet, mellow taste.

BRAISED RED CABBAGE

Delicious with roast pork and traditional with roast goose or duck, braised red cabbage improves if cooked ahead and then reheated just before serving. The sweet flavour of red cabbage marries well with tangy apple and rich comforting spices and it has a great affinity with beer, honey, chestnuts and caraway seeds. Braised red cabbage also looks very attractive.

If not serving at once, cool the cabbage, then refrigerate until ready to reheat for serving. This is an ideal supper dish for vegetarians. Serves 6.

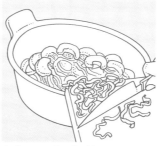

1 Quarter 1 red cabbage, weighing about 1kg (2lb). Cut out the core and shred (page 45). Place the cabbage in a flameproof casserole with 1 sliced onion and 1 large cored and sliced cooking apple, such as a sharp but firm Bramley or 2 Granny Smith apples or other cooking apples.

2 Pour over 600ml (1 pint) chicken or vegetable stock or water, or try half water and half light ale. Add 1 tablespoon honey, 1 teaspoon caraway seeds, 1 cinnamon stick, salt and freshly ground pepper. Cover and braise for 50 minutes at 160°C, 325°F, Gas Mark 3 or until tender.

STUFFED VEGETABLE DISHES

It was my first visit to Turkey, where it seems as if almost every ingredient is stuffed, which fired my enthusiasm for stuffing vegetables. Stuffed vegetables always provide an element of surprise and ingenuity, and can be a wonderfully dense mingling of flavours. Served cold and dribbled with good olive oil, stuffed vegetables make a perfect first course. Several vegetables like sweet peppers, large onions, tomatoes, aubergines, every type and shape of the squash family and crisp, cup-like leaves of Iceberg lettuce and radicchio, are natural containers for stuffings, but round root vegetables can also be hollowed out and stuffed. Large leaves such as cabbage, spinach, spring greens and vine leaves can be softened and wrapped around stuffings.

Stuffings for juicy containers such as tomatoes should be absorbent enough, for instance containing breadcrumbs, to incorporate the juices which will exude during the cooking. Denser vegetables, however, should be given a more juicy or buttery stuffing to help enrich and moisten them. As well as butter, you can also include a little double cream or extra virgin olive oil.

SPICY STUFFED PUMPKIN

A pumpkin makes a good edible cooking container for a spicy meat or vegetable stuffing. A stuffed pumpkin looks extremely impressive but is easy to make and is less fiddly than smaller, stuffed vegetables. Ideal for lunch or supper, it can be served by scooping out pieces of the soft, sweet pumpkin flesh and combining it with a spicy stuffing. It makes a delectable dish for lunch or supper. This recipe includes a vegetable stuffing but as an alternative use a minced meat stuffing.

To prepare a vegetable stuffing, mix thoroughly 500g (1lb) blanched and drained chopped spinach and 1 finely chopped small red pepper with 250g (8oz) soft, medium fat white cheese, such as curd or grated Mozzarella cheese, 2.5–5cm (1–2in) piece fresh ginger, chopped, 1 large crushed clove of garlic, 2 teaspoons ground mace, 1 teaspoon ground cinnamon, ½ teaspoon cayenne pepper, 2 teaspoons caster sugar and a good sprinkling of sea salt. These quantities serve 4.

1 *Cut the top off a 1.7–2kg (3½–4lb) pumpkin using a large, sharp knife; reserve the top. Scrape out the seeds and stringy area with a large spoon. Spoon in the stuffing.*

2 *Place the lid on top, smear with oil and put into a roasting tin. Roast at 180°C, 350°F, Gas Mark 4 for 45–60 minutes until the pumpkin feels tender when tested with a skewer.*

STUFFED MUSHROOMS

Large flat mushrooms make lovely containers for stuffing. Trim the stalks from 4 large mushrooms and reserve. Fry a small chopped onion and a crushed garlic clove in 2 tablespoons olive oil with 2 chopped celery stalks, 2 rashers chopped Tendersweet bacon, the chopped stalks and 1 skinned and chopped tomato for 5 minutes until softened. Season well, add 1 tablespoon chopped fresh oregano or sage and 2 tablespoons double cream.

The spicy spinach and soft white cheese stuffing of the whole pumpkin contrasts nicely with its tender, sweet flesh.

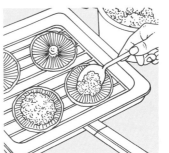

1 *Brush the outside of the mushrooms with more oil and grill on each side for about 5 minutes. Add the filling to the cups, spreading it out.*

2 *Top with sliced Mozzarella cheese. Return to the grill until just melted, then serve sprinkled with chopped herbs on 4 rounds of hot buttered brown toast.*

BAKED STUFFED VEGETABLES

Baked stuffed vegetables are an exciting and mouthwatering fusion of taste and texture. You can serve small, stuffed vegetables as a first course, and larger ones such as marrow and pumpkin as a more substantial main course. When baking stuffed vegetables in a roasting tin, you should put about 1cm (½in) water or olive oil in the bottom of the tin. For courgettes, cut in half lengthwise, scoop out the centres (which you can use in a salad or in the filling) and boil in salted water for 3–4 minutes before stuffing. Bake as for tomatoes (below). All stuffed vegetables are equally good hot or cold. Use the stuffing ideas in the box below or try well-seasoned curd cheese mixed with chopped nuts, herbs, spices, sautéed onion slices and so on.

Rice and pine kernel-filled dolmades (front) with a stuffed mushroom, a stuffed pepper and a stuffed tomato.

To stuff tomatoes, *slice the tops off very large ones. Carefully scoop out the inside flesh with a teaspoon, leaving the tomato shells as your containers. Fill with your chosen stuffing (see box below), including the tomato pulp. Place in a roasting tin and bake at 200°C, 400°F, Gas Mark 6 for about 15 minutes.*

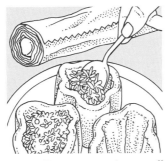

To stuff peppers, *cut the tops off the peppers and scoop out the core and seeds (page 49). Cook the scooped-out peppers and tops in boiling water for 5 minutes, then drain. Stuff the peppers, replace the tops, place in a roasting tin, loosely cover with foil and bake at 190°C, 375°F, Gas Mark 5 for 35–45 minutes.*

DOLMADES

An Eastern Mediterranean appetizer, dolmades are vine leaves enclosing a rice filling. Buy the vine leaves in brine in packs or jars. One pack (227g) makes about 35 dolmades. Make a filling of 1 chopped onion fried in olive oil and mixed with 125g (4oz) long grain rice, 3 tablespoons currants, 1 tablespoon each chopped fresh mint and fresh or dried dill, 2 tablespoons pine kernels, 150ml (¼ pint) water, 1 teaspoon salt and pepper. Boil for 5 minutes.

1 *Drain and rinse the vine leaves in brine, then lay them out rib side up on a board. Put 1 teaspoon of filling at the stalk end of each leaf. Fold in the 2 sides to meet in the centre.*

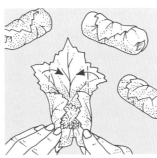

2 *Roll the vine leaf up, starting from the stalk end. Place join side down in a large shallow pan with a lid. Repeat with the remaining leaves, fitting the rolls close together in a single layer.*

3 *Pour over water just to cover and the juice of ½ lemon and 4 tablespoons olive oil. Weigh down with a heatproof plate, cover and simmer 1 hour. Cool in the pan, then transfer to a plate.*

VEGETABLE STUFFINGS

• Spicy, minced meat stuffing is suitable for all kinds of vegetables and leaves. Fry minced beef, pork, veal, lamb or turkey, pressing with a wooden spoon to separate it. Add flavourings such as chopped garlic, sliced onions, chopped tomatoes, tomato purée, pesto sauce, curry paste, miso paste, chopped mushrooms, pine kernels, chopped walnuts, grated citrus rind, or herbs or spices.
• Minced meat mixtures or finely chopped and fried vegetables can be mixed with cooked rice – I always prefer basmati for its nutty flavour and texture (page 108).
• Fruit like chopped fresh apricots, apples, pears and plums can also be mixed with well-seasoned rice, finely grated lemon rind and chopped spring onions for a stuffing.
• Breadcrumbs can be an alternative to rice when you want to make stuffings more solid and absorbing. Grated cheese – a combination of Gruyère and Parmesan is good – can be mixed with a stuffing, or sprinkled on top.
• Two vegetable purées of contrasting colours can be used for stuffing hollowed-out roast vegetables, especially if topped with grated cheese.
• One of the most homely but satisfying stuffed dishes, which can make a complete meal, is a whole cabbage. Hollow out the centre and fill with a vegetable, rice or minced meat-based stuffing, putting stuffing between the remaining leaves as well as the centre. Cook slowly in a covered casserole with butter and a little stock.

HOT AND COLD SALAD *(40)*

This special salad is wonderful for a summer lunch, and I like to serve it with smoked fish or cold poached chicken. The hot and cold effect, part raw and part cooked, brings out much more flavour than a salad would normally have. Shiitake mushrooms, when available, are ideal.   *SERVES 4*

  250g (½lb) dwarf green beans, topped
    and tailed
  125g (4oz) chestnut mushrooms, sliced
    not too thinly
  1 small radicchio
  2 Little Gem lettuces
  7 tablespoons extra virgin olive oil
  2 large cloves garlic, chopped finely
  8–10 fresh basil leaves, sliced thinly
  25g (1oz) pine kernels
  2 tablespoons sherry vinegar
  Sea salt
  Black pepper

Steam or boil the beans until just tender but still with a slight crunch to them. Drain and leave on one side. Add the sliced mushrooms to the beans. Separate the leaves of the radicchio and of the Little Gem lettuce and arrange alternately around the outside of a fairly shallow large serving bowl or dish.

Very shortly before you want to eat, put 3 tablespoons olive oil in a large frying pan over a medium heat, add the finely chopped garlic and stir around for 30 seconds or so.

Add the cooked beans and the mushrooms to the frying pan and stir around for 2–3 minutes until the mushrooms have softened. Season well with crushed sea salt and plenty of black pepper, then turn the mixture, including any oil and juices, into the serving bowl or dish surrounded by the lettuce leaves. Stir the sliced basil leaves roughly into the hot green bean and mushroom mixture.

Put the empty frying pan back over a high heat and stir the pine kernels in it for a minute or so just to brown them, then scatter the pine kernels on to the salad. Dribble the remaining 4 tablespoons olive oil all over the salad, including the lettuce leaves, followed by the sherry vinegar. Serve as soon as possible.

GRILLED COURGETTES AND GOAT CHEESE WITH WALNUTS *(40)*

Goat cheese is the best cheese for grilling there is. I also find grilled courgettes acquire a wonderful smoky flavour, so the two combined are unbelievably delicious. You can serve this simple quick recipe either as a hot first course or as a side dish, or, accompanied by some crusty bread, as a light lunch or late supper. Small grilled courgettes can be served with drinks.   *SERVES 4*

  750g (1½lb) medium courgettes, topped,
    tailed and halved lengthwise
  Extra virgin olive oil
  175g (6oz) round white goat cheese,
    sliced fairly thinly
  2 teaspoons dried oregano
  25g (1oz) walnut pieces, chopped finely
  Salt
  Black pepper

Preheat the grill to its highest heat. Steam or boil the courgettes (page 52) for only 3–4 minutes until bright green but still fairly firm. Drain the courgettes thoroughly and put them into a bowl, then sprinkle with olive oil and salt and toss around to coat well.

Arrange the courgettes on a grill pan, skin sides upwards, and put under the preheated grill until the skins are well speckled with blackened bits all over.

Lay the charred courgettes in a large, shallow flameproof earthenware dish, cut sides upwards, and arrange the slices of goat cheese on top. Sprinkle with the dried oregano and plenty of freshly ground black pepper, and scatter the chopped walnuts all over.

Put the dish back under the hot grill for just a minute or two until the cheese is melted and browned; be sure to watch carefully while it browns.

Just before serving, trickle a little olive oil over each courgette half.

AUBERGINE AND OKRA STEW WITH MINT AND PINE KERNELS *(49)*

This dish always reminds me of my childhood in the Middle East where I first grew to like the unique tastes and textures of both aubergine and the elegant pointed okra (known to me then by its alternative name of ladies' fingers). This is an easily made dish which can be eaten hot or cold, as an accompaniment to roast meat or chicken, or on its own, served with a green salad and crusty bread to help mop up the juices. There is no need to salt and drain the aubergines. Many people think they do not like okra because they may have had large ones which have been overcooked and become fibrous and slippery but I find they often change their minds when the okra is small, fresh and not overcooked as in this dish.   *SERVES 4*

  750–875g (1½–1¾lb) aubergines
  White wine vinegar
  300ml (½ pint) water
  3 rounded tablespoons tomato purée
  4 tablespoons lemon juice
  4 tablespoons extra virgin olive oil
  397g (14oz) can chopped tomatoes
  2 teaspoons ground coriander
  1 rounded teaspoon paprika
  1 rounded dessertspoon honey
  3 large cloves garlic, sliced across finely
  1 large handful fresh mint leaves, chopped
    finely
  25g (1oz) pine kernels
  250g (8oz) fresh small whole okra, tops
    trimmed (page 49)
  2–4 pinches cayenne pepper
  Salt

Cut the aubergines across in 1cm (½in) slices, then cut the slices in half, sprinkling with wine vinegar as you do so and put to one side. Pour the water into a large, heavy-based saucepan and add the tomato purée, lemon juice, olive oil, chopped tomatoes, spices and honey. Bring to the boil, stirring well to melt the honey. Mix the ingredients thoroughly together.

Rinse the aubergines, pat dry and stir into the boiling liquid with the sliced garlic and chopped mint. Cover the pan, reduce the heat and leave to simmer as gently as possible, stirring around once or twice, for about 30 minutes until the aubergines are very soft.

Meanwhile, heat a dry frying pan over a medium heat. Toss the pine kernels around in it just until golden brown, then transfer to a plate and set aside until ready to serve.

When the aubergines are soft, remove the pan from the heat and season the juices to taste with cayenne pepper and salt. Return to the heat and bring to bubbling again, then mix in the prepared okra, cover the saucepan and bubble for 5–10 minutes or just until the okra feel soft when you insert a small, pointed knife, but are still bright green.

Transfer the mixture to a warm serving dish and scatter the toasted pine kernels on top, mixing some of them into the stew.

POTATOES AND FENNEL COOKED WITH CHEESE AND CREAM (57)

This is inspired by the classic *pommes dauphinoise*, where potatoes are cooked in a gratin dish with milk, cheese, cream and a hint of garlic. Cooked fennel is also wonderful with all these ingredients, and this recipe is quicker than most versions of *pommes dauphinoise* as you mix the ingredients together instead of layering them. The nutty taste of Gruyère cheese is an important element. Close-textured salad potatoes or new potatoes (page 43) are the best to use. For a real treat, use saffron-infused cream, which is made by putting a pinch of saffron threads into the cream, bringing it just up to bubbling and then leaving it to cool while the saffron infuses before using.　　　　*SERVES 6*

1kg (2lb) new potatoes, well scrubbed but not peeled and sliced about 2.5mm (⅛in) thick
1 large bulb fennel, trimmed, quartered and thinly sliced
75g (3oz) butter, cut into small pieces, plus a little extra
1 large clove garlic
125g (4oz) Gruyère cheese, cut into very small pieces
300ml (½ pint) whipping cream
1 tablespoon grated Parmesan cheese
Sea salt and black pepper

Steam or boil the potato and fennel slices together for about 10 minutes until half cooked and beginning to soften. You may need to do this in two batches depending on the size of your steamer or saucepan. Drain and put into a mixing bowl. Stir the butter into the vegetables with a wooden spoon, then crush the garlic into the mixing bowl. Mix in the Gruyère cheese together with a seasoning of crushed sea salt and black pepper.

Spoon into a large, shallow ovenproof dish and pat level. Pour over the cream slowly. Dot the top with a little more butter and sprinkle with the grated Parmesan cheese. Put the dish towards the top of a preheated oven, 180°C, 350°F, Gas Mark 4 for 40–50 minutes until the surface is browned in patches.

SPINACH AND PEPPERS IN A SWEET POTATO AND PARSNIP BOWL (53)

This dramatic-looking dish is an exciting way to serve your accompanying vegetables all in one – or, make it into a main course for a lunch or a light supper by arranging anchovy fillets alternately with the strips of red pepper.　　*SERVES 4–6*

1–1.2kg (2–2½lb) orange-fleshed sweet potatoes, peeled and chopped roughly
625–750g (1¼–1½lb) parsnips, peeled and chopped roughly
1 large red pepper, cored, halved lengthwise and deseeded (page 49)
50g (2oz) butter
¼–½ whole nutmeg, grated
500g (1lb) spinach, well washed, thick stalks removed (page 45), leaves chopped up roughly if large
2–3 tablespoons extra virgin olive oil
Sea salt
Black pepper

Steam or boil the chopped sweet potatoes and parsnips together until very soft (page 52). Meanwhile, in order to skin the peppers later, put the pepper halves skin side upwards, under a very hot grill until the skins are charred black (page 55). Remove the peppers from the grill and wrap in a tea towel or place in a paper bag until cool enough to handle.

Meanwhile, purée the sweet potatoes and parsnips with the butter in a food processor (you may have to do this in two or three goes, depending on the capacity of your food processor). Whizz in the freshly grated nutmeg with sea salt and black pepper to taste.

Spoon the sweet-potato mixture into a wide, shallow, ovenproof serving bowl, spreading it out and up the sides of the bowl with a rubber spatula so as to roughly form a bowl shape within the bowl. Cover the bowl loosely with foil and put into the lowest possible oven to keep warm while you skin the cooled peppers.

Remove the blackened skin from the pepper halves with your fingers, then cut the flesh lengthwise into thin strips with a sharp knife. Wrap these pepper strips in a piece of foil and keep warm in the oven with the bowl.

Shortly before you are ready to serve, steam or boil the spinach until soft (page 52), then drain in a colander and squeeze out the excess water.

Remove the bowl with the sweet-potato purée from the oven and spoon the cooked spinach into the centre of the root purée. Sprinkle with sea salt and freshly ground black pepper. Remove the pepper strips from the oven and arrange them fanning out like a starburst on top of the spinach, adding the anchovy fillets if wanted. Then dribble the extra virgin olive oil all over the top and serve at once.

CARROT SALAD WITH ORANGES AND SPRING ONIONS *(40)*

This carrot salad was originally designed for my vegetarian daughter but meat-eaters also always enjoy it with roast duck or pork. *SERVES 4–6*

> *375–500g (12oz–1lb) carrots, grated*
>   *coarsely*
> *1 tablespoon orange flower water*
> *1 tablespoon caster sugar*
> *½ teaspoon salt*
> *½ teaspoon cayenne pepper*
> *4 tablespoons lemon juice*
> *2 small oranges, peeled with white pith*
>   *removed and sliced thinly*
> *1 bunch spring onions, trimmed and sliced*
>   *(use as much of the green part as*
>   *possible)*
> *Handful flat-leaved parsley, chopped*
>   *roughly*

Put the grated carrots in a salad bowl. Mix the orange flower water, sugar, salt, cayenne pepper and lemon juice together. Mix thoroughly with the carrots. Arrange the orange slices among the carrots and then sprinkle the salad with the spring onions and chopped parsley.

EGG, FENNEL AND TOMATO PIE *(40)*

As the puff pastry lid cooks quickly the poached eggs underneath surrounded by fennel and tomatoes magically retain their softness in this delicious vegetarian main course. Serve with a green vegetable such as spinach, brussels sprouts or crisply steamed cabbage. *SERVES 6*

> *6 large eggs (size 1)*
> *50g (2oz) butter*
> *2 tablespoons olive oil*
> *4 large bulbs fennel, trimmed and sliced*
>   *fairly thinly*
> *3 large cloves garlic, chopped*
> *1 rounded teaspoon paprika*
> *397g (14oz) can chopped tomatoes*
> *2–3 sprigs fresh tarragon or mint leaves,*
>   *chopped roughly*
> *250g (8oz) packet puff pastry, thawed if*
>   *frozen*
> *1 egg yolk*
> *Salt*
> *Black pepper*

Poach the eggs for about 2 minutes (page 69) until softly done. Carefully transfer them with a slotted spoon to a bowl of cold water so that they stop cooking at once and remain soft.

Melt 25g (1oz) of the butter and the olive oil together in a large, deep heavy-based saucepan over a fairly low heat. Add the fennel pieces and cook, stirring often, for about 10 minutes until soft. Then add the chopped garlic cloves and the paprika and stir around for another minute. Stir in the chopped tomatoes with their liquid and bring to bubbling for a minute or so stirring around. Stir in the remaining 25g (1oz) butter.

Remove the saucepan from the heat and leave until the mixture is cool, then season well with salt and freshly ground black pepper and stir in the roughly chopped tarragon or mint leaves.

Spoon half the fennel and tomato mixture into a pie dish or rectangular ovenproof dish. Lift the eggs from the bowl of cold water with a slotted spoon, one by one, and let any extra water drip off. Lay the drained, poached eggs on top of the mixture. Spoon the remaining fennel and tomato mixture on top, covering the eggs.

Roll out the puff pastry on a lightly floured surface to roughly the size of the top of the pie dish. Dampen the edges of the pie dish and lay the pastry on top. Trim the edges and use the scraps to roll out and make decorations for the top of the pie (page 245). Make 2 small slits in the pastry to allow steam to escape while baking. Refrigerate the pie for at least 30 minutes or until about 30 minutes before you want to eat.

To make the glaze, stir ½ teaspoon of salt into the egg yolk and then brush all over the decorated pastry lid. Bake the pie just above the centre of a preheated oven, 220°C, 425°F, Gas Mark 7 for 20–30 minutes until the pastry has risen and is a darkish golden brown. Serve the pie at once.

SPINACH AND PEA PURÉE WITH CABBAGE AND PARMESAN *(40)*

This contrast of a smooth, rich vegetable purée topped with a crunchy green vegetable is always appreciated. Serve with new potatoes. *SERVES 6–8*

> *500g (1lb) spinach, washed and stalks*
>   *removed if coarse*
> *250g (8oz) frozen peas*
> *125g (4oz) butter, cut up roughly*
> *750g (1½lb) green cabbage, shredded*
> *50–75g (2–3oz) Parmesan cheese, grated*
>   *coarsely*
> *Salt*
> *Black pepper*

Steam or boil the spinach until soft. Add the peas and cook for 4–5 minutes. Drain thoroughly in a colander, pressing the spinach to get rid of excess liquid. Put the spinach and peas into a food processor with the butter and whizz to a purée. Season with salt and black pepper. Put the mixture into a wide ovenproof serving bowl, cover loosely with foil and keep warm in a very low oven.

Just before serving, slice the cabbage up fairly thinly (page 45) and steam or boil for 3–6 minutes just until bright green and still crisp. Drain the cabbage, pile on top of the green purée and sprinkle all over with grated Parmesan and freshly ground black pepper.

BRAISED LEEKS WITH TOMATOES AND BALSAMIC VINEGAR *(59)*

When leeks are cooked slowly in this way, a lovely sweet, mellow flavour emerges, which is enhanced in this recipe by the almost syrupy juices of tomatoes, balsamic vinegar and olive oil. Serve this with roast meats, chicken or game. *SERVES 4*

> *500g (1lb) thin leeks, trimmed (retain as*
>   *much of the green part as possible) and*
>   *halved lengthwise*
> *4 tablespoons olive oil*
> *2 tablespoons balsamic vinegar*
> *2 teaspoons fennel or dill seeds*
> *2 large tomatoes, skinned (page 48)*
> *Sea salt*
> *Black pepper*

Lay the leek halves in a heavy, fairly shallow flameproof casserole, respectable-looking enough to be brought to the table. Add the olive oil, balsamic vinegar, fennel or dill seeds and a sprinkling of sea salt and plenty of black pepper.

Chop up the tomatoes thoroughly and spoon the tomatoes and any juicy mush on top of the leeks roughly, but don't mix in. Sprinkle with a little more salt and pepper. Cover the casserole and cook over a very low heat for about 30 minutes, or until the leeks are very soft indeed. Remove the lid of the casserole, increase the heat and bubble fiercely until the juices are thick and syrupy. Serve in the casserole.

SAUTÉED POTATOES WITH CHOPPED GINGER AND SPICES (40)

Potatoes with a close texture such as red-skinned Desirée are particularly good for this recipe. If you want to sauté the potatoes in advance, they will keep warm without spoiling for several hours, but remember to stir in the chopped parsley and salt only just before serving. _SERVES 4_

1kg (2lb) largish potatoes, scrubbed but
not peeled and cut into 2.5cm (1in)
pieces
3 tablespoons olive oil or groundnut oil
25g (1oz) butter
2–3 large cloves garlic, chopped finely
5cm (2in) piece fresh root ginger, peeled
and chopped finely
3 teaspoons ground cumin
4 teaspoons caraway seeds
Generous bunch parsley, chopped
Black pepper
Crushed sea salt

Steam or boil the potatoes until they are just cooked but not breaking up. Drain well and set aside.

Heat the oil and butter together in a large frying pan or wok over a medium heat. Add the garlic and ginger and stir around for 1 minute, then add the ground cumin and caraway seeds and stir for another minute. Add the potatoes and sauté, stirring occasionally, over a medium heat for about 8 minutes until brown. Sprinkle with black pepper. Before serving, stir in a sprinkling of crushed sea salt and the chopped parsley. Turn into a warmed serving dish.

LEEK AND CELERIAC COBBLER (40)

As a main dish, accompanied by a tomato salad (page 51), this cobbler pie is a delicious alternative to meat, fish or poultry, even for non-vegetarians. _SERVES 4_

FOR THE TOPPING
600ml (1 pint) milk
¼ whole nutmeg, grated
125g (4oz) semolina
90g (3½oz) mature Cheddar cheese,
grated
25g (1oz) butter, plus extra
1 large egg (size 1), lightly beaten
Grated Parmesan
3–4 pinches cayenne pepper
Salt
FOR THE FILLING
50g (2oz) butter
2 tablespoons olive oil
375g (12oz) celeriac, peeled and diced
750g (1½lb) leeks, well washed and cut
into 2.5cm (1in) slices
2 teaspoons caraway seeds
Sea salt
Black pepper

Lightly grease a 23 x 30cm (9 x 12in) Swiss roll tin. Make the gnocchi topping at least 2 hours in advance. Pour the milk into a saucepan with the nutmeg and season with the cayenne pepper and salt. Stir in the semolina. Bring the milk to the boil, then simmer for 3–4 minutes, stirring until thick. Remove from the heat and add the Cheddar cheese, butter and egg. Return to a low heat and stir for 1 minute more. Spread the semolina mixture evenly all over the bottom of the tin. Leave to get completely cold, then chill for at least 30 minutes.

Meanwhile, make the filling. Melt the butter with the olive oil in a large frying pan over a high heat. Add the celeriac and stir for 2–3 minutes, just to brown slightly. Add the leeks and caraway seeds, then cook gently, stirring often, until the leeks are soft. Season with sea salt and plenty of black pepper. Turn into a heated, shallow flameproof dish.

Preheat the grill to high. Cut the gnocchi mixture into 5 x 2.5cm (2 x 1in) fingers or into circles.

Arrange in an overlapping pattern all over the leek and celeriac mixture, then dot with butter, sprinkle generously with Parmesan cheese and put under the grill until golden brown.

ARTICHOKES WITH YELLOW MYSTERY SAUCE (47)

Artichokes always seem rather a treat – especially if they are prepared as cups in this way with the hairy choke and small leaves removed. In this simple recipe, they are eaten cold as a first course and can be prepared several hours in advance. See if anyone can guess what the subtle sauce is made of. If you drink water while eating artichokes, even tap water will taste as if it comes from a mountain spring. _SERVES 8_

8 large artichokes
4 tablespoons lemon juice, plus extra for
cooking artichokes
1–1.2kg (2–2½lb) pumpkin, seeds and
skin removed and flesh chopped roughly
1 tablespoon caster sugar
75ml (3fl oz) extra virgin olive oil
200g (7oz) 8% fat fromage frais
Salt
Cayenne pepper

Remove the artichoke stalks and for a neat presentation trim the leaves with scissors (page 47). Cook in simmering, lightly salted water with a little lemon juice for 40–45 minutes, until the base leaves separate easily. Drain and cool the artichokes upside down in a colander. Pull out the purple leaves revealing the hairy choke. Scoop out the choke with a teaspoon and discard, rinse the artichokes and drain upside down.

To make the sauce, steam or boil the pumpkin until soft. Then cool under cold water and drain. Put the flesh into a food processor with the lemon juice and caster sugar and whizz until smooth, then gradually whizz in the olive oil. Lastly whizz in the fromage frais and season to taste with salt and cayenne pepper. Pour into a bowl and leave until cold.

To serve, put the artichokes on individual plates, spoon some yellow sauce into the centre of each one and sprinkle a little cayenne pepper on top.

EGGS

When we talk about eggs we nearly always mean hens' eggs, but many other eggs are worth trying, too. Duck eggs, with their blue-tinted whites and distinctive taste, are much liked by some people; and are very popular in the Far East. I have never been offered a goose egg, perhaps because geese are not such prolific layers as hens and ducks, but their eggs are said to be excellent and milder in flavour than ducks' eggs. Both duck and goose eggs make deliciously rich sponge cakes.

One of the best eggs I have ever eaten was a pheasant's egg, which was delicate and creamy. And, I wish I could try pigeons' eggs, which, I am told, are absolutely delicious. After hens' eggs, quails' eggs now seem to be the most readily available commercially. Although quails' eggs are nearly always eaten hard-boiled, soft-poached quails' eggs, either served plain in a salad or dropped into a clear soup, are truly magical. Fried quails' eggs make lovely canapé toppings.

We can now choose between battery eggs and free range. I think most people would rather pay more if they can for free range because, even if they can not distinguish any difference in taste and consistency, they prefer the idea of an egg which comes from a happier chicken. Real free-range eggs, which means the chickens have roamed over an open area where they pecked at grass and plants as well as corn, certainly do taste much better.

Very fresh eggs from home-kept chickens, as I knew so well until a fox visited mine one night, are superlative, with whites like whipped cream. My eggs were alluringly dark speckled brown, though the colour of the eggshell has no relevance to the quality. Deep yellow yolks, however, are usually a sign that the chicken has been picking at plenty of greenery.

Whatever theories come and go about eating eggs there can be no doubt that they are a highly nutritious food. Their pure nourishment is not surprising when you think that eggs are, after all, designed to feed the chick until it is strong enough to survive outside the egg. As well as protein eggs contain several important minerals including iron and calcium, and vitamins A, B and D.

Quite apart from the nutritional contribution of eggs to our diet they must also be about the most versatile food. Speedy breakfast-time favourites such as boiled, poached and scrambled eggs, spectacular dinner-party roulades and Sunday's essential Yorkshire pudding are just a few examples of the adaptability of eggs. Then there are the various types of omelettes and pancakes just waiting for exciting fillings to transform them into satisfying family meals or more extravagant special-occasion dishes. Hard-boiled eggs make wonderful picnic food.

Eggs are also the ultimate magic ingredient in cooking. It is helpful to remember that egg whites stiffen and lighten, whereas egg yolks thicken and enrich. Egg whites also have a wonderful ability to hold air. Whisked whole eggs bind together stuffings, meatballs and purées. Eggs are, of course, vital to many classic cakes, puddings and sauces too, and these are described in separate chapters.

Without eggs the ever-popular soufflé would not exist. A soufflé has the effect of a brilliant firework – it causes amazement and excitement for a few intense moments. A good classic cheese soufflé (page 76) illustrates perfectly the supreme qualities of eggs; the golden appearance, the rich yolky flavour and the miraculously risen light foam of the whisked whites which dissolves tantalizingly in your mouth.

Clockwise from top left: Hot Cheese, Egg and Anchovy Roulade, an adaptation of the basic soufflé mixture (page 78), served here with a mixed green salad; Very Special Toad-in-the-Hole (page 78) made with delicious homemade spicy sausages; Stuffed Rice Pancake (page 79) with a light oriental-flavour filling; Soft Eggs on a Vegetable Curry (page 79), a variation of poached eggs and garnished with fresh dill; and finally one of the most simple and versatile of all egg dishes, creamy scrambled eggs, here served with slices of smoked salmon and garnished with the feathery leaves of fresh dill. Dill is one of the most successful herbs for accompanying egg dishes.

BOILING *and* POACHING

'Can't even boil an egg' implies that someone can't cook at all. Yet many people can cook very well without managing to boil an egg successfully. Boiling and poaching are two ways of cooking eggs, that, although very simple, do require a bit of practice to get the exact result you want. Always use the freshest possible eggs.

Soft-boiled eggs, where the white is only just opaque and set and the yolk is still runny, are usually served in the shell in an egg cup with slivers of toast or 'soldiers' to dip into them. Medium-boiled eggs, or *oeufs mollets*, have a firm but not rubbery white, becoming softer towards the centre with a semi-soft yolk. They are used, as are poached eggs, in many more elaborate egg dishes. Hard-boiled eggs are set all through but are nicest when they have not been cooked so long that the whites become tough and the yolks powdery. Apart from being staples of packed lunches or picnics, hard-boiled eggs are often sliced for salads. Remember that an egg should not, in fact, be boiled but simmered. It is easier to achieve the consistency you like if you soft boil eggs using the hot-water method as they can be timed more exactly. But when cooking hard-boiled eggs start them off in cold water as this is less likely to result in rubbery whites. Never cook eggs straight from the refrigerator – they should be at room temperature so they cook more quickly and are less likely to crack.

HANDLING AND HYGIENE
Store eggs in a cool place. Buy them as fresh as possible and use within three weeks of the packing date. Make sure your hands, the work surfaces, utensils and containers are clean, and do not use any eggs that are cracked. Egg dishes should be eaten as soon as possible after preparation or cooled and then put in the refrigerator.

BOILING EGGS

The hot-water method *is best for soft-boiled eggs. Lower the eggs into a small saucepan of gently boiling water. Reduce the heat to a simmer and time from the moment the water returns to the boil (see chart right).*

The cold-water method *is less likely to cause cracked shells if the eggs are cold. Put the eggs in a pan with cold water to cover and bring to a simmer. Start timing when the water bubbles (see chart right).*

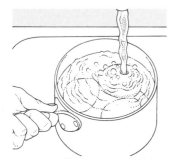

Use the cold-water method *for hard-boiled eggs. Time carefully (see chart right) and when cooked, cool immediately under cold running water to stop the cooking and to prevent black rims forming round the yolks.*

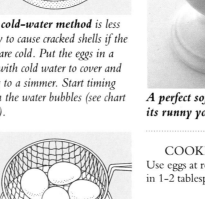

The easiest way *to boil several eggs at once is to use a wire basket. Lower the basket of eggs into a large pan of water, then lift out when the eggs are ready. Remember, the more eggs the longer the water will take to boil.*

A perfect soft-boiled egg with its runny yolk and soft white.

SHELLING EGGS
To make hard- or medium-boiled eggs easier to shell put them into cold water as soon as they are cooked (as you do anyway for hard-boiled eggs) and leave until cold. Tap the shells all over on a hard surface before peeling.

Shelling the eggs under cold running water also helps remove the membrane between the shell and the egg.

Keep the shelled eggs in a bowl of cold water or in a polythene food bag in the refrigerator until needed, as this prevents the whites going tough. Pat dry with kitchen paper before using.

COOKING TIMES FOR BOILED EGGS (in minutes)
Use eggs at room temperature. If the eggs crack in the pan, quickly stir in 1-2 tablespoons vinegar to 'seal' the cracks.

Hot-water method (time from when water returns to boil)

Egg size	Soft	Medium	Hard
1, 2 and 3	3½	5–6	12
4 and 5	3	4–5	10
Quails' eggs	2	3	5

Cold-water method (time from when water first boils)

Egg size	Soft	Medium	Hard
1, 2 and 3	3	4	10
4 and 5	2	3	8

POACHING EGGS

Use a large frying pan as the more boiling water there is, the less the temperature drops when the eggs are added. Vinegar in the water also helps prevent the whites from spreading. Poached eggs should be cooked until the whites are just set and turn opaque but the yolks are still soft – test by pressing the yolk gently with your finger.

To keep poached eggs warm put them in a basin of warm water. If you are going to use the eggs cold put them in a basin of cold water so the whites stay supple.

1 Bring a large pan of water and 2–3 tablespoons vinegar to a rolling boil in a deep frying pan. (I like to use a flavoured vinegar such as dill which imparts a little of its taste to the eggs.) Break the egg into a cup, then slide it into the pan.

2 Gather the white round the yolk with two spoons if it is spreading too much. Reduce the heat to a simmer, cover and poach for 3–5 minutes.

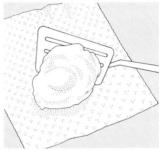

3 Lift out the egg using a slotted fish slice or large spoon. Drain well on kitchen paper if eating at once, otherwise keep in warm or cold water until ready to serve.

USING A POACHER

Butter the cups, set them over simmering water and break in the eggs. Cover and cook gently until the whites are just set but the yolks still soft.

Alternatively, put buttered metal scone or biscuit cutters in a frying pan of simmering water. Break an egg into each one and cover the pan. When the eggs are cooked lift them out using a fish slice.

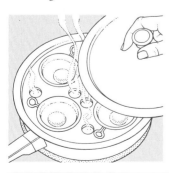

USING BOILED AND POACHED EGGS

• Eggs go famously well with spinach, as in *oeufs à la Florentine*: poached eggs served on a bed of chopped cooked spinach and topped with a well-flavoured cheese sauce (page 196).

• Medium-boiled eggs and poached eggs can be served hot or cold with a variety of sauces: with a good hollandaise sauce (page 200), a purée of grilled and skinned yellow peppers (page 49) mixed with a little soured cream or with a creamy béchamel sauce (page 196) flavoured with cheese and grated nutmeg, fresh chopped tarragon, chopped anchovy and a little crushed garlic or well-drained spinach purée and fennel seeds.

• Medium-boiled eggs, poached eggs or sliced hard-boiled eggs can be served cold with homemade mayonnaise (page 202) on a bed of salad leaves. You can flavour the mayonnaise with, for example, spices or curry paste or with a little finely chopped spinach.

• For stuffed eggs scoop out the yolks of halved hard-boiled eggs and mix with chopped herbs and anchovies, or with spicy mayonnaise, or with finely chopped spring onions and seasoning, then spoon the mixture back in the whites, mounding the mixture.

• As a first course I love cold soft-poached eggs with fresh herbs set in aspic in little dishes – add a little wine or sherry to the aspic for flavour (page 33).

• Add whole raw eggs in their shells to a slow-cooked spicy casserole. During the long cooking the eggs absorb the flavours around them and become creamy textured. Before serving shell the eggs, halve them and return them to the dish.

• It is great fun to make tea eggs for salads. Boil the eggs in water with some aromatic tea leaves and whole spices for 3–4 minutes, then remove the eggs, reserving the liquid. Crack the shells all over and continue boiling the eggs in the liquid for another 10 minutes. When shelled the eggs will be beautifully marbled and taste faintly spicy.

• To make a quick egg curry, cover warm medium-boiled eggs with a creamy sauce; boil double cream with mild curry paste added to taste or ground turmeric and other Indian spices, then stir in 1 tablespoon thick Greek yogurt and chopped fresh coriander leaves or flat-leaved parsley.

A delicate Poached Egg on Green Cushion (page 78), with its soft yolk and just-firm white, makes an ideal starter or light meal served with the chilli-flavoured spinach sauce.

FRYING, SCRAMBLING *and* BAKING

These three methods of cooking eggs all involve oil or fat, and which oil or fat you use makes a great difference to the flavour of the eggs. Good olive oil such as extra virgin is hard to beat, but you can mix it with sunflower or groundnut oil for greater economy. Olive oil and butter together not only taste marvellous but do not burn as quickly as just butter. Bacon fat adds a lot of flavour for frying, and duck or goose fat, if you have any, are also delicious. Butter should be used for scrambling and baking, and you can add a little good oil when baking, too – try hazelnut oil or olive oil that has had cheese and spices infused in it for adding flavour to the eggs.

Fried eggs can vary enormously. The whites can be gently set and white or they can be crisp, frilly and browned at the edges. If you add more oil and fat the eggs will bubble up in a way that I specially like. They can be cooked 'sunny side up'– the 'sunny' bit is the yolk which still shows because the egg hasn't been turned over – or 'easy over', which simply means turned over.

Frying and scrambling eggs must be the easiest and most convenient way of quickly producing a tasty meal. As the heat needs to be transmitted rapidly and evenly to fried foods, pans for frying eggs should be heavy based and made of a heat-conducting metal such as iron or, best of all, stainless-steel lined copper. Non-stick pans are usually not heavy enough and the non-stick surface wears away quickly. The pan should be fairly shallow with sloping sides so that you can remove the cooked eggs easily. A new egg pan should be seasoned before use (page 19) and then wiped after each time it is used rather than washed.

FRYING EGGS

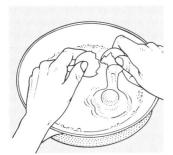

1 *Heat a little oil or fat in a heavy-based frying pan over a medium heat until hot but not smoking. Break the egg directly into the frying pan.*

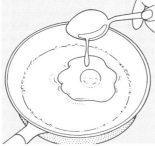

2 *Gently baste the egg with spoonfuls of fat, tipping the pan if necessary, until the top of the egg just begins to set.*

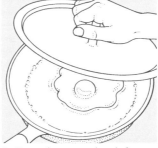

3 *Cover the pan and cook for about 1 minute until the white is set but the yolk is still soft. Lift the egg out of the pan using a slotted fish slice. Serve at once.*

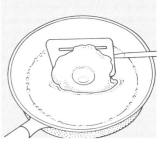

For an 'easy-over' egg *turn it over carefully using a slotted fish slice when the top is set and cook it briefly on the other side. Serve at once.*

An egg frying in hot fat with bright yolk and set white.

SERVING FRIED, SCRAMBLED AND BAKED EGGS

• **Fried eggs** are good served on top of full-flavoured ingredients, for example a rich ratatouille (page 59) or a purée of root vegetables such as parsnip and celeriac with nutmeg (page 53). When you cut into the egg the yolk mingles with the food beneath and makes a nice rich 'instant' sauce. Another combination is sweet potatoes either mashed or sautéed with sliced onions.
• Enhance plain fried eggs by sprinkling them with a little soy sauce, freshly chopped herbs (try oregano) or spiced salt.
• **Creamy scrambled eggs** become extra special with any smoked fish mixed in. Smoked salmon with fresh dill makes a delicious addition but add the salmon at the very end so it doesn't become tough.
• Sliced truffles or chopped sorrel sautéed in a little butter is excellent, too.
• For a Far Eastern touch stir a little thick coconut milk (made from creamed coconut dissolved in hot water) into an egg mixture as it scrambles. Season with a pinch or two of chilli powder and stir in some chopped fresh coriander leaves when you take the scrambled eggs off the heat.
• **Baked eggs** are very versatile. As a variation on plain baked eggs make depressions in a wide dish containing a cooked spicy mince and onion mixture, drop in the eggs and top with cheese or cream. Return to the oven until the eggs are just set.
• For a different kind of baked egg with an Italian flavour, drop the yolk into a buttered ramekin dish, season and sprinkle with oregano, then cover with the stiffly whisked white and grated Parmesan cheese before putting into the oven to bake.
• Eggs can also be baked inside vegetables such as a baked potato (page 56), the inside mashed with cream and seasonings and put back, making an indentation to hold the eggs and a sprinkling of grated cheese on top.

SCRAMBLING EGGS

The creamiest scrambled eggs (page 66) are cooked over a very low heat for at least 5 minutes. The pan should be heavy based for even heat distribution. For a really gentle heat cook the eggs in a bowl set over simmering water.

Before cooking whisk the eggs until they are frothy and season with salt and pepper, adding some fresh chopped herbs such as parsley, tarragon and chives, if you like. Allow 2–3 eggs per person.

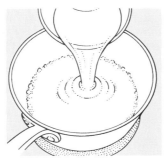

1 *Melt about 1 teaspoon unsalted butter per egg in a pan. When it stops foaming reduce the heat to low and add the whisked eggs. Stir with a wooden spoon.*

2 *Cook over a very gentle heat, stirring the cooked eggs from the sides of the pan into the liquid egg in the middle. (For softly 'set' eggs, don't stir too much.)*

3 *Remove the pan from the heat while the eggs are still lightly set (they will go on cooking in the hot pan) and continue to stir until thickened. Serve at once.*

BAKING EGGS

Eggs can be baked in several ways. *Oeufs en cocotte* are eggs baked in buttered little ramekins or cocotte dishes. The eggs are seasoned, topped with butter or a little cream and baked in a roasting tin half full of hot water.

Oeufs sur le plat are eggs baked in a shallow dish (right). You can cook ingredients such as bacon, mushrooms and tomatoes in the dish before adding the eggs, or cook others such as ratatouille beforehand and spoon them into the dish before breaking the eggs on top.

1 *To make oeufs en cocotte generously butter the inside of individual ramekin dishes or cocotte dishes using a small piece of greaseproof paper. It helps if the butter is soft at room temperature. Preheat the oven to 180°C, 350°F, Gas Mark 4.*

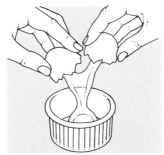

2 *Break 1 or 2 eggs into each ramekin. Season and top with butter and/or cream (season underneath the eggs if only adding butter so as not to speckle the tops). You can also add other flavourings such as finely chopped herbs or chopped anchovies.*

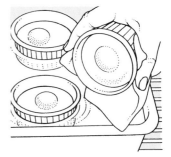

3 *Stand the ramekins in a roasting tin with enough boiling water to come half way up the sides. Bake for 6–8 minutes until the whites are just set and the yolks still very soft. Test by tipping the ramekin a little; the white of egg should just hold.*

BAKED EGGS IN A DISH

Melt about 15g (½oz) butter in a medium-sized gratin dish in a preheated oven, 200°C, 400°F, Gas Mark 6. Add 2 eggs, spooning the butter over them. Season, cover with a little cream and return to the oven for 5–6 minutes until the whites are set but the yolks are still soft.

If you are combining the eggs with other ingredients that need cooking it is best to cook the other ingredients first, either in the same dish or separately. Then break the eggs on top of the cooked ingredients. Eggs cooked in this way will take slightly longer to cook.

Double cream and chives quickly and easily turn these baked eggs in a dish into a light meal.

OMELETTES

There are at least three very different kinds of omelette. A classic French omelette is light, soft and creamy. It is cooked very quickly and folded. It is served either folded over a filling such as cheese or mushrooms, or with added herbs, or completely plain. A fluffy soufflé omelette is much lighter than a classic omelette as the egg whites are whisked separately and folded into the beaten yolks before it is cooked. It is served as a sweet or savoury, and can have a variety of fillings.

Both classic and soufflé omelettes must be eaten immediately after they are cooked or else they will lose their qualities of being fresh and very light.

Flat omelettes are quite a different thing and even more versatile. With these the eggs do not provide the whole texture of the dish but hold a wide variety of fillings together. These omelettes are like a complete meal. Flat omelettes are best cooked slowly and can be served warm or lightly cooled. They are very useful to take on picnics, cut into wedges like a cake. There are several different types. The Italian *frittata* is about 2.5cm (1in) thick and can either be plain or mixed with vegetables in the pan. The Spanish *tortilla* is a thicker, heartier dish – it is usually packed with cubes of cooked potato and fried onion, though it can also contain other ingredients. The Arabian *eggah* is even more like a cake with fillings of vegetables, noodles, meat and spices.

The pan used for French and soufflé omelettes should not be larger than 23cm (9in) in diameter as handling a bigger omelette is very difficult. This size pan is just right for a four to five egg omelette. Allow two or three eggs per person. The pan should be made of cast iron with sloping sides so you can slide the omelette out easily.

SEASONING AN OMELETTE PAN

A new omelette pan should be seasoned to prevent sticking before it is used: cover the base with a little oil and coarse salt and heat slowly until the oil is hot, then wipe the pan dry with crumpled kitchen paper (page 19). The pan should be simply wiped out, not washed, each time it is used and kept only for omelettes or plain fried eggs.

CLASSIC FRENCH OMELETTE

Serve a classic French omelette as soon as it is cooked. Gently flip the omelette out of the pan on to a plate. Finely grated cheese can be spread over the cooked omelette just before it is folded over.

1 *Heat 15g (½oz) butter per 2 eggs in a hot pan until foaming. Add the beaten, seasoned eggs and stir with a fork for 8–10 seconds until they start to thicken.*

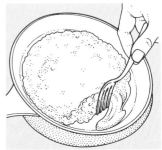

2 *Working quickly, pull back the egg that sets and tip the pan so that the uncooked egg pours to the sides of the pan. Continue until the mixture is lightly set.*

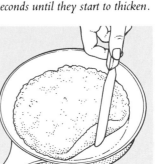

3 *Let the omelette cook for a minute or so until the bottom is slightly browned and the top lightly set; test with a palette knife. If using a filling, spoon it over half the omelette.*

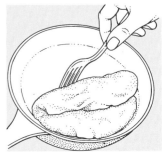

4 *Tilt the pan to one side and use a fork or palette knife to roll up or fold the omelette. Slide the omelette carefully out of the pan on to a warm plate and serve immediately.*

SOUFFLÉ OMELETTE

Separated eggs can be whisked up into a light, fluffy soufflé omelette. Allow 2 or 3 eggs per omelette.

Separate the eggs. Beat the yolks with some pepper until thick. In another bowl, whisk the egg whites with the salt until softly stiff. Fold the whites carefully into the yolks, using a large spoon.

Heat an omelette pan, then add 15g (½oz) butter per 2 or 3 eggs. When it has stopped foaming, pour in the egg mixture. Cook gently over a low heat, without stirring, for about 3 minutes until the underside of the omelette is pale golden and the top lightly set. Check by lifting the edge

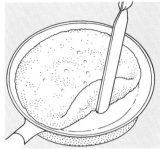

carefully with a palette knife.

Tipping the pan, fold over the omelette and slide it out on to a warm plate. For a firmer set flash the omelette under a hot grill before folding. Serve at once. If you like, add a sweet or savoury filling just before folding the omelette over. Have the filling warm and ready.

FLAT OMELETTE

This needs more filling than a classic French omelette. The following recipe is an example of what you can do but there are endless possible variations. Use fresh-cooked ingredients or leftover foods such as sliced potato, peas, cauliflower, spinach and ham.

To make the filling, fry the potatoes in half the oil in a heavy-based frying pan, turning until well browned, then remove. Fry the onions and pepper in the remaining oil for 5–7 minutes until softened, then cool a little. Beat together the eggs,

grated Parmesan cheese, onions and pepper, herbs and seasoning. Serves 3.

375g (12oz) cooked potatoes, peeled and diced
4 tablespoons olive oil
2 red onions, sliced thinly
1 red or green pepper, cored, deseeded and sliced thinly (page 49)
6 eggs, beaten
25g (1oz) Parmesan cheese, grated
1 tablespoon chopped fresh parsley or marjoram
25g (1oz) butter
Salt and ground black pepper

OMELETTE FLAVOURINGS AND FILLINGS

• Classic fillings for French omelettes such as cheese and mushrooms can hardly be bettered, but there is still plenty of room for improvisation. I like onions sautéed in good olive oil until soft, or thin slivers of Parma ham, or salami or ham.
• Add colour to a French omelette with red onion rings and sautéed and buttered, lightly blanched tiny broccoli florets.
• Fromage frais mixed with fresh chopped herbs, skinned and chopped tomatoes with fresh basil, or flakes of poached smoked cod all taste good in omelettes.
• Try cooked pumpkin mashed with butter, grated Parmesan cheese, caraway seed to taste and plenty of black pepper for an omelette filling.
• Ratatouille, finely chopped sautéed aubergine with cumin seed, grated courgettes seasoned and sautéed in butter for 30 seconds with 1 tablespoon of pine kernels, slivers of cooked chicken breast with fresh tarragon, chopped hard-boiled eggs with plenty of fresh dill or fresh coriander and cooked, well-drained spinach mixed with a little olive oil all add a slight Mediterranean flavour to omelettes.
• Some chopped fresh sorrel or a little sprinkling of whole spices added to the uncooked egg mixture also makes a more unusual omelette – caraway, fennel and dill seeds all go well with eggs.
• The classic way to serve a light fluffy soufflé omelette is

with warm jam, but a delicious savoury alternative is to surround it with a pool of fresh tomato sauce (page 206) flavoured with parsley and basil or marjoram.
• For an Italian flavour for flat omelettes add fried aubergine cubes with Feta cheese cubes, black olive slivers and dried oregano.
• Cooked potatoes mixed with well-drained spinach, crushed garlic, mild curry paste and chopped fresh mint make an Indian-flavoured flat omelette.
• To me, the nicest Spanish *tortillas* are filled to bursting with waxy potatoes and onions with perhaps the odd piece of chorizo sausage embedded among them. They are wonderful for a beach picnic. These omelettes can also contain bacon, sweet peppers, tomatoes, spinach and peas and are a useful way to use up cooked chicken meat.
• Middle Eastern *eggahs* are cooked gently in a covered frying pan and are filled with either vegetables – often a single vegetable rather than a mixture in one omelette – such as aubergine, broad beans, leeks, courgettes and spinach, or spiced meats. Cook spiced mixtures in the pan – minced or sliced chicken with potatoes or noodles – and mix the eggs into them or pour the eggs over them. Suitable spices to use are ground cumin, coriander, caraway, cardamom and paprika, with plenty of chopped fresh herbs – mainly mint, flat-leaved parsley or coriander leaves.

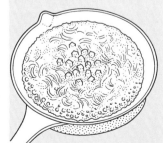

1 Melt the butter in the pan and when it stops foaming add the egg mixture, stirring lightly as you pour. Reduce the heat and scatter the fried potatoes over the egg.

2 Cook the egg mixture slowly for 10–15 minutes. When nearly set, cover the pan with a large heatproof plate and invert the omelette on to the plate.

3 Slide the omelette back into the pan and cook the other side. Or, if the omelette sticks to the bottom of the pan, flash it under a hot grill to brown the top.

4 Remove from the heat. Cut the omelette in wedges and serve it warm straight from the pan, or cool slightly and serve with a salad or take on a picnic.

BATTERS

A batter is basically a mixture of flour and liquid with a pouring consistency. For most pancakes and crêpes eggs are vital to add richness, flavour and air for a slightly risen texture. Add melted butter for even more richness. Water makes the batter lighter and milk makes it smoother.

Mixing flour with water and a little oil and folding in a stiffly whisked egg white makes a very light, crisp coating batter for deep-frying vegetables. For a richer coating batter the egg yolk can be mixed into the flour and water or milk first. Using lager or beer instead of the water in a Yorkshire pudding batter not only makes the pudding rise more dramatically but also adds extra crispness and some subtle flavour, too.

A food processor makes batter far more swiftly than whisking by hand. However, a batter should never be over beaten – which can happen in the processor – as the gluten in the flour develops and makes the batter tough when cooked. Clarified butter or concentrated butter for cooking is often recommended for cooking pancakes as it does not burn but if you do not have any, use a mixture of oil and butter, which won't burn as quickly as butter alone. Pancakes can be made ahead and frozen between sheets of greaseproof paper ready to thaw when needed.

USING THE RIGHT PAN
A crêpe pan should be shallow with sloping sides. Ideally, the pan should be made of cast iron but light enough to let you turn the pancake over by tossing it in the air if you like, though turning it with a wide palette knife is perfectly satisfactory and much less risky. A new pan should be seasoned and then cared for in the same way as an omelette pan (page 72).

PANCAKES

The secret of making good wafer-thin pancakes is to heat the pan first and to use batter the consistency of single cream. Plain wheat flour produces the soft pancakes we are most used to and buckwheat flour the thin, lacy crêpes of Brittany. Makes 15 18–20cm (7–8in) pancakes.

125g (4oz) plain flour
Pinch of salt
1 egg
300ml (½ pint) milk or milk and water mixed
Butter or oil for greasing

1 *Sift the flour and salt into a large bowl. Make a well in the centre and break in the egg. Using a whisk or wooden spoon beat the egg, gradually drawing in flour from the sides and slowly adding the liquid.*

2 *When the batter is smooth heat a crêpe pan or small- to medium-sized flat frying pan steadily until hot but not smoking. Grease it lightly with butter or butter and oil mixed, using a pastry brush or kitchen paper.*

3 *Hold the pan in one hand and with the other ladle about 2 tablespoons batter into the hot pan, immediately swirling the pan to coat the base with a thin layer of batter. Cook the pancake until set and small holes start to appear on the surface.*

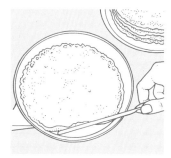

4 *Loosen the pancake with a palette knife and flip over. Cook the second side until lightly browned. Remove from the pan and stack under a tea towel. Reheat the pan, regreasing as necessary and repeat with more of the mixture.*

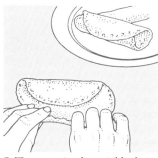

5 *To serve, simply sprinkle the pancakes with sugar and lemon juice and roll up. Alternatively, spoon a favourite filling in the centre of each, then fold in half, quarters or thirds. If made in advance, the pancakes can be served at room temperature.*

YORKSHIRE PUDDING

Using a strong bread flour gives a better rise and crisper texture, while a second egg makes the pudding richer.

This recipe makes six 10cm (4in) or 18 bun-tin puddings.

125g (4oz) strong or plain flour
½ teaspoon salt
1 or 2 eggs
300ml (½ pint) milk and water mixed half and half
Oil, dripping or lard

Mix the batter *as for pancakes (left). Letting the batter stand for 30 minutes after making helps make lighter puddings. Put a little oil or fat in each tin and place in a preheated oven, 220°C, 425°F, Gas Mark 7 until just smoking. Three-quarters fill each tin with batter. Bake for 20–25 minutes until risen and golden brown.*

SCOTCH PANCAKES

These are made with a thicker batter than pancakes and traditionally are cooked on a griddle or you can use a heavy-based frying pan. Flavourings such as honey, grated lemon rind, mixed spice, grated apple or sultanas can be added. This recipe makes about 20 pancakes.

250g (8oz) plain flour
Pinch of salt
½ teaspoon bicarbonate of
  soda
1 teaspoon cream of tartar
1 egg
300ml (½ pint) milk
1 tablespoon caster sugar
Oil for greasing

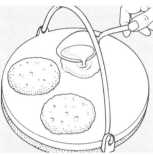

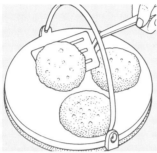

1 *Mix the batter as for pancakes (opposite). Heat a griddle or frying pan until hot but not smoking. Grease lightly with oil. Drop 2 or 3 tablespoons batter on to the griddle at a time.*

2 *Cook until holes appear on top and the batter has set. Flip the pancakes over and cook the other side for about 1 minute. Remove to a wire rack. Reheat the griddle and repeat with more batter.*

WAFFLES

To make about 10 waffles, mix the batter as for pancakes (opposite) using 250g (8oz) self-raising flour, 2 egg yolks, 300ml (½ pint) milk, 1 tablespoon vanilla sugar (page 235) and 50g (2oz) melted butter. Quickly fold in 2 stiffly whisked egg whites with a large metal spoon to make a consistency like double cream.

Grease and heat the waffle iron on a gas flame or on an electric element, or use an electric waffle iron, following the manufacturer's instructions; turn the non-electric iron over so both sides are very hot. Manual irons made of aluminium will heat quicker than those made of cast iron. Spoon in the batter without overfilling. Cook for 1½–2 minutes or until it stops steaming, turning once. If the iron does not open easily, cook for ½–1 minute longer.

PANCAKE FILLINGS AND FLAVOURINGS

• For savoury pancake fillings I especially like cooked vegetables, such as spinach or broccoli, added to seasoned cream cheese or fromage frais, or try chopped leeks sautéed slowly in butter with plenty of freshly ground black pepper and chopped chives stirred in at the last moment.

• Try skinned chopped tomatoes cooked in butter to a thick mush with cubes of crisp fried bacon stirred in at the end, or thinly sliced and softly sautéed bulb fennel mixed with fennel leaves and grated Parmesan cheese.

• Softly sautéed onions with 1 teaspoon of sugar added with the seasoning.

• Sliced chestnut or shiitake mushrooms and chopped walnuts fried with chopped garlic and fresh ginger and a little ground coriander or cardamom.

• Fish and meat fillings include cooked and flaked smoked haddock or cod either mixed with chopped herbs or watercress or in a thick, creamy white sauce; pieces of smoked salmon or chopped anchovy stirred into fromage frais with plenty of chopped dill.

• Try mixtures of seafood such as fresh mussels, prawns and scallops, or ham in a thick cheese sauce (page 196).

• Filled pancakes can be covered with a sauce. Béchamel (page 196) is always adaptable with added cream, grated cheese, puréed sweet peppers, tomato purée and paprika, chopped spinach and herbs.

• A simple sauce of double cream, seasoned and boiled for 2–3 minutes to thicken slightly, with or without fresh herbs, can also be poured over filled pancakes.

• Seasoned fromage frais, creamed smetana and Greek yogurt all make quick sauces, but do not let them boil.

• A quick Italian-style filling is crumbled Gorgonzola cheese with slivers of Parma ham.

Feathery light pancakes can be folded or rolled to enclose a savoury or sweet filling. Here, they are folded in quarters around a filling of sautéed mushrooms, bacon and tomatoes with fresh basil.

SOUFFLÉS

The dramatic rise of a soufflé and its brief moment of exquisite glory are unparalleled. The magic is caused by hot air expanding with stiffly whisked egg whites, which once whisked must be folded very carefully into the base sauce to produce maximum volume. Resist the temptation to open the oven door until five minutes before the end of the cooking time or your soufflé may collapse before your eyes!

Either savoury or sweet flavourings can be used in soufflés. The flavouring ingredient must be intense as it will be diluted by the eggs, and it must be the right consistency – just soft enough to fall from the spoon, neither thicker nor thinner. The base sauce should be thin but not running, and easily drop off a spoon. The volume of the strongly flavoured base should never be more than half the volume of the whisked egg whites and there should ideally be roughly one-third more egg whites than yolks. Whisked egg whites can also be combined with gelatine to make chilled sweet soufflés (page 229).

If you want to serve a soufflé at a dinner party you can prepare it up until after the egg yolks are stirred in well beforehand so that you only have to whisk and fold in the egg whites and put it in the oven after your guests have arrived. You can even fold in the whisked egg whites an hour or two beforehand and keep the prepared, uncooked soufflé in the refrigerator until you are ready to cook it.

Roulades, which can be made with the same soufflé mixture, are baked in Swiss roll tins, then rolled around a filling. Roulades are even more adaptable than hot soufflés as they can also be served cold.

CLASSIC CHEESE SOUFFLÉ

Use a 1.2 litre (2 pint) soufflé dish. Serves 2 people as a main course or 3–4 as a starter.

25g (1oz) butter
3 tablespoons plain flour
½ teaspoon curry powder,
    English mustard or ground
    nutmeg
Pinch of cayenne pepper
200ml (7fl oz) milk
50g (2oz) mature Cheddar
    cheese, grated
25g (1oz) Parmesan cheese,
    grated
4 eggs, separated
1–2 extra egg whites (optional)
Salt and black pepper

1 To make the base sauce melt the butter in a medium-sized saucepan, then stir in the flour and the curry powder, English mustard or ground nutmeg and cayenne pepper. Cook for 1 minute, stirring constantly until the roux has a sandy texture.

2 Gradually add the milk, stirring until the sauce thickens, then simmer for 2 minutes. Remove from the heat, mix in all but a spoonful of the 2 cheeses until melted, then beat in the egg yolks. Season well with salt and black pepper.

3 Whisk the egg whites until they form stiff, but not dry, peaks. (Include the extra egg whites if you want a very high soufflé.) Beat 1 tablespoon of egg white into the sauce to loosen it. This makes it easier to fold in the whites without losing any air.

Few dishes make such an impressive start to a dinner party as a well-risen golden classic cheese soufflé. Adding extra egg whites helps to lift the soufflé further above the dish's rim.

4 With a large metal spoon, gently fold in the rest of the beaten egg whites, turning the spoon in a figure-of-eight movement. Butter the soufflé dish and coat the sides with dry breadcrumbs to help the soufflé 'climb' up the side of the dish as it rises during cooking.

5 Spoon the soufflé into the prepared dish and sprinkle the top with the reserved cheese. Bake in a preheated oven, 190°C, 375°F, Gas Mark 5 for 20–25 minutes, until well risen and golden brown – the soufflé should wobble very slightly when shaken. Serve instantly.

ROULADE

The classic cheese soufflé mixture (opposite) can also be used to make a savoury roulade. Unlike a soufflé, a roulade can be made in advance and cooled to serve with a filling at room temperature. If you do this, roll up the roulade while still hot, incorporating the bottom piece of greaseproof paper inside. Before serving unroll the roulade, discard the paper, add the filling, then re-roll.

Use a medium-sized Swiss roll tin (35 x 27cm/14 x 10½in). Serves 4–6.

1 *Cut a sheet of greaseproof paper about 5cm (2in) larger than the tin and snip the corners diagonally. Grease the tin and fit in the paper, folding in the corners. Grease the paper. Spread the soufflé mixture in the tin.*

2 *Bake the roulade in a preheated oven, 190°C, 375°F, Gas Mark 5 for 15–17 minutes, until just firm to the touch. Turn out on to a large sheet of greaseproof paper. Peel off the lining paper carefully in strips and discard.*

3 *Trim the long edges with a knife. Cover with a clean tea towel and allow to cool slightly. Spread with the chosen filling (see box). Fold over one edge of the roulade then roll up, holding the paper firmly underneath. Transer to a serving plate and serve sliced.*

WHISKING EGG WHITES

Soufflés rise to their impressive heights because of the air trapped in whisked egg whites. Using a food processor to whisk egg white will not produce enough volume for a soufflé, though electric whisks or rotary beaters give excellent results. The best-textured egg whites, however, are produced by whisking with a balloon whisk in a large copper bowl. Lift the whisk out of the whites each time, using large circular sweeps of your arm to incorporate as much air as possible. A small amount of salt helps to make the white more stable and so able to trap the air longer.

FLAVOURINGS AND FILLINGS

• Stir wholegrain mustard, chopped fresh chives and cayenne pepper into a cheese soufflé base before you fold in the egg whites.
• Puréed root vegetables, especially parsnips, make a delicious soufflé base if mixed with Indian spices.
• Chopped smoked fish or shellfish such as crabmeat or fresh mussels added to the egg yolk base are excellent in a soufflé.
• Red peppers boiled until soft with several whole cloves of garlic and then puréed and added to the egg yolks and flour with a little paprika and cayenne pepper make a lovely coloured soufflé.
• Sauces can often be very good finishing touches for soufflés – try heated cream with a soft white garlic cheese melted in, a very smooth vegetable purée with added cream, a curried or cheese béchamel sauce (page 196) with added cream, or a traditional rich hollandaise sauce (page 200).
• Put a little sauce such as homemade fresh tomato sauce (page 206) in the bottom of the prepared dish before adding the soufflé mixture.
• Easy and impressive roulades can be made by substituting a vegetable purée (page 53) for the butter, flour and egg mixture of the classic soufflé recipe. Fill with a hot mushroom béchamel sauce (page 196) or a garlic and herb cream cheese and serve with a fresh tomato sauce (page 206).
• Cream and curd cheeses, fresh soft goat cheeses and seasoned fromage frais make excellent fillings for roulades.

HINTS AND TIPS

Any trace of grease in the whisking bowl will prevent the egg whites from rising properly, so wash it out before use with very hot water and a drop of detergent or wipe with a little vinegar. Dry the bowl thoroughly. Whisked egg whites should form slightly soft peaks. If the whites are beaten too much, they will be dry and will not fold well into the sauce.

The classic cheese soufflé recipe (opposite) can be cooked in individual ramekin dishes instead of one large dish: place the ramekins on a baking sheet and cook for about 12 minutes only. Individual unbaked soufflés can be frozen in freezerproof ramekin dishes but add an extra egg white when whisking. Thaw at room temperature for 1 hour, then bake as usual.

Egg whites for adding to soufflés should be stiffly whisked until the peak just slightly falls over when the whisk is lifted. If they are not whisked enough the soufflé will not rise.

VERY SPECIAL TOAD-IN-THE-HOLE (66)

Instead of using commercial sausages, make your own spicy ones out of minced pork and red and yellow peppers.   *SERVES 4*

FOR THE SAUSAGES
500g (1lb) minced pork
1 each small–medium red and yellow peppers, cored, deseeded and chopped finely (page 49)
1 clove garlic, chopped finely
2 teaspoons ground coriander
1 teaspoon caraway seeds
1 small egg (size 4–5)
Olive oil
Sea salt and black pepper
FOR THE BATTER
150ml (¼ pint) milk
150ml (¼ pint) lager
125g (4oz) plain flour
½ teaspoon salt
2 large eggs (size 1–2)
Black pepper

Put the pork into a mixing bowl. Add the peppers, garlic, and coriander and caraway seeds and season generously with salt and pepper. Mix together thoroughly. Whisk the egg lightly, then mix into the meat mixture.

Using wet hands form the mixture into sausage shapes. Smear them all over with a little olive oil. Spoon 2 tablespoons olive oil into a roasting tin and add the sausages in a single layer. Put the tin just above the centre of a preheated oven, 220°C, 425°F, Gas Mark 7 for 10–15 minutes, turning the sausages once so they begin to brown.

Meanwhile, make the batter. Mix the milk and lager together. Sift the flour and salt into a food processor and add the eggs and half the liquid. Whizz until smooth, then gradually pour in the remaining liquid and whizz again thoroughly. Season with pepper. When the sausages are ready pour the batter around them. Bake for 40–45 minutes until the batter is well risen and golden brown.

HOT CHEESE, EGG AND ANCHOVY ROULADE (66)

Serve this light cheesy roulade either as a hot first course or as the main course of a light meal accompanied by a mixed salad. The roulade can be made, filled, then reheated just before serving so you can prepare it ahead, only having to put it briefly in the oven before serving. Use a 35 x 27cm (14 x 10½in) Swiss roll tin.   *SERVES 6*

FOR THE ROULADE
Butter
Grated Parmesan cheese
50g (2oz) fresh white breadcrumbs
175g (6oz) mature Cheddar cheese, grated finely
4 large eggs (size 1–2), separated
150ml (¼ pint) single cream
3 pinches cayenne pepper
2 tablespoons warm water
Salt
FOR THE FILLING
250g (8oz) curd or cream cheese
4 medium-boiled large eggs (size 1–2), chopped
2 50g (2oz) cans anchovy fillets
Large handful of chopped parsley
2 tablespoons chopped fresh oregano or 2 teaspoons dried oregano
Black pepper
Olive oil

Butter the Swiss roll tin. Line with greased greaseproof paper or baking parchment (page 77) and sprinkle with grated Parmesan cheese.

Mix the breadcrumbs and Cheddar cheese together, then add the egg yolks and cream. Mix lightly but thoroughly and season with the cayenne pepper and salt to taste. Stir in the warm water.

Put the egg whites in a large bowl. Add a pinch of salt and whisk until they stand in soft peaks, then gradually fold into the cheese and yolk mixture using a metal spoon. Spoon into the prepared tin and bake in the centre of a preheated oven, 200°C, 400°F, Gas Mark 6 for 10–15 minutes until risen and just firm to a light touch. Remove and cool slightly – it will shrink a little – then cover with a clean, damp tea towel and leave the roulade until cool.

Meanwhile, make the filling. Put the curd or cream cheese in a bowl and soften slightly with a wooden spoon, then stir in the chopped eggs. Pour the oil from the anchovy cans into the mixture. Chop the

anchovies finely, then mix them in thoroughly with the herbs. Season with plenty of freshly ground black pepper – the anchovies should make the mixture salty enough already.

When the roulade is cool loosen the edges with a knife. Sprinkle a large sheet of greaseproof paper or baking parchment evenly with Parmesan cheese and turn out the roulade on to the paper. Using a palette knife or spatula spread the filling over the roulade to within 1cm (½in) of the edges, then roll up from a short end by folding over one edge, then rolling, holding the paper underneath. Again with the help of the paper push the roll gently on to a large flat ovenproof dish. Brush all over with olive oil and sprinkle with Parmesan cheese.

Shortly before you are ready to eat put the roulade in the centre of a preheated oven, 190°C, 375°F, Gas Mark 5, for 20 minutes. To serve cut across in thick slices using a sharp knife.

POACHED EGGS ON GREEN CUSHIONS (69)

The 'green cushion' in this cold first course is a subtle purée of spinach and green pepper with just a bite of fresh green chilli.   *SERVES 6*

5 tablespoons extra virgin olive oil
1 large green pepper, cored, deseeded and chopped finely (page 49)
1 small fresh green chilli, stemmed, deseeded and chopped roughly (page 49)
500g (1lb) spinach, stemmed and washed
1 clove garlic, crushed
1 teaspoon caster sugar
1 tablespoon white wine vinegar
6 large eggs (size 1–2)
300ml (½ pint) creamed smetana
Salt
6 sprigs flat-leaved parsley, coriander, fennel or dill leaves to garnish

Put 2 tablespoons of olive oil into a heavy frying pan over a medium heat. Add the green pepper and chilli and fry fairly gently, stirring often, until the pepper is completely soft but not browned. Leave on one side in the pan.

Steam or boil the spinach leaves until soft, then drain and press out as much liquid as possible. Put into a food processor with the garlic, the fried peppers and their oil and the sugar and whizz to a smooth purée. Finally, whizz in the wine vinegar and the remaining olive oil. Season to taste with salt and leave until cold.

Meanwhile, poach the eggs for about 2 minutes until soft (page 69) – the yolks should be opaque but still feel soft to touch in the centre. (I would poach the eggs one by one to get them right.) Put them straight into a bowl of cold water to stop them cooking any further.

Not more than an hour or so before you eat drain the eggs and gently pat dry with kitchen paper. Spoon the spinach and pepper purée on to individual plates, then swirl a little creamed smetana on top. Place a poached egg in the centre and garnish with a herb sprig.

STUFFED RICE PANCAKES (66)

Using ground rice instead of flour makes light, bubbly pancakes ideal for this stuffing with its delicate Far Eastern character. Serve the pancakes with a crisp green vegetable such as broccoli.   *SERVES 6*

FOR THE PANCAKES
150g (5oz) ground rice
25g (1oz) plain flour
1 level teaspoon salt
3 pinches cayenne pepper
1 large egg (size 1–2), beaten
450ml (¾ pint) milk
Groundnut oil
FOR THE FILLING
50g (2oz) butter
2 cloves garlic, chopped
2.5cm (1in) piece fresh root ginger, peeled and chopped
75g (3oz) creamed coconut, broken roughly into pieces
250ml (8fl oz) milk
Cayenne pepper
125g (4oz) frozen petits pois
6 hard-boiled large eggs (size 1–2), chopped fairly finely
Generous handful of fresh coriander leaves
3–4 tablespoons natural yogurt
Salt

To make the pancakes put the ground rice, flour, salt and cayenne pepper in a bowl and mix thoroughly. Stir in the beaten egg and a little milk. Continue to add the rest of the milk, stirring, until you have a smooth, thin batter.

Pour just enough groundnut oil into a heavy 20cm (8in) frying pan to coat the bottom. Put the pan over a high heat until the oil is smoking then reduce the heat a little. Stir the batter – it must be stirred before cooking each pancake otherwise the ground rice sinks to the bottom – and ladle about 2 tablespoons into the pan, swirling the pan immediately to coat the base. Cook until the batter is set and small holes start to appear, then loosen with a palette knife and flip over. Cook the second side until lightly browned. Continue with the rest of the batter, laying the pancakes on a plate under a clean tea towel when they are ready. Add a little oil to the pan as necessary and adjust the heat if the pancakes are browning too quickly.

To make the filling, put half the butter in a small pan over a low heat. Add the garlic and ginger and stir for a minute or so, then add the creamed coconut and the milk. Stir over a low heat until the coconut has dissolved. Remove from the heat and season with cayenne pepper and salt. Boil the petits pois for 2–3 minutes. Put them in a bowl with the chopped eggs, add the coconut milk and stir together. Taste and adjust the seasoning if necessary. Reserve a few whole coriander leaves to garnish. Chop the rest roughly and stir into the mixture.

Butter a large shallow ovenproof dish. Lay the pancakes out on a flat surface and divide the filling evenly among them. Roll up the pancakes round the filling. Lay them close together in the dish and dot with the remaining butter. Cover with foil.

About 30 minutes before you want to eat put the dish in the centre of a preheated oven, 190°C, 375°F, Gas Mark 5 for 25 minutes. Just before serving spoon the yogurt down the centre of the pancakes and sprinkle with the reserved coriander leaves.

SOFT EGGS ON A VEGETABLE CURRY (66)

Eggs go well with spices, and the sweet flavour of parsnips, the main vegetable here, also lends itself specially well to spicing. Dill is not a typically Indian herb but I find it goes well with this dish.   *SERVES 4*

6–8 cardamom pods
2 teaspoons coriander seeds
1 teaspoon cumin seeds
75g (3oz) butter
2 red onions, chopped finely
500g (1lb) parsnips, diced
1 fresh green chilli, stemmed, deseeded and chopped finely (page 49)
2 large cloves garlic, chopped finely
500g (1lb) tomatoes, skinned and chopped roughly (page 48)
2 teaspoons caster sugar
Good handful of fresh dill, chopped
4 large eggs (size 1–2)
Salt

Grind the cardamom pods and coriander and cumin seeds finely in a coffee grinder or a pestle and mortar. Melt the butter over a medium heat in a large, heavy-based pan. Add the onions and stir for a few minutes until softened, then add the parsnips, ground spices, chilli and garlic and stir for a further minute or two.

Stir in the tomatoes and sugar, then cover and simmer over a fairly low heat for 15–20 minutes until the parsnips are soft. Remove the lid and increase the heat. Stirring all the time, let the mixture bubble for a few minutes until it is very thick. Remove from the heat and season to taste with salt.

Just before you want to eat reheat the vegetable curry over a medium heat until just bubbling. Stir in half the chopped dill. Quickly break in the eggs, spaced apart, then cover and cook for about 3 minutes until the egg whites are set but the yolks still soft. Sprinkle the remaining dill on top and serve straight away.

PASTA and PIZZA

Legend has it that pasta was invented in China and introduced to the West by Marco Polo but Chinese historians maintain that it came to them from the West. Whatever the truth, pasta has been eaten for centuries, and a form of pasta was even recorded at the time of the ancient Greeks. Now, above all, pasta is the gastronomic god of Italy, but noodles are just as popular in Asia, and there are the *udon* of Japan, the *pierogi* of Poland, the *spätzel* of Germany, the *nouilles* of France, even the *tel 'meni* of Siberia – and many, many more.

Pasta must surely be the world's most versatile food since it marries happily with almost any added ingredient and combination of flavours, seasonings and spices. Pasta can be – and has always been – eaten by paupers and princes: an excellent inexpensive food which can be elevated to luxurious sophistication according to what ingredients you combine with it.

Just as versatile are the small Italian dumplings called *gnocchi*. Often served simply with butter and Parmesan cheese, they are equally good with all pasta sauces.

I have never met anyone who didn't like pasta, but for the Italians it inspires real passion. This is shown by their unending fund of often affectionate names for different shapes of pasta – approximately 300 names for about 100 pasta shapes. The word *maccheroni* is thought to have evolved from *ma, che, carini!* which can be roughly translated as 'but what pretty little things!'. Then there are *amorini*, little loves; *tira baci*, kiss stealers; and *ziti*, bridegrooms, as well as all the familiar names such as tortellini, tagliatelle, fettucini, ravioli and so on.

Pasta is also the perfect convenience food. A packet of dried pasta can always be kept in the cupboard, and even if you only have olive oil or butter and seasoning to add to it you will have a satisfying meal. Add a handful of fresh herbs, a few canned anchovies and a sprinkling of grated Parmesan cheese and it will be quite special. And any leftover pasta also tastes good cold.

Throwing together a pasta dish at the last minute is ideal for informal occasions but if you are expecting several guests one of the baked, stuffed or layered pasta dishes is more practical. These dishes, such as the many varieties of lasagne and cannelloni, can be made in advance and then simply put in the oven just before you are ready to eat, allowing you to relax before your friends arrive. Usually only a salad and some bread is needed as an accompaniment, which makes preparing the meal even easier.

Although today there are countless pasta restaurants and pizzerias to choose from which provide an informal, inexpensive outing, it is still worthwhile making the dishes at home. Making your own pasta may be time-consuming but it is also very satisfying. The ingredients are basic and cheap yet the reward is rich and delicious. In your own home, too, there need be no rules about the combinations of ingredients you use for sauces or toppings – this is a chance to exercise your creative instincts and experiment to produce something really personal.

Tomatoes are often paired with pasta dishes and pizza although it is important to realize there are endless possibilities for pizza toppings and for pasta sauces which do not include them.

During this century pizza has followed pasta and broken through the Italian frontiers. Now pizzas seem to be an everyday food almost all over the world. I was amazed to see little pizza restaurants when I was travelling through a remote rural area of India recently. In fact, several of the Indian breads, topped with spiced meat, onions and herbs are like a form of pizza, and in Egypt and the Middle East there are delicious pizza-like breads topped with whole eggs and spices and sometimes meat. It is useful to remember that combinations of Indian and Middle Eastern spices go particularly well with pasta dishes and with pizzas.

Clockwise from top left: Salmon and Crab Cannelloni (page 92) is made with spinach lasagne wrapped around seafood; Pasta Bows with Spiced Meatballs (page 91); Spaghetti with Walnuts, Parsley and Gorgonzola (page 91) elevates spaghetti to dinner party status; a golden Cheddar cheese sauce tops spinach and tagliatelle in Noodle Pie (page 90); Tagliatelle Verdi with Squid and Green Cream Sauce (page 93); delicate pieces of poached salmon complement the smoked fish flavour in Sea Shell Pasta with Salmon, Smoked Haddock and Broccoli (page 90); Chick Pea, Mushroom and Leek Pizza (page 92) served with a mixed green salad. Centre: Pasta with Parsnips and Kabanos Sausages (page 93) with skinned yellow pepper strips.

PASTA

Pasta – the Italian word for dough – is simply flour and water, sometimes combined with an egg and other added flavouring. Italian dried pasta is made from hard durum wheat, and it can be bought made with egg or simply with water. Although fresh pasta is supremely light and delicate, you should not feel that dried pasta is inferior; it is simply different. Good-quality dried pasta has a mellow flavour and a strength of texture which homemade pasta cannot achieve. Where homemade pasta does triumph is in the coloured and flavoured pastas.

For homemade pasta strong white bread flour with its high gluten content is best and eggs are almost always added. Pasta can also be bought or made with wholemeal flour. Personally, I think wholemeal flour is too heavy for pasta as lightness should be one of its most attractive features. The stronger flavour of the flour is also quite dominant. I prefer a mixture of buckwheat and plain flours.

It is very important to cook pasta al dente, which means that you still need to bite it slightly with your teeth. Prolonged cooking can make it soft and mushy. It is impossible to give an exact time for achieving the texture you want as pasta varies so much: always test it two or three times while it is cooking. Homemade pasta cooks extremely quickly – it is ready almost as soon as the water comes back to the boil in just two to three minutes – so watch it like a hawk!

MAKING FRESH PASTA

Making your own pasta may be time consuming, but it is very satisfying. The ingredients are basic and cheap, yet the result is so rich and delicious. Either make pasta dough by hand, as shown here, or whizz all the ingredients together in a food processor until the dough comes away from the sides of the bowl, sprinkling in extra flour if needed.

You can either cut the pasta by hand into the required shape or shapes or use a pasta rolling machine (opposite). Serves 6 as a starter or 4 as a main course.

1 *Sift 300g (10oz) strong white bread flour on to a clean work surface with 1 teaspoon salt. Make a well in the centre. Break in 3 eggs and add 2 teaspoons olive oil (optional) to help keep the dough pliable while you work with it.*

2 *Using the tips of your fingers or a fork mix the eggs and oil lightly together, then start to mix the flour into the eggs drawing in more and more flour until you have a thick dough. If the dough is moist and too sticky add a little more flour and mix in.*

3 *With a flour shaker at the ready, knead the dough for 5–10 minutes until smooth, adding more flour as necessary. Put the dough into a polythene bag or wrap in foil and leave it at room temperature for about 1 hour to rest before the next stage.*

4 *Divide the dough into 3 portions and work with 1 at a time, keeping the remaining pieces of dough covered with a clean tea towel. Lightly flour a work surface and roll out the dough to the thickness of a 10 pence piece. Fold over four times, give a quarter turn and re-roll. Repeat 4 times until the dough is smooth and no longer feels sticky.*

To cut into noodles, *lightly flour the rolled dough and fold it into a long, loose roll, slightly flattened. Cut across into thin slices with a sharp knife. Open out and dry the noodles on a tea towel over the back of a chair; this will take 30 minutes to 2 hours, depending on how warm the room is. Dust, if necessary, with flour to prevent them sticking together.*

To cook pasta, *bring a large saucepan of salted water to the boil. Add about 1 tablespoon oil, then add the pasta and stir so it does not stick together. Cook until al dente (above). Drain and rinse under cold running water. Return to the pan a little wet and reheat with your chosen sauce, or toss in oil and butter with seasoning to taste.*

COLOURING PASTA
Homemade pasta can be coloured in a number of ways which also give flavour and texture: finely chopped or puréed spinach for vibrant green pasta; tomato purée for orangy-red pasta; grated cooked beetroot for pink to crimson pasta (depending on how much you add); saffron and extra egg yolks for yellow pasta; and squid ink for black pasta. You can also add flavour by adding chopped herbs, ground spices or a little pesto sauce or olive paste from a jar. Add the extra ingredients at the same time as the eggs. You may need to use more flour as you knead.

USING A PASTA MACHINE

If you make pasta often it is well worth getting a pasta rolling machine. Hand-operated machines, as illustrated below, are reasonably priced, easily available and quite robust. There is a little technique involved – it is simply a matter of holding one end of the pasta dough while turning the handle.

Make the dough (steps 1–3 opposite). Have a clean tea towel spread out at the ready and feed the dough through the rollers in pieces the size of a large egg, keeping the remaining dough under a tea towel or wrapped in a polythene bag or foil to stop it drying out.

The machine works like a mangle – you feed the dough in at one end, turn a handle with your other hand and the dough comes out as a sheet of pasta. Repeat this a number of times with the same piece of pasta, progressively reducing the thickness each time. (There are usually six thickness settings.)

The dough will cut more cleanly and not stick if it is allowed to rest briefly after rolling and before cutting and again before cooking. To make lasagne or cannelloni, instead of noodles, simply cut the rolled-out dough (step 3 below) into the required lengths by hand and leave to rest before using.

Creamy Pasta with Chicken and Tarragon Cream Sauce (page 91) is made here with a mixture of spinach and egg noodles.

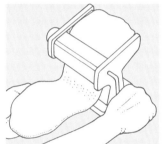

1 *Feed a small piece of dough through at the widest setting, holding the rolled-out end of the dough as it comes through. Fold in half and feed through again. Repeat this 4 more times. If the dough is at all sticky or breaks dust it with a little flour.*

2 *Set the rollers one setting thinner and feed the dough through again about 4 times. Reset the rollers to the next thinner setting and repeat. For pasta of normal thickness stop at this stage; for thinner pasta feed the dough through again.*

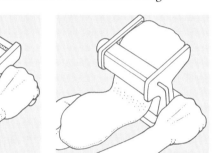

3 *Lay the sheets of rolled pasta out to rest on a clean dry tea towel, making sure they don't overlap otherwise they will stick together. Leave the pasta for about 1 hour at room temperature to dry it slightly so it will cut cleanly.*

4 *To cut into noodles or spaghetti, fit the appropriate cutting rollers on the machine and refit the handle, if necessary. Feed the dough through as before, turning the handle with one hand and supporting the strands as they come out of the machine.*

SIMPLE SAUCES FOR PASTA

• Melted butter with plenty of freshly ground black pepper and chopped fresh herbs is one of the simplest pasta sauces you can make. I love it.
• Try slivers of sautéed fresh vegetables such as mushrooms, shallots and courgettes, or cooked ham or fish, tossed with single or double cream.
• Chopped walnuts or almonds or pine kernels sautéed in olive oil with garlic and plenty of chopped parsley adds a crunchy texture to pasta.
• Brightly coloured sweet peppers fried until soft in oil and butter, then puréed, are a good

topping for noodles.
• For a lower-fat sauce, mix boiled and puréed sweet peppers with fromage frais.
• Mix prawns into hot pasta with butter, seasoning and lots of chopped fresh dill.
• Canned tuna, cockles, mussels, crab meat or anchovies can be combined with olive oil or cream and fresh herbs.
• Fresh mussels, squid and scallops, cooked for just a minute or two and then mixed with cream and a small amount of the pasta cooking water makes a delicious light sauce.
• Try cubed Mozzarella or

crumbled blue cheese stirred into a cream, tomato or oil-and-butter sauce until the cheese just begins to melt.
• Cream with a little mild curry paste, lemon juice and chopped fresh coriander or mint stirred in gives an Indian taste.
• And, of course, tomato sauce is always popular. Use canned chopped tomatoes for a quick tomato sauce (page 89) and add strips of fresh basil just before serving. Or, use the fresh tomato sauce recipe (page 206) without reducing it too much. Stir in some chopped fresh basil or dried oregano.

5 *Dry the noodles on the back of a chair and leave for 30 minutes to 2 hours. To make individual serving nests hold the noodles up, then curl them on to a tea towel; you should have about 3–4 nests per serving. Cook the noodles in a saucepan of boiling water until al dente (opposite).*

LAYERED *and* STUFFED PASTA

Baked layered and stuffed pasta dishes such as cannelloni and lasagne, and little filled parcels of pasta such as ravioli and tortellini, offer enormous scope for different ingredients and treatments.

The dough for filled pasta shapes should be fairly moist so it seals easily. Spinach pasta usually stays moist but if you are using egg pasta add a little oil to the dough. Roll out the dough thinly so the shapes will not be heavy, but not so thinly that they will tear when stuffed. You must not overfill them either or they may burst while cooking. After forming the little parcels arrange them spaced apart on a floured clean dry tea towel for an hour or so, turning them over once so they dry on both sides.

Dried cannelloni which do not need precooking are useful but still can be fiddly to deal with. If you use the sort which have to be boiled before stuffing, take care not to overcook them or they may split when filled.

Cannelloni are, in fact, easiest to prepare if you use homemade fresh pasta sheets. Cut the pasta dough into rectangles like lasagne, and simply roll up round the filling, then lay the cannelloni join side down in a shallow, rectangular ovenproof dish and cover with a sauce before baking. Always arrange them in the dish close together but in a single layer so they have the sauce both on and around them and don't dry out.

Stuffed pasta shapes are a boon for the home cook because they offer such scope for variety with different coloured and flavoured pastas (page 82) and tasty fillings.

CLASSIC LASAGNE

Called *lasagne al forno*, this is a classic baked pasta dish layered with a ragù or minced beef sauce (page 213), pasta sheets, béchamel sauce (page 196) and finely grated fresh Parmesan cheese. *Lasagne verdi* is made from spinach-flavoured lasagne sheets. Homemade pasta sheets make the best lasagne of all but you can save yourself a great deal of time if you buy the dried 'no precooking' variety. These sheets will be even more successful if you soak them briefly in a large bowl of hot water before you assemble your lasagne, as this softens them slightly. It is also now possible to buy fresh lasagne sheets, making the whole process simpler still. When assembling lasagne, do not use more than 4 layers of pasta as too many layers with too little filling and sauce make a stodgy dry lasagne.

To serve 6–8 people, you will need 8–10 lasagne sheets, 900ml–1.2 litres (1½–2 pints) béchamel sauce and 900ml–1.2 litres (1½–2 pints) minced beef sauce and grated Parmesan cheese. The exact quantities, of course, depend on the size of your ovenproof dish.

1 *Cook dried lasagne sheets that need precooking in a large pan of boiling salted water with a few drops of oil until al dente. Add the sheets a few at a time. Remove with a slotted spoon and drain on a clean tea towel, spacing well apart.*

2 *Spread a thin layer of meat sauce in a greased ovenproof dish. Add a layer of pasta sheets, then a layer of meat sauce, a layer of béchamel sauce and a sprinkling of Parmesan. Add a second layer of pasta and continue layering, finishing with pasta.*

3 *Top with a thick layer of béchamel sauce sprinkled with more grated Parmesan cheese. Cook in a preheated oven, 180°C, 350°F, Gas Mark 4 for about 45 minutes until the top is golden brown.*

Bubbling Parmesan cheese tops classic lasagne.

STUFFED PASTA

As well as ravioli and tortellini there are numerous other small stuffed pasta shapes you can make just as easily. It's worth making your own because the pasta is more delicate in texture and the filling can be more varied and personal. *Lunette* are one of the easiest shapes to make. Just cut out circles of dough and place the stuffing along one side. Moisten the edges with water and press to seal, creating the distinctive half-moon shape.

Cook all fresh stuffed pasta in boiling salted water with a little oil for 5–7 minutes, or until *al dente*. Dried pasta shapes will take slightly longer to cook. Serve either with a sauce or simply with butter and grated Parmesan cheese.

MAKING RAVIOLI

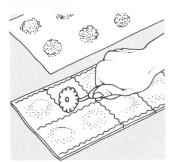

Spoon mounds of filling (about ½ teaspoon each) on to a sheet of rolled pasta dough, about 5cm (2in) apart. Brush between the mounds with water. Lay a second sheet on top, then press with your fingers to seal between the mounds. Cut into squares with a fluted pastry wheel. Dry for about 1 hour before cooking (right).

If using a ravioli mould lay a sheet of rolled dough over the moulds, pressing the dough into the hollows. Place a small amount of filling in each hollow, moisten and top with a second sheet of dough. Run a rolling pin over the top to cut. Cook in boiling salted water for 5–7 minutes, until al dente.

SHAPING TORTELLINI

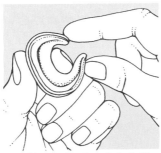

1 *Thinly roll out the pasta until it is about 2.5mm (⅛in) thick. Cut out circles of dough, about 6cm (2½in) in diameter, using a pastry cutter. Put about 1 teaspoon of filling on one half of each circle and moisten the edges of the dough with a little water.*

2 *Fold each dough circle in half over the filling and press the edges together firmly to seal. Carefully curve the half-moon shape round your forefinger, turning up the sealed edges like a hat brim. Pinch the pointed ends together. Repeat with the rest of the circles of dough. Cook the tortellini in the same way as ravioli (above).*

Creamy cheese-flavoured béchamel sauce tops Cannelloni Stuffed with Turkey and Fennel (page 90). Using fresh or 'no precooking' dried lasagne sheets makes this an easy dish.

PASTA FILLINGS AND FLAVOURINGS

- A vegetable lasagne makes a complete and ideal meal for vegetarians. Use cooked vegetables and a suitable sauce such as yogurt stabilized with cornflour so it doesn't curdle when heated instead of the usual béchamel sauce.
- With a yogurt sauce you can crumble over Ricotta or other white cheese.
- Sautéed sliced bulb fennel, aubergine, leeks, spinach or pumpkin and fresh tomatoes can all be layered with plain or cheesy béchamel sauce for a lasagne with a difference.
- Toast pine kernels (see pesto page 207) or chopped walnuts and add to the lasagne layers. Scatter more untoasted ones on top before baking.
- Chestnut mushrooms, which are more solid and keep their texture, are best for lasagne.
- Smoked fish goes well with a cheesy béchamel sauce, as do mussels and other shellfish.
- For a light chicken lasagne filling, spread a creamy béchamel sauce containing slivers of sautéed chicken breast and roughly chopped tarragon between the pasta sheets.
- As a change from minced beef try minced veal, pork, chicken or turkey in stuffed pasta or for a meat sauce.
- Chopped ham or salami can be mixed with Parmesan cheese and Ricotta or fromage frais.
- Smoked haddock or cod mixed with fromage frais and chopped dill or fennel is delicious in ravioli.
- A mixture of spinach and Ricotta cheese – probably the best known pasta filling – is ideal for tortellini. Or, try Ricotta mixed with cooked leeks, kale or broccoli.
- Spinach on its own can be an excellent filling for stuffed pasta, served with a cream or tomato sauce. Season with freshly grated nutmeg.
- Pumpkin mashed with butter and nutmeg is a popular Italian filling. Try mashed parsnip with ground and fresh coriander as an alternative.
- Sauté some onions and bacon in butter until soft, then mix with Ricotta and season with freshly grated nutmeg.
- Another favourite pasta filling of mine is goat cheese with chopped walnuts.
- Sprinkle crumbled crisply fried bacon over the stuffed pasta just before serving.
- Ricotta cheese with slivers of fresh basil or a little pesto sauce (page 207) makes a simple filling for pasta.

NOODLES *and* GNOCCHI

Noodles in various shapes and forms are eaten all over the world, and are particularly popular in Asia. Most noodles are made from some kind of wheat flour, with or without egg, but they can also be made from rice or buckwheat flour and from vegetable starches: mung bean, soya bean, chick pea, potato, yam and even seaweed.

Asian noodles range in shape from fairly thin egg noodles to wide flat rice noodles. Most can be boiled like European noodles but both rice and bean noodles must be soaked first to soften them before cooking. Very thin rice noodles can be deep-fried straight from the packet – they puff up into a crisp and delicious tangle that goes well with salads or stir-fried vegetables.

Gnocchi or 'little dumplings' vary greatly but are all irresistible. They can be made from potato and flour, from semolina and cheese (*gnocchi alla romana*) or even from spinach and Ricotta or curd cheese. Lightness should be one of the main characteristics of gnocchi, which is why potato gnocchi should be made with the driest main-crop potatoes, and not too much flour which would make the mixture heavy. Avoid adding eggs as this only means having to add more flour, and although eggs may bind the mixture they will also make it rubbery.

Chopped fresh herbs can be added to a potato gnocchi mixture to give it added flavour and pretty green specks, or you can make a beautifully coloured version using orange-fleshed sweet potatoes. Serve gnocchi piping hot with plenty of grated Parmesan cheese and butter.

ORIENTAL-STYLE STIR-FRIED NOODLES

It is so easy to stir-fry precooked Chinese egg noodles with finely shredded vegetables and slivers of meat, fish or shellfish to make a variety of quick dishes.

As with all stir-fry recipes, the key to success is preparation. Have everything ready before you start cooking. Wash, peel and slice thinly the vegetables as appropriate. Cutting the vegetables into equal-sized pieces will help ensure even cooking. Cut any meat or fish into thin slivers.

Make sure the oil in your wok or pan is hot and constantly stir all the ingredients while they are cooking. It is best to use sunflower or groundnut oil for stir-frying.

To prepare the noodles precook them in a large pan of boiling salted water for about 3 minutes until tender, then drain and rinse under cold water. If you want to cook the noodles in advance, keep them in a polythene bag in the refrigerator.

To serve 4, use about 500g (1lb) finely shredded vegetables and 250g (8oz) precooked noodles.

1 *Heat 3 tablespoons sunflower or groundnut oil in a wok or frying pan over a medium-high heat. Add 2 finely chopped garlic cloves and fry until light brown, then stir in 2 teaspoons Chinese five-spice powder.*

2 *Add the prepared vegetables and stir-fry for 2–5 minutes, taking care not to overcook the vegetables, then add 75g (3oz) bean sprouts and the precooked noodles. Stir-fry for about 2 minutes more.*

Chinese Egg Noodles with Aromatic Vegetables (page 93) includes stir-fried garlic, root ginger, sliced tomatoes and courgettes, fresh bean sprouts and chopped fresh coriander leaves.

3 *When the vegetables are just tender but still slightly crisp, stir in 1 teaspoon soft brown sugar, 3 tablespoons soy sauce and a small bunch of finely chopped spring onions and just warm through. Season with salt and freshly ground black pepper and serve immediately. If you like you can sprinkle a little toasted sesame oil on top for extra flavour.*

POTATO GNOCCHI

These light 'dumplings' make a welcome alternative to pasta as a first course. Cooking the potatoes in a steamer before you mash them will make them extra dry, contributing to the desired lightness. Mash the potatoes by hand, because if you use a food processor it will turn them into unusable glue (page 53).

For every 1kg (2lb) mashed potatoes knead in about 200g (7oz) plain flour and salt and pepper to taste. Avoid adding eggs as they tend to make the gnocchi rubbery. These quantities serve 4–6.

1 *Knead together the mashed potatoes, flour and seasoning to make a smooth, elastic dough on a work surface. Divide the dough into 3 pieces. Sprinkle each portion of dough with flour and roll into sausage shapes about 1.5cm (¾in) wide.*

2 *Cut the 'sausages' across into 2.5cm (1in) lengths. Press each piece of dough against the back of a large, curved fork. At the same time pull it along the fork, then flick it off on to a floured surface. The gnocchi should look like ribbed shells.*

3 *Drop the gnocchi into a large pan of boiling, salted water. When cooked they will float to the surface. Lift out with a slotted spoon, drain well, then put into a warm, buttered serving dish. Add butter and grated Parmesan cheese or a sauce.*

SERVING NOODLES AND GNOCCHI

• Parsnip cubes browned in groundnut oil with a little chopped garlic and ginger until almost soft with chopped fresh coriander leaves added at the end are delicious with noodles.

• Noodles of any kind can be added to a broth or good chicken stock (page 29) or to a can of consommé. Include finely shredded vegetables to cook for a minute or so and slivers of cooked chicken, meat or fish for a quick soup. Soy sauce and finely chopped ginger can be added for a more Chinese flavour.

• Simply toss cooked noodles in a little oil with chopped garlic and ginger and some soy sauce for a really quick dish.

• Roughly chopped fresh coriander and briefly fried chopped garlic add an instant oriental character to noodles.

• You can buy oriental sauces in jars – oyster sauce is one of my favourites – to add to stir-fried noodles, or you can make up a quick mixture of soy sauce, Chinese five-spice powder, tomato purée, some brown sugar and seasoning.

• Potato gnocchi are delicious served just with butter and grated cheese. Or, add a sprinkling of chopped fresh chives or dill for extra flavour.

• A rich fresh tomato sauce (page 206) combined with strips of basil is excellent to serve with gnocchi.

• You can make a variety of creamy sauces to serve with noodles and gnocchi by heating double cream and adding either crumbled Gorgonzola or a mixture of Parmesan and other cheeses, or finely chopped walnuts and parsley combined with chopped spring onions.

• A green sauce for potato gnocchi can be made from chopped or puréed cooked spinach, fromage frais and a little heated cream.

• Butter and cream warmed with tomato purée and seasoning make a pretty pink sauce for spinach gnocchi.

• As well as sea salt and freshly ground black pepper, grated nutmeg works well in all the above sauces. Try caraway seeds for a different flavour.

• Very light gnocchi can be made with Ricotta mixed with spinach. Mix together 500g (1lb) cooked, drained and finely chopped spinach, which has been lightly sautéed in butter, with 175g (6oz) Ricotta, 75g (3oz) plain flour, 2 egg yolks and 125g (4oz) grated Parmesan cheese. Season with salt, pepper and freshly grated nutmeg. Form the mixture into small 1cm (½in) balls and cook in boiling water in the same way as potato gnocchi (left) for 3–4 minutes.

BAKED SEMOLINA GNOCCHI

Semolina gnocchi are the easiest gnocchi to make, and are served here baked with cheese. Make the mixture at least 2 hours in advance, so it cools before you cut it. Boil 600ml (1 pint) milk with 125g (4oz) semolina and grated nutmeg, salt and black pepper, stirring. Simmer gently, still stirring, until the mixture is very thick. Remove from the heat and stir in 75g (3oz) grated Parmesan, 25g (1oz) butter and 1 egg plus 1 egg yolk whisked lightly together. Return to a low heat and stir for 1 minute. Serves 4–6.

1 *Using a palette knife spread the hot semolina mixture about 1cm (½in) thick over a cool work surface or in a buttered large shallow dish and leave until solid and cold. Take care not to burn your fingers on the hot mixture while you are spreading it.*

2 *Cut the cooled semolina mixture into 5cm (2in) rounds with a pastry cutter, then arrange in an overlapping pattern in a buttered shallow flameproof serving dish. Dot the tops with butter. Place any misshapen ones on the base underneath.*

3 *Bake towards the top of a preheated oven, 220°C, 425°F, Gas Mark 7 for 15 minutes or grill until the gnocchi are golden brown at the edges. Sprinkle with finely grated fresh Parmesan cheese and serve at once, straight from the dish.*

PIZZA

Making a pizza must be one of the easiest ways to produce a complete and balanced meal. The variety of suitable toppings is endless, and you can invent toppings for all manner of occasions or to cater for the particular tastes of your family and friends.

A pizza base is simply made with a bread dough using strong white flour. You can, of course, use brown or wholemeal flours but I find that these stronger-flavoured flours compete too much with the toppings, and also they do not produce the thin, light and crisp Neapolitan-style crust which is ideal. Many commercially bought pizzas have a thick doughy base of bread, but, personally, I much prefer the original Neapolitan crust. Since part of the point of making a pizza is that it is quick and easy, I always use easy-blend dried yeast (page 282).

Part of the crunchiness of a truly authentic Neapolitan pizza base is the result of baking it on the floor of a traditional brick-lined bread oven at a very high temperature. You cannot do this at home but a similar effect can be achieved by putting a baking stone or unglazed terracotta tiles on the oven shelf to bake the pizza on without using a pizza tin.

Make sure you only use prime-quality ingredients for pizza toppings, and remember that seasoning is also important. Too much topping, however, can weigh down and dampen the crust. It is also important that the topping is not too wet or the crust will become soggy.

Eat your pizzas as soon as they come out of the oven because they lose much of their appeal as they become cold. If you do want to take a pizza on a picnic, I suggest wrapping it in foil and several layers of newspaper so it stays warm and delicious.

Classic pizza Napoletana with golden crusts and a bubbling topping made from fresh tomato sauce, Mozzarella cheese, canned anchovies and a sprinkling of oregano.

CLASSIC PIZZA NAPOLETANA

This is the most famous of all pizzas, and you can use the basic recipe as a guide to making others with different toppings. The quick tomato sauce (opposite) should be made in advance and left to cool before using.

To make the dough, follow the white bread dough recipe, (page 282), but add 2 tablespoons extra virgin olive oil with the water. When the dough has risen divide it into 8 pieces to make 8 pizzas, each about 20cm (8in) wide, or make into 2 large pizzas. Use 2 baking sheets, if necessary.

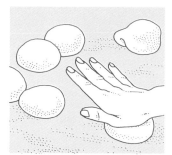

1 *Roll each piece of dough into a ball, then flatten into 20cm (8in) rounds about 2.5mm (⅛in) thick using the heel of your hand. Use your fingers to make the rounds a little thicker at the edges so the sauce does not run off the pizza during baking.*

2 *Place the pizzas on oiled baking sheets and leave to rise again, covered with lightly oiled clingfilm. Brush each one with olive oil, then top with tomato sauce, sliced Mozzarella cheese, a lattice of drained canned anchovies (optional) and dried oregano.*

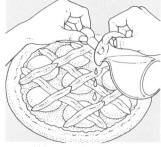

3 *Dribble over a little more olive oil, then bake the pizzas towards the top of a preheated oven, 230°C, 450°F, Gas Mark 8 for 10–15 minutes, rotating the baking sheets halfway through, until the edges are golden brown and the cheese bubbling.*

QUICK TOMATO SAUCE

A good, rich tomato sauce is essential for pizza toppings. My favourite sauce can quickly be made by mixing in a saucepan 2 tablespoons extra virgin olive oil, 1 finely chopped clove of garlic, 397g (14oz) can chopped tomatoes, 2 tablespoons tomato purée, some black pepper and a little salt. Heat the mixture until bubbling strongly, stirring constantly until it is reduced to a thick sauce. Cool before using. Alternatively, make a fresh tomato sauce (page 206).

A calzone, here filled with Gorgonzola cheese, sautéed thinly sliced onions and slivers of Parma ham, makes an excellent light lunch or supper dish served with a simple salad.

MAKING CALZONE

Calzones are the natural evolution of the pizza. The same white bread dough is used (opposite) but instead of being baked flat the dough is folded over a filling, like a Cornish pasty.

Calzones can be filled with any of the topping mixtures suggested for pizzas (see box right) but remember the filling must not be too wet initially. Be careful not to overfill the calzone or it may burst during cooking. Set the dough aside to rise before adding the filling.

1 *Divide the risen dough into 8 balls. Using the heel of your hand flatten each one on a lightly floured work surface to form a round as symmetrical as possible about 20cm (8in) in diameter and 2.5mm (⅛in) thick.*

2 *Brush the rounds with olive oil, then place about 3 rounded tablespoons filling on one half of each round. Brush the edges of the dough with beaten egg, then fold the rounds over the filling, making sure none of it seeps out. Press the edges to seal together firmly.*

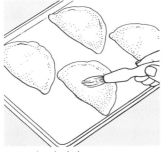

3 *Brush a little beaten egg over each calzone for a shiny glaze. Place on an oiled baking sheet, or use 2 sheets if necessary, and bake in a preheated oven, 220°C, 425°F, Gas Mark 7 for 10–15 minutes until the dough is crisp and golden. Cool slightly before serving.*

IDEAS FOR PIZZAS AND CALZONES

• Use thinly sliced Mozzarella cheese. If you do not have any Mozzarella, use slices of Gruyère, Emmental or mature Cheddar cheese.

• Goat cheese or Gorgonzola or other blue cheese mixed with Ricotta makes a good pizza topping.

• My family likes pizza topped with very thinly sliced onions covered with grated cheese or with well-drained cooked spinach, greens or kale and slices of Mozzarella cheese.

• Strips of grilled, skinned peppers (page 55), sliced tomatoes and thin slices of courgettes with cheese on top.

• Sautéed thinly sliced onions, especially the red-skinned variety, with crumbled Gorgonzola and a few slivers of thinly sliced Parma ham.

• Briefly sautéed thin slices of fennel with goat cheese on top. If the tomatoes are too juicy they can make a pizza too wet.

• Nuts are a good garnish for pizzas – frisée lettuce sautéed in olive oil with a few capers and chopped stoned black olives, topped with pine kernels or chopped walnuts and crumbled goat cheese, makes a delicious topping. Alternatively, spread pesto sauce on the dough and top with pine kernels and grated Parmesan cheese.

• Thinly sliced chestnut mushrooms, plenty of chopped garlic, ground and fresh coriander, a little chopped chilli and generous dribblings of olive oil. I recommend this type of mushroom because they are less watery than others.

• Thinly sliced dessert apples with Ricotta cheese.

• Fresh pineapple with Gorgonzola cheese.

• Well-drained canned tuna with plenty of crushed garlic and freshly chopped herbs. Dill is specially good.

• Cockles, mussels, prawns, crab meat and briefly sautéed thinly sliced squid. (I always use plenty of chopped parsley and herbs with a seafood topping.)

• Thinly sliced dried sausages – salami, chorizo, kabanos – with cheese.

• Miniature calzones made from 10cm (4in) circles of dough can be deep-fried in olive oil, making good snacks for picnics or parties. The quantity of white bread dough (opposite) makes 8–10.

• If you have time use fresh tomatoes when they are in season to make a tasty tomato sauce (page 206). Just remember to bubble the sauce until it reduces to the correct consistency.

• Sun-dried tomato paste enriches the flavour of the tomato sauce. It can also be spread on to pizza before adding other toppings.

SEA SHELL PASTA WITH SALMON, SMOKED HADDOCK AND BROCCOLI (80)

This pretty mixture of colours tastes every bit as good as it looks. It would not really be appropriate to add Parmesan cheese.   SERVES 6

375g (12oz) broccoli florets, trimmed and
  sliced thinly
375–425g (12–14oz) small pasta shells
  (depending on appetites)
2 tablespoons extra virgin olive oil
40g (1½oz) butter
2 large cloves garlic, chopped finely
2.5cm (1in) piece fresh root ginger, peeled
  and chopped finely
425g (14oz) salmon tail, filleted, skinned
  and sliced into 2.5cm (1in) pieces
300–375g (10–12oz) smoked haddock
  fillets, skinned and sliced into 2.5cm
  (1in) pieces
3 tablespoons double cream
2 heaped tablespoons fromage frais
Sea salt and black pepper

Cook the broccoli in boiling salted water for 3–4 minutes, then drain and leave on one side. Cook the pasta in plenty of boiling salted water until *al dente*.

Meanwhile, put the olive oil and butter in a deep frying pan over a medium heat. Add the chopped garlic and ginger and cook for 2 minutes, then add the sliced salmon and haddock and stir around gently with a wooden spoon for 4–5 minutes until just cooked. Stir in the cooked broccoli, then the cream and fromage frais and season to taste with plenty of black pepper and some sea salt. Remove the pan from the heat.

Drain the pasta and rinse under cold running water. Reheat in the rinsed-out saucepan, then turn it into a warm serving bowl. Add the sauce, mix it roughly into the pasta with a wooden spoon and serve at once.

CANNELLONI STUFFED WITH TURKEY AND FENNEL (85)

This recipe uses lasagne sheets which are not layered but instead wrapped round a filling of minced turkey, fennel and red pepper. The result is light, rather fat cannelloni in a rich cheese sauce.   SERVES 4

3 tablespoons olive oil
1 large red pepper, cored, deseeded and
  chopped finely (page 49)
1 large bulb fennel, trimmed and
  chopped finely (page 46)
8 lasagne sheets (the 'no precooking' type)
2–3 large cloves garlic, chopped
1 heaped teaspoon ground mace
500g (1lb) minced turkey
25g (1oz) butter
25g (1oz) plain flour
600ml (1 pint) milk
125g (4oz) mature Cheddar cheese,
  coarsely grated
1 tablespoon grated Parmesan cheese
Salt and black pepper

Lightly oil a rectangular ovenproof dish. Put the olive oil in a large, deep frying pan over a medium heat. Add the chopped pepper and fennel and stir around, then cover and leave to cook, stirring occasionally, for 10–15 minutes.

Meanwhile, put the lasagne sheets into a sink of hot water into which you have sprinkled a few drops of oil. Leave for 8–12 minutes until the pasta is just soft enough to bend but not so soft that it will tear easily. Drain the sheets separately on a flat surface.

When the vegetables are soft add the chopped garlic and stir for another 1–2 minutes, then increase the heat and stir in the mace, followed by the minced turkey. Stir around with a wooden spoon over a high heat until the turkey meat has separated, then cook for about 5 minutes. Season to taste with salt and black pepper. Turn the mixture into a bowl and allow to cool slightly.

Spoon some of the cooked turkey and vegetable mixture on to the centre of each lasagne sheet, then roll the pasta loosely round the filling and place the rolls carefully in the dish join side down.

To make the sauce, gently melt the butter in a saucepan. Remove from the heat and using a wooden spoon stir in the flour until smooth. Gradually stir in the milk, return to the heat and bring to the boil. Stir all the time until thickened. Remove the pan from the heat, add the grated Cheddar cheese and stir until melted, then season with plenty of black pepper and a little salt if necessary.

Gradually pour the sauce over the pasta rolls, letting it sink down to the bottom of the dish. Sprinkle the Parmesan cheese over the top. Bake just above the centre of a preheated oven, 190°C, 375°F, Gas Mark 5 for 35–40 minutes until speckly brown.

NOODLE PIE (80)

I made this pasta pie during one of the school holidays and it has remained a family favourite ever since. It is a practical family dish as you can prepare it in advance and reheat when necessary.   SERVES 6

125g (4oz) tagliatelle or other
  wide flat egg noodles
500g (1lb) spinach, stalks removed,
  washed and drained
1 tablespoon sunflower oil
500g (1lb) lean minced beef
1 tablespoon tomato purée
2 large cloves garlic, chopped finely
8–10 sage leaves, chopped finely
3–4 pinches cayenne pepper
40g (1½oz) butter
2 teaspoons ground mace
40g (1½oz) plain flour
900ml (1½ pints) milk
125g (4oz) grated Cheddar cheese
Salt and black pepper

Cook the pasta in plenty of boiling salted water until *al dente*. Drain and rinse under cold running water, then keep on one side. Meanwhile, cook the spinach in a little boiling water in a covered pan for 1–2 minutes, just until limp. Drain, press out the moisture thoroughly and leave on one side.

Heat the sunflower oil in a frying pan over a high heat. Add the minced beef and stir around until browned, then add the tomato purée, chopped garlic and sage leaves. Bubble the mixture, stirring, for another 3–4 minutes, then season rather more than to taste with the cayenne pepper and salt. Transfer to a large, shallow ovenproof dish, spread level and cover evenly with the cooked spinach leaves.

Melt the butter in a saucepan, stir in the mace and remove from the heat, then stir in the flour until smooth. Gradually add the milk. Return to the heat and bring to the boil, stirring all the time. Bubble, still stirring, for about 3 minutes, then remove from the heat and season to taste with salt and black pepper. Pour half the sauce over the spinach leaves. Spread the cooked noodles over the sauce and pour the remaining sauce over the top. Finally sprinkle with the grated Cheddar cheese. Bake in a preheated oven, 200°C, 400°F, Gas Mark 6 for 25–35 minutes until the surface is rich golden brown.

PASTA WITH CHICKEN AND TARRAGON CREAM SAUCE (83)

The classic combination of chicken, cream and fresh tarragon is always a success. For extra interest, use half egg pasta and half a coloured pasta, such as spinach or tomato.   *SERVES 6*

375g (12oz) noodles or pasta shapes
1 tablespoon olive oil
40g (1½oz) butter
1 red onion, halved and sliced very thinly
375g (12oz) skinless chicken breast fillets, sliced very thinly
125g (4oz) button mushrooms, halved if large
300ml (½ pint) double cream
Small handful fresh tarragon leaves, chopped roughly
2 teaspoons white wine vinegar
Salt and black pepper
Grated Parmesan cheese to serve

Cook the pasta in plenty of boiling salted water until *al dente*. Meanwhile, heat the olive oil and butter in a large, deep frying pan over a medium heat. Add the sliced onion and stir until softened, then add the chicken slices and cook for another 3 minutes. Add the mushrooms and toss around for a further minute.

Add the cream and the chopped tarragon and bring just up to boiling point, then remove from the heat. Gradually stir in the vinegar and season to taste with salt and black pepper.

When the pasta is ready drain it and rinse under cold running water. Reheat in the rinsed-out pan, then put it into a warm serving bowl. Pour the chicken sauce over the pasta, mix in lightly and serve immediately with a bowl of grated Parmesan cheese.

SPAGHETTI WITH WALNUTS, PARSLEY AND GORGONZOLA (80)

This is an example of how the most simple pasta dish, produced in minutes, can achieve a degree of excellence. The walnuts and Gorgonzola complement each other and plenty of chopped parsley adds a fresh element.   *SERVES 4*

5 tablespoons extra virgin olive oil
2 cloves garlic, chopped finely
50g (2oz) walnuts, ground coarsely
2 handfuls fresh parsley, chopped finely
2 tablespoons very hot water
125g (4oz) Gorgonzola cheese, crumbled roughly
250–300g (8–10oz) spaghetti
Salt and black pepper
Grated Parmesan cheese to serve

Gently heat 2 tablespoons of the olive oil in a pan. Add the garlic and stir around for 30 seconds over a low heat, then add the ground walnuts and chopped parsley and stir around for not more than 1 minute.

Add the remaining oil and the hot water followed by the Gorgonzola cheese. Stir around for a moment until the cheese starts to melt. Season the sauce with a little salt and plenty of black pepper, then remove from the heat, cover and leave on one side.

Cook the spaghetti in plenty of boiling salted water until *al dente*, then drain and rinse under cold running water. Return to the rinsed-out pan, reheat, then add the sauce and mix together thoroughly. Transfer to a warm serving bowl and serve with grated Parmesan cheese.

PASTA BOWS WITH SPICED MEATBALLS (80)

This pasta dish is practical for a main course at a dinner party as you can make the meatball sauce in advance and all you need to do is reheat the sauce when you cook the pasta. For greatest ease you need only serve a green salad with the pasta, but broad beans or french beans also go well with it.   *SERVES 3–4*

375g (12oz) lean minced pork or veal
2 teaspoons ground coriander
1 teaspoon dill seeds
8–10 sage leaves, chopped finely
4 pinches cayenne pepper
3 cloves garlic, crushed
2 tablespoons olive oil
25g (1oz) butter
397g (14oz) can chopped tomatoes
1 tablespoon tomato purée
Small handful fresh basil or lovage leaves, sliced into thin strips
375–425g (12–14oz) pasta bows
Salt and black pepper
Grated Parmesan cheese to serve

Pound the minced meat in a bowl to make it as soft as possible. Add the ground coriander, dill seeds, chopped sage leaves, cayenne pepper, about half the crushed garlic and a sprinkling of salt. Mix together thoroughly with a wooden spoon. Then, using wet hands, form the mixture into very small balls.

Heat the olive oil and butter in a large frying pan over a high heat. Add the meatballs and stir them about until browned all over. Reduce the heat to medium and add the remaining garlic, the chopped tomatoes and the tomato purée. Season with salt and freshly ground black pepper and let the sauce bubble gently for 4–5 minutes. Remove the frying pan from the heat.

Shortly before you are ready to eat, cook the pasta bows in plenty of boiling salted water until *al dente*, then drain and rinse under cold running water. Return to the rinsed-out pan, reheat gently, then tip into a warm serving dish.

Reheat the meatballs and sauce gently and add the sliced basil or lovage at the last moment. Spoon the sauce and meatballs on top of the pasta and serve at once with a bowl of grated Parmesan cheese.

CHICK PEA, MUSHROOM AND LEEK PIZZA (80)

The dough base for this vegetarian pizza is made with easy-blend yeast which is mixed directly into the flour, needs only one rising and so is useful if you haven't much time. Bake the pizza on your largest baking sheet or shallow ovenproof dish. A rectangular-shaped pizza made in a shallow ovenproof dish is easier to cut and share out than a round one. The chick pea and mint topping has a Middle Eastern flavour to it and has the advantage of tasting good when eaten cold, which is not the case with most pizzas.   *SERVES 4–5*

FOR THE DOUGH
375g (12oz) strong plain flour
3 teaspoons crushed sea salt
1 sachet easy-blend dried yeast
250ml (8fl oz) lukewarm water
About 2 tablespoons olive oil

FOR THE TOPPING
432g (14oz) can chick peas, drained
1 large handful fresh mint leaves, chopped finely
2 cloves garlic, chopped finely
2 tomatoes, chopped
125g (4oz) chestnut mushrooms, sliced thinly
1 teaspoon cumin seeds
2 tablespoons tomato purée
About 2 tablespoons olive oil
2 thin leeks, trimmed and sliced very thinly
50g (2oz) Feta cheese
Salt and black pepper

Grease a very large baking sheet or shallow ovenproof dish. Put the flour into a bowl and add the sea salt and yeast. Stir in the water and olive oil with a wooden spoon, then gather the dough together and knead on a floured work surface with the palms of your hands for 5–10 minutes until the dough is smooth and elastic. Using a heavy rolling pin roll out the dough firmly and thinly into a piece the same size as the baking sheet or dish. Lay in the dough and put the baking sheet or dish inside a puffed-up large polythene bag or bin liner in a warmish place for 45–60 minutes until the dough has risen moderately.

Meanwhile, prepare the topping. Using a fork roughly crush the drained chick peas in a bowl, then add the chopped mint leaves, chopped garlic, chopped tomatoes, sliced mushrooms, cumin seeds, tomato purée and olive oil. Season with salt and black pepper. Mix together with a large spoon.

When the dough is ready brush it all over with olive oil. Spread the chick pea mixture evenly over the dough, leaving a 1.5cm (¾in) border around the edges, then sprinkle the sliced leeks over the chick pea mixture and crumble the Feta cheese on top. Cook at the top of a preheated oven, 230°C, 450°F, Gas Mark 8 for about 15 minutes until the edges of the dough are browned.

SALMON AND CRAB CANNELLONI (80)

For this luxurious dish of fish and crab wrapped in spinach pasta and enveloped in a creamy béchamel sauce the cannelloni are formed in an easy way using softened lasagne sheets. It is a perfect dinner party dish as it can be prepared in advance and needs only a crisp vegetable such as french beans or mange tout peas as an accompaniment. If you are serving it as a first course and your family or guests don't have gigantic appetites (unlike my family) this quantity will serve 6.   *SERVES 4*

8 sheets lasagne verdi (the 'no precooking' type)
250g (8oz) mixed brown and white crab meat (fresh or canned)
750g (1½lb) tail piece of salmon, filleted, skinned and cut into 1cm (½in) chunks
3–4 teaspoons capers
3–4 pinches cayenne pepper
1 egg, separated
40g (1½oz) butter
2 large cloves garlic, chopped finely
40g (1½oz) plain flour
450ml (¾ pint) milk
300ml (½ pint) double cream
Salt and black pepper
Grated Parmesan cheese

Butter a fairly large, shallow ovenproof dish. Fill a sink with hot water and sprinkle in a few drops of oil. Lay the lasagne sheets in the water and soak for 8–12 minutes until the pasta is soft enough to bend but not so soft that it will tear easily. Remove the pasta sheets, drain well on a flat surface and lay separately on one side while you prepare the filling.

Put the crab meat in a bowl with the salmon chunks and capers, season with the cayenne pepper and a little salt, then add the egg white and stir in thoroughly using a wooden spoon.

Pile the fish mixture evenly in lengthwise strips down the centre of each lasagne sheet, then roll the pasta round the filling to make a tubular cannelloni shape. Arrange the tubes carefully, close together in a single layer in the buttered dish, join side down.

To make the sauce melt the butter gently in a fairly large saucepan, add the garlic and cook for 1–2 minutes, stirring it around, then remove from the heat. When the bubbles subside stir in the flour with a wooden spoon. Gradually add the milk, only a little at a time at first, stirring very thoroughly until smooth. Stir in the cream. Return the pan to a higher heat and bring to the boil, stirring vigorously all the time. Bubble gently, still stirring, for 3–4 minutes. Remove from the heat, season the sauce generously with salt and freshly ground black pepper and stir in the egg yolk.

Spoon this thick sauce all over the cannelloni and sprinkle generously with grated Parmesan cheese. Bake just above the centre of a preheated oven, 180°C, 350°F, Gas Mark 4 for 40 minutes until golden brown.

TAGLIATELLE VERDI WITH SQUID AND GREEN CREAM SAUCE (80)

Squid is a perfect ingredient for pasta sauces as it cooks so quickly – in fact, it must never be cooked for more than a few minutes or it will become rubbery. However, if cooked very briefly, it is tender and delicious. People are sometimes alarmed at the idea of preparing squid but once you have learned how it is not difficult and I even find it quite fun. *SERVES 6*

500–625g (1–1¼lb) smallish squid
425g (14oz) tagliatelle verdi
125g (4oz) fresh spinach, stalks removed,
*   washed and drained*
175ml (6fl oz) double cream
3 tablespoons olive oil
125ml (4fl oz) dry white wine
2 cloves garlic, sliced very thinly
Good handful fresh dill, chopped roughly
Salt and black pepper

Clean and prepare the squid as shown on page 126, reserving the tentacles and slicing the bodies across into very thin rings. Set aside.

Cook the tagliatelle verdi in plenty of boiling, salted water until *al dente*.

Meanwhile, prepare the sauce. Put the spinach leaves into a food processor and whizz until chopped as finely as possible, then add the double cream and whizz again.

Heat the olive oil in a large, deep frying pan over a medium heat, then add the wine, sliced squid and tentacles and the sliced garlic and stir around for 30 seconds only. Pour the spinach cream into the pan, bring to the boil and bubble for 1 minute, then season to taste with salt and plenty of freshly ground black pepper and remove from the heat. Cover the pan with a lid or foil to keep the sauce warm.

When the tagliatelle is ready drain it and rinse well under cold running water, then return it to the rinsed-out pan with a spoonful of olive oil to stop it sticking together and reheat. Stir in the squid and cream sauce and the roughly chopped dill. Turn the mixture into a warm serving bowl and serve immediately.

CHINESE EGG NOODLES WITH AROMATIC VEGETABLES (86)

Serve this fresh-tasting stir-fry dish as an unusual vegetarian main course. You can cook the noodles and prepare all the vegetables beforehand so that it takes only minutes to prepare before your meal.   *SERVES 4*

250g (8oz) Chinese egg noodles
2 tablespoons groundnut oil, plus extra for
*   coating the noodles*
2 large cloves garlic, chopped finely
2.5cm (1in) piece fresh root ginger, peeled
*   and chopped finely*
2 teaspoons Chinese five-spice powder
500g (1lb) small tomatoes, coarsely
*   chopped*
3–4 pinches cayenne pepper
375–500g (12oz–1lb) courgettes, cut into
*   fairly thin 2.5cm (1in) strips*
175g (6oz) fresh bean sprouts
2 teaspoons soft light brown sugar
2 tablespoons soy sauce
Handful fresh coriander leaves, chopped
*   very roughly*

Cook the Chinese egg noodles in plenty of boiling, salted water, for about 3 minutes until tender, then drain, rinse well in cold water, and tip into a bowl. Stir in a little groundnut oil to stop the noodles sticking together and leave on one side.

Put the groundnut oil in a wok or large, deep frying pan over a medium heat and add the chopped garlic and ginger and the Chinese five-spice powder. Stir around for 1 minute, then add the chopped tomatoes, cayenne pepper and courgettes. Stir over the heat for about 5 minutes until the strips of courgette are bright green and just cooked but still slightly crunchy.

Add the cooked egg noodles, the bean sprouts, soft light brown sugar and soy sauce. Stir around for 1 minute, just to heat through the noodles and bean sprouts. Finally stir in the chopped coriander leaves. Transfer to a warm serving dish and serve at once.

PASTA WITH PARSNIPS AND KABANOS SAUSAGES (80)

Parsnips are far more versatile than you would imagine, as this easy recipe shows. With the smoky sweet additions of grilled peppers and kabanos (thin Polish sausages with a spicy smoked flavour) and the light oniony taste of the leeks this is a wonderful combination.   *SERVES 4*

2 large yellow peppers, halved lengthwise
*   and deseeded (page 49)*
250–300g (8–10oz) pasta shapes,
*   noodles or spaghetti*
4 tablespoons olive oil
250g (8oz) kabanos sausages, sliced very
*   thinly*
375g (12oz) thin leeks, sliced into thin
*   rings*
375g (12oz) parsnips, sliced very finely
Salt and black pepper
Parmesan cheese to serve

Put the pepper halves under a hot grill, skin side upwards, until blackened in patches all over. Wrap in a tea towel until cool enough to handle. Peel off the skin using your fingers, then cut the peppers lengthwise into thin strips. Cook the pasta in plenty of boiling, salted water until *al dente*.

Meanwhile, heat 2 tablespoons of the olive oil in a large, deep frying pan over a fairly high heat. Add the sliced kabanos and toss around for 1–2 minutes. Add the remaining olive oil and the sliced leeks and stir around for 1–2 minutes until they begin to soften, then add the sliced parsnips and stir for another minute. Lastly stir in the sliced, grilled peppers and season to taste with salt and plenty of black pepper.

Drain and rinse the pasta well under cold running water. Return it to the rinsed-out pan and reheat gently. Place the pasta in a warm serving bowl. Pour the sauce on top and serve with grated Parmesan cheese.

PÂTÉS and TERRINES

In French the word *pâté* means pastry; and originally all pâtés were pork mixtures wrapped in pastry, whereas terrines were the same kind of mixture without the pastry, cooked in an earthenware dish called a terrine. Nowadays, the distinctions are somewhat blurred, but I think of a pâté as a smoothly puréed mixture, not always cooked in a dish, and a terrine as a more homely affair with layers of coarsely chopped meats and pork fat, often wrapped entirely in strips of streaky bacon, which both adds flavour and stops the meat drying out during the cooking. Cooking the sealed terrine in a bain-marie (page 216) also helps keep in the moisture, and a certain amount of fat is necessary for both succulence and flavour. When onions or other vegetables are added to a terrine, they must be gently fried in butter first to soften them.

Long ago, terrines were a way of preserving pork, and although pork fat and liver are still the most usual ingredients, all sorts of other things are now added to make the terrine more interesting, and more decorative, too. A variety of birds, including chicken, turkey, duck, pheasant and pigeon, lend their different colours and flavours. Venison and hare add their assertive character to game terrines, but pig's and ox liver should be presoaked in milk to lessen their strong taste.

For a first course, smooth pâtés are more suitable than chunky terrines, which I really prefer for a light lunch or supper, accompanied by good crusty bread and a salad. Terrines are best pressed with weights after cooking to make them easier to slice, and can be arranged beautifully on a large plate for a buffet party.

Rather different to meat and poultry concoctions are fish and vegetable pâtés and terrines. These are ideal as a first course, or as part of a cold lunch, and they can also be far less rich than meat and liver pâtés since you can add ingredients, such as low-fat fromage frais and yogurt. Some softer, smooth fish and vegetable pâtés seem more like dips than pâtés.

Smoked fish pâtés, such as mackerel, trout, kipper, bloater and salmon, are very easy to make, and always popular; they can also be used as a stuffing for hard-boiled eggs and tomatoes, or other vegetables. Fresh fish can be made into terrines and cooked in a bain-marie rather like meat terrines, but the fish is usually puréed and mixed with egg white, and often cream, (when it is called a mousseline) so the finished result is much lighter and more suitable for a first course.

Vegetable terrines have also become extremely fashionable; they can be very pretty indeed, but they can also be laborious to assemble as the vegetables have to be carefully prepared. I would rather have a jumbled mixture of vegetables that tasted really appetizing than a perfect work of art. Seasoning really is crucial, as vegetable pâtés and terrines which are not seasoned well can be far from a pleasure to eat.

Pâtés, terrines, and the lighter puréed mousselines and mousses produce a wide range of different effects, depending on the ingredients used, and how they are cooked. It is quite possible to deviate from the basic methods to produce different, exciting tastes and textures, which is what can make this an especially interesting and personal area of cookery.

Pâtés and terrines in a variety of textures and flavours, clockwise from top: Glazed Terrine in a Case of Herb Pastry (page 105) encases veal, pork, turkey and chicken livers in a crisp rosemary-flavoured pastry; Hot Fish Terrine with Mace and Pink Peppercorns (page 105) is made with smoked haddock, plaice and salmon and here served with a light saffron-flavoured cheese sauce and fresh tarragon; Parsnip and Garlic Mousse with Green Coriander Sauce (page 104) is a hot, baked mousse flavoured with honey and mace, served with a simple sauce made from yogurt and fresh coriander; a medley of lightly blanched fresh vegetables set in a wine-flavoured aspic in Glossy Vegetable Terrine (page 104), with a lettuce garnish; Duck, Chicken and Pork Terrine with Prunes and Pistachios (page 104), flavoured with orange liqueur, orange juice and ground mace and coriander, is served here with sliced lettuce and cucumber.

SMOOTH PÂTÉS

Smooth pâtés can be made from livers, chicken, game, marinated meats, fish or vegetables. They can either be cooked in an earthenware container in a bain-marie (page 216) or by lightly cooking the ingredients in a frying pan, then puréeing and spooning into a dish to seal with clarified butter. Instead of clarifying your own butter (below) you can also use concentrated butter for cooking which has been refined and had much of the liquid removed. Simply melt some and bubble it for a minute before pouring it through a fine sieve on top of the pâté.

In cooked mixtures, herbs, cream or cream cheese, which will enrich and lighten the pâté, can be added to the puréed mixture before it goes in the oven, and as always with all pâtés, careful seasoning is vital.

But I prefer making the pan-prepared smooth pâtés, as they are so quick; flavour contributors such as mushrooms and bacon can be softened in the pan before adding the main quick-cooking ingredients, such as chopped chicken livers and slivers of chicken breast, tossing them around to cook lightly in the butter. To lighten the consistency after puréeing, add cream, or for a less rich effect, natural yogurt, fromage frais or other milk products. With this method it is easier to get the seasoning right as you can taste the mixture in the final stage and adjust it if needed.

QUICK CHICKEN LIVER PÂTÉ

A smooth, rich chicken liver pâté is one of the quickest pâtés to make, but tastes even better if you take time to soak the livers in milk for at least an hour beforehand to give them a milder flavour. Other ingredients can be added which will also enhance the pâté. I like to add mushrooms, onions, bacon, or even slightly sweet ingredients like finely chopped parsnips – but they must be softened properly in the pan before adding the livers, which must be cooked only briefly.

A delicate mildness should be one of the characteristics of chicken liver pâté, so garlic should only be added if it has been cooked long and gently beforehand, to remove strength and induce sweetness, either by frying or by boiling the cloves in their skins. Blending the livers after cooking with unsalted butter and/or cream will make the mixture taste even milder. For flavouring, 1–2 tablespoons brandy, sherry or Marsala can be used according to taste.

To serve 4 use 250g (8oz) chicken livers, soaked in milk. Serve the pâté with some delicious crusty bread.

1 *Melt 50g (2oz) unsalted butter in a pan over a gentle heat, then add 1 teaspoon ground coriander and 1 finely chopped small onion. Stir until softened, then add the drained and roughly chopped chicken livers and 1–2 tablespoons brandy.*

2 *Stir for about 5 minutes until the livers are lightly cooked. Turn the mixture into a food processor and add another 25g (1oz) soft unsalted butter and 2 tablespoons double cream. Whizz to a smooth purée. Season to taste with sea salt and black pepper.*

3 *Spoon the chicken liver pâté in to an earthenware dish, about 900ml (1½ pints) capacity, or 6 small ramekin dishes and spread level. Melt 25–50g (1–2oz) clarified butter (right) and pour carefully over the top of the pâté to seal it. Chill the pâté for up to 3 days before serving to give the flavours time to mature.*

CLARIFYING BUTTER

Butter that has been clarified of its milk solids not only raises the temperature at which it can be cooked without burning, it also helps the butter last longer (up to 1 month) and so is useful for sealing. It is worth clarifying reasonable amounts of butter at a time, remelting as required. First melt the butter slowly in a heavy-based saucepan. Pour the melted butter carefully through a sieve lined with muslin into a bowl, leaving as much of the milk sediment behind as possible. Allow to settle then pour gently again into another bowl or jug or pour on top of pâtés as required.

A homemade chicken liver pâté is always popular; it is one of the quickest and easiest pâtés to make, and inexpensive too.

AUBERGINE PÂTÉ

I learned to make this delectable purée years ago in a little Turkish restaurant above the covered market in Istanbul. The aubergine skin is burnt black to impart a subtle smoky taste to the soft flesh within. This aubergine pâté is far softer than most pâtés, and makes a good first course piled on to thin toast. As the flavour is so delicate, it is better to use sunflower rather than olive oil which can be overpowering. This quantity serves 4.

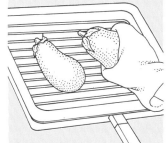

1 *Put 2 medium-sized, unpeeled aubergines under the hottest possible grill for 15–25 minutes, turning them once or twice until the skin is charred. Plunge the hot aubergines into cold water.*

Aubergine pâté (left) and smoked salmon trout pâté are both easy to prepare and ideal for informal meals.

2 *Peel off the skins with your fingers and discard. Put the flesh into a fine nylon sieve and press with a wooden spoon to push out as much liquid as possible. Put the drained flesh into a food processor and add 1 tablespoon lemon juice.*

3 *Whizz together, adding 3–5 tablespoons sunflower oil, a little at a time until smooth. The more oil you add, the lighter the texture. Season with salt and black pepper. Spoon into a dish and chill until ready to serve. Sprinkle with chopped herbs.*

MAKING THE MOST OF SMOOTH PÂTÉS

• Adding some finely chopped and sautéed red onions, fennel or wild mushrooms, or a smattering of finely chopped ready-to-eat dried apricots, prunes or pistachio nuts to chicken liver pâtés makes them more interesting and adds extra flavour too.

• When topping pâtés with melted clarified butter, it looks pretty if you lay a few whole leaves, such as flat-leaved parsley or bay leaves on top so they set in the butter.

• Ground spices such as coriander, mace, allspice and cinnamon go particularly well with meat mixtures.

• Finely grated lemon or orange rind is another good flavouring for most pâtés.

• Make chicken liver pâté even milder and lighter by sautéing a few slivers of boneless chicken breast with, or in place of, some of the livers.

• I think smoked fish pâtés and puréed vegetable or dried pulse pâtés look more impressive if you stuff them into containers such as halved red peppers or hollowed-out tomatoes, or into avocado shells, incorporating the avocado flesh mixed with lemon juice into the pâté.

• A quick smoked salmon pâté can be made by finely chopping scraps of smoked salmon and mixing them into softened cream cheese or 8 per cent fat fromage frais with plenty of finely chopped fresh dill, 1–2 teaspoons of wholegrain mustard and a dash of lemon juice.

SMOKED FISH PÂTÉ

If you use a food processor or blender, smooth pâtés made from smoked fish are very easy to make.

To make the pâté more impressive for a dinner party, serve it in hollowed-out lemon or orange shells instead of a terrine dish. It also looks pretty simply spooned on to cups of crisp lettuce leaves with a scattering of fresh herbs on top. You can use any skinned and filleted smoked fish, including mackerel, kipper, bloater, trout, salmon and salmon trout. Instead of fromage frais you can use curd or cream cheese. Serves 6.

1 *Put 375g (12oz) roughly flaked smoked fish into a food processor with 75g (3oz) soft unsalted butter, 125g (4oz) fromage frais, 4 tablespoons double cream, 1 teaspoon caster sugar and 1 small clove crushed garlic (optional). Whizz to a smooth purée.*

2 *Gradually whizz in 1 tablespoon lemon juice and then season to taste with salt and cayenne pepper. Stir in 1 tablespoon chopped fresh dill or fennel, reserving a few unchopped sprigs for garnishing.*

3 *Spoon the pâté into a small terrine dish or else use hollowed-out lemon or orange shells. Cover the pâté loosely with foil and chill until ready to serve. Before serving, garnish the top with fresh sprigs of dill or fennel.*

COARSE-TEXTURED TERRINES

I love making this kind of terrine because, without the need for any skill, you can make it look so beautiful. You really can't go wrong – simply by arranging different-coloured meats and livers, and sometimes other ingredients, such as nuts, dried fruits or olives, within the mixture, an intriguing mosaic of varying shapes and shades will be revealed when the terrine is sliced.

The meat for a terrine is usually cut up by hand into small pieces or long strips (though you can process some of it in a machine to vary the textures) and is best marinated for two or three days in a wine, oil and seasoning mixture to make it more tender, succulent and full of flavour. After cooking, weigh down the terrine while cooling, so the meats become pressed together and easier to slice.

The compactness of terrines makes them a supremely portable food, ideal for picnics or to take friends as a present when you go to stay. Terrines are also perfect for occasions like Christmas when you have a houseful of people who may become hungry at any time. They can be made well ahead as their taste is at its best two or three days after cooking. You can keep the terrine in the refrigerator, but it should be eaten at room temperature.

MAKING COARSE TERRINES

Any shape of container or dish can be used to make this terrine – in fact, it looks very attractive made in a pie dish and turned out. Lining the dish with strips of bacon is not essential but it helps to add moistness to the strips of lean meat within it.

Alternatively, instead of turning out the terrine make it in a special terrine dish (page 25) and garnish the top attractively with bay leaves, juniper berries and maybe at Christmas time with a few cranberries. For an appetizing gloss, brush the top with some cooled chicken aspic (page 33). Serves 8–10.

1 Mix together in a large bowl 500g (1lb) minced or chopped braising pork, 250g (8oz) chopped pig's liver, 1 chopped onion, 2 crushed cloves of garlic, 3 tablespoons brandy or sherry, ½ teaspoon ground allspice, 1 teaspoon dried sage, salt and black pepper. Marinate for 4–8 hours or overnight.

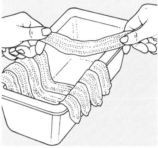

2 Cut 2 duck, pheasant or chicken breasts into strips and season. Mix in a bowl and cover. Stretch 250g (8oz) derinded streaky bacon rashers with the back of a knife (page 149) and line in strips across a greased 1.5 litre (2½ pint) loaf tin or terrine dish, leaving a little on each side as an overlap.

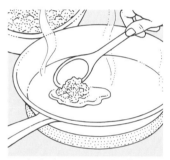

3 Check the seasoning by frying a small amount of the marinated meats first, tasting, then adding more salt, pepper or spice if necessary. Spoon into the bacon-lined tin, alternating layers of marinated meats and the strips of poultry or game. Fold back the overlapping strips of bacon. Cover with greased foil.

A coarse terrine (left) and pâté en croûte can be made with your favourite flavourings and ingredients.

4 Place in a bain-marie (page 216) and cook at 180°C, 350°F, Gas Mark 4 for 1½ hours. Remove from the bain-marie and cool, then chill, placing a board and some weights on top; leave to 'mature' in the refrigerator for about 2 days. To serve remove the foil and unmould by dipping the tin briefly in hot water. Cut in thin slices.

PÂTÉ EN CROÛTE

Wrapping a delicious and colourful mixture of meats (especially game, such as venison, pheasant, rabbit or hare), herbs, nuts and dried fruits in a free-standing rich shortcrust pastry case makes for a very special pâté, ideal for parties. Make sure, though, there are no cracks in the pastry for any juices to escape, and although the pastry case may sag a bit on the base this adds to the lovely homemade feel of the pâté. When cool, pour well-flavoured aspic (page 33) mixed with extra gelatine through one or two small holes in the pastry to fill in any little gaps and hold the pâté and pastry together better.

For this recipe, to serve about 8, you will need shortcrust pastry made with 375g (12oz) plain flour, ½ teaspoon salt, 175g (6oz) butter and 3–4 tablespoons water (page 246).

First of all prepare the ingredients for marinating: mix together 500g (1lb) minced game meat or pork or veal, 250g (8oz) diced uncooked ham or gammon, 250g (8oz) pork fat cut into thin strips, 1 chopped onion, 2 cloves crushed garlic, salt and freshly ground black pepper and 1–2 tablespoons chopped fresh herbs, and a splash or two of brandy or sherry.

1 *Place the well-mixed meats and other flavouring ingredients in a large glass bowl and marinate overnight, stirring when possible. Check the seasoning by frying a small amount of the marinated mixture first, tasting, then adding more salt, or freshly ground black pepper if necessary.*

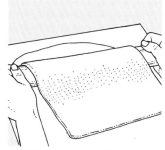

2 *Add flavourings such as green peppercorns, pistachio nuts, stoned olives or chopped ready-to-eat dried apricots to the marinated ingredients. Make the pastry and roll out slightly less than half to a large oblong about 5mm (¼in) thick and place on a greased flat baking sheet.*

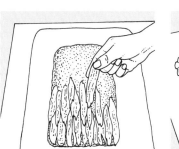

3 *Cut into strips an additional 175g (6oz) lean game or meat such as breast of pheasant or pigeon, fillets from a hare saddle or pork tenderloin. Spoon the marinated ingredients into a long tall mound in the centre of the rolled-out pastry, layering as you go with the strips of additional lean meat.*

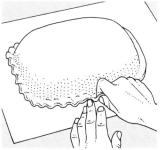

4 *Roll out the remaining pastry to an oblong large enough to cover the pâté easily. Lay it on top, glaze the edges with beaten egg, trim and press the edges to seal. Make 2 steam holes in the top. Reroll any trimmings for decorations such as leaves or cut out letters spelling PÂTÉ or even EAT ME! (page 245).*

5 *Glaze the top with beaten egg yolk, attach the decorations and glaze again. Chill for 20 minutes. Cook the pâté at 200°C, 400°F, Gas Mark 6 for 15 minutes, then reduce the temperature to 180°C, 350°F, Gas Mark 4 and cook for another hour. Remove from the oven and cool the pâté on the baking sheet.*

6 *Make up 300ml (½ pint) of aspic by dissolving 2 teaspoons powdered gelatine in 300ml (½ pint) hot pork or chicken stock (page 28). Allow to cool before pouring carefully through the holes in the top of the pâté. Chill for at least 1 day before serving. Transfer to a serving dish and cut into slices with a serrated knife.*

ADDING COLOURS AND FLAVOURS TO COARSE-TEXTURED TERRINES

• Coarse-textured meat terrines are a joy for the imaginative or artistically inclined cook. You can use different coloured meats such as a combination of duck, turkey and pigeon breast fillets, pork, uncooked ham and pork fat, either arranged in simple layers or in more complicated patterns. Long strips of meat can be wrapped in blanched spinach leaves which will give a pretty effect of green circles when the terrine is sliced.

• You can also stud the meat with pistachio nuts, walnuts or almonds, and with ready-to-eat dried apricots, peaches, prunes, black or stuffed olives, water chestnuts, cranberries, strips of coloured peppers or pieces of blanched orange or lemon rind.

• Try pieces of lychee in a pork and chicken terrine, marinating the meat first in sherry with plenty of fresh ginger slivers.

• Green or pink peppercorns add aroma to terrines, and juniper berries are good with hare.

• I like to use Tendersweet bacon to wrap around terrine mixtures because of its unsalty taste.

• Marinades can be made up with some kind of alcohol – red or white wine, sherry, vermouth, brandy or port – or with fresh fruit juices. Mix the alcohol or juice with olive oil and seasonings which can include herbs, onions, garlic, ginger and spices such as ground cloves, allspice, mace, coriander and cinnamon.

• If you like, you can marinate the meats in different mixtures; for example, the dark meats such as hare in a wine mixture and the paler ones, such as turkey or chicken, in a yogurt marinade.

• Chopped chicken livers mixed among coarsely chopped meats in a terrine will add softness to the overall texture.

• A certain amount of minced or finely chopped pork fat should be included in all meat and game terrines to stop them becoming too dry and solid and to improve the consistency.

• To serve a thin slice of prettily patterned terrine on individual plates as a first course, I think it is nicest to lay it on some smoothly puréed sauce; try fresh tomatoes stewed and puréed with orange juice, or a savoury fruit like red or golden stewed plums mixed with sherry vinegar.

SAVOURY MOUSSES

Cold and hot savoury mousses and mousselines are variations on a theme whose main characteristic is a delicate lightness. As long as the flavour is right, they can be a wonderful, sensual pleasure to eat. They are each made with a base of smooth purée which can be made from cooked or raw meats or poultry, fish or vegetables. In hot mousses, these purées are often enriched by egg yolks and lightened with whisked egg white or sometimes cream, too. Hot mousses are usually cooked, but they can also be steamed, or, in the case of quenelles, poached. Cold mousses are purées mixed with mayonnaise (page 202), or with a béchamel sauce (page 196), lightened with whipped cream and set with either a small amount of gelatine dissolved in stock or ready-made aspic – they should never be rubbery.

Whisked egg whites are sometimes added to lighten the mixture further. As in fish and vegetable terrines (page 102), the smoothly puréed mixtures of both hot and cold mousses can be dotted with pieces of vegetables, nuts, seafood, fish or simply with chopped fresh herbs.

A mousseline mixture is a purée of raw fish (either smoked or unsmoked), poultry or pale meat into which unwhisked egg whites and cream are gradually beaten. All the ingredients must be chilled to make a stiff mixture. It is often used as the basis of terrines, either layered or covered with whole ingredients, or the mousseline can be spooned into ramekins and cooked like a terrine in a bain-marie (page 216) in the oven before serving hot with a sauce. Use a mousseline mixture also for making quenelles.

COLD SAVOURY MOUSSE

Cucumber mousse is perhaps one of the most popular cold buffet dishes. To make other mousses, use this technique and substitute about 300ml (½ pint) of mashed fish, grated carrot or chopped tomatoes for the cucumber. Always season cold mousses well as chilling weakens flavours. The decorated shimmering aspic top is purely optional, but is a good way of showing off.

The mousse can be set in a 1.2 litre (2 pint) pretty glass dish or divided between 8 individual ramekin dishes or moulds. Serve with a pretty salad garnish for a spectacular effect. Serves 8.

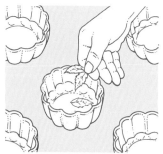

1 *Make up 300ml (½ pint) aspic (page 33) and use half to line eight 150ml (¼ pint) individual moulds, or a 1.2 litre (2 pint) mould. Chill until set, then place a few mint leaves on top of the aspic. Pour over the rest of the aspic and chill again until set. Alternatively, use feathery dill, chervil or parsley instead of mint.*

2 *Meanwhile, peel, halve and deseed 2 cucumbers. Coarsely grate into a bowl, then mix in 2 tablespoons each chopped spring onion tops and chopped fresh mint. Mix in 150g (5oz) of softened low-fat soft cream cheese or 150g (5oz) fromage frais, 2 tablespoons lemon juice and season well.*

3 *Dissolve 1 sachet of powdered gelatine in 3 tablespoons hot water, then mix in. Add to the cheese and cucumber mixture. Whip 200ml (7fl oz) whipping cream and fold in, then pour the mixture into the moulds. Chill until set. Loosen the sides, dip the moulds briefly in hot water and turn out.*

A cucumber savoury mousse served with carrot matchsticks tossed with shredded fresh mint, sesame seeds and a light vinaigrette.

FLAVOURING SAVOURY MOUSSES

• Add tomato purée or sun-dried tomato paste, or olive, garlic, anchovy or curry pastes or roughly crushed green or pink peppercorns to the basic mousse mixture to strengthen or enhance taste.
• Instead of a classic, creamy velouté sauce, such as sauce Nantua (page 197) to serve with quenelles, use a smooth cheese or curry-flavoured béchamel sauce (page 196).
• If you grow sorrel in your garden, a sauce made by wilting sorrel leaves in a little unsalted butter in a pan and then puréeing and heating again with a little cream, is delicious to serve with savoury mousses. Improve the sauce's colour by including a leaf or two of spinach with the sorrel.
• Quick cold sauces can be made using creamed smetana or Greek yogurt with thin vegetable purées (page 53) stirred into them.
• Make a garlic and saffron sauce by boiling 300 ml (½ pint) double cream with 2 halved garlic cloves and a pinch of saffron. Cool and remove the garlic before serving.

MAKING MOUSSELINE

Food processors have made it possible to produce lovely, light fish mousselines, as well as smooth terrines without long arduous pounding and beating by hand with a wooden spoon. But if you want your purée to be extra smooth, you can press it through a sieve or pass it through a food mill.

Most firm fish, such as sole, haddock and salmon, is suitable, although oily fish like herrings and mackerel are too rich and some shellfish, such as scallops, too watery. The other ingredients are simply double cream, egg white and lots of seasoning, ideally with sea salt and white pepper and maybe a good pinch of paprika. As it is difficult to season the mousseline after cooking, check by cooking a small spoonful of the mixture first, by poaching in a little stock or water.

The secret of a light mousseline is to keep the mixture well chilled while you beat in the cream. This helps the mixture maintain a firm texture and yet cook to a delicate lightness. Be sure to have crushed ice ready to use in step 2. Mousselines can be cooked simply in buttered moulds or ramekins, with a delicious surprise base of chopped, lightly cooked asparagus, tomatoes, peppers or mushrooms, if you like. Serves 6.

1 *Trim 500g (1lb) skinless, fish fillet of membranes and stray bones. Cut into cubes, then whizz in a food processor until smooth. Add 2 egg whites and season more generously than you would think. Process until well mixed and spoon into a bowl.*

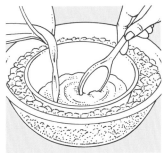

2 *Place the bowl in a larger one containing crushed ice cubes, then gradually beat in 200–300ml (7–10fl oz) chilled double cream, depending on the fish; firmer fish need more cream. The mixture should be thick and smooth and hold its shape.*

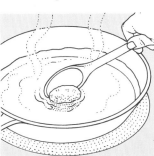

3 *Check the seasoning by poaching a spoonful in simmering water for 3 minutes and tasting. Spoon the mixture into a 900ml (1½ pint) ovenproof dish or into 6 individual 150ml (¼ pint) ramekins, on top of a base of lightly cooked vegetables if liked, and cover with greased foil.*

4 *Cook in a bain-marie (page 216) at 180°C, 350°F, Gas Mark 4 for 25–30 minutes until just firm in the centre. Run a knife round the outside and unmould on to small serving plates. Serve warm with hollandaise or other hot buttery sauce (page 200).*

QUENELLES

A delicate light mousseline mixture can be shaped into small 'dumplings' called quenelles and then poached for a few minutes until firm. Make up the mousseline mixture as left, then shape the individual quenelles using 2 dessertspoons.

As quenelles only take a few minutes to cook and are nicest served freshly cooked, the mixture can be kept chilled in the refrigerator until nearly ready to serve. Prepare a wide, shallow pan of simmering fish stock (page 31) before you start shaping the quenelles. Cook the quenelles in batches of about 6 at a time. Serve with a hot, buttery sauce (page 200). Makes about 18 quenelles.

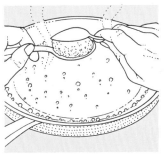 

1 *Using 2 dessertspoons, scoop up a spoonful of mousseline with 1 spoon and smooth over the top with the other spoon. Work over the pan of simmering stock while you continue shaping the quenelle. Scrape the other spoon down, scooping off the mixture towards you in one quick movement.*

2 *Then repeat the same movement with the first spoon. Repeat this twice more and finally drop the shaped quenelle straight in to the stock. Poach for about 5 minutes until firm, shaking the pan gently to roll the quenelles. Lift out with a slotted spoon and keep warm.*

Attractive fish quenelles (left), here served with a creamy sauce Nantua (page 197), can be made from any fresh white fish. The hot salmon mousselines are served with a creamy, rich hollandaise sauce (page 200) and fresh dill.

FISH *and* VEGETABLE TERRINES

Fish and vegetable terrines are lovely for first courses and summer lunches. Unlike meat, game and poultry terrines which improve with a day or two of maturing, these should be eaten very fresh. If the ingredients are not perfect and the seasoning not well thought out and adjusted, vegetable terrines can taste very dull.

Spinach is often used to line the mould for a vegetable terrine and make a pretty green edge to each slice – in this case, I oil the dish instead of buttering it, so that the leaves look glossy when the terrine is turned out.

A light and delicate fish terrine is one of my favourite preludes to a rich, meaty meal. I like hot fish terrines best of all, and these can also be served as the main course of a light meal. Fish terrines are made in the same kind of way as meat terrines, using uncooked ingredients, but the time taken to cook the fish, with the dish usually set in a bain-marie, is far less, so as not to overcook and lose the succulence of the fish. Most fish terrines, as below, are assembled in the dish using a mixture of fish mousseline (page 101) and pieces of fish or seafood added either in neat layers or at random which I think looks just as good.

Something not made in this way are potted shrimps, which can be served like a terrine when they are turned out of the pot. They are one of my great favourites. Despite the laborious peeling, it tastes far better if you use real shrimps instead of prawns; with a combination of clarified unsalted butter (page 96) and a little mace and cayenne pepper for seasoning. It is an irresistible dish.

FISH TERRINE

An attractive mousseline terrine to be served warm or lightly chilled can be made with one or two coloured mousseline mixtures. Terrines also look very pretty layered with strips of lightly cooked vegetables or long strips of a contrasting firm fish. The variations of colour and flavour are endless.

For a special mousse or terrine, line a buttered mould with thin fillets of sole, skinned side facing inwards, and make a smoked fish mousseline speckled with chopped herbs or even pistachios or coloured with a spice such as turmeric or paprika. Alternatively, line the mould with blanched spinach leaves and stir into the mousseline some finely chopped herbs or 1–2 tablespoons sherry. Serve warm fish terrines with a hot fresh tomato sauce (page 206).

For cold terrines, line the container with blanched spinach leaves, cool and then chill until ready to serve.

Chopped pistachio nuts and chopped coriander are mixed with a turmeric-flavoured smoked fish mousseline and white fish fillets.

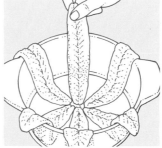

1 *Lightly oil a 1.5 litre (2½ pint) round ovenproof dish and line the base with a greased disc of greaseproof paper. Arrange about 6 long thin fillets of sole or plaice in a pattern, extending from the centre to the top edges. Let the fillets overlap a little to allow for shrinkage.*

2 *Make a double quantity of mousseline mixture (page 101) from smoked fish, such as haddock. Stir in 2 teaspoons turmeric to give the mousseline a yellow colour, then add some roughly chopped pistachio nuts and finely chopped fresh coriander leaves to taste.*

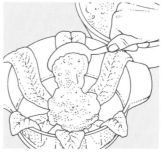

3 *Spoon the golden mousseline into the fish-lined dish, making sure it fills the gaps between the sole 'spokes'. Tap gently on the work surface to make sure the mousseline works its way down to the bottom. Use a wet spatula to smooth the top. Fold over the overhanging fillets.*

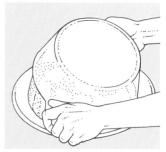

4 *Cover with greased foil, then place in a bain-marie (page 216) and cook at 180°C, 350°F, Gas Mark 4 for about 50 minutes until the centre of the terrine feels firm when tested with a skewer. Allow to stand for a few minutes before inverting on to a warm serving plate. Serve cut in wedges.*

VEGETABLE TERRINE

A pretty layered vegetable terrine can be served lightly chilled and cut into elegant slices. The 'binding base' is a delicate cheesy savoury custard holding colourful cooked vegetables together. Choose vegetables of contrasting colours such as carrots, leeks, red pepper, green beans, asparagus spears and button mushrooms, and arrange them either randomly or symmetrically in layers. For best effect, line the base and sides of the tin with blanched spinach leaves.

Distinctive vegetable flavours and freshly grated nutmeg make this spinach-wrapped terrine with an egg custard base a popular first course or light main course.

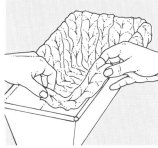

1 *Blanch 250g (8oz) large spinach leaves until just wilted. Refresh and cool. Carefully line the base and sides of an oiled 1kg (2lb) loaf tin, slightly overlapping so that there are no gaps.*

2 *Boil a selection of about 500g (1lb) mixed vegetables until tender. Add in stages, the harder ones first, to cook the vegetables to the same degree of tenderness. Drain the vegetables together.*

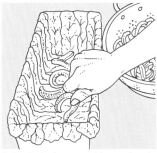

3 *Refresh the vegetables and cool. Arrange the vegetables in the loaf tin in a glorious jumble lengthwise along the tin; mixing the colours and shapes and seasoning well in between the layers of vegetables.*

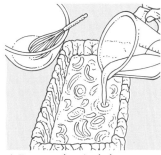

4 *Beat together 1 whole egg, 2 egg yolks and 300ml (½ pint) single cream with salt, pepper and freshly grated nutmeg. Add 50g (2oz) grated Cheddar cheese. Pour over the vegetables. Fold back the spinach leaves.*

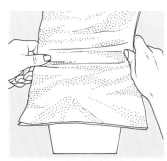

5 *Cover with a double thickness of greased foil and bake in a bain-marie (page 216) at 180°C, 350°F, Gas Mark 4 for 1–1¼ hours until the centre is just set.*

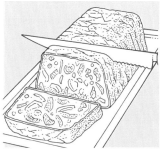

6 *Remove the tin and cool, then chill before turning out on to a serving plate. If the custard has seeped out a little, scrape it off. Cut carefully into slices.*

IDEAS FOR FISH AND VEGETABLE TERRINES

• One of the most beautiful dishes is a vegetable terrine set in clear aspic; a simple and successful aspic can be made by dissolving gelatine in warmed dry wine diluted with a little mineral water, and seasoned well. Sometimes I add a little sherry vinegar. Different colours of steamed vegetables should be arranged in layers in a loaf tin, covering each layer with aspic and allowing it to set in the refrigerator before adding another layer. If you are in a hurry, you can simply pack the layers of vegetables closely together and spoon the aspic gradually into the filled dish until it has reached the top. Fresh herbs can be put on the bottom of the tin so that it looks pretty when it is turned out (see Glossy Vegetable Terrine page 104).

• Pumpkin purée with a small amount of butterbean purée, seasoned with nutmeg and a little mustard, bound with eggs, makes a nice autumn terrine.

• Use different colours of fish when making fish terrines – the yellow of smoked fish looks very pretty with the pink of salmon, and, of course, shellfish add a lot of colour. Whiting, cod or plaice can be used for the white fish, and I particularly like haddock.

• Pieces of seafood such as mussels, scallops (with their coral), prawns and lobster, add both colour and texture to delicate fish mixtures.

• Both vegetable and fish terrines are nicest served with a sauce such as a purée of peppers, tomatoes or courgettes, with a little oil and vinegar added. Or try something simple like Greek yogurt, creamed smetana or soured cream with seasoning and chopped fresh herbs.

• For an excellent simple sauce for fish terrine season double cream with a trace of crushed garlic and a few threads of saffron, bring to the boil and then leave to cool and infuse, before stirring in 1–2 teaspoons sherry vinegar at the end.

• Individual moulds or timbales made from a well-seasoned vegetable purée, such as parsnip, courgette or spinach bound with whole eggs or egg whites, are lovely hot with a sauce as a first course.

GLOSSY VEGETABLE TERRINE (94)

This is my favourite kind of vegetable terrine. The key to a good terrine is that both the aspic and the vegetables should have real flavour – it is worth using organic vegetables if possible.   *SERVES 6–8*

> 600ml (1 pint) white wine
> 2 bay leaves
> ½ teaspoon caraway seeds
> 1 large clove garlic, chopped
> 2.5cm (1in) piece fresh root ginger, peeled and chopped roughly
> 250g (8oz) broccoli florets, halved lengthwise
> 300g (10oz) small courgettes, trimmed and sliced thinly lengthwise
> 375g (12oz) small carrots, sliced thinly lengthwise
> 250g (8oz) cauliflower florets, sliced fairly thinly lengthwise
> 250g (8oz) frozen broad beans
> 1½ sachets powdered gelatine
> Sprigs flat-leaved parsley
> 1 large yellow pepper, cored, deseeded and chopped as finely as possible (page 49)
> Salt
> Cayenne pepper

Boil the wine with the bay leaves, caraway seeds, garlic and ginger, then cover and simmer for about 25 minutes.

Meanwhile, blanch the broccoli, courgettes, carrots and cauliflower separately in boiling salted water. Immediately drain and refresh under running cold water. Put the broad beans in a bowl, pour boiling water over them and immediately begin popping the beans out of their skins and into a bowl on one side.

When the wine mixture is ready strain it through a fine sieve into a bowl. Season to taste with salt and cayenne pepper. To make the aspic sprinkle in the powdered gelatine and stir until it has fully dissolved. Don't start to assemble the terrine until the aspic has cooled almost completely.

Pour a thin layer of the cooled aspic over the bottom of a 1kg (2lb) loaf tin. Arrange sprigs of flat-leaved parsley in the bottom of the tin and chill until the aspic has set. Arrange the vegetables in alternating layers, interspersed with broad beans and yellow pepper. Pour in the remaining aspic, letting it seep through the vegetables and cover them.

Chill the terrine for several hours until well set. To serve, dip the tin briefly in a bowl of hot water, then turn out on to a serving plate, giving the tin a shake against the serving plate. Use a very sharp serrated knife to cut into slices.

PARSNIP AND GARLIC MOUSSE WITH GREEN CORIANDER SAUCE (94)

Here is a delicious example of how well-cooked garlic becomes mild and sweet.   *SERVES 6*

> 500g (1lb) parsnips, chopped roughly
> 1 large head garlic cloves, separated but unpeeled
> 1 teaspoon paprika
> 1 large egg (size 1)
> 1 large egg white (size 1)
> 300ml (½ pint) double cream
> 1 teaspoon honey
> 1 teaspoon ground mace
> Salt and black pepper
> *FOR THE SAUCE*
> 300ml (½ pint) creamed smetana or Greek yogurt
> 3 teaspoons white wine vinegar
> 1 good handful chopped fresh coriander
> Salt
> Cayenne pepper

Cook the parsnips in salted water with the garlic cloves until soft, then drain.

Generously oil a 1.2 litre (2 pint) mould or bread tin. Sprinkle the paprika on to the bottom, mainly in the centre. Put a roasting tin of hot water in the oven and heat to 160°C, 325°F, Gas Mark 3. Pop the garlic cloves out of their skins into a food processor with the parsnips, egg and egg white, cream, honey and mace. Whizz until very smooth, then season to taste with salt and black pepper. Pour slowly into the prepared mould and put into the roasting tin of water in the oven. Cook for 30–40 minutes until firm to a light touch in the centre. Remove and leave until almost cold, then loosen the sides carefully, using a knife if necessary, and turn out on to a serving plate.

To make the sauce, simply mix the creamed smetana or yogurt, vinegar and chopped coriander together and season to taste with salt and a little cayenne pepper. Put in a bowl and serve with the mousse, which should be served at room temperature, not chilled.

DUCK, CHICKEN AND PORK TERRINE WITH PRUNES AND PISTACHIOS (94)

Make this at least two days before you plan to eat it as it will keep for 10 days in the refrigerator. It is an ideal standby accompanied by crusty bread and salad. The duck skin adds the good flavour of duck fat and so keeps the terrine moist – just as you often add pork fat to a terrine, only duck has a richer taste.   *SERVES 8–10*

> 2 duck breast fillets, about 300g (10oz)
> 2 skinless chicken breast fillets, about 300g (10oz)
> 500g (1lb) belly of pork, derinded and diced
> 2 cloves garlic, crushed
> 1 teaspoon ground mace
> 1 teaspoon ground coriander
> Finely grated rind and juice of 1 orange
> 150ml (¼ pint) Cointreau or brandy
> 125g (4oz) soft pitted prunes, quartered
> 50g (2oz) shelled pistachio nuts
> 375g (12oz) thinly sliced rindless smoked bacon
> Whole peppercorns
> Salt and black pepper

Skin the duck breast fillets. Cut up the skin into very small pieces, then cut the duck and chicken flesh into 1cm (½in) cubes. Mix together the flesh and duck skin, and the pork in a small bowl with the garlic, mace and coriander, orange rind and juice, Cointreau and a generous sprinkling of black pepper. Cover and chill for at least 8 hours.

Put a roasting tin of water in the centre of the oven and heat to 150°C, 300°F, Gas Mark 2. Stir the prunes, pistachio nuts and a sprinkling of salt into the meat mixture. Line the bottom and sides of a medium-sized earthenware bowl or soufflé dish with about half the bacon, then spoon in the mixture with any juices and pack level. Lay the remaining bacon neatly all over the top and scatter 1 teaspoon of peppercorns in the centre of the bacon for garnish. Cover with foil, stand in the roasting tin and cook for about 2 hours until the terrine comes away from the sides of the dish.

When the juices and fat have started to cool, put a heavy weight on top of the foil and put the dish in the refrigerator. Remove the dish at least 30 minutes before you plan to serve the terrine.

GLAZED TERRINE IN A CASE OF HERB PASTRY (94)

A wonderful fusion of flavours combined with a luxurious appearance makes this a perfect terrine for a lunch party, accompanied by a green salad and crusty bread in summer, or during colder weather, a bowl of hot new potatoes. Including herbs in the pastry is an easy way of adding extra flavour.   *SERVES 6–8*

FOR THE TERRINE
  250g (8oz) boneless stewing veal, finely diced
  175g (6oz) boneless pork, such as leg, finely diced
  175g (6oz) skinless turkey breast fillets, finely diced
  250ml (8fl oz) dry white wine
  125ml (4fl oz) dry sherry
  125g (4oz) chicken livers, chopped finely
  Milk
  125g (4oz) pork fat, chopped finely
  2 teaspoons drained capers
  1 teaspoon juniper berries, crushed, plus extra for garnishing
  2 teaspoons green peppercorns
  3–4 large cloves garlic, chopped finely
  50g (2oz) can anchovy fillets
  Several bay leaves
  Olive oil
  1 sachet powdered gelatine
  Sea salt
  Black pepper
FOR THE PASTRY
  250g (8oz) strong white flour
  1 teaspoon salt
  1–2 sprigs fresh rosemary, chopped finely
  2 teaspoons dried oregano
  1 teaspoon dried thyme
  150g (5oz) butter
  5 tablespoons water

Place the veal, pork, turkey, white wine, sherry and a generous sprinkling of freshly ground black pepper in a large bowl and mix together thoroughly. Cover the bowl and place in the refrigerator for 12–24 hours. About halfway through the marinating time put the chopped chicken livers in a second bowl, cover with milk and chill.

While the meat is marinating, butter an 18cm (7in) deep cake tin with a loose base. To make the pastry, sift the flour and salt into a bowl and mix in the rosemary, oregano and thyme. Put the butter and water in a small saucepan and melt over a gentle heat, then pour on to the flour and herbs and stir until you have a smooth, thick dough. Put the ball of dough into the tin and press the dough evenly over the base and up the sides of the tin to just beyond the rim. Refrigerate until needed.

Drain the meat and marinade mixture in a sieve over a bowl, then pour the liquid through a fine sieve into a small saucepan. Drain the chicken livers and discard the milk. Put the meat and chicken livers in a bowl and mix in the pork fat, capers, juniper berries, green peppercorns and garlic. Drain the oil from the anchovies and add it to the bowl. Season with sea salt and a little black pepper.

Spoon the mixture into the tin and spread level. Arrange a star pattern of alternate anchovy fillets and bay leaves on top, pressing them into the meat mixture. Brush with olive oil. Lay a piece of foil loosely on top and cook at 160°C, 325°F, Gas Mark 3 for 1¾–2 hours.

Towards the end of the cooking time, boil the sieved marinade mixture for 1 minute, then pour into a bowl through a fine sieve lined with muslin. Sprinkle in the powdered gelatine and stir until it has fully dissolved. When the terrine is cooked, you can replace the bay leaves with fresh ones for a more colourful effect if you wish. Spoon the slightly cooled gelatine liquid over the top of the meat so that it sinks into any gaps where the meat has shrunk away from the pastry. Leave until cold.

To unmould, stand the tin on top of a jar and press the terrine up out of the sides. Carefully remove the base before putting the terrine on to a serving plate. Serve cool, but not straight from the refrigerator.

HOT FISH TERRINE WITH MACE AND PINK PEPPERCORNS (94)

I serve this terrine as a main course with a cheese sauce which I make slightly thinner than usual, adding threads of saffron and a clove of crushed garlic right at the beginning so that they infuse into the sauce as it cooks. New potatoes and either a green vegetable or salad are good accompaniments.   *SERVES 4*

  425g (14oz) smoked haddock fillet, skinned and cut up roughly
  1 teaspoon ground mace
  2 eggs
  2 egg whites
  150ml (¼ pint) double cream
  1 teaspoon chopped fresh tarragon leaves
  1 teaspoon pink peppercorns
  3–4 pinches cayenne pepper
  1 plaice fillet, 175–250g (6–8oz), skinned and cut into thin strips lengthwise
  1 salmon tail, 625–750g (1¼–1½lb), filleted, skinned and cut into 1.5–2.5cm (¾–1in) pieces
  Salt

Purée the smoked haddock in a food processor. Add the mace, then one at a time, the eggs and egg whites, whizzing very thoroughly after each addition. Gradually whizz in the cream. Turn the mixture into a bowl, stir in the tarragon and peppercorns and season with the cayenne pepper and salt. Cover and refrigerate for at least 30 minutes. Put a roasting tin of hot water in the oven and heat to 160°C, 325°F, Gas Mark 3.

Butter a 1.2 litre (2 pint) terrine dish generously and lay a piece of buttered greaseproof paper on the bottom, then layer the strips of plaice fillet across the terrine and up the sides, leaving a space between each strip. Stir the pieces of salmon fillet into the chilled haddock mixture and spoon into the terrine dish. Top with a piece of buttered foil, pressing the edges to seal. Pierce 2 holes in the top of the foil to let the steam escape.

Set the terrine dish in the roasting tin and cook for 60–70 minutes until the edges have slightly shrunk from the sides and a small knife inserted in the centre comes out clean. Remove the foil and pour off any liquid around the terrine. (You can use this in your cheese sauce.) Leave to stand for 5 minutes before turning out on to a warm serving dish.

RICE, GRAINS and PULSES

Rice, grains and pulses have kept man alive and healthy for thousands of years, and still form the staple diet of more than half the world's population. Now, as a result of the high cost of meat and a growing number of vegetarians, the Western world is returning to a diet which previous generations might have scorned as peasant food. If you are a real vegetarian, a variety of pulses and grains, which are full of protein, vitamins and minerals, with the bonus of fibre too, can provide all the nutrients you need. Non-vegetarians can also benefit from the healthy properties of grains and pulses, and once you have realized their versatility in the kitchen, it is very possible you will not need to eat as much meat as you did before.

In any case, grains and pulses provide a huge and important area of cookery, and can be made into a wide variety of dishes, ranging from hearty stews to delicate purées trickled with the best olive oil. They should be eaten for their taste, texture and adaptability, as much as for their low cost and nutritious qualities.

If you have never had rice well-cooked, it is easy to be bored by it. I still find that rice served as an accompaniment to meat or fish in restaurants is frequently dull, bland and stodgy. But basmati rice, with its aromatic grains, or a real risotto made with Italian arborio rice, can be ambrosial. The Egyptian way of cooking rice by the absorption method and then raising the heat and letting the grains on the bottom of the pan toast golden to dark brown before stirring them up into the rest of the rice is my favourite rice dish. Dark, spicy wild rice although not a true rice but the seed of an aquatic grass grown in North America, can also be used cold in salads, or in stuffings.

Most dried pulses should be soaked in cold water for several hours – I usually leave them overnight, which makes the cooking time shorter. If you have a pressure cooker, it is much the quickest way to cook them, and it also preserves the valuable B vitamins.

Among the countless possibilities for using pulses, you can make wonderful soups, subtle purées, or delectable cassoulet-type stews with a variety of these beans. When I am feeding large crowds during the holidays some kind of bean stew is one of the most useful and popular dishes to make. It can be simply beans: kidney, haricot, cannellini or chick peas in particular, slowly cooked with vegetables added at different stages, or more luxuriously, like a real cassoulet with pieces of goose or duck, smoked sausages and chunks of bacon – in either case the beans have to cook long and gently to become meltingly soft, absorbing the flavours of ingredients cooked with them, and forming creamy, self-thickened juices around them.

Grains and pulses, the first foods to be discovered by man, were also the first 'store cupboard' food and offer enormous scope for nutritious and also more unusual meals. One great advantage is their keeping properties; rice can be kept in a dry atmosphere more or less indefinitely, and pulses and grains will last well for at least a year, after which they are still usable, but they become harder with time, so taking longer to cook.

Clockwise from top: My Cassoulet (page 114), a hearty stew of haricot beans, pork, duck, sausages under a golden oregano-flavoured breadcrumb topping; Basmati Rice with Crisped Grains (page 114) is flavoured with cinnamon sticks; Kidney Bean and Grilled Pepper Salad (page 115) combines red kidney beans with yellow peppers, spring onions and flat-leaved parsley; Saffron and Chilli Rice Cooked in Coconut Milk (page 115) makes a flavourful, golden accompaniment to curries and grilled meats; Golden Lentil Rolls Wrapped in Bacon (page 114) are baked with finely grated Parmesan cheese and served here with friseé lettuce.

RICE

There are literally thousands of varieties of this vital grain, all with different characteristics that lead to many ways of cooking. Yet in our cuisine rice remains a much underrated food, relegated to the side of the plate as a boring accompaniment, which it can be if not cooked properly. This is a great pity as rice's ability to absorb and enhance flavourings and textures makes it ideal to produce some unusual and even glorious dishes.

Rice comes in two main grain types – long (*indica*) and round (*japonica*). Round grains cook to either a creaminess or a light glutinous stickiness (ideal for chopsticks), depending on the variety. Light, long grains that stay separate and have real flavour are essential for spicy pilaffs or for simply elegant fluffy rice as a side dish. Short round grains cooked long and slowly become a comforting pudding; medium round grains also with the same creamy quality make the memorable Italian classic risottos or colourful Spanish paellas. Brown rice with the outer bran layer intact gives a deliciously nutty taste but does take longer to cook. Readily available easy-cook rices have been refined by par-boiling, which slightly hardens the outside layer and reduces the risk of overcooking. These rices are ideal for cooking in one-pot meals and casseroles as occasional stirring will not break up the grains.

PREPARING AND COOKING RICE

Most modern brands of rice have much of the loose starch removed so it is not necessary to rinse or soak. The cooking times given here are for unsoaked rice. There is no need to rinse or soak easy-cook rices. Rinsing and soaking, though, is traditional for basmati rice and gives a lighter, more delicate texture. To rinse, tip the rice into a large bowl with cold water, swilling the grains round with your hand. Let it settle, then pour off the water. Repeat 2–3 times more until the water becomes clearer, then soak with more fresh water for 30–60 minutes, drain and cook. Soaked rice needs less water and shorter cooking times than unsoaked.

Do not cook more than 500g (1lb) raw rice at a time (that's 8–10 portions). Allow 50g (2oz) raw rice per person for a side dish and 75g (3oz) for a main dish. Most rice absorbs at least 3 times its weight in liquid making this a generous serving. To test if rice is cooked scoop out some grains and press 1 or 2 between your thumb and forefinger. If a small hard core remains allow a few minutes extra. After cooking, rice continues to absorb moisture and it fluffs up even more if allowed to stand for a few minutes before stirring and serving.

ABSORPTION METHOD
In this method the rice simmers slowly in a measured amount of water or stock in a covered pan and the rice should be cooked when the liquid has been absorbed and there are small holes between the grains.

Use the same measuring jug for the rice and water or stock. For long grain rice use double the amount of water or stock, 1¼–1½ times the amount of liquid for basmati and 2¼ times the amount of liquid for brown rice. Add any seasoning before cooking although basmati or Thai rices taste delicious unseasoned.

Place the water or stock and rice in the pan, season and bring to the boil. Lower the heat to simmer, then cover tightly and cook for 15–20 minutes for long grain rice, 10 minutes for basmati and 30–35 minutes for brown rice. Remove from the heat without uncovering and leave for 5 minutes. Toss with oil or butter.

OPEN PAN METHOD
Many cooks have their own favourite ways of cooking rice. One method is the open pan or excess water method, boiling it in a lot of water like pasta. Allow 1.5 litres (2½ pints) water to 250g (8oz) rice. Season with 1 teaspoon of salt either during cooking or afterwards, remembering that rice absorbs salt very easily. Long grain rice takes 12–15 minutes; brown rice 30–35 minutes; basmati rice 8–10 minutes. Easy-cook rice needs a few minutes extra cooking time and because of its slightly harder outside layer doesn't spoil if overcooked.

Bring a large pan of water to a good rolling boil. Add the measured rice, stir and return to a medium boil. Cook, uncovered, stirring once or twice with a large wooden spoon, according to the timings (left), then drain in a sieve and rinse with hot water if liked. Toss with a little oil or melted butter.

MICROWAVE METHOD
Rice cooks beautifully in a microwave. Do not cook more than about 375g (12oz) rice at a time and you need a deep bowl for the water as it bubbles up. Use the same proportions of long grain and brown rice to water as in the absorption method (left), and 1½ times the amount of water for basmati rice. Use these times: for long grain rice cook 7 minutes on High, then 8 minutes on Defrost; for basmati cook 6 minutes on High, then 4–6 minutes on Defrost; for brown rice cook 7 minutes on High, then 25 minutes on Defrost.

Cover the bowl with microwave clingfilm pierced several times. Cook on High (100%) for the specified time (left), then stir, re-cover and cook on Defrost (30%) for the remaining time. Remove from the microwave and leave for 5 minutes before removing the wrap and forking through the rice. Toss with a little oil or butter.

MAKING A PILAFF

A pilaff is oil- or butter-enriched rice, cooked until the liquid, usually stock, has been absorbed, and then a few other cooked or sautéed ingredients such as prawns, mushrooms or peas, are added. The rice is never stirred during the main cooking period.

Pilaff can either be cooked on top of the stove, as here, or cooked, covered, in the oven at 180°C, 350°F, Gas Mark 4. Rinse and soak the rice in water for at least 1 hour before cooking. These quantities serve 4.

1 Melt 25g (1oz) butter in a heavy-based pan and fry 1 finely chopped onion until golden. Add 250g (8oz) basmati rice and spices to taste and stir to coat with butter. Cook for 1–2 minutes until the grains are opaque.

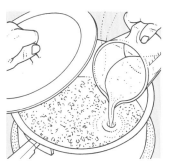

2 Add 300ml (½ pint) chicken stock and bring to the boil, stir, then cover the pan and simmer as gently as possible for about 12–15 minutes until tender but still with a slight bite to it. Test for doneness (opposite).

3 If the rice is still too firm, and all the liquid has already absorbed, add a little more liquid, stir in the prepared ingredients and continue cooking until the rice is done. Fluff the rice with a fork and season. Mound on a serving dish.

MAKING A RISOTTO

A real risotto is luxuriously creamy; this is achieved by stirring in small amounts of hot stock during the cooking process, and only adding more after the previous amount has been absorbed. The best risottos are made freshly to order so they retain their delicious creaminess. Use short grain Italian arborio rice. The method here is for a basic risotto; other prepared ingredients such as sautéed vegetables or fresh herbs can be added 5 minutes before the end of cooking. Serves 4.

1 Melt 40g (1½oz) butter and 2 tablespoons olive oil in a large saucepan over a medium heat. Add 1 finely chopped onion and fry until golden. Add 375g (12oz) arborio rice and stir for 1–2 minutes until a pale opaque colour.

2 Heat 1.2–1.8 litres (2–2½ pints) of chicken stock and add a ladleful, stirring until absorbed. Continue adding stock, a ladleful at a time, and stirring for 20–25 minutes until the rice is cooked but still firm.

3 After adding the stock stir in any prepared ingredients and warm through. Stir in 25g (1oz) butter and season to taste. Spoon on to individual plates and serve at once, topped with coarsely grated Parmesan cheese.

SERVING RICE

• Paella, ideally using a medium round grain rice, is cooked with chopped tomatoes, onions, garlic, meat and fish in a stock, but the pan is shaken during cooking rather than stirred so the grains separate more.

• Good ingredients to add to both pilaffs and risottos are sliced, sautéed slices of bulb fennel, parsnips, aubergines, mushrooms, courgettes or broccoli, as well as grilled, skinned and finely sliced peppers, pieces of smoked fish, prawns, crab meat, crispy fried cubes of smoked bacon, smoked or raw ham, chicken, and always plenty of fresh herbs. Squid ink can be added to risotto to make it a shimmering black colour, which looks wonderful with chopped flat-leaved parsley, and beetroot juice will turn the rice pink.

• Rice mixtures but not easy-cook types are excellent for stuffing vegetables (page 61), pastry or sometimes fish or packing into moulds to serve either hot or cold.

• Rice for salads should be dressed with vinaigrette (page 204) after draining and rinsing while still hot. Leave to cool before serving.

A risotto flavoured with prawns, asparagus and dill.

GRAINS

Grains can be the basis of much innovative cooking. Wheat in many forms, buckwheat, corn, rye, barley and millet are all dried grains which offer nourishment, taste and variety once they have absorbed liquid and softened. They are an invaluable way of stretching more expensive ingredients such as pieces of meat or fish without producing a dish which is in any way stodgy.

Wheat could be called the king of grains, as it is the essential ingredient for most of our daily bread. There are also several forms of cracked wheat, including bulgar, which have been cracked by preboiling so only need soaking for use in salads, croquettes, stuffings and so on. Semolina and couscous are also forms of wheat.

Cooked whole grains are ideal cold and can be used in salads to provide a chewy element. Like rice, other grains are perfect vehicles for all kinds of sauces, and for added herbs, spices, garlic and other seasonings. Buckwheat, which you can buy either roasted or not, cooks more quickly than most grains: roasted buckwheat is particularly good and buckwheat flour make the laciest, crispest pancakes possible (page 74). Millet is another quick-cooking grain which can be used for making rissoles, or in stews. Polenta, simply the Italian name for cornmeal, can be cooked until thick, cut into wedges when cold, then fried and served with a sauce.

One of the things I look forward to when the weather gets colder is eating porridge again. As well as for porridge, oatmeal can be used in biscuits or as an addition to bread dough as it has a wonderful flavour and gritty texture. Oatcakes made with oatmeal are another of my favourites.

PREPARING COUSCOUS

The staple grain of North Africa and becoming better known elsewhere, couscous is a form of semolina made from durum wheat and rolled into little pellets. Traditionally, it is cooked in a couscoussière (page 24), which looks like a steamer, and is put over a pot of a simmering spicy meat or vegetable stew. If you don't have a couscoussière, use an ordinary steamer with a tight-fitting lid. Allow 250g (8oz) couscous to serve 4.

Couscous grains, except the instant variety, benefit from a certain amount of preparation before cooking to lighten them.

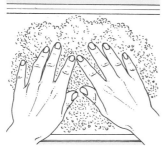

1 Soak the couscous grains in cold water for 10 minutes to swell and soften them. Drain in a fine sieve, not a colander, shaking well. Spread the couscous evenly on a clean tray with your fingertips. Allow to dry for about 15 minutes, then run your fingers through the grains to separate them and break up any lumps.

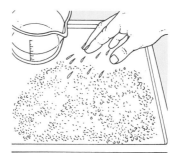

2 Sprinkle the couscous with more cold water, flicking it on with your fingers. Leave to dry again, spreading the grains evenly on the tray, then stir with your fingers to separate the grains. Repeat this process 1 more time. The grains continue to swell and lighten as they absorb more water and are thoroughly stirred.

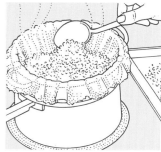

3 Meanwhile, fit the top half of a steamer lined with a clean cloth over a pan of boiling vegetable, meat or chicken stock (pages 28–31). Spoon in the couscous, cover tightly and steam for 15 minutes until the grains are light and fluffy. Fork through before serving with a spicy meat or vegetable stew.

MAKING TABBOULEH

Tabbouleh is one of the most famous of the Middle Eastern *mezze*, meaning appetizers, which cover the whole table with countless little dishes. Serve it as a salad, making it part of a cold summer meal.

The grain used is bulgar, which is preboiled, cracked wheat. The only preparation it needs is soaking. Traditionally, tabbouleh is made with chopped tomatoes, onion, parsley and mint leaves. Serves 6.

125g (4oz) bulgar soaked for
    15–20 minutes and drained
6 tablespoons lemon juice
75–125ml (3–4fl oz) extra
    virgin olive oil
3 large handfuls flat-leaved
    parsley, chopped finely
2 large handfuls mint leaves,
    chopped finely
1 red onion, chopped finely
4–5 firm tomatoes, cubed
Salt
Black pepper

1 Use your hands to transfer the soaked and drained bulgar to a bowl, squeezing out all the water. Marinate with the lemon juice and salt and pepper for 30 minutes.

2 Stir in the remaining ingredients and mix together well with a wooden spoon. Spoon into a shallow serving dish. Stir again just before serving.

POLENTA

Yellow cornmeal, or polenta, is a classic of Italian cooking. Freshly cooked polenta looks like a cross between semolina pudding and porridge. In Italy it is eaten in many different ways from a simple first course with butter and Parmesan cheese to an accompaniment for game casseroles. Or serve with fresh tomato sauce (page 206) or grilled meat.

You need 300g (10oz) polenta to serve 4–6. In Italy, polenta is lovingly and continually stirred for up to an hour, but I find frequent stirring for 20 minutes is quite sufficient. If allowed to set in a shallow layer, polenta can be cut up and grilled, making it even more delicious.

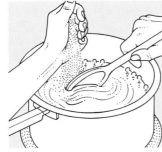

1 Bring 1.8 litres (3 pints) milk and water mixed to boil in a large, heavy-based saucepan. Season with salt. Weigh out 300g (10oz) polenta. With a long-handled spoon in one hand for stirring, drizzle the grains into the saucepan with your other hand. Stir briskly, but not too vigorously, always in only one direction to avoid lumps, as you add the polenta.

Grains make a hearty start to the day – try homemade muesli or hot, creamy porridge with yogurt and brown sugar.

2 Continue to stir rapidly until smooth and thick, then turn down the heat to simmer and cook for 20 minutes. Ideally you should stir all the time, but as long as you stir frequently to stop the polenta burning on the base of the saucepan it should be fine. Check the seasoning and stir in a good knob of butter and grated Parmesan cheese.

***To serve polenta** as grilled slices pour the cooked polenta into a large, shallow ovenproof dish and spread out evenly. Cool and chill until set solid, then cut into narrow rectangles. Preheat a grill until very hot and grill the slices until browned and crispy on both sides. Spread with butter to serve with stews or grilled meats or simply buttered on its own.*

USING GRAINS

• Boiled whole wheat, barley or rye grains are enhanced by stirring in some butter-sautéed onions or mushrooms to serve with roasted game birds, duck and chicken. You can also sprinkle the grains with soy sauce just before serving.
• Bulgar, so quick to prepare, can be made into various stuffings for vegetables, vine leaves or poultry. Mix it with spiced minced lamb, nuts or chopped sautéed vegetables.
• Cooked grains are also good served with vegetable sauces, such as pumpkin cooked with plenty of garlic, butter and spices until it becomes a mushy sauce, or a fresh tomato sauce (page 206) with strips of basil added at the end.
• Grains can be added to vegetable soups and stews to add body to the juices as well as texture and flavour.

PORRIDGE

Traditional Scots porridge is made with oatmeal and often cooked overnight in a very low oven. The method below takes only a few minutes to cook on top of the stove.

I like using jumbo or 'traditional' large flaked oats, which only take a little longer to cook than quick or rolled oats, and have much more texture. To serve 4 allow 125g (4oz) jumbo oatflakes.

***Place the oatflakes** and 600ml (1 pint) water in a small saucepan and bring to the boil, stirring. Simmer gently, stirring constantly, for 3–5 minutes until it is the thickness you like. Season to taste with salt. Spoon the porridge into bowls and serve with milk, cream or Greek yogurt, and brown sugar, honey or molasses.*

MUESLI

This mixture of uncooked grain flakes and dried fruit was introduced by a Dr Bircher at his clinic in Switzerland at the end of the nineteenth century. Today it is almost as familiar as cornflakes on the breakfast table and often more popular.

Making muesli at home means you can put in more of your favourite ingredients and vary them each time. The following mixture is my personal choice: 1 mug ready-to-eat dried apricots, ½ mug each dried apples and ready-to-eat prunes, ½ packet dried bananas, ¼ mug hazelnuts, ¼ mug almonds in their skins, 2 mugs jumbo oatflakes, 2 mugs barley flakes, 3 teaspoons ground cinnamon, 1 tablespoon sesame seeds and ½ mug sultanas.

Chop the dried fruit and nuts fairly small. Put into a bowl with the grains, cinnamon, sesame seeds and sultanas, mixing well with a wooden spoon. Transfer to an airtight container for storage, and serve with milk, fruit juice or natural yogurt, and add pieces of fresh fruit and some brown sugar if you like.

PULSES

Pulses are the dried seeds of an enormous variety of bean and pea pods, many possessing very different flavours and characters. Whenever I travel abroad and discover pulses I haven't seen before I cannot resist bringing them home to try. The flavouring of pulses is very important; although they do not have a definite taste of their own, the long, slow cooking they need allows them to take on the flavours of the ingredients they are cooked with. Some pulses, such as butter beans and lentils, break up more easily than others, making them more suitable for soups, purées or very mushy, comforting stews. Chick peas, however, never break up, however long they are cooked, although they can also be puréed to make hummus, the classic Middle Eastern appetizer.

Although pulses can make irresistible stews and casseroles, they can also be used for lighter dishes. Carefully seasoned and butter-enriched puréed pulses are excellent alternatives to potatoes or rice as a side dish, and cold purées make delicate dips or appetizers. Pulses of all kinds can be added to salads. As well as being convenient, canned pulses hold their shape and colour well and this makes them ideal for salads (you may prefer to rinse them first).

SOAKING PULSES

Almost all dried pulses require presoaking to speed up the cooking process, and soaking is also supposed to help to reduce any tendency to flatulence. Although not essential, pulses intended for the pressure cooker are best presoaked as this cuts down on foaming. Pulses can be soaked in cold water for up to 8–12 hours. Smaller pulses, such as lentils, can be cooked without soaking, particularly red lentils which can be tipped straight from the pack into the cooking pot and only take 20 minutes or less to cook. Thicker green and brown lentils, however, cook far quicker if soaked for a couple of hours beforehand. If you forget to start soaking larger pulses well in advance, then you can cut the soaking time to 1–2 hours by covering in boiling water and then cooking them a little longer.

Remember, pulses yield about double their weight when cooked, so take that into account when calculating quantities. For 4 servings, use 125g (4oz) dried pulses. As cooked pulses can be stored in the refrigerator for up to 4 days, it is sensible to cook double the quantity and use them for another meal.

Cover pulses with at least 4 times the amount of cold water. Swish around with your hands and leave to soak (see chart below). Drain and rinse under cold water. Cook pulses with added flavourings (but not salt) in more fresh cold water (right).

COOKING PULSES

It is important to boil some pulses for the first 10 minutes to destroy any potential toxins that may be present, but after that reduce the heat to a gentle simmer so they soften without breaking up. Simmering times in the chart are approximate because older pulses take longer to cook. Aduki, black-eyed, borlotti, kidney and soya beans specifically require vigorous preboiling to destroy toxins but it does no harm to preboil all pulses.

Put the soaked pulses into a saucepan and cover with at least 4 times the volume of cold water. Add herbs, onion slices or diced carrots. Bring to the boil. Boil hard for 10 minutes and skim off any scum. Reduce to a simmer, cover and cook until tender (left). Top up with boiling water, if necessary. Drain, discard the flavourings and season. Toss with olive oil or vinaigrette (page 204) if serving cold in salads.

SOAKING AND COOKING CHART

Use these times as guidelines; how long the pulses have been soaked and stored will affect the cooking times. Older pulses and those that have not been soaked long, take longer to cook. First preboil the pulses for 10 minutes, then reduce the heat to a simmer.

Variety of pulse	Soaking time	Approximate simmering time after 10 minutes' preboiling
Aduki bean	At least 8 hours	40 minutes
Black-eyed bean	At least 8 hours	50 minutes
Borlotti bean	At least 8 hours	50 minutes
Broad bean	At least 8 hours	50 minutes
Butter bean	At least 8 hours	1 hour
Chick peas (garbanzos)	At least 8 hours	1 hour
Haricot bean (navy bean, cannellini and flageolet)	At least 8 hours	50 minutes
Kidney bean, black	At least 8 hours	50 minutes
Kidney bean, red	At least 8 hours	1 hour
Lentils, green	Not necessary	45 minutes
Lentils, red	Not necessary	20 minutes
Mung bean	At least 8 hours	25 minutes
Peas, split	Not necessary	30 minutes
Peas, whole	At least 8 hours	1–1¼ hours
Pinto bean	At least 8 hours	1 hour
Soya bean	12 hours	1¾ hours

SPROUTING BEANS AND SEEDS

Watching beans, peas and seeds sprout over a few days is quite magical. Fresh homegrown sprouts are also very nutritious, and an excellent inexpensive way of taking in fresh vitamins. The sprouting and germination process renders the beans digestible and all they need is time and water. Most pulses will sprout, but not split beans and split lentils, and it is a good idea to have 2 or 3 types growing at once. Sprouts can be used in pasta sauces, pilaffs, homemade burgers, stir-fries, stews and even sandwich fillings as well as in salads.

1 *Soak about 3 tablespoons of pulses in at least 4 times the amount of fresh water for 12 hours. Drain, rinse in cold water and place the pulses in a clean glass jar. Cover with a piece of muslin, secured with an elastic band. Pierce the top a few times with a skewer. Lay the jar on its side on a light, but not sunny, windowsill away from draughts.*

2 *Rinse well with tepid running water each morning and night to wet the seeds and remove waste gases. It should not be necessary to remove the top. When sprouted (usually within 3 days), rinse and drain again, then store in a polythene food bag in the refrigerator and eat within 2 days. If the pulses do not sprout this means they are too old so discard.*

MAKING PURÉES AND DIPS

Pulse purées can be either hot or cold, loosely mushy or thick enough to form a solid cake. Hot purées should be made with pulses that break up easily, such as lentils, butter beans and haricot beans. After draining the cooked pulses, you can simply mash them with a fork, adding butter and flavours as you mash, or use a food processor. Serve hot purées as a side dish instead of potatoes, or cold to serve with crisp vegetables as a dip.

For extra-smooth purées *use a food processor. Put the drained, cooked pulses in the machine with spices or extra flavourings as you like. Whizz until the purée is smooth and creamy.*

For a runnier purée *add a little olive oil, nut oil or natural yogurt to the drained cooked pulses. Either add through the top of a food processor or beat in by hand with a fork after puréeing.*

IDEAS FOR PULSES

• Spices such as turmeric, cumin, coriander, caraway, nutmeg, cinnamon and mace all go well with pulses, as do herbs such as oregano, thyme, rosemary, coriander leaf, basil, mint, garlic, fresh ginger and chilli.

• Butter beans are specially good for puréeing to form the basis of soups or pâtés. A purée of butter beans and carrots in a well-seasoned chicken stock makes a wonderful soup. Top with a swirl of cream and fresh dill or basil.

• Thick lentil, chick pea, haricot or kidney bean purées can be formed into rissoles or balls and shallow-fried until crisp all over. Mix with finely chopped fried onions or mushrooms, chopped spring onions or simply with lots of chopped parsley and chopped garlic, adding spices if you like, or a spoonful of curry paste. The balls can be rolled in fresh breadcrumbs, and deep fried for an extra crispy exterior.

• I think long and gently simmered stews and casseroles are perhaps the most satisfying way of cooking pulses. I always boil beans for a stew separately in unsalted water, until they are soft but not breaking up, and then cook them again with the other ingredients, long and gently. Seasoning should be adjusted at the end.

• Try haricot and cannellini beans in stews, particularly with chunks of smoked bacon, tomatoes, onions and plenty of garlic. They are delicious but they do tend to break up more than kidney beans.

• Nutty-flavoured chick peas are lovely in a chicken casserole with turmeric or saffron, garlic and bulb fennel with a handful of chopped fresh herbs such as coriander or tarragon thrown in at the end.

• Pale green flageolet beans or green lentils are excellent as a salad on their own mixed with finely chopped, raw red onion, plenty of chopped parsley and a vinaigrette dressing (page 204).

• Crunchy ingredients such as bulb fennel, celery, parboiled thin slices of parsnip, radishes and blanched slivers of broccoli, as well as plenty of fresh herbs, combine well with beans in a salad.

Clockwise from top: Crusted Butter Bean Purée with Onions and Garlic (page 115), chick pea purée with turmeric and fresh coriander and a hot green lentil purée topped with melting butter.

MY CASSOULET (106)

There is a lot of argument about what a true cassoulet consists of, but it seems to me that as long as it is a richly satisfying fusion of beans and meats, it is really up to personal taste, what ingredients you can get, and how much time you have. There is no point in thinking you can't make a cassoulet if you haven't got any preserved goose or Toulouse sausages. The crust of breadcrumbs on top of the cassoulet is an authentic touch worth doing. Serve with a green salad. *SERVES 8*

> 500g (1lb) dried haricot beans, soaked
>   overnight in cold water
> 25g (1oz) butter
> 4 tablespoons olive oil
> 3 large onions, cut into 5mm (¼in) slices
> 6–8 large cloves garlic, chopped
> 2 large red peppers, halved, deseeded and
>   cut into 1cm (½in) slices (page 49)
> 2 large bulbs fennel, trimmed, halved and
>   cut into 1cm (½in) slices (page 46)
> 1kg (2lb) stewing pork, cut into chunks
> 4 unboned breast joints of duck, halved
> 500g (1lb) kabanos sausages, cut into
>   2.5cm (1in) pieces
> 500g (1lb) tomatoes, cut up roughly
> 1 tablespoon chopped fresh rosemary
> 2 rounded teaspoons green peppercorns
> 600ml (1 pint) dry cider
> 2 tablespoons tomato purée
> 6 slices 2-day-old bread, made into crumbs
> 3 teaspoons dried oregano
> Extra olive oil
> Salt and black pepper

Drain the soaked haricot beans and put them in a saucepan. Cover generously with cold water. Bring to the boil for 10 minutes, then cover and simmer gently for 20–35 minutes until just soft but not breaking up. Drain and set aside.

Melt the butter with 2 tablespoons olive oil in a large, deep frying pan over a medium heat. Add the onions and cook, stirring, until soft and browned, then add the garlic and stir for 1 minute.

Transfer the onions and garlic to a large bowl. Add another tablespoon of oil and the sliced peppers and fennel to the pan and fry until beginning to soften, then add to the bowl of onions. Add the final tablespoon of oil and fry the pork until just browned all over. Add it to the mixture in the bowl, then fry the duck pieces just to brown them.

Put the beans in a large casserole and add all the ingredients from the bowl, the duck and any fat from the pan, the sausages, tomatoes, rosemary, green peppercorns, cider and tomato purée. Mix together and season with salt and black pepper. Cover the casserole and cook at 230°C, 450°F, Gas Mark 8 for 20–25 minutes, then reduce the heat to 140°C, 275°F, Gas Mark 1 and cook for a further 2½–3 hours.

Mix the breadcrumbs and oregano together. Stir the cassoulet, then thickly sprinkle the breadcrumb and herb mixture all over the top. Dribble olive oil all over the top and return the cassoulet to the oven, uncovered, for another 30 minutes.

BASMATI RICE WITH CRISPED GRAINS (106)

Basmati rice has a unique elegant, fragrant flavour. This method of cooking is based on the Egyptian way of almost burning the rice on the bottom of the pan and then scraping up the toasted grains to mix them with the rest. *SERVES 6*

> 250g (8oz) basmati rice, rinsed and
>   soaked in salted water for 1 hour
> 50g (2oz) butter
> 3 cinnamon sticks, each about 2.5–5cm
>   (1–2in) long
> 300–450ml (½–¾ pint) water
> 1 teaspoon salt

Drain the soaked rice. Melt the butter in a heavy-based saucepan, add the cinnamon sticks and rice and stir. Stir in the water and salt, then bring to the boil. Cover the saucepan tightly, reduce the heat to as low as possible and cook for 10–14 minutes until the rice has absorbed the liquid and is tender but still has a slight bite to it. Put a tea towel between the lid and the top of the rice, tying the corners together on top of the lid so that they don't burn. Increase the heat to as high as possible – this is to toast the bottom layer of rice and takes about 8–12 minutes, occasionally more depending on individual stoves. Don't try to stir the rice to see if the bottom is browning. Instead look at the top rim of the rice – when you see that the sides are beginning to brown, it will be ready. In my experience it hardly ever burns too much.

Remove the pan from the heat and leave on one side for 10 minutes. Fork the rice out on to a serving plate, scraping out all the toasted bottom and forking the crisp, brown grains among the rest of the rice.

GOLDEN LENTIL ROLLS WRAPPED IN BACON (106)

Serve this lovely supper or lunch dish with a crisply cooked green vegetable like broccoli, or just a salad. It can be made well ahead so that you can simply put it in the oven to bake shortly before the meal. *SERVES 6*

> 175g (6oz) split red lentils
> 450ml (¾ pint) milk
> 1 onion, chopped finely
> 75g (3oz) strong cheese, grated
> 25g (1oz) butter
> 2 teaspoons dried oregano
> 1 egg, beaten
> About 175g (6oz) thinly sliced, rindless
>   smoked streaky bacon
> Grated Parmesan cheese
> Salt and black pepper

Place the lentils, milk and finely chopped onion in a saucepan and bring to the boil, then simmer very gently, stirring now and then, for 20 minutes or until thick and mushy. Remove from the heat and add the cheese, butter, oregano and salt and black pepper to taste. Stir in the egg, then leave to become cold.

Butter a fairly large, shallow, ovenproof dish. Using floured hands, roll small handfuls of the lentil mixture into 6cm (2½in) long sausage shapes. Wrap a piece of bacon around each one, leaving gaps of lentil still exposed.

Lay the rolls closely together in the dish and sprinkle all over with grated Parmesan cheese. Bake at 230°C, 450°F, Gas Mark 8 for 20–30 minutes until the rolls are golden brown and crispy.

CRUSTED BUTTER BEAN PURÉE WITH ONIONS AND GARLIC *(113)*

Butter beans really do have a rich buttery flavour, and as they tend to break up when they cook, a purée or a soup is the best thing you can do with them. This simple purée is wonderful, and goes perfectly instead of potatoes or rice with any roast or grilled meats or birds, or as part of a vegetarian meal. Butter beans combine specially well with the flavour of bay so for extra flavouring add a bay leaf or two to the water when cooking the beans.   *SERVES 6*

300g (10oz) dried butter beans, soaked
 for 8 hours or overnight in cold water
75g (3oz) butter
2 tablespoons olive oil
1 onion, sliced thinly
2 teaspoons caster sugar
2 cloves garlic, crushed
2 tablespoons fresh white breadcrumbs
1 tablespoon grated Parmesan cheese
Extra butter
Salt and black pepper

Drain the soaked butter beans. Put them in a saucepan and cover generously with cold water. Bring to the boil, boil for 10 minutes, then cover and simmer for 1–1½ hours until very soft, skimming the surface as necessary to remove any scum.

Meanwhile, melt 25g (1oz) of the butter with 2 tablespoons olive oil in a frying pan over a medium heat. Add the sliced onion and fry, stirring until it is soft and dark golden brown. Stir in the caster sugar, then remove from the heat and put on one side.

Drain the cooked butter beans and place in a food processor with the crushed garlic and remaining butter. Whizz thoroughly to a smooth purée. Season to taste with salt and black pepper, then stir in the fried onion with its butter and oil. Spoon the mixture into a shallow earthenware or gratin dish.

Mix the breadcrumbs with the grated Parmesan cheese, sprinkle all over the top and dot with little bits of butter. Cook at 200°C, 400°F, Gas Mark 6 for 20–30 minutes until speckled golden brown on top – if you already have meat or poultry roasting in the oven at a different temperature, just put in the dish and leave it for either more or less time until the surface has browned.

SAFFRON AND CHILLI RICE COOKED IN COCONUT MILK *(106)*

Rice cooked in this way has such a lovely discreet exotic flavour that I like serving it with grilled chicken or fish instead of a dish with a lot of sauce, so that the rice can be tasted separately.   *SERVES 6*

8–10 strands saffron
1 rounded teaspoon salt
300ml (½ pint) boiling water
40g (1½oz) creamed coconut
250g (8oz) basmati rice, rinsed and
 soaked in salted water for at least 1 hour
40g (1½oz) butter
1–2 fresh red chillies, stemmed, deseeded
 and chopped finely (page 49)

Put the saffron and the salt in a jug with the boiling water and stir. Crumble in the creamed coconut and stir until dissolved. Cover and set aside for 10 minutes or so to infuse.

Drain the soaked rice. Melt the butter in a large, heavy-based saucepan over a low heat, add the rice and finely chopped chillies and stir. Then pour in the saffron-coconut milk, including every strand of saffron. Bring to the boil, cover the saucepan tightly and reduce the heat to as low as possible for 10–14 minutes until the rice is tender but still has a slight bite to it when tested. Remove the saucepan from the heat.

If you aren't ready to eat immediately, put a cloth between the rice and the lid and leave on top of the stove, with the heat turned off, for up to 20 minutes. To serve fork out the rice on to a warmed serving dish.

KIDNEY BEAN AND GRILLED PEPPER SALAD *(106)*

With its combination of smoky, grilled peppers, this is a salad which can be prepared well ahead. When you can find them, black beans look particularly effective. Cooking dried beans with a selection of herbs and a roughly chopped onion will add to their flavour when you want to use them for a salad, as here. It is much better to put on the dressing while the beans are still hot so that they will absorb it.   *SERVES 6*

250g (8oz) red or black kidney beans,
 soaked overnight in cold water
2 bay leaves
2–3 sprigs rosemary
1 onion, chopped roughly
3 yellow peppers, halved, cored and
 deseeded (page 49)
l bunch spring onions, finely chopped
2 good handfuls flat-leaved parsley,
 chopped roughly
FOR THE VINAIGRETTE
 1 tablespoon sherry vinegar
 2 tablespoons lemon juice
 1 teaspoon caraway seeds
 1 small clove garlic, crushed
 2 teaspoons clear honey
 6 tablespoons extra virgin olive oil
 Salt and black pepper

Drain the soaked beans and put in a saucepan with the bay leaves, rosemary sprigs and roughly chopped onion. Cover generously with water and bring to the boil. Boil for 10 minutes, then lower the heat, cover and simmer very gently for 40–60 minutes, skimming as necessary, until the beans are soft but still holding their shape.

Meanwhile, grill the pepper halves until the skins have blackened (page 55). Wrap them in a tea towel and set aside to cool. Put all the vinaigrette ingredients into a jam jar, cover and shake to mix thoroughly.

When the beans are cooked, drain them, discarding the herbs and onion, and put them in a large bowl. Shake the vinaigrette again and pour over the beans, mixing gently. Set aside to cool.

Meanwhile, peel the grilled peppers and slice thinly. When the beans are coolish, mix in the peppers, chopped spring onions and roughly chopped parsley. Serve the salad warm or at room temperature, not chilled.

FISH and SHELLFISH

Only a short time ago many fishmongers used to say it was not worth their while stocking a wide variety of fish. Customers, they said, dared not budge from old faithfuls such as cod and plaice. Now, happily, more and more kinds of fish are available, including tropical, Mediterranean and freshwater fish, different varieties of smoked fish and fresh shellfish of all kinds. Perhaps because we are more aware of healthy eating, and perhaps because there is an increased interest in cooking, we are beginning to be more imaginative and daring with what fish we buy, and what we do with it. Many people are discovering for the first time in their lives how glorious fish can be.

Fish is exciting to buy because it is so beautiful to look at. I find it almost impossible to pass the fish counter without buying something, even if I have not planned to eat fish that day. Fish is quick and interesting to cook, adapting itself to all sorts of wonderful sauces. The character of fish can become decidedly sophisticated when it is lightly poached with a delicate sauce, or comfortingly homely in something like really good fish cakes or a fish pie. For anyone who insists they hate fish and cannot bear that 'fishy' taste, the more meaty fish now available, like tuna, monkfish, shark and swordfish, are a good way to start converting them.

When shopping for fish the characteristics of freshness are easy to spot. The fish should look as much as possible as if it is still swimming in the sea; shining bright, the gills deep pink to red and the eyes protruding and glossy, never sunken and cloudy. The flesh should be slippery and firm – if you can press it with your finger and it leaves no indentation you can be sure of freshness. Fish should smell of the sea but the smell should never be 'fishy' and strong. The exception to this is skate, which can smell very faintly of ammonia; this fish will be at its sweetest and is more tender about two days after it is caught.

When you are buying fish fillets the flesh should look translucent and succulent with no sign of discoloration. If possible ask the fishmonger to fillet the fish freshly for you, or do it for yourself at home, as fish deteriorates more quickly once it has been filleted.

Different methods of cooking fish produce very different results. Many people are put off trying to cook fish at all because they have chosen a tricky method for their first attempt, with disastrous results. I think the best way to gain the confidence and feeling that is needed to bring out the best in fish is by simply wrapping either a whole fish or steaks in foil with butter, lemon juice and seasoning and baking the package in the oven (page 132). In this way the fish can cook gently and never dries out, while producing a delicious sauce of its own. I still like this way of cooking fish more than any other. When you are much more confident you can try poaching which, as long as the heat is kept low enough, is a wonderfully delicate way of producing supreme texture and taste. Frying fish takes more practice but there are times when one longs for a piece of fried fish – juicy inside and with a golden crust – so it is worth learning how.

To overcook fish is to ruin it; moisture and flavour will be lost and texture destroyed. With such different kinds and shapes of fish, cooking times and methods vary, but the golden rule remains: do not overcook. To tell if a fish is cooked, gently pull back the flesh with a knife: it should be just opaque right through and flake easily. With filleted fish a soft curd-like white substance oozing out is a sign that it is cooked.

Clockwise from top right: with its golden orange top of mashed sweet and ordinary potatoes Golden Fish Pie (page 141) is a variation of the traditional fish pie ; Marinated Scallops with Avocado and Tomatoes (page 138) is a simple summer salad; The Emperor's Fan (page 141) is poached skate wing with a delicate sauce of citrus juices, fresh ginger and coriander leaves; the pretty colours of Stuffed Salmon Fillets with Yellow Pepper and Saffron Sauce (page 140) make it a perfect treat for a dinner party; a fine mixed seafood platter with fresh oysters, mussels and large and small prawns set on crushed ice. Centre: red mullet with their distinctive colour grilled simply with olive oil and fresh herbs.

PREPARING ROUND FISH

Round fish include some of the most familiar fish such as cod, haddock, mackerel and herring, as well as Mediterranean fish like red mullet and tropical fish, such as the beautiful parrot fish with its brilliant colours. As well as an enormous variety of species, there is a wide range of flavours and textures.

Oily round fish, such as mackerel, with pale brown flesh, in particular, are as different to white fish as beef is to chicken. The flesh is richer with a more pronounced flavour which responds well to stronger seasonings and spices, and to full-bodied sauces. All fish are rich in pro-tein, minerals and vitamins, but oily fish have the added bonus of healthy fish oil.

Many round fish are large and often sold cut into steaks or filleted. When possible buy a whole fish and ask for it to be scaled, trimmed, gutted and cut or filleted on the spot, or prepare it yourself at home. With smaller fish that I want to cook whole I always ask the fishmonger to pre-pare and gut the fish, but to leave the head on as I think the appearance is better for serving. Even if you have an obliging fishmonger it is useful to learn the following techniques for times when you are given fresh fish.

SCALING, TRIMMING AND GUTTING

Most fish need scaling, otherwise the scales loosen during cooking and spoil the flesh. But, be warned, scaling is messy and it's best to work at the sink with cold running water and a trap fitted over the plug hole.

Some fish may need additional trimming of fins, tails and heads, although it is quite acceptable to present scaled fish looking more natural. All fish, except for very small fish like whitebait, need gutting. You can do this by slitting the belly or pulling the guts out through the gills.

1 *Cut off all fins. Hold the fish by the tail, gripping with hands dipped in coarse salt, and scrape towards the head using the back of a large knife or a special fish scaler. Rinse frequently under cold running water. Some scales can cut, so take care.*

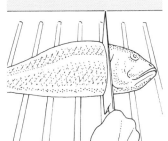

2 *Cut off the head, if desired, just behind the gills. The head can be saved for using in the stockpot (page 31); if you do not want to make stock at the moment, just freeze the head and any other bones until you have more time or need the stock.*

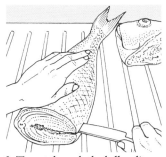

3 *To gut through the belly, slit from the head end to the vent just before the tail, then scrape out the innards. Wash thoroughly and using your finger or a teaspoon, scrape out any dark blood, especially along the backbone, which could make the fish bitter.*

• Fish is a highly perishable food so needs to be kept in peak condition if you are to get the best from it. An attractive, well laid out fish counter indicates a certain amount of care and attention on the part of the fishmonger – someone who cares about what he or she sells and prepares for you.
• Fresh fish have shiny, moist skin and firm flesh. Heads, where left on, will have bright eyes that do not appear sunken, and bright red or pink gills. A really fresh fish will remain stiff when you pick it up.
• White fillets should be a good translucent colour, while smoked fish should look glossy, bright and have a healthy, subtle smoky aroma.

HANDLING SEAFOOD
• After buying fish, simply rinse, pat dry, cover loosely in clingfilm and refrigerate.
• Cook fresh fish within 24 hours of purchase.
• The supply of fresh fish is dependent on a number of variables, not least the weather. If good fresh fish is not available or does not look appetizing, try frozen. Often, as it is frozen at sea within hours of catching, it can be even 'fresher' than some fresh fish.
• Frozen fish should be sold frozen hard in well-sealed, untorn packaging without any ice crystals.
• Thin fillets of frozen fish can be cooked from frozen, but thicker fillets and steaks and also whole fish are best thawed before cooking (page 313).
• Thaw fish either quickly at room temperature and cook immediately, or thaw overnight in the refrigerator. Do not thaw fish in cold water.
• When thawing fish in the refrigerator place it on a large plate with a lip so none of the juices drip on other foods.
• For fast thawing use a microwave on the Defrost (30%) setting, then cook the fish as soon as possible. Watch fish thawing in the microwave so the thin parts do not cook before the other parts thaw.
• While you can freeze freshly caught fresh fish, do not refreeze frozen fish unless it has been thoroughly cooked first, such as in a pie filling.

GUTTING THROUGH THE GILLS
A fish with its head left on and stuffed whole makes an attractive presentation, and for the fish to keep its shape it is gutted through the gills. This technique is also useful if you want the fish to keep its round shape when you cut it into steaks.

To gut through the gills push your finger down inside the fish, through the gills. 'Hook' your finger around the innards, then pull them out and snap off the gills. Rinse the fish out thoroughly with cold running water. Pat dry inside and out with kitchen paper, stuffing it down inside the body cavity and then pulling it out.

FILLETING ROUND FISH

It is easier to fillet round fish before skinning, giving 1 meaty fillet on each side of the backbone. These can then be skinned (right) and coated and fried or cut into strips for goujons, which are simply small pieces of fried fish.

Check that all the small 'pin' bones around the back fins are removed, as these can be annoying to come across when you are eating the fish. Begin by cutting off the head.

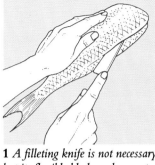

1 *A filleting knife is not necessary but its flexible blade makes neater fillets. Place the fish with its head end away from you and its back towards you. Cut through the backbone down to the tail, keeping the blade as close as possible to the bone.*

2 *Using a gentle sawing motion, starting from the head end, cut the flesh from the fine rib bones. Hold back the freed flesh with one hand and use your other hand to keep the knife's blade scraping back and forth in a gentle sawing motion against the bones, working as quickly as possible. This filleting technique gets easier the more you practise.*

3 *Turn the fish over and remove the fillet from the other side in the same way. Check both fillets for any stray bones and pull them out with your fingers or tweezers. Skin the fillet (right) if you like. Save the bones for making stock (page 31). They can be put in a polythene food bag together with the head and frozen until you wish to make the stock.*

SKINNING FISH FILLETS

Round and flat fish fillets (page 120) are skinned in the same way. Like filleting (left), perfecting this technique really is just a matter of practice.

Lay the fillets skin side down on a board. Dip your fingers in coarse salt for a better grip or hold the tail with a cloth to prevent it slipping away.

Use a large-bladed knife and make a small cut through to the skin at the tail end and loosen the flesh just a little.

Pull the tail skin tight *and, holding the knife at a right angle to the flesh, use a gentle sawing motion to work the knife towards the other end.*

Jock's Grilled Stuffed Mackerel (page 140) has a simple breadcrumb stuffing with chopped almonds and fresh tarragon.

BONING ROUND FISH FOR STUFFING

Stuffing a whole boned round fish makes an interesting and attractive meal. This can either be done by boning from the back (keeping the fish attached at the belly), or, as is more usual, by boning from the belly, shown here. You can either leave the head on or remove, as you like.

Use this technique for herring, mackerel, haddock, whiting and trout. Rinse the fish well with cold running water after boning, taking care to remove all the dark blood along the backbone, which causes a bitter taste.

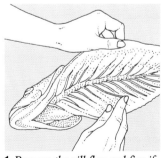

1 *Remove the gill flap and fins if you have not cut off the head. If the fish has not been gutted, cut it along the belly to the tail and open it up. Rinse well with cold running water. Use your fingers or a small sharp knife to free each of the long rib bones.*

2 *When the rib bones are free on each side, run a sharp knife down either side of the backbone, scraping it free of flesh and not cutting through the skin. Make sure all small bones are removed. Along the backbone it is easier to free the flesh with your fingers.*

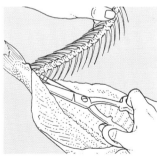

3 *Cut the backbone at each end with a sharp pair of scissors. Lift out the bone and save it for using in the stockpot (page 31), if you like; do not use bones from oily fish, such as mackerel, for making fish stock as the flavour is too strong and the stock could be oily.*

PREPARING FLAT FISH

Flat fish, which include plaice, sole, halibut, turbot and brill, all swim on their side – in fact, rather than swim they mostly lie on the seabed with both eyes on one side of their twisted faces looking for prey. Skates and rays also lie on the seabed and look like flat fish but they are actually cartilaginous fish, related to sharks.

Most flat fish are sold whole or in fillets, but large halibut and turbot can also be cut into steaks.

Flat fish fillets are versatile. They can also be fried gently in butter, cut into strips and sautéed with fresh herbs, ginger or mild spices, covered in a sauce and baked or covered in a light batter and deep fried. Fillets are also ideal for stuffing and rolling, then poaching gently before finally covering with a sauce made with the thickened poaching liquid (page 130). Whole flat fish, because of their characteristic thinness, can also be fried, grilled or baked.

Sole and turbot are the kings of flat fish; they are expensive but you are paying for real quality and a flavour which should never be disguised. Although there are countless recipes for sole, many with elaborate sauces and accompaniments, it is a fish of such delicate, sweet taste and fine, firm texture that it seems a pity to mask it with anything more than lightly seasoned butter or a light creamy sauce. I like sole grilled on the bone best of all and it is the easiest fish there is to separate from its skeleton on your plate. Because of turbot's large size it is less practical to grill, but its flesh is sweet, firm, moist and beautifully white. You can buy fillets or steaks and simply grill or poach them.

FILLETING FLAT FISH INTO FOUR FILLETS

A flat fish on the fish counter, complete with skin and head, can be a somewhat daunting sight if you are unsure of how to prepare it for the table. The price per pound is less than ready prepared fillets, so it can be worth doing the preparation yourself. You can either cut the fish into 4 fillets, 2 from the top and 2 from the underside, as shown here, or 2 large fillets, one each from the top and the underside, as shown opposite.

Flat fish have a light side and a dark side that provides good camouflage against inquisitive predators. When filleting flat fish, it is easiest to cut the fillets from the skeleton first and then skin them if you want. Use the same technique for skinning flat fish fillets as for round fish fillets (page 119).

A filleting knife is not absolutely necessary, but its flexible thin, blade makes the job easier than if you use a cook's knife with its firm blade.

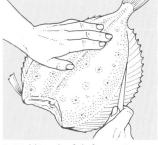

1 *Place the fish head towards you. Remove the head, cutting in a half circle just behind the gills, which removes all the insides from a flat fish. Discard the innards which are much smaller in a flat fish than a round one but save the head for the stockpot (page 31).*

2 *Holding the fish firm so it doesn't slide about, slice around the edge of the flesh where it meets the fins to cut an outline for the fillets. It is not necessary to cut off the fins. Slice along the backbone from the head end to the tail, cutting down to the bone.*

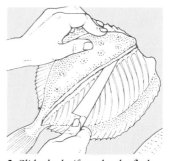

3 *Slide the knife under the flesh, almost flat along the rib bones. Use a gentle sawing motion to cut away the first fillet, keeping the knife as flat as possible and scraping firmly against the bones. Repeat this action on the other side of the backbone, to remove the second fillet.*

4 *To remove the remaining fillets, turn the fish over and repeat steps 2 and 3, making 4 fillets in total. If you want, remove both the dark and light skins from the fillets or just the dark upper skin if you are pressed for time (page 119). Save the skeleton for using in the stockpot (page 31).*

A fillet of plaice can be coated in batter and deep fried quickly in oil so it becomes golden and crisp on the outside and the flesh remains moist and juicy on the inside.

FILLETING INTO TWO FILLETS

For more generous-looking helpings keep the top and bottom fillets whole. This technique requires more practice than the technique for making 4 fillets (opposite).

Cut the head behind the gills and remove. Make a slit across the tail end and slice around the edge of the flesh where it meets the fins. Insert the knife flat along the backbone between the rib bones and flesh. Use a sawing motion to cut to one side, keeping the knife flat .

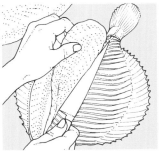

Take the knife back to the backbone and repeat on the other side, making 1 large fillet. To make the second fillet, turn the fish over and use the same procedure on the other side.

SKINNING A WHOLE FLAT FISH

This technique requires a great deal of strength, but it does yield a skinned whole fish suitable for boning and stuffing, as shown below. Alternatively, remove only the top dark skin and then shallow fry the fish (page 128) so the unskinned side has a crispy finish.

It is easiest to skin the smaller flat fish, such as plaice and sole, by this method. Turbot and halibut will be more difficult because of their large size.

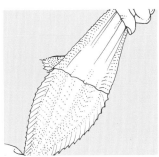

Cut a nick at the tail end. Hold the tail firmly with fingers wrapped in a cloth or dipped in salt. With your other hand, hold the skin and pull it back towards the head end in one swift tear.

POCKET-BONING A FLAT FISH FOR STUFFING

Medium to large flat fish, such as sole and plaice, can be partially skinned, boned and left whole for stuffing, and then either baked as here, or crumbed and fried (page 128).

Remove the head and gills (opposite). Trim the fins, if you like, and remove the dark skin (above).

To make the stuffing for 4 sole, cut 2 carrots, 2 well-washed leeks and 1 small bulb fennel into matchsticks, then stir-fry in 75g (3oz) butter with 2 teaspoons grated fresh ginger for 2 minutes. Add 3 tablespoons dry sherry and cook for 2 more minutes. Season well.

Any variety of ingredients can be used to make a stuffing for pocketed fish. Here, stir-fried ginger-flavoured vegetables are used, and the fish is served with boiled new potatoes with thyme.

1 Cut down one side of the backbone on the skinned side, starting 1cm (½in) from head end. Cut the flesh away in a sawing motion, keeping the knife flat to the rib bones. Do not remove the fillets. Repeat along the other side of the backbone.

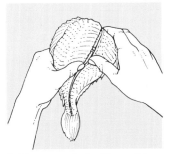

2 To remove the backbone slide the knife in from the head end between the flesh and the backbone, to loosen the flesh on the other side of the bones. Fold the fish over and crack the bone in 2 or 3 places to make it easier to remove.

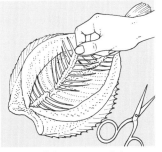

3 Snip all the way round the edges of the bones and across the tail and head ends of the backbone with small scissors. Using your fingers, pull the backbone and rib bones out and discard. Double check that no small stray bones are still in the flesh.

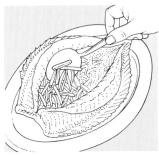

4 Divide the stuffing between the boned sole. Place in a roasting tin, cover with foil and bake at 180°C, 350°F, Gas Mark 4 for 20 minutes. Serve with the cooking juices blended with a little cream and spooned on top, if you prefer a richer sauce.

PREPARING MOLLUSCS

It is extremely important that all seafood is fresh when you buy it and particularly so with molluscs, the group of shell-fish which includes mussels, scallops, oysters, clams and cockles. To ensure freshness the shells should be tightly closed before eating raw or cooking, or, if the shells are open, they should close quickly when tapped. Discard any that remain open or have cracked shells.

Scallops are often sold shelled, but if you can get them in the shell, use the shells as serving containers. I have never understood why many chefs do not use the scallop's orange 'coral' – I think it is just as delicious as the white part, with its contrasting rich taste and smooth texture.

Some people, including my husband, are passionate about oysters – if he wants a real treat oysters will be top of

his list. Pacific oysters are the most readily available and are cheaper than the smooth-shelled native variety which are said by some to be superior. Nowadays, the high price of oysters makes people think it a shame to cook them so their flavour and texture are not fully appreciated. To eat them raw, just hold your head back and slip the oyster and juices down your throat, with or without chewing. The choice is yours.

Clams are becoming more available and are a delightful surprise and easy to prepare. Cockles are hardly ever sold fresh in their shells and if you do find them you should treat them like mussels, though you will have to wash them far more thoroughly as they are apt to be full of sand. Most cockles are usually sold preserved in vinegar.

MOULES MARINIÈRE

Mussels are richly flavoured, succulent and not expensive. The golden rule is to discard any not tightly closed or that do not close when tapped before cooking, and any that remain closed after cooking. Simply steam mussels until their shells open up.

This is my version of *moules marinière*, the classic dish of steamed mussels with flavoured cooking juices. Allow 500g (1lb) of mussels per person; the shells take up bulk and there will probably be some to discard.

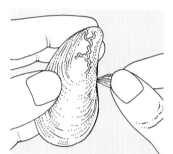

1 *Discard any mussels that are cracked or open and stay open when tapped. Wash the mussels in plenty of cold running water to remove any trapped sand. Scrape off any barnacles, pull off the beards and scrub well.*

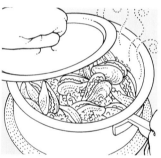

2 *Put 2 chopped shallots and some parsley stalks in a large pan with 300ml (½ pint) dry white wine, black pepper and the mussels. Cover and shake over a high heat until the shells open; it will take less than 2 minutes.*

3 *With a large spoon, transfer the mussels to a colander set over a bowl. Discard any mussels that remain closed. Put the remaining ones into a large warm serving bowl. Cover with foil and keep warm and moist.*

SERVING MOLLUSCS

• A richer version of *moules marinière* (above) can be made by reducing the juices as in step 4, then adding double cream and a little lemon juice, which will also thicken the sauce.
• Alternatively, for extra flavour add chopped garlic at the initial stage of steaming open the mussels.
• A peeled and finely chopped tomato added to the wine will give the resulting sauce a pretty pink tinge.
• Shelled mussels can be added to pasta and the juices reduced with cream to make the sauce.
• 'Stuffed' mussels on the half shell are, in fact, not really

stuffed but covered with a variety of toppings. These can include garlic and parsley butter, cheese and breadcrumbs, or chopped spinach and Parmesan.
• Scallops with their delicate taste are best served simply: they need hardly any cooking and are also excellent served raw as a first course either with a vinaigrette-type dressing, or briefly marinated.
• Scallops are wonderful lightly poached in a little seasoned cream with fresh dill.
• Stir-fry slices of scallop quickly with thin slivers of fresh ginger and a crunchy green vegetable, shredded lettuce, thin slices of

mushrooms or simply a generous handful of fresh herbs.
• Cockles which have not been soaked in vinegar can be used as an alternative to clams in soups like chowder.
• Clams and cockles are excellent with pasta or any seafood mixtures.
• Add clams or mussels at the last moment to any kind of fish stew or soup so they do not overcook.
• All kinds of fresh, tender herbs can be used with seafood. Feathery fennel is a good additional or alternative herb to parsley. Mild spicing with spices such as coriander or fennel seed can also be delicious.

4 *Strain the cooking liquid into a saucepan and reduce over high heat by about one third. Whisk in 50g (2oz) unsalted butter, a large handful of chopped parsley and some black pepper and adjust the seasoning if necessary. Pour over the mussels and serve. Chunks of good crusty bread are the only accompaniment necessary.*

PREPARING SCALLOPS

Scallops, particularly the smaller queens, are available fresh or frozen throughout the year, although they are best bought fresh in their shells.

Scallops have 2 parts – the ivory-coloured main body and orange-pink coral. They can be poached, baked, fried or steamed, and are excellent grilled if you wrap them in derinded bacon rashers before putting under the fierce heat. Take care not to overcook scallops or the sweet white meat will toughen. Add corals at the end of cooking. Scallops are cooked when they turn opaque but are still translucent in the centre.

Served in the half shell on a bed of crushed ice with plenty of lemon wedges, raw oysters make an impressive and wonderful starter for a dinner party.

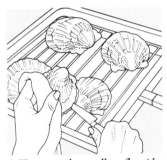

1 To open, place scallops flat side down under a grill or in a warm oven. As soon as the shells open remove the pan from the heat. Insert a sharp knife and cut the muscle which holds the top and bottom shells together. Carefully separate the 2 shells.

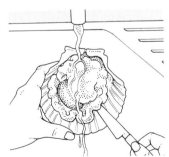

2 Hold the lower shell under cold running water and scrape away the yellow-brown membrane or 'frill'. Discard this and the black intestine, then loosen the flesh and coral; the scallops are ready for cooking. Wash the shells if using as serving containers.

SHUCKING OYSTERS

Live native or European oysters are traditionally available in any month containing the letter 'r'. Farmed Pacific and American oysters are sold throughout the year. Only buy ones with tightly closed shells and keep in a bowl covered with a damp cloth in the refrigerator for up to 2 days. Open the oysters only just before serving or cooking.

Oysters are usually eaten raw, served on a bed of crushed ice with lemon wedges, and either hot pepper sauce to sprinkle on top, or horseradish or Worcestershire sauce. Allow 6–8 oysters per person.

Cooked oysters are usually served on their bottom shell with a sauce or breadcrumb topping. Grill or cook in the oven at 220°C, 425°F, Gas Mark 7 for 2–3 minutes until the edges curl back but the centre is still soft.

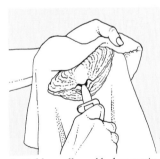

1 Hold a well-scrubbed oyster in a thick cloth, flat side up. Stick an oyster knife, or short-bladed knife, into the hinged edge of the shell, and twist to prise open.

2 Still holding the shell firmly, cut through the muscle and lift off the top shell, taking care not to spill any of the liquid inside.

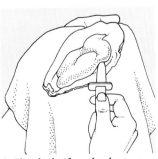

3 Slip the knife under the oyster to separate it from the lower shell, and flip it over still in the shell, if liked, to show the smooth side.

PREPARING CLAMS

Clams vary greatly in size and variety, and, depending on their size, should be dealt with like mussels or oysters.

Smaller clams can be steamed open like mussels and then cooked in a light tomato sauce to make *vongole*, a classic Italian pasta sauce. Larger clams should be treated like oysters and can be eaten raw, although they are also delicious cooked barbecue-style on an open outdoor grill. You can also add them to soups and seafood salads.

To steam small clams, place them in the top of a steamer over boiling water. Cover and steam until the shells open This should not take more than 2 minutes. Discard any that do not open. For extra flavour replace the water with wine or add herbs and lemon slices to the water.

PREPARING CRUSTACEANS

Lobsters, crabs, prawns, shrimps, crawfish and scampi, known collectively as crustaceans, have the sweetest flavour of all shellfish. Some of these are relatively expensive, but if you choose, prepare and present shellfish well the quality of their delicate flesh make them well worth their cost. These shellfish always seem like a real treat.

It is vitally important that shellfish are very fresh as they deteriorate quickly. Shellfish should really smell of the sea and still feel springy within the shell – not limp, which is an indication of staleness. If you buy cooked prawns it is best to buy them in their shell – the shells are, in any case, valuable for making excellent stock (page 31) or for sauce Nantua (page 197). When you are able to buy large prawns and cook them yourself, it is worth the expense because the taste and texture are wonderful. Uncooked prawns and the smaller shrimps look grey when you buy them raw but they become pink when cooked, although the tiny, delectable Morecombe Bay shrimps are brown.

When choosing lobster or crab go by weight rather than size; the size of the shell can be far bigger than the flesh within it which may have shrunk. There should not be any sound of water when you shake a crab. Male crabs and lobsters are larger than the females but females often contain eggs or a coral which tastes wonderful and can also be used for garnishing.

Crab is my favourite shellfish, and it has the great advantage of being comparatively cheap. Picking at a whole freshly cooked crab, simply accompanied by good fresh brown bread and lemon juice or, perhaps, home-made mayonnaise, creates an intimate, friendly atmosphere at a relaxed meal. Ready picked crab meat, both white and brown, can also be bought either fresh or frozen.

PREPARING A CRAB

PREPARING PRAWNS

You can buy whole cooked crabs to prepare at home. Choose one that feels heavy for its size, because it will be full of meat. A dressed crab makes a very special cold dish, with both brown and white meats attractively presented. Each of these meats have very different textures and flavours; the white is sweet and pure, and the brown is rich and creamy. The brown meat is also excellent added to pâtés or sauces. A 500g (1lb) crab serves 1 person as a main course, or 2 people as a starter.

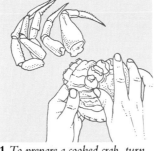

1 *To prepare a cooked crab, turn it on its back and pull off its claws and legs. Discard the legs unless they are big and contain lots of meat. Hold the crab bottom side up and twist off the tail, which you can discard.*

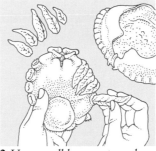

2 *Use a small hammer to crack the shell on the bottom around the body. Pull the central body part out of the shell. Discard the grey lungs which look like tentacles, and pull away the spongy stomach. Discard.*

Half the joy of eating really fresh cooked prawns is in peeling them yourself.

On the fish counter you will find prawns of varying sizes, ranging from the common prawn to the large Dublin Bay prawns. Cooked prawns with their rosy orange shells are ready for eating or using in dishes such as Italian risotto or Spanish paella.

3 *Cut the central body in half with a heavy knife. With a metal skewer scoop out the white meat into a bowl. Using a spoon, scoop out the meat from the main shell, under where the body was, keeping the brown and white meats separate.*

4 *Crack the claws with the hammer and extract any meat with the skewer. Mix brown meat with a little mayonnaise and seasoning and white meat with fresh lemon juice. Arrange separately and serve with brown bread and butter.*

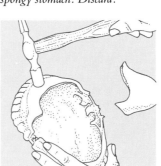

If you want to use *the crab shell as a serving container, lightly tap the line around the opening of the shell with a small hammer or rolling pin and pull away the shell to enlarge the opening. Wash well with soap and hot water, then dry.*

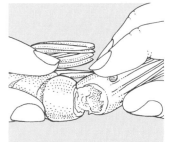

To peel whole prawns *pull the heads from the bodies and discard. Pull off the legs first, then remove the body shell, leaving on the tail if you like. With larger prawns you have to remove the thin black intestinal vein that runs along the back with the tip of a small knife. Sometimes the vein is clearly visible and at other times you have to slice along the whole back to find it and pull it out.*

PREPARING LOBSTER

In season from April to October, a fresh lobster is a real treat and it can usually be bought ready cooked. Be sure to check that both the claws are attached and that the lobster feels heavy for its size. If it is too light it means it is not fresh and the meat has had time to dry up a little. A 1.2kg (2½lb) lobster is ample for 2 servings with homemade mayonnaise (page 202) and a salad of mixed leaves.

You will need a heavy sharp kitchen knife to cut through the shell or you can use a heavy Chinese-style cleaver.

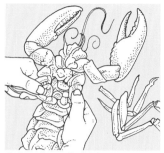

1 *Lay the cooked lobster on its back and pull off the legs and claws. For presentation purposes keep the attractive long wispy antennae. Small legs can be discarded because they do not contain much meat but keep the larger claws.*

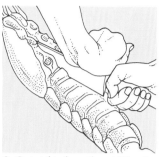

2 *Cut right along the middle of the lobster, stretching out the tail and pressing down firmly on the back of the knife blade. If pressing on the knife back is uncomfortable then press down on a clean, folded cloth.*

3 *Remove the 'sac' at the head end, and the long thin black intestine which runs down to the tail. Discard any feathery gills and stray bony bits, too. The greenish liver, called a tomalley, and the pink coral in the female can be eaten.*

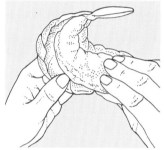

4 *Carefully pull the tail meat out of each lobster half. Clean out and wash the shells with plenty of hot soapy water if you plan to use them for serving. Rinse and dry the shells and arrange them on a bed of pretty salad leaves, ready for filling.*

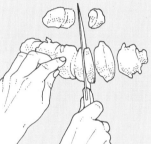

5 *Cut the tail meat neatly into chunks. Any pink coral, which is delicious, can be served on its own or used as a garnish. The tomalley or liver can be mixed with sauce for serving with the lobster meat.*

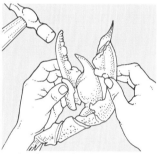

6 *Crack open the claws and pull out the firm pinky white meat. Cut this into chunks and mix with the tail meat. Pile the mixed meat into the shells, adding the antennae, if you like. Garnish with lemon quarters.*

SERVING CRUSTACEANS

• The most obvious way to serve prawns, crab and lobster is to include them in a salad. Arranged among pretty leaves and dressed simply with a good vinaigrette, they look beautiful, and their sweet, delicate flavour can be appreciated for what it is.
• Fresh herbs which go well with shellfish are dill, fennel and coriander.
• Crab meat, both brown and white, makes wonderful sandwiches, particularly if you mix in fresh coriander leaves.
• I like to add crab meat to fish cakes and sauces.
• When adding prawns to fish stew, a sauce or a soup, do so only at the last moment or they will shrink and be tough.
• Prawns, especially the larger ones, and scampi are delicious grilled in their shells and served with really garlicky butter, or shelled and coated first with garlic and fresh herbs, then quickly fried in butter and served with lemon.
• There are many elaborate recipes for lobster but I think that if it is really fresh and meaty it is a pity to mask the flavour with any sauce other than homemade mayonnaise or melted butter, depending on whether you are serving the lobster cold or hot. Add dill to the mayonnaise.

A luxurious individual Scallop, Crab and Prawn Tart (page 139) served with a simple green salad makes a delicious seafood starter or light lunch.

PREPARING SQUID *and* OCTOPUS

Squid are widely available and extremely good, as well as being inexpensive. They are also far easier to prepare and cook than is often imagined. When my children were very young their favourite meal used to be 'squid and chips'. This was after eating it every day in Spain, where they also watched with great fascination the octopuses being beaten on the rocks to make them tender.

Smaller squid are perfectly tender as long as you don't cook them either too long or too fiercely. Slices of squid literally need no more than a minute or two of fairly gentle cooking, just until they turn an opaque white.

I needed no encouragement from my children to cook squid frequently because I love that sweet, clean taste and

texture, and their adaptability to so many flavourings and preparation methods. They are actually far easier to deal with and cook than most other fish and shellfish. If the squid you buy still contains its ink sac intact (this is what holds the ink which the creature squirts out in a thick black cloud if it wants to deter attack), save the rich and flavourful liquid to make a sauce for the squid.

Octopus are tough and need tenderizing before cooking; this is usually done by the fishmonger. Stewed gently and slowly with root vegetables, bulb fennel, tomatoes and lots of garlic, octopus produces an excellent, rich flavour and wonderful juices. I like to sprinkle chopped flat-leaved parsley over the mixture just before serving.

PREPARING SQUID

Don't be alarmed either by the appearance of uncooked squid or by the prospect of preparing them. The removal of the bone and innards is intriguing and, once you know what to do, very easy. It is certainly easier than preparing ordinary fish, and much cleaner and more pleasurable, too.

The most important thing to remember once you have prepared your squid is not to ruin its tender texture by cooking it too long or with too fierce a heat. If deep-frying, the cooking time must be even shorter.

1 *Rinse the squid well. Cut the tentacles away from the head, discarding the beak-like mouth found in the centre of the tentacles, just below the eyes. Reserve the tentacles which can be cooked with the main body meat or finely chopped and mixed with stuffing ingredients.*

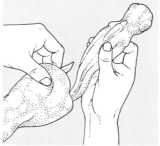

2 *Hold the body of the squid in one hand and pull the head gently with the other hand, which brings out the innards. Discard the head and innards but carefully retain the ink sac if needed in the recipe – it is pearly coloured with a blue tinge. It is often used in pasta sauces.*

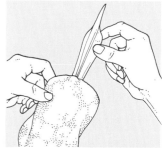

3 *Pull the transparent quill-like bone out from the body pocket and discard. Use your fingers to check for any residual innards and pull out and discard.*

USING SQUID AND OCTOPUS

• I like to stir-fry squid because of the short cooking time. Try squid slices stir-fried with red pepper, broccoli, mange tout and sliced spring greens with ground coriander.
• Squid always makes a fish stew seem more exotic. Add the slices only at the very last minute, just long enough for the heat to turn the pearly flesh an opaque white.
• Pasta with squid is wonderful. While the pasta is cooking toss slices of squid and chopped garlic briefly in a generous mixture of extra virgin olive oil and unsalted butter and stir in

lots of chopped parsley before mixing into the drained pasta.
• If you want to barbecue larger pieces of squid, marinate the pieces in olive oil, lemon juice and herbs or spices for an hour or so beforehand. Grill very briefly over a high heat.
• As well as making an excellent stew, thin slices of octopus can be simmered gently in a little stock or water until very tender – they will turn pink and can be drained, cooled and then dressed with olive oil, lemon juice, garlic, lots of flat-leaved parsley and served as a first course.

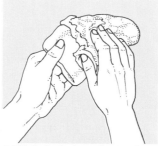

4 *Wash the body pocket inside and out thoroughly under cold running water, getting rid of any traces of innards that may remain. Peel and rub off the purply mottled skin from the outside. Pat dry with kitchen paper.*

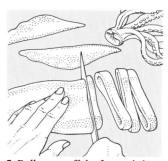

5 *Pull or cut off the fins and slice into strips for cooking with the main body meat. Slice the body across into fairly thin rings or leave whole if stuffing the squid (opposite). Divide the reserved tentacles into 2 or 3 pieces if the squid are fairly large and you are using them for stuffing.*

STUFFING AND COOKING SQUID

You can stuff squid of all sizes; with larger squid slice the stuffed body across in thick slices after cooking, then arrange them on a serving plate surrounded by the sauce. With smaller squid serve a whole one to each person. You can even stuff very small squid and then poach them in a sauce so each serving contains several squid. If you like add the ink sac to the sauce you cook the squid in, to make it rich and black.

Clean and prepare the squid (opposite), leaving the bodies whole. Chop up the fins and tentacles to use in the stuffing.

To make the stuffing for 4 small to medium-sized squid, put 3 tablespoons olive oil in a frying pan over a medium heat. Add 2 large finely chopped cloves of garlic, a finely chopped 2.5cm (1in) piece of fresh root ginger and the chopped squid fins and tentacles, then stir for 1 minute only. Stir in 50g (2oz) can finely chopped anchovies, 250g (8oz) blanched and finely chopped spinach, 2 tablespoons fresh brown breadcrumbs and remove from the heat. Season with salt and freshly ground black pepper to taste.

Squid Rings with Leeks and Spinach (page 139) on a dramatic bed of red sauce.

1 *To stuff squid, spoon an equal amount of stuffing into each one, taking care not to fill them so full that they burst during cooking. For smaller squid you may find it easier to press the stuffing into the body cavity through a plastic funnel, or use a piping bag without the nozzle attached.*

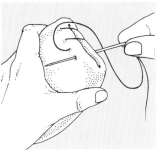

2 *Sew the ends up, using a trussing needle and kitchen string, or secure with wooden cocktail sticks. Put 2 tablespoons olive oil and 25g (1oz) butter in a flameproof casserole over a medium heat. Add 2 finely chopped large cloves of garlic and 1 small deseeded and chopped red pepper. Stir for 1 minute.*

3 *Add 397g (14oz) can chopped tomatoes, 1 tablespoon tomato purée, 4 tablespoons fresh orange juice, salt and pepper. Add the stuffed squid, cover and simmer very gently for 35–45 minutes until tender. Place the squid in a serving dish. Stir plenty of chopped parsley into the sauce and serve with the squid.*

PREPARING OCTOPUS

Most of the octopuses sold today have already been cleaned and tenderized. They can become tough when cooked, so try to find the variety with small heads and long tentacles as these are generally the most tender. If the octopus is not already cleaned you will have to gut it, remove the eyes, beak and skin and tenderize it before cooking, as shown here.

Octopuses can be fried, stuffed and stewed or grilled over a barbecue. Little ones are best fried in olive oil.

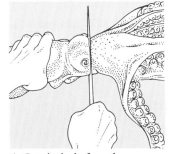

1 *Cut the body from the tentacles, and discard the contents of the body sac, including the innards and ink bag, if you are not using it for a sauce.*

2 *Push the body inside out and cut away the eyes and beak and discard. Wash the head and tentacles under cold water, then blanch them in boiling water for 5–10 minutes.*

3 *Drain and rinse well under cold water, then peel off the skin and the thin membrane underneath. Tenderize the octopus by beating it against the sink or on a large chopping board about 40 times. It is now ready for cooking.*

FRYING

Frying fish can produce delicious results when carefully and attentively. For small fish and fillets, shallow frying (also called pan frying), sautéing or stir-frying are the quickest and simplest methods to do at home. Deep-frying in breadcrumbs, seasoned flour or batter, however, produces irresistible results; a crisp crunchy coating on the outside, succulent fish on the inside.

Batters are useful for protecting deep-fried food during cooking. The correct temperature of oil is important in frying, especially deep-frying. If the temperature is too low the coating will not seal and will break up, and if it is too high the outside will burn before the inside is cooked. It is important to reheat oil between batches.

For sautéing and stir-frying, which involves constant stirring, use even-sized pieces of close-textured firm fish. Monkfish, tuna, shark and prawns are among the best.

As with all frying remember to watch the stove constantly and adjust the temperature when necessary.

SHALLOW FRYING

For shallow frying use vegetable oil or concentrated butter for cooking or make your own clarified butter (page 96). Both butters are good to use because they have no sediment to burn, while ordinary butter is unsuitable unless it is mixed with oil.

Use any thin fillet of fish, preferably skinned, or cut across into strips for goujons. A crisp homemade breadcrumb coating, ideal for shallow frying, is delicious and quite simple. Prepare three plates – one with seasoned flour, another with beaten egg and the third with dried breadcrumbs.

1 *Dip the fish pieces in the flour, then in the egg and finally in the crumbs, making sure the fish is well coated. Shake off the excess. Chill for 10–20 minutes.*

2 *Heat enough oil in a frying pan to cover the base by 5mm (¼in). Fry the fish in a single layer until golden, then turn over and fry the other side. Drain on kitchen paper.*

DEEP-FRYING

Fish coated in batter and fried quickly in hot deep oil is light and the flavour of the fish is preserved. The choice of oil is important not only for the flavour but also because the higher the temperature an oil can reach without developing a 'burnt' taste, the better. Vegetable oils are best to use, notably sunflower and groundnut.

For deep-frying fish, the temperature of the cooking oil should be between 180°C and 190°C (350°F and 375°F) or until a cube of white bread browns in about 30 seconds.

To make a simple batter for 4 cutlets or fillets, mix 1 egg and 300ml (½ pint) milk or water with 125g (4oz) seasoned flour until smooth. Milk makes a thicker batter than water.

1 *Prepare the batter and place in a relatively deep bowl. Dip each piece of fish into the batter, then allow the excess batter to drip off. It is best to cook the fish as soon as it is coated, so prepare and dip in batches, depending on how many pieces of fish fit in your frying basket at one time.*

2 *Use a deep heavy-based saucepan only one-third full with oil. Heat the oil steadily to the correct temperature, testing with a deep-frying thermometer or bread cube (above). Place the fish in a frying basket that fits the pan comfortably, then lower it in gently. Cook until golden brown and crisp. Drain the fish well on absorbent kitchen paper and keep it warm in a low oven, until all the pieces have been fried and you are ready to serve.*

*For special occasions these **Salmon Fish Balls** (page 138) make the lightest fish cakes, with no mashed potatoes, just plenty of fish bound together in a rich béchamel sauce.*

PRAWN TEMPURA

Tempura must be one of the most universally popular of all the Japanese dishes – tender morsels of fresh fish and seafood, or vegetables, coated with the lightest batter and deep-fried for only a few minutes.

The secret of a good tempura is to make up the batter just before you use it and not to beat the mixture – it should be made with either a fork or chopsticks and left lumpy. To make the batter, use 1 beaten egg, 75g (3oz) plain flour, 25g (1oz) sifted cornflour and 100ml (4fl oz) water.

Prawn tempura served with an oriental dipping sauce (page 207).

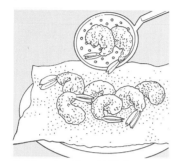

1 *Prepare raw prawns (page 124). Score the undersides so they do not curl during frying. Rinse well and pat dry. Just before frying, dip each prawn in the batter, holding it by its tail and shaking off the excess. Prepare in batches, if necessary.*

2 *Heat the oil to 180°C (350°F) or until a cube of white bread browns in about 30 seconds. Fry the prawns in batches until the batter is pale golden and crisp and bubbling. Drain well on kitchen paper and keep warm until ready to serve.*

FISH CAKES

I adore fish cakes as long as they are made with plenty of fish, never less than the amount of potato, and seasoned well. Use any filleted white fish, mackerel, smoked haddock or cod. A mixture of smoked and unsmoked fish is excellent.

To serve 6, mash together 500g (1lb) boiled potatoes, adding 25g (1oz) butter and set aside. Simmer 500g (1lb) skinned fillets in 150ml (¼ pt) milk in a covered saucepan for about 5 minutes until the fish flakes easily. Strain the milk into the potatoes and mix together. Flake in the fish with 2 tablespoons chopped fresh chives, 1 beaten egg and salt and pepper. Mix well and chill.

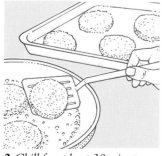

1 *Using floured hands form the mixture into balls about the size of a small orange. Flatten slightly, then brush with a little beaten egg and coat with 50g (2oz) fresh breadcrumbs.*

2 *Chill for at least 30 minutes. Shallow fry in vegetable oil (opposite), turning once until golden brown on each side. Drain on kitchen paper and serve with fresh tomato sauce (page 206).*

FLAVOURING FRIED FISH

• Flour for a coating can be seasoned with herbs and spices.

• Make red devilled fish by adding paprika and cayenne pepper to the coating flour.

• Nutty flavoured oatmeal is the traditional coating for fried herring and mackerel, but you can also use ground nuts, cornmeal, ground rice and semolina, all of which give a nice crunchy crust.

• A basic batter can be varied in many ways, including folding in whisked egg whites for lightness.

• Beer in a batter in place of the water or milk, and sometimes in place of the eggs, produces a lightness with a slightly bitter tang. I find it enhances the taste of the fish.

• Whole spices such as fennel, dill and caraway seeds are effective in various batters for deep-fried fish, as are herbs.

• Add colour and spice to a batter by adding paprika or turmeric with other ground spices.

• Fish cakes are nicest coated with coarsely crumbled fresh white breadcrumbs.

• The mixture for the fish cakes themselves can vary as far as your imagination takes you. Mashed salt cod (page 137) makes very good fish cakes.

• Flavour fish cakes with either saffron, capers, crushed garlic, grated lemon rind, spices such as cardamom, coriander, cumin and turmeric, fresh herbs or chopped spring onions.

• Fish cakes made in a saffron-flavoured béchamel sauce (page 196) are light and sophisticated enough to serve as a starter.

• Finely chopped hard-boiled eggs, anchovies or firm tomatoes can also add interest to a fish cake mixture.

• I sometimes add some nut-flavoured oils to vegetable oil when frying for extra flavour. Try hazelnut or walnut oil.

• Bacon or duck fat both add a delicious flavour to any fish fried in it.

POACHING *and* STEAMING

The important thing about poaching as a cooking method is its gentleness. It achieves exquisite results of succulent, tender, evenly cooked fish. Poaching means cooking in a liquid, but it must never mean boiling; if fish is agitated in bubbling liquid the flesh begins to fall apart, succulence escapes, tenderness is lost and the appearance is destroyed. The very most that the liquid should do is just to tremble on the surface. There shouldn't be any bubbles.

When poaching whole large fish you will need a receptacle big enough, ideally a fish kettle (page 18). If you are going to eat fish cold you should start it in cold liquid and bring it slowly up to just bubbling; then, after about 1 minute, remove it from the heat and leave it to become completely cold in the liquid. For eating hot, poach the fish, let it sit in the hot water for 15–20 minutes, then test to see if it is done by inserting a thin skewer or trussing needle; if it meets no resistance in the flesh it will be ready. The fish will feel firm if you press it lightly with your finger.

Steaming, as well as poaching, is a healthy, virtually fat-free way of cooking. Many types of inexpensive steamer are sold, including the excellent tiered Chinese baskets and a steaming rack to fit inside a wok.

Lightly steamed green vegetables and poached Fillets of Cod with Creamy Prawn and Dill Sauce (page 141) make a luxurious main course for a dinner party.

POACHING FISH

Cutlets or fillets should be poached in a court bouillon (page 30), then after poaching, use the liquid to make a delicate sauce; strain and reduce the liquid, then whisk in small pieces of unsalted butter for extra richness.

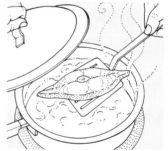

1 *Place the fish in barely simmering, just trembling, liquid to cover in a shallow pan that holds the fish in a single layer. Cover and poach for 5–10 minutes, depending on the thickness of the fish.*

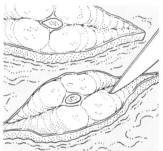

2 *When cooked, the fish will be opaque and the flesh will flake if tested with the tip of a knife. Drain well on kitchen paper. Keep covered and warm in a low oven while you make a sauce out of the poaching liquid.*

SHAPING FISH FILLETS

Skinned fillets (page 119) can be rolled or folded into various shapes before poaching or steaming. Put the skinned side on the inside for a neater appearance when serving.

Enclosing a contrasting stuffing adds flavour and colour. Although the fillets can be cooked plain, a stuffing, which can be as simple as chopped herbs and melted butter, helps compensate for the loss of flavour when the flesh is removed from the bones.

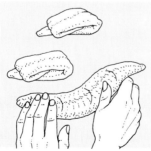

A very simple *presentation is to fold a fillet in half, tucking in the thin end. Lightly slash the skinned inside before folding, so the flesh does not contract during cooking and lose its shape.*

A 'turban' *is half a flat fish fillet rolled from the wide end to the thin end. Secure with wooden cocktail sticks or poach the 'turbans' close enough together so they do not uncurl during cooking.*

Two long thin *fillets of contrasting coloured fish, such as salmon and lemon sole, look striking twisted together like a barley sugar twist. Secure with cocktail sticks for poaching.*

STEAMING FISH

Steaming is a delicate way of cooking, ideal for cooking fish, but steamed fish can taste bland. To avoid this, lay flavourings such as herbs and vegetables underneath the fish and sprinkle other aromatics over the top. The fish can also be lightly marinated before steaming to add extra flavour.

If you want, after steaming reduce the liquid slightly to thicken and make a sauce for the fish. Or, you can serve the fish simply sprinkled with flavourings, such as fresh herbs, lemon juice or soy sauce. Pieces of steamed fish are also excellent cooled and then used in salads.

Delicate shellfish *such as scallops are ideal for steaming. Less gentle methods can make scallops tough, while steaming leaves them tender. Place the shelled scallops in a steamer over bubbling water, cover and steam for 2–3 minutes until opaque but still translucent in the centres and just lightly firm to the touch.*

Use 2 heatproof plates *to make an impromptu steamer for cooking thin fillets. Place a fillet over some herbs, if you like, on a lightly buttered heatproof plate. Cover with the second plate, turned upside down. Place over a saucepan of boiling water and steam for 5–10 minutes until the flesh flakes lightly.*

PERKING UP POACHED AND STEAMED FISH

• For someone on a diet, pieces of fish steamed with fresh ginger and served with soy sauce and crisp bean sprouts should not provoke complaints of deprivation.
• Flavourful quick sauces for poached or steamed fish can by made by reducing the poaching or steaming liquid and then whisking in butter or adding flour and egg yolks to thicken.
• You can also add cream to reduced cooking juices, or, if you want a low-fat sauce, use Greek yogurt, but make sure you don't boil the sauce or the yogurt will curdle.
• A mixture of natural yogurt and fromage frais makes a thicker sauce.
• Bland fish which has been given added flavour by being poached in a court bouillon (page 30) is excellent to use for fish cakes – then you can keep the court bouillon for soup or

reduce it and freeze it in ice cube trays in order to have a concentrated stock for sauces and soups at any time.
• Cold poached fish is most often served with mayonnaise, and you can vary this by adding fresh herbs such as dill, fennel and tarragon, a little cooked and well-drained spinach purée to make it green, sun-dried tomato paste and tomato purée, or spicy Indian paste, such as tikka paste, or even lime pickle and mango chutney.
• If time is short use a good commercial brand of mayonnaise mixed with whipped cream and well seasoned.
• For both poached and steamed fish fresh tomato sauces are excellent, or sauces made with puréed peppers and other vegetables. Steamed fish pieces can be mixed into these thick sauces, then spooned into a dish and sprinkled with herbs.

HEARTY FISH STEW

In this stew, all the ingredients except the fish and tarragon are cooked first, then these are added so the fish is gently poached only for the last few minutes of the cooking time.

To serve 4 people, you will need 500g (1lb) peeled and chopped potatoes, 3 sliced garlic cloves, 2 bay leaves, 5 skinned and chopped tomatoes, 1 sliced yellow pepper, 4 tablespoons lemon juice, 150ml (¼ pint) cider, 4 tablespoons olive oil, 500–625g (1–1¼lb) skinned and filleted white fish, cut into large chunks, 1 tablespoon chopped fresh tarragon, salt and pepper.

1 *Mix together the potatoes, garlic, bay leaves, tomatoes and yellow pepper in a large saucepan or flameproof casserole. Season and pour over the lemon juice, cider and olive oil. Cover and cook gently for about 30 minutes until the potatoes are tender.*

2 *Carefully add the fish to the pan with the tarragon, cover again and gently poach over a low heat for 5–10 minutes until the fish is just opaque and flakes when tested with the tip of a knife. Serve at once, ladling into individual bowls.*

To make this simple hearty fish stew, fillets of monkfish are set on a bed of vegetables and poached in cider with chopped fresh tarragon and bay leaves.

BAKING *and* GRILLING

If you are nervous about cooking fish the most uncomplicated and foolproof method is baking. Baking is a loose term generally meaning to cook in the oven; it can mean that the fish is wrapped in greaseproof paper or foil or that you bake it in a dish, basting with the juices. Bake large fish at a lower temperature and small fish at a higher one because then the cooking time is so short that they will not have time to dry out.

Steaks or pieces of meaty fish such as tuna, shark and swordfish can be cooked gently and comparatively slowly in a covered casserole with vegetables all round them to make a complete and full-flavoured dish. Whole fish can be stuffed with all sorts of good things or simply a bunch of

fresh herbs which flavour the flesh during baking.

Grilling brings out the real flavour of fish in a unique way, and can be done either under or over a fierce heat. The flavour imparted to fish grilled over charcoal or some aromatic wood is best of all. Oily fish such as mackerel or herring, and larger fish like salmon and bass which have full, rich flavours, are specially good for grilling. Large uncooked prawns cooked in their shells and basted with garlicky oil are wonderful.

All fish, whether whole, steaks or fillets should be basted several times during grilling to keep them moist. Use either the fish juices which collect beneath the fish, or spoon or brush over a marinade when you are barbecuing.

PAN-BAKED FISH

This style of baked fish can be a complete meal if it is cooked with vegetables, or you can just cook the fish in a little wine with olive oil, which effectively bastes the fish.

Cook stuffed whole fish (pages 119 and 121) or steaks in this way, but medium-sized steaks should be covered with foil to keep the moisture in. Large fish won't dry out so they don't need covering.

Place sliced, skinned tomatoes, mushrooms and thinly sliced onions in a buttered ovenproof dish, and season well. Rub the fish with butter and seasoning and place on top of the vegetables.

Add 175ml (6fl oz) *white wine and 3–4 tablespoons of olive oil and season with salt and pepper. Cover the dish loosely with foil and bake at 180°C, 350°F, Gas Mark 4 for 30–40 minutes for a medium-sized fish. The fish is cooked when the flesh looks opaque and flakes easily when tested with the tip of a knife.*

FOIL-BAKED FISH

After preparing the fish (right), lay the foil package on a large baking sheet and bake steaks at 150°C, 300°F, Gas Mark 2 for about 15 minutes or until firm to the touch. Bake whole fish at the same oven temperature for 12 minutes per 500g (1lb) for fish between 1–2.5kg (2–5lb) in weight and 8 minutes per 500g (1lb) for fish over 2.5kg (5lb) in weight. After cooking leave the fish in the foil for a few minutes before serving with the cooking juices.

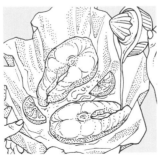

Generously butter *a piece of foil. Dot the fish with butter and seasonings such as herbs and lemon slices. Bring the foil up round the fish, add the juice of 1 lemon and wrap up securely.*

BAKING FISH IN PAPER CASES

Chunky fillets or steaks of fish are delicious baked in greaseproof paper or foil with knobs of butter, sprigs of fresh herbs, wafer-thin strips of vegetables or toasted split almonds and splashes of wine, sherry or vermouth.

The fish makes its own delicious juices while it cooks, then the parcels are unwrapped at the table by each diner. As each parcel is opened it releases the most wonderful aroma.

Either simply wrap up in rectangles of greaseproof paper with a double fold on top, tucking the sides under, or try this more striking presentation.

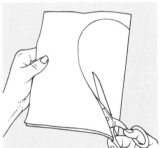

1 *Fold a square of greaseproof paper in half and cut out a half heart, which when opened out forms a heart shape large enough to comfortably enclose the fish and any flavourings. Lightly brush the paper with melted butter or olive oil. (To cut out a number of hearts at once, fold several pieces of paper together.)*

2 *Place the fish steak or fillet on one side of the paper heart, with any finely chopped vegetables, almonds and/or fresh herbs as you like. Season to taste with salt and freshly ground black pepper. For extra flavouring, 1 tablespoon of dry white wine or vermouth can be added as well, if you like.*

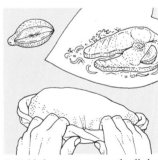

3 *Fold the paper over and roll the sides in on themselves to seal in the juices. Place on a baking sheet and bake at 190°C, 375°F, Gas Mark 5 for about 20 minutes until the fish is cooked. Check by pressing the fish through the paper with your finger; it should be just firm.*

FLAVOURING BAKED AND GRILLED FISH

• You can transform the character of baked fish very easily by varying the flavours you add. The combination of tomatoes for their sweetness and lemon juice for its sharpness is always good, especially if it mingles with some well-flavoured olive oil.

• A sprinkling of finely chopped garlic and fresh ginger is a favourite combination for baked fish in my family.

• Ground spices or Indian curry pastes can be smeared all over the outside of the fish, and into gashes in the skin before baking. If you do this it is a good idea to wrap the fish and leave it to absorb the seasoning for a few hours before cooking.

• I like spiced grilled fish with fresh coriander butter.

• Robust whole fish can also be stuffed before baking. Chopped vegetables such as onions, leeks, peppers, aubergines and mushrooms should be softened first in butter or oil and cooled before spooning inside the fish and then baking.

• Chopped nuts, particularly hazelnuts, and chopped black olives and anchovies are a good addition to a stuffing for grilled or barbecued fish.

• Add chopped ready-to-eat dried apricots to stuffing for mackerel and herring for a sweet-and-sharp taste.

• Fresh apricots and gooseberries contribute their lovely juices to the sauce surrounding a foil-baked fish.

BUTTERFLYING PRAWNS

Butterflying large uncooked Mediterranean and Dublin Bay prawns is an attractive way to prepare them for grilling or barbecuing. The prawn is opened flat to expose the translucent and pale grey flesh which turns white during cooking.

To keep the prawns flat while cooking, skewer several prawns side by side on soaked long wooden sticks with 1 stick just above the tail ends and another near the head ends. Alternatively, coat the butterflyed prawns in breadcrumbs or cornmeal and then shallow fry (page 128) so they curl slightly.

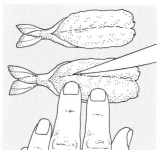

To butterfly a prawn *take off the head and remove the shell (page 124). Cut along the outer curve from the head end to the tail, leaving the tail intact and without cutting all the way through. Flatten and use the tip of the knife to remove the black intestine that runs along the length of the prawn's back.*

GRILLING FISH

To preserve succulence and fresh flavour fish should never be grilled for too long: the grill must be preheated and very hot so as to cook the fish swiftly, producing tender flesh and a crisp outside.

To grill fillets, the flesh side should always be grilled first, and thick fillets or steaks are the most successful. With a large whole fish it is best to make deep, slanting cuts in the skin at 2.5–5cm (1–2in) intervals so the heat penetrates all the way through the flesh, cooking it evenly.

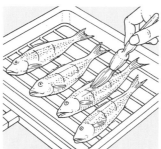

To grill fish *brush the rack with oil, then brush the fish before cooking so the flesh remains moist and the skin crisps. Carefully turn the fish over halfway through the estimated cooking time and brush again.*

BARBECUING FISH

For successful barbecuing choose rich-flavoured or meaty fish such as mackerel, sardines, shark, tuna, salmon, monkfish or bass.

With large fish you can leave the scales on so the skin is protected, then lift off the skin in one piece after cooking. Another trick is to wrap the fish in wet newspaper; then when the paper is peeled off after cooking the skin comes with it. White fish cubes can be wrapped in bacon if being made into kebabs so they don't fall apart.

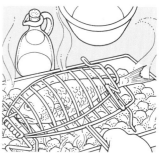

Use a fish rack *for easy turning of whole fish during barbecuing. Oil the rack thoroughly before use, then place the fish in it, with some herbs either side, if liked. Put the rack on the barbecue grill, turning once halfway through cooking.*

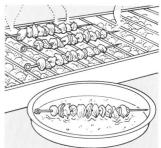

To make kebabs *cut the fish into 3–5cm (1½–2in) pieces, then marinate in a mixture of lemon juice, oil and seasonings for at least 30 minutes. Skewer and cook on an oiled rack, turning 2 or 3 times until the flesh flakes.*

Grilled Grey Mullet in a Spiced Coating (page 140) makes a fine sight and is easy to prepare.

SALMON *and* SALMON TROUT

It seems only a few years ago that salmon ranked with lobster as one of the fish 'treats' for special occasions. Now, as a result of being farmed very successfully on a large scale, it is becoming cheaper than many other fish and is available, of consistently good quality, all year round.

Between February and August wild salmon is sometimes available; its flesh is a much paler pink, delicate and succulent, and should be cooked very simply to make the most of its flavour and texture.

Salmon trout is a family of several species of brown trout which, like salmon, leave their rivers for the open sea and develop pink flesh – though not as orangy pink as salmon – as a result of the crustaceans they eat. Salmon trout is one of my favourite fish, even more smooth fleshed and moist than salmon, paler pink and less oily. Salmon trout is smaller than salmon with a more rounded stomach and stubbier tail.

Both salmon and salmon trout can be cooked in the same way; whole or cut into steaks or fillets, and served hot or cold. They are delicious baked or poached whole, but large steaks or fillets are also excellent grilled. The one thing to guard against, as with all fish, is overcooking. When perfectly cooked the pale pink flesh will still be slightly dark towards the centre, but will come away from the bone easily.

POACHING AND SERVING A WHOLE SALMON

Especially if you are going to eat salmon cold I think this is the best way to produce cooked but still extremely moist flesh, particularly next to the bone. The poaching liquid can either be a flavoured court bouillon (page 30), or simply salted water as salmon has such a unique flavour of its own.

Because salmon is a rich fish, 125–175g (4–6oz) per person is an adequate portion. When calculating what size fish to buy don't forget the head, tail, bones and entrails amount to about 500g (1lb) wastage during cleaning.

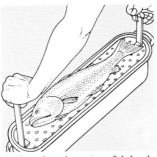

1 *Place the salmon in a fish kettle and cover with cold poaching liquid. Cover and bring to the boil on top of the stove. Poach for 1 minute for fish up to 2.5kg (5lb) and 2 minutes for larger fish. To serve hot, leave it for 15–20 minutes. To serve cold, leave the fish overnight in the liquid.*

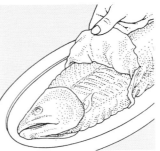

2 *Remove the fish from the kettle. To skin, score around the head and gills, then around the tail with a sharp knife. Carefully peel back the skin in long strips and discard. Scrape off any brown spots with the back of a knife, without disturbing the pink flesh underneath.*

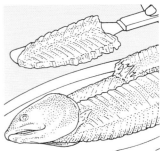

3 *To serve hot or cold salmon, cut along the backbone, then carefully slide a thin-bladed knife under the flesh to separate it from the rib bones. Use a fish server to lift off individual portions. After the top half of the fish has been served, lift off the bones and discard. Continue with remaining fish.*

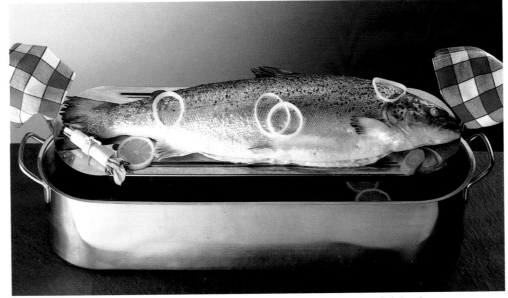

A whole poached salmon with flavourings ready to serve after cooling in a fish kettle.

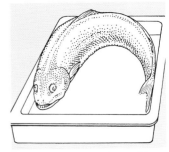

Use a roasting tin *for poaching a whole salmon if you do not have a fish kettle (page 18). Place the fish in a half-moon position and pour in the poaching liquid. Cover with foil and cook as in step 1 (above). After cooking, skin the fish. Serve hot salmon simply garnished with lemon and cold salmon on a bed of shredded lettuce leaves.*

BAKING SALMON

Whole gutted salmon and salmon trout can also be baked in the oven, wrapped in a well-buttered sheet of foil like other fish (page 132). If serving hot, smear generously with butter which will mingle with the fish juices and a little lemon juice to produce a good sauce. If you want to serve the fish cold, however, smear the foil with olive oil instead of butter before baking because butter leaves a cloying taste when cold.

Leave the fish in the foil for 10 minutes after cooking and before serving. If you plan to eat the fish cold, it will be easiest to remove the skin while it is still warm.

MARINATING RAW SALMON

Now that gravad lax (below) is beginning to rival smoked salmon and there are more Japanese restaurants serving sashimi (thinly sliced raw fish), people are getting used to the idea of eating raw fish. Lightly marinated raw salmon can be delicious, as it has such a smooth, dense texture. To marinate salmon begin a few hours before serving and use olive or hazelnut oil and lemon juice, a wine or spirit, such as brandy, plus seasoning.

Salmon for eating raw should be the freshest fish possible. Serve it filleted, skinned and thinly sliced on a plate with salad leaves. Or, serve with soy sauce and Japanese horseradish (wasabi) powder mixed to a paste for dipping the salmon in. For something a bit adventurous serve marinated raw fish as a main course with warm new potatoes and spinach.

GRAVAD LAX

Gravad lax is a wonderful Scandinavian way of mildly pickling raw salmon, and is extremely easy to prepare at home. A salmon tail piece (approximately 1kg/2lb), cut into two pieces, will produce a considerable amount. Serve with plenty of brown bread and a sweetened mustard and dill-flavoured mayonnaise (page 202). The salmon should be filleted but left unskinned.

SERVING SALMON

• A rich homemade mayonnaise (page 202) is the classic sauce for cold salmon, but you can vary it in many ways by adding herbs, crushed garlic, spices and other flavourings. The most effective fresh herbs for fish are dill, fennel, tarragon, basil, lovage and chervil, and chopped blanched watercress. A purée of cooked and well-drained spinach and sorrel produces a really green mayonnaise.

• Thick Greek yogurt with whipped cream and any of the above flavourings also makes a good sauce for cold salmon.

• Of course, you can serve non-mayonnaise type sauces with cold salmon, too; skinned chopped tomatoes cooked to a mush in olive oil with the addition of garlic and a little sherry or balsamic vinegar, and served cold, is excellent.

• For an oil-based green sauce you can use blanched and chopped spinach and sorrel with extra virgin olive oil.

• An easy sauce to make to serve with poached salmon is puréed avocado with lemon juice, a little oil and seasoning.

• Make salmon tartare the same way as steak tartare, mixing finely chopped raw salmon with olive oil, capers and herbs. Add some finely chopped onion as well, if you like.

• Flavoured butters melt delectably on to hot salmon. Try butter softened with fresh parsley or other herbs, pounded anchovies, lemon rind and juice, crushed garlic or mustard.

• Peeled whole garlic can be sautéed gently until soft, golden and sweet and then puréed and stirred into cream to be heated and seasoned for an easy sauce to serve with salmon.

• Hollandaise sauce (page 200) is a favourite with me and can have many of the flavourings suggested for mayonnaise (left) added to it.

• Smoked salmon is also effective as a wrapping for fish pâtés or terrines or for stuffings of shellfish, or vegetables such as spinach or broccoli.

• Make scrambled eggs for a special occasion with slivers of smoked salmon stirred in at the last moment. Dill or chives are good flavourings for the eggs.

• Pasta with cream and slivers of smoked salmon tossed in at the last moment is a dreamy dish.

SLICING SMOKED SALMON

Although smoked salmon is expensive, a little goes a long way. Good-quality smoked salmon should be quite oily, slightly sweet and have a peachy pink colour. Sliced smoked salmon is readily available but if you are serving it for large numbers it is more economical to buy a whole side and slice it yourself. Serve with lemon wedges and brown bread and butter.

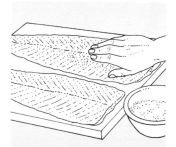

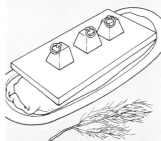

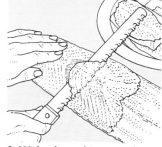

1 *Mix together 1½ tablespoons each crushed sea salt and caster sugar and 1 teaspoon crushed peppercorns. Rub the mixture in to the flesh of both salmon pieces and place 1 piece skin side down in a shallow glass or china dish. Cover with plenty of finely chopped fresh dill. Place the second fillet on top, skin side up, and surround with more chopped dill.*

2 *Cover the salmon pieces with greaseproof paper and wrap tightly, then place a weighted board on top and chill for 2–3 days. Turn the fish and baste with the juices twice a day. Scrape off the pickling mixture before serving. Slice very thinly as for smoked salmon (right) or slightly thicker, in the Scandinavian style, which I prefer.*

1 *To slice your own smoked salmon lay the side of smoked salmon skin side down on a board or other flat surface. Check for any stray small bones, removing them with your fingers or a pair of clean tweezers.*

2 *With a long, thin serrated knife, cut wafer-thin slices starting at the tail end. Use your free hand to hold the uncut salmon firm. Lay the slices on non-stick paper, interleaving the paper between each layer.*

SMOKED, DRIED *and* SALTED FISH

Smoking, drying and salting are early methods of preserving fish that we still use. Each has survived because of the particular flavour it gives to food. Smoking only preserves for a limited period but it must have been realized early on what wonderful results it can have on fish. Fish is either hot smoked, which lightly cooks the fish as well as flavouring it, or cold smoked, which leaves the fish raw as with smoked salmon (which is salted before smoking). Hot smoked fish include mackerel, trout and eel. As a rule look for plump, pale-coloured fish.

Kippers and Finnan haddock are both soaked in brine before smoking, then dried and lightly cold smoked. Buckling and bloaters are salted and then smoked; the buckling thoroughly hot smoked and the bloater only very lightly cold smoked.

The kind of wood used for cold smoking and the length of time (anything from two to twenty days) both affect the final flavour of the fish. Cod and haddock are normally cold smoked and it is sometimes possible to buy cold smoked mackerel as well. Other smoked delicacies to look out for are smoked halibut, Arbroath smokies, tuna, mussels and monkfish. Smoked cod and haddock fillets are by no means always genuinely smoked, but dyed, salted and given an artificial smoky flavour; they are not as good as the real thing but can be used in fish cakes, pies and kedgeree.

There are different kinds of salted fish; some of them salted and dried, others packed in a salt brine or simply closely packed in salt, which produces its own brine around them. Anchovies, for example, can be salted or brined. There are also fish which are simply dried in the sun or in drying sheds. The Spanish and Portuguese have what seems to me an almost obsessive passion for salt cod although they live in countries which abound with many types of wonderful fresh fish.

PREPARING KIPPERS

Although traditionally associated with a good British breakfast, kippers make excellent suppers or light lunches, too. They are cured herrings, preserved further by cold smoking so they still need cooking before eating. You can buy whole or filleted kippers. Fillets have been boned, although fine bones may still be present. Look for plump, firm flesh with a good sheen.

There are three ways of cooking kippers. Whole or filleted kippers can be grilled, cooked by the jug method or in a microwave. To cook kippers in a microwave, place them on a lightly greased microwaveproof plate. Cover with microwave clingfilm and pierce, then cook on High (100%) for 3–5 minutes. Leave to stand for 3 minutes, then serve.

Regardless which method you use, they are cooked when the flesh flakes easily. Serve with a squeeze of lemon juice, freshly black ground pepper and plenty of brown bread and butter.

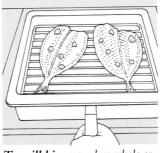

To grill kippers, *place whole or filleted kippers on a grill pan, flesh side up. Dot with butter and grill for about 5 minutes until the flesh flakes easily.*

For the jug method *fill a tall heatproof jug with boiling water. Immerse the kipper fillets and leave for 5–10 minutes until tender. Drain well and serve.*

USING PRESERVED FISH

• Thinly sliced or flaked smoked fish mixed with salad vegetables or leaves make wonderful salads. Toss with a herb, garlic or mustard vinaigrette (page 204) just before serving.
• Any filleted smoked fish can be made into a pâté (page 97) but smoked mackerel and kipper are the most usual; they can be made with added butter, cream, curd cheese or fromage frais – if you have a blender or food processor this takes only minutes to make, and not much longer by hand. Season to taste with herbs, spices or even a drop of alcohol such as Pernod.

• Stuff taramasalata into edible receptacles such as hollowed-out tomatoes and hard-boiled eggs or little pastry cases. Choux buns stuffed with taramasalata are delicious, too.
• For a first course, wrap taramasalata in smoked salmon parcels.
• Smoked haddock can be very delicious when cooked in milk and then made into a soup or served with lightly poached eggs and spinach or used for fish cakes.
• I love anchovies, fresh or salted. The anchovies which are most easily available are salted fillets in cans: these are a boon for adding to pasta dishes, to

pizzas, to stuffings for lamb or chicken, for flavouring butter and for all manner of sauces.
• I make my favourite potato salad by mixing hot, boiled potatoes with a mixture of finely chopped anchovies with their oil and extra olive oil, crushed garlic, a little balsamic vinegar and lots of black pepper, then leaving the potatoes to cool and absorb the flavours.
• Cooked gently, soaked dried cod can be treated like its fresh counterpart. It goes well with the strong Mediterranean flavours of garlic, olives and tomatoes.

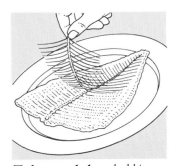

To bone a whole *cooked kipper, place the fish flesh side up, and loosen the main bone. Slowly pull it up and discard. Even if the kipper is skinned and ready filleted there may still be fine bones on the skinned side so use a fish knife to loosen them and pull away.*

PREPARING SMOKED COD'S ROE

Smoked cod's roe can be eaten as it is or as thin slices on toast, but the strength of its flavour and saltiness makes it more suitable for taramasalata. This Greek and Turkish speciality is traditionally made from tarama, salted grey mullet roe, but smoked cod's roe is often used because of its availability.

Homemade taramasalata is much more delicious than the suspiciously bright pink concoction you get in the average Greek taverna. When you buy uncoloured smoked cod's roe taramasalata will be a more appetizing creamy pale pink. If you do not have a food processor pound the ingredients in a pestle and mortar, beating in the oil and lemon juice. Using a food processor, however, you can make taramasalata in minutes. To serve 4 people, you need 250g (8oz) smoked cod's roe.

Pasta Spirals with Smoked Haddock (page 138) is an easy-to-prepare family dish that makes the most of smoked haddock's full flavour. Fresh basil is used as the garnish here but you can, of course, use any fresh herb in season.

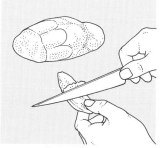

1 *Pour a little milk over 125g (4oz) stale white bread with crusts removed and set aside until the milk is absorbed. Pour boiling water over the smoked cod's roe, leave for 1 minute, then drain. Cut pieces off the large roe and scrape the flesh away from the skin, then coarsely chop up the remaining roe.*

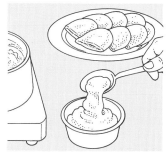

2 *Put all the roe flesh, the soaked bread and 1–2 large cloves of crushed garlic into a food processor or blender and whizz, gradually adding 150–250ml (5–8fl oz) olive oil and 4–8 tablespoons lemon juice to taste. Season with black pepper. Spoon into a small bowl and serve with hot pitta bread (page 292) or toast.*

PREPARING SALT COD

Salt cod is mainly eaten in southern Europe along the shores of the Mediterranean and the Atlantic, and in the West Indies. It needs a little forward planning as it should be soaked for at least 24 hours before cooking.

Look for fish with a beige-grey colour with a dusting of salt, and ideally choose from the thicker middle of the fish.

One simple way to serve cooked salt cod is in pieces with plain boiled potatoes and a good garlicky mayonnaise.

My favourite way of serving it is in a brandade – a creamy purée of salt cod, garlic, olive oil and even cream – popular along the Mediterranean.

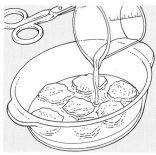

1 *With a very strong pair of scissors or a heavy kitchen knife, cut the salt cod into pieces to fit in a single layer in a large flat bowl. Cover the salt cod pieces with cold water and leave to soak for 24–48 hours, changing the water every 8 hours or so. This preparation is necessary so the cod loses its salty taste yet still retains a unique, firm texture.*

2 *Drain the salt cod pieces and place in a large saucepan with fresh cold water to cover. Add a bouquet garni and whole black peppercorns. Bring slowly to the boil. Cover the pan and simmer gently for 10–20 minutes, depending on the thickness of fish, until the salt cod is tender and flakes easily when tested with the tip of a knife.*

3 *Remove the salt cod from the cooking liquid with a slotted spoon and set aside until cool. Remove the skin and flake the flesh into meaty chunks. Serve with a sauce or mash and use for fish cakes or a brandade mixed with garlic and olive oil (left). You can also use it like ordinary flaked fish in pies or in casseroles mixed with chunks of potatoes.*

MARINATED SCALLOPS WITH AVOCADO AND TOMATOES (116)

Queens, the small scallops, are the best to use for this delectable first course. They are meltingly tender, and it is really pointless to cook them. They are much nicer either marinated and eaten cold as here, or simply warmed in a sauce or soup.

In this simple summer dish the scallops are marinated with lemon juice and then served with chopped fresh dill and basil and a lemon vinaigrette, accompanied by sliced avocados and tomatoes. If you can't find queens, use the larger scallops, but slice them into thirds before adding the marinade. *SERVES 4*

500g (1lb) little scallops, preferably queens, thawed if frozen
125ml (4fl oz) lemon juice, preferably freshly squeezed
Extra virgin olive oil
Small bunch of fresh dill, chopped fairly finely
2 large avocados
Lemon juice for sprinkling
375g (12oz) tomatoes, skinned and cut across into thin slices
8–10 fresh basil leaves, cut across into thin strips
Salt and black pepper
Fresh dill sprigs to garnish (optional)

Put the scallops in a bowl and pour over the lemon juice – it should be enough to cover the scallops. Sprinkle with black pepper. Cover the bowl and leave in the refrigerator for 30 minutes, or a little longer if convenient.

Pour the marinade off the scallops into a jar or jug and add olive oil and seasoning. Shake or whisk to make a vinai-grette dressing. Mix the chopped dill with the scallops.

Shortly before you want to eat cut the avocados in half, remove the stones and peel off the skins carefully. Slice across thinly in half-moon slices. Sprinkle with lemon juice as you slice them to prevent the flesh browning.

Arrange the avocado slices alternately with the tomato slices on a serving dish, overlapping slightly. Spoon the scallops alongside. Sprinkle the basil strips over the avocado and tomato slices and finally spoon the vinaigrette dressing over the whole dish. Garnish with fresh dill, if liked, and serve at once.

PASTA SPIRALS WITH SMOKED HADDOCK (137)

You can use any of the pasta shapes which hold sauces well for this mouthwatering and quickly made supper dish. Smoky-flavoured, succulent haddock blends well with this creamy sauce. *SERVES 4*

375g (12oz) pasta spirals
50g (2oz) butter
375g (12oz) smoked haddock fillet, skinned and cut into chunks
2 teaspoons paprika
1 tablespoon tomato purée
450ml (¾ pint) double cream
2 bunches spring onions, trimmed and chopped finely (including the green parts)
3–4 tablespoons lemon juice
Cayenne pepper
Salt
Fresh basil to garnish
Grated Parmesan cheese to serve (optional)

Cook the pasta in plenty of boiling salted water until *al dente* (page 82).

Meanwhile, melt the butter in a large frying pan over a medium heat. Add the fish and stir around gently for about 3 minutes until the fish is opaque, then stir in the paprika followed by the tomato purée. Add the cream and bring up to the boil. Stir in the chopped spring onions and bubble gently for 1 minute, then remove from the heat and gradually stir in the lemon juice. Season with cayenne pepper and salt to taste.

When the pasta is ready drain it, put it into a warmed serving dish and roughly mix in the haddock and cream sauce. Garnish with fresh basil and serve at once, with or without grated Parmesan cheese.

SALMON FISH BALLS (128)

These fish balls are very light and creamy as they contain no potato and instead have a base of béchamel sauce. They are sophisticated enough to serve at a dinner party either as a hot first course or as a main course, accompanied by a mixed green salad. Prepare the mixture well in advance as it must chill thoroughly so you can form the fish balls easily. A mixture of salmon and smoked haddock is also delicious. *SERVES 4–6*

75g (3oz) butter
2 cloves garlic, chopped finely
75g (3oz) plain flour, sifted
300ml (½ pint) milk
500g (1lb) lightly poached salmon (page 130)
3–4 pinches cayenne pepper
Bunch of fresh watercress leaves, chopped finely
About 5 tablespoons fresh white breadcrumbs
Groundnut oil for frying
Salt

Melt the butter in a saucepan and add the chopped garlic. Remove from the heat and stir in the sifted flour. Gradually stir in the milk. Put the pan back on the heat and bring to the boil, stirring all the time with a wooden spoon. Bubble gently, still stirring, for about 4 minutes until very thick. This also cooks the flour so it does not taste raw in the fish balls.

Remove the pan from the heat and flake in the poached salmon flesh. Season well with salt and the cayenne pepper and stir in the chopped watercress. Turn the mixture into a shallow dish or roasting tin and leave until cold. Cover with clingfilm and chill thoroughly in the refrigerator for at least 1 hour.

Put the breadcrumbs in a bowl, and flour your hands. Take up small amounts of the chilled salmon mixture and lightly roll into round shapes, a little bigger than ping-pong balls. Dip the balls in the breadcrumbs, one by one, and set aside until all are coated.

Heat groundnut oil in a deep frying pan until very hot and fry the balls, a few at a time, over a high heat for a short time, until golden brown all over. Take out using a fish slice and drain well on kitchen paper. Arrange the cooked fish balls on a serving dish and keep warm in a low oven, until ready to serve.

SQUID RINGS WITH LEEKS AND SPINACH (127)

This is a wonderful way of serving larger stuffed squid; when cooked the squid is sliced and laid on a rich red sauce. When preparing the squid save the fins and tentacles and chop to include in the stuffing. *SERVES 4*

1 tablespoon olive oil
15g (½oz) butter
375g (12oz) leeks, trimmed and cut into
*   1cm (½in) rings*
5cm (2in) piece fresh root ginger, peeled
*   and chopped*
1 large clove garlic, chopped
750g (1½lb) large squid, washed and
*   prepared for stuffing (page 126)*
125g (4oz) fresh spinach, stalks removed,
*   washed, well drained and chopped*
50g (2oz) pecan nuts, chopped
1 small egg (size 4), beaten lightly
Salt and black pepper
FOR THE SAUCE
1 large red pepper, halved, deseeded and
*   cored (page 49)*
25g (1oz) butter
1 clove garlic, chopped finely
375g (12oz) tomatoes, skinned and
*   chopped roughly (page 48)*
2 teaspoons caster sugar
Salt and black pepper

Heat the olive oil and the butter in a large, deep frying pan over a medium heat. Add the leeks and stir occasionally until softened – don't let them brown. Add the ginger and garlic, the chopped squid fins and tentacles and the spinach with only the water that clings to the leaves after draining. Stir around over the heat, just until the spinach is limp – if there is a lot of liquid increase the heat and bubble for a minute to reduce it slightly. Remove from the heat and add the pecan nuts, with a good sprinkling of salt and black pepper. Turn into a bowl and leave the stuffing mixture until cool, then stir in the beaten egg.

Hold the squid firmly and spoon the stuffing mixture in, working it down to the bottom. Still holding the squid, stitch or skewer to enclose the stuffing (page 127).

Smear the stuffed squid with a little oil, place in a roasting tin and cover tightly with foil. Bake at 160°C, 325°F, Gas Mark 3 for 1–1¼ hours.

Meanwhile, make the sauce. Whizz the red pepper in a food processor until very finely chopped. Heat the butter in a large saucepan over a medium heat, then add the chopped garlic, the red pepper and its juices, the chopped tomatoes and the caster sugar. Cover the pan and cook, stirring now and then, over a very low heat for 20–25 minutes until you have a fairly thick mush. Remove from the heat and leave on one side.

When the squid is cooked transfer carefully to a chopping board and pour any pan juices into the tomato and pepper sauce. Bring the sauce to the boil, bubble for a minute or two and season to taste with salt and black pepper. Pour into a fairly shallow, warm serving dish. Using a very sharp knife cut the squid across into 1–1.5cm (½–¾in) rings. Using a spatula, carefully arrange the squid rings, slightly overlapping, on top of the tomato sauce. If necessary, cover with foil and keep it warm in a low oven.

SCALLOP, CRAB AND PRAWN TART (125)

If you can get the little queen scallops, they are the sweetest of all, and cheaper, too. To make 8 individual tarts, instead of 1 large one, use 10cm (4in) tartlet tins and increase the quantities of scallops, crab meat and prawns slightly. Bake the pastry blind for only 15–20 minutes. *SERVES 6–8*

FOR THE PASTRY
250g (8oz) strong plain flour
½ teaspoon salt
25g (1oz) semolina
175g (6oz) chilled butter, cut into small
*   pieces*
1 egg
1 tablespoon cold water
FOR THE FILLING
250g (8oz) scallops, sliced fairly thinly
*   and corals halved if large*
250g (8oz) mixed crab meat
75g (3oz) peeled prawns
1 fresh red chilli, deseeded and chopped
*   finely (page 49)*
1 clove garlic, crushed
1 tablespoon roughly chopped fresh
*   tarragon*
1 teaspoon ground mace
300ml (½ pint) double cream
1 egg, beaten lightly
2 tablespoons lemon juice
1 teaspoon paprika
Salt and black pepper
Lemon slices and extra tarragon to garnish

To make the pastry, sift the flour and salt into a bowl. Stir in the semolina, then rub in the butter lightly with your fingertips until the mixture resembles coarse breadcrumbs. Lightly whisk the egg with the water and mix it into the flour and semolina with a knife until the mixture starts to stick together.

Gather the pastry mixture into a ball and roll it out on a lightly floured surface into a piece large enough to line a 25–28cm (10–11in) loose-bottomed flan tin. Line the tin with the pastry, pressing a rolling pin round the edges to cut off the excess neatly.

Refrigerate the pastry case for at least 30 minutes. Take the pastry-lined tin out of the refrigerator, and line it with grease-proof paper and dried beans (page 245). Bake the pastry blind at 200°C, 400°F, Gas Mark 6 for 20–25 minutes until lightly golden. Remove the greaseproof paper and beans and leave the tart to cool in the tin on a wire rack.

To prepare the filling, place the thinly sliced scallops and their corals in a bowl with the crab meat and peeled prawns. Mix in the chopped chilli, the crushed garlic, the chopped tarragon and the ground mace. In another bowl whip the cream until beginning to thicken, then add the lightly beaten egg, the lemon juice, salt and freshly ground black pepper. Continue beating until thick, then stir lightly into the fish mixture.

Pour the fish and cream mixture into the cooled pastry case and sprinkle a dash of paprika across the centre.

Bake the tart in the centre of a pre-heated oven, 190°C, 375°F, Gas Mark 5 for 15–20 minutes, until the filling is set and lightly browned. Remove the tart from the oven and leave to cool a little, then carefully remove from the tart tin and place on a serving plate.

Garnish the tart with lemon slices and extra sprigs of fresh tarragon if you like, then serve. Serve lukewarm or at room temperature but never straight from the refrigerator.

JOCK'S GRILLED STUFFED MACKEREL (119)

I dream of landing a plump sea bass but the only fish I catch in Devon is the humble mackerel. However, very fresh mackerel tastes like a prince of fish. It has a beautiful soft yet dense texture and a characteristic flavour which is at its best when grilled so that the blackened skin adds a hint of smokiness. The inspiration for this recipe comes from a family friend who visits every summer.   SERVES 4

75g (3oz) blanched almonds, chopped
A few sprigs of fresh tarragon
2 cloves garlic, chopped finely
2 tablespoons fresh brown breadcrumbs
1 small egg (size 4), beaten lightly
4 small–medium mackerel, gutted through
   the gills and heads removed (page 118)
Salt and black pepper
Lime or lemon wedges and tarragon to
   garnish

Toast the almonds in a dry frying pan over a high heat. Put in a bowl. Pull the leaves off the tarragon, chop roughly and add to the almonds with the garlic. Stir in the breadcrumbs and egg and season.

Preheat the grill to the highest possible heat. Using a sharp knife, make 3 or 4 diagonal cuts on the side of each mackerel. Spoon the stuffing mixture into the body cavities of the fish and lay the fish on a grill rack. Cook under the preheated grill for about 5 minutes on each side until the flesh of the fish is opaque. Garnish and serve at once.

STUFFED SALMON FILLETS WITH YELLOW PEPPER AND SAFFRON SAUCE (116)

These are a perfect treat for a small dinner party and the mixture of pink, yellow and green is alluring. The filleted tail pieces of salmon are stuffed with prawns (for a very special occasion you could use pieces of lobster) and plenty of fresh dill and coriander. They are then cooked in a creamy yellow sauce which goes especially well with Jersey new potatoes and mange tout.   SERVES 4

2 tail pieces of salmon, about 625–750g
   (1¼–1½lb) each before filleting and
   skinning
Bunch of fresh dill, chopped
Generous handful of fresh coriander leaves,
   chopped
175g (6oz) peeled cooked prawns
Black pepper
FOR THE SAUCE
200ml (7fl oz) white wine
2 good pinches saffron strands
2 small–medium yellow peppers, halved,
   deseeded and cored (page 49)
300ml (½ pint) double cream
4 tablespoons balsamic or sherry vinegar
Salt and black pepper

Lay out the fillets of salmon and sprinkle generously with black pepper. Press the chopped dill and coriander all over one side of the pieces of salmon. Place the prawns in the centre of each piece. Roll over the salmon lengthwise to enclose the prawns and hold the rolls together with wooden skewers or wooden cocktail sticks. Leave on one side while you prepare the sauce.

In a small saucepan, heat 6 tablespoons of the white wine with the saffron strands until bubbling, then remove from the heat and leave on one side to infuse. Preheat a hot grill. Put the pepper halves, skin side upwards, under a hot grill until the skin has burned black nearly all over (page 55). Place in a tea towel until cool enough to handle, then peel off the skins using your fingers. Put the flesh in a food processor with the remaining white wine and whizz until as smooth as possible (press the purée through a fine sieve if not absolutely smooth).

Put the pepper purée into a flame-proof casserole which will be wide enough to hold the rolled fillets of fish side by side. Stir the cream into the pepper purée with the infused saffron and wine. Place the rolled fish fillets on top of the sauce and cover with a lid.

Very shortly before eating put the casserole over a high heat on top of the stove. Bring the sauce just up to bubbling, then lower the heat and poach the fish very gently for 6–8 minutes – the salmon should not be left to overcook and should still be a slightly darker pink in the centre if you gently test by sticking in the tip of a knife. Lift out the salmon fillets with a fish slice and put carefully on to a heated serving plate.

Add the balsamic vinegar or sherry to the sauce, season to taste with salt and freshly ground black pepper, then bring up to bubbling again. Stir for 1 minute, then sieve before pouring it over the fish. Serve at once.

GRILLED GREY MULLET IN A SPICED COATING (133)

Grey mullet is an inexpensive fish which grills and bakes well, and is particularly successful when spiced. I always find this way of cooking very useful when time is short but if possible start early in the day so that the spices permeate the flesh. Ask the fishmonger to gut the fish through the belly, leaving the head on, and to scrape off the scales, or do it yourself (page 118).   SERVES 4

1 grey mullet, about 1.75kg (3½lb)
2 rounded tablespoons natural yogurt
2 teaspoons paprika
1 teaspoon ground cinnamon
½ teaspoon cayenne pepper
1 large clove garlic, crushed
Sea salt
Flat-leaved parsley, bay leaves and lemon
   wedges to garnish
1 tablespoon olive oil

Put the yogurt in a bowl and stir in the paprika, cinnamon, cayenne pepper, garlic, olive oil and a little sea salt. Cut diagonal deep slashes at 2.5cm (1in) intervals on each side of the fish. Rub the yogurt and spice mixture on to the fish outside and in, pressing it down into the slashes. If possible leave in the refrigerator for 30 minutes or more before cooking.

Preheat a very hot grill. Cook the fish under the preheated grill for about 6–8 minutes on each side until blackened in patches. Garnish and serve.

FILLETS OF COD WITH CREAMY PRAWN AND DILL SAUCE (130)

Cod is an often underrated fish, not associated with more sophisticated dishes. Cooked carefully, however, its large flakes should be moist and smooth with a delicate flavour. These fillets are poached lightly in a white wine and prawn stock, which then becomes part of the creamy prawn sauce, making it a luxurious dish. Serve with new potatoes and a green vegetable.   *SERVES 4*

375g (12oz) prawns in their shells
3 large cloves garlic, sliced roughly
2 rounded teaspoons paprika
300ml (½ pint) dry white wine
300ml (½ pint) water
4 thick pieces cod fillet, about
   250g (8oz) each
250ml (8fl oz) double cream
2 teaspoons white wine vinegar
1 rounded tablespoon roughly chopped
   fresh dill
Salt and black pepper

Peel the prawns, putting the shells and heads into a saucepan and the prawns into a bowl. Add the sliced garlic and paprika to the prawn shells and pour in the white wine and water. Cover the saucepan and bring to the boil, then lower the heat and simmer very gently for 20 minutes. Strain the liquid through a sieve into a wide saucepan into which the pieces of cod fillet will fit close together in a single layer.

Lay the fillets skin side upwards in the prawn stock. Cover the saucepan, put over a medium to low heat and keep only just trembling for 8–10 minutes until the fish is opaque white all through. Using a wide slotted fish slice carefully lift out the fillets and put on to a warmed serving dish. Again carefully, peel off the skin and discard. Keep the fish loosely covered in a low oven or warm place while you make the sauce.

Bubble the poaching liquid fiercely over a high heat for about 3 minutes until slightly reduced. Stir in the cream and bubble fiercely for 1 minute until the sauce has thickened. Remove from the heat. Stir in the vinegar and season to taste with salt and freshly gound black pepper if necessary, then add the prawns and the chopped dill. Spoon the sauce over the cod fillets and serve at once.

THE EMPEROR'S FAN (116)

My husband named this dish at first glance. You wouldn't think there was anything very imperial about skate, but the fan-shaped wings, glazed with a clear sauce flavoured with orange and lemon juices, fresh ginger and coriander is certainly evocative of the Far East.   *SERVES 4*

1 orange
600ml (1 pint) fish or chicken stock
   (pages 28–31)
4 tablespoons lemon juice
2.5cm (1in) piece fresh root ginger, peeled
   and sliced roughly
4 skate wings
2 rounded teaspoons arrowroot
1 tablespoon water
125g (4oz) button mushrooms, sliced
A good handful of fresh coriander leaves,
   chopped roughly
Salt and cayenne pepper (optional)
Orange wedges and extra rind and
   coriander sprigs to garnish (optional)

Remove a few strips of peel from the orange and squeeze the juice. Pour the stock and orange and lemon juices into a large frying pan which has a lid with the ginger and orange peel. Warm the stock, then add 2 skate wings. Cover, bring the liquid up to barely simmering and poach for 5–6 minutes until the skate is just opaque. Remove the skate and arrange on a shallow serving dish, like overlapping fans. Cover with foil and put into a low oven while you poach the rest.

Then bring the liquid to the boil for 5 minutes. Strain through a fine sieve into a saucepan. Mix the arrowroot with the water until smooth, then stir into the strained liquid. Bring to the boil, stirring all the time, then bubble, still stirring, for 3 minutes. Season if necessary with a little salt and cayenne pepper. Add the mushrooms and cook for another minute. Stir in the coriander. Pour over the skate wings, garnish if liked and serve.

GOLDEN FISH PIE (116)

We often have variations of fish pie for a family supper, and this one is popular with its golden orange top of mashed sweet and ordinary potato. For an extra treat, you can add a few shelled mussels to the fish. Serve with a simple green salad.   *SERVES 4–5*

500g (1lb) sweet potatoes (the large,
   orange-fleshed kind), peeled
375g (12oz) potatoes, peeled
75g (3oz) butter
2–3 pinches cayenne pepper
750g–875g (1½–1¾ lb) haddock or cod
   fillets, skinned
2 heaped tablespoons cornflour
2–3 tablespoons water
600ml (1 pint) milk
150ml (¼ pint) double cream
375g (12oz) smallish tomatoes, skinned
   and quartered (page 48)
1 rounded teaspoon of Dijon mustard
2 good tablespoons chopped fresh dill
Salt and black pepper

Steam or boil the sweet potatoes and the ordinary white potatoes until very soft. This takes approximately 20 minutes. Mash the potatoes together with 50g (2oz) of the butter and season to taste with salt and the cayenne pepper.

While the potatoes are cooking steam the fish fillets until just cooked (page 131) – this should not take more than 5 minutes so keep checking so as not to overcook. Leave the fish and potatoes on one side.

Preheat the grill to high and put a shallow ovenproof serving dish in a low oven to keep warm. Put the cornflour and water in a cup and stir until smooth. Pour into a saucepan and gradually stir in the milk and the cream. Bring to the boil, stirring all the time, then bubble, still stirring, for about 3 minutes.

Add the tomatoes and bubble for another minute. Stir in the mustard with salt and black pepper to taste. Lastly add the steamed fish and chopped fresh dill (and mussels if using). Remove immediately from the heat and pour into the warm serving dish.

Using a spatula carefully distribute the mashed potatoes all over the fish mixture and spread gently to form a topping. Dot with the remaining 25g (1oz) of butter and put under the grill for 5–10 minutes until the surface is darkly speckled all over – the speckles should look black against the orange of the potato.

MEAT and GAME

Although I can very well go without meat for days I cannot imagine I will ever become a vegetarian. Meat adds enormous scope to both cooking and eating – a family Sunday lunch is epitomized by a large juicy joint, the appetizing smell of which fills the house during the morning. In winter a slowly cooked meat casserole with its rich juices and meltingly soft vegetables is a great comfort, while a rare, tender fillet of beef wrapped in pastry is a luxurious treat. Another experience I would hate to miss out on in life is the pleasure of eating meat cooked out of doors. Given a beautiful garden or picnic spot, lamb grilled outside, ideally over a bundle of rosemary twigs whose aromatic smoke infuses into the meat and scents the air, can induce a sense of ecstasy, and should taste as good as anything the most exclusive restaurant could produce. As it is the juices of meat which are so wonderful it is important not to overcook and dry out grilled or roast meat – in slow-cooked casseroles and stews it is these juices which literally make the dish.

The cheaper cuts of meat often have the most flavour, and if cooked with thought and time they produce a supremely satisfying meal. Mince is sometimes scorned, probably because it can be so badly cooked, resulting in a grey and tasteless mess. But seasoned well, with added herbs or spices, and cooked carefully, it can be transformed into an enormous variety of dishes. Even shepherd's pie can be made into a dish fit for a dinner party, not to mention lasagne, moussaka, stuffed peppers and courgettes and countless different meatballs.

The meats most widely eaten are beef from the ox, lamb from the sheep and pork from the pig. In our household, and I suspect in many others, lamb is the meat we eat most although the occasional treat of a large rib joint of beef, on the bone and properly hung in the traditional way, is well worth paying for. Both fresh and frozen lamb can be excellent, but fresh, really young spring lamb is sweet, mild and succulent and needs no added flavourings. As pork is bred so much leaner nowadays, which gives it a tendency to dryness, it must be cooked in a way which will add moisture; I find it a perfect meat for casseroles. Goat is often served in Mediterranean countries and baby kid is wonderfully tender and succulent. Venison, hare and rabbit are classed as game even though they are not always wild. Farmed venison can be so tender that you can treat it exactly like the best cuts of beef and cook it rare. Many people even prefer its milder flavour.

A light marbling of fat gives tenderness and flavour to pieces of meat which are to be grilled, roasted rare or lightly cooked, while leaner cuts of meat develop tenderness and flavour with long, slow cooking. But the texture and taste of the meat also vitally depends on the hanging of the animal – all meat except veal should have been hung, for varying amounts of time. Luckily, meat is now beginning to be hung for longer in the traditional way. Often this is indicated on the joint but if in doubt always check before buying.

All meat is muscle, and the harder the muscle works the tougher the meat is likely to be, yet the flavour will tend to be better, especially on an older animal. Many wonderful slowly cooked stews and casseroles with intense juices can be made with the tougher parts of the animal. And then there is offal, which some love and some hate; I am an offal lover for its wonderful flavours. But, once again, careful cooking is essential.

Clockwise from top right: The flavourings used in Roast Veal with Prunes, Ginger and Pistachio Nuts (page 168) keep the meat moist and tender; Pork Chops Stuffed with Roquefort and Baked with Pears (page 170) are served with lightly steamed savoy cabbage; Grilled Lamb Fillets with Mint and Yogurt Sauce (page 170) are quick and easy to make using boned lamb neck fillets, and served here with creamy purées of carrot, and spinach and potato; buttered Chinese noodles give an oriental touch to the more traditional combination of pork and apple in Stir-fried Pork Fillet with Fruit and Lettuce (page 169); and the rich, strong flavour of hare is complemented by a smooth red pepper and tomato sauce in Casseroled Hare with Quinces (page 171), accompanied by steamed potatoes.

BEEF *and* VEAL

Beef is the meat of the ox, and veal is the meat of the young ox or calf, yet the characters of these meats are so different it is as if they come from two different animals. Beef is eaten fresher than it used to be, as the traditional longer hanging takes up space and raises the price of the meat. But now once again butchers are beginning to realize the virtues of hanging, which are increased flavour and tenderness. Look for darker red beef which indicates that it has been well hung, or look out for information to indicate that the meat has been matured in the traditional way.

Beef is, above all, an extremely versatile meat which suits either the most lavish or the most economical meal. Although cuts such as fillet and sirloin are expensive they are never wasteful, and they are usually very simply cooked. Beef that is marbled with thin strands of creamy coloured fat has more flavour. Some inexpensive joints of beef, such as brisket, have a marvellous flavour, but are very fatty; look for the least fatty piece you can find, then cook it long and gently, skimming off as much fat as you can from the surface. Richly delicious casseroles can be made with the cheapest cuts of beef, providing the meat is cooked gently for a long time – at least three hours.

Veal comes from calves up to five months old, but the best veal is from really young animals which have been fed entirely on milk. The flesh should be a very pale pink, soft and moist. Veal is nearly always tender but it has little fat so it is not ideal for grilling or roasting at a high heat. A gently roasted joint of veal produces the most intense gravy juices of all meat and the gelatinous bones make the best stock, thus pot-roasted and slowly casseroled veal is delicious.

TYING MEAT WITH A BUTCHER'S KNOT

Meat is tied not only for a neater appearance, but also because it enables more even cooking and easier carving. Boned joints, with or without a stuffing, obviously need tying, but it also helps to tie joints with one large muscle, such as silverside, so they retain their shape.

Professionals use this knot because of the control it gives over tightness. If you've boned a joint, or have an unrolled one for stuffing this knot at regular intervals gives a neat shape for even cooking.

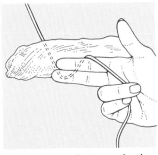

1 *Pass a piece of string under the joint, with the short end towards you. Make the shape of a pair of scissors with your right hand and pass the short end of string over the palm and hold it firm with your third and little finger.*

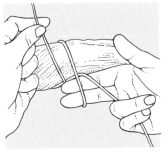

2 *Take the long end of string with your left hand and pass it over and behind the first two fingers of your right hand, parallel to the first piece of string. Pull with the left hand to keep the required tension.*

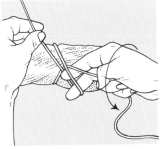

3 *Keeping your right hand in the scissor shape twist from the wrist in an anticlockwise direction towards you and out so that the back of the hand is uppermost. Keep the left hand holding on to the long end.*

HANDLING MEAT AND GAME

• Refrigeration prevents the growth of and cooking destroys bacteria which can cause food poisoning. You must take great care, however, that bacteria in raw meat do not cross-contaminate other foods.
• Your refrigerator should not be any warmer than 5°C (42°F) for safe storage of meat.
• Refrigerate meat as soon as you get it home. Meat sold on plastic trays can be left as it is; other meat should be put on a dish with a lip to catch any juices.
• Do not let juices from raw meat drip on any other foods.

• Never prepare raw and cooked meat on the same chopping board, unless it is thoroughly washed and dried in between. This cuts down on bacterial cross-contamination.
• Always wash your hands and utensils thoroughly after handling raw meat.
• All frozen meats are best thawed slowly and thoroughly before cooking. Unwrap, put on a plate with a lip or in a shallow container, cover loosely with foil or a food bag and, ideally, thaw in the refrigerator slowly to cut down on moisture loss.

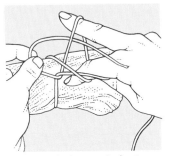

4 *Thread the long end of string through the loop made by the 'open scissors'. Remove these fingers from the loop carefully and draw the knot slightly closer, pulling the left hand end up tightly to close the loop and pull the string closer around the joint.*

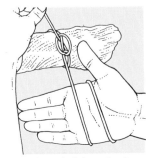

5 *Wrap the end of the string in the right hand around your palm, then yank the knot tight pulling the right hand towards you and down. This locks the knot. Finish with a right over left, left over right knot and cut off excess string with a pair of scissors or a sharp knife.*

STUFFED BONED VEAL BREAST

BEEF OLIVES

A boned and stuffed breast of veal makes a delicious and economical mid-week joint.

The stuffing flavour variations are endless, using breadcrumbs or rice, herbs, spices, chopped dried fruit, nuts and lemon. For a 1.2kg (2½lb) piece of meat before boning you will need about 250g (8oz) stuffing. Bind the stuffing with an egg if necessary.

Trim the joint well and remove the thick skin first. Lay skinned side down on a chopping board.

1 *Pull back the half flap of meat which covers the bones. Cut out the L-shaped rib bones singly, cutting back the meat flap until all bones are removed. Do not cut through to the other side. Open up the meat and press flat.*

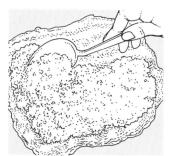

2 *Spread your chosen stuffing on the boned side of the breast. Be careful not to add too much stuffing or the joint will be difficult to roll up neatly.*

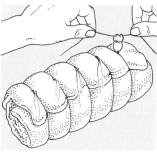

3 *Roll up the joint and tie firmly with 4–6 butchers' knots (opposite). Weigh and roast join side down according to the chart on page 157.*

For this popular dish the meat must be cut into slices like thin steaks so it can be rolled up round a stuffing. To serve 6 you will need 875g–1kg (1¾–2lb) stewing beef, such as topside, sliced into 12 large, thin slices, tomato purée to taste, a handful finely chopped fresh sage leaves, 3 chopped cloves garlic, 50g (2oz) can anchovies, drained and sliced, 75ml (3fl oz) dry red wine, 1 rounded tablespoon cornflour, 150ml (¼ pint) soured cream and salt and black pepper.

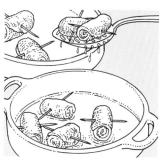

1 *Lay the beef slices between 2 sheets of wet greaseproof paper and bash the slices with a rolling pin or meat mallet until very thin. Smear each slice generously with tomato purée, then pat on some chopped sage leaves, garlic and anchovies. Season well with black pepper. Roll up and secure each slice with a wooden cocktail stick. Lay in a flameproof casserole, pour over the wine and enough water to three-quarters cover the beef.*

2 *Bring to the boil, then cover and cook in a preheated oven, 150°C, 300°F, Gas Mark 2 for 1¾–2½ hours until tender. Remove beef olives with a slotted spoon and keep warm in a low oven. Pour the cooking juices into a saucepan. Mix the cornflour with a little water until smooth, then stir into the juices. Bring to the boil for 3 minutes, stirring, constantly until thickened. Season, pour the sauce over the beef and top with soured cream.*

BEEF CUTS

Allow 250–375g (8–12oz) meat on the bone and 125–175g (4–6oz) meat off the bone per person.

Cooking method	Cuts
Roast	Aitchbone cut, topside, forerib on bone, top rib, back rib, wing or prime rib, fillet, sirloin, top rump, silverside
Casserole/Pot roast	Chuck, blade, leg, shin, topside, skirt, brisket, clod, flank, silverside, neck
Grill/Fry/Barbecue	Steaks (T-bone, fillet, sirloin, rump, minute, porterhouse), spare rib

VEAL CUTS

Allow 250g (8oz) meat on the bone and 175g (6oz) meat off the bone per person.

Cooking method	Cuts
Roast	Shoulder, middle neck, loin, fillet, end of leg, rump, silverside, boned breast
Casserole	Flank, neck, shin, rib, breast, middle neck cutlets, shoulder
Grill/Fry/Barbecue	Boned best end of neck, loin chop, rump, medallions, escalopes (not barbecue)

These gently stewed beef olives are rolled around a piquant anchovy and garlic filling and topped with soured cream.

LAMB

Lamb is my favourite meat. Living in the Middle East as a young child, it was the only meat I knew, and I still love cooking it with coriander, cumin, yogurt, mint and even dried fruit – all accompaniments to lamb which I became used to at the time.

Lamb is sold when it is under one year old; pale pink flesh indicates young lamb, and the flesh darkens to light red as its age increases. As a general rule, the younger the lamb, the more tender it is. The best lamb easily available is usually spring lamb of under six months old; preferably its flesh should still be pale and its fat creamy white, never yellow. A blue tinge in the knuckle and rib bones also indicates a young animal. Flavour, however, develops with age; mutton (sheep over two years old) can have a wonderful gamy flavour, but needs slow cooking to make it tender. It is difficult to obtain nowadays but if you ever come across any mutton, try it. To me, young lamb is most delicious when it is cooked slightly rare, pink rather than actually bloody. I think an expensive leg of lamb is wasted if it is overcooked but a larger shoulder can have great appeal when it is spiced, garlicked and roasted very gently. Shoulders have, in fact, a sweeter flesh than the leg. If you can't face the more difficult task of carving a shoulder you can have it boned and rolled. Boning takes away a little of the flavour but you can make up for this by stuffing the joint.

The most impressive joint of lamb for entertaining is the crown roast – literally a beautiful spiked crown of succulent cutlets which should always be roasted slightly rare, and the centre filled with an interesting stuffing of vegetables, nuts, herbs and so on. The cheapest cuts can be made into a wide variety of stews and casseroles with all sorts of seasonings and other ingredients, including fruit.

POCKET-BONING AND STUFFING A SHOULDER OF LAMB

A shoulder has two bones – a wide blade bone and a long shank bone. Pocket-boning is removing the blade bone only. The 'pocket' left behind is then stuffed. Alternatively, you can remove both bones and roll the whole joint up with stuffing or flavouring inside. If you plan to do this method it really is just as easy to buy a boned joint.

To stuff a fully boned 1.6kg (3½lb) rolled joint you will need 250g (8oz) of stuffing. For stuffing a pocketed joint, as explained here, allow about 300g (10oz) stuffing.

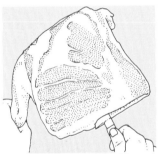

1 *Place the unboned shoulder skin side down on a chopping board with the knuckle on the left side. Hold the knuckle firmly and stick a boning knife horizontally into the bottom edge of the shoulder so the knife lies flat on top of the blade bone.*

2 *Still holding the knuckle firmly, cut to the left, scraping the flesh from the bone, then to the right, scraping and freeing the flesh as you go. Do not cut through the flesh on the side. Lift the freed flesh to check underneath and cutting any flesh not already freed.*

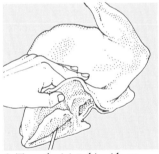

3 *Turn the joint skin side up, with the knuckle pointing to the right. Insert the knife as in step 1 and free the flesh from the bone to the right and left, working the knife around the bone. Again, take care not to cut the sides of the joint or nick the skin.*

Stuffed Shoulder of Lamb wrapped in Pastry (page 168) *with its spinach stuffing makes the most of a fully boned joint.*

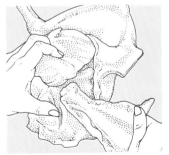

4 *Turn the joint back skin side down with the knuckle on the left. Use both hands to push the meat back, then twist the blade bone out of the socket. Cut any tendons to free the blade bone. Discard the bone.*

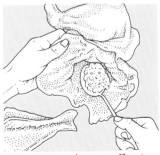

5 *Spoon your chosen stuffing into the 'pocket', without packing it too full. Stitch the edge fairly tightly closed with a trussing needle and kitchen string. Weigh the joint and roast according to the chart on page 159.*

PREPARING A BEST END OF NECK

This cut (also called a rack of lamb) is popular with cooks because it is sweet, tender and easy to carve between the cutlets. It is also very versatile to present, from impressive-looking crown roasts and guards of honour to simple plain roasted racks.

Best end comes from between the loin and middle neck, with tender pieces of meat attached to elegant rib bones. The ribs are often left attached but scraped clean down to the eye of meat for a more elegant presentation. Each end of neck contains six or seven ribs.

The backbone, called the 'chine' bone, needs to be sawn, or 'chined' where the vertebrae meet the ribs. For traditional British roasting, leave the chine bone attached, just removing it before carving. For crown roasts, guards of honour and racks of lamb it is removed before roasting.

For a crown roast, if the fat layer is thick, trim it slightly before curving inside. Both guards of honour and crown roasts can be roasted with a stuffing – between the racks for a guard of honour and in the centre for a crown roast. You can also cook a crown roast hollow and then fill the centre afterwards with a pretty medley of crisp buttery vegetables or a spicy pilaff (page 109).

You can let your imagination loose when making a guard of honour by varying the stuffing each time. Here, red peppers, celery and onions have been softened in butter with turmeric and then mixed with breadcrumbs and a lightly beaten egg.

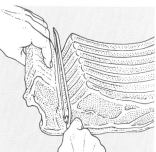

1 *To chine use a small saw or cleaver. Cut just through the bone, leaving the meat underneath uncut, and just loosening but not cutting off. For guards of honour and crown roasts remove completely. Cut off the skin, leaving the fat underneath.*

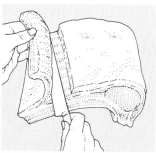

2 *For attractive presentation cut the fat and flesh off the end of the rib bones, leaving about 7cm (3in) of bones.*

3 *Use a small sharp knife to scrape the rib bones clean, cutting and scraping between each one. Scrape as clean as possible.*

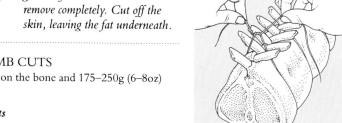

For a guard of honour, choose 2 matching racks. Remove the chine bones and prepare as in steps 1–3. Stand the racks upright and interlink, then tie. Score the fat in a criss-cross and stuff if you like. Roast according to the chart on page 159.

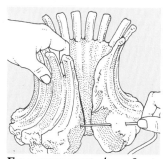

For a crown roast, choose 2 matching racks. Remove the chine bones and prepare as in steps 1–3. Curve them round with the bones facing outwards and place end to end. Stitch together with kitchen string. Roast according to the chart on page 159.

LAMB CUTS

Allow 250–375g (8–12oz) meat on the bone and 175–250g (6–8oz) meat off the bone per person.

Cooking method	Cuts
Roast	Leg , shoulder, loin, saddle, best end of neck, breast, guard of honour, crown roast
Casserole	Scrag end, best end of neck, chump, breast, middle neck, shoulder
Grill/Fry/Barbecue	Shoulder (boned), saddle, neck fillet, cutlets, noisettes, chump or loin chops, best end of neck

PORK, HAM *and* BACON

More food products are derived from the pig than from any other animal; they include pork, ham, bacon and an endless variety of fresh and cured sausages, and smoked or cured pieces of meat and fat. Almost every bit of the pig is edible, and it is the only animal whose skin we eat.

Pigs have been bred leaner and leaner over the years, and, although the meat is generally quite tender, it is very important to cook it in a way that doesn't lose moisture, such as in stews, casseroles, pies or pot roasts. When you roast or grill it you should cook it gently and rather slowly, basting often – slightly sweet liquids such as cider are good for basting, and beer is also excellent.

Real ham is the salted and matured back leg of the pig, although cured and pressed shoulder is known as ham, and cooked gammon, the leg cured like bacon, is often used as ham. Only a real ham keeps for any length of time and some are eaten raw, such as the delicious Italian Parma or Spanish Serrano hams.

The smell of sizzling bacon is one of the most mouth-watering smells of all cooking. Bacon comes from the sides of the pig which have been soaked in brine and then may be smoked. The bacon I love is Tendersweet, which is literally sweeter and milder because it is cured with less salt – both rashers and boneless joints are delicious.

Sausages are another of my favourites – best of all I love spicy, meaty ones, and whenever I travel I search for the best local sausage. Pork is at its most succulent when it is used in a sausage, and a simple meal of good sausages, carefully cooked cabbage and buttery mashed potatoes never seems ordinary to me.

BONING AND ROLLING A LOIN OF PORK

Loin is as an excellent special-occasion joint roasted boned or whole with or without crackling. It is often difficult to roast the sides and bottom of a rolled pork joint successfully so that the rind becomes crisp, therefore it is best to remove the rind before cooking. The advantage of a boned joint is that it is so much easier to carve, making it ideal for a tableful of hungry guests.

For a thicker rolled joint, buy a loin with rib bones still attached so you have a long belly flap after boning to roll round the loin and stuffing.

To stuff a 1kg (2lb) joint after boning you will need about 250g (8oz) stuffing, or spread with 125g (4oz) of a savoury buttery paste such as herb and garlic.

PORK CUTS

Allow 375g (12oz) meat on the bone and 175g (6oz) meat off the bone per person.

Cooking method	Cuts
Roast	Spare rib, fillet and knuckle ends of leg, loin, shoulder, belly, tenderloin, blade, hand and spring
Casserole/Braise	Hand and spring, blade, spare rib, tenderloin, chops, shoulder, belly
Grill/Fry/Barbecue	Spare ribs, belly slices, tenderloin, medallions, fillet and leg steaks, chops (loin, chump, shoulder)

BACON AND HAM CUTS

Allow 375g (12oz) meat on the bone and 175g (6oz) meat off the bone per person.

Cooking method	Cuts
Boil	Gammon: hock, corner, middle, collar, forehock
Bake	Gammon
Grill/Barbecue	Gammon steaks; bacon: back, streaky

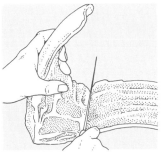

1 *Remove the kidney, if present, if you want, or leave it to be roasted with the joint. Remove the rind if you do not want crackling. Place the joint ribs side up. Insert a boning knife between the meat and the bones at the tip of the rib bones.*

2 *Holding firmly with your free hand, cut downwards against the rib bones until you reach the chine bone on the bottom, releasing the meat as you go. Scrape as much meat away from the bones as possible, holding the knife very close to the bones.*

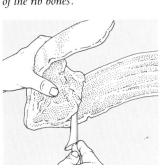

3 *Turn your knife in a right angle to the left and cut off the chine bone. The chine bone and rib bones will come away in one piece. It is not worth scraping meat from between the rib bones. Discard all the bones or save to make stock (page 28).*

4 *Flatten out the belly flap where the ribs were and spread with a stuffing or paste and roll up. Tie at regular intervals (page 144). Score the fat or rind and stick with garlic slivers or herbs, if you like. Weigh and roast according to the chart on page 159.*

PREPARING BACON

Bacon is the collective name for pork that has been preserved or cured. It is either sold 'green' or smoked. Nowadays, bacon is available in a variety of lighter sweeter cures, and many joints do not need any presoaking.

Gammon and bacon joints are sold sliced into rashers or thicker chops. Lean back and middle rashers are from the loin of the animal, streaky rashers from the belly and collar slices from the shoulder end. Streaky bacon is most attractive rolled up as a classic accompaniment to roast turkey.

This country-style Smoked Bacon with Spiced Garlic Potatoes (page 169) uses a bacon joint that does not require presoaking to make a filling dish for colder weather.

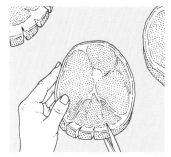

Because of the round shape of gammon steaks they curl up when cooked. To prevent this from happening, snip or cut the rind at 2.5cm (1in) intervals with scissors before cooking. Bacon chops may need snipping, too, if they have the rind still attached. Extra large gammon steaks can be cut into half-moon shapes for cooking.

To make bacon rolls or to stretch rashers for lining terrines (page 98), remove the rind from the rashers, then check for stray bones and lay flat on a board. Run the back of a knife along the rasher holding one end firm. This stretches it and makes rolling up neater. Use a wooden cocktail stick to fasten each bacon roll.

TENDERLOIN

Turn a piece of lean pork tenderloin into a quick rolled joint by slicing lengthwise and beating out thinly. Spread with a stuffing of chopped herbs, nuts, spinach and herbs or simply a spicy, garlicky paste, then roll up, tie, weigh and roast, according to the chart on page 159, basting well with oil or butter. For a 300–375g (10–12oz) tenderloin you will need about 4 tablespoons stuffing or 2 tablespoons garlic paste.

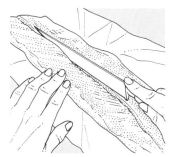

1 Place the piece of tenderloin on a sheet of wet greaseproof paper. Slit down the centre from one end to the other without cutting all the way through the meat. Open out and place another sheet of wet greaseproof paper on top.

2 Using a rolling pin or meat mallet, beat and flatten the meat. Uncover, spread the joint with a fine stuffing or paste and roll up. Tie at regular intervals, then weigh and roast according to the chart on page 159.

Type	SAUSAGES Ingredients	Cooking method
Beef	Minced beef, bread, seasoning	Fry, grill
Black Pudding (blood sausage)	Pig's/sheep's blood, cereal, onion, spices	Slice and fry
Breakfast sausage	Finely minced pork, spices	Boil, fry, grill
Cambridge	Pork (twice lean to fat), herbs, spices	Fry, grill
Chipolata	Minced pork or beef, cereal (half normal width)	Fry, grill
Cumberland	Coarsely chopped pork, spices, black pepper (in continuous link)	Bake, fry or grill
Haggis	Liver, lungs, heart of sheep, oatmeal, parsley, onions and seasonings, (all stuffed in the paunch of the animal)	Boil, fry, bake
Oxford	Minced veal, minced pork, beef, suet, herbs, spices	Fry, grill
Lincolnshire	Minced pork, fat, cereal, sage and spices	Fry, grill
Pork	Minced pork, fat, cereal	Fry, grill
Pork and Beef	Minced pork, minced beef, seasonings, bread	Fry, grill
Saveloy	Minced cured pork, often sold ready cooked or spiced	Deep fry
Venison	Four parts minced venison to one part pork or veal, spices	Fry, grill
Vienna	Minced kosher beef	Warm in hot water

OFFAL

Offal offers an enormous variety of different meats and possible ways of cooking them. It includes all the bits of the animal's carcase that are not straightforward cuts of meat, fat and bone, including the head, tail, feet and internal organs. Although some are squeamish about offal, do not ignore it because it is highly nutritious and economical. It is a rich source of iron which is used by our bodies to make healthy red blood cells. Calf's and pig's trotters are also wonderful for gelling stock.

Lamb's liver and kidneys are the most popular bits of offal; both can be ruined by overcooking but are a delicacy when lightly cooked and juicy. Calf's liver is more expensive but worth it for its mild flavour and melting smoothness.

Generally speaking, lamb's and calf's offal needs just quick light cooking, whereas pig's and ox offal is stronger and needs slow cooking with sweet ingredients such as onions.

PREPARING OFFAL

Offal is somewhat slippery so one of the key pieces of equipment is a good sharp knife. These are very lean types of meat – any fat will be on the outside and easily removed. Some offal contains tubes and membranes and therefore needs more careful preparation than straightforward muscle meats. Offal, however, encompasses such a wide variety of taste and texture that the delicious results more than compensate for the extra labour involved.

KIDNEYS

When you buy kidneys they should have just a mild smell and no discoloured patches. They are sometimes sold with a layer of hard fat, called suet, around them that acts as a protective cushion while the animal is alive. It can be easily peeled off with your fingers. Either discard the fat or grate it to use in suet puddings, such as Special Steak and Kidney Pudding (page 259).

Lamb's kidneys are small while pig's are large.

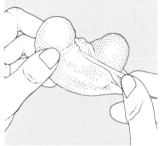

1 *Use the tip of a knife to cut any fine membrane surrounding the kidney, being careful not to cut the flesh. Then peel off and discard the membrane.*

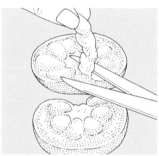

2 *Cut the kidney in half lengthwise through the core, then snip out the tubes and discard. Alternatively, keep the kidney whole and cut across in slices.*

USING OFFAL

• One of my favourite quick supper dishes is a sauté of kidneys with a slightly spicy sauce – with the addition of a little liquid kidneys make an instant, rich sauce of their own. I often add a little wine or brandy with ground spices (cinnamon is good) or some cream or soured cream and fresh herbs.

• I use whole lamb's kidneys as a stuffing for a boned joint of lamb which I am going to cook slightly pink – then the kidneys in the centre remain lightly cooked and add their wonderful flavour. The same technique is used in Saddle of Venison with Spinach and Lamb's Kidneys (page 171).

• Soak sliced pig's or ox liver and kidneys in milk and then cook in the oven at a gentle heat with tomatoes, garlic and a little sherry for at least 2 hours until tender.

• Make quick sauces for grilled or fried lamb's or calf's liver by adding dry sherry, marsala, orange juice or Worcestershire sauce to the pan just as the liver finishes cooking. Remove the liver and let the liquid bubble up, then pour over the liver.

• Another sauce to try with liver is made by stewing a few fresh gooseberries or apricots with sugar to taste and a little sherry vinegar.

Kidneys complement the subtle flavour of veal in Veal and Kidney Rissoles with Fresh Tomato Sauce (page 168), served here with fresh noodles and broccoli.

LIVER

The best liver is calf's liver, sweet and meltingly tender. Lamb's liver is also sweet but firmer when cooked.

Liver is generally sold ready prepared. If not, run your fingers over the surface to check for any tubes and remove. When buying lamb's and calf's liver I look for the palest colour as experience has taught me it is milder and more tender. As well as being shallow fried, calf's and lamb's livers are excellent stir-fried.

Pig's liver is ideal for braising gently in a sauce or for using in pâtés and terrines. Ox liver is best for long, slow cooking. Both pig's and ox livers have strong flavours which can be mellowed by presoaking in milk for about 30 minutes.

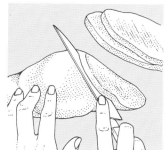

Calf's and lamb's liver are best sliced very thinly for quick shallow or stir-frying. If the liver is sold as one piece, use a sharp knife and cut thin slices across the grain at a slight diagonal, firmly holding the piece of liver steady with one hand while cutting. As you will be cooking the liver so briefly, it is important to cut the liver into even-sized slices so no part of it remains raw or becomes overcooked.

Grilled calf's liver is served here with a delicious sauce made from the pan juices and a little sherry, fresh orange juice and parsley.

SWEETBREADS

Sweetbreads are lamb's or calf's thymus glands from the throat and heart. They are quite fiddly to prepare but have a delicate flavour and creamy soft texture that is a rich reward in itself. After preparing the sweetbreads (below) they can be either shallow fried in butter and oil, or coated with beaten egg and breadcrumbs and deep fried. You can also braise them in stock with chopped onion, carrot and celery, sherry and fresh herbs. Cook at 200°C, 400°F, Gas Mark 6 for about 45 minutes until tender.

For a delicious sweetbread curry, fry sweetbreads and sliced onions with butter and Indian spices over a low heat, stirring frequently until both are very soft. Then add some double cream and fresh coriander leaves and bubble for a minute.

1 *Sweetbreads are easier to peel if soaked and blanched first. Soak sweetbreads in cold salted water for 30 minutes to 4 hours to remove any blood, changing the water whenever it becomes pink. Place in a saucepan of fresh cold water, bring to the boil and simmer for 2 minutes.*

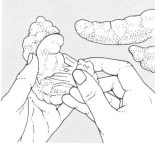

2 *Drain the sweetbreads and rinse well. Use your fingers to peel off the thin membrane and any small amount of fat and the tubes. If you want sweetbreads with a firmer texture, place a weight on top of the sweetbreads for 30 minutes, then cut thinly or chop before cooking.*

HEART

The heart is a muscle that works hard all the animal's lifetime so will be quite tough. Therefore, before cooking, all tubes and sinews need to be removed. Because heart is so lean, it needs a sauce to keep it moist during cooking.

Small lambs' hearts are the best and most tender but still need long gentle cooking. Chopped kidneys are good in stuffing for a lamb's heart, together with fresh breadcrumbs and a little chopped spinach. A lamb's heart stuffed with sage and onions is also very good. Calf's heart is also very tender. As well as being good roasted, it is also good braised or stewed. Ox hearts are good cut up and slowly casseroled with rich ingredients such as red wine, garlic and onions, with a parsnip purée to thicken the sauce. They are also delicious stuffed and braised with vegetables and stock.

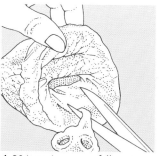

1 *Using scissors, carefully snip out all tubes and sinews. Wash the heart well inside and out and pat dry with absorbent kitchen paper. Soak in lightly salted water for up to 1 hour before cooking, then drain well.*

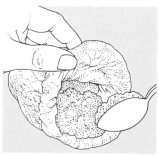

2 *To cook whole, make up a rich, moist and tasty stuffing (above). Spoon it into the heart taking care not to pack too much in and stitch up with kitchen string. Brown well on all sides in hot fat before braising slowly.*

MINCE

The most important thing to realize about minced meat is that it does not have to become grey, granular and tasteless in a glutinous, floury sauce; on the contrary, it is extraordinarily versatile, and when cooked properly minced beef can be as pink and succulent as the best steak. Mince, in fact, can be said to be one of the most useful ingredients for creative cookery. It is possible to buy a very lean mince but a small proportion of fat adds flavour and tenderness. Adding extra flavour to mince is crucial and must not be forgotten – spices, herbs and many other additions make all the difference to the final cooked dish.

Mince can be served in many ways from the most homely cottage pie to the sophisticated steak tartare which is lean, raw seasoned minced beef. The Greek moussaka is rather like a shepherd's pie of minced lamb with tender aubergines and a cheese custard on top instead of potatoes. I love meatballs and make them in many different ways, not only from minced beef but also using pork, lamb and veal, with different seasonings and flavourings to suit the character of the meat and sometimes surprise stuffings too.

I use mince mixtures to stuff vegetables, pancakes and boned joints, fill little pastry pies and to make sauces for spaghetti, including the well-known Bolognese sauce or ragù (page 213). I also love making meat loaves, sometimes striped with two varieties of mince. The possibilities are endless and most of them don't take much time.

MINCING MEAT

Mincing meat yourself is well worth the effort for inexpensive special occasion dishes, for memorable homemade burgers or if you want to use a different meat such as pork or lamb that is not available as ready prepared mince. You also know exactly what meat has been used and can choose lovely, lean juicy cuts. For best results only mince up meat just before cooking, because once minced it deteriorates rapidly.

Mincing can be done in a home mincing machine (hand or electric as an attachment to a mixer), in a food processor or by chopping finely using two very sharp, large, heavy knives. Each method gives a different texture. Mincer mince is ground and slightly twisted, processor mince is more pulverized and some say more tender, while chopped mince is firmer.

After mincing, season well and add additional flavours such as fresh herbs, garlic or onion. As one of the advantages of making your own mince is using good quality meat, however, do not mask it with flavours that are too strong.

To make mince *in a hand mincer or food processor, cut the meat into cubes. Feed the cubes of meat into the mincer in stages. Alternatively, use a food processor and push the meat in stages through the tube with a plunger.*

To mince by hand, *place the meat on a large chopping board and work 2 very sharp, heavy knives up and down on the meat like drumsticks, until the meat is thoroughly chopped.*

MAKING THE MOST OF MINCE

• Try cumin, coriander, cardamom, cinnamon, paprika, allspice, nutmeg and whole caraway seeds to flavour mince.
• Fresh chopped herbs in mince both taste and look good, as does finely chopped red pepper.
• Tomato purée or sun-dried tomato paste adds a lot of flavour to all minced meats, and spoonfuls of mild curry pastes, pickles or even pesto sauce (page 207) can be very effective.
• Chopped raw nuts and grated Parmesan cheese are delicious with lots of garlic in a minced pork mixture.
• A meat loaf can be delicious; I like to use a combination of pork

and veal flavoured with plenty of garlic, tomato purée, chopped capers, chopped fresh rosemary and some grated cheese.
• The taste of shepherd's pie can also be varied by adding spices and herbs and the mashed potato top substituted by other root vegetables; golden sweet potato is delicious and so is celeriac or parsnip. All these vegetable toppings can be sprinkled with grated cheese.
• Fill meatballs with surprise fillings which can include a cube of cheese. This melts within as the meatball cooks. Whole nuts, dried fruits, whole dill seeds, lots of chopped fresh dill and wholegrain mustard are good inside pork meatballs.

Never dismiss hamburgers as mere junk food. When homemade with fresh accompaniments, such as blue cheese, capers and tomatoes, crispy lettuce and green peppers, burgers become a filling meal especially if you have minced the meat yourself.

MAKING MEATBALLS

Meatballs are one of the natural things to make with minced meat, and, not surprisingly, they are popular around the world. In the Middle East, koftas are highly spiced meatballs shaped around skewers, and in India meatballs are often the only tender meat available. Although the spicy, exotic meatballs are usually made with lamb or mutton, you can also use beef and pork, or a combination. The meat should be top quality and more finely minced than for hamburgers. Meatballs can be round, oval-shaped or slightly flattened, but never very big.

For about 8–14 meatballs, use 625–750g (1¼–1½lb) finely minced lamb, 2 teaspoons ground cumin, 3 teaspoons ground coriander, 2 peeled and finely chopped cloves garlic, 1 handful finely chopped fresh mint and salt and black pepper. Serve with natural yogurt mixed with chopped cucumber and mint.

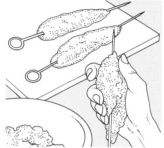

1 *Put the finely minced lamb into a bowl, add the ground spices, the chopped garlic and chopped mint leaves and season generously with salt and freshly ground black pepper. Mix together thoroughly either with your hands or with a wooden spoon until all the ingredients are well combined.*

2 *Using wet hands, take up bits of the mixture and shape, moulding around skewers for koftas or forming into walnut-size meatballs. Either grill (smearing with oil first) or fry in a little oil in a pan, over a medium heat for 8–12 minutes, turning the meatballs often until browned.*

An ideal dish for an informal meal is small cumin-flavoured lamb meatballs as in Aromatic Meatballs with Spinach and Mushrooms (page 170). Just before serving, the meatballs are topped with smetana or soured cream and dusted with paprika.

THE BEST HAMBURGERS

All hamburgers are extremely simple; they should taste of unadulterated meat so must not be bound with egg or coated with flour. Unlike meatball mixtures which can benefit from all manner of spices and additions, hamburgers should be seasoned only with black pepper and sea salt, and possibly a little finely chopped onion and capers. I add some fresh green peppercorns and a little ground coriander seed, or a spoonful of tomato purée if I am not sure of the beef's quality. Ideally it should be top quality and fairly lean, and it must be coarsely minced.

Hamburger flavourings and accompaniments which are added after cooking between meat and bun, or simply as a topping instead of a bun, provide lots of scope for experiment. Classic combinations are excellent; tomato slices and lettuce, pickles and sauces of various kinds, cheese which melts on to the hot meat, thin pieces of grilled streaky bacon, avocado slices, mayonnaise and so on.

If you have a charcoal grill, hamburgers become especially delicious, but in any case the grill or griddle should always be at its hottest so that the meat becomes black in patches on the outside and remains succulent inside – there is nothing good about a dry, grey hamburger.

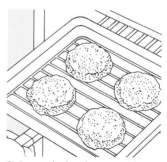

1 *To make 4 burgers, put 750g (1½lb) coarsely minced lean beef into a bowl and mix in coarsely ground black pepper, a little sea salt and finely chopped onion and/or capers, if desired. Using wet hands form the meat into 4 balls, then flatten each slightly to form hamburgers about 2.5cm (1in) thick. If there is time, refrigerate them for 30 minutes.*

2 *Smear the hamburgers with a little oil. Place on a grill pan and grill under the highest heat or on a charcoal grill or barbecue for about 3 minutes each side for rare hamburgers, and 5 minutes for medium. Lightly toast the hamburger buns, then put the cooked hamburger between the bun halves with any additions or relishes on the hamburger.*

GAME

Venison, rabbit and, to a slightly lesser extent, hare are now readily available and reasonable in cost, but they still make a special and often impressive meal. Because rabbit is bred domestically and most venison is farmed they are beautifully tender, even if they lack the intensity of flavour of the wild animals. Venison is also the leanest of all red meats, which is a healthy bonus.

All game should have been hung for a certain amount of time to develop its flavour and tenderness; after a few days hanging, enzymes in the flesh cause a chemical change which tenderizes the meat while strengthening the taste. Very young venison needs hanging most of all as it has the least flavour but older animals with more flavour can be very tough; they should be marinated for at least 24 hours and it is not unusual to marinate large joints for up to four days. The best venison comes from animals aged between 18 and 24 months. When roasting, grilling or frying the meat should never be cooked too long as it is so lean and will become dull and dry – ideally it should be cooked fairly swiftly so it remains pink and juicy inside.

Domestic rabbit is not hung and is very mild in flavour, but has a lovely smooth-textured tenderness. It can be cooked exactly like chicken, using the same recipes, but it should be marinated first for added flavour, or it can be used as a vehicle for absorbing the character of strong ingredients which are cooked with it. As it is so lean it needs to be cooked with other moist ingredients.

Hare cannot be bred domestically and has dark, gamy flesh. When it is hung the blood is often saved to thicken the sauce it is cooked in, as in jugged hare. The strong character of hare makes it ideal for cooking with assertive seasonings, particularly a combination of sweet and sour.

PREPARING VENISON JOINTS

Venison is the name for all deer meat. Most venison now is farmed and when cooked becomes deliciously tender, but that also means it lacks a strong gamy flavour which may disappoint some people. I, in fact, prefer it milder. The choicest cuts of venison are haunch or leg, loin and saddle, and they are best served slightly pink and juicy.

Venison fat is strongly flavoured so it should be removed before roasting. But because venison is so lean, it is advisable to bard joints (page 156) and baste frequently during roasting, or smear with vegetable oil before putting in the oven.

The fuller flavour of venison means it takes beautifully to exciting marinades, which also help to keep the meat moist and tender during roasting.

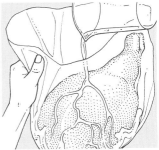

1 *Prepare the marinade in a large jug by mixing together 300ml (½ pint) wine vinegar, 150ml (¼ pint) olive oil, 2–3 crushed garlic cloves, 2 tablespoons crushed juniper berries and fresh herb sprigs. This makes enough marinade for a 1.5kg (3lb) joint.*

2 *Trim the joint, here a haunch, of any fat, membranes or gristle. Place the joint in a large polythene roasting or food bag. Pour in the marinade, then securely close the bag with plastic tags or tie with a knot if the bag is long enough.*

3 *Rub the joint all over in the bag, so it is well covered with the marinade. Place on a large dish and refrigerate for 4–5 days, turning every 8 hours or so. This allows the marinade flavours to permeate the meat.*

4 *To prepare for roasting, remove the joint from the marinade and place it on a rack in a roasting tin. Bard the joint (page 156) or smear it with oil. Weigh and roast it according to the chart (opposite).*

Saddle of Venison with Spinach and Lamb's Kidneys (page 171) is served with a mustard and cream sauce.

VENISON CUTS

Allow 250g (8oz) meat on the bone and 175g (6oz) meat off the bone per person. Begin roasting in a preheated oven, 230° C, 450°F, Gas Mark 8 for 10 minutes, then at the temperature below:

Cooking method	Temperature	Time
Roasting joint on bone		
Haunch (leg), saddle	180°C, 350°F, Gas Mark 4	Rare: 12 minutes per 500g (1lb) plus 12 minutes if necessary Medium: 15 minutes per 500g (1lb) plus 15 minutes if necessary Well done: 20 minutes per 500g (1lb) plus 20 minutes if necessary
Roasting boned rolled joint		
Leg, shoulder	180°C, 350°F, Gas Mark 4	Medium: 20 minutes per 500g (1lb) plus 20 minutes if necessary Well done: 25 minutes per 500g (1lb) plus 25 minutes if necessary
Casserole		
Shoulder, boned and diced	180°C, 350°F, Gas Mark 4	1½–2 hours
Grill/Fry		
Tenderloin chops or steaks	Medium heat	20–30 minutes

RABBIT AND HARE CUTS

A cleaned and skinned rabbit weighing 1.7kg (3½lb) will serve 4 people; a 2kg (4½lb) hare will serve 6 people.

Cooking method	Temperature	Time
Roast		
Saddle	180°C, 350°F, Gas Mark 4	35–40 minutes for up to 1kg (2lb) 40–50 minutes up to 2kg (4½lb)
Casserole		
All joints including saddle	160°C, 325°F, Gas Mark 3	1–1½ hours, depending on age

FLAVOURING GAME

• Olive oil mixed with lemon juice, black pepper, garlic and a few herbs (but never salt which draws the juices out) is an easy and excellent marinade for game. A little sherry vinegar is also an effective addition.

• Marinades can be liquid or more like a thick paste of seasonings – this can be a generous mixture of spices and herbs moistened with a little lemon juice, red wine or fruit vinegar and oil, which is smeared on to a joint and left for the flavours to be absorbed before roasting.

• Joints of game can be immersed for several hours or days in liquid marinades containing not only oil, lemon juice and seasoning but wine as well and will become substantially tenderized and fuller flavoured.

• More complicated liquid marinades can be made rather like a stock by cooking vegetables such as carrots, onions and celery with herbs and seasonings in an oil and wine mixture, then leaving to cool before using.

• The strong taste of hare benefits from a rather sweet but garlicky marinade and then by casseroling gently with both sweet and sharp ingredients – dried apricots, onions, yellow peppers and crushed juniper berries are a good combination, with ground cinnamon and a teaspoon of whole caraway seeds, and a little orange juice as the liquid.

• Rabbit is often cooked with mustard and cream – I casserole joints with whole shallots or pickling onions, wholegrain mustard, green peppercorns and a glass of sweet cider. When the rabbit is cooked I add double cream and bubble up the sauce for a minute.

JOINTING RABBIT AND HARE

Rabbit and hare are best served jointed, if only because they don't look too appetizing roasted whole, although they can be roasted with a stuffing in the cavity. The saddle or loin is the most tender cut and can be roasted, but the joints are best cooked slowly as in a flavourful casserole such as my recipe for Rabbit and Pumpkin with Mustard (page 171), pictured below.

Jointing a skinned and gutted rabbit or hare by this method will give 7 pieces.

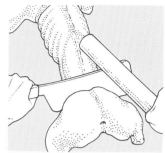

1 *Place the skinned and gutted rabbit or hare belly side down. Using a rolling pin and meat cleaver cut crosswise to remove the hindlegs, and again to remove the forelegs, leaving the back whole.*

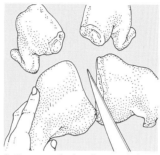

2 *Separate the hindlegs and the forelegs into 2 pieces each. On adult hares the massive hindlegs can be cut into several more pieces.*

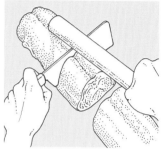

3 *Cut the saddle into 3 equal-sized pieces crosswise depending on the size of the saddle, using a rolling pin to help push the meat cleaver through the bones.*

The classic combination of rabbit and mustard is enhanced with caraway in casseroled Rabbit and Pumpkin with Mustard (page 171).

ROASTING BEEF *and* VEAL

Roasting is a wonderful cooking process for larger pieces of meat, producing a tempting smell as the joint sizzles in the oven. The most important thing to remember if you want to produce a perfect roast is that it needs care and attention. All too often a roasted joint is treated as a convenience food: brought straight out of the refrigerator and put, unseasoned, into the oven for an allotted time during which it is forgotten – this will do nothing for the meat except to cook it.

Meat should always sit at room temperature for two hours or more before roasting. Because both ovens and the meat itself are unpredictable you must never rely entirely on timing charts and suggested temperatures – you must check constantly during the cooking and adapt timing and heat, if necessary. I invariably like to start the meat off in the hottest part of the oven for 10 minutes and then lower the heat for the remainder of the cooking, somtimes lowering it even twice.

Basting the meat is also vital for succulence and to create a beautiful gloss. Vital, too, is the resting of the joint before carving. All joints should be left in a warm place, or in the turned-off oven with the door open for 15–20 minutes after cooking – this will tenderize the meat and give it a better texture which will be easier to carve.

RIB ROAST

A joint of beef, to my mind, should always be roasted so the flesh remains pale to dark pink within a glossily browned crust – those who insist on eating only grey meat can have the outside slices but they will miss out on the succulence. Flavour joints off the bone with garlic cloves or herb sprigs inserted into small slices in the flesh. I don't usually add extra flavouring to prime joints of beef, particularly when they are on the bone, except some olive oil and freshly ground black pepper and a bit of crushed sea salt for those who enjoy the fat (as I confess I do).

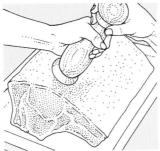

1 About 2 hours before roasting smear the skin side of the beef joint generously all over with olive oil or softened butter, then grind on black pepper to taste. Set the joint aside in the roasting tin and covered loosely in a cool place, but not the refrigerator, until you are ready to put it in the oven to roast.

2 Weigh and calculate the cooking time and preheat the oven (see chart opposite). Keep in mind that long, thinner joints tend to take less time than a smaller, tall joint, regardless of weight. Season the meat with freshly ground black pepper and rub coarse sea salt into the fat. Place the tin in the oven.

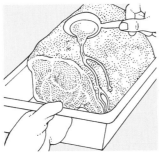

3 During roasting baste occasionally with a large metal spoon, spooning over the pan juices. Remove from the oven, transfer the meat to a warm serving plate and keep warm for 15–20 minutes while you make the gravy. After 10 minutes pour off any cooking juices from the serving plate and add to the gravy.

BARDING LEAN JOINTS

Barding is a simple technique of covering a lean joint with thin sheets of pork fat or rashers of fatty bacon. (This is different from larding where strips of fat are actually threaded through the joint with a larding needle.) The fat bastes the joint as it roasts so it does not dry out. This technique can be used for venison and game birds as well as for beef and veal joints. Pork fat is used because of its blander flavour and more pliable texture.

Season or flavour the joint as normal, then wrap the fat over the top. Tie at intervals with kitchen string. Weigh the joint, roast and baste as normal. Discard the fat before serving, if you like.

IDEAS FOR ROASTING BEEF AND VEAL

• The flavour and succulence of a good joint of roast beef on the bone is so good that it needs little extra seasoning or complicated accompaniments. Leaner, boneless joints such as topside, can be enhanced by making deep slits in the meat with a knife, inserting well-crushed garlic and green peppercorns, capers or wholegrain mustard and then pot-roasting (page 160). Wholegrain mustard can be smeared with olive oil on to any beef joint before roasting.

• Roast beef can be served with horseradish stirred into whipped cream, béarnaise sauce or simply Greek yogurt seasoned with finely chopped capers and black pepper.

• As an alternative to gravy for beef, heat double cream with the de-fatted pan juices, adding sea salt and crushed green peppercorns.

• Joints of veal are invariably boned and stuffings can play an important part. Fresh herbs such as marjoram, sage, thyme or rosemary added to breadcrumbs with finely chopped butter, sautéed mushrooms, onions, peppers, aubergines or even dried apricots. Bind the stuffing ingredients with egg, or alternatively with curd cheese.

• Joints of veal produce intensely flavoured juices; add a little vermouth, sherry or cider to the pan and bubble on top of the stove, stirring in all of the veal juices and residue, then add double cream and bubble again for a delicious sauce.

BEEF IN PASTRY

In the classic Beef Wellington the beef fillet is surrounded by a mixture of chopped and sautéed onion and mushroom and a good liver pâté, but you can simplify this, as I often do by using only pâté with extra flavourings. You can make your own flaky pastry (page 250) or use ready-made puff pastry. Serve with béarnaise sauce (page 200) or creamed horseradish.

For a 1kg (2lb) fillet of beef to serve 6–8 people you will need a mixture made from 2 teaspoons crushed green peppercorns, 1 tablespoon finely chopped fresh parsley and 175g (6oz) liver pâté.

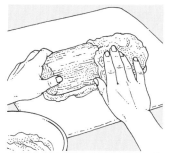

1 *On a lightly floured surface roll out 500g (1lb) pastry fairly thinly to a rectangle large enough to enclose the beef. Spread about one-third of the pâté mixture down the centre of the pastry making sure it is as wide and as long as the fillet. Place the beef on top, then cover the top and sides with the remaining mixture.*

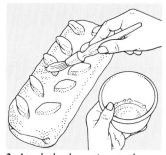

2 *Trim the corners and the long edges of the pastry so that the long edges meet on top of the fillet and fold up to enclose. Moisten the edges with water and press to seal. Fold up the end pastry, moisten with water and seal to make a neat parcel. Cut out decorations from the pastry trimmings (page 245).*

3 *Attach the decorations to the pastry with water, using a pastry brush. Pierce 2 holes for the steam to escape. Place the parcel join-side down on a baking sheet and chill for at least 30 minutes. Brush on beaten egg yolk. Cook at 220°C, 425°F, Gas Mark 7 for 45 minutes for rare; let stand for 10 minutes before carving.*

QUICK GRAVY

I never make a thickened gravy (page 199), which I know some people like. Instead, about 30 minutes before the end of cooking I add a glass of liquid to the roasting tin. While the joint is resting on its serving plate I bubble the juices in the roasting tin, reducing or adding a little water or stock as necessary. To make an instant sauce, stir in double cream and bubble until reduced.

Place the roasting tin *on the stove and bubble up the juices, scraping the bottom. Add extra liquid or reduce and then season.*

A tender, juicy fillet of beef wrapped in an egg yolk-glazed crust of puff pastry is an impressive sight.

ROASTING CHART

Beef

All timings are guidelines only. Longer, thinner joints may need less time, so it is best to check about three-quarters of the way through the calculated cooking time; it may not need the extra time. Internal temperature on a meat thermometer (page 159) should be: rare, 60°C (140°F); medium, 70°C (160°F); well done, 80°C (175°F). Stuffed joints need an extra 5–10 minutes per 500g (1lb). Begin roasting in a preheated oven, 230°C, 450°F, Gas Mark 8 for 10 minutes, then at the temperature below:

Cut	Temperature	Time per 500g (1lb)
Joint on bone		
Forerib, sirloin, wing rib	180°C, 350°F, Gas Mark 4	Rare: 10 minutes plus 10 minutes if necessary Medium: 12 minutes plus 12 minutes if necessary Well done: 20 minutes plus 20 minutes if necessary
Boned rolled joint		
Fillet, rolled rib, top rump, topside	180°C, 350°F, Gas Mark 4	Rare: 12 minutes plus 10 minutes if necessary Medium: 15 minutes plus 15 minutes if necessary Well done: 20 minutes plus 20 minutes if necessary

Veal

Internal temperature on a meat thermometer (page 159) should be: medium, 70°C (160°F); well done, 80°C (175°F). Stuffed joints need an extra 5–10 minutes per 500g (1lb). Begin roasting in a preheated oven, 230°C, 450°F, Gas Mark 8 for 10 minutes, then at the temperature below:

Cut	Temperature	Time per 500g (1lb)
Boned rolled joint		
Fillet, shoulder, topside	180°C, 350°F, Gas Mark 4	Medium: 20 minutes plus 20 minutes if necessary Well done: 25 minutes plus 25 minutes if necessary

ROASTING LAMB *and* PORK

Lamb can be roasted in two equally delicious ways; either gently and long so it begins to fall apart and becomes meltingly tender but dark and crisp on the outside, or for a shorter time at a higher heat so the flesh is pale pink to a darker pink in the centre and very juicy, as the French like it. The second method is best for a leg, saddle or crown roast, but a shoulder, which has the sweetest flavour, can be cooked either way. As it is a difficult joint to carve, a shoulder is a good choice for boning, stuffing and rolling. All lamb is delicious flavoured with garlic.

Pork provides lots of dense meat and therefore works out relatively inexpensive for a roast joint. As pigs are now bred so lean it is most important to keep the flesh moist, especially as it has to be thoroughly cooked. Stuffings are a good idea for pork joints and can be flavoured similar to those suggested for roast veal (page 156).

Roasted joints should never be wrapped in foil as it simply steams rather than roasts the joint, and there will be none of the glossy crispness on the outside which comes from frequent basting in an open roasting tin.

ROASTING A LEG OF LAMB

A leg of lamb is a lean joint with a delicate flavour and should always be cooked so it is still pink inside to retain its succulence. Prepare the joint at least 2 hours before roasting so the flesh absorbs the flavours of this light coating: mix 2 cloves of crushed garlic with fresh thyme or oregano, black pepper and a little lemon juice. Make small, deep slits in the meat and push the mixture in with your finger. Smear the whole joint with a little lemon juice mixed with olive oil and leave at room temperature.

1 *Just before roasting smear a little more olive oil all over the prepared joint, then rub the outside skin with crushed sea salt, if you like, and put into a roasting tin. Weigh and roast according to the chart (opposite), basting frequently.*

2 *About 20 minutes before the end of cooking add about 75ml (3fl oz) dry vermouth to the roasting tin. After roasting, leave the joint to rest on a warm serving plate in a warm place for 15–25 minutes. Use the pan juices to make gravy (page 157).*

SHOULDER OF LAMB

A completely boned shoulder of lamb is ideal for stuffing and is easy to carve. Bone it yourself (page 146) or ask the butcher to do it for you.

A 1.2kg (2½lb) boned and stuffed joint is enough to serve 6 people.

1 *Prepare a stuffing (see box). Open up the meat, skin side down, and evenly pat in the stuffing, making sure you press it into any pockets.*

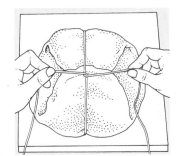

2 *Roll up the meat and tie with kitchen string. Smear the skin with olive oil and crushed sea salt and place in a roasting tin, join side down. Weigh the joint and roast according to the chart (opposite).*

FLAVOURINGS AND STUFFINGS FOR LAMB AND PORK

• To stuff a 1.2kg (2½lb) boned shoulder of lamb mix together a good handful of finely chopped blanched spinach, 2 chopped garlic cloves, 50g (2oz) can anchovies, 2 teaspoons dried oregano, 50g (2oz) chopped walnuts and 1 beaten egg with black pepper to taste.
• An old-fashioned stuffing for lamb is a mixture of crab meat and breadcrumbs.
• Vary basic olive oil and wine marinades for lamb by adding some soy sauce, mustard or mild curry paste.
• Yogurt is a good marinade in itself as it tenderizes the meat. You can mix it with chopped mint and cumin or with tomato paste, crushed garlic and ground coriander.
• Lamb does not need a substantial stuffing; insertions of

herbs, garlic and aromatics are usually enough.
• Lamb has a particular affinity with thyme and rosemary, and also with dried oregano.
• A mixture of mint and cumin adds a Middle Eastern touch to a lamb stuffing.
• Roast a boned piece of lamb rolled round some halved lamb's kidneys, which will remain pink and succulent in the centre. The wonderful juices of the kidneys add to the flavour of the lamb and to the pan juices.
• For joints of pork I smear thick yogurt marinades on the flesh but not on the skin of the joint. I often add a sweeter element such as orange juice. Beer is a good liquid to add to the pan to baste the joint with as it cooks.
• Sage and juniper berries are classic flavourings for pork.

• Finely chopped spinach spread on to a boned piece of pork, then seasoned and rolled before roasting, will add moisture to the flesh.
• For an easy, creamy sauce to serve with roast pork or lamb reduce the juices until they are almost sticky, then add double cream and bubble up in the pan, seasoning to taste. A little sherry or balsamic vinegar, stirred into the cream sauce gradually at the end is often a good idea, and tomato purée is another.
• Fresh chopped herbs added to a gravy or sauce at the last moment always improves the appearance.
• Redcurrant or rowan berry jelly stirred into lamb or pork gravy with a splash or two of port and a few shakes of soy sauce is wonderful.

ROASTING A LOIN OF PORK

It is advisable to cook pork thoroughly – that is until just done with no pinkness but still tender and juicy. A meat thermometer (below) helps you determine more accurately if the meat is cooked all the way through.

Leg and loin joints are the prime cuts for roasting, and they can be roasted on or off the bone. If unboned ask the butcher to cut the chine bone from loin joints for easier carving.

Be sure the oven is preheated according to the chart (below) before you put the joint in if you want really crisp crackling.

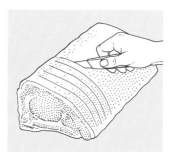

1 *To make perfect crackling, deeply score the rind and fat without cutting into the meat. The scores should be about 5mm (¼in) apart. You will need a very sharp knife – I use a Stanley knife that I keep just for use in the kitchen. If the crackling is not evenly scored, you will find it difficult to cut when carving.*

2 *Wipe the rind with a clean, damp cloth, then sprinkle liberally with crushed sea salt and rub it into the rind.*

3 *Place the joint on a rack in a roasting tin. Remove from the oven 3 or 4 times during roasting and splash with water.*

USING A MEAT THERMOMETER

One way of ensuring thoroughly cooked meat is to use a meat thermometer, shaped like a metal spike. Using one certainly takes all the guesswork out of calculating the roasting times.

Different meats are cooked at certain temperatures. Stick the thermometer's spike into the thickest part of the joint. While the joint is roasting watch the dial move up until it reaches the required internal temperature (see charts right and page 157). Or, insert the thermometer towards the end of the estimated cooking time to check the temperature inside the joint.

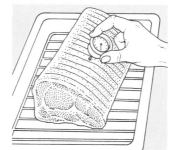

When putting *a meat thermometer in a large joint of meat avoid hitting the bone as this can give a false high reading. Once the thermometer is in position, do not move it or too many juices will escape. Try and buy a thermometer with a thin spike so it does not create a large hole in the joint's flesh.*

Apple rings quickly sautéed in butter and fresh sage are the traditional accompaniments for a golden roasted loin of pork.

ROASTING CHART

Lamb

All timings are guidelines only. Longer, thinner joints may need less time, so it is best to check about three-quarters of the way through the calculated cooking time. Internal temperature on a meat thermometer should be: rare, 60°C (140°F); medium, 70°C (160°F); well done, 80°C (175°F). Stuffed joints need an extra 5–10 minutes per 500g (1lb). Begin roasting in a preheated oven, 230°C, 450°F, Gas Mark 8 for 10 minutes, then at the temperature below:

Cut	Temperature	Time per 500g (1lb)
Joint on bone		
Best end, crown roast, guard of honour, loin, saddle, shoulder	180°C, 350°F, Gas Mark 4	Medium: 15 minutes plus 15 minutes if necessary Well done: 20 minutes plus 20 minutes if necessary
Boned rolled joint		
Leg, loin, shoulder	180°C, 350°F, Gas Mark 4	Medium: 25 minutes plus 25 minutes if necessary Well done: 30 minutes plus 30 minutes if necessary

Pork

Internal temperature on a meat thermometer should be 80°C (175°F). Stuffed joints need an extra 5–10 minutes per 500g (1lb). Begin roasting in a preheated oven, 230°C, 450°F, Gas Mark 8 for 10 minutes, then at the temperature below:

Cut	Temperature	Time per 500g (1lb)
Joint on bone		
Hand, leg, loin, shoulder	180°C, 350°F Gas Mark 4	25 minutes plus 25 minutes if necessary
Boned rolled joint		
Leg, loin, shoulder	180°C, 350°F, Gas Mark 4	30 minutes plus 30 minutes if necessary

CASSEROLING *and* POT-ROASTING

The toughest joints of meat often have the richest flavour; braising, pot-roasting and casseroling are long, gentle methods of cooking in a pot which not only bring out the flavour to the full but also transform the meat to a melting tenderness. Vegetables and other ingredients cooked in the same pot add their goodness to the wonderful juices.

Braising and pot-roasting are similar in that they both involve cooking with small amounts of liquid with chopped vegetables. As a rule, however, pieces of meat are braised but whole joints can be pot-roasted or braised. Likewise there is little difference between casseroling and stewing, where pieces of meat cook in gently simmering liquid. The cooking liquids of casseroles, however, are often thickened after cooking. None of the terms are very exact, which is partly why these methods of cooking are so versatile and pleasing.

It is useful to know that it is not really necessary to seal the meat before cooking; browning the meat does not improve the dish but it will deepen the colour of the sauce if that is what you want. Vegetables, however, do seem to take on a sweeter flavour if they are sautéed in a little fat in the pot first. Although marinating adds moisture to dry, lean meats, it is also not essential unless you feel you have a really tough piece of meat; if you add liquid such as wine, and also aromatics to the pot the meat will absorb their goodness during the long, slow cooking.

BEEF CASSEROLE

Beef needs longer and gentler cooking than other stewing meats to become tender, but it can produce a most satisfying, rich flavour. I like to use plenty of garlic which becomes sweet and mild during the extended cooking. Onions are also necessary, I feel, for their sweet softness. You can experiment with different vegetables such as celery and root vegetables, adding them when you add the onions. This quantity serves 4–5.

25g (1oz) plain flour
1kg (2lb) stewing steak, such as
  chuck, cut into large chunks
3 rounded tablespoons meat
  dripping or lard
2 large onions, chopped roughly
4 large cloves garlic, chopped
  roughly
300ml (½ pint) beef stock or red
  wine
397g (14oz) can chopped
  tomatoes
3 teaspoons wholegrain mustard
1 teaspoon sugar
Chopped fresh parsley
Salt and pepper

1 *Put the flour and salt and pepper into a polythene food bag, add the beef and shake to coat evenly in the flour. Melt the fat in a flameproof casserole over a fairly high heat. Add the beef.*

2 *Cook the beef until browned on all sides. Remove and set aside. Add the chopped onions to the casserole, with more fat, if necessary. Stir until softened and slightly browned, then add the garlic. Stir in any surplus flour from the bag and cook for 3 minutes, then return the meat and any juices to the casserole.*

3 *Gradually stir in the stock or wine, tomatoes and mustard. Continue stirring until bubbling and thickened, then season with salt, black pepper and sugar. Cover and cook at 150°C, 300°F, Gas Mark 2 for 3–3½ hours until tender. Before serving add a handful of chopped parsley.*

Few things can be more welcoming on a cold day than a hearty beef casserole with tender chunks of meat and tasty root vegetables such as baby parsnips.

POT-ROASTING A PORK JOINT

Blades, shoulders, hands and springs are ideal pork joints for long, slow, delicious pot-roasting where the result is a meltingly tender joint with a tasty sauce at the same time. If liked, bone the meat first. Have a selection of chopped vegetables ready as a base for cooking the meat on.

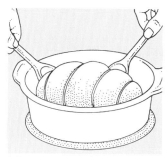 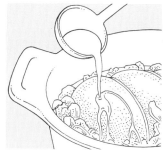

1 *Remove any rind and tie the joint into a neat shape (page 144). Stud with slivers of garlic at intervals, if liked. In a large flameproof casserole, brown the meat in hot oil, turning frequently. Remove the joint and set on one side, then brown a selection of roughly chopped vegetables. Return the joint to the pan on top of the browned vegetables, together with any juices.*

2 *Add enough hot stock or water to a depth of about 4cm (1½in), and bring to the boil. Season, cover and cook gently over a low heat, or in the oven at 160°C, 325°F, Gas Mark 3 for 45–50 minutes per 500g (1lb). After cooking, discard the vegetables and flavourings, strain the juices into a small pan and thicken with a little cornflour or arrowroot to make a sauce (page 199).*

FLAVOURING POT ROASTS AND CASSEROLES

• All pot-roasted and casseroled meat and game is improved by a certain sweetness in the ingredients: peeled and chopped parsnips lend a delicious flavour and at the same time often disintegrate and thicken the liquid; dried fruit such as prunes and apricots are often cooked with lamb and spices in Middle Eastern or North African dishes, and they also go particularly well with pork and veal.

• Slivers of orange peel and orange juice for the cooking liquid go particularly well in a beef casserole, combined with a pinch or two of ground cloves and some crushed juniper berries.

• Lamb, veal and pork are enhanced by cumin, coriander, cardamom and paprika, while beef can take on cloves and allspice. Cinnamon goes well with all meat.

• If you don't want to thicken your dish with flour but would rather the sauce has some body, include either very finely chopped onion, root vegetables or even sweet red pepper (for a beautiful scarlet effect). These will cook to such softness that they amalgamate with the thin liquid and so thicken it.

• Liquids added to stews, pot-roasts and casseroles can be mixtures of stock and wine, beer and stout, marsala, sherry, citrus juices or even flamed brandy, in varying quantities depending on the style of the finished dish.

• Vegetables which do not suit long cooking, such as most green vegetables, can be added 20–30 minutes before the end of the cooking so that they don't lose their freshness. Apart from vegetables and fresh or dried fruits there are other things which add flavour and character to slow-cooked dishes; for example, black olives, walnuts, canned chestnuts, dried mushrooms, pickled lemons or simply a little grated orange zest.

SIMPLE LAMB CURRY

Ideally the spices for a curry, a simple braised dish, will be at their most aromatic when bought whole and freshly ground but when you are in a hurry a good curry, like this one, can be made by using a bottled curry paste. Fresh ginger and garlic, however, cannot be replaced, and fresh coriander makes all the difference. This quantity serves 4–5 people.

2 tablespoons groundnut oil
25g (1oz) butter
1 large onion, puréed
2–3 teaspoons mild curry paste
3 large cloves garlic, chopped
5cm (2in) piece fresh ginger, peeled and chopped finely
1kg (2lb) lamb neck fillet, cubed
1 tablespoon tomato purée dissolved in 300 ml (½ pint) water
Juice of 1 lemon
Handful fresh coriander leaves
Salt

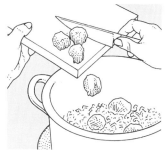 

1 *Heat the groundnut oil and butter in a flameproof casserole over a fairly high heat. Add the puréed onion and cook, stirring occasionally, until slightly brown. Stir in the curry paste, chopped garlic and ginger and pieces of lamb fillet. Cook for 2 minutes, stirring until the meat cubes are browned all over.*

2 *Add the tomato purée and water and lemon juice, season with salt and bring up to bubbling. Cover and cook in the oven at 160°C, 325°F, Gas Mark 3 for 1½–2 hours until the lamb is very tender, stirring around once or twice. Stir in roughly chopped coriander leaves and serve with basmati rice.*

Fresh coriander leaves add colour and flavour to this simple lamb curry, served here with puppodums and spiced basmati rice.

GRILLING *and* FRYING

Only the more expensive cuts of meat should be used for grilling, as the heat is fierce, which combined with the short cooking time, makes tough meat tougher. Lean meat such as veal and pork should ideally be marinated before grilling, and basting while grilling or barbecuing also helps meat remain moist.

Good quality, carefully grilled meat can be delicious – charred on the outside and succulent inside. Grilling on a barbecue over charcoal or wood, with its added aromatics, is best of all. Meat for grilling, or for roasting, should be at room temperature before beginning.

Frying is a more versatile method of cooking as it can be done in several ways with or without other ingredients. For tender meat, frying should either be done quickly over a high heat so that the meat remains pink inside, or over a low heat for much longer – anything in between will be inclined to produce tough meat, as meat toughens after the first minutes of fierce cooking and then becomes tender again with time and gentle cooking.

Sautéing or stir-frying in a little oil or melted butter are the quickest methods, but are only successful with small, even-sized, thin slices of boneless meat – marinating the meat before cooking is best, and thinly sliced vegetables can be added.

Shallow frying in oil, butter or fat in a heavy-based pan is better for larger pieces of meat such as chops and steaks. It is also possible to dry fry chops and steaks, starting in a cold pan with no added fat, so that those on a low-fat diet can pour away almost every scrap of fat which comes out of the meat during cooking.

GRILLING CHOPS

Use only prime quality chops, such as loin or best end of neck for grilling as the meat can toughen and dry out quickly with the fierce heat. Brush liberally with fat or oil before cooking or for leaner cooking baste frequently with a marinade while grilling. The other essential hint is to preheat the grill well so the meat seals quickly. Use tongs or two wooden spoons to turn the meat rather than a fork so the flesh isn't punctured, allowing the juices to seep out.

You can tell when a chop is cooked by pressing it with the flat edge of a knife. If the chop is slightly springy and soft it is still pink inside; a firmer texture indicates the chop is just done. Be careful not to overcook.

Grilled chops are delicious spread with a little honey or currant or mint jelly and popped back under the grill quickly, or topped with pats of herb and garlic or mustard butter.

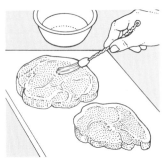

1 *If you like, marinate the chops before grilling for extra flavour and reserve the excess marinade for brushing on the chops during grilling. Preheat the grill to high. Brush the chops with oil or melted butter. Season with black pepper only and spices. Pork chops with rind will need to have the skin and fat snipped at 2.5cm (1in) intervals to keep the chops flat during grilling.*

2 *Place the chops on a lightly greased grill pan and quickly brown to seal on both sides. Turn down the heat to medium and continue cooking the chops until done as desired, turning the chops once more during grilling. Brush any marinade on the chops while grilling. Check for doneness by pressing with the flat edge of a knife. Season with salt and extra pepper if liked, and serve.*

FRYING VEAL ESCALOPES

Veal escalopes are thin slices cut across the grain from the fillet or cushion end of the leg. The usual way to treat escalopes is to coat them in egg and breadcrumbs (preferably made from 2-day-old bread) before frying. I also like to sauté the uncoated meat gently in butter, adding lemon juice and fresh herbs, and often some cream at the end of basting to form a delectable sauce.

Take care never to cook escalopes too long or the lean meat will dry out and become tough. Escalopes can also be cut in slivers for stir-frying.

1 *Place the escalopes well spaced apart on a wet sheet of greaseproof paper and cover with a second wet sheet of greaseproof paper. Use a rolling pin or meat mallet to beat out the meat evenly until the escalopes are very thin. Peel off and throw away the pieces of paper.*

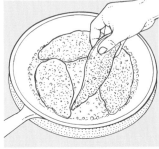

2 *The escalopes can either be fried with or without a breadcrumb coating. If liked, dip the escalopes first in a bowl of beaten egg, then in one of breadcrumbs. If coated, chill the escalopes for at least 15 minutes before frying to let the coating set.*

3 *Melt a small amount of olive oil and butter together in a large heavy-based frying pan. Add the escalopes in a single layer and fry for 2–4 minutes on each side, turning only once. Serve at once, sprinkled with lemon juice and salt and pepper.*

COOKING STEAKS

Beef and lamb are the best meats for steaks as they are nicest served slightly pink. Beef fillet and sirloin steaks are the most tender and rump (from the top of the leg) has the most flavour. Lamb steaks are either leg fillet, or from the loin, or lean shoulders. 'Frying steak' is from less tender parts of the animal which have been beaten to tenderize.

With practice you can tell how well a steak is cooked by pressing it with your finger, rather than cutting it open and letting juices escape. Use this guide: blue/very rare – when meat is simply browned on the outside and feels very soft when pressed; rare – meat feels springy when pressed and drops of blood and juices appear on the outside; medium rare – meat feels quite firm and just a little springy and pinkish juices are visible; well done – meat quite firm to touch.

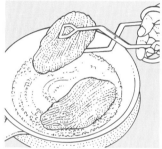

1 *Preheat a heavy-based frying pan or grill until very hot. Add a small amount of olive oil and butter to the pan, or use a brush if grilling. Add the steaks and cook for 1–4 minutes on each side, turning once with tongs.*

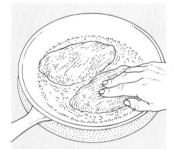

2 *Test for doneness (above) and remove the steaks from the pan or grill. If frying, add wine or stock to the pan juices, swirl, season and add a little cream or knob of butter. Pour over the steaks and serve at once.*

A perfectly fried fillet steak with its well-browned exterior and a still pink interior is served here with some homemade chips (page 43) and a simple salad with grilled tomatoes.

FLAVOURING GRILLED AND FRIED MEAT

• Marinades give grilled and fried meats many different flavours. The marinades can be a simple mixture of olive oil with lemon juice and coarsely ground pepper. Or, add flavourings such as herbs, spices, crushed garlic, juniper berries, capers, green peppercorns or fresh ginger.
• Liquids I like to use for marinades include lemon, orange, lime or pineapple juices, soy sauce, wine and sherry and other alcohols, including whisky.
• Thicker marinades, ideal for grilled meats, can be made from seasoned natural yogurt. These are more like a paste, which softens the meat's texture if rubbed in and left for several hours or overnight. Stir spices such as cumin, coriander and cinnamon into the yogurt with lemon juice and chopped garlic. I add a great deal of chopped mint, thyme or rosemary for lamb or pork.
• Make a thick sauce from grilled, skinned and puréed sweet peppers to serve with grilled meat – after puréeing reheat with a generous amount of butter, a little lemon juice and plenty of chopped fresh herbs, seasoned well.
• Grilled kebabs are popular in my family. Ideally, use prime quality cuts of beef, lamb, pork or veal, but less tender cuts can be used if marinated first. For lamb kebabs cut long neck fillets into small medallions. Marinate in a mixture of yogurt or olive oil flavoured with crushed garlic, grated ginger, lemon juice, ground cumin and seasoning, turning occasionally for at least 2 hours.
• Add chopped fresh herbs to bottled Chinese marinades.

BARBECUING SPARE RIBS

Chinese-style spare ribs (as distinct from the bigger British shoulder spare rib chops) are, as the name suggests, the leftover rib joints leading off from the loin. Normally pork ribs are used for this party-style dish but lamb riblets are equally suitable and can be treated in the same way.

The secret of successful spare ribs that are deliciously flavourful and tender enough to almost fall from the bones is to cook them long and slowly, then finish them under intense heat to caramelize the outside.

The Chinese have a saying 'the nearer the bone, the sweeter the meat' and nowhere is this truer than with their style of cooking very bony ribs. The sauce, a lovely blend of sweet and savoury flavours, is almost as important as the meat itself.

Marinate the spare ribs overnight in a barbecue sauce made from a mixture of soy sauce, sherry, vinegar, sugar or honey, chopped garlic, ginger and Chinese five-spice powder. Transfer the ribs and the marinade to an ovenproof dish, cover and cook at 160°C, 325°F, Gas Mark 3 for about 1 hour. Either increase the oven to 200°C, 400°F, Gas Mark 6 and roast, uncovered, for 30 minutes, skimming off excess fat, or transfer the ribs to a barbecue or preheated grill, spooning over excess marinade, to brown and caramelize the outside.

BOILING *and* POACHING

Boiling and poaching meat are methods which cannot really be distinguished; the most accurate term would be poaching, which implies gentleness, as meat should never be boiled. Instead, merely bring it slowly to the boil in cold water and then simmer as gently as possible to prevent the flesh from becoming tough. It is often a refreshingly pure experience to have a dish of tender, boiled meat with a green sauce such as they serve in Italy.

Cuts of meat which poach most successfully are brisket and silverside of beef, neck and knuckle of veal, breast and stewing cuts of lamb, the leg, belly or hand of pork, and,

of course, gammon, ham and bacon joints. A certain amount of fat is nicer, particularly with salted and cured meats as the curing gives it a unique texture and taste.

I love salted and cured meats; beef, pork, ham and bacon joints, either to eat hot or cold. If we are going to have a boneless joint cold I wrap it in foil after poaching while it is still hot and leave it to cool overnight under some weights. This presses the meat together which gives it a finer consistency and makes it much easier to carve. Although salted and cured meats are soaked before poaching the liquid is seldom suitable for stocks.

BOILED SALT BEEF AND DUMPLINGS

This is one of the great classic recipes and a marvellous winter warmer. Beef cuts sold ready salted are very lean silverside and the slightly fattier, but better flavoured rolled brisket. Both cuts are sold tied in a neat compact shape to fit a large saucepan.

Salt beef and salt pork, too, if you can find it, and hams are now available in lighter and sweeter cures that do not require long soaking times. If sold wrapped follow the instructions. Generally, however, only a few hours soaking, say 4–8, will be necessary. Traditional salt cure meats will need to be soaked for at least 24 hours and have the water changed two or three times to remove excess saltiness. Although the cooking liquid will still be too salty to use for stock, you can mix some with unsalted stock to make a ham and pea soup.

If serving with dumplings, prepare the dumpling mixture just before cooking and then cook on the lowest simmer so they don't break up.

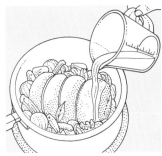

1 *After soaking place the joint in a saucepan with sliced carrots, onion, celery, a few bay leaves, whole black peppercorns, and juniper berries or cloves. Add fresh water to cover.*

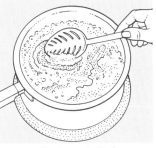

2 *Bring slowly to the boil, skimming as necessary, then lower to a gentle simmer, cover and cook for 25 minutes per 500g (1lb) plus 30 minutes, or 1½ hours for joints less than 750g (1½lb). When cooked, remove beef and set aside to rest in a warm place while you cook the dumplings.*

To make dumplings, *mix self-raising flour with half as much shredded suet, salt and pepper, herbs and just enough water to bind to a firm dough. Shape the dough into small balls. Carefully drop the balls into the pan, cover and cook on a very gentle simmer for 15–20 minutes until cooked and fluffy. If the dumplings start to break up the simmer is not gentle enough.*

Mustard is the only accompaniment necessary to serve with boiled salt beef and herb dumplings.

BOILING AND PRESSING AN OX TONGUE

The best-flavoured tongue is ox and it is usually cooked and pressed to serve cold. It makes an impressive dish for a buffet table and carves easily. Ox tongues are usually sold salted and need soaking before cooking. Boiled tongue served hot without pressing is delicious, too, served with a spicy Cumberland sauce (page 206).

A 2kg (4lb) ox tongue is enough to serve 8 people if served hot and more if pressed and served cold.

To prepare a salted tongue for cooking soak for 12–24 hours in cold water, changing the water 2–3 times.

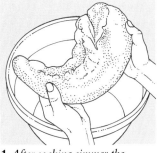

1 After soaking simmer the tongue in a large saucepan of clean water for about 3 hours until tender, adding a little more boiling water if necessary to keep the tongue covered. Check with a fine skewer. Drain, reserving 450ml (¾ pint) of the cooking liquid, and plunge the tongue into a bowl of cold water.

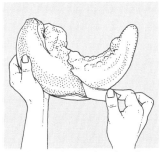

2 When cool enough to handle, remove the tongue from the bowl and discard the water. With a small sharp knife loosen the skin on the underneath and then peel away the remaining skin using your fingers.

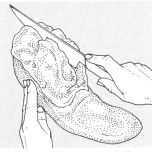

3 Hold topside down with the tongue pointing towards you. Cut lengthwise along the middle. Cut away any gristle and tiny bones from the thick end. If serving hot, slice and drizzle with a little of the cooking liquid.

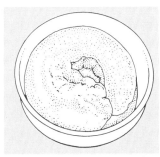

4 Using a 18cm (7in) round deep loose-bottomed cake tin (lined with foil if liked), curl one half tightly into the base of the tin, cut side downwards. Curl the other half on top in the other direction, cut side up. Heat a small amount of the reserved cooking liquid and stir in 1 sachet powdered gelatine.

5 When dissolved add to the rest of the reserved cooking liquor and pour in to the tin around the tongue. Place a small plate on top to fit inside the tin with weights on top. Cool, then chill overnight. Unmould by dipping the tin briefly in hot water and shake out. Serve cut in wafer thin slices.

MAKING THE MOST OF BOILED MEATS

• Salt brisket of beef is a great favourite of mine, as the flavour of both the meat and the fat is excellent. I often press green peppercorns and sometimes finely chopped yellow pepper deep into any cracks or cavities in the meat before cooking as this both looks and tastes interesting when the meat is sliced.

• An economical collar of bacon joint can be transformed for eating cold by first soaking well, then removing the rind and rubbing with a mixture of dark brown sugar and spices. Wrap well in foil and cook slowly at 180°C, 350°F, Gas Mark 4 for about 35 minutes per 500g (1lb) plus 30 minutes.

• The poaching liquid for salt meats can be plain water or an unsalted stock. Add whole spices such as blades of mace, cloves, allspice berries, bay leaves and sticks of cinnamon for extra flavour. Juniper berries and slivers of fresh ginger or chilli are also good.

• Other sauces for boiled or poached meats are a delicious green sauce of chopped spinach, sorrel and parsley and a little wine vinegar, with or without chopped anchovies or a simple mixture of double cream bubbled with chopped capers or green peppercorns.

• Alternatively, I sometimes make a creamy béchamel sauce (page 196) and add chopped anchovies and parsley to it.

• Another quick sauce can be made by puréeing sweet peppers that have been cooked with the meat.

• Sweet and sour sauces for salt meats and ham – such as apricots and slivered orange rind stewed in orange juice and sugar, with a little wine vinegar added at the end – can make a lively difference.

• When pressing a tongue stir chopped fresh parsley or other herbs into the gelatined cooking liquid before pouring into the tin.

BOILING A HAM

Hams, gammons, collar joints and salted hands or knuckles can all be cooked until tender by gentle poaching. Leaner, more prime cuts can be almost cooked, then removed from the saucepan, the rind peeled off and the ham roasted with breadcrumbs or a sugary glaze. If the joint is not wrapped with cooking instructions on the label weigh and cook it for 20 minutes per 500g (1lb).

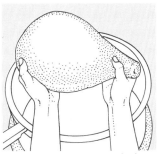

***After soaking, remove** the ham and discard the soaking water. Place the ham in a large saucepan and add fresh cold water to cover and any flavourings (above). Bring the water to the boil, then cover the pan and turn down the heat to a gentle simmer. When the ham has simmered for the calculated cooking time, allow it to cool in the water until tepid.*

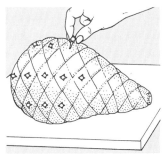

***To finish if baking,** simmer for two thirds the calculated cooking time, and cut off the skin. Score the fat in a neat criss-cross pattern and stud the centres of alternate diamonds with cloves. Sprinkle with soft brown sugar, pressing well in. Bake at 180°C, 350°F, Gas Mark 4 for the remaining time until a tempting golden brown glaze is formed.*

CUTTING *and* CARVING

A truly sharp knife is vital to the carver, and one which is the right shape for the type of joint you are carving. Knives for carving should be slightly flexible, and should have a pointed end for joints with a bone in to cut the meat away from the bone (page 16).

The other crucial point to remember for successful carving of roasted meat is that you must always leave it to rest in a warm place, such as the turned-off oven with the door open, for 15–20 minutes after cooking. During this time, the juices, which move to the centre of the meat while it is cooking, will filter back evenly through the joint so it won't be dry at the edges. The meat's texture will also become relaxed, softer and, therefore, far easier to carve and more tender to chew.

Meat should always be carved across the grain to shorten the fibres and make them more tender. The direction of the blade should never be altered in mid-slice as this will produce ragged pieces, and tougher cuts of meat should be sliced as thinly as possible.

Badly carved meat can destroy all its virtues – the texture, taste and the luscious appearance. It is probably better to carve away from the table so that you are not inhibited by the scrutiny of others hungrily waiting for their helping, and it is easier to carve if you can find a surface slightly higher than a dining table like the kitchen worktop.

Don't forget to save all the juices that seep out during carving for adding extra flavour to the gravy or any accompanying sauce. If you have cooked an expensive joint of meat to perfection but are not entirely confident of your carving don't hesitate to ask if someone else will do it for you – some people are proud of their carving skills and will enjoy performing for you and your guests.

CARVING LARGE BEEF JOINTS

Beef joints with large rib bones are each basically carved in the same way. The idea is to loosen the meat in a piece from one end of the bones and cut across the grain in neat slices. Traditionally, beef is carved thinly.

As with all carving an extra-sharp knife is essential so the meat is cut, not torn. Once you are experienced with sharpening knives with a steel (page 16) keep the steel handy so you sharpen after every several slices or so.

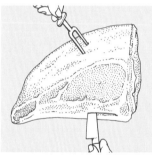

1 *To carve a wing rib of beef, lay the joint fat side up and the side with the long bones down on a board. Slide the carving knife between the flesh and rib bones and loosen.*

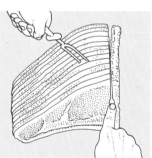

2 *Carve down the joint in neat slices, then loosen all the slices at the chine bone. To keep the meat juicy only carve as much as you need at a time and serve the carving juices over the slices.*

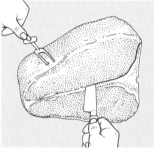

To carve a sirloin *on the bone run a carving knife between the bone and meat and then carve down to the bone in thin slices. Turn the joint over and repeat on the other side.*

CARVING ROLLED JOINTS

Small, round, rolled joints are best laid meat side down on the board and carved horizontally. You will have to cut off the pieces of string as you come to them. If the joint has been barded (page 156), it is best to remove the fat before carving.

Larger rolled joints which would be too tall to carve horizontally, are best laid fat side down on the board. Cut thin vertical slices down across the joint, holding the joint still with a carving fork.

Lay the joint *meat side down on a flat surface. Hold securely in position with a carving fork and cut horizontally across the grain into thin slices with a sharp carving knife.*

ACCOMPANIMENTS FOR CARVED MEATS

• Mix grated horseradish with whipped cream or a mixture of whipped cream and yogurt with chopped cucumbers and capers for a quick accompaniment to roast beef.
• Add a can of peeled chopped tomatoes to the pan juices of roasted veal with double cream and bubble up a quick sauce.
• Very few things taste better with roast lamb than a simple homemade mint sauce (page 207). For a creamed mint sauce (page 207) stir in a little cream.
• A small bowl of redcurrant or rowan berry jam is one of the easiest accompaniments for a tender, pink leg of lamb.
• My family like freshly made mustard or wholegrain mustard with rare roast beef or ham slices. Mustards with many different flavourings are widely available, so it is easy to ring the changes without any effort.
• For a lovely sauce intensify the flavour of the cooking juices by reducing them until almost sticky while the meat is resting, then add double cream and bubble. Season to taste and add a little sherry or balsamic vinegar. Some freshly chopped herbs added at the end improves the appearance and taste.

CARVING A LEG OF LAMB

For successful carving, it helps to remember how the bones lie in a joint. In legs the bones will be down the centre with one side of the joint more fleshy than the other, so start carving on the fleshy side, turning the joint over after all the meat is removed from the top. Hold the bony shank with a clean napkin to keep the joint steady as you carve. If the shank has been cut off by the butcher use a carving fork instead to steady the joint while you carve.

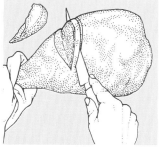

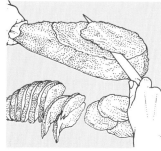

1 *With the rounded side of the leg uppermost, make a wedge-shaped cut in the middle of the joint, cutting through to the bone. Lift out a slice. Continue cutting slices on each side of this first cut.*

2 *Turn the joint over and hold the shank end as in step 1. Cut down the joint in long oblique slices to free and remove the rest of the meat.*

Here is a selection of simple accompaniments suggested in the box (opposite) to serve with carved roasted meats. Experiment with flavoured mustards and jellies to find your favourite.

CARVING A SHOULDER OF LAMB

A shoulder of lamb is ideal for roasting because of its succulent, tender meat, yet for some, this is the trickiest joint to carve because of the wide flat blade bone. It helps to loosen the blade bone before roasting (page 146), then it is easy to remove after cooking before carving. Step 3 below, however, shows how to carve the joint with the blade bone still in.

As shoulders are generally roasted until well done and tender, take care not to pull the meat into shreds.

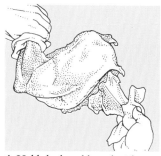

1 *Hold the knuckle end with a napkin and with the other hand twist the blade bone from its socket and pull clear. Carve the meat across the grain in thin slices, working towards the knuckle end.*

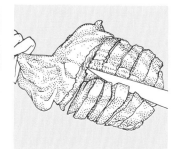

2 *Turn the joint over and, still holding the knuckle end, cut oblique horizontal slices from the underside of the shoulder. Continue cutting round the sides back to the knuckle.*

If the blade bone *is left in, make vertical cuts down the meatiest part of the centre of the joint, cutting down to the bone. Cut down across the middle of the slices to halve them. Run the knife horizantally under the slices along the blade bone to free them. Turn the joint over and carve the meat on the underside in long oblique slices.*

CARVING A WHOLE GAMMON

On a buffet table or at a large family lunch, a whole joint of gammon looks impressive. One of the advantages of gammon for a party is that it is delicious served hot or cold, which means you can prepare it well in advance.

Gammon is a large joint usually served in thin slices. For this reason, it is best to carve a whole joint with a long thin ham knife with a slightly serrated edge. Although not essential, it does make for easier carving.

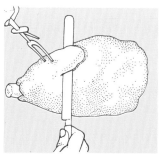

Remove a small slice *of meat from the knuckle end of the gammon joint and then carve with the knife at an angle in long thin oblique slices down as far as the bone.*

ROAST VEAL WITH PRUNES, GINGER AND PISTACHIO NUTS *(142)*

Although veal produces the best juices of all meat when roasted, the lean flesh can be slightly lacking in flavour. If you press flavourings deep into the cracks of a rolled, boned joint, it becomes something far more sophisticated. The juices combine with apple juice and cream to make a wonderful sauce.   *SERVES 8*

3 large cloves garlic, chopped very finely
5cm (2in) piece fresh root ginger, peeled and chopped very finely
75g (3oz) stoned prunes, sliced into 3 or 4 pieces
50g (2oz) shelled pistachio nuts
1 rolled, boned joint of veal, about 2kg (4lb), such as loin or leg
Olive oil
250g (8oz) tomatoes, skinned and chopped finely (page 48)
300ml (½ pint) unsweetened apple juice
150ml (¼ pint) double cream
Sea salt
Black pepper

In a small bowl, mix together the garlic, ginger, prunes and pistachio nuts. Untie the veal and lay out flat, flesh side up. Spread the filling over, re-roll and tie again (page 144). If you don't want to untie the joint, press the garlic and ginger into the cracks in the meat from both ends and from the sides, as deep as you can with your fingers, then poke in the slices of prune and the pistachio nuts. Rub the joint generously all over with olive oil and sprinkle with plenty of pepper.

Spoon the chopped tomatoes into the centre of a roasting tin and place the veal on top. Cook the meat in the centre of a preheated oven, 160°C, 325°F, Gas Mark 3 for 2½–3 hours, basting with the juices now and then. About 15 minutes before the end of the cooking time pour the apple juice into the roasting tin. When the meat is done, turn off the oven, transfer the joint to a carving board and leave it to rest in the oven with the door ajar for about 20 minutes.

Meanwhile, add the cream to the juices and tomato residue in the roasting tin and bring to the boil, stirring, on top of the stove. Still stirring, bubble the sauce for about 2 minutes. Season to taste with sea salt and black pepper and pour into a sauceboat to serve with the veal.

VEAL AND KIDNEY RISSOLES WITH FRESH TOMATO SAUCE *(150)*

Use veal kidneys if possible but lamb's kidneys will still give these rissoles a lovely softness and enriched flavour. I like the rissoles best when they are served with spinach and egg noodles and sprigs of bright green and still very slightly crisp steamed broccoli.   *SERVES 4*

FOR THE SAUCE
3 tablespoons extra virgin olive oil
50g (2oz) butter
500g (1lb) tomatoes (the plum variety if available), skinned and chopped roughly (page 48)
2 large cloves garlic, chopped finely
1 tablespoon tomato purée
Salt
Black pepper
FOR THE RISSOLES
750g (1½lb) minced veal
2 veal or 4 lamb's kidneys, skinned and chopped very finely (page 150)
Good handful chopped fresh dill, or 1 level tablespoon dried
2 teaspoons ground coriander
Plain flour
Groundnut oil for frying
Salt
Black pepper
Fresh dill for garnishing (optional)

Prepare the sauce first. Heat the olive oil and butter in a saucepan over a medium heat, add the chopped tomatoes and garlic and season with salt and black pepper. Cover the pan, reduce the heat and cook very gently for about 20 minutes until

the tomatoes are completely mushy. Stir in the tomato purée and adjust the seasoning if necessary. Remove the pan from the heat and leave on one side while you prepare the rissoles.

Put the minced veal in a bowl with the chopped kidneys and dill, the ground coriander and a generous seasoning of salt and black pepper. Mix together thoroughly with a wooden spoon. Put some plain flour into a separate bowl.

Shape the meat mixture with your hands into slightly flattened balls rather bigger than a ping-pong ball. As you shape them dip the balls into the bowl of flour so that they are generously covered – this helps them hold together during cooking. To cook, heat a little oil in a large, heavy-based frying pan over a fairly high heat. Add the rissoles carefully and cook for 4–5 minutes on each side, turning once with a fish slice.

Meanwhile, gently reheat the tomato sauce. Carefully transfer the rissoles to a shallow serving dish, pour over the reheated sauce and serve, garnished with fresh dill, if you like.

STUFFED SHOULDER OF LAMB WRAPPED IN PASTRY *(146)*

This is an impressive piece for a large dinner party. It can be prepared well ahead, even the day before, and simply put in the oven shortly before the meal to cook the pastry. As the meat is boned, the serving is simple, providing you use a large, well-sharpened knife.   *SERVES 8–10*

1 boned shoulder of English lamb, weighing about 1.2–1.5kg (2½–3lb)
4 tablespoons lemon juice
250g (8oz) spinach or kale, thick stalks removed, washed and drained
125g (4oz) chestnut mushrooms, chopped finely
2 large cloves garlic, chopped finely
50g (2oz) shelled walnuts, chopped finely
75g (3oz) mature Cheddar cheese, grated coarsely
500g (1lb) packet puff pastry, thawed if frozen
1 egg, beaten
Salt and black pepper
FOR THE SAUCE
3 tablespoons brandy
300ml (½ pint) double cream
Salt and black pepper

If the lamb has been tied up, undo the string and lay the meat out flat. Smear the flesh with the lemon juice. To make the stuffing, put the spinach leaves into a food processor and whizz until very finely chopped. Turn into a mixing bowl and add the finely chopped mushrooms, garlic, walnuts and the grated cheese. Season with a little salt and freshly ground black pepper, then mix together thoroughly with a wooden spoon.

Press the stuffing mixture on to the lamb and into any pockets in the meat. Roll up the lamb loosely to enclose the stuffing as much as possible, pressing it back in with your fingers as it falls out. Secure in as neat a shape as possible with string and/or skewers and put into a roasting tin. Rub the joint all over with sea salt.

Cook the meat in a preheated oven, 180°C, 350°F, Gas Mark 4 for 1½–2 hours according to the size of the joint and how well done you like your lamb, basting occasionally with the pan juices. Remove the meat from the oven and leave in the tin until cold.

When the meat is completely cold, remove and discard any solidified fat. Press any of the stuffing which may have oozed out of the joint back into the meat and carefully remove the string and/or skewers. Pour the pan juices into a small bowl and reserve in the refrigerator.

On a lightly floured surface roll out the pastry thinly into a piece big enough to completely enclose the meat. Wrap up the meat in the pastry like a parcel, moistening the pastry edges to seal and cutting off any excess pastry at the corners to make decorations.

Place the joint with the join of pastry underneath in a greased roasting tin. Roll out the pastry trimmings and cut out decorations for the joint (page 245). Attach them with water. Cut 3–4 small slits in the pastry for the steam to escape. Refrigerate the pastry-covered meat for at least 30 minutes before cooking.

Brush the pastry all over with the beaten egg and cook in the centre of a preheated oven, 200°C, 400°F, Gas Mark 6 for 30–40 minutes until a glossy, rich brown. Leave the joint in the oven with the heat turned off while you make the sauce.

Bring the reserved meat juices to the boil in a saucepan with the brandy and cream and bubble for a minute or two. Season to taste with salt and black pepper and pour into a sauceboat to serve with the meat. Cut the joint into slices to serve.

SMOKED BACON WITH SPICED GARLIC POTATOES (149)

This is a simple but delicious dish. The smoky taste and succulence of a Tendersweet bacon joint permeates the potatoes which cook underneath it in a mixture of olive oil, garlic, cumin and mace, with onion and tomato to make a rich juice. Only a simple green vegetable, such as steamed cabbage, is needed as an accompaniment.   *SERVES 6*

750g–1kg (1½–2lb) firm-textured potatoes, scrubbed but unpeeled
4 large cloves garlic, chopped finely
3 teaspoons cumin seeds
About 6 blades mace
1 large onion, chopped roughly
250–375g (8–12oz) tomatoes, chopped fairly finely
2 bay leaves
3 tablespoons extra virgin olive oil
1 tablespoon wine vinegar
1–1.2kg (2–2½lb) back or loin smoked Tendersweet bacon roasting joint
Salt
Black pepper

Cut the potatoes into 1cm (½in) thick slices and lay them in the bottom of a large, deep casserole dish. Add three-quarters of the chopped garlic, 2 teaspoons of the cumin seeds, the mace, chopped onion and tomatoes, bay leaves, olive oil and the wine vinegar and mix together. Season with a little salt and plenty of black pepper.

Put the rest of the chopped garlic in a small bowl with the remaining teaspoon of cumin seeds and season with plenty of freshly ground black pepper. Smear this mixture all over the bacon joint, then place it on top of the potatoes. Cover the casserole and cook in the centre of a preheated oven, 180°C, 350°F, Gas Mark 4 for 1¾–2 hours.

To serve, lift the joint on to a carving board and cut into thin slices with a sharp knife. Serve the potatoes and their juices straight from the casserole.

STIR-FRIED PORK FILLET WITH FRUIT AND LETTUCE (142)

This is ideal for an informal supper after a busy day, as it takes very little time to prepare. It has the familiar English combination of pork and apple but with a Chinese character. Serve it with buttered Chinese noodles or with rice.   *SERVES 3–4*

375–500g (12oz–1lb) pork tenderloin, cut across into 1cm (½in) slices
3 tablespoons sunflower or groundnut oil
3 Granny Smith apples, washed but unpeeled
2.5cm (1in) piece fresh root ginger, peeled and cut into thin slivers
2 large cloves garlic, sliced thinly
75g (3oz) ready-to-eat dried apricots, halved lengthwise
1 small–medium Cos lettuce, sliced across fairly thinly
4–5 pinches cayenne pepper
Salt
Soy sauce

Place the slices of pork, spaced apart, between two large sheets of wet grease-proof paper. Bash with a rolling pin until thin. Heat 1 tablespoon of sunflower oil in a wok or large frying pan. Fry the pork pieces over a high heat until lightly browned on both sides then, using a slotted spoon, transfer to a dish and keep warm in a low oven.

Core the apples, then cut in half and slice thinly in half-moon pieces. Put a second tablespoonful of oil into the wok or frying pan over a high heat. Add the ginger and garlic and stir around for a minute, then add the apple slices and stir for another minute or so until the apples are tinged with brown. Stir in the halved apricots and add the mixture to the pork in the oven.

Lastly, put the remaining tablespoon of oil in the wok or pan, add the lettuce and stir over a high heat for about 30 seconds or so until the lettuce is limp. Add to the pork mixture. Season with cayenne pepper and salt and turn into a warmed serving dish. Sprinkle with soy sauce and serve immediately.

GRILLED LAMB FILLETS WITH MINT AND YOGURT SAUCE (142)

Lamb neck fillets are a marvellous buy when you want boned lamb; they are specially good when marinated and grilled, as this produces aromatic meat which remains pink and juicy inside. Puréed vegetables (page 53) are ideal accompaniments.　　*SERVES 4*

2 tablespoons olive oil
4 tablespoons lemon juice
3 cloves garlic, crushed
3 rounded teaspoons ground cumin
1 tablespoon tomato purée
Black pepper
750–875g (1½–1¾lb) lamb neck fillets
Mint leaves to garnish
FOR THE YOGURT SAUCE
1 rounded teaspoon coriander seeds
2 teaspoons sesame seeds
Generous handful of fresh mint leaves,
　chopped very finely
8 tablespoons Greek yogurt
Salt and black pepper

At least 4 hours in advance make the marinade mixture. Put the olive oil, lemon juice, crushed garlic, ground cumin and tomato purée in a bowl and mix together. Season generously with black pepper. Lay the lamb fillets in a shallow dish and smear all over with the marinade. Cover the dish and leave in a cool place, but preferably not the refrigerator, for 4 hours or more – all day or overnight if possible.

Before cooking the lamb prepare the yogurt sauce. Put a dry frying pan over a high heat and toss the coriander and sesame seeds around in it for a minute or two just to toast. Turn the seeds into a small mixing bowl. Add the chopped mint and the yogurt. Mix well, season with salt and black pepper and spoon into a serving bowl.

To cook the meat preheat the grill to its highest. Grill the fillets for about 10 minutes until dark brown all over, turning once or twice and spooning over any excess marinade. When cooked remove from the heat but leave the fillets on the grill pan for a few minutes before putting them on a board and slicing across into 1cm (½in) slices. To serve, arrange the lamb slices on a warm serving plate, garnish with a few fresh mint leaves and serve with the spicy yogurt sauce.

AROMATIC MEATBALLS WITH SPINACH AND MUSHROOMS (153)

This is a popular family dish in my house, full of goodness and lovely aromas. Serve with new potatoes or buttered noodles.　　*SERVES 4*

500g (1lb) lean minced lamb or beef
2.5–5cm (1–2in) piece fresh root ginger,
　peeled and chopped finely
2 teaspoons cumin seeds
1 tablespoon tomato purée
1–2 tablespoons groundnut oil
50g (2oz) butter
1 onion, chopped roughly
500g (1lb) spinach, stalks removed,
　washed and chopped roughly
175g (6oz) mushrooms, sliced thinly
4 large cloves garlic, sliced lengthwise
4 tablespoons creamed smetana or soured
　cream
Sea salt
Black pepper
Cayenne pepper to garnish

Put the meat into a mixing bowl and season well with sea salt and black pepper. Add the chopped ginger, cumin seeds and tomato purée and mix thoroughly with a wooden spoon. Using damp hands, form the mixture into small balls the size of a large marble or walnut.

Put the groundnut oil in a large frying pan over a high heat. When the oil is hot, add the meatballs and turn around carefully with a wooden spoon just to brown all over. Remove the pan from the heat and leave on one side.

Melt the butter in a large flameproof casserole over a medium heat. Add the chopped onion and cook until soft and translucent. Pile in the roughly chopped spinach, cover the casserole and cook for a few minutes, opening the dish and stirring around once or twice. Stir in the sliced mushrooms and garlic and season with salt and black pepper.

Using a slotted spatula, take the meatballs from the frying pan and arrange them on top of the spinach and mushroom mixture. Cover the casserole again and continue to cook over a gentle heat for 15 minutes. Remove the lid of the casserole, increase the heat and bubble vigorously for 5–8 minutes until the juices have reduced by about half. Just before serving, spoon the creamed smetana or soured cream roughly over the top then dust with a little cayenne pepper.

PORK CHOPS STUFFED WITH ROQUEFORT AND BAKED WITH PEARS (142)

Both pork and onions call for a little sweetness, and this is a delicious way of combining them. The onions are given extra zip with fresh ginger, while the salty flavour of Roquefort mingles into the juices.　　*SERVES 4*

4 thick boned loin or spare rib pork chops
125g (4oz) Roquefort cheese
Olive oil for frying
3 onions, chopped roughly
2 cloves garlic, chopped finely
5cm (2in) piece fresh root ginger, peeled
　and chopped finely
1 rounded tablespoon dark marmalade
2 firm large dessert pears
Caster sugar
Salt and black pepper
Finely chopped fresh parsley to garnish

Using a sharp knife, slice a wide, deep pocket in each pork chop. Crumble the Roquefort into a bowl and season well with black pepper. Press the Roquefort into the chops, then press to enclose the cheese. Smear with olive oil and set aside.

Heat about 1 tablespoon olive oil in a shallow flameproof casserole over a medium heat, then add the onions and stir constantly until softened. Add the garlic and ginger and stir for another minute. Finally stir in the marmalade and season with salt. Lay the stuffed chops on top.

Cook in the open casserole in the centre of a preheated oven, 160°C, 325°F, Gas Mark 3 for 1–1¼ hours. Meanwhile, peel the pears, then halve them and carefully cut out the cores. About 30 minutes before the end of cooking lay a pear half on each chop, smear with olive oil and sprinkle with a little caster sugar, salt and black pepper. Sprinkle with parsley to serve.

CASSEROLED HARE WITH QUINCES (142)

These joints of spiced hare in a smooth red pepper and tomato sauce are perfect accompanied by boiled potatoes, rice or buttered noodles, and a crisp green salad or vegetable. Quinces contribute a unique flavour which is excellent with meat but if they are difficult to find use hard pears instead.   *SERVES 6*

2 red peppers, cored, deseeded and
*   chopped roughly (page 49)*
500g (1lb) tomatoes (the plum variety if
*   available), chopped roughly*
1 very large onion, chopped roughly
1 rounded tablespoon caster sugar
600ml (1 pint) medium or dry cider
2 tablespoons sherry vinegar
2 tablespoons groundnut oil
1.5–1.7kg (3–3½lb) joints of hare (page
*   155)*
3 large cloves garlic, peeled and chopped
*   finely*
½ teaspoon ground cloves
1 teaspoon ground mace
1 whole nutmeg, grated
500g (1lb) quinces, washed but unpeeled
Handful of chopped fresh parsley
Salt and black pepper

Put the roughly chopped peppers, tomatoes and onion in a large saucepan with the sugar, cider and sherry vinegar and season to taste with salt and black pepper. Place the pan over a high heat and bring to the boil, then cover the saucepan and simmer gently over a medium heat for about 30 minutes. Remove the saucepan from the heat and leave on one side.

Heat the groundnut oil in a large frying pan over a high heat, and fry the joints of hare on both sides just to brown them. Remove the joints from the frying pan with a slotted spoon and transfer them to a large casserole dish. Sprinkle the hare with the chopped garlic and the other spices.

Pour the contents of the saucepan into a food processor and whizz until smooth. Work the purée through a fine sieve, taste and adjust the seasoning with more salt and black pepper if necessary. Pour the purée over the joints of hare. Cover the casserole and cook in the centre of a preheated oven, 240°C, 475°F, Gas Mark 9 for 15 minutes, then reduce the oven temperature to 160°C, 325°F, Gas Mark 3 and cook for another 1½ hours

or until the hare is tender.

Finally, cut the washed quinces into quarters, cut out the cores and add the quince pieces to the casserole dish, mixing them in roughly. Cover the dish and continue cooking for another 30 minutes or until the quinces are just soft. Scatter with the chopped fresh parsley just before serving.

RABBIT AND PUMPKIN WITH MUSTARD (155)

The mild tenderness of domestic rabbit is perfect for this lovely autumn dish. The pumpkin softens to form a delicious pale orange sauce, rich yet mild, and the mustard and green peppercorns add zest. *SERVES 4*

1 tablespoon olive oil
2 teaspoons caraway seeds
1–1.1kg (2–2¼lb) joints of rabbit (page
*   155)*
4 cloves garlic, chopped roughly
125g (4oz) butter, cut into pieces
1kg (2lb) piece pumpkin, peeled, deseeded
*   and chopped into small pieces*
2 teaspoons bottled green peppercorns,
*   drained and crushed roughly*
4 teaspoons Dijon mustard
150ml (¼ pint) white wine or cider
150ml (¼ pint) double cream
Salt
Flat-leaved parsley sprigs to garnish

Heat the olive oil in a large flameproof casserole over a medium heat. Add the caraway seeds and stir around for a minute, then add the rabbit joints and seal on both sides. Next add the chopped garlic and stir around for 30 seconds. Remove from the heat and add the butter, then, when the butter has melted in the hot casserole, add the chopped pumpkin, the crushed green peppercorns, the mustard, the white wine or cider and a sprinkling of salt. Stir with a wooden spoon to mix thoroughly.

Cover the casserole with a tight-fitting lid and cook in the centre of a preheated oven, 180°C, 350°F, Gas Mark 4 for 1¼ hours. Stir with a wooden spoon to break up the pumpkin until it becomes a purée, then replace the lid and continue cooking for another 20–30 minutes.

Just before serving, pour the double cream over the top and garnish with parsley sprigs.

SADDLE OF VENISON WITH SPINACH AND LAMB'S KIDNEYS (154)

A saddle of venison looks splendid and the moist and piquant spinach lining with its pink and juicy kidneys is an added bonus.   *SERVES 6–8*

1.7–2kg (3½–4lb) piece of saddle of
*   venison, boned*
4 tablespoons lemon juice
Olive oil
500g (1lb) spinach, stalks removed and
*   washed*
2 rounded teaspoons bottled green
*   peppercorns, drained and crushed*
2 rounded teaspoons wholegrain mustard
4–5 lamb's kidneys, skinned (page 150)
Pork fat for barding (optional)
1 tablespoon sherry or balsamic vinegar
2 teaspoons Dijon mustard
300ml (½ pint) double cream
Sea salt
Black pepper

Lay the venison skin side down in a roasting tin. Smear the flesh with the lemon juice and olive oil and sprinkle liberally with pepper. Cover and leave in a cool place for several hours or overnight.

Steam or boil the spinach leaves until very soft. Rinse with cold water and drain thoroughly, pressing out as much liquid as possible. Leave to cool.

Put the crushed green peppercorns in a bowl with the wholegrain mustard. Mix in the spinach and press on to the inside of the venison joint, then place on the lamb's kidneys and bring the sides of venison flesh up round them. If any spinach oozes out as you do this press it back in. Carefully turn the joint over, and either smear the top with olive oil and sprinkle with sea salt or if using, wrap the top half of the joint in the pork fat. Tie the joint at regular intervals (page 144). Put the joint in a preheated oven, 220°C, 425°F, Gas Mark 7 and cook for 45–60 minutes.

Meanwhile, put the vinegar and mustard in a bowl and stir in the cream. Season with salt and black pepper. When the venison is cooked, transfer it to a warm serving dish. Pour off any fat from the tin, then add the cream and mustard mixture into the roasting tin with the meat juices. Put over a high heat and bring the sauce to bubbling, stirring all the time. Bubble for a minute and then pour into a sauceboat to serve with the venison.

POULTRY and GAME BIRDS

Poultry – which includes chickens, turkeys, ducklings, ducks and geese – offers enormous scope in the kitchen and is becoming increasingly popular. Chicken and turkey are also the most economical of meats, and are ideal for entertaining because you can transform them into almost any type and character of dish. Chicken is a wonderful vehicle for flavours, sauces and enhancing ingredients; this applies particularly to frozen birds as they often need added taste and texture. Fresh free-range birds have enough flavour, as a result of their more varied diet and roaming lifestyle, to be cooked simply. This applies to free-range turkeys just as much as to chickens.

The wide variety of poultry available is relatively inexpensive and is low in fat (except ducks and geese). Chicken and turkey, almost universally popular with both young and old, are therefore supremely practical for family meals. But there is no need to bore your household with repetitive chicken dishes as the basic bird can be transformed by different ways of cooking and seasoning and by different sauces. Boned chicken breasts, for example, offer enormous scope. They can be grilled, roasted or steamed whole but I think they are far more exciting when sliced across thinly for quick stir-fry style dishes or put between sheets of greaseproof paper, bashed thin and rolled round a stuffing. Small poussins are perfect for a single serving and fun to serve.

Chickens which are yellow skinned have been corn fed though they are not necessarily free range; they usually have a good flavour and a moist, tender texture because they have a little more fat under the skin than other varieties.

Ducklings, ducks, and geese do not offer value for money in the same way as chickens and turkeys because they have shallow breasts with not much meat on them,

and altogether a lot of bone in proportion to meat. They do, however, offer real character, and few foods seem more festive than a roast goose with a good fruit and nut stuffing. Aylesbury ducks have a thick layer of fat under the skin which stops the meat from drying out or becoming tough. I particularly like the French Barbary duck which has less fat but as much meat, of a slightly darker red and fuller flavour. I also love the little mallard, or wild duck, which has an even stronger, more gamy taste and the darkest flesh.

Duck breast is best and most succulent when eaten pink but as the legs should be more thoroughly cooked it is difficult to roast a bird like this. Individual breast fillets, however, are now widely available and they can be cooked briefly under a hot grill producing tender slivers of pink and juicy meat. Duck breast joints are also available sometimes and can be roasted or grilled slightly rare. Quails were once considered a game bird but because they are now only available farmed they are considered poultry. Try them for their subtle taste and delicate texture.

All sorts of game birds are now farmed and, although they may not have been hung enough to develop a really gamy flavour, it is exciting to be able to buy them so easily. Pigeons always taste good and are very inexpensive, but are best casseroled as they can be tough if roasted. Similarly, pheasants, which can also be dry, are excellent in a casserole, their flavour enhanced by other ingredients. Partridges have a delicate taste and texture and can be beautifully juicy when not overcooked; but of all game birds plump grouse are my favourite birds to eat, as they have a distinctive flavour and a lot of succulence. All game birds take very well to slightly sweet, fruity accompaniments and also, which fewer people realize, to aromatic spices.

Clockwise from top: A thick honey and apricot sauce with fresh mint tops duck joints in Dark Glossy Fruited Duck (page 192); Chicken in Almond and Coconut Milk (page 190) served with saffron-flavoured rice; Poussins with Fresh Coriander and Lime (page 191) are roasted with flavoured cream cheese under the skins and bacon rashers over the breasts, then served with a sauce made from pan juices; Steamed Chicken in Yellow Pepper and Dill Sauce (page 190); Duck Fillets in Pastry with Leek Sauce (page 193) with potatoes; Roast Grouse with Mystery Sauce (page 193) accompanied by steamed baby carrots.

PREPARATION

When choosing a whole fresh bird, look for one with a compact and rounded shape, plump breasts, dry and unmarked skin and pliable legs. Chickens, turkeys, guinea fowl, ducks and geese should smell fresh, which means very little smell at all; if they have been stored too long an off-putting smell is easily distinguishable, even through plastic. Always remove tight plastic wrapping when you get home and leave the bird in the refrigerator on a large plate for no more than three days, covered only loosely with greaseproof paper so plenty of air can circulate around it. If the bird comes with its giblets be sure to save them for the stockpot (page 29); they can be frozen until you are ready to use them.

Poultry pieces do not need cleaning before cooking but whole birds should be well rinsed. Whether you truss the bird or not is a matter of personal preference but I like the neater shape it guarantees. Although there are traditional ways of cooking certain birds, almost all poultry and game is more versatile than you would think. It can be roasted, pot-roasted, boiled, steamed, casseroled, barbecued, grilled or fried.

Duck is best either roasted or grilled as this achieves a delicious crispy skin, but it is also good jointed and casseroled, with some starchy ingredient such as dried beans to absorb its delicious fat.

I think roast goose is a fine sight for a special occasion, especially if it is served with a moist and aromatic fruity stuffing. Turkey is also traditionally roasted but it can be dull and dry. You can add far more character to turkey by casseroling joints or fillets or using diced meat in stir-fries. Game birds are usually roasted but are also good casseroled, especially pheasant and pigeon.

CLEANING AND TRUSSING CHICKEN

Most prepared birds are sold ready trussed so it is not always necessary to undo the string or elastic thread unless you wish to stuff the bird (page 176). Trussing helps keep the bird in a good compact shape for even cooking, easier carving and to retain meat juices for more tender flesh. A simple method is to pull up the legs and tie together. Make sure the neck skin is pulled under the bird and wings tucked underneath.

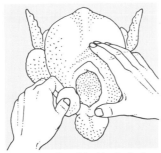

1 *Put your hand inside the body cavity and pull away the pad of fat just inside. Wash the bird inside and out under running water and dry with kitchen paper.*

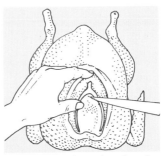

2 *Working at the neck end, pull back the neck flap. Cut out the wishbone, if liked, for easy carving. Pack stuffing, if used, in neck end and pull down the skin.*

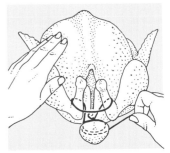

3 *Using a piece of string 5 times the bird's length anchor one end around the parson's nose and loop the long end around one leg and then the other and back around the parson's nose to draw the legs and nose together.*

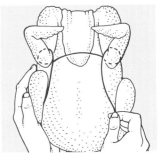

4 *Take the string to the back, passing between the thigh and body, then turn the bird over. Loop around one wing and across to the second wing, securing the neck flap. Loop again and pull up the wings to the body. Pass string back to parson's nose and tie.*

Chicken joints are so versatile and can be combined with endless ingredients. Here Aromatic Chicken on a Mattress (page 191) combines apple, onion, chicory and bulgar to make a purée.

JOINTING CHICKEN

Jointing a bird yourself is quite straightforward if you have a good sharp knife. A pair of poultry shears is useful but not essential. Be sure to allow plenty of time when you try this the first time.

One of the advantages of cutting up a whole bird yourself is that you get a selection of pieces, such as the breasts and thighs. The other advantage is that you do not lose the 'oysters', two tender pieces of meat along the backbone. These small pieces of dark meat are traditionally known as the 'chef's treat'.

This method of jointing makes 8 pieces.

HANDLING POULTRY AND GAME BIRDS

• I cannot over-emphasize the importance of safe handling of poultry, particularly chickens and turkeys. All foods contain bacteria, some of which can cause food poisoning if allowed to grow at room temperature and not destroyed by thorough cooking.

• Buy birds that are well wrapped. Check the use-by date and avoid any with torn packaging.

• Get the birds home as soon as possible, then store in the refrigerator or freezer until required. Cook fresh birds within 3 days.

• Frozen birds must be completely thawed before cooking. Follow instructions on the packaging. You can check the thawing by putting your hand inside the cavity. If some ice is still present, it needs further thawing. Cook as soon as the bird has thawed.

• It is best to thaw birds as slowly as possible to produce the most tender flesh, so thaw them in the refrigerator on a plate with a lip. This prevents the juices dripping on to other food. Place on a shelf below cooked meats.

• Do not put frozen birds in hot water to thaw.

• Do not refreeze thawed poultry meat, even after it has been cooked.

• Always wash hands and utensils after handling raw poultry. Scrub chopping boards well in hot soapy water – don't just wipe them with a damp cloth. This cuts down on the chance of cross-contamination.

• Do not allow raw and cooked meats to come into contact with each other.

• Cook all poultry thoroughly. Potential problem bacteria such as salmonella thrive and grow in warm temperatures. If food is only half cooked, this is an ideal breeding ground for germs. Salmonella bacteria grow slowly in temperatures less than 10°C (50°F) but cannot survive in temperatures above 70°C (160°F) for 2 minutes. These temperatures are reached when food is properly cooked. At this temperature, poultry juices will run clear. Any hint of pinkness indicates further cooking is needed.

• When boiling a mixture with raw poultry meat in it, bring the mixture to the boil as quickly as possible and boil for 30 seconds to kill the bacteria.

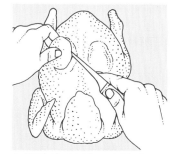

1 *With the bird breast side down locate the 2 oysters either side of the backbone. Loosen them with a sharp knife, putting the tip of the blade underneath and cutting them free from the skeleton without completely cutting the oysters off.*

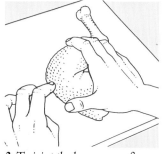

2 *Turn the bird over breast side up. To remove the legs cut through the skin between the legs and breast, pulling the legs away and cutting through each joint to the backbone and including the oyster. The oysters should come away with the thighs.*

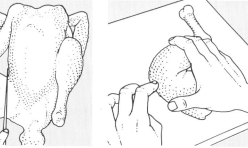

3 *To joint the leg use your finger to locate the joint between the drumstick and thigh on one side, then cut straight through the joint with a sharp knife; repeat with the other leg. Cut off the lower legs and discard or save for use in the stockpot (page 29).*

JOINTING DUCK

The jointing technique for a duck is different to that for a chicken because ducks have different shapes and so much less meat in relation to bone.

It is also easy to remove breast fillets. Remove the backbone as if jointing, then cut off the leg and thigh portions. Cut along the breastbone, and use the knife's tip to cut away the meat.

4 *Turn the bird round with the neck end facing you, then cut through the wing joints, cutting off some of the breast flesh with each joint for more generous portions. Cut off the wing tips and discard or save for use in the stockpot with the lower carcase.*

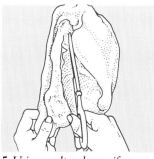

5 *Using poultry shears, if available, split the carcase, cutting away the backbone from the breast, then reserve the lower carcase and save for use in the stockpot.*

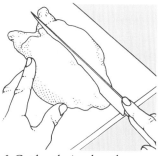

6 *Cut lengthwise along the breastbone with a knife, then remove the bone, if liked, giving 2 portions. Add the bones to the stockpot.*

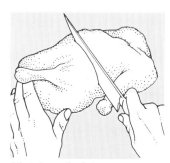

To joint a duck into quarters *cut through and discard the bony backbone which can be used for making stock (page 29). Then turn the duck over so it is breast side up. Split the duck in half through the breast, then cut each half again crosswise making 4 quarters, allowing bigger portions at the wing ends.*

BONING AND STUFFING

I love stuffed dishes, whether they are vegetables, fish or meat, so I am always inspired by a boneless bird. Years ago I used to buy whole boned chickens so I could stuff them with good things, tie them up into neat parcels and then roast them. Nowadays, although it is far easier to find boned pieces of chicken, it is more difficult to find boned whole birds. A stuffed boned chicken, either to roast and eat hot or to poach, press and eat cold as in a galantine, can be such a delicious pleasure to create that it is worth learning to bone poultry yourself.

Open- and tunnel-boning are the two techniques for boning birds before stuffing. Open-boning, where the bird is cut open and the bones scraped out from the inside is the easiest technique to learn. Tunnel-boning, which leaves the skin and flesh whole, is most suitable for larger birds such as duck but it takes more practice.

Using different coloured ingredients for stuffing a whole bird and arranging them in a definite pattern produces impressive-looking slices that can be beautifully arranged on a serving plate. The flavours of the stuffing also enhance the meat and help avoid blandness. Include ingredients with striking colours such as red, green or yellow peppers, black and green olives, spinach leaves, pistachio nuts, dried fruit and so on. In a galantine you might add minced meat. Stuffings are not always a solid mixture of ingredients; in chicken Kiev, for example, a boned chicken breast is stuffed with flavoured butter, then breaded and sealed before cooking.

OPEN-BONING AND STUFFING CHICKEN

A boned bird has endless possibilities for stuffing and serving, and, hot or cold, a stuffed boned bird is easy to cook through evenly.

Boning a whole chicken may seem tricky at first, but with practice it will soon become easier. Three things help – a good, short-handled, sharp, thin-bladed boning knife, a pair of poultry shears and some knowledge of the bird's anatomy so you can work out where the bones lie. Do not nick the skin while you are working as the stuffing may burst through during cooking.

1 *Untruss the bird and lay it breast side down. Cut a line along the backbone, beginning at the neck end. Working the blade under the skin, shave the flesh away from the backbone in a back and forth motion. Pull the flesh away with one hand while you cut with the other.*

2 *Work your way down round the leg and wing joints, carefully scraping and shaving as you go. Cut through the joints with poultry shears to free them so you can get at the rest of the flesh. Sometimes you can ease the flesh from the bones simply with your fingers.*

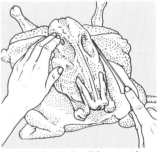

3 *With the bird still breast side down work your way along the rib cage, shaving and scraping close against the bones. Take care not to cut the skin over the breastbone where the flesh is very thin. The carcase should now lift out in one piece and can be used in the stockpot (page 29).*

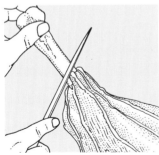

4 *Cut off the lower legs and discard or save for use in the stockpot. Working from the inside remove the leg bones on either side by scraping away the flesh first from the thigh bone, then from the drumstick. Sever the white ligaments, pull the bones free and remove.*

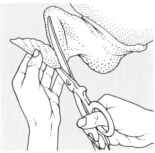

5 *Cut off the wing tips. To remove the wing bones hold each joint and carefully scrape away the flesh. Twist the bones free and remove. Cut off the parson's nose and discard. Lay the bird flat, skin side down, and turn the leg and wing flesh in to the centre to make a neat shape.*

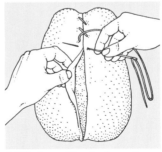

6 *Pile the stuffing in the centre and wrap the sides around it, taking care not to overlap the skin too much. Secure with kitchen string, using a trussing needle. Weigh the stuffed bird and roast as normal (page 178) but for 25 minutes per 500g (1lb) plus 25 minutes extra.*

BONING A CHICKEN LEG

An easily boned chicken leg (the drumstick and thigh together) can be stuffed and baked or coated in crumbs and deep fried.

Scrape the flesh away from the top of the thigh, working your way down the bone. Do not cut the skin. Pull the flesh down and outwards as you scrape. Cut through the joint and discard the thigh bone. Stuff the thigh cavity only, leaving the drumstick bone in and stitch the top closed.

TUNNEL-BONING DUCK

A duck has a much higher bone to meat ratio, so it is worth boning and stuffing one, if only because it makes it easier to carve. Boning and stuffing are also a good way to stretch a duck to feed a larger number of people.

Normally only the breastbone and backbone are carved out in this style of boning. The legs and wings are left to add shape to the boned and stuffed bird.

A good boning knife and poultry shears are essential. Take care not to nick the skin, so the juices and stuffing do not escape during cooking, resulting in a dry bird.

A tunnel-boned duck stuffed with a mixture of yellow peppers, red onions, chopped walnuts, raw spinach and stewed apricots, and then roasted makes an impressive easy-to-carve party dish.

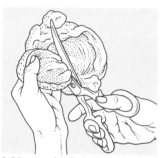

1 *Untruss the duck if necessary and cut off the wing tips and lower legs. Rinse the duck inside and out with cold running water and pat dry with kitchen paper. Stand the duck upright on its neck end. Cut off the parson's nose and discard.*

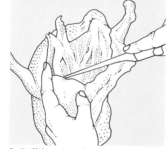

2 *Still keeping the bird upright, carefully scrape the knife against the bone structure, and start to cut the flesh away from the bones, pulling back the freed flesh with one hand as you cut with the other.*

3 *When you get to the legs and wings, cut through the joints from the inside with poultry shears. Leave the legs and wings alone as they are not boned in this method, unlike open-boning. This makes the stuffed bird look more natural.*

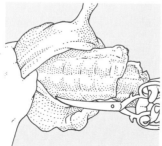

4 *Use poultry shears to cut the rib cage from the main whole carcase, then pull out the skeleton and discard or use in the stockpot (page 29). Trim and stuff the bird. Using a trussing needle and string stitch up the neck end for a neat roasting shape.*

STUFFING AND SERVING BONED POULTRY

• One of the simplest and most successful poultry stuffings is a mixture of fresh herbs, such as tarragon, dill or coriander leaf with finely chopped ginger, garlic, finely grated lemon rind and a little soft butter or olive oil. Use it to stuff boned thighs, breasts and whole birds.

• Flatten boneless legs, thighs and breasts for rolling up or folding around a stuffing by putting them under wet greaseproof paper and bashing with the side of a meat mallet, heavy flat knife or rolling pin. This way you can put a chunkier stuffing of chopped ingredients in the centre and bring the meat round it to enclose like a parcel.

• Ingredients particularly good for stuffing mixtures are pieces of grilled and skinned peppers (page 55), sautéed onions, chopped mushrooms (especially chestnut or shiitake), pine kernels, pistachio nuts and walnuts, cooked wild rice, grated carrot, grated cheese, grated citrus rind, chopped tomatoes, chopped ready-to-eat dried apricots, peaches or prunes and chopped spinach.

• A little root vegetable purée (page 53), such as parsnip or celeriac, is a good binder for the more chunky ingredients,

such as vegetables, in stuffing.

• Another excellent stuffing is cream cheese, particularly the kind with garlic and herbs, or blue cheese – use this instead of the traditional butter in a chicken Kiev.

• There are all sorts of flavour enhancers you can stir into stuffing mixtures including tomato purée, sun-dried tomato paste, olive paste, finely chopped anchovies, and, for an exotic stuffing, a little tikka paste.

• Boned thighs and breasts can be stuffed and wrapped in puff pastry, then decorated with scraps of pastry and glazed with egg yolk. Cook in a preheated oven, 220°C, 425°F, Gas Mark 7 for the first 20 minutes, then at 160°C, 325°F, Gas Mark 3 for another 20 minutes. Decorated with scraps of pastry and glazed with egg yolk, these exciting little parcels are perfect for dinner parties as they can be prepared well ahead, and kept in the refrigerator before cooking. They will even keep warm for a short while in a low oven before serving.

• Use thinly sliced rindless streaky bacon to wrap round stuffed and rolled boned pieces of poultry for extra flavour.

ROASTING

The smell of a roasting bird never fails to excite the taste-buds. Roasting is one of the simplest ways of cooking, and carefully done it can produce exquisite results. Even though a roast chicken is nowadays perhaps the meal we are more used to than anything else, a glistening, golden bird still has an aura of feasting about it.

When done thoughtfully, roasting is probably in the end the most satisfying way of cooking chicken, turkey, guinea fowl, duck, goose and most game birds. Chicken, turkey and guinea fowl should be cooked until all the flesh has turned from pink to white, but it is equally important that they should not dry out, losing both tenderness and flavour. For smaller birds a medium or high heat is best and there are various ways to make sure that moisture is not lost, particularly from the breast. With most birds olive oil or butter, spread either on top of or pushed under the skin, or a few rashers of streaky bacon over the breasts, will do, but some larger birds need basting during roasting. Duck and goose have so much fat that they do not need any extra to keep them moist.

Game should be cooked at a fiercer heat and must never be overcooked so that it remains juicy and slightly pink inside, particularly as with small birds it is only the breast that is fleshy enough to eat.

ROASTING TURKEY OR CHICKEN

Basting and careful timing are essential if turkey legs are not to dry out before the breast meat is cooked. With the larger birds, it is sometimes recommended to cut off the legs and roast them separately. Using a baster during roasting also helps keep the meat tender and juicy. If you put the bird on a rack or trivet the juices are easier to get to.

Nowadays, birds should only be stuffed in the neck end, with any leftover stuffing roasted in an ovenproof dish.

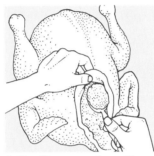

1 *If stuffing, spoon the stuffing into the neck end and truss (page 174). Add an onion, lemon halves or herb sprigs to the body cavity for flavour. Weigh and calculate cooking time (opposite).*

2 *To keep the breast moist during cooking, cover it with rashers of rindless streaky bacon or lift the breast skin and, using your fingers, smear the flesh with butter or cream cheese (opposite).*

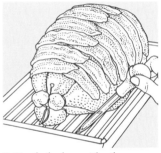

3 *Brush the legs with oil or smear with butter. Using a baster or spoon, baste the bird in its own juices 2 or 3 times during roasting. Any bacon needs to be removed for the last 20 minutes of roasting to brown the breast to an attractive golden colour.*

4 *Check the bird for doneness by piercing between the thigh and breast. Clear juices should run out. If there is even a hint of pink, return the bird to the oven for further cooking.*

Roast Pheasants Indian Style (page 192) served with okra and a curried mushroom sauce. A spicy marinade is smeared over the birds before roasting.

ROASTING DUCK OR GOOSE

Because these birds are so fatty they do not need extra fat to keep them moist but they do need basting during cooking. For a rich, dark glaze and crisp skin on roasted duck or goose I often rub the skin with honey or caster sugar as well as salt about 30 minutes before the end of cooking.

For a flavoursome gravy to serve with roast duck, I nearly always put 2 orange halves in the body cavity. This way the mingled juices can be poured out at the end of cooking to be added to the gravy.

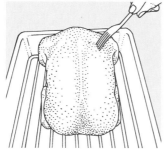

Place the duck or goose on a rack in the roasting pan and prick the skin all over with a fork. This allows the fat to run out during roasting and helps the skin become crisp and golden. Save the fat for roasting potatoes (page 57).

ROASTING CHART

All timings are guidelines only. Check for doneness by piercing the bird between the thigh and breast. For just cooked birds, the juices should run clear. (Alternatively, use a meat thermometer which should reach 70°C, 160°F.) If not return the bird to the oven. Juices from just pink birds such as ducks should have a slight pinky hue. Allow an extra 10 minutes cooking time for stuffed birds. After roasting, allow the bird to sit for 10–15 minutes to firm up for easier carving.

Bird	Temperature	Time
Chicken	190°C, 375°F, Gas Mark 5	Allow 20 minutes per 500g (1lb) plus 20 minutes
Poussin	190°C, 375°F, Gas Mark 5	40–45 minutes total cooking, depending on size
Duck	200°C, 400°F, Gas Mark 6	Allow 20 minutes per 500g (1lb) for 'just pink' and 25 minutes for 'just cooked'
Goose	180°C, 350°F, Gas Mark 4	Allow 20 minutes per 500g (1lb) plus 20 minutes
Pheasant	200°C, 400°F, Gas Mark 6	50 minutes total cooking
Guinea fowl	200°C, 400°F, Gas Mark 6	20 minutes per 500g (1lb) plus 25 minutes
Wild duck	200°C, 400°F, Gas Mark 6	1 hour total cooking
Grouse	220°C, 425°F, Gas Mark 7	35 minutes total cooking
Quail	220°C, 425°F, Gas Mark 7	30 minutes total cooking
Partridge	220°C, 425°F, Gas Mark 7	40 minutes total cooking
Turkey 3.6–4.5kg (8–10lb)	160°C, 325°F, Gas Mark 3	3½–3¾ hours
5–5.4kg (11–12lb)		3¾–4 hours
5.4–6.3kg (12–14lb)		4–4¼ hours
6.3–7.2kg (14–16lb)		4¼–4½ hours
7.2–8.1kg (16–18lb)		4½–4¾ hours
8.1–9kg (18–20lb)		4¾–5 hours

FLAVOURING AND SERVING ROAST BIRDS

• For flavouring butter to smear under the skin of a bird while roasting you can include fresh herbs, particularly tarragon, crushed or finely chopped garlic and fresh ginger, or ground aromatic Sichuan pepper and five-spice powder for a Chinese flavour. Ground Indian spices or tikka paste with chopped fresh coriander leaves add an Indian touch.

• For a more elaborate result also try pesto sauce, finely chopped anchovies with garlic, finely chopped rockét or watercress with cinnamon, finely grated lemon and orange rind, sun-dried tomato paste with fresh chopped basil and even slices of black truffle.

• A mixture of butter and an equal quantity of Brie or garlic and herb cream cheese is also very effective for putting under a bird's skin.

• With guinea fowl and game birds I often put some garlic and herb cream cheese inside the body cavity – when emptied out at the end of roasting and mixed with the juices this makes the most delicious gravy, particularly with the addition of a little dry or medium sherry.

• Stuffings add both flavour and a different dimension to a roast bird. A stuffing should be simply a mixture of good flavours and textures. Eggs can be used to bind the mixture if it is dry but moist ingredients usually hold together well.

• For ducks and geese fruit and nut stuffings are ideal with combinations of apple, dried apricots, peaches or prunes, fresh plums, walnuts, pecans, hazelnuts, almonds and pistachio nuts.

• Pistachio nuts also go well in a well seasoned, minced veal or pork stuffing mixture.

• Wholemeal breadcrumbs make a good stuffing mixed with lemon juice and rind and plenty of fresh herbs.

• Game chips (page 43), which are really homemade crisps, are traditional with game but many people want to steer clear of the smell and labour of deep-frying; as an alternative buy the best crisps you can find and heat them up spread out on a baking sheet in the oven.

• Mashed potatoes also go well with the juices of roast birds – try infusing a few threads of saffron into hot milk or cream before mixing it into the cooked potatoes when you mash them (page 53).

KEEPING BIRDS MOIST

Buttering under the skin is an excellent way of stopping the breast meat from drying out and at the same time adding flavour. I also smear the skin with olive oil or butter and sprinkle it with sea salt to produce a crisp golden appearance when cooked. Another way of keeping the bird moist is to lay a large sheet of buttered foil over it, but not wrapped tightly, or you simply produce a steamed, rather than roasted, bird.

Another way I sometimes use for large birds is to drape the bird with muslin dipped in plenty of melted butter which you remove for the last 30 minutes of the cooking for a brown finish.

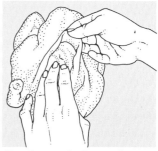

Gently ease the breast skin from the flesh, working between them with your fingertips and being careful not to tear the skin. Smear a generous amount of flavoured butter at room temperature evenly over the flesh and around the breast area of the bird. Finally, smear the skin with olive oil or a little more butter. The bird is now ready for roasting (see chart left).

FRYING *and* STIR-FRYING

Ever since I treated myself to a heavy copper frying pan sautéing and stir-frying have become my favourite ways of cooking. As it has deep sides the pan is perfect for both sautéing and shallow frying or pan frying, which are the best ways of retaining the succulence of larger pieces of poultry with the bonus of an enticingly golden, crisp exterior. It is much easier to control the heat of the oil when frying by gas as the heat can be changed instantly if you see that it is becoming too hot or cool. With most electric rings it is a question of moving the pan off the heat briefly while the ring cools a little. With all frying it is important to watch and adjust the temperature the whole time you are frying, and never to leave the stove.

For deep-frying the temperature of the cooking oil should be high and more exact – between 180°C and 195°C (350°F and 385°F). Butter is not suitable for high or deep-frying temperatures so use a vegetable oil. One of the things people have against deep-frying is the smell of the oil, so I like to use groundnut oil which has practically no aroma. The pieces of poultry are usually dipped in a coating of egg and breadcrumbs and should not be too large or they will burn on the outside before cooking through. The temperature of the oil will fall when you add the pieces and from then on you must watch and regulate the heat so that a normal chicken joint will turn a rich golden brown in 7–10 minutes.

Duck and goose are so fatty that they should only be dry pan-fried, and you will have to pour off the fat which will emerge from them. Slivers of skinless duck or goose can be successfully sautéed.

FRYING CHICKEN

Fried chicken either with a crisp crumb or a light flour coating is quite delicious and most suitable for young birds. Deep-frying is best for crumb coatings, shallow frying, also called pan frying, and sautéing are best for flour-coated birds. Natural colour dried breadcrumbs give the most attractive colour coating, but you can also use matzo meal or polenta (cornmeal). White breadcrumbs, which I prefer, give a golden coating.

It is important to fry at the correct temperature. If the oil is too hot, the skin and coating will start to burn while the centre is still raw. If the oil is not hot enough, the coating will not crisp enough to form a barrier between the oil and the meat and the cooked chicken will be too greasy.

Joint a chicken into 8 pieces (page 175) and remove the skin to lower the overall fat content, if liked.

Tasty-looking shallow-fried chicken drumsticks with moist juicy flesh inside a rich golden brown coating of paprika-seasoned flour. Using paprika or other spices adds extra flavour and colour to the flour coating.

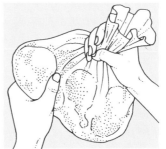

1 *To prepare chicken pieces for deep-frying toss the chicken first in seasoned flour in a polythene food bag until well coated. Shake off the excess flour. Have a bowl of beaten egg and one of breadcrumbs at the ready.*

2 *Dip floury pieces first in egg, then in crumbs, spooning the crumbs over evenly. For a thicker crunchier crumb repeat the egg and crumbing. Lay on a plate and chill for 1 hour. This helps the coating stick to the flesh.*

3 *Half fill a deep-frying pan with oil. Heat the oil to 190°C (375°F) or until a cube of white bread browns in 30 seconds. Lower in 3 or 4 pieces at a time in a basket, and cook for 7–10 minutes depending on size. Drain well on kitchen paper. Repeat with the remaining pieces, reheating the oil first.*

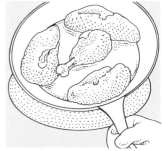

To shallow fry *toss chicken pieces in seasoned flour in a polythene food bag. Shake off the excess flour. Heat 4–6 tablespoons vegetable oil in a heavy-based frying pan until nearly smoking, then add the pieces, shaking the pan to stop them sticking. Cook over a medium heat for 12–15 minutes, turning once.*

STIR-FRYING

Stir-frying in a wok is a traditional Chinese way of cooking meats and vegetables, although a wok is not strictly necessary. Any large, deep, heavy-based frying pan will do.

Chicken, being lean and tender, is the ideal meat for stir-frying. Very thinly sliced duck's breast is also successful, especially if you remove the fatty skin and cook the slivers of meat quickly so they remain pink and juicy.

Ingredients for stir-frying should be cut into thin, even-sized slices or strips, cubes or dice – some small vegetables such as mange tout peas can be added whole. Vegetables, such as courgettes, which only need brief cooking are excellent.

At the end of the cooking you can add some liquid and cornflour to form a shiny thickened sauce, but I frequently find that the cooking juices with a little extra liquid are all that are necessary. Quantities for stir-frying need not be exact but for 4 people you will need about 500g (1lb) boneless chicken, depending on the quantity of other ingredients. Use about 2 tablespoons of oil for each 500g (1lb) ingredients.

Thinly sliced duck's breast is an excellent choice for a stir-fry dish. Slices of shiitake mushrooms, yellow pepper, fresh root ginger and garlic add delicate flavourings, and thinly sliced spring onions are delicious stirred in at the last moment before serving.

1 *Slice skinless poultry breasts across in thin slices and marinate (page 182). Slice vegetables to roughly the same size, leaving small ones whole, and lay them out in the order of cooking. Prepare flavourings such as peeled and chopped garlic and ginger, chopped herbs or ground spices.*

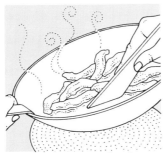

2 *Heat the oil in a wok or large frying pan over a high heat. Stir in the drained marinated poultry slices (reserving the marinade) and cook for 3–4 minutes, stirring constantly. Then add the ginger and garlic, or spices, but no fresh green herbs yet. Stir constantly for 1 minute.*

3 *Stir in the prepared vegetables, starting with those that take longest to cook and adding the remainder at 30 second intervals. Cook, tossing and stirring the vegetables for a few minutes, until all the vegetables are tender but still crunchy. It helps to shake the wok occasionally.*

4 *Pour in the marinade and a little extra soy sauce, sherry, lemon juice or stock. If you like a shiny sauce mix 1 teaspoon cornflour with 1–2 tablespoons of water until smooth, then stir in. Bubble the juices, stirring for 1 minute until thickened. Stir in chopped spring onion or fresh herbs. Serve at once.*

MAKING THE MOST OF FRYING

When making up an egg and breadcrumb coating first season the breadcrumbs, which can be either white or brown, white making the most golden crust. As well as sea salt and black pepper, dried herbs, particularly oregano, are a good addition. Ground spices such as coriander, cinnamon or whole cumin or caraway seeds are also excellent for adding extra flavour to the coating.

• Finely grated fresh Parmesan cheese and paprika, mixed with breadcrumbs give the browned chicken a reddish tinge.

• Extra-crunchy ingredients to add to flour include finely chopped nuts, matzo meal, cornmeal, ground rice and, a favourite of mine, semolina.

• A little semolina added to a normal egg and breadcrumb coating also adds crunchiness.

• Boned turkey and chicken breasts are ideal to cut into nugget-sized pieces, then coat with batter and deep fry. They are also perfect to cut in thin slivers for stir-frying; in this case they need no coating, only seasoning, and if more flavour and tenderness are needed, marinate them beforehand (page 182).

• I often finely chop skinless chicken and turkey fillets in the food processor, or mince them. The flesh can then be formed into small balls and sautéed. Because chicken and turkey breast meat tends to be dry and bland seasoning and extra moisture are important. Extra finely chopped fresh herbs, spinach, courgettes, tomato, finely grated lemon rind or grated cheese will all add moisture.

• A very successful way of using the above balls is to press a cube of cheese into the middle of each one. The cheese melts during cooking so that the ball reveals a delicious liquid centre. Try blue cheese, Mozzarella or goat cheese.

• With shallow frying or sautéing, the small amount of oil and butter you use really makes a difference to the flavour of the sauce so use extra virgin olive oil, creamy unsalted butter or, for a nutty flavour, walnut or hazelnut oil. With Chinese-style seasonings, try using a very little toasted sesame oil.

• Be sure to save the fat that accumulates in the frying pan after frying pieces of duck or goose to make the best roast potatoes (page 57).

GRILLING *and* BARBECUING

There are moments when one longs for the natural taste of food which grilling brings out. The only drawback to grilled poultry and game birds is that the pieces can dry out, and this is why marinating is particularly suitable for ingredients you are going to grill. Marinating keeps in and adds natural moisture and flavour, as well as being a tenderizer. A yogurt marinade alters the texture of the meat most noticeably as you will realize when eating Indian grilled and baked tandoori meats. As well as yogurt, marinades can be made from a simple mixture of oil and lemon juices, or wine for a more pronounced taste.

Whole chicken breast fillets are too bland and lean to grill well – they can be extremely dry and dull. If you cut them up into pieces, marinate them well and use skewered and flanked by vegetables for kebabs, however, they will have tenderness, moisture and flavour.

Joints of chicken, duck and guinea fowl all grill well. Quails and poussins are extremely tender so they just need seasoning but not marinating, and must be spatchcocked before grilling to make them the right thickness for evenly cooking all the way through.

The best tastes of all are those of food barbecued over the embers of a wood fire, particularly if you use aromatic fruit woods like apple wood. Charcoal is also wonderful, with a smell which transports me instantly to the Mediterranean or Middle East. But the smell of marinated birds grilling under an ordinary gas or electric grill can be almost as evocative, if lacking the romance of an outside meal.

MARINATING POULTRY

There are several simple ways to marinate poultry. A liquid marinade is oil with another liquid such as lemon juice, wine, fruit juice or various alcohols plus seasoning. Or, a moist marinade can be simply a seasoned yogurt mixture.

Flavours can also be added to the meat with a dry marinade; simply rub spices and herbs directly into the skin and leave overnight. Keep marinating pieces in a covered, non-metallic dish in the refrigerator and spoon with the marinade from time to time. Leave at least 1 hour.

Yogurt marinades *should be rubbed into the meat. Deep slashes help the marinade penetrate and tenderize the meat. Place the meat in a shallow, non-metallic dish, spoon over any remaining marinade, cover and place in the refrigerator.*

GRILLING POULTRY BREASTS

When grilling you must watch carefully and adjust the heat if the outside of the breasts are browning too quickly, giving no time for the centres to cook properly. Grilled duck breast fillets are a great favourite in my house. They are simple and quick to do, and when thinly sliced lengthwise into pink juicy strips, look and taste sophisticated.

For either duck or pigeon breasts I usually make a slightly sweet marinade which could be a mixture of olive oil, orange juice, a little sherry or balsamic vinegar, with finely chopped garlic and fresh herbs such as tarragon, dill or oregano. Season the marinade with plenty of black pepper and sea salt and lie the breasts flesh side down in a dish in which they fit closely so that the marinade juices are all round them. Spoon the marinade over the breasts from time to time.

Before grilling smear the skin with either honey or caster sugar and salt so that the skin blackens and crisps under the hot grill and forms a dark border to the pink flesh when the breasts are sliced. A certain amount of charring adds a smokiness I like.

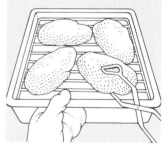

Place marinated duck breasts *under the hottest grill for 3–5 minutes until the skin is dark brown, then turn over and repeat on the other side. The flesh inside will be pink and juicy.*

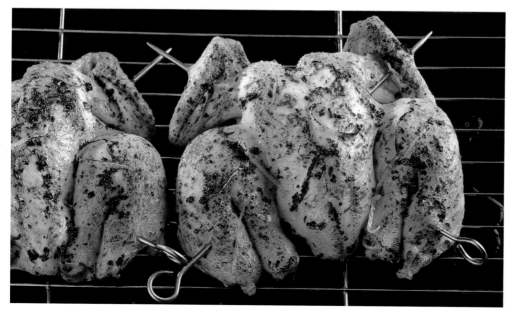

Spatchcocking is always an attractive way of grilling poussins for even cooking.

KEBABS

Kebabs made with various pieces of boneless turkey or chicken, interspersed with colourful vegetables, look pretty and are simple and fun to put together. Marinate skinless pieces of meat for extra tenderness and flavour.

Grilled kebabs are usually served with a sauce, which could be an Indonesian satay sauce made with spiced peanut butter, or one like Japanese yakitori, based on soy sauce. Or make yogurt-based sauces with an Indian touch by stirring in a little tikka paste and chopped fresh coriander.

Colourful kebabs Fill kebab sticks with marinated 5cm (2in) cubes of boneless meat, alternating with vegetables all roughly the same size. Brush with oil and grill under a hot grill or on a barbecue, turning once or twice, basting with leftover marinade.

Threaded kebabs are skewered concertina-style on to wooden sticks, which should be soaked in water beforehand to prevent them from burning. Cut skinless and boneless pieces of poultry into long strips about 1cm (½in) wide and marinate before skewering.

Marinated pieces of skinless chicken are threaded on to kebab sticks with strips of yellow and red peppers, button mushrooms, slices of courgette and fresh herbs to make colourful tasty kebabs.

BARBECUING TIPS

• One of the things it is easy to forget when there is suddenly a fine day and you are filled with enthusiasm about having a barbecue is to start in good time. Charcoal or wood must be left until the flames have subsided to produce just smouldering, white-looking charcoal or glowing embers before starting to cook. This process will take at least 30 minutes.

• Precook whole birds or 2 large halves to save time barbecuing. Finishing over the charcoal or wood adds the authentic smoky taste but the meat may not be quite so aromatic or succulent.

• To cook a whole bird or large poultry pieces entirely on the barbecue you can make a loose hood of foil (some sophisticated barbecues have their own lid) which keeps in the heat so that cooking is more even and makes the poultry even smokier in flavour.

• When cooking over wood remember that fruit woods will add their aroma to the meat, as will pieces of woody herbs such as rosemary or bay added to the embers or to charcoal. Juniper wood produces the most wonderful aroma.

• Let marinades add variety to barbecued food. Oil-based marinades can be olive, sesame or other vegetable and nut oils, mixed with lemon juice, wine, sherry or other alcohols, aromatic vinegars and soy sauce or various fruit juices.

• Add chopped garlic and fresh ginger, spices of all kinds, herbs and pastes such as tomato, and aromatic peppers such as green peppercorns and Sichuan pepper to a liquid marinade.

• Yogurt, seasoned with herbs, spices or Indian pastes is a very effective marinade as it tenderizes the toughest meat if left for several hours.

• Sesame seeds mixed with a marinade add crunchiness and extra flavour.

SPATCHCOCKING

This is a most attractive and tasty way of grilling or barbecuing small birds such as poussins, quails and guinea fowls. The birds are opened out flat, then stopped from curling back to their original shape during cooking by being held in position with two long criss-crossed skewers.

The term 'spatchcock' comes from an Irish expression for preparing an impromptu meal for unexpected guests. A chicken was 'dispatched', or killed, before being quickly split in half and then fried.

Cook the birds simply basted with oil and seasoning or marinated with spices and herbs which will give an attractive speckled appearance to the cooked birds. Grill them for 5–10 minutes on each side according to size, basting during cooking. Sprinkle with fresh lemon juice to serve, if you like.

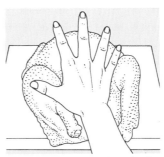

1 *Using a large very sharp knife or poultry shears, cut through the backbone and open out the bird, flattening it firmly with the palm of your hand.*

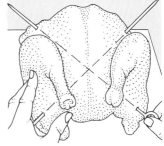

2 *Stick metal skewers or long wooden satay sticks diagonally through the bird to hold it flat. Quails can be skewered side by side, 2 birds on 1 skewer.*

CASSEROLING *and* POT-ROASTING

Casseroling and pot-roasting are long, gentle methods of cooking in a covered pot, which need minimum attention but can produce the most delectable results. With slow cooking the meat gradually becomes meltingly tender and absorbs the flavours of ingredients and flavourings with which it is cooked. These methods are ideal for older poultry and game birds which might otherwise be rather tough and dry. Pigeon, pheasant and mallard are ideal candidates, as well as chicken.

Casseroles are usually made from joints or smaller boneless pieces of meat and cooked in a covered casserole dish. The liquid in which casseroles cook is plentiful and often thickened, and vegetables are usually added during cooking. Stews are like casseroles but usually have unthickened juices, and can also be cooked on top of the stove. Pot-roasting and braising are very similar as the ingredients are cooked with little or no liquid and vegetables are usually added so the meat juices flavour the vegetables and vice versa. Pot-roasting is for whole birds, whereas whole and jointed birds can be braised.

Preliminary frying of the meat adds both colour and flavour but is by no means obligatory if you have little time. After the frying, liquid is added in which the ingredients cook; this can include wine, good stock, the marinade mixture if the meat has been marinated, fruit juices or even cream.

The most important thing about slow cooking is that it really is slow; the liquid should be barely trembling. Too high a temperature toughens the meat, and the flavours of meat, vegetables and flavourings merge better without the turbulence of boiling. Vegetables should be added at different moments, depending on how long they take to cook. Add green vegetables, such as broccoli or mange tout, at the end of cooking so they remain bright green.

Casseroled Quails in a Pear Tree (page 192): quails cooked slowly with pears and tomatoes. Quails are ideal birds for casseroling as it prevents their delicate flesh from drying out.

CASSEROLING PIGEON

I always casserole or braise pigeons, and you can adapt this method for any poultry or game birds with vegetables of your choice. First quarter lengthwise 2 fennel bulbs, finely chop 3 cloves garlic and a 5cm (2in) piece fresh ginger and skin and chop 500g (1lb) tomatoes (page 48). Have ready 4 pigeons, 3 strips orange rind, 1 teaspoon ground mace, 1 tablespoon plain flour, 150ml (¼ pint) stock and the juice of 1 orange. Serves 4.

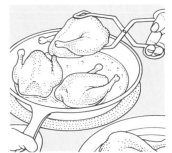

1 *Heat a small amount of olive oil and butter in a heavy-based frying pan over a high heat. Brown 4 whole or halved pigeons all over, then remove from the pan and set aside.*

2 *Fry the fennel until golden, then add the garlic and ginger for 1 minute. Transfer to a flameproof casserole with the tomatoes, orange rind and mace. Stir in the flour, add the stock and orange juice and season. Then return to the heat.*

3 *Bring to the boil, stirring until the sauce has thickened. Add the pigeons on top of the vegetables, cover and cook in a preheated oven, 150°C, 300°F, Gas Mark 2 for 2½–3 hours until the pigeons are very tender when tested with the tip of a knife.*

POT-ROASTING PHEASANT

This is an excellent method for cooking older birds, such as pheasants, which can be tough and dry. If you cook a few vegetables in the dish, too, they will also add flavour. The liquid of a pot roast, gently reduced by long simmering, turns into an intense sauce. Before cooking, slice 2 onions and have ready 2 teaspoons caster sugar, 1 teaspoon crushed juniper berries, 2 teaspoons ground coriander and 500g (1lb) well-scrubbed whole small carrots. One pheasant serves 2–3.

Alternatively, use your favourite vegetables for other birds. Parsnips and turnips with a little added honey are successful, as are skinned and chopped tomatoes.

In late autumn older grouse are best cooked by a slow method such as pot-roasting. Slices of pumpkin and small onions are cooked with the birds to give added flavours.

1 *Heat 2 tablespoons olive oil and 25g (1oz) butter in a flameproof casserole over a fairly high heat. Fry 1 pheasant on all sides until browned. Remove the pheasant using wooden spoons so the skin isn't pierced; set aside.*

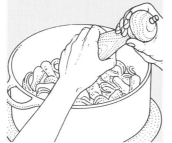

2 *Add the sliced onions and stir until browned. Stir in the caster sugar, juniper berries, ground coriander and carrots. Season with salt and pepper. Return the browned pheasant to the casserole on top of the vegetables.*

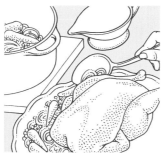

3 *Add 75ml (3fl oz) dry vermouth or white wine, cover and cook in a preheated oven, 160°C, 325°F, Gas Mark 3 for 2–3 hours until tender. Transfer to a warm serving dish.*

4 *Remove the vegetables and arrange round the pheasant. To make a sauce add 150ml (¼ pint) double cream to the casserole juices and bring to the boil for about 2 minutes, stirring.*

FLAVOURING CASSEROLES AND POT ROASTS

• Fresh herbs should always be added to casseroles at the very end of cooking. If a bouquet garni was added at the beginning of cooking discard it and replace with fresh herbs for serving.

• Sweetness brings out savoury flavours and sweet vegetables such as carrots, parsnips and sweet potatoes can be very effective cooked with game birds.

• Fruit such as pears, apples and plums are excellent with pheasants, but need only be added halfway through the cooking or they become too mushy.

• Dried fruits, particularly apricots and prunes, are excellent in a game casserole.

• Cinnamon has a special affinity with chicken.

• Game is good cooked with a few whole cloves and some caraway seeds. Coriander seems to go well with almost everything, and you can experiment with many other spices, including Chinese five-spice powder.

• Soy sauce, as well as wines, spirits, liqueurs, citrus and other fruit juices, tomato juice and purée and good stocks can all be used for the liquid in casseroles and pot roasts.

• Cream stirred into a casserole at the end, or used to make a sauce for pot-roasted birds, always adds a luscious sophistication to a dish. Soured cream, smetana or thick yogurt can also be used. Do not boil the juices after adding smetana or yogurt or they will curdle.

• Apart from soft, sweet onions, some of the other vegetables I particularly like in casseroles and pot roasts which take well to slow cooking are leeks, bulb fennel, aubergines, parsnips and, of course, carrots and tomatoes.

• Courgettes can be cooked slowly, too, but I prefer them added towards the end of the cooking so they are still crunchy and bright in comparison to the other soft, mellow-coloured ingredients.

• Chestnut mushrooms, which have more body than the ordinary button variety, are the best to use for long cooking. For a special treat, try fresh shiitake mushrooms or soaked dried mushrooms for their intense flavours.

POACHING *and* STEAMING

Poaching and steaming are simple, healthy and efficient ways of cooking which retain moisture, tenderness and flavour in a bird. Both these methods have the advantage of using no added fat. Poaching is particularly good for boiling fowl and older game birds which could be tough.

Poaching is often confused with boiling but 'poaching' is a far better term because the important thing to remember is that although the liquid surrounding the bird is brought up to the boil initially, it should thereafter barely simmer, retaining only a gentle shuddering instead of bubbling. This is because strong boiling toughens birds and makes them stringy; it is the gentleness of simmering which results in the tender fine texture characteristic of poached poultry. Game birds, which tend to be dry, are also very good poached, especially with whole spices and fruit juices in the liquid.

For poaching, it is important that a bird is completely immersed in the liquid but since the flavours will dilute too much in a large quantity of water use a casserole in which the bird, and vegetables if using, fit closely. Apart from being eaten as a main course with its vegetables, the meat from a poached bird is excellent in pies or for sandwiches, salads, or any dish which requires cold poultry or game. After removing the bird the flavourful liquid can be eaten as a delicate broth on its own or reduced and thickened and used to make a sauce or soup.

Steaming is a slower cooking process than poaching and is excellent for boned chicken or turkey breasts and other pieces of boneless poultry. Steaming can be done on any rack or tray suspended over boiling water as long as it is tightly covered. If you do not have a steamer it is possible to improvise by using two heatproof plates large enough to fit over the top of a saucepan. Place thin slices of poultry on the surface of one plate over a pan of simmering water. Top with an upside-down plate and leave for about 5 minutes until the meat is cooked through.

POACHING A WHOLE CHICKEN

As well as whole birds, poultry joints can also be poached successfully to keep the flesh moist and tender. The Chicken Breast Rolls with Wine and Parsley Sauce recipe (page 190) uses chicken breast fillets which are wrapped up like a Swiss roll round a flavourful filling and then poached.

Poach the bird with a selection of coarsely chopped vegetables and other flavourings such as fresh herbs and spices for 20–25 minutes per 500g (1lb), according to the age and size of the bird. Time from when the water comes to the boil. Good vegetables for adding flavour to the poaching water are chopped onions, carrots, leeks or celery.

Test the bird for 'doneness' as you would do for roasting (page 178), and if the juices run clear the bird is cooked through. If you intend dicing the meat you can actually cut into the leg to check whether it is cooked or not.

If you are eating the bird cold, for a moister texture, allow the cooked bird to cool in the liquid. This is not, however, recommended in warm weather when the bird should be cooled out of the stock as quickly as possible, then stored well covered in the refrigerator for up to 3 days.

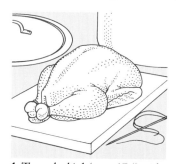

1 *Truss the bird (page 174) with kitchen string before poaching, if you like, so it retains its shape after cooking. Place the bird in a close-fitting saucepan filled with water. Add the coarsely chopped vegetables of your choice and any other flavourings.*

2 *Scatter over fresh herbs and spices, as you choose, then bring to the boil. Skim any scum that rises to the top, then partially cover, lower the heat and simmer gently until cooked and the juices run clear when tested with the tip of a knife.*

STEAMING

Steaming is an ideal method for cooking tender pieces of poultry breast, especially if they have been marinated beforehand in Chinese- or Japanese-style sauces.

You can use a traditional metal steamer that fits on top of a saucepan, or a modern electric one, but perhaps the most attractive way to steam is using an oriental bamboo steamer that fits into a wok.

The most suitable cuts of poultry for steaming are breasts, or small whole birds such as quails or poussins. Old birds can be tenderized by first steaming them whole, and patting them dry before rubbing with aromatic flavourings and roasting.

Steaming oriental-style, using an attractive bamboo steaming basket and flavourings such as whole star anise, finely sliced spring onions and fresh coriander leaves. Far from being a bland method of cooking pieces of poultry steaming can impart some exciting flavours to the lean flesh as well as keeping it moist.

1 *Marinate chicken breasts for steaming oriental-style in light soy sauce, dry sherry and a few drops of sesame oil for 10 minutes. Slash the breasts each side for even heat penetration. Place in the top of a steamer.*

2 *Half fill the bottom of the steamer with water and bring to the boil over a high heat. Add a selection of fresh herbs or other flavourings to the water. This will give extra flavour to the steamed poultry.*

3 *Place the top half of the steamer over the water, making sure no water comes through the holes. Sprinkle sliced spring onions, shredded ginger or spices over the poultry. Cover and steam about 10 minutes until the juices run clear when tested with a knife.*

Adapt a collapsible metal steamer so you can steam marinated food without losing all the delicious juices into the boiling water below. Remove the central handle from the steamer and place the poultry on a small heatproof plate in the base.

POACHING AND STEAMING TIPS

• To preserve a chicken's white flesh rub it all over with lemon juice before poaching in water with lemon juice or white wine vinegar added to it.

• Additions to poaching water can be whole spices of all kinds, bay leaves, rosemary, tarragon, thyme or other strong herbs, roughly chopped garlic, lemon and orange rind, whole peppercorns including green and Sichuan, tamarind pods, saffron and, for extra bite, 1 or 2 dried red chillies.

• I like to poach chicken pieces in aromatic tea such as Earl Grey which produces a delicate and interesting flavour, as well as a darkly stained exterior.

• Liquid additions to poaching or steaming water can be wine, sherry, Pernod for its aniseed taste, and fruit juice.

• There are ingredients you can add to the cooking liquid which will colour the eventual sauce when poaching. Tomatoes will add a light orangy red colour, but you can also add 2–3 teaspoons paprika and some tomato purée to strengthen this. Saffron gives a yellow colour, at a cost, but if the sauce is to be spicy you can add turmeric instead.

• If you grow marigolds in your garden the flowers will add a yellow colour but no discernible taste.

• To make the liquid green you can either use spinach leaves or wrap compressed spinach leaves up in muslin like a large bouquet garni so that the green juices seep out during the cooking. The spinach should not be in the water for more than 1 hour or it will lose its bright green colour.

• If there is not much cooking liquid left after the bird has been removed you can reduce it after straining it through a fine sieve and to make an excellent sauce without extra thickening, simply stir in double cream and bubble for a minute or two. As a last touch, add chopped fresh green herbs.

• In addition to marinating pieces of poultry before steaming, you can also flavour the simmering water underneath with slivers of onions, fresh root ginger, carrots or celery. This water can then be used to make sauces, as with poaching liquid (opposite), but it will probably not have such a full flavour. Or place poultry pieces on a base of tasty lovage or mint leaves to impart more flavour.

CARVING *and* CUTTING

One of my earliest memories is of my father sharpening the carving knife with a steel. Being a jazz enthusiast, and an old-fashioned English eccentric, the sharpening process was always done to a jazz rhythm and, in fact, the sliding and clicking noises of steel against steel fitted it perfectly and produced a marvellously sharp knife as well.

An important step towards successful carving is to rest the bird in a warm place for 10–15 minutes after taking it out of the oven – this 'sets' the flesh and makes it easier to slice neatly. Remember to include this resting time when you calculate what time to start cooking the bird for a particular meal (page 179). Also, always remember the supreme importance of the knife's sharpness for successful carving; a blunt carving knife can induce fury and result in a wrecked bird. Slices should be as thin as you can manage and arranged on the plate rather than just thrown haphazardly on to it. Leg and wing joints should be cut off as neatly as possible.

There are some people who never really take to carving and others who pride themselves on it. If you are the cook there are so many other things such as the vegetables or the gravy to attend to at this stage in the meal that it is worth asking if any of your guests, or a member of the family, would like to carve.

CARVING ROAST TURKEY OR CHICKEN

There is actually nothing difficult or mysterious about carving but a really sharp knife, ideally sharpened by a proper steel, is a must (page 16). Remember to cut across the grain of meat. This requires a little simple knowledge of anatomy and which way the meat fibres run. Cutting across the grain of meat shortens muscle fibres and means more tender meat. It is also worth remembering that white meat comes from the breast and dark meat from the rest of the body and the legs. Ideally you should serve a selection of both to your guests.

Don't be tempted to carve too far ahead or you may lose valuable meat juice. It is better to serve good juicy slices freshly cut than to try and save a few minutes.

Turkey and chicken are carved in the same way, while ducks and geese require a slightly different technique because of their different body shapes (opposite).

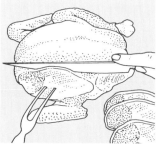

1 *Before starting to carve, remove all the trussing strings if the bird was trussed. Work on one side of the bird at a time. Cut through the thigh and breast skin, then prise the thigh away from the body. Locate the socket joint and pull the leg away from the body, cutting through the joint. There is no need to cut through the actual bone.*

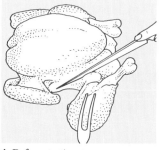

2 *Cut down across the breast in 5mm (¼in) slices, including stuffing if possible, otherwise spoon out the stuffing. Cut enough for 1 portion, then cut some leg meat. If you are carving a large turkey, you can save time by slicing the breast in advance and putting it back on the carcase before bringing the bird to the table.*

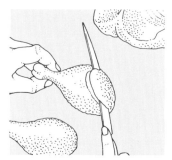

3 *Next, separate the thigh from the drumstick, slicing down between the joint. If the bird is small, however, you can leave the leg whole. For a better presentation cut or pull off the scaly knuckle at the end of the drumstick and discard.*

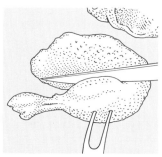

4 *The legs of larger chickens and turkeys should be carved into further pieces. For darker leg meat, hold the drumstick away from you and cut off slices. Cut the thigh across into several pieces. Discard the wing tip and only serve the wing joint if you are running out of other meat.*

If carving a cold turkey for a large number it is worth thinking about attractive presentation. Arrange the carved slices in piles of white meat, dark meat and stuffing on a large plate with a garnish. Here, a few fresh cranberries, pieces of fresh fig and some coriander leaves make a simple finishing touch.

CARVING DUCK OR GOOSE

Small ducks can be simply jointed into quarters for serving but I prefer the long, narrow slices of breast meat achieved by normal carving. Larger ducks and geese are carved as below. Remember that because of the high bone content on these birds there is much less meat on them than on other poultry.

To carve a stuffed boned duck (page 177) remove the trussing strings and cut crosswise in neat, thin slices. If you make the stuffing with colourful ingredients this looks attractive presented on a pretty plate on a buffet table.

A roast goose is a traditional bird to serve on festive occasions and makes an impressive sight.

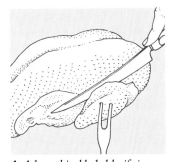

1 *A long thin-bladed knife is useful for carving a duck or goose. Pull the wings and legs away from the body and cut firmly through the joints. Put the legs to one side for carving later. Wings on ducks have little meat and are not usually served.*

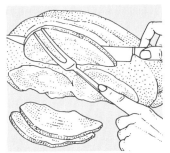

2 *Neatly cut the breast meat in long thin slices, working the full length of the carcase from the sides up towards the breastbone. Remove the slices carefully holding them between the carving knife and fork.*

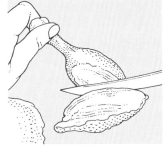

3 *Large duck and goose legs can be carved into further pieces as for larger chickens or turkeys (opposite). Cut the leg into 2 pieces, thigh and drumstick, by slicing down between the joint. Cut slices off the drumstick and cut the thigh into several pieces.*

SMALL BIRDS

Pheasants can be carved in the same way as small chicken. For small guinea fowls, partridges and wild duck half a bird is usually just the right amount for each serving. Cut it before you bring it to the table. Poussins and quails are served whole. Allow 1 poussin or 2 or 3 quail per person, depending on how large appetites are. Even young game birds can be tougher than farmed poultry and will need to be cut on plates after serving with sharp or serrated steak-style knives.

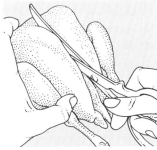

Simply cut the bird *in two through the breast- and backbones with sharp poultry shears, then to serve place cut side down on individual plates. If you don't have poultry shears, use a sharp cook's knife.*

PRESENTING CARVED POULTRY AND GAME BIRDS

• Some poussins are a bit too big to serve 1 per person, so instead of serving them on individual plates I usually halve the cooked birds and arrange them on a large serving plate with sprigs of fresh herbs or a cream sauce poured over them.

• Pigeons look wonderful all together on a serving plate with a glaze of seasoned honey warmed with a little balsamic vinegar spooned over them. This glaze can also be used with grouse on individual plates.

• A plate of cold carved meat is greatly enhanced by greenery. Lay the pieces on a bed of pretty leaves such as the oak leafed or curly lettuces, feathery frisée, or simply watercress. If you grow it in your garden lovage leaves make a dashing border.

• You can also scatter fresh herbs such as dill, fennel or chopped parsley over carved meat.

• I often make a mixture of lemon juice or good, fruity wine or sherry vinegar with extra virgin olive oil and plenty of chopped herbs, seasoned with sea salt and black pepper, and spoon it over the arranged meat – this both adds flavour to the meat and prevents it from drying out.

• Another way of presenting cold chicken or turkey is to arrange a wide border of thinly sliced breast edged with leaves around the plate and then mix the small pieces of meat with either thick yogurt or mayonnaise and plenty of chopped fresh herbs and seasoning, and spoon it into the middle of the plate.

• A quick way of making Indian-style cold chicken or turkey, which is particularly useful for a party, is to stir tikka pasta into yogurt then mix with the carved meat and plenty of chopped fresh coriander leaves.

CHICKEN IN ALMOND AND COCONUT MILK (172)

The character of this dish is Indian but you would be most unlikely to find almonds in the dishes of southern India or coconut milk in those of the north. My recipe combines both. It is quick to make, and convenient too, as it can be made ahead and reheated when required. Serve with saffron-flavoured rice or Basmati Rice with Crisped Grains (page 114). *SERVES 6*

> 75g (3oz) desiccated coconut
> 450ml (¾ pint) boiling water
> 1 tablespoon sunflower oil
> 25g (1oz) butter
> 2 onions, chopped finely
> 1 teaspoon ground cardamom
> 1 teaspoon ground coriander
> 1 teaspoon ground cumin
> 2.5cm (1in) piece fresh root ginger, peeled and chopped finely
> 1 large clove garlic, chopped finely
> 75g (3oz) ground almonds
> 3–5 pinches chilli powder
> 6 boned and skinned chicken thighs
> Handful of fresh coriander leaves, chopped roughly
> Salt

Put the desiccated coconut in a bowl, pour over the boiling water and leave for at least 30 minutes.

Heat the oil and butter in a flameproof casserole over a fairly high heat. Add the chopped onions and fry, stirring occasionally, until richly browned. Add the ground spices and the chopped ginger and garlic. Stir occasionally, then add the ground almonds and stir over the heat for another minute until mushy and brown. Remove the casserole from the heat.

Strain the water from the soaking coconut into the casserole through a sieve. Using your hand squeeze the coconut in the sieve over and over again until all the liquid has been squeezed out of it. Discard the leftover coconut. Stir the coconut liquid into the casserole and season to taste with chilli powder and salt.

Add the skinned pieces of chicken. Bring the mixture to the boil, cover and leave to simmer gently over a very low heat for about 1 hour. Remove from the heat and stir in the chopped coriander leaves just before serving.

STEAMED CHICKEN IN YELLOW PEPPER AND DILL SAUCE (172)

I devised this recipe for a visiting friend on a low-fat diet. The pepper and dill sauce tastes almost creamy so it has none of the austerity of a slimmer's dish. *SERVES 4*

> 2 yellow peppers, deseeded and chopped roughly (page 49)
> 3–4 large cloves garlic, halved
> 150ml (¼ pint) water
> 4 chicken breast fillets, skinned and cut across into thin slices
> Generous handful of fresh dill, chopped
> 3 tablespoons Greek ewes' milk yogurt
> 3–4 pinches cayenne pepper
> Salt
> Fresh dill to garnish

Put the chopped peppers and garlic in a saucepan with the water and sprinkle in a little salt. Bring to the boil, cover and simmer gently for about 20 minutes until the pepper is very soft. Remove from the heat. Put the pepper, garlic and water in a food processor and whizz to a smooth purée. You can then strain through a fine sieve if you want an extra-smooth purée, but I don't think this is necessary.

Place a fairly shallow serving dish into a low oven to warm. Put the slices of chicken breast in a steamer and steam over boiling water for about 5 minutes until the slices are white all through. Arrange the chicken pieces in the warm serving dish, cover loosely with foil and keep warm in the oven.

Spoon the pepper purée into a saucepan and heat gently, stirring. Stir in the chopped dill and yogurt, then remove the sauce from the heat without allowing it to boil. Season to taste with cayenne pepper and salt. Pour the sauce over the chicken and garnish with more fresh dill. Serve at once.

CHICKEN BREAST ROLLS WITH WINE AND PARSLEY SAUCE (186)

Here chicken breast fillets are wrapped round a thin layer of lemon rind, curd cheese and capers in this delicious and easily made dish. The chicken rolls are then gently poached in the oven and served with a delicate, translucent sauce made with the cooking juices. Serve with hot new potatoes or buttered noodles and a green vegetable such as french beans. *SERVES 4*

> Finely grated rind of 2 lemons
> 3 teaspoons capers, chopped finely
> 1 tablespoon curd cheese
> 1 teaspoon caster sugar
> 4 large chicken breast fillets, skinned
> 4 tablespoons lemon juice, strained
> 150ml (¼ pint) white wine
> 2 teaspoons cornflour mixed with a small amount of water
> 1 teaspoon flower honey
> Large handful of parsley, chopped finely
> Sea salt and black pepper

Put the grated lemon rind, chopped capers, curd cheese and caster sugar in a small bowl and mix together thoroughly. Season well with crushed sea salt and black pepper.

Cut the chicken breast fillets in half crosswise and lay spaced apart on a large sheet of wet greaseproof paper or baking parchment on a firm work surface. Put another sheet on top and beat the fillets evenly with a rolling pin or heavy flat implement until the pieces of breast are spread out and fairly thin.

Spread the lemon rind, curd cheese and caper mixture thinly on each piece of chicken, then roll up fairly loosely like a Swiss roll.

Lay the rolls, join side down, in a fairly shallow ovenproof dish in which they fit closely in a single layer. (By putting the chicken rolls close together you prevent them from unrolling during cooking.) Pour the lemon juice and wine over the rolls.

Cover the dish with foil and leave to marinate for at least 1 hour before cooking. If you have time to marinate the chicken for several hours, put the dish in the refrigerator but bring it out to return to room temperature 30 minutes before cooking.

Cook the chicken rolls, still covered

with foil, in the centre of a preheated oven, 190°C, 375°F, Gas Mark 5 for 35–40 minutes until white and just lightly cooked all through. Test with the tip of a knife; there shouldn't be any pink juices. Carefully pour all the juices off into a saucepan and leave the dish of rolls in a warm place while you make the sauce.

Stir the cornflour and water mixture into the juices. Bring to the boil, stirring as the sauce bubbles and thickens for at least 5 minutes. Stir in the honey and season to taste with salt and black pepper. Finally stir in the chopped parsley and remove from the heat. Pour any juice that has emerged from the chicken rolls while you made the sauce into the finished sauce and stir in before spooning over the rolls and serving.

AROMATIC CHICKEN ON A MATTRESS (174)

In this aromatic dish joints of chicken are cooked on top of the purée (or mattress) of apples, onion, garlic and chicory mixed with bulgar, also called cracked wheat. The mixture produces a wonderful combination of contrasting flavours and textures, and the 'mattress' is made even tastier by the juices of the chicken which run into it as it cooks. Serve with a crisp green vegetable such as broccoli, and with sautéed potatoes or a bowl of buttered noodles.   *SERVES 6*

75g (3oz) bulgar
2 tablespoons olive oil
1 large onion, sliced
5–6 whole allspice berries
3 large cloves garlic, chopped roughly
2.5cm (1in) piece fresh root ginger, peeled and chopped roughly
4 large dessert apples, unpeeled, cored and sliced fairly thinly
4 heads chicory, sliced
6 chicken joints, such as breasts, drumsticks or thighs
Extra virgin olive oil
3 tablespoons natural yogurt
1 clove garlic, chopped finely
25g (1oz) pine kernels or split almonds
Salt and black pepper

Put the bulgar in a bowl, cover with plenty of cold water and leave to soak for at least 10 minutes.

Meanwhile, put the olive oil in a large, deep frying pan over a medium heat. Add the sliced onion and stir for 1–2 minutes, then add the allspice berries, garlic and ginger, apples and chicory. Cook, stirring often, for 10–20 minutes or until the apples and onions are soft but not browned. Sprinkle with a little black pepper and salt.

Spoon the mixture into a food processor, picking out the whole allspice as you do so. Whizz until smooth, then check the seasoning again – the purée should be strongly seasoned as it is to be mixed with the bland-tasting bulgar.

Drain the bulgar, squeezing out the excess water with your hand, then stir it into the purée. Spoon the mixture into a large, wide ovenproof casserole and spread level.

Rub each of the chicken joints with a little extra virgin olive oil and sprinkle with salt and black pepper.

Arrange the joints on top of the mattress of the purée and bulgar, then cover the dish and cook in the centre of a preheated oven, 190°C, 375°F, Gas Mark 5 for 1 hour. Remove the casserole from the oven and increase the temperature to 240°C, 475°F, Gas Mark 9.

Put the yogurt in a bowl and mix in the garlic. Using a pastry brush apply this mixture thickly over the chicken joints. Scatter the pine kernels or split almonds on top all over.

Return the uncovered casserole back to the oven at the very top for 10–20 minutes until the joints are tinged with brown. Remove from the oven and serve straight from the casserole or on individual plates.

POUSSINS WITH FRESH CORIANDER AND LIME (172)

One poussin per person is generous but half of one, is, I think, definitely skimping. A whole bird on your plate also looks more impressive so serve this for a small dinner. Flavourful cheese under the skins and bacon on the breasts keep the birds tender.   *SERVES 4*

75g (3oz) full-fat white cheese
1 tablespoon lemon juice
Large bunch of fresh coriander leaves
5cm (2in) piece fresh root ginger, peeled and chopped very finely
Finely grated rind and juice of 2 limes
4 poussins
12–16 rashers rindless smoked bacon
300ml (½ pint) double cream
Salt and black pepper

Put the white cheese into a bowl with the lemon juice and work with a wooden spoon to soften and mix. Reserve about 2 tablespoons of the smallest coriander leaves and chop the remaining leaves roughly. Stir the chopped coriander, ginger and grated lime rind into the white cheese mixture.

Lift up the skin of the poussins from the neck end and carefully insert your fingers to separate the skin from the flesh. Cut a small slit in the skin of the inside leg of each bird and stick a finger in to loosen the skin from the thighs, too. Using your fingertips place the cheese paste under the skin of the birds and press from the top to distribute the paste all over the breasts and the thighs. Place the rashers of bacon over the breasts and thighs of the poussins, cutting the bacon to fit. Put the poussins in a roasting tin and cook in a preheated oven, 190°C, 375°F, Gas Mark 5 for 40–45 minutes. Transfer the birds to a warmed serving dish or individual plates.

Add the lime juice to the cooking juices in the roasting tin, then place it over a fairly high heat. Bring the juices to the boil and stir for 1 minute. Stir in the cream and boil again, still stirring, for 2–3 minutes until the sauce has thickened quite a bit. Remove from the heat and add the reserved coriander leaves with salt and black pepper to taste.

Pour the sauce into a sauceboat to serve with the poussins or, if they are already on individual plates, spoon the sauce on to each plate.

DARK GLOSSY FRUITED DUCK *(172)*

This is a dish evocative of Morocco where meats, spices and fruits are often mixed together – with delicious results. It is very simple to prepare and so it is perfect for a dinner party. Serve with saffron-flavoured rice or Basmati Rice with Crisped Grains (page 114) and a green salad.   *SERVES 4*

4 joints of duck or 1 large duck, jointed
*   (page 175)*
Sunflower oil
75g (3oz) ready-to-eat dried apricots
2 large cloves garlic, chopped finely
3 teaspoons paprika
2 teaspoons ground cinnamon
¾ teaspoon cayenne pepper
150ml (¼ pint) apple juice
2 tablespoons honey mixed with 150ml
*   (¼ pint) warm water*
4 tablespoons lemon juice
50g (2oz) unskinned whole almonds
Good handful of fresh mint leaves,
*   chopped roughly*
Salt

Prick the skin of the duck joints all over with a fork. Heat a little oil in a large frying pan and fry the duck joints over a fairly high heat on both sides until they are just brown. Transfer the joints to a large saucepan and add the apricots, garlic, spices, cayenne pepper, apple juice, honey and water mixture, lemon juice and almonds. Bring the liquid to the boil, then cover and simmer gently for about 45 minutes or until the duck is tender and just cooked through, but still slightly pink.

Using a slotted spoon, remove the joints of duck, the apricots and almonds and arrange on a serving dish with the almonds mostly on top. Keep the dish warm in a very low oven.

Boil the remaining saucepan juices fiercely until they are much reduced, thickened and glossy. Add salt and more cayenne pepper to taste. Just before serving, reheat the sauce, stir in the chopped mint leaves and spoon the sauce over the duck joints.

CASSEROLED QUAILS IN A PEAR TREE *(184)*

In the autumn when my garden is full of rather hard pears I find this simple casserole a marvellous way to make use of them. They seem made for the delicate flavour of quails, which have more flesh on them than you would think. Don't be alarmed by the quantity of garlic – cooked long and gently it becomes sweet and mild.   *SERVES 4*

1 tablespoon olive oil
25g (1oz) butter
8 quails
1 small red pepper, deseeded and sliced
*   finely (page 49)*
1 large bulb fennel, trimmed and sliced
*   thinly (page 46)*
1 teaspoon fennel seeds
6–8 cloves garlic
4 firm pears, peeled, quartered and cored
397g (14oz) can chopped tomatoes
Salt and black pepper

Put the olive oil and butter in a large flameproof casserole and heat to a fairly high heat. Add the quails, in batches if necessary, and turn until lightly browned all over. Remove the birds to a plate and keep on one side. Reduce the heat to medium, then add the sliced pepper and fennel to the casserole and cook, stirring often, until softened. Add the fennel seeds and the whole cloves of garlic. Cook for another minute or two, then remove from the heat.

Arrange the pear pieces among the vegetable mixture and season with salt and black pepper. Place the quails on top, in 2 layers if necessary, and spoon the chopped tomatoes evenly over each quail. Season again with a little salt and black pepper. Cover the casserole and cook just above the centre of a preheated oven, 190°C, 375°F, Gas Mark 5 for 1–1¼ hours. Transfer to a serving dish or serve straight from the casserole.

ROAST PHEASANTS INDIAN STYLE *(178)*

If you roast pheasants without seasoning them they can be dry and bland, and so one of the best ways to treat them is to use a spicy marinade. Serve with saffron-flavoured rice and a green salad.   *SERVES 6*

FOR THE PHEASANTS AND MARINADE
2 oven-ready pheasants
2 large cloves garlic, chopped very finely
3 tablespoons groundnut oil
2 tablespoons tomato purée
1 tablespoon wine vinegar
2 teaspoons ground cumin
3 teaspoons ground coriander
1 teaspoon ground cardamom
½ teaspoon each ground cloves and
*   cayenne pepper*
4 tablespoons lemon juice
Juice of 1 orange
FOR THE SAUCE
50g (2oz) butter
2 teaspoons each ground cumin, ground
*   cardamom and ground coriander*
250g (8oz) mushrooms, sliced thinly
4 tomatoes, skinned and chopped finely
2 large cloves garlic
5cm (2in) piece fresh root ginger, peeled
*   and chopped finely*
1 heaped tablespoon tomato purée
300ml (½ pint) hot water
50g (2oz) creamed coconut, crumbled
Cayenne pepper
Handful of fresh coriander leaves, chopped
*   roughly*
Salt

Using a small sharp knife, cut 3 slits in the skin on each side of the pheasants' breasts and 1 slit in each thigh. Put the chopped garlic in a bowl with the groundnut oil, tomato purée, vinegar, ground spices and cayenne pepper. Mix thoroughly, then smear the mixture over the birds pushing it into the slits and under the breast skin, too. Put the birds in a roasting tin, cover the tin tightly with foil and leave at cool room temperature for several hours or overnight.

Add the lemon and orange juices to the roasting tin, cover with foil again and roast in the centre of a preheated oven, 160°C, 325°F, Gas Mark 3 for 1½ hours, basting occasionally with the juices. Remove the foil and continue roasting, uncovered, for another 30 minutes until the birds are browned.

Meanwhile, melt the butter in a large saucepan over a medium heat. Add the ground spices and stir, then add the sliced mushrooms, chopped tomatoes, garlic and ginger and stir around until the mushrooms have softened and the tomatoes are mushy. Mix the tomato purée with the hot water and add to the mushroom and tomato mixture.

Cover the saucepan and simmer very gently for 20–30 minutes, then add the creamed coconut and stir in until it dissolves and thickens the sauce. Season to taste with cayenne pepper and salt and remove from the heat.

Transfer the cooked pheasants to a carving board. Pour the juices from the roasting tin into the saucepan of sauce, stir and reheat. Check for seasoning and add the chopped coriander leaves. Pour the sauce into a jug and serve with the carved pheasants.

DUCK FILLETS IN PASTRY WITH LEEK SAUCE (172)

The first *magrets de canard* (duck breast fillets) I ever ate were in a little restaurant in Paris; they were grilled pale pink, succulent and tender and it seemed to me to be the greatest luxury to be eating just the breast of the duck without struggling to get the meat off the bones of a leg joint. This recipe is another way of using breast fillets. If you like, you can make the rolls without using the fatty duck skin, though it does add extra flavour. *SERVES 4*

4 duck breast fillets
Good handful of fresh mint leaves, chopped
5–6 stalks fresh tarragon leaves, chopped
5cm (2in) piece fresh root ginger, peeled and chopped very finely
1 tablespoon Seville marmalade
250g (8oz) packet puff pastry, thawed if frozen
2–3 long leeks, trimmed and sliced thinly (include the green parts)
Juice of 1 orange, strained
4 tablespoons lemon juice, strained
4 teaspoons caster sugar
250ml (8fl oz) double cream
1 egg yolk, beaten
Salt and black pepper

Pull the skin off the duck fillets and if using, prick each one all over deeply

with a fork. Keep on one side. On a large, flat surface lay out 2 large sheets of wet greaseproof paper. Put 2 fillets on each piece of paper spaced well apart. Wet 2 more large sheets of paper and lay them on top. Beat very hard with a rolling pin or heavy flat implement until the fillets have spread out and are as flat as you can get them. Repeat this procedure with the fatty duck skin, beating it out to roughly the same size as the fillets.

Put the herbs, ginger and marmalade in a bowl and mix together thoroughly. Season with salt and black pepper. Spread the mixture on to each breast fillet then, roll up fairly loosely like a Swiss roll. Wrap a piece of skin round each roll.

Cut the pastry into 4 equal-sized pieces and roll out thinly until big enough to wrap up the rolled duck breasts. Wrap each duck roll in pastry like a neat parcel, cutting off the excess uneven pieces and moistening the edges of the pastry to seal.

Roll out the trimmings and cut out a leaf or two to decorate each parcel if you like (page 245). Pierce a small hole in the top for the steam to escape. Put the parcels in the refrigerator until 30 minutes before you plan to eat.

Meanwhile, prepare the sauce. Put the leeks in a saucepan with the orange and lemon juices and the sugar. Cover and bubble over a low heat for 15–20 minutes until the leeks are soft. Put the leeks and juices in a food processor and whizz until very smooth. Add the cream and whizz again. Lastly season with salt and black pepper. Transfer into a saucepan and keep on one side.

Brush the parcels all over with egg yolk and bake in the centre of a preheated oven, 220°C, 425°F, Gas Mark 7 for 20–25 minutes until a rich golden brown all over. Reheat the sauce shortly before the duck parcels are ready. Bubble it for 2–3 minutes and pour into a warmed serving jug.

ROAST GROUSE WITH MYSTERY SAUCE (172)

Young grouse really are a treat but a total waste of money if you overcook them. The flesh must be pink and therefore still juicy. The dark sauce in this recipe is a mystery because no one can ever guess what it is made from. Serve the grouse with new potatoes and either mange tout or broccoli. *SERVES 4*

1 small–medium parsnip, peeled and cut into smallish pieces
4–5 large cloves garlic, chopped roughly
250g (8oz) mushrooms, chopped roughly (include the stalks)
300ml (½ pint) freshly squeezed orange juice
4 tablespoons soy sauce
4 young grouse
50g (2oz) unsalted butter
1 heaped tablespoon fresh tarragon leaves
Salt and black pepper

Put the parsnip, garlic and mushrooms in a saucepan with the orange juice, soy sauce and a sprinkling of black pepper. Bring to the boil over a high heat, then cover and simmer gently for about 45 minutes until soft, mushy and dark in colour. Then whizz the mixture to a purée in a food processor. You should have a thickish sauce. Taste for seasoning and leave on one side while you roast the grouse.

Wipe the birds inside and out, sprinkle with salt and pepper and put a generous knob of butter inside each bird. Smear the remaining butter on the base of a roasting tin and add the birds breast side down. Cook in the centre of a preheated oven, 220°C, 425°F, Gas Mark 7 for 25 minutes, basting occasionally and turning the birds on to their backs for the last 10 minutes of the cooking time. Remove the birds from the roasting tin (making sure that the juices from inside the bodies empty into the pan) and put them on warmed individual serving plates while you finish the sauce.

Pour the sauce into the roasting tin with the buttery juices, put it over a medium heat and bring the sauce to the boil, stirring constantly. Lastly, stir in the tarragon leaves, boil for a moment more and either pour the sauce into a sauceboat to serve with the grouse or spoon it directly next to the grouse on the individual plates.

SAUCES and DRESSINGS

Sauces are the most important, yet, perhaps the most daunting area of cookery. The day I made my first flour-based white sauce, however, I suddenly realized the creative possibilities that cooking held, and how exciting it could be. For this reason, I would always advise new cooks to learn to make this most reliable of sauces as soon as possible. Flour-based sauces have sometimes been out of favour but they should not be scorned; they are the perfect base for variation, and can be adapted to suit all kinds of dishes; once mastered they also give you confidence to attempt the more tricky, emulsified sauces. Good sauces can transform and enhance your cooking, can raise humble or leftover ingredients to sublime heights, and can widen your repertoire immeasurably. Confidence is the vital first step to making them.

I think people are often alarmed by the long list of impressive sounding names for sauces, implying endless time-consuming and complex methods. If you understand that all sauces stem from a very few basic methods, and that different names often mean only a change of ingredient rather than technique, this should encourage you to become a saucemaker.

Since the textures and flavours of sauces are so crucial to the wonderful final results, they do need constant attention. Depending on the type of sauce the consistency can range from satin-smooth to frothy, and from transparently thin to creamily thick, but the texture must always be as much of a pleasurable characteristic of the sauce as the flavour. Taste your sauce constantly as you make it, and feel it against your tongue – there are many adjustments you can make along the way if it

doesn't seem right; lumps can be destroyed by pressing the sauce through a fine sieve, a sauce which is too thick can be thinned by beating in cream, milk or stock or a very thin sauce can be reduced by boiling to a thicker consistency.

The point of a sauce is to enhance and complement the flavours of the ingredients it is served with, sometimes very subtly and sometimes by being in complete contrast. The seasoning of the sauce itself needs to be both careful and thoughtful; you must bear in mind the sauce's final destination – sauces should always have an additional last minute seasoning, and therefore it is best to add seasoning at several points during cooking. Season only lightly at first in the case of sauces where the basic mixture is reduced at the end to thicken the texture and intensify the taste.

Although a sauce should have a much more concentrated flavour than say a soup or the juices of a stew, it should contain no individual seasoning or ingredient which dominates enough to obliterate the taste of the food it is eaten with. Remember, too, that all flavours become more assertive as they cool, so care must be taken when making a cooked sauce which is then to be served cold. The taste of a sauce, of course, also depends on the basic ingredients, which need to be top quality and really fresh because although a good sauce can transform dull ingredients, nothing can redeem a bad sauce. The techniques of even the trickiest sauce-making can be learnt, practised and perfected, but in the end it is the tiny and personal adjustments to its seasoning by the cook which can make the entire meal memorable for long afterwards.

Clockwise from the to left: Plum and Shallot Sauce with Fresh Mint (page 212), flavoured with freshly squeezed orange juice, to serve with pork, duck, ham or game; Best Bread Sauce (page 212) is made with wholemeal bread and spiced with cloves and grated nutmeg; Red Velvet Sauce (page 213) combines tomatoes, red peppers and green peppercorns to complement vegetables, meat, poultry and pasta; Kumquat Sauce with Dill (page 212) includes apple juice and raspberry vinegar ; Indian Spiced Mushroom Sauce (page 212) made from mushrooms, spices and cream; Ragù (page 213) is a classic Italian meat sauce for serving with pasta. Centre: Coconut Sauce (page 213) uses creamed coconut to make an accompaniment for exotic fruits.

BASIC WHITE SAUCES

White sauces provide a neutral base which can be varied for many purposes. The two classic white sauces are both flour-based; basic white sauce made with milk, and velouté sauce made with stock. These sauces are made from a roux – equal amounts of butter (or oil) and flour, cooked together. It is important the roux is cooked for a few minutes before the liquid is added, so the final sauce does not taste of raw flour. You can avoid a lumpy sauce by sprinkling in the flour to make a smooth and soft roux that is easy to beat the liquid into. It is safest to add cold milk to the hot roux for white sauces. Although cold milk takes longer to come to the boil, hot milk can be beaten in quickly with a balloon whisk. It also helps to stir the sauce constantly as you add the liquid. If the sauce does go lumpy, you can try beating out the lumps with a whisk or whizz it in the food processor until smooth.

Make these sauces ahead, then reheat for serving. To prevent a skin forming, melt a little butter on the surface, then whisk it in while reheating. Store, covered, for 2–3 days in the refrigerator.

BASIC WHITE SAUCE

The quantities of flour and fat used to make this versatile sauce are varied to produce different consistencies for different uses. For 300ml (½ pint) thin pouring sauce use 15g (½oz) each butter and plain flour; for a medium sauce for coating use 20g (¾oz) each butter and plain flour; and for a thick binding sauce for making soufflés, 25g (1oz) each butter and flour.

1 *Melt the butter in a heavy-based saucepan. Whisk in the flour until the roux is blended and sandy coloured. Cook for 2 minutes, whisking constantly. Remove the pan from the heat.*

2 *Gradually whisk in 300ml (½ pint) milk. Return to the heat and whisk until the sauce thickens and boils, then simmer for 2–3 minutes, whisking occasionally. Season to taste.*

For a quick version, *use the classic quantities (above) and put the fat, flour, milk and seasoning into the pan in one go. Bring to the boil, stirring constantly with a wooden spoon, until thickened. Simmer for 2 minutes, season well, then use as required.*

To make a parsley sauce *make a medium coating white sauce (above) and stir in a finely chopped large bunch of parsley. Simmer gently for 1–2 minutes, then season to taste. Serve with boiled meats, steamed chicken breasts, fish cooked in any way or with vegetables.*

BÉCHAMEL SAUCE

This classic French sauce is identical to a basic white sauce, except it is made with milk infused with herbs and spices for more flavour. It is also made in varying consistencies like the basic white sauce (left). Use for layered pasta dishes, such as lasagne (page 84). Once made it is important to simmer the sauce until reduced down and fully thickened, stirring frequently. Makes about 300ml (½ pint).

Many ingredients, including pre-cooked ones, can be stirred into a béchamel sauce at the end of cooking. The cheese sauce (below) is good with fish, eggs and vegetables.

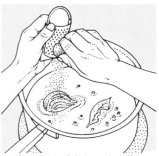

1 *Place 300ml (½ pint) milk in a heavy-based saucepan with ½ onion, 8–10 black peppercorns, 1 bay leaf and a pinch of freshly grated nutmeg. Bring the milk to the boil, then remove the saucepan from the heat, cover and leave it on one side for 10–12 minutes for the flavours to infuse into the milk.*

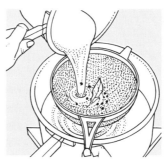

2 *Meanwhile, in another saucepan, prepare the roux (left), then remove from the heat. Strain the milk into the roux, whisking immediately, and discard the flavourings. Return the saucepan to the heat and bring to the boil, whisking constantly until the sauce thickens, then simmer gently for 2–3 minutes, still whisking. Season to taste with salt and pepper.*

To make a cheese sauce, *make a thin béchamel sauce; remove the saucepan from the heat. Stir in 125g (4oz) grated Parmesan or Cheddar cheese and 1 teaspoon Dijon mustard, stirring until the cheese melts; do not return to the heat again or the cheese may turn stringy. For extra flavouring, add either grated nutmeg or a sprinkling of caraway or cumin seeds and stir in.*

VELOUTÉ SAUCE

A good, flavourful stock is the most important ingredient in a velouté sauce. This stock need not be specially made; usually it is the cooking liquid of the ingredient the sauce is to be served with, such as poached fish, chicken or veal. Skimming during cooking gives this sauce its distinctive velvety appearance, hence its name which is derived from the French word for 'velvet'.

The mushroom and cream variation (below) is often used to make a chicken stew and the shellfish variation (below) uses leftover shells to enhance the flavour of shellfish poaching liquid. It is an ideal sauce to serve with poached crab, lobster or prawns.

To make 300ml (½ pint), bring 400ml (14fl oz) fish, chicken or veal stock (pages 28–31) or shellfish cooking liquid to the boil, skimming the surface. Meanwhile, prepare a roux (opposite) with 20g (¾oz) each butter and plain flour and cook for 2 minutes until grainy and golden coloured. Remove from the heat and cool slightly.

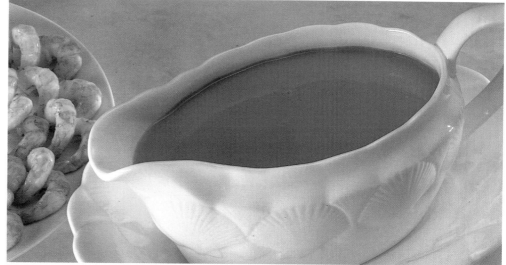

Shellfish sauce, also called sauce Nantua, is one of many variations of basic velouté sauce and is flavoured by shellfish using the reserved shells and poaching liquid.

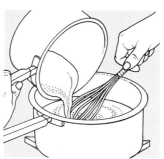

1 *Gradually whisk about three-quarters of the boiling stock or cooking liquid into the slightly cooled roux. Return the pan to the heat and bring the mixture to the boil, whisking constantly, until the sauce thickens.*

2 *Lower the heat and simmer the sauce gently for at least 15 minutes to concentrate the flavour, stirring from time to time. Skim occasionally with a large slotted spoon until the surface of the sauce is clear.*

3 *Use the sauce as it is, or pass it through a fine sieve into a clean saucepan. Whisk in 1–2 tablespoons double cream or cold butter and season to taste. Thin down with the remaining hot stock, if necessary.*

FLAVOURING WHITE SAUCES

• Transform a quickly made white sauce by adding spices with the butter at the beginning and a little lemon juice or wine vinegar at the end.
• Add cream and fresh tarragon to a white sauce to serve with grilled chicken. Or, if you roast the chicken, stir the pan juices into the tarragon sauce just before serving.
• Season a white sauce to coat cauliflower, broccoli or baby carrots with freshly grated nutmeg, and add whole caraway or dill seeds.
• For a delicious and quick accompaniment to hot, fresh beetroot add soured cream and chopped fresh parsley to a white sauce at the end.
• To make a white garlic sauce, add 1–2 cloves crushed garlic

to the butter before adding the flour for the roux, and stir it for 2–3 minutes over a low heat.
• I stir curry paste into white sauce with a little lemon juice to make an instant dish of curry when I'm in a hurry. Just pour the sauce over pieces of cold chicken or turkey in a saucepan and heat them together before turning into a serving dish – chopped fresh coriander stirred in just before serving makes the dish even better.
• Many additions to a velouté sauce are the same as for a white sauce, but added ingredients taste more intense in a velouté sauce. Shellfish butter, smoked cod's roe, pounded crab or chopped lobster and prawns stirred in at the last minute, are wonderful.

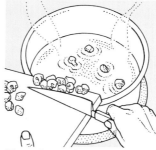

To make mushroom *and cream sauce (or sauce suprême) use chicken stock (page 29) to make the velouté sauce (above), adding 125g (4oz) chopped mushrooms after the boiling stock is incorporated into the roux. Complete steps 1 and 2, then strain the sauce through a sieve, as in step 3, and whisk in 50ml (2fl oz) double cream. Season with salt, pepper and a squeeze of lemon juice.*

To make shellfish-flavoured *sauce (or sauce Nantua) to serve with poached shellfish save the shells and liquid from when you poach the shellfish. Make the roux and add 400ml (14fl oz) boiling poaching liquid, as in step 1 (above). Add the reserved shells and simmer for 15 minutes. Strain the sauce into a clean saucepan. Return to the heat and for an extra rich sauce whisk in 1–2 tablespoons cold butter.*

BROWN SAUCES *and* THICKENERS

Brown flour-based sauces are made in the same way as white velouté sauces (page 197), but they depend on a well-browned roux and brown stock (page 28) for their colour, as well as for their very rich flavour. They most often accompany roast or sautéed meat and game.

The most classic brown sauce is espagnole sauce, so called because it was originally made with a fine, cured ham from Spain. Traditionally, this was a complicated sauce, often taking days to prepare. It is still time-consuming to make but is an essential part of many of the traditional rich sauces we associate with fine French cooking.

Nowadays, however, most people only have time to make simple brown sauces with a basic browned roux and brown stock. Probably our most popular 'brown sauce' is basic brown gravy, made from the dripping and juices of roasted meat, game or poultry and thickened with flour.

BASIC BROWN SAUCE

A good stock is essential for a brown sauce. Bring 900ml (1½ pints) beef or veal stock (page 28) to the boil and simmer until slightly reduced to concentrate the flavour. This recipe makes about 600ml (1 pint). Freeze any extra you don't want.

1 *Melt 25g (1oz) butter in a heavy-based saucepan and stir in 25g (1oz) plain flour. Cook the roux for 3–4 minutes over a medium heat until it is well-browned, stirring constantly so as not to burn the roux.*

2 *Off the heat, gradually stir in the slightly reduced hot stock and 1½ tablespoons tomato purée. Return the pan to the heat and bring to the boil, then simmer for 20–30 minutes, uncovered, skimming occasionally. Season.*

A basic brown sauce gets its deep colour and full flavour from a brown roux and reduced brown stock.

CLASSIC ESPAGNOLE SAUCE

To make about 1.2 litres (2 pints) espagnole sauce, use approximately 2.4 litres (4 pints) rich brown meat stock which should have a full flavour and colour, as well as plenty of gelatine from the bones (page 28). Espagnole sauce is rarely served on its own, because it takes several hours to make, but instead, is used as a base for other sauces. (See hunter's sauce in box opposite.)

Because it does take so long to make, it is worth making a large quantity and freezing some for later use. Freeze in 300ml (½ pint) blocks and reheat from frozen, slowly stirring occasionally, then boiling for 2 minutes.

1 *Bring 2.4 litres (4 pints) beef or veal stock (page 28) to the boil. Simmer and skim the stock until it reduces to about half its original volume. In a second saucepan, heat 75ml (3fl oz) vegetable oil. Add 125g (4oz) diced smoked bacon and cook for 2 minutes. Add 2 diced onions and 2 diced carrots to the saucepan and cook gently until the vegetables begin to soften.*

2 *Sprinkle over 50g (2oz) plain flour and stir until well blended. Cook for 4–5 minutes, stirring frequently, until the roux becomes a rich brown colour, taking care not to let it burn. Remove the pan from the heat. Stir three-quarters of the hot stock into the roux and softened vegetables. Return to the heat and bring to the boil, stirring constantly, until the sauce thickens.*

3 *Add 1 large bouquet garni (page 10), 2 halved small tomatoes, 2 tablespoons tomato purée, and simmer for 2–3 hours, uncovered, skimming often. Reheat the remaining stock and add little by little to the saucepan as the sauce thickens and reduces. Strain the sauce, if you like, before using. Stir in 25–40g (1–1½oz) diced chilled butter and season if necessary.*

QUICK SAUCE THICKENERS

Sometimes a sauce needs thickening at the last minute and there are several traditional methods that do not require great skill. A beurre manié, simply equal amounts of flour and butter kneaded to a paste, added just before the end of cooking, thickens and enriches. As the butter melts it distributes the flour throughout the liquid. Other thickeners are cornflour, arrowroot or potato starch. These thicken with very little cooking as they work more quickly than wheat flour. Egg yolks and cream are used to thicken and enrich velouté sauces.

To make a beurre manié, knead together about 20g (¾oz) each plain flour and butter with a fork. Bring 300ml (½ pint) sauce to the boil, then flick in small knobs of beurre manié, stirring until the sauce thickens. Beurre manié can be stored in the refrigerator for several weeks and used as necessary.

A simple way to thicken sauces is by stirring in equal amounts of butter and flour, called a beurre manié.

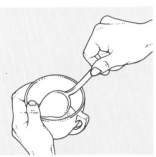

To use cornflour, arrowroot or potato starch to thicken 300ml (½ pint) sauce, bring the sauce to the boil. Mix 2 teaspoons thickener with 1½ tablespoons cold water or stock, then whisk into the hot sauce, whisking until lightly thickened.

To thicken and enrich 300ml (½ pint) hot velouté sauce, mix 1 egg yolk and 1–2 tablespoons double cream in a cup, then stir in a little hot sauce. Whisk this mixture into the sauce over a low heat, whisking constantly until thickened. Do not boil.

TRADITIONAL GRAVY

Although I prefer an unthickened gravy many people consider a traditionally thickened brown sauce an essential part of Sunday lunch. When you make a roast either use my quick gravy (page 157) or this more traditional method. Be sure the flour cooks until brown so it doesn't taste uncooked when the gravy is served.

After roasting, pour off all but 2 tablespoons fat from the roasting tin and place the tin over a medium heat.

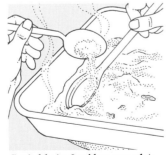

Sprinkle in 2 tablespoons plain flour. Stir for 4 minutes until rich brown. Add 450ml (¾ pint) hot stock or vegetable water, stirring up all the bits off the base, and cook until thickened. Season.

FLAVOURING BROWN SAUCES

• Sauté thin slices of sharp red plums or firm, fresh apricots to add to a basic brown sauce to serve with duck, pork or game. Or simmer coarsely grated orange rind in the sauce when you are making it.

• For a piquant brown sauce, sauté 1 small finely chopped onion in butter when you make the roux until very soft, adding 2–4 pinches of cayenne pepper and 2 teaspoons paprika half way through the sautéing, then stir in 50ml (2fl oz) red wine vinegar at the same time as adding the stock.

• A spicy brown sauce is excellent with game birds, chicken or turkey – add curry paste, 1 finely chopped onion and 2 crushed garlic cloves to the roux and cook slowly for at least 5 minutes before pouring in the hot brown stock. Just before serving, stir in a handful of roughly chopped fresh coriander leaves. Alternatively, use individual ground Indian spices such as cardamom and coriander for a spicy sauce.

• Finely chopped fresh ginger is a good addition with garlic to a roux. Thicken and enrich a spicy brown sauce at the end of cooking with about 25g (1oz) broken up creamed coconut.

• To make hunter's sauce or sauce chasseur soften 2–3 chopped shallots and 125g (4oz) chopped mushrooms in 15g (½oz) butter. Add 200ml (7fl oz) dry white wine and reduce by half. Add 250ml (8fl oz) basic brown or espagnole sauce and 2 tablespoons tomato purée and simmer for 15 minutes. Stir in 2 tablespoons diced cold butter and 1 tablespoon chopped parsley. Serve with grilled or roasted meat or game.

• I also love the flavour of roughly chopped capers added to a brown sauce at the end.

• Meat glazes, which are simply meat, poultry and game stock boiled until reduced to a thick, syrupy consistency, with an extremely concentrated flavour, add great finesse when stirred into a brown sauce after cooking. For extra richness, finish by whisking in 15–25g (½–1oz) diced cold butter.

• The appearance of a brown sauce is often improved, and a refreshing element given, if you stir a handful of chopped fresh herbs such as dill, tarragon, basil, chives or flat-leaved parsley into the sauce just before serving. Chopped sorrel loses its bright colour and seems to dissolve into the sauce when bubbled for a minute or two, but it adds a delicious sharpness.

HOT EMULSIFIED SAUCES

Hollandaise, béarnaise and butter sauces are my favourite sauces; they are all hot emulsified sauces made by whisking two or more ingredients into an emulsion. All these sauces are light, yet rich and have many variations, such as orange-flavoured hollandaise. These sauces have a reputation of being difficult because the egg yolks can easily curdle and ruin the sauce. This can be overcome by using a food processor, although the technique of making them by hand can easily be mastered with a little practice.

When making these sauces by hand you must take time to heat the yolks and butter sufficiently. Heat slowly over a low heat in a heavy-based saucepan because too high a heat will cause them to curdle. The safest way to make them by hand is to use a heatproof bowl set over a pan of simmering water (below) or use a double boiler (page 18).

Each egg yolk will absorb about 50g (2oz) of butter. Using clarified butter (page 96) also helps prevent curdling but for less experienced cooks it is probably easier to use softened butter rather than melted butter. Use unsalted butter if possible. Start by adding the butter in small spoonfuls, then when the sauce thickens it can be added in larger amounts until the sauce is smooth and creamy.

CLASSIC HOLLANDAISE SAUCE

If the sauce separates or curdles, remove from the heat and immediately whisk in an ice cube. This lowers the temperature and usually saves the sauce. If not, start again with 2 fresh yolks, slowly whisking in the curdled sauce until a new emulsion forms.

You should make hollandaise sauce just before serving, but it will keep for about 30 minutes in a bowl set over simmering water if you stir often. Serve with poached eggs, fish and vegetables. Makes about 300ml (½ pint).

1 *Whisk 3 egg yolks with 1 teaspoon caster sugar, 1 tablespoon water, 1 tablespoon white wine vinegar and 1 tablespoon lemon juice in a heatproof bowl set over a saucepan of simmering water until well mixed and foamy.*

2 *Over a very low heat, continue whisking the egg yolk mixture until the whisk leaves a trail on the surface. This should take about 3 minutes. Be careful the bottom of the bowl doesn't actually touch the water or the yolks may scramble.*

3 *Remove from the heat and whisk in 175g (6oz) softened butter, cut into pieces. Add piece by piece at first, then several at a time until the hollandaise sauce is thick but still light enough to pour. Season to taste with salt, pepper and more lemon juice.*

BÉARNAISE SAUCE

Béarnaise sauce uses the same technique as hollandaise, but it is slightly thicker and has a much more concentrated and pronounced flavour because the flavourings are reduced. Serve with grilled or roasted lamb, beef and full-flavoured fish like salmon or monkfish.

For 300ml (½ pint), boil 3 tablespoons each white wine vinegar and dry white wine, 10 crushed peppercorns, 2–3 chopped shallots and 1 tablespoon chopped fresh tarragon until reduced to 1–2 tablespoons. Strain, cool slightly and place in a heatproof bowl set over a pan of simmering water.

Whisk 2 egg yolks *into the reduction until foamy. Continue whisking over a low heat for about 3 minutes until the whisk leaves a trail on the surface. Remove from the heat and whisk in 125g (4oz) softened butter, a small piece at a time, until the sauce is thick. Stir in 1 tablespoon chopped fresh tarragon.*

FLAVOURING HOT EMULSIFIED SAUCES

• For an orange-flavoured hollandaise sauce, which goes well with broccoli, asparagus or cauliflower, whisk a little finely grated orange rind into the egg yolks, followed by the lemon juice, wine vinegar and 3–4 tablespoons fresh orange juice. Omit the water. Add a little more butter if necessary to thicken the sauce as desired.

• Reduce 150ml (¼ pint) fish stock made with white wine (page 31) to 2 tablespoons and use instead of lemon juice in a hollandaise sauce to serve with simply cooked fish.

• Flavour hollandaise sauce by stirring in chopped fresh herbs just before serving – try dill, tarragon and basil.

• For a good sauce to serve with egg dishes, grilled fish or new potatoes, stir 2–3 tablespoons of smooth puréed seafood, cooked and puréed soft herring roe or grilled, skinned and puréed red or yellow peppers into a hollandaise sauce.

• If you are not a purist, there is no reason why you should not try many of the variations mentioned above for béarnaise sauce as well.

• For a tomato-flavoured béarnaise, I like adding tomato purée (made from fresh, butter-sautéed tomatoes, if possible) and strips of fresh basil leaves to the finished sauce, leaving out the tarragon in the classic recipe – this goes beautifully with grilled chicken.

QUICK METHODS

WHITE BUTTER SAUCE

The food processor and microwave oven can both be used to make foolproof hollandaise and béarnaise sauces in minutes. The eggs, however, are not as well cooked as in the classic methods (opposite) and the butter is melted not softened, so the sauce is not quite as creamy and silky. However, I don't think there is anything wrong with using these modern methods, especially as it encourages people to make sauces they might otherwise be apprehensive about.

This version of hollandaise sauce, like the classic version, becomes an almost ethereal sauce if you fold in 2 or 3 stiffly whisked egg whites just before serving. This lightens the sauce, as well as increasing the volume. Béarnaise sauce can also be made by these quick methods, using the quantities opposite.

I love this simple butter sauce, often known by its French name of *beurre blanc*; it makes an elegant accompaniment to fish, vegetables and egg dishes. Because this sauce does not contain any egg yolks it is more likely to separate than the other hot emulsified sauces, and it really should be made just before serving. It only takes a few minutes to make.

When adding the butter in step 2 be sure to whisk vigorously so it emulsifies before melting and becoming oily. If the sauce does separate, it cannot be rescued unlike the sauces that contain egg yolks, so you will have to start again. It is important to use unsalted butter. Makes about 300ml (½ pint).

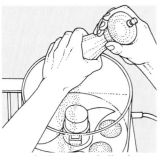

1 *For food processor hollandaise, use the same ingredients as for classic hollandaise (opposite). Melt the butter in a pan, taking care not to let it burn by stirring as it melts and then leave it on one side. Put the egg yolks, salt and pepper in the processor and blend for 15 seconds until the yolks are creamy and lightened.*

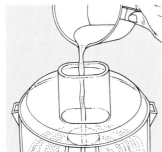

2 *In another pan, heat the sugar, water, vinegar and lemon juice. With the machine still running, add the warm sugar, water, vinegar and lemon juice and whizz in. Add the melted butter in a slow steady stream until the mixture emulsifies and forms a smooth creamy sauce. Adjust the seasoning if necessary.*

1 *Boil 2–3 finely chopped shallots with 3 tablespoons each white wine and white wine vinegar in a heavy-based saucepan until reduced to 1–2 tablespoons and thick and syrupy. Add 1 tablespoon double cream and boil again until reduced to 1–2 tablespoons. (This step can be done ahead.) Adding the cream helps to stabilize the sauce before the butter is whisked in.*

2 *Over a low heat, whisk in 300g (10oz) diced chilled butter, little by little until incorporated. Increase the heat and bring just to the boil, whisking constantly and vigorously to stabilize the emulsion. You can either strain out the shallots or leave the sauce as it is. Season with salt and pepper to taste, using white pepper to avoid any black specks, and serve at once.*

For microwave hollandaise, *cut 125g (4oz) cold butter into large pieces and soften on Defrost (30%) for 1½ minutes. Remove from the microwave. In another bowl, beat 2 egg yolks with 1 tablespoon lemon juice, 1 teaspoon French mustard, and salt and freshly ground black pepper. Heat on Full (100%) for 40 seconds. Remove the bowl from the microwave and stir well, then beat in the softened butter in pieces until creamy and thickened.*

Rich hollandaise sauce is a traditional accompaniment for delicately poached salmon with fresh dill.

COLD EMULSIFIED SAUCES

Mayonnaise is the most popular and well known cold emulsified sauce. It should be thick and creamy and the key to making it successfully is to have the ingredients at room temperature. Although there is no worry of eggs scrambling as in a hot sauce, a mayonnaise can easily curdle if the oil is too cold or if it is added too quickly.

Making mayonnaise by hand is easily mastered, but with a food processor it is magically quick. I think making the sauce by hand is very satisfying and enables the cook to feel the texture thicken, but using a food processor means that a homemade sauce with a flavour so different from commercial variations can be produced in minutes.

The flavours of mayonnaise, as well as other salad dressings, derive mainly from the oil used – so use good-quality oil and experiment with the wide variety of oils now available. In France, mayonnaise and salad dressings are often made entirely with olive oil but this is sometimes too overpowering for a delicate fish or vegetable dish. A good idea is to use half vegetable oil, such as sunflower, and half olive or other flavoured oil. You can also vary the taste by using different-flavoured vinegars, such as a herb vinegar or a wine vinegar. If you are making a tomato mayonnaise by adding tomato purée, it is a good idea to use the slightly sweet and thick balsamic vinegar.

CLASSIC MAYONNAISE

Make mayonnaise with a whisk, or, for the faint-hearted, a hand-held electric mixer to beat in the oil. Adding a small amount of Dijon mustard to the yolks, along with the lemon juice and seasoning, helps the sauce to emulsify as well as flavouring it. The proportion of oil to egg yolk can be varied, depending on the consistency desired, but in general, 1 egg yolk 'holds' about 150ml (¼ pint) oil; if too much oil is added or if you add it too quickly, the sauce separates.

If the sauce does separate or curdle, there are several ways to save it. Begin with a clean bowl and another beaten egg yolk and a pinch of salt and slowly whisk the curdled mixture into the new egg yolk until it emulsifies again. You can also whisk the curdled mixture into a little mustard, lemon juice or vinegar, but be careful the flavour does not become too strong.

Store in the refrigerator for 2–3 days, but bring it to room temperature before stirring or it could curdle. Mayonnaise is the ideal sauce to serve with cold fish, poultry, vegetables, eggs and salads. There are many popular variations too, such as aïoli, a garlic-flavoured mayonnaise. Makes 300ml (½ pint).

1 *Set a small bowl on a folded tea towel or kitchen cloth to prevent the bowl moving about as you whisk vigorously. Whisk 2 egg yolks with a little salt, white pepper, 1½ tablespoons lemon juice or white wine vinegar and 2–3 teaspoons Dijon mustard until the mixture is well blended and lightened. This stage takes about 1 minute.*

2 *Gradually add up to 300ml (½ pint) oil, drop by drop, whisking constantly. It is easy to add the oil drop by drop if you just let it drip off a spoon. Do not add the oil too quickly or the mixture may curdle. When the sauce begins to thicken, pour the oil in a very slow stream until the mayonnaise reaches the desired consistency. Season to taste.*

FOOD PROCESSOR MAYONNAISE

Using a food processor saves time and there is little risk of curdling, but it does make a lighter texture and colour. Use the quantities as for classic mayonnaise (left), using 1 whole egg instead of the 2 egg yolks to help lighten it. Once you have added about 300ml (½ pint) oil, stop the machine and check the texture. If the mayonnaise is too thin, continue adding oil, and if too thick add 1–2 tablespoons lemon juice, single cream or natural yogurt. Makes 300ml (½ pint).

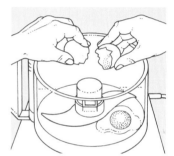

Process the whole egg, *salt, white pepper, lemon juice and Dijon mustard in a food processor for 15 seconds. With the machine running, add the oil drop by drop at first, then in a steady stream. Adjust the seasoning.*

AÏOLI

Aïoli is a garlic mayonnaise, used to accompany the classic French Provençal dish called *aïoli* – a large dish of poached salt cod, boiled meats and vegetables. It is also delicious served with cold poached fish and shellfish, salads, hard-boiled eggs and cold meats.

If you are in a hurry, add 3–5 cloves crushed garlic to classic mayonnaise (left), although it doesn't take much longer to make aïoli from scratch in a food processor (above). Just add the garlic with the egg and flavourings. It is important to use a fruity extra virgin olive oil. Makes about 300ml (½ pint).

To make aïoli by hand, *crush 3–5 cloves of garlic into a bowl with 2 egg yolks and a pinch of salt and beat together. Add 300ml (½ pint) oil, drop by drop at first using a teaspoon, then in a gradual steady stream, as if making mayonnaise, until the sauce is thick. Aïoli should be quite thick and glossy.*

TARTARE SAUCE

Homemade tartare sauce is well worth making as it bears no resemblance to the bottled variety, and is delicious with all sorts of things, especially cold or hot fish, poultry, vegetable and egg dishes. It is made by emulsifying mashed hard-boiled egg yolks with oil, then adding capers, gherkins and the chopped hard-boiled egg whites.

For a quick version of tartare sauce add gherkins, capers and finely chopped herbs to classic mayonnaise (opposite).

Tartare sauce will keep covered for 2–3 days in the refrigerator. Makes about 300ml (½ pint).

Mash 3 hard-boiled egg yolks with 1 tablespoon Dijon mustard, salt and pepper. Gradually beat in 300ml (½ pint) sunflower oil, as if making mayonnaise, until the sauce is thickened. Stir in 1–2 tablespoons lemon juice, 2 tablespoons each chopped gherkins, capers, tarragon and the chopped egg whites.

Golden homemade mayonnaise, with a tarragon-flavoured variation and rouille (see box below), a piquant chilli-flavoured mayonnaise, served with fish soups in France.

COATING WITH MAYONNAISE

Although mayonnaise is often used to bind fish, poultry, vegetable, pasta and egg dishes and salads, it can also be thinned to coat cold foods. Adding a little lemon juice, wine vinegar, warm water, Greek yogurt, whipped cream or milk thins mayonnaise to a coating consistency for dressing salads made with raw or lightly cooked vegetables and other ingredients.

If the mayonnaise needs to be thin, but still keep its shape for coating fish or poultry pieces, gelatine can be added. Use ½ sachet gelatine dissolved in 3–4 tablespoons hot water, wine or stock. Dissolve completely and allow to cool to room temperature, then whisk the gelatine mixture into 300ml (½ pint) mayonnaise. If you like, decorate the coated fish or poultry with fresh herbs sprigs and chill to set before serving.

NO-EGG 'MAYONNAISE'

A mayonnaise-like sauce, excellent with cold or grilled fish and meat, can be made by adding oil to a base of a light vegetable purée instead of the egg yolks used in mayonnaise. This sauce can also be made with a base of smooth fish purée or smoked cod's roe to make a delicious accompaniment to egg dishes and chunky salads, including potato salad.

I like using sweet peppers for this kind of sauce, or puréed aubergine as in aubergine pâté (page 97). Purées made from root vegetables also work well. The amount of oil you need depends on what base you use for the sauce, as these obviously vary in density and texture. For strong-flavoured purées, I use olive oil, and for more subtle ones, sunflower, grapeseed or a mixture of oils. Makes about 450–600ml (¾–1 pint).

FLAVOURING MAYONNAISE

• My favourite additions to mayonnaise are finely chopped anchovies and crushed garlic; sun-dried tomato paste mixed with tomato purée and strips of fresh basil; chopped capers; fresh dill and wholegrain mustard; roughly crushed green or pink peppercorns; garlic which has been roasted in its skin until soft, then skinned and crushed to a purée; the juice of fresh ginger squeezed through a crusher and chopped fresh coriander; and many chopped fresh, tender herbs such as tarragon, dill, chervil, savory and lovage.

• I particularly like green mayonnaise, made by mixing in chopped, blanched and well drained spinach (adding sorrel leaves, too, if you have them) or blanched and chopped watercress to the mayonnaise. If using a food processor, whizz in the blanched leaves to make the sauce a uniform green.

• The delicious red chilli sauce, rouille, which is spooned in small quantities into hot soups and stews, can be made by first pounding a fresh red chilli and several cloves of garlic in a mortar and then continuing as for classic mayonnaise (opposite), but using extra virgin olive oil and adding tomato purée instead of vinegar or mustard.

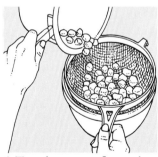

1 *To make a pepper-flavoured no-egg 'mayonnaise', deseed and chop roughly 375g (12oz) yellow peppers (page 49). Place in a saucepan with just enough water to cover. Bring to the boil, then simmer for about 10 minutes until the peppers are very soft. Drain, discarding the water, and set aside until the peppers are cool or rinse in cold water to cool.*

2 *Put the peppers in a food processor with 1 tablespoon white wine vinegar, 2 teaspoons caster sugar and 1–2 teaspoons Dijon mustard and whizz all together to a purée. With the machine running all the time, add 7–9 tablespoons sunflower or grapeseed oil, drop by drop, until fairly thick. Season and chill until ready to serve.*

SALAD DRESSINGS

It is well worth making your own salad dressings, especially since it is now so easy to make such exciting salads. Many lettuces that were once only available abroad are now sold here, adding to the appeal of salads.

Classic vinaigrette contains mostly oil, so choose the oil you use carefully. Many interesting types of high-quality oils are available, so the combination of flavours is almost endless, but the choice usually depends on the salad to be dressed. Olive oil, for example, is a natural partner for a tomato and Mozzarella cheese salad, and a nut-flavoured oil goes well with salads containing nuts, mushrooms or bitter leaves, while a plain sunflower oil is many people's choice for a simple tossed green salad.

A good basic formula for an oil-and-vinegar dressing is about 3–5 parts oil to 1 part vinegar or lemon juice, depending, of course, on how sharp you like your dressing and the flavour of the ingredients. If dressing a leafy green salad, be sure the leaves are clean and dry so the dressing coats the leaves and clings to them.

For convenience, dressings can always be made ahead in a large quantity, but they do taste best when freshly made. The quick way to make most dressings is to put all the ingredients in a screw-top jar and shake. Although it's best to toss a salad at the last minute to avoid wilted soggy leaves, an alternative for a simple dressing is to toss the leaves with oil alone a short time ahead. Then when you are ready to serve the salad, toss the oiled leaves with a little flavoured vinegar or lemon juice and season well.

VINAIGRETTE DRESSING

A few plain lettuce leaves can be turned into a gastronomic delight with a good vinaigrette dressing. Opinions vary as to how sharp it should taste, but I prefer a little more oil than the classic proportions of 1 part vinegar to 3 parts of oil, and I like to use extra virgin olive oil as its fruity flavour can be really appreciated. All sorts of different oils and vinegars can be used for a variety of results, and lemon juice can be used instead of vinegar. Dark, matured balsamic vinegar, which is sweet and rich-tasting, makes a very special vinaigrette, as does delicious sherry vinegar which is also slightly sweet and not strong.

For a smoothly emulsified vinaigrette, it is best to add powdered mustard, but I often use Dijon mustard and personally like mild wholegrain mustards best of all. It is not necessary to use mustard at all if you don't like it. Traditionally, vinaigrette is made by whisking the oil gradually into the vinegar and mustard mixture, but I find vigorous shaking of all the ingredients in a screw-top jar successful, and far easier. Makes about 300ml (½ pint).

1 *Put 2 tablespoons wine vinegar, 1 teaspoon caster sugar and 2 teaspoons powdered or Dijon mustard into a screw-top jar. Replace the lid securely and give the jar a really good shake. If making dressing to store for any length of time, choose a jar with a plastic-coated inner lid so the vinegar doesn't affect it.*

2 *Add 6–7 tablespoons extra virgin olive oil to the jar, replace the lid securely again and shake vigorously until the dressing has lightly emulsified. Season to taste. Store, covered, in the refrigerator. Before using, bring the jar to room temperature for at least 30 minutes before the dressing is needed and shake again.*

VINAIGRETTE VARIATIONS

There are endless variations of vinaigrette dressing (see box opposite), but here are 3 of the most usual ones. You can, of course, add other flavourings as well to any of these suggestions.

The taste of garlic in a salad dressing should not be overpowering, but in moderation I think crushed garlic is a wonderful addition for many salads.

I almost always use a little mustard in any vinaigrette and very often chopped fresh herbs, too. Wholegrain mustard is my favourite and I often add a little soy sauce with the vinegar to add extra flavour.

Usually 1 small *crushed garlic clove is enough to add a garlicky flavour to the vinaigrette unless you want a much stronger taste. Shake the dressing before using. If you don't want to bite on tiny bits of raw garlic, you can leave the dressing standing with the garlic for a bit, then strain the vinaigrette through a sieve when ready to use.*

Add 2 tablespoons *chopped, fresh herbs such as dill, fennel, chervil, savory, mint, tarragon and lovage for a stronger flavour, and shake up in the dressing. This herb variation is useful with meat, poultry and fish salads.*

For a honey and mustard *variation, add 2–3 teaspoons wholegrain or Dijon mustard or 1 teaspoon mustard powder and 1 teaspoon clear honey to the vinegar and mix together before adding the oil.*

YOGURT DRESSING

Natural yogurt is a fantastically useful ingredient for salad dressings. It can simply be used on its own, seasoned to taste and freshly chopped herbs such as mint added, or you can mix it into a vinaigrette base with very little olive oil or into creamed smetana or soured cream. For a mousseline-style dressing, add some whipped double cream.

Use either low-fat natural yogurt, or the thick Greek yogurt for a richer, thicker dressing. Or, try fromage frais. Makes about 300ml (½ pint).

A classic vinaigrette is the ideal dressing for a simple salad of sliced tomatoes with sliced black olives and finely shredded leaves of fresh basil.

Strain the juice of 2 small lemons into a bowl and mix in 300ml (½ pint) natural yogurt with a wooden spoon. Season with salt and freshly ground black pepper and add finely chopped fresh mint or other herbs. A mint-flavoured yogurt dressing is a good alternative to traditional mint sauce or jelly with roast lamb. It is also ideal for dressing potato salads.

CHEESE DRESSINGS

Because cheese dressings are fairly strong in flavour and heavy in consistency use them to coat crisp greens and vegetables. Use Iceberg, Cos, spinach and radicchio leaves with cucumber, radishes, fennel and other crisp vegetables. Soft leafy greens and delicate flavours are just overpowered by these cheese dressings.

The most popular cheese dressings are made with a blue cheese, preferably French Roquefort or Italian Gorgonzola for a more exciting taste, but for economy use Danish blue.

To make a blue cheese dressing, make 300ml (½ pint) vinaigrette (opposite). Mash or crumble 50g (2oz) Roquefort, Gorgonzola or other blue cheese in a small bowl, then whisk in the vinaigrette dressing. This is especially good with spinach salad and for very finely sliced red cabbage.

To make a cream cheese dressing, beat 75g (3oz) softened cream cheese until creamy. Add 2 finely chopped spring onions and 2 tablespoons chopped parsley, then beat in 250ml (8fl oz) vinaigrette dressing (opposite). Serve with sliced hard-boiled eggs and tuna fish.

EASY WAYS TO ADD FLAVOURS TO SALADS

• Different oils, vinegars and mustards make it possible to achieve a great variety of flavours from a vinaigrette; for cooked vegetables and substantial mixed salads with crunchy ingredients, I like the rich, fruity taste of extra virgin olive oil, but for more delicate, leafy salads, it can be made less assertive by diluting with grapeseed or sunflower oil or using light olive oil.
• Walnut and hazelnut oils are strongly flavoured and should be mixed with a blander oil; they are delicious for leafy salads, especially those containing Feta or goat cheese and bitter leaves such as chicory and frisée combined with nuts.
• Wine vinegar can be either white or the richer red, which I prefer for most dressings, but fruit vinegars such as raspberry, which smell almost scented, can be effective in delicate, subtle or slightly sweet salads.
• Sweetness is an important ingredient in a salad dressing to bring out all the flavours; I usually use a little clear honey (opposite) or soft light brown sugar instead of the more classic caster sugar.
• Try adding aromatic crushed green or pink peppercorns, or even a little chopped fresh red chilli, for a piquant dressing.
• For an oriental vinaigrette to serve with Chinese leaf and bean sprout salads, use sherry vinegar and add crushed garlic and fresh ginger with soy sauce and a mixture of sunflower with a little toasted sesame oil.
• Apart from yogurt dressings, seasoned creamed smetana and soured cream are very useful for dressing potato and other cooked vegetable salads. Add all sorts of ingredients, including chopped fresh herbs, wholegrain mustard, crushed green peppercorns, grated horseradish, chopped anchovies, onions and gherkins or capers, and curry pastes with chopped fresh coriander. These dressings also make effective coatings for cold chicken and fish, instead of mayonnaise.

FRUIT *and* VEGETABLE SAUCES

Savoury fruit and vegetable sauces are based on the cooked reduced purée of the fruit or vegetable, and are usually used in small quantities as a condiment rather than as a covering sauce. A fresh tomato sauce, for example, can accompany soufflés, gratins, fried fish or vegetable cakes as well as many pasta dishes to complement the dish's flavour.

Tomatoes are so versatile they are used as the base for many of these sauces. A cooked tomato sauce is classic and can be made all year round. Mexican-style salsas (relishes) and American-style barbecue sauces are also based on tomatoes or tomato sauce. Almost any cooked vegetable, however, can be softened with butter or oil, natural yogurt, fromage frais or cream and used as a sauce or as a base for another sauce, soup or soufflé. Herbs are also used as a base for many savoury sauces, such as basil for pesto sauce, a traditional Italian accompaniment to pasta, and mint sauce, always a favourite for serving with roast lamb.

Fruit purées are also used as the base for creating sauces which are classic with certain dishes; apple sauce with pork, cranberry sauce with chicken, turkey and ham, Cumberland sauce with roast game and pâtés and plum sauce with duck, ham or pork.

Fruits or vegetables for these savoury sauces do not have to be puréed however – I often prefer, particularly with fruit sauces, to leave pieces of fruit soft and mushy to give texture to the sauce and I like to stir in chopped fresh green herbs at the end which add a fresh taste to the sauce and glamorize its appearance.

FRESH TOMATO SAUCE

This is one of the most useful and also one of the best tasting sauces of all. This recipe is a simple version I have devised, and I think it is hard to beat. It can either be used on its own or as a base for other sauces. A good tomato sauce goes with every kind of ingredient from meat, fish and vegetables to pasta. When you don't have time to make this sauce, use the quick tomato sauce (page 89) that uses canned tomatoes.

The best fresh tomatoes for cooking are the plum variety, if you can get them, and I only use the ones that are really ripe and deep red; when plum tomatoes are in season, make a large quantity of sauce and freeze it in separate containers. Mix in 25–50g (1–2oz) butter at the end for a richer sauce. And, if the tomatoes you are using are not really ripe and full of flavour, stir in 1 tablespoon tomato purée.

It doesn't make much difference to the colour of the finished sauce if you substitute white wine for red. Finely shredded fresh basil is a wonderful addition stirred in just before serving. Makes about 1.2 litres (2 pints).

1 *Melt 50g (2oz) butter with 4 tablespoons olive oil in a large saucepan. Add 3–4 large chopped garlic cloves, 1kg (2lb) skinned and chopped tomatoes (page 48), 150ml (¼ pint) red wine, 2 teaspoons caster sugar and a little salt.*

2 *Bring to the boil, then simmer over a low heat, stirring often, for 20–30 minutes until the tomatoes are completely mushy and the sauce thickens as desired. Season to taste with crushed sea salt and plenty of freshly ground black pepper.*

CUMBERLAND SAUCE

Cumberland sauce, more like a glaze than a thin pouring sauce, is basically a redcurrant jelly sauce flavoured with orange and/or lemon rind and port. Traditionally served at room temperature with venison, this sauce is equally delicious with lamb, ham, beef, tongue and especially with pâtés and terrines.

To make about 300ml (½ pint) sauce, you will need 250g (8oz) good-quality or homemade redcurrant jelly (page 301) and a ruby port to provide a deep rich colour.

1 *Remove the rinds of 1 orange or ½ orange and ½ lemon. Cut the rinds into fine julienne strips. Bring the rind and 150ml (¼ pint) water to the boil in a pan for 2–3 minutes. Drain and refresh under cold water.*

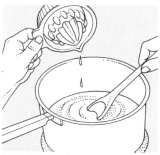

2 *Melt the redcurrant jelly in a small saucepan. Squeeze the juice from the fruit and add to the pan. Stir in ¼ teaspoon each ground cinnamon or ginger, dry mustard, 1 finely chopped shallot and 50–75ml (2–3fl oz) ruby port.*

3 *Simmer the sauce for 3–4 minutes until the jelly is melted and the shallot softened. Strain. Stir in the julienne and set aside to cool until thickened and syrupy. For a clear sauce, simmer with the julienne and then strain.*

MINT SAUCE

I never really liked mint sauce as a child, but I think it must have been because I had only tasted a bottled variety made with strong malt vinegar and too much sugar. Home-made mint sauce, using really fresh mint and good wine vinegar is quite a different thing. I also like using sherry vinegar for its rounded flavour or cider for its mildness. For variation add 1 teaspoon ground cumin, which has a great affinity both with lamb and mint. Serves 4–6.

Put a handful of finely chopped fresh mint and 1 teaspoon caster sugar in a bowl. Stir in 2 tablespoons boiling water. Add 2 tablespoons white wine vinegar and leave for at least 1 hour.

SAVOURY FRUIT SAUCES

All sorts of fruits can be used to make enhancing sauces for serving with pork, ham, duck, goose and game, and gooseberry sauce is traditionally served with mackerel.

Either simply stew the fruit with a little sugar until soft and thick, or sharpen it with vinegar or lemon juice as a little acidity cuts the fattier meat. I prefer apple sauce to be cooked until mushy, but not smoothly puréed. If you like, stir in 1 heaped tablespoon Greek yogurt before the sauce cools. Serves 4–6.

To make apple sauce, put 500g (1lb) peeled and sliced cooking apples in a saucepan with 25g (1oz) caster sugar and 2 tablespoons lemon juice. Cook, stirring, until mushy. Remove the pan from the heat and leave the sauce to cool.

IDEAS FOR FRUIT AND VEGETABLE SAUCES

• Make vegetable purée sauces from red or yellow peppers, spinach, watercress, parsnips, carrots, leeks, courgettes, fennel or aubergines. Cook the vegetables by boiling, grilling or sautéing in butter, then purée and thin with cream, yogurt or stock if necessary.
• For the smoothest possible vegetable sauce, pass the purée through a fine sieve after blending in a food processor.
• Fresh plums, blackcurrants, apricots, gooseberries, whole kumquats or chopped satsumas and, of course, cranberries, can all be stewed with a small amount of sugar, and a little water or orange juice to make thick, shiny sauces which are delicious served cold or hot with pork, ham, duck and game. Sharpen these sauces with lemon juice or wine, cider or raspberry vinegar.
• To make an oriental-style dipping sauce, boil together 2 tablespoons lemon juice, 125ml (4fl oz) soy sauce, 1 tablespoon cider vinegar, 2 tablespoons sugar, a grated 2.5cm (1in) piece fresh ginger and 2 cloves finely chopped garlic for 1–2 minutes. Cool, then strain and stir in 2–3 tablespoons finely sliced spring onions. Serve with prawn tempura (page 129).

Pesto, a traditional Italian sauce for pasta, is made with fresh basil, olive oil and toasted pine kernels.

PESTO SAUCE

In Liguria, Italy, where this basil sauce for pasta originated, there are vast fields of basil plants stretching as far as the eye can see. The smell as the basil is picked in the warm sun is exquisite. You can recapture this fantastic smell if you make pesto at home, particularly if you pound the leaves and other ingredients in a pestle and mortar, which is the best way of making the sauce if you have time. For speed, however, whizz all the ingredients in a food processor, adding the cheese last. Keep in well-sealed jars in the refrigerator or freeze. If you haven't enough basil use some parsley. Makes about 300ml (½ pint).

1 Toast 25g (1oz) pine kernels in a high oven or toss in a dry frying pan for 1–2 minutes. Put about 50g (2oz) roughly sliced fresh basil leaves, 2 roughly chopped garlic cloves, the toasted pine kernels and a good pinch of salt in a mortar. Press and grind with the pestle until the mixture becomes a paste.

2 Beat in 150–175ml (5–6fl oz) olive oil, starting with a drop at a time and gradually increasing to a steady stream, as if making mayonnaise (page 202). Stir in 4 tablespoons freshly grated Parmesan and 2 tablespoons grated Pecorino cheese, or use all Parmesan cheese if you can't obtain Pecorino.

SWEET SAUCES *and* SYRUPS

Sweet fruit sauces are usually based on fruit purées, or jams and jellies, and can be cooked or uncooked. In general, they are thinner than savoury fruit sauces (page 207) as they are intended to be served with or to coat puddings, pies or tarts. Fruit-based purées can be sweetened and are sometimes thinned and flavoured with a liqueur or lemon juice. Both these ingredients help to bring out the flavour of the fruit and prevent discoloration.

I think the most popular sauce for puddings is chocolate – it is usually used with ice cream and other frozen puddings, but is also delicious with poached fruit, especially pears. Vanilla, coffee and brandy, along with orange, almond, cherry and other flavoured liqueurs can be stirred in for extra flavour or to complement a particular pudding. Cinnamon also has a special affinity with chocolate.

Another type of sweet sauce is based on sugar syrups. To make these syrups, sugar and water are cooked together to a certain density which is calculated by the proportion of water to sugar or measured on a special thermometer (page 23). A sugar syrup can be flavoured with vanilla, cinnamon, ginger, mint and many liqueurs to serve with a wide array of puddings.

UNCOOKED FRUIT PURÉES

A fruit sauce for pouring, also called a coulis, can be made in minutes in a food processor. Soft fruits and fruit pulps are the easiest as they need little preparation and tend to have the brightest colours. Raspberries, strawberries, blackberries, blackcurrants, blueberries, kiwi and mango all make vividly coloured purées which look spectacular on a plate with other sliced fruit arranged on top. The amount made depends on how liquid the fruit is.

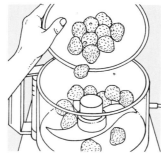

To make a strawberry purée, whizz hulled berries in a food processor or blender with a little fresh orange juice and water until smooth. Strain and sweeten the sauce if you want.

RASPBERRY SAUCE

The most famous fruit sauce is Melba sauce, a raspberry sauce prepared especially for the opera singer Nellie Melba by Escoffier while he was working at the Savoy Hotel in London in 1892. It was intended to coat a poached peach served on vanilla ice cream, which is still a wonderful combination of flavours known as Peach Melba.

When fresh raspberries are not in season, use frozen ones. Makes about 300ml (½ pint).

Purée 300g (10oz) raspberries with a little lemon juice, water and sifted icing sugar. Strain through a fine nylon sieve and stir in 2 tablespoons framboise (raspberry liqueur), if liked.

SUGAR SYRUPS

A simple solution of sugar dissolved in water is very useful for a number of sweet recipes, from soaking fruit, sponges and savarins and rum babas, to making sorbets and sauces. The technique is easy but needs a little care.

It is vital that all grains of sugar are dissolved in the water before boiling, otherwise the solution may crystallize around the remaining grains. To prevent this, use a heavy-based saucepan, preferably copper-based or aluminium for even heat distribution, and brush down the sides of the pan while the sugar grains dissolve, using a pastry brush dipped in cold water.

Syrups are measured in terms of densities according to its final use. The boiling hard in step 2 evaporates the water away, so concentrating the density. A low-density or light syrup of 500g (1lb) sugar to 1 litre (2 pints) water is used for fruit salads, poaching fruits, soaking sponges, rum babas and savarins; a medium-density syrup of 500g (1lb) sugar to 500ml (1 pint) water is used for candying fruits; a high-density or heavy syrup of 500g (1lb) sugar to 450ml (¾ pint) water is used for making sorbets and ice creams.

If you wish to keep sugar syrup for a couple of weeks in the refrigerator, add 1 teaspoon of liquid glucose, obtainable from chemists, after it has cooled. This stops it crystallizing.

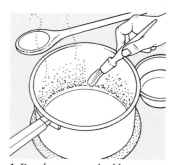

1 Put the sugar and cold water into a large heavy-based saucepan and heat slowly to dissolve the grains, stirring occasionally with a wooden spoon. As the sugar dissolves, brush down the insides of the pan using a pastry brush dipped in cold water to remove any stray grains of sugar. It is very important not to allow the water to boil until every grain of sugar has dissolved.

2 Increase the heat and bring to a foaming boil, without stirring at all. Boil for about 2 minutes or until the syrup is clear. Remove the pan from the heat and leave to cool. For an orange- or lemon-flavoured syrup add orange or lemon juice at this stage. When the syrup is cold use as required or store in the refrigerator in a screw-top jar, adding 1 teaspoon liquid glucose if necessary.

SWEET WHITE SAUCE

Here is a simple steamed pudding sauce to which you can add all sorts of flavourings – grated lemon, lime or orange rinds, brandy, sweet sherry, almond essence, vanilla essence and so on.

For an economical chocolate version, mix 1 tablespoon cocoa powder with the cornflour before cooking and add some plain chocolate, broken in pieces.

You can make this useful sauce in advance, then just gently reheat it when ready to serve. Makes about 300ml (½ pint).

Mix 1 tablespoon cornflour with a little milk from 300ml (½ pint). Bring the remaining milk to the boil with 1 tablespoon vanilla sugar (page 235). Pour the hot milk on to the cornflour paste, beating well, then return to the heat, stirring, until thickened.

Thick and glossy Hot Spiced Chocolate Sauce (page 213) complements the fresh taste of a pear poached lightly in syrup.

HOT CHOCOLATE FUDGE SAUCE

Very simple to make, this chocolate fudge sauce is wickedly good and ideal to serve over homemade ice cream. Try it with coffee, chocolate, strawberry or traditional vanilla ice cream (page 235). It is particularly good poured over bananas or sliced fresh pears, topped with chopped, toasted nuts. It keeps well in the refrigerator for about a week and still stays quite runny, although it thickens a bit. Before serving, reheat gently in a saucepan without boiling. Makes about 450ml (¾ pint) to serve 4–6.

1 Melt 50g (2oz) butter in a small saucepan with 50g (2oz) plain chocolate, broken in pieces. Stir until smooth, then beat in 2 tablespoons cocoa powder. Beat in 125g (4oz) soft brown sugar or muscovado sugar for a stronger, more fudgy taste.

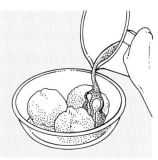

2 Slowly add 200ml (7fl oz) evaporated milk, 1 teaspoon vanilla essence and a pinch of salt. Boil for 1 minute, then set aside to cool slightly. Serve while still warm over scoops of ice cream, fresh fruit, such as strawberries, or a hot sponge pudding.

BRANDY BUTTER

When I was a child, brandy butter was the only thing which would make me eat Christmas pudding. I still adore this rich mixture of sugary, brandy-flavoured butter which melts over the steaming pudding. For a very smooth butter, all icing sugar can be used, but I think a combination of sugars is best to give the texture a slight crunchiness. Cover and store in the refrigerator for up to 1 week but remove about 1 hour before serving. Makes about 400g (13oz).

FLAVOURING SWEET SAUCES

• Butterscotch is one of my favourite sweet sauces to pour over ice cream, or over soft fruit. I make it with 75g (3oz) unsalted butter, 150g (5oz) soft light brown sugar and 2 tablespoons light honey such as orange blossom or clover. Melt the ingredients together in a saucepan and then boil for 1 minute; for a finishing touch stir in a little lemon juice or double cream at the end.
• Chopped toasted hazelnuts can be stirred into butterscotch, hot fudge or chocolate sauces just before serving.

• For a fresh orange sauce, sweeten 300ml (½ pint) freshly squeezed orange juice and the juice of 1 lemon with a little honey or sugar in a saucepan. Stir in 1 teaspoon arrowroot mixed with 1 tablespoon water. Bring to the boil and stir constantly for 2 minutes until the sauce has thickened. This is a good sauce for steamed puddings served with or without cream as well.
• I often dress fruit salads, particularly those containing strawberries, or it could be simply a bowl of strawberries,

with a fresh orange syrup: dissolve 175g (6oz) caster sugar in the strained juice of 3 oranges and 1 lemon, then bring to the boil and bubble rapidly for 3 minutes. Leave to cool before pouring over the top.
• Yogurt, creamed smetana and the thicker fromage frais are a boon for making quick sweet sauces. For mocha sauce, stir in strong black coffee and grated chocolate. Other good additions are chopped, toasted nuts, fresh fruit purées and caramel or a little concentrated orange juice and finely grated rind.

Put 250g (8oz) soft diced unsalted butter into a bowl and beat in 75g (3oz) sifted icing sugar and 50g (2oz) fine demerara sugar. Little by little, beat in 4–6 tablespoons brandy according to taste. Use rum instead of brandy if you prefer.

CUSTARD *and* CREAM SAUCES

Sweet egg custard is a wonderful sauce as well as being the base for many other puddings, ice creams and mousses. Although you can flavour it with endless variations such as lemon or orange rind, coffee, chocolate and a variety of liqueurs, the flavour of real vanilla from an infused vanilla pod is hard to match. Pastry cream, also called *crème patissière* or confectioner's custard, a rich filling for fruit tarts, cakes, éclairs and profiteroles, is simply thickened custard.

A sweet sabayon, or the Italian version, zabaglione, is a rich mousseline sauce, so special it can even be served as a pudding on its own. Really an emulsified sauce of beaten egg yolks, sugar and a liqueur, usually Marsala, it is cooked carefully over a low heat, like hollandaise sauce. It can also be poured over fruit and then glazed under a grill at the last minute.

Sweetened and flavoured whipped cream, also called *crème Chantilly*, has many uses. As a sauce it can be spooned over puddings and served with fresh fruit but it can also be used for a pastry filling like pastry cream. Flavour it the same way as custard and pastry cream (see box opposite).

REAL VANILLA CUSTARD

This really is a luxurious treat. It is so good that the French recognize its worth with the name of *crème anglaise*. In traditional custard recipes, the milk and eggs are stirred for ages in a bowl set over a saucepan of simmering water, but I find if you just scald the milk and pour it from a height on to the eggs, then stir it over the lowest heat possible you can speed up the process without running the risk of curdling.

To obtain the flavouring of true vanilla split a vanilla pod lengthwise and remove the seeds with a pointed knife. (The seeds intensify the vanilla taste.) Place the pod and seeds in a saucepan and add 300ml (½ pint) each milk and single cream. Bring just to the boil and remove from the heat. Set aside, covered, for 15–20 minutes to infuse the flavour. This is delicious hot or cold served with puddings, pies, fruit salads and best of all, treacle tart (page 220). Makes about 600ml (1 pint).

1 *Beat 4 egg yolks (or 1 whole egg and 2 yolks) together in a bowl. If planning to serve the custard thickened and cold, beat in 2 teaspoons sifted cornflour.*

2 *Reheat the vanilla-flavoured cream and milk just until tiny bubbles appear around the sides of the saucepan but do not boil. Remove at once and pour gradually on to the eggs from a height, beating hard until all the milk and cream are added. Strain the mixture through a fine sieve back into the saucepan.*

3 *On the lowest possible heat, stir constantly until the custard thickens to the consistency of single cream: if you draw your finger across the back of the wooden spoon it should leave a clear line. Pour the custard immediately into a jug to cool and serve warm or cover with a piece of clingfilm so a skin doesn't form. This will keep for up to 2 days in the refrigerator.*

Real vanilla-flavoured custard sauce elevates a homemade apple pie to a very special pudding.

PASTRY CREAM

More hardy than whipped cream or *crème Chantilly*, (below) pastry cream has numerous uses as a filling for éclairs or profiteroles (page 255) and fruit tart bases.

Although quite simple to make, pastry cream does need swift stirring to avoid any lumps forming. If it does go lumpy beat it well when cold or whizz it in a food processor. You can flavour it in the same way as custard (see box right). Pastry cream will keep for up to 2 days covered in the refrigerator. Beat well before using. Makes about 300ml (½ pint).

1 *Blend together 3 egg yolks, 50g (2oz) caster sugar, ½ teaspoon vanilla essence and 25g (1oz) each cornflour and plain flour in a heavy-based saucepan over a low heat. Gradually mix in 450ml (¾ pint) milk, stirring constantly as you pour.*

2 *Slowly bring to the boil, stirring constantly until thickened. It will look alarmingly lumpy at first but keep stirring and the sauce will become smooth. Cook for 1 minute.*

3 *Remove the saucepan from the heat. Leave to cool, stirring occasionally to prevent a skin from forming. For a touch of luxury, beat in 2 tablespoons brandy, rum or sherry.*

FLAVOURING CUSTARD AND CREAM SAUCES

• You can flavour a custard sauce with flavourings other than vanilla; infuse grated orange, lime or lemon rind in the milk and cream instead of the vanilla pod for citrus custards; stir in 2–3 teaspoons instant coffee to the hot milk and cream as well as the vanilla pod for a coffee sauce; grate 75g (3oz) plain chocolate into the hot vanilla-flavoured milk and cream and stir until melted for a chocolate sauce.
• For honey custard sauce, sweeten the milk and cream with 2 tablespoons well-flavoured honey instead of sugar and stir until melted.
• Liqueurs, such as rum, brandy, kirsch or an orange liqueur, can be stirred into the custard at the end of cooking.
• A little ground cardamom enhances an orange custard, and ground nutmeg or cinnamon are good with a plain vanilla custard.

• Other ingredients can also be added to the custard such as chopped toasted nuts, crushed macaroons or finely chopped prunes, raisins, ready-to-eat dried apricots or stem ginger.
• To make a light mousseline custard sauce, whisk 2 egg whites with a pinch of salt until they hold soft peaks and then fold them gently but thoroughly into the sauce just before serving.
• If, like me, you love lemon and orange curd, you can make a delicious citrus sauce by following the recipe for custard sauce but omitting the vanilla and using fresh, strained orange and lemon juice for the liquid instead of milk and cream – this sauce is wonderful for steamed puddings (page 218), upside-down pudding cakes (page 221) or hot sponges (page 220).
• Coarsely grated chocolate is good folded into crème Chantilly and looks pretty too.

CRÈME CHANTILLY

This is simply sweetened and flavoured whipped cream, which can be lightened with a little whisked egg white. Sometimes, 1–2 tablespoons brandy are folded in. Whip whipping or double cream with vanilla sugar (page 235), using 2 dessertspoons sugar for each 300ml (½ pint) cream, or to taste. If you are using double cream, fold in 1 whisked egg white. Use like pastry cream (above), or spoon over puddings or serve with fresh fruit.

SABAYON SAUCE

In France, this light and frothy mousseline sauce is known as sabayon and is spooned over fruity puddings. When freshly made and warm it is delicious served with a light sponge pudding. In Italy, when flavoured with sweet rich Marsala and extra sugar it becomes the classic pudding zabaglione.

For a sauce, allow 1 tablespoon caster sugar to each egg yolk. For zabaglione, allow 25g (1oz) sugar and 1 tablespoon of Marsala per yolk. The method of making is almost the same. Makes about 300ml (½ pint).

1 *To make sabayon sauce, put 4 egg yolks and 4 tablespoons caster sugar in a heatproof bowl and beat until frothy, ideally using an electric mixer. If making zabaglione whisk in the Marsala at this stage. Scrape down the sides of the bowl with a rubber spatula.*

2 *Set the bowl over a saucepan of gently simmering water and continue beating the mixture until thick. Make sure the bottom of the bowl does not touch the water, or the eggs could scramble. It helps to lift the bowl occasionally to check the water underneath.*

3 *The sauce is thick enough when the beaters leave a ribbon trail on the surface when lifted. For sabayon sauce, stir in 2 tablespoons sherry or sweet white wine and cool, beating occasionally. Zabaglione is usually served hot straight from the pan in tall, elegant glasses.*

PLUM AND SHALLOT SAUCE WITH FRESH MINT (194)

Plums, with their natural sharpness, are ideal to serve with pork, duck, ham or game. Like apricots, they are a fruit which often has more flavour when cooked, and they go well with the slight sweetness of shallots. Serve hot or cold.   *SERVES 4–6*

175g (6oz) shallots, peeled but left whole
500g (1lb) red plums, stoned and sliced
300ml (½ pint) freshly squeezed orange juice
50g (2oz) caster sugar
1 tablespoon sherry vinegar
Salt and black pepper
Handful of fresh mint, finely chopped

Put the shallots and plums into a saucepan with the orange juice and caster sugar. Bring to the boil, then cover and simmer very gently for about 30 minutes until the shallots are completely soft and the plums are mushy. The juiciness of plums varies, so if you feel the sauce should be thicker, uncover the pan and bubble to reduce the juices slightly, then stir in the vinegar and season to taste with salt and black pepper. Just before serving, stir in the chopped mint.

BEST BREAD SAUCE (194)

To me, the best bread sauce is made out of brown bread rather than the more traditional white bread and includes meltingly soft pieces of onion. It should also be rich with cream and butter and have a definite hint of cloves and nutmeg. The sauce must be cooked slowly either on top of the stove in a pan or in a covered dish in a low oven, stirring now and then. As some bread absorbs more liquid than others, adjust the thickness of the sauce towards the end by adding more milk or more crumbled bread.   *SERVES 6–8*

1 onion, chopped finely
125–150g (4–5oz) wholemeal or brown bread, torn into pieces, including crusts
50g (2oz) unsalted butter
6–8 whole cloves
600ml (1 pint) milk
300ml (½ pint) double cream, plus a little extra (optional)
¼ whole nutmeg, grated
Sea salt and black pepper

Put the onion into a heavy-based saucepan with the pieces of bread and butter. Tie the cloves up in a piece of muslin, and add to the pan. Add the milk and double cream. Season with a little salt and freshly ground black pepper and stir to mix. Cover the saucepan and put over the lowest possible heat, stirring now and then to break up the bread and to stop any of it sticking to the bottom of the pan, for 1–1½ hours until the sauce is thick and soft.

Remove the bag of cloves, add the grated nutmeg and season with more salt and pepper if needed. If you like, stir in a little more double cream.

If you prefer, cook the sauce in the oven. Follow the recipe but put the ingredients into a casserole dish, cover and cook at 120°C, 250°F, Gas Mark ½ for 2–2½ hours.

KUMQUAT SAUCE WITH DILL (194)

I once visited kumquat orchards in Israel and the little trees massed with their brilliant orange fruit were a charming sight, like a miniature world. Kumquats have a pleasantly sharp and piquant flavour and the edible skin is quite thin. This is the perfect sauce for serving with roast or grilled duck.   *SERVES 4*

250g (8oz) fresh kumquats, cut in half lengthwise and pips removed
300ml (½ pint) unsweetened apple juice
1 heaped tablespoon caster sugar
2 teaspoons raspberry vinegar
2 teaspoons arrowroot
About 1 tablespoon chopped fresh dill
Salt
2–4 pinches cayenne pepper

Put the kumquats into a saucepan with the apple juice, and bring to the boil, then simmer gently for about 20 minutes until they are very soft. Stir in the caster sugar, then remove from the heat and stir in the raspberry vinegar.

Put 1 tablespoon of water in a cup, add the arrowroot and mix until smooth, then stir the mixture into the softened kumquats and return to the heat. Bring to the boil, stirring, then simmer gently, still stirring, for about 2 minutes until the sauce has thickened and translucent. Stir in the chopped dill and remove the saucepan from the heat. Season to taste with salt and cayenne pepper and serve the sauce warm.

INDIAN SPICED MUSHROOM SAUCE (194)

Cultivated mushrooms are greatly improved by spices, and this creamy sauce transforms roast and grilled chicken or lamb. It is quite piquant despite the cream. Serve the sauce with pasta dishes. Alternatively, you can make a delicious egg curry by slicing hard-boiled eggs and mixing them in with the sauce. The meatier chestnut mushrooms are ideal for this sauce if available.   *SERVES 6*

50g (2oz) butter
1 tablespoon groundnut or sunflower oil
2 teaspoons ground coriander
1 teaspoon ground cumin
1 teaspoon ground cinnamon
5cm (2in) piece fresh ginger, peeled and chopped finely
3 large cloves garlic, chopped finely
175g (6oz) mushrooms, chopped finely including stalks
2 tablespoons tomato purée
125ml (4fl oz) water
4 tablespoons lemon juice, strained
300ml (½ pint) double cream
Salt
2–4 pinches cayenne pepper
Handful of fresh coriander or mint leaves, chopped roughly

Melt the butter and oil in a heavy-based saucepan over a medium heat, then add the ground coriander, cumin and cinnamon and the chopped ginger and garlic. Stir the spices for a minute or so and then add the chopped mushrooms. Toss around until beginning to soften, and then add the tomato purée, the water and the strained lemon juice.

Mix the contents of the saucepan thoroughly and bring to the boil, then lower the heat and simmer very gently in the open pan, stirring now and then, for 15–20 minutes. Bring to the boil again (if the mushroom mixture is very liquid bubble for a few more minutes to reduce it slightly) and add the double cream.

Stir and bubble the mixture for about 2 minutes, then remove the saucepan from the heat. Add salt and cayenne pepper to taste and stir in the roughly chopped coriander or mint leaves just before serving.

If you want to make the sauce well in advance, which you can, add the fresh herbs after you have reheated it gently.

RED VELVET SAUCE (194)

Peppers are a marvellous ingredient for sauces and you can vary the colour of the sauce according to the pepper used. But I use red peppers again and again for their vibrant scarlet which you can make even more dramatic with a sprinkling of roughly chopped flat-leaved parsley when the sauce is on the plate. This is a lovely, light sauce and is excellent with meat, poultry, vegetables and pasta. I particularly like it with grilled lamb or chicken. *SERVES 4*

> *2 tablespoons olive oil*
> *1 tablespoon lemon juice*
> *4 tablespoons water*
> *1 tablespoon tomato purée*
> *1 large red pepper, halved, deseeded and finely sliced (page 49)*
> *1 large onion, sliced roughly*
> *3–4 cloves garlic, sliced roughly*
> *2 teaspoons bottled green peppercorns, drained and crushed*
> *Salt*
> *1–3 pinches cayenne pepper*

Put the olive oil, lemon juice, water and tomato purée into a heavy-based saucepan and add the sliced pepper, onion and garlic and a little salt. Cover the pan and bring to the boil, then lower the heat and simmer gently for 15–20 minutes, stirring now and again, until all the ingredients are completely soft.

Pour the contents of the saucepan into a food processor and whizz to a smooth purée, then spoon the sauce back into the saucepan. Add the crushed green peppercorns and bring the sauce just up to the boil again. Remove from the heat, add salt and cayenne pepper to taste and serve hot in a sauceboat or bowl.

RAGÙ (194)

Ragù, or Bolognese sauce, is a meat sauce to serve with all sorts of pasta including lasagne (page 84). If it is cooked long and very gently, it becomes rich, almost creamy, and aromatic with the addition of herbs and grated nutmeg. Make the sauce in advance and keep it in the refrigerator for up to 4 days, or freeze it, and then reheat from frozen while you cook the pasta. To make it really creamy, you can stir in a little double cream before serving. *SERVES 4*

> *50g (2oz) butter*
> *2 tablespoons olive oil*
> *1 onion, chopped finely*
> *1 stick celery, chopped finely*
> *1 carrot, chopped finely*
> *375g (12oz) extra lean minced beef*
> *3 large cloves garlic, chopped finely*
> *250ml (8fl oz) dry red wine*
> *150ml (¼ pint) milk*
> *397g (14oz) can chopped tomatoes*
> *1 teaspoon dried oregano*
> *2 bay leaves*
> *¼ whole nutmeg, grated*
> *1 rounded tablespoon tomato purée, dissolved in 75ml (3fl oz) water*
> *Handful of fresh parsley, finely chopped*
> *Salt and black pepper*

Melt the butter with the olive oil in a wide, heavy-based saucepan over a medium heat. Add the chopped onion, celery and carrot and stir around until the vegetables are beginning to brown, then add the minced meat and the finely chopped garlic and stir around briefly just until the meat has broken up and lost all of its redness.

Pour in the wine, increase the heat and bubble, stirring frequently, for a few minutes until the wine has evaporated. Then add the milk and boil, stirring all the time, until that has evaporated, too.

Stir in the chopped tomatoes, oregano, bay leaves, nutmeg and the tomato purée and water. Season carefully with salt and black pepper.

Stir the mixture and bring to the boil, then cover the saucepan and leave to barely simmer over the lowest possible heat for at least 2 hours, stirring now and then and adding a little water if the mixture looks dry at all. Finally, remove from the heat and adjust the seasoning to taste. Before mixing with the pasta, stir the chopped parsley into the sauce.

COCONUT SAUCE (194)

Making coconut milk from fresh coconut is a laborious business, but a block of creamed coconut makes it very easy. This thick, creamy sauce is a wonderful accompaniment for fruit salads made out of mainly exotic fruits, such as mangoes, lychees, passion fruit or star fruit. *SERVES 6*

> *50g (2oz) creamed coconut, broken*
> *75ml (3fl oz) milk*
> *½ teaspoon salt*
> *2 tablespoons golden caster sugar*
> *300ml (½ pint) double cream*

Put the coconut into a saucepan with the milk and stir to dissolve over a medium heat. Add the salt and caster sugar and stir until all the sugar has dissolved, but don't allow to boil. Remove from the heat and stir in the cream, then pour into a bowl and chill before serving.

HOT SPICED CHOCOLATE SAUCE (209)

I love watching a hot chocolate sauce solidifying as it runs down ice cream. The sauce must be pure chocolate and a little added soured cream and cinnamon brings out the best in it. Be careful when you melt the chocolate that the hot water beneath never bubbles. If the chocolate does get too hot and it 'seizes' and thickens, briskly stir in a little warm water. *SERVES 4–6*

> *175g (6oz) plain chocolate, broken into pieces*
> *2 teaspoons vanilla essence*
> *75ml (3fl oz) soured cream*
> *1 teaspoon ground cinnamon*

Put the chocolate into a heatproof bowl set over simmering water or in the top of a double boiler. Add the vanilla essence, soured cream and cinnamon and stir until melted and smooth.

PUDDINGS

I have to admit that this is the chapter closest to my heart. I have always loved puddings – I love making puddings, I love eating puddings, I even love just looking at puddings. I do have a sweet tooth, but I don't enjoy things which taste only of sweetness – there must either be an exceptional texture, or an element of sharpness, usually provided by the addition of lemon juice, to temper the sweetness.

My friends say they can always recognize my puddings by their sweet but sharp character, exemplified by the Hot Lemon and Passion Fruit Soufflé in the Recipe Collection on page 238. I also love chocolate; dark, moist chocolate pudding cakes, served either with crème fraîche or an intense fruit coulis, are a great favourite. I often bring lemon in with chocolate, too; a sharp lemon tart glazed with melted chocolate is wonderful. With fruit I also enjoy the sharp intensity of flavour which you can find in passion fruit and blackcurrants, but delicate combinations, such as lightly cooked fresh apricots with the flowers from two or three elderflower heads are absolutely magical, too.

Cream, I feel, has to be used judiciously; too much cream without a strong taste to cut it, can make a pudding sickly, which I hate. I often mix a little natural yogurt into whipped cream to temper the richness or I use crème fraîche or creamed smetana, which is delicious and far less expensive than cream. For those wishing to cut down on fat, the virtually fat-free fromage frais is useful in puddings as an alternative to cream, because it actually tastes more creamy than even whole milk natural yogurt.

Making puddings is one of those areas of cookery which can often give you the feeling that you have really raised a magic wand at some stage in the preparation. Results can be ethereal as with the lightest soufflés or melt-in-the-mouth mousses; they can also be warm and reassuring, like treacle tart or an old-fashioned steamed pudding oozing with butter and syrup. They can be light and dreamy like a pavlova filled with cream and summer fruit; rich and luxurious as in the darkest chocolate mousse or real vanilla ice cream; frosty and cooling as in delicately perfumed sorbets, and fruit ice creams; or tangy and refreshing as in fruit jellies or fools. The last course sets the seal on the meal and must never be a disappointment.

As a pudding should echo the season, the weather and the mood of the occasion, it must also complement the main course to the advantage of both. A heavy meat course such as a hearty pie is best followed by something juicy and fruity like stewed fruit or a refreshing sorbet. A rich fish like salmon is also better followed by a really good salad of summer berries, whereas spicy foods, however rich, somehow make the taste buds appreciate creamy, milky puddings.

A pudding can be a truly artistic creation, and those inclined can spend a lot of time and thought on the final appearance. It is also important to realize, however, that just a swift sprinkling of nuts, grated chocolate, sugar crystals or flower petals, or a dusting of sieved icing sugar or cocoa powder, can transform an ordinary looking dish into something really special. I certainly prefer simple decorations to swirls of piped cream.

Clockwise from top: Quince Pudding Brûlée (page 240) with sweetened cream cheese and quinces under a caramelized top; luscious fresh raspberries encased in a fromage frais and chocolate mixture in Chocolate Ripple Heart with Raspberries (page 241); ever-popular Summer Pudding (page 238) with a hint of orange; Passion Fruit and Orange Puddings (page 239) with a creamy sauce; Banana and Pecan Pie with Cranberry and Orange Coulis (page 241) uses puff pastry for the top and bottom crusts; Queen of Puddings with Fresh Poached Apricots (page 239); and an individual Crème Brûlée (page 240).

MILK *and* EGG PUDDINGS

People often talk of milk puddings in a slightly disparaging way as reminiscent either of school or the nursery. It should not be forgotten that they can also be delicious. Rice (either whole, ground or flaked and brown as well as white), semolina, tapioca and sago are the most usual grains to use for milk puddings.

The best rice pudding I have ever had was made by my grandmother (who must have been one of the first health-food enthusiasts); she used brown rice and muscovado sugar and gentle, slow cooking to produce a nutty, creamy, caramel-flavoured pudding with a wonderful, shiny brown skin. But other ways of cooking and flavouring milk puddings can have their charms, too. An excellent and often somewhat lighter rice pudding can be

made by cooking the rice on top of the stove, stirring it often. This pudding will not form a skin like baked rice pudding and is excellent eaten cold. You can add cream and flavouring such as cinnamon to taste while you are cooking the rice, and you may stop cooking it the moment the rice is the exact texture you want. You can also stir in natural yogurt or whipped cream at the end.

Baked egg custards should be rich and yolky (add an extra egg yolk or two) with an intriguing light smoothness which I find irresistible. They can be baked in a dish like a rice pudding or in moulds with a sauce which tops them when they are turned out, as in crème caramel. Egg custard is also responsible for the creamy layers in bread and butter pudding.

TRADITIONAL BAKED RICE PUDDING

This classic old-fashioned pudding should be rich and creamy – never a solid white lump of rice.

I always use soft brown sugar for flavour, and finely grated lemon rind to make it even better.

Because the character of the pudding is to be creamy there is no point in using skimmed or semi-skimmed milk – use full-fat milk.

To make enough for 4 people you will need 50g (2oz) short grain white rice and 600ml (1 pint) milk.

1 *Rinse the rice and put it in a buttered 900ml (1½ pint) ovenproof dish. Stir in 2 tablespoons soft light brown sugar, the finely grated rind of 1 small lemon, a pinch of salt and 600ml (1 pint) milk.*

2 *Dot the top of the pudding all over with little pieces of butter and freshly grated nutmeg and bake, uncovered, in a preheated oven, 150°C, 300°F, Gas Mark 2 for 1–1½ hours, stirring once after the first 30 minutes.*

Creamy baked rice pudding.

BREAD AND BUTTER PUDDING

The best bread and butter puddings have a golden crusty top, rich creamy egg custard, plumped-up fruit and not too much bread.

To serve 4 you will need 4–6 slices well-buttered crustless bread, cut into triangles, about 50g (2oz) sultanas or raisins and 2 tablespoons candied peel.

To make the custard whisk together 2 eggs plus an extra egg yolk with 40g (1½oz) caster sugar, then whisk in 300ml (½ pint) milk and 150ml (¼ pint) double cream and set on one side.

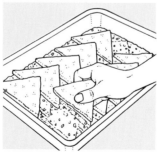

1 *Arrange the bread buttered sides up in layers in a 1.2 litre (2 pint) buttered ovenproof dish, sprinkling sultanas or raisins and candied peel between the layers. End with a layer of bread. Alternatively, dot with marmalade instead of fruit.*

2 *Strain the custard mixture on top of the bread and leave to soak for 30–60 minutes. Bake, uncovered, in a bain-marie (right) in the centre of a preheated oven, 150°C, 300°F, Gas Mark 2 for 1–1¼ hours until the pudding is golden and slightly risen.*

USING A BAIN-MARIE
A bain-marie, or water bath, is a roasting tin of hot water for cooking food slowly at a low temperature. The hot water prevents the pudding from overheating and curdling. Steam rising from the water keeps the food moist and prevents it drying out. For baking egg custards and egg puddings put the tin of water in the oven when you preheat it, so the water heats up before you set the dish in it. The water should come halfway up the sides of the dish.

BAKED EGG CUSTARD

It is easy to forget the pure and simple goodness of this dish. Crème caramel (below) is a variation with a caramel sauce topping.

If possible use a vanilla pod in the custard, as the flavour of real vanilla makes all the difference, but, if necessary, substitute 2 teaspoons vanilla essence. You can make a baked egg custard simply with 3 or 4 eggs but I prefer a richer version made using 3 whole eggs plus 2 extra yolks with 600ml (1 pint) milk. These quantities serve 6.

IDEAS FOR MILK AND EGG PUDDINGS

• Ground nutmeg, cinnamon and mace are spices which enhance milk puddings, and a crushed cardamom pod or two boiled with the milk to flavour it is wonderful.
• For something deliciously exotic dissolve creamed coconut in the milk you use to make the milk pudding and flavour it with cardamom.
• Brown rice can also be used for puddings and produces a nice, nutty flavour and texture but cook the pudding slower and for longer with about a quarter more milk than normal to prevent it becoming too solid.
• I once made a wonderful bread and butter pudding using slices of Italian panettone, a light, dry yeasted cake with fruit and peel.
• Saffron, infused in the milk for rice pudding first, is a luxurious addition which will give a pudding a rich yellow colour and distinctive taste.
• Crème caramel can be varied by substituting orange juice for the water.
• A little ground vanilla pod adds extra vanilla flavour to milk or cream.
• Prepare individual baked egg custards or crème caramels by dividing the mixture among 4–6 ramekin dishes. Cook in a bain-marie for 30–40 minutes.

1 *Put the milk in a saucepan with 75g (3oz) caster sugar, a split vanilla pod and a sliver of lemon rind. Bring just to the boil, then cover, remove from the heat and set aside for 10 minutes for the flavours to infuse.*

2 *Whisk the whole eggs and egg yolks together to mix, then pour on to the warm milk, whisking all the time. Strain the custard mixture through a sieve into a buttered 1 litre (1¾ pint) ovenproof dish.*

3 *Put the dish in a bain-marie (opposite) in the centre of a preheated oven, 160°C, 325°F, Gas Mark 3 and bake for about 1 hour or until firm and a knife tip inserted in the centre of the custard comes out clean.*

CRÈME CARAMEL

 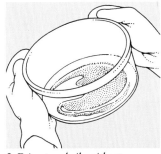 

1 *Stir 125g (4oz) sugar with 150ml (¼ pint) water in a small saucepan over a low heat until dissolved. Brush any sugar crystals from the sides of the pan with a wet pastry brush.*

2 *Bring to a boil, without stirring, and bubble until golden. Tip the pan to make an even colour, then pour the caramel into a 1 litre (1¾ pint) soufflé dish and tilt to coat the base.*

3 *Prepare the baked egg custard mixture (above). Strain the mixture into the soufflé dish and bake in a bain-marie as above. Set aside to cool, then invert the caramel on to a serving dish.*

Coconut Cream Custard (page 241) makes an excellent pudding to follow a spicy meal, and can be accompanied by fresh exotic fruits such as star fruit, mango and kumquat, as here.

STEAMED PUDDINGS

Steamed puddings are sometimes forgotten or dismissed as a thing of the past but they are very well worth making. Neither dull nor heavy, as some people think, they can have a wonderful flavour. Traditionally they were cooked by wrapping the pudding mixture in a cloth and boiling it in a preserving pan, but nowadays they are usually made by gently cooking the mixture for a few hours in a basin set in a steamer or saucepan half filled with boiling water.

The pudding mixture is quick to prepare, and, if you have a pressure cooker or a microwave, it won't take long to cook. For convenience a steamed pudding can be cooked in advance and left in its basin to be reheated in the steamer or saucepan shortly before the meal.

You can make sweet steamed puddings using suet crust pastry as you would in a Sussex pond pudding (page 257). Fill the pudding with apples or other fruit. When making steamed puddings, such as a jam or syrup sponge, I like to use butter instead of suet for its inimitable taste.

Moisture and softness are the key to a good steamed pudding and those cooked with a sauce in the bottom of the basin, some of which becomes absorbed in the pudding, are specially delicious. Even when they have a sauce steamed puddings should always be served with plenty of cream or custard.

BASIC STEAMED SPONGE PUDDING

Use a large saucepan or preserving pan and put a metal trivet, an old saucer or metal pastry cutter in it to keep the base of the pudding basin off the bottom of the pan. The saucepan should be half filled with water and put on to boil while you prepare the pudding mixture. While the pudding is cooking remember to keep an eye on the water level and top it up with more boiling water if necessary. To serve 6 you will need a 1.2 litre (2 pint) pudding basin.

A moist steamed sponge pudding before turning out.

1 *In a large bowl beat together 125g (4oz) butter and 125g (4oz) caster sugar until soft and fluffy, then stir in the grated rind of 1 lemon. Slowly beat in 3 beaten eggs. Sift in 75g (3oz) self-raising flour and 1 teaspoon baking powder. With a large metal spoon fold in 75g (3oz) fresh white breadcrumbs. Add just enough milk to give the pudding mixture a dropping consistency.*

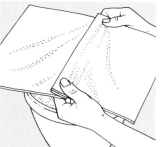

2 *Line the base of the pudding basin with a piece of buttered greaseproof paper cut to fit. Butter the sides of the basin well. Spoon in the pudding mixture. Top the basin with 2 layers of greaseproof paper, the bottom sheet buttered, and pleated together across the middle. Cover with a sheet of foil much larger than the top of the basin, mould it round the basin, then tie the greasepaper and foil securely round the rim with string.*

3 *Draw up the 4 corners of the foil and twist and scrunch together in the centre to make a handle for lifting the basin in and out of the saucepan. Steam in the covered pan for about 2 hours, with the water boiling gently. Carefully lift out the pudding basin, remove the foil and greaseproof paper and leave to cool just slightly. Turn out on to a warm serving plate and serve with cream or custard.*

IDEAS FOR STEAMED PUDDINGS

• Using fresh white breadcrumbs instead of all flour gives steamed puddings an extra lightness.
• For a delicious topping to a steamed pudding, I spoon about 3 tablespoons jam, golden syrup or honey into the basin before adding the pudding mixture.
• Add plenty of grated lemon rind to a steamed sponge pudding and mix the juice with honey as a sauce in the bottom of the pudding basin.
• Try mixing some lemon curd into a lemon sponge mixture or some marmalade into an orange sponge mixture before steaming.
• Ground spices such as cinnamon and nutmeg can often be added to a sponge mixture.
• When making a steamed sponge I sometimes press slivers of orange rind, split cherries and raisins or toasted flaked almonds against the buttered pudding basin before adding the mixture.
• Small individual steamed puddings can be made by using buttered dariole moulds or deep ramekin dishes. Cover with buttered foil, and then arrange in a steamer or on a rack in a large saucepan and steam for 30–40 minutes before removing and turning out.
• Christmas pudding can, of course, be made with butter, but as it is such a strong-flavoured pudding I don't think there is much point. I prefer to use vegetable suet.
• With steamed sponge puddings to which you have added extra egg yolks for richness, use the whites to make a light mousseline custard sauce (page 211), a light accompaniment to a homely pudding.

SUET ROLY-POLY PUDDING

Steaming a traditional long suet roly-poly is not easy in today's smaller saucepans. Baked suet dough can be tough though, so this baked/boiled method is a good compromise. You need a rack or an oval ovenproof plate that fits inside a roasting tin.

To make this pudding for 4–6, use 250g (8oz) self-raising flour, 125g (4oz) shredded beef or vegetable suet, about 150ml (¼ pint) milk or stout and some jam, marmalade or mincemeat as filling. Grated apple also adds extra flavour to the filling.

1 *Put the flour and suet in a bowl with 1 tablespoon caster sugar and 1 teaspoon ground mixed spice (optional) and mix to a firm dough with the milk or stout. Knead lightly, then roll out on a lightly floured surface to a rectangle about 1cm (½in) thick.*

2 *Spread the rolled-out dough with your chosen filling and sprinkle with grated apple if you like. Roll up fairly loosely and place on a double sheet of greased foil. Fold in the ends, then draw up the sides and fold over, pressing down to seal.*

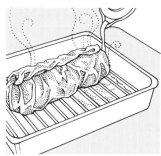

3 *Place the pudding on a rack or an oval ovenproof plate in a roasting tin. Add boiling water just to the base of the pudding, cover the tin with foil and bake in a preheated oven, 180°C, 350°F, Gas Mark 4 for 1 hour. Unroll from the foil and serve hot.*

ROUND CHRISTMAS PUDDING

I have evolved this recipe over the years to achieve what I feel is the perfect pudding – dark and rich but light in texture. For the perfect spherical shape I have experimented with cooking the pudding in a floured cloth and wrapping it in foil, but my rice steamer lined with foil is ideal. Round steamed-pudding moulds are also available. The quantities here will also fill two 1.2 litre (2 pint) pudding basins. You can make the pudding either 3 months or 1 week ahead. On Christmas Day all you need do is steam the pudding for an hour before turning out.

75g (3oz) glacé cherries, chopped roughly
175g (6oz) soft pitted prunes, chopped roughly
175g (6oz) candied peel
175g (6oz) seedless raisins
175g (6oz) sultanas
175g (6oz) currants
75g (3oz) pecan or walnut pieces, chopped roughly
250g (8oz) fresh breadcrumbs
250g (8oz) shredded vegetable suet
6 eggs, beaten
150ml (¼ pint) stout
3–4 tablespoons brandy, rum or whisky

1 *Put the dried fruit, nuts, breadcrumbs and suet in a large bowl and mix with a wooden spoon. Stir in the eggs, then the stout and enough spirit to make a mixture which just drops from the spoon. Leave for a few hours.*

A round Christmas pudding with sprigs of holly gives the look and feel of a real old-fashioned Christmas.

2 *Line both halves of the rice steamer with buttered foil, letting it overlap the edges. Fill both halves, then clamp shut and press the foil edges together. Put the steamer on a metal trivet in a large saucepan and pour in hot water to come half way up the bottom half of the mould.*

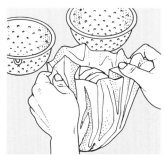

3 *Cover and steam for about 6 hours, topping up with more boiling water as necessary. Remove from the pan and allow to cool. When cold uncover the pudding, then rewrap it in a layer of fresh greaseproof paper, followed by one of foil. Keep in a cool place until required.*

TARTS, PIES *and* PUDDING CAKES

A pie or tart always seems like a treat to me, whether it be an old-fashioned top-crust pie in a traditional pie dish with a thick but crumbly pastry top over fruit such as apples, plums or gooseberries cooked in their juices, or an elegant open tart with the most delicate wafer of pastry as a base.

Pies and tarts provide endless scope for experiment and new ideas and can suit all seasons, all occasions and a wide variety of ingredients. On the whole, a fruit filling for a plate pie or an open tart should be precooked – either baked, stewed or fried – and cooled. You can reduce the juices to intensify the flavour and to stop them making the bottom of the pastry soggy.

Top-crust pies offer many opportunities for the artistic or for those who simply want this part of the meal to be very personal or to have a special message. Pieces of the leftover pastry can be cut into decorations such as simple leaf or flower shapes (page 245). I often cut out letters in order to write appropriate names or words on the pie, even if all I can think of is 'EAT ME!'

Pudding cakes are really just cakes which are moist and delicious enough to be served as puddings accompanied by pouring cream or a fruit, chocolate or caramel sauce. An upside-down cake, with its shining layer of slightly caramelized fruit on top of soft sponge, is a favourite variation of mine. Pudding cakes can be served straight from the oven or at room temperature but are best warm.

OPEN TART

Treacle tart is a good example of the technique for making an open tart. Before 1885 when golden syrup first appeared this would have been made using black treacle with its very strong flavour. Golden syrup, its sweetness cut by lemon juice and rind, makes an irresistible evolvement of an old recipe. You can replace a little of the golden syrup with honey if you like.

To serve 6 use a 23cm (9in) loose-bottomed flan dish or tart tin. Serve the tart warm with thick cream.

1 *Make shortcrust pastry using 250g (8oz) plain flour and 175g (6oz) butter and bind with 1 beaten egg yolk and the juice and rind of 1 lemon instead of water (page 246). Line the flan dish with the pastry, trim, and prick the base all over with a fork.*

2 *In a bowl mix together 5 rounded tablespoons golden syrup, the juice and finely grated rind of 1 lemon and 125g (4oz) fresh white breadcrumbs until well combined. Spoon the mixture into the prepared pastry case and spread it around with a knife.*

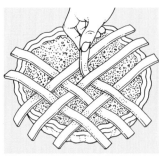

3 *Use the pastry trimmings to make 1cm (½in) wide strips. Arrange in a lattice pattern over the tart. Trim off the edges and press to seal. Glaze pastry with milk. Bake in a preheated oven, 200°C, 400°F Gas Mark 6 for 25–30 minutes.*

TOP-CRUST FRUIT PIE

A top-crust pie should be made with slightly thicker pastry than that for an open tart. For covering a 1.2 litre (2 pint) oval dish, you will need shortcrust pastry made with 300g (10oz) flour, 200g (7oz) butter, 1 teaspoon salt and 2-3 tablespoons well-chilled water (page 246). Using a pie funnel prevents the pastry from falling in on to the fruit filling.

Spoon about 1kg (2lb) stewed fruit or 1–1.2kg (2–2½lb) fruit filling, sugar and any flavouring, such as spices, around the funnel.

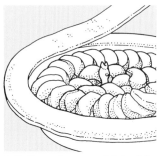

1 *Roll out about one eighth of the pastry into a strip as wide as the rim and long enough to go right round the edge of the pie dish. Carefully lay the strip in position all along the rim of the dish, pressing the edges with your fingers to seal them together.*

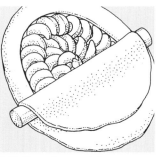

2 *Roll out the remaining pastry to cover the pie dish. Brush the pastry strip with water, then lay the large piece of pastry on top, using a rolling pin so it doesn't stretch. Cut a small hole for the funnel. Press the edges to seal. Chill for 20 minutes.*

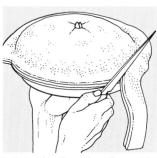

3 *Trim the edges, then glaze with milk or egg yolk beaten with a little water. Bake at 200°C, 400°F, Gas Mark 6 for 20–30 minutes until the pastry is golden. If the filling is uncooked, continue baking at 160°C, 325°F, Gas Mark 3 for another 20 minutes.*

PLATE PIE

A plate pie is cooked on a shallow metal, enamel or china plate. For a 20cm (8in) pie to serve 4–6 use pastry made from 375g (12oz) plain flour, 3 tablespoons caster sugar and 250g (8oz) butter. Make it by the rubbing-in technique (page 244), then stir in the sugar and bind it with 1 beaten egg plus a little well-chilled water, if needed. As well as helping to make the pastry short, the egg adds richness and flavour.

The filling should never be soggy – a thick mixture of precooked or stewed fruit sweetened to taste is the most successful. Gooseberries, apricots and blackcurrants make three good fillings. You will need about 500g (1lb) of fruit filling.

1 *Roll out a little over half the pastry and use to line the plate. Add the filling, mounding up well. Roll out the remaining pastry to cover the pie, moistening the edges, press to seal and decorate the edge with fork prongs (page 245). Chill for 20 minutes.*

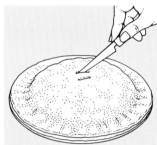

2 *Pierce 2 holes in the pastry to let steam escape. Glaze with milk and place on a preheated baking sheet. Bake in a preheated oven, 200°C, 400°F, Gas Mark 6 for 45–60 minutes. If browning too quickly cover it loosely with foil after the first 30 minutes.*

UPSIDE-DOWN PUDDING CAKE

For a 20–23cm (8–9in) pudding cake to serve 6–8 you will need about 500g (1lb) fruit. You can use almost any fairly firm fruit such as peaches, pears or apples. Make the sponge cake mixture for the pudding using 175g (6oz) plain flour, 1 teaspoon baking powder, 175g (6oz) butter, 3 eggs and a little milk (page 264). Prepare a fluted ovenproof dish by spreading it generously – especially the bottom – with 50g (2oz) butter, then sprinkling evenly with 50g (2oz) caster sugar. Pudding cakes are best served warm with pouring cream.

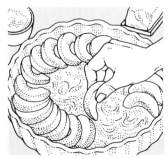

1 *Prepare and slice the fruit thinly, then arrange it in overlapping slices in the base of the prepared dish. Spoon the sponge mixture on top.*

2 *Bake in a preheated oven, 180°C, 350°F, Gas Mark 4 for about 50 minutes until well risen. Invert the pudding cake on to a serving plate.*

FLAVOURING TARTS, PIES AND PUDDING CAKES

• I use dessert rather than cooking apples for both apple pies and tarts, as dessert apples hold their shape better and have a fuller flavour. For an open tart or plate pie fry peeled apple slices in butter until soft, adding sugar and spices if liked and a little lemon juice which will form a caramel-flavoured sauce around the apples.

• Remember that plums and berries produce much juice during cooking so it is a good idea to precook them with sugar but no extra liquid and evaporate some of the juice by bubbling down until it is syrupy and strongly flavoured.

• Spices often enhance a fruit pie. Apples and pears take well to cinnamon, cloves or nutmeg.

• In the summer, chopped fresh mint goes well with all soft fruit pie fillings.

• To vary the flavour of a pudding cake add a little soft brown sugar or honey to the sponge mixture or replace some of the flour with ground nuts, such as ground almonds.

• Upside-down tarts are similar to upside-down cakes, but use shortcrust (page 246) or puff pastry or sweet hot butter crust pastry (page 249) instead of a cake mixture. They look so beautiful with glossy fruit on a crisp caramelized base. Brush the pastry with water and caster sugar just before baking. It is important to remember that after cooking the pastry you should reduce the oven temperature to 160°C, 325°F, Gas Mark 3 for the last 30 minutes or so so that the fruit is mellow-tasting and soft enough.

• For upside-down apple cakes and tarts I don't peel the thin slices of apple – the coloured border of skin both looks and tastes better.

This Caramelized Orange Tart (page 238) is cooked upside down so that the pastry is extra crisp and the thin seedless orange slices, honey, butter and cinnamon combine to make a wonderful caramel filling.

FRESH *and* DRIED FRUIT SALADS

Fruit is beautiful to look at, wonderful to taste, simple to serve and good for you. With modern methods of cold storage and swift refrigeration, fruit from all over the world is now available at any time of year. But despite the choice all year round, seasonal fruit still holds a special charm and attraction.

When choosing fruit, inspect it very carefully. Colours should be bright, even sparkling; the skins taut but the fruit slightly soft to the touch, and a light aromatic smell should be noticeable. Hard fruit which has to ripen further at home should be arranged at room temperature on a dry surface and not touching each other.

Ever since I first tasted 'apricot leather' – a sheet of compressed dried apricot purée – in the Middle East as a young child, dried fruit has been one of my passions. It is altogether different from fresh fruit. Stewed with a little water, brown sugar and lemon juice, dried fruits such as prunes or apricots make a lovely simple pudding with cream or custard, or they can be made into full-flavoured fruit fools, ice creams, purées and sauces as well as fillings for tarts and pies. They are also good in many spiced savoury dishes.

Fruit salads can be made with either fresh or dried fruits or a mixture of both. Always think of a combination of colour and texture as well as taste when composing a fruit salad. I like to make an orange- and lemon-flavoured fruit juice syrup for fruit salad instead of just sprinkling the fruit with sugar. Soft fruits are nearly always a marvellous ingredient but I think that apples are far better kept to eat whole or to cook in other puddings.

PREPARING FRESH FRUIT

Many fruits need no more preparation than just rinsing in cold water, though apples and pears may need a good scrub. Soft fruits deteriorate very quickly after contact with water, so they should not be rinsed.

Many fruits such as apples, pears, quinces and peaches swiftly discolour when cut and exposed to the air but you can prevent this by rubbing the cut surfaces with lemon juice or put the pieces into a bowl of water with lemon juice added to it, or in a light sugar syrup (page 208).

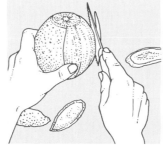

Peeling an orange *One of the simplest ways is to cut off the very top and bottom of the fruit, then cut off the skin and pith carefully in vertical strips, using a small serrated knife. Trim off any of the remaining bitter white pith and discard.*

Segmenting an orange *Slice down between the membrane and flesh on either side of a segment with a sharp knife, working over a plate or bowl to catch the juices. Repeat on the other side and pull away the segment. Continue with the remaining segments.*

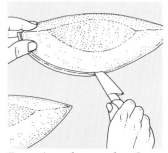

Preparing a large melon *Cut the melon in half lengthwise and scrape out the seeds. Cut each half into wedge-shaped slices. Loosen the flesh from the skin with a knife, then cut the flesh into pieces. Or use a melon baller to scoop out the flesh into balls.*

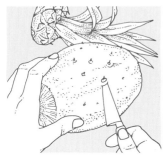

Peeling a pineapple *Cut off the crown and base, then hold the pineapple firmly upright on a chopping board and cut off the peel in vertical strips. Poke out the remaining eyes with the tip of a sharp knife. Cut across into slices or chunks, cutting out the central core.*

Preparing a mango: **1** *Cut through the mango horizontally as close as possible to the stone on each side. Peel the centre section containing the stone and cut the flesh away from around the stone as neatly as possible. Cut the flesh into pieces or cubes as required.*

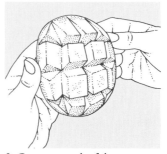

2 *Cut across each of the remaining side sections of the mango in a chequer pattern, cutting down as far as the peel but without piercing it. Then push up the skin from the centre base so that the cubes of flesh are exposed. Cut them away from the peel with a sharp knife.*

Stoning fruit *Using a small sharp knife cut along the groove in the fruit through the flesh to the stone, then use both hands and give a sharp twist to each half of the fruit to loosen the stone. If the flesh still clings to the stone use a teaspoon to lever out the stone and discard.*

FRESH FRUIT SALAD

Some of the fruit salads I had as a child put me off for many years. Over-sweet and with dull combinations of fruit, including the inevitable canned cherries, they gave no hint of how inspired a fruit salad can be. Think of the colour of the fruit and how the flavours will complement each other. I usually use syrup made from freshly strained orange juice sharpened with strained lemon juice and mixed with a dash of liqueur (page 209). Allow about 300ml (½ pint) syrup for about 1kg (2lb) fruit. Except when soaking fruits in wine or in liqueur beforehand, it is best to make up fruit salads only shortly before serving.

A colourful fresh fruit salad made with nectarines, raspberries and bilberries. A fresh orange juice syrup gives an extra gloss to the fruit and prevents discoloration.

1 *Wash and dry any firm fruit not being peeled. Prepare the fruit, by hulling berries and slicing or cutting larger fruit into chunks. Apples and pears discolour very quickly so it is best to leave their preparation until last.*

2 *Gently mix the pieces of fruit together in a bowl and sprinkle with lemon juice or liqueur, and caster sugar to taste if not adding syrup later. Cover the bowl tightly with clingfilm without touching any fruit and chill in the refrigerator.*

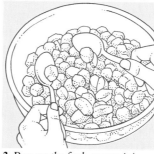

3 *Prepare the fresh orange juice syrup mixture (page 209) and chill well. Shortly before serving, pour the chilled syrup over the fruit and gently toss to coat all the pieces of fruit thoroughly. Serve in a pretty glass bowl to show off all the fresh fruit colours.*

DRIED FRUIT SALAD

A dried fruit salad is not so much a salad as stewed fruit. Presoak the fruit if necessary so that it softens. Place fruit and liquid together in a saucepan and cook gently on top of the stove for about 20–30 minutes until soft and plump. Strain off the juices and reduce them in a small saucepan. Put the fruit in a bowl, pour over the reduced glaze and mix, then chill before serving.

USING FRESH AND DRIED FRUIT SALADS

• Fresh fruit can make the easiest but often the most welcome end to a meal. If you are serving a selection of whole fruit it simply has to be well washed and arranged prettily in a bowl or a serving platter.
• Classic fruit combinations include peaches or nectarines with redcurrants, melon and strawberries with orange juice or orange segments, and redcurrants with raspberries.
• Prunes and apricots make a good combination for a dried fruit salad.

• Mixtures of soft fruit can be excellent simply sprinkled with lemon juice and caster sugar and chilled briefly before serving.
• When in season the juice of blood oranges makes a beautiful fruit-juice syrup (page 209) to use for fresh fruit salads.
• Wine or fruit liqueurs are often used to steep fruit in, so that the fruit absorbs the flavour before the fruit salad is assembled. The steeping liquid can be reduced and made into a thin syrup.
• Whipped cream mixed with liquid yogurt, smetana or soured

cream is an excellent low-fat alternative to pouring cream for serving with fruit salads.
• A smooth fruit purée or coulis (page 208) of raspberries, blackcurrants or other soft fruits can be lovely for serving with fruit salads, too.
• For a mango salad sprinkle the slices or cubes of fruit with lemon juice, and then make a coconut cream dressing by dissolving a chunk of creamed coconut in warmed single cream with a pinch of salt and sugar to taste. Chill before using.

• A mixed citrus salad is nice with slivers of caramelized rind and a clear honey dressing.
• My favourite fruit salad is a generous mixture of soft berries: fresh raspberries, redcurrants and other berries combined with blackcurrants which have been sweated in a saucepan with caster sugar to bring out their juices and then cooled.
• Garnishes for fruit salads can include slivers of nuts, strips of fresh mint leaves, grated fresh coconut and raisins or sultanas soaked in wine or liqueur.

FRUIT PUDDINGS *and* JELLIES

Stewed and poached fruit can be cooked either on top of the stove or in a covered dish in the oven. Stewed fruit, cooked over a higher heat and stirred while cooking, becomes soft and mushy. Poached fruit is lowered into a flavoured sugar syrup and cooked gently until just soft enough to pierce through easily with a knife while still holding a perfect shape. Fruit can also be sautéed in butter and eaten warm: the sugary juices become caramelized and the flavour of the fruit is enriched by the butter.

Fruit fools, one of the simplest puddings of all time, are usually made by adding cooled puréed stewed fruit to whipped cream. Low-fat alternatives to cream include creamed smetana, natural yogurt, crème fraîche and fromage frais. Egg custard can be used, too. Fruit purée is also good served with double cream simply poured over it.

Finally don't forget fresh fruit jellies and terrines. Cool and refreshing, they make a simple but impressive end to a meal when made in a decorative mould.

STEWING FRUIT

Stewing is a simple technique of softening fruit so it can be made into a smooth purée, used as a pie filling or simply eaten with just plain cream or thick Greek yogurt. Stewed fruit purées are so versatile as they can be served on their own or slightly sweetened to make a 'natural' sauce for other fruit, or combined with whipped cream to make a fruit fool.

Only very hard fruits such as under-ripe pears, apples or plums need much liquid for stewing. Most ripe fruits contain enough juice to cook in the syrup formed by added sugar dissolved in their own juices. A little lemon juice added with the sugar sharpens the taste, and you can use honey instead of sugar.

Apricots are the best dried fruits to stew: soak and simmer gently in just enough orange and lemon juices sweetened with brown or white sugar to half cover the apricots.

Put the fruit for stewing into a saucepan with sugar and little or no liquid. Stir over the heat until the sugar has dissolved, then cover and simmer until the fruit is soft and mushy.

POACHING FRUIT

Poached fruit is cooked very gently in a light syrup (page 208) so it still holds its shape. It can be eaten hot or cold, with or without its syrup and makes a simple but elegant pudding. Firm fruit such as pears, apples and plums hold their shape best when poached, but with juicy fruits you can use a heavier sugar syrup which delays the moment when they begin to collapse. Lemon juice added after cooking counteracts the sweetness.

1 *Place a single layer of sliced or whole peeled fruit carefully in a wide saucepan of hot syrup. Make sure that the fruit is fully covered by the syrup.*

2 *Cover and poach very gently until the fruit is just soft when pierced with a small knife. Remove from the heat, cover and leave for several minutes.*

MAKING A FRUIT PURÉE

For the smoothest purée, whizz the stewed fruit in a food processor, then push through a fine nylon sieve using the back of a ladle. Or you can simply use either the sieve or processor alone for a slightly less smooth result.

For a fruit fool, whip double cream until it forms soft peaks and is about the same consistency as the purée, then gently fold the same amount of stewed or puréed fruit into the cream. Chill well before serving.

MAKING EXTRA-SPECIAL FRUIT PUDDINGS

• Fools are nicest when they have a little texture, so I tend to use very mushy stewed fruit for fools without puréeing it. Smooth purées are better for sorbets and ice creams, or for a fruit coulis sauce (page 208) to accompany fresh fruit.

• If making a fool from strong-coloured fruits such as blackcurrants you can achieve a marbled effect by mixing in the whipped cream only very roughly in swirls.

• Gooseberries or apricots stewed with elderflowers take on a scented muscatel flavour and make irresistible fools. If you have some muscat wine, such as Beaumes-de-Venise, add a little to the gooseberry purée before combining it with the whipped cream.

• Decorate fools with strips of fresh mint leaves, feathery fennel and dill leaves, curls of plain chocolate or toasted, flaked or chopped nuts.

• Flavour syrups for poaching fruit with fruit juice or wine and whole spices such as mace, cinnamon, black peppercorns and cloves if appropriate.

• A simple compôte of poached fruit can seem more sophisticated if the syrup contains an interesting liqueur. Experiment with what you have at home. Stir it at the end of the cooking for the strongest flavour.

• As well as using fruit juices, you can also make fruit jellies with sweetened wine or lemon juice or with the cooled juices of stewed fruits.

• Fresh pineapple and kiwi fruit contain an enzyme which destroys the setting power of gelatine. If you want to use fresh pineapple juice in a jelly you must boil it for 3 minutes.

MAKING FRUIT JELLIES

Fruit jellies are usually made with powdered gelatine which comes in sachets: 1 sachet, equivalent to 3 teaspoons or 1 tablespoon, will normally set 600ml (1 pint) liquid, except in very hot weather when you will need a little extra gelatine. You should also use a little more gelatine for a firmer set when you have a tall or complicated mould. Vegetarians can set jellies with agar-agar instead of gelatine, using the same quantity. A jelly made from 600ml (1 pint) fresh fruit juice serves 4–6.

1 *Put 300ml (½ pint) fresh fruit juice in a saucepan with 50g (2oz) caster sugar and warm gently to dissolve the sugar. Sprinkle 1 sachet powdered gelatine on to the liquid and stir until dissolved. Do not allow to boil or the gelatine will not work.*

2 *Pour the warm liquid into a measuring jug containing another 300ml (½ pint) cold fruit juice and stir thoroughly to mix before pouring into a jelly mould. Cool completely, then chill in the refrigerator for several hours until the jelly is firmly set.*

3 *To turn out, gently loosen the edges by pulling them back with your fingers. Dip the mould into a bowl of hot water for just 1–2 seconds. Place a wet serving plate on top, then holding firmly with both hands, invert the mould and give a strong shake.*

MAKING A FRUIT TERRINE

Gleaming fruit terrines are easy to make, especially when the fruit is added randomly. To make one with set layers of fruit you must allow the jelly to set between each layer. Using slightly sweet hock instead of fruit juice makes a crystal clear, delicious jelly.

To serve 6–8 use 600ml (1 pint) fruit juice such as freshly squeezed orange juice sweetened with 2 tablespoons clear honey and a selection of prepared fruits such as redcurrants, the segments of 6 oranges and about 500g (1lb) fresh raspberries.

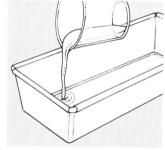

1 *Make up 600ml (1 pint) fruit juice jelly with 1 sachet powdered gelatine (above), and pour a small amount into a 1kg (2lb) loaf tin or ring mould to coat the base. Chill for about 15 minutes until set. Do not chill the leftover jelly.*

2 *Add the prepared fruit in random layers, pressing down well as you go, then slowly pour in the remaining jelly in a slow trickle until the tin is full. As you pour tap the tin on the base so the jelly works its way down round all the pieces of fruit.*

3 *Chill until well set. Unmould by loosening the edges, pulling them back with your fingers. Dip the tin in a bowl of hot water for 1–2 seconds only, then invert on a wet serving plate and give a strong shake. Reposition the jelly if you want. Slice to serve.*

This glistening fresh fruit terrine uses slices of orange, seedless grapes and raspberries to make a decorative pudding. To set the fruit, a jelly was made from hock, coloured with raspberry cordial. Like all fruit terrines, it can be served with cream or a fruit purée.

MERINGUES

The sculptural, overblown and fragile appearance of meringues never fails to thrill and they are an easy way to impress. Simple, old-fashioned meringues baked slowly at a very low heat until the edges turn slightly brown always bring me nostalgic memories of childhood.

Meringue can be used to great effect as a topping for old-fashioned jam and custard puddings, for lemon meringue pie and other tarts, or to transform a plain dish of stewed fruits (page 224). Pudding cakes (page 221) can be made using meringue discs instead of sponge cake or pastry. A meringue topping is cooked at a high heat more quickly than individual-shaped meringues so it is soft and frothy inside. The peaks or swirls with sugar sprinkled on at the last moment on top are attractively browned and give a sparkling effect.

Like other apparently tricky culinary techniques, making meringues successfully is really quite straightforward. There are three basic methods, Swiss meringue being the easiest, but Italian meringue is the most stable and useful. I use Italian meringue to make ice cream (page 234).

SWISS MERINGUE

Swiss meringue is used for making simple shells or for topping a pie. A balloon whisk and copper whisking bowl will produce the most voluminous egg whites of the lightest and finest texture (page 77), however an electric beater works quite well. Be careful not to overwhisk the egg whites or else the meringue might 'weep' during baking. Any trace of yolk in the egg whites will prevent the whites from forming stiff peaks.

Two egg whites will make 12–16 shells or will top a 20cm (8in) pie.

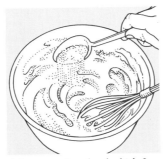

1 *In a very clean bowl whisk 2 egg whites until they hold their shape and form a slightly floppy point. Whisk in 2 tablespoons caster or vanilla sugar (page 235), whisking until the meringue is smooth and glossy. With a large metal spoon gently fold in 75g (3oz) more sugar.*

2 *To top a pie, spread the mixture over a cooled, baked tart, being careful to leave no gaps. Use a palette knife to make decorative peaks. Bake in a preheated oven, 160°C, 325°F, Gas Mark 3 for 20 minutes or until lightly tinged. Serve warm or at room temperature.*

COOKED MERINGUE

Also known as meringue cuite this type is used for making petits fours, discs and meringue baskets, as well as for topping pies. Although difficult to work, its main advantage is that it keeps in the refrigerator, covered, for up to 1 week before using.

Put 2 egg whites *and 125g (4oz) icing sugar in a heatproof bowl set over a pan of simmering water and beat until the mixture forms a very stiff meringue. Remove from the heat and continue beating the meringue for a further 10–15 minutes until cool. These quantities make enough to cover one large pie.*

A sumptuous Raspberry and Chocolate Meringue Cake (page 240). Light meringue rounds flecked with toasted hazelnuts are sandwiched with raspberries, cream and a rich chocolate filling. Cocoa powder and caster sugar are sifted on top as a final decoration.

ITALIAN MERINGUE

Similar to American cake frosting, Italian meringue is most often used for topping puddings and for piping. Boiling sugar syrup is poured on to whisked egg whites, which, as a result, are partially cooked, making the mixture more stable and versatile than Swiss meringue.

This meringue holds its foam for a few hours before use or baking, which is why it is excellent for piping into shapes or making into baskets or discs. Italian meringue also forms the basis of some of the lightest and most successful ice creams (page 234).

To make the sugar syrup (page 208), use 250g (8oz) granulated sugar and 125ml (4fl oz) water.

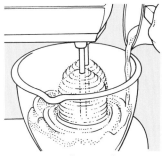

Beat 3 egg whites with ½ teaspoon salt in a clean bowl until stiff and glossy. (For ease, use an electric mixer but not a food processor.) Pour the boiling sugar syrup on to the egg whites in a steady, thin stream, beating constantly until the mixture is smooth, very stiff and glossy. Allow the meringue to cool before using. These quantities are enough to make two 23cm (9in) discs or baskets.

Piping decorative meringue fingers and stars. Use plain or fluted nozzles and allow a little space between the shapes for expansion.

SHAPING AND FLAVOURING MERINGUES

- Use Swiss meringue for making individual shapes, and Italian or cooked meringue for making pavlovas, baskets or discs for meringue cakes.
- Homemade meringue shells sandwiched with cream make a delicious tea-time treat.
- You can vary meringues and meringue toppings for pies, tarts and stewed fruit by adding toasted flaked or chopped nuts, grated fresh coconut, citrus fruit rind or grated chocolate.
- Coarsely grated chocolate or chopped pieces can either be incorporated in the meringue mixture or sprinkled on top – the chocolate melts lusciously into the meringue as it cooks.
- Add cocoa powder to a meringue mixture and then grate chocolate on top for all-chocolate meringues.
- Extra caster sugar sprinkled over a meringue topping will make it colour attractively and glisten. Demerara sugar or coffee sugar crystals are especially effective as they remain crunchy.
- As a topping for a large mince pie or an apple tart add ground mixed spice or cinnamon to the meringue mixture. You can also fold in a handful of currants and candied peel.
- When filling a meringue case do so only very shortly before you want to eat, and if possible spoon a layer of whipped cream, cream cheese or pastry cream on to the meringue before adding the fruit to prevent the juices soaking into the meringue and softening it.
- To make one of my favourite puddings, *oeufs à la neige* or floating islands, poach blobs of meringue mixture in simmering water, then chill and serve on a sea of cold vanilla egg custard made with the egg yolks (page 210).
- A meringue mixture incorporating ground nuts can make the lightest pudding cake to sandwich with cream or with a vanilla or lemon custard made from the egg yolks (page 210).
- Two circles of meringue sandwiched with fresh soft fruit and whipped cream or lemon curd (page 302) makes a spectacular summer pudding.
- Meringue can also be used to add a contrast of texture to smooth dishes. You can crumble a crisp meringue and fold it into a smooth ice cream before freezing.

SHAPING AND COOKING MERINGUE

Before shaping meringues prepare a baking sheet with baking parchment or greased greaseproof paper.

To cook meringue shapes bake at the lowest oven setting, 110°C, 225°F, Gas Mark ¼ for 2½–3 hours until the meringue dries out and peels off the paper easily. If the meringue sticks to the paper after baking it hasn't been baked enough. Cool on a wire rack to crisp up.

***To make shells** gently mould the mixture by shaping between 2 dessertspoons and place on a prepared baking sheet.*

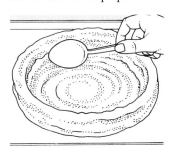

***To make a pavlova** or basket shape, pile a mound of Italian or cooked meringue on a prepared baking sheet. Use the back of a large spoon to form a rim around the edge of the basket.*

***To make a meringue disc** draw a circle on paper on a baking sheet. Use a piping bag fitted with a plain nozzle and pipe the meringue in coils in a continuous circle, beginning in the centre.*

SWEET SOUFFLÉS *and* MOUSSES

The experience of chilled cream poured over a light, steaming hot sweet soufflé is heavenly. You can make a hot soufflé with fruit purée, melted chocolate or lemon, orange or other strong-tasting fruit juices blended with flour and milk to make a sauce base just as you do when making a savoury soufflé (page 76).

Because of the large quantity of bland egg whites in hot sweet soufflés, and egg whites and cream in chilled soufflés and mousses, use flavourings strong enough not to get lost. Puréed and stewed apricots, for example, are excellent base flavourings. Lightly cooked fresh blackcurrants are one of the strongest tasting fruits to use in a soufflé, and gooseberries are one of my favourite tastes.

Chilled soufflés are, in fact, not really soufflés but actually mousses with plenty of whisked egg whites incorporated into them then set with gelatine. They are called soufflés because of their high soufflé-like appearance, the result of the mousse mixture being spooned into a soufflé dish with a foil or greaseproof paper collar rising above the rim. When the collar is removed after chilling the pudding has the appearance of a dramatically risen soufflé.

Chilled mousses can be flavoured with fruit, fruit juices, liqueurs or chocolate. They are richer than chilled soufflés because they contain more egg yolks than whites and have a more velvety texture. They are not necessarily set with gelatine, unlike chilled soufflés.

HOT SWEET SOUFFLÉ

Hot Lemon and Passion Fruit Soufflé (page 238) here made as individual soufflés. The dark golden tops, dramatically speckled with the black fruit pips, are lightly dusted with icing sugar just before serving.

A hot sweet soufflé is made on the same principle as a savoury soufflé (page 76), with a sweetened white sauce base to which you add the egg yolks and your chosen flavouring. The desired consistency is like a thick custard but not so thick that all the air will be knocked out of the egg whites when they are folded in. If you are using a fruit purée or fairly liquid mushy fruit as flavouring, you will need to add less milk when making the sauce base than if you are making a savoury soufflé. The base of a hot sweet soufflé can be prepared well ahead, leaving only the whisking and folding in of the egg whites to do just before cooking the soufflé.

This Grand Marnier soufflé is a classic pudding. To serve 3–4 make a white sauce from 50g (2oz) butter, 40g (1½oz) plain flour, 2 teaspoons grated orange rind and 200ml (7fl oz) milk (page 196). You also need 4 separated eggs and 1 egg white.

Stir 3–4 tablespoons Grand Marnier into the sauce, then beat in the egg yolks thoroughly. Whisk the egg whites until they stand in soft peaks and fold into the soufflé mixture. Spoon into a buttered 1.5 litre (2½ pint) soufflé dish that has been coated with sugar or ground almonds. Cook in a preheated oven, 190°C, 375°F, Gas Mark 5 for about 25 minutes until well risen but still slightly wobbly. Dust the top of the soufflé with a little icing sugar and serve at once.

IDEAS FOR SOUFFLÉS AND MOUSSES

• Puréed exotic fruits such as mangoes (with added lemon juice) and passion fruit also make a good base for soufflés and mousses (see Hot Lemon and Passion Fruit Soufflé page 238).
• Of all the soft summer fruits, raspberries and strawberries can be crushed or puréed and sieved with a little lemon juice to bring out their flavours. Redcurrants make a nice addition to raspberries. Toss both fruits briefly with caster sugar over the heat in a saucepan until the sugar just dissolves and the juices start to run. Then purée and sieve the fruit to use as the base in mousses and soufflés.
• For chocolate mousses or chilled soufflés the chocolate tastes at its most dark and luxurious if it is melted with a little strong black coffee.
• Adding a liqueur, rum or brandy to a fruit purée makes the resulting soufflé or mousse taste more sophisticated. An apple purée made with lemon juice to keep the apples white, and flavoured with Calvados is excellent in a cold soufflé. Or, use Curaçao for an orange soufflé decorated with caramelized orange rind, or instead of rum or brandy in a chocolate mousse.
• Decorate the chilled lemon soufflé (opposite) with chocolate curls (page 231), an edging of crystallized violets, or prettiest of all, fresh violets, primroses or rose petals.
• The chilled lemon soufflé (opposite) can be set in a jagged-edge chocolate bowl (page 231) instead of using a soufflé dish.
• Caramelized nuts for decorating chilled soufflés and other puddings are easy to do; simply rinse the slivered, chopped or whole nuts to dampen, stir them in some caster sugar to coat and toss in a very hot dry pan for 1–2 minutes until they caramelize. Turn them at once on to baking parchment and separate them as much as possible before the caramel hardens.

CHOCOLATE MOUSSE

Chocolate never goes out of fashion; a chocolate mousse is always popular, and rightly so. Serve it well chilled in pretty glasses or individual ramekin dishes or little pots.

Chocolate mousse is usually piped with whipped cream but I prefer a sharper mixture of whipped cream and yogurt, which I spoon smoothly over the top of each serving. For decoration add glazed orange rind or grated chocolate.

To make 4–6 mousses use 175g (6oz) plain chocolate and 4 eggs, separated.

1 *Break the chocolate into a heatproof bowl and add 2 tablespoons strong black coffee. Put the bowl over a saucepan of gently simmering water and stir with a wooden spoon until the chocolate is melted.*

2 *Remove the bowl from the heat and beat in the 4 egg yolks followed by 1 tablespoon soft butter and ½ tablespoon rum or brandy. Whisk the egg whites with a pinch of salt until they stand in soft peaks.*

3 *Fold the egg whites quickly but thoroughly into the chocolate mixture with a large metal spoon. Spoon the mixture into ramekin dishes or small glasses and chill for at least 4 hours or overnight before decorating.*

CHILLED LEMON SOUFFLÉ

This light and refreshing pudding looks very dramatic rising well up above the edge of the dish. This was the first pudding I ever made; it seemed like a miracle to me then, and I still think it is excellent and refreshing. If you like a particularly sharp lemon taste, as I do, dissolve the gelatine in extra lemon juice instead of the water. To serve 4–6 use 4 large eggs (size 1–2), separated, 125g (4oz) caster sugar, the finely grated rind and juice of 3 lemons and 150ml (¼ pint) double or whipping cream. Use a lightly buttered 900ml (1½ pint) soufflé dish.

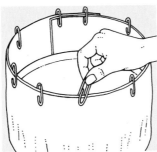

1 *Cut a strip of foil or greaseproof paper which when folded in half lengthwise is twice the depth of the dish and will fit round the sides with an overlap. Oil one side of the folded foil or paper, then mould it round the outside of the dish, cut edges uppermost. Secure with paper clips or tie with kitchen string.*

A rich chocolate mousse always makes an attractive pudding. Served here in individual glasses, the mousse is decorated with thick Greek yogurt and curls of glazed orange rind.

2 *Put a heatproof bowl over a saucepan of simmering water. Add the egg yolks and sugar and mix well. Add the lemon rind and juice and beat thoroughly until pale and thick enough to leave a trail on the surface.*

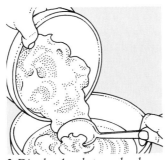

3 *Dissolve 1 sachet powdered gelatine completely in 3 tablespoons of hot water. Fold into the egg yolk mixture. Whip the cream until it holds soft peaks, then fold into the mixture with a large metal spoon.*

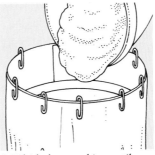

4 *Whisk the egg whites until fairly stiff, then fold in to the lemon and egg yolk mixture gently but evenly with a large metal spoon. Pour into the prepared soufflé dish and level the surface carefully with a spatula.*

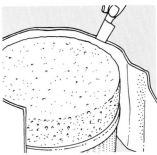

5 *Chill well for at least 4 hours. When set, remove the paper clips or string and run a palette knife dipped in hot water between the 2 layers of paper or foil. Carefully peel away from the mixture. Decorate before serving.*

USING CHOCOLATE

Chocolate makes the most popular puddings of all. Hot, cold, or frozen, any chocolate pudding is always welcome – as long as you have not stinted on a generous concentration of chocolate. Good-quality plain dark chocolate should be used in all chocolate cookery. The most important thing is that it should contain a high proportion of cocoa solids – at least 50 per cent. Milk chocolate can only be used for coating or decoration as it will not add enough flavour in baking and is too sweet for most recipes.

Unsweetened cocoa powder is the solid brown part of the cocoa bean with the cocoa butter removed. The darkest, most chocolaty cakes of all can be made with plenty of plain chocolate and a tablespoon or two of cocoa powder replacing some of the flour or ground nuts. In fact, chocolate can replace flour altogether – a hot chocolate soufflé is the only soufflé that doesn't need flour. For baking, cocoa powder added to chocolate intensifies both colour and taste but don't add it to melted chocolate to make a cake covering as it makes the chocolate grainy.

White chocolate has the consistency but not the taste of chocolate as it is made only with cocoa butter, milk and sugar. It can be used to make a good chilled mousse, set with gelatine, which you can serve with a dark chocolate sauce – but it is not easy to melt (except in a microwave) and use for coating.

MELTING CHOCOLATE

Melting chocolate can be tricky, even for experienced cooks. As the cocoa butter content varies so much with different kinds of chocolate, it is extremely difficult to gauge just how long it will take to melt. If left a moment too long, or if the heat is too fierce, the mixture can easily turn into a hard, dry lump. Usually the damage will have been done and the smooth glossy consistency lost but you can try to retrieve the situation by adding butter, milk, cream or water and beating it again.

To melt chocolate break it into small pieces. Put the pieces in a completely dry heatproof bowl and set over a pan one-third filled with hot, but not boiling, water. Do not let the bowl touch the water, or the chocolate will become lumpy. Leave, uncovered, for 6–12 minutes, stirring until the chocolate is completely melted and smooth.

Melting chocolate should be done very slowly and with a watchful eye or it may scorch.

MAKING THE MOST OF CHOCOLATE

• There are a few ingredients which complement chocolate particularly well and seem to bring out its flavour even more; strong black coffee and cinnamon are two of them. Ground cardamom is also extremely effective. Vanilla is another compatible flavour but ideally it should be vanilla from a vanilla pod or use vanilla sugar (page 235).

• Gooey chocolate cakes (page 273) are marvellous sandwiched together with soft fruit – raspberries are ideal. You can also make a fresh citrus curd (page 302) filling using orange or lemon juice.

• During the summer months complement a simple bowl of soft fruit with a jug of chocolate sauce (make this by melting plain chocolate with a little water and then stirring in soured or single cream). Pour over the fruit, or on to each plate before you arrange a serving of fruit on top.

• Chocolate flakes or grated chocolate can be incorporated into ice creams with dramatic results. Make a lemon or vanilla bombe (page 237) and fill the hollow in the centre with grated chocolate. Pack down and cover with extra ice cream and refreeze. When you spoon into the turned-out bombe the chocolate tumbles out.

• Chop chocolate into smallish pieces and add it to steamed puddings, as well as to lemon or orange cake mixtures – it will melt into the cake in a delicious way as it cooks.

• Sprinkle grated pieces of chocolate on to cakes as soon as they come out of the oven so the chocolate melts in a haphazard pattern on top.

• A smooth chocolate coating looks beautiful on a cake or poured over a moulded pudding. Before it has set you can decorate it further with chocolate curls (opposite).

• Melting 125g (4oz) chocolate with 15–25g (½–1oz) unsalted butter makes a good coating consistency for covering cakes. For a less rich coating substitute 2 tablespoons of soured cream, creamed smetana or natural yogurt for the butter.

• A good chocolate filling for a sponge cake can be made by melting chocolate and adding to butter whisked with a little icing sugar, then whisking in chopped toasted hazelnuts.

• Make a sauce of melted chocolate and water to serve with chilled lemon soufflé (page 229) instead of cream.

• If making an ice cream by the Italian meringue method (page 227), pour a thin stream of melted chocolate onto the mixture at different points before freezing to produce swirls of hard chocolate in the smooth ice cream.

• A thin layer of melted chocolate makes a delicious topping for a cheesecake.

CHOCOLATE DECORATIONS

Chocolate decorations are surprisingly easy to make and can transform almost any pudding or cake into a spectacular, professional-looking showpiece (see box opposite). A good-quality plain chocolate will produce excellent results.

Any leftover chocolate can be melted again and used in a sauce or cake filling or coating.

This jagged-edged chocolate bowl, filled with fresh strawberries, makes a simple but dramatic pudding.

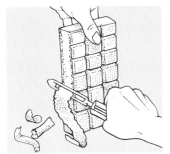

Making curls *Use a swivel-bladed vegetable peeler to shave off curls from the side of a block of well-chilled chocolate.*

Grating chocolate *Gently rub a lightly chilled bar of chocolate along the coarse edge of a standard vegetable grater.*

Coating fruit *Leaving the stalks on, wash and pat dry fruits such as strawberries, cherries and grapes. Dip each fruit halfway into a bowl of melted chocolate and leave to set on a tray lined with a sheet of baking parchment.*

Coating leaves *Brush melted chocolate on the shiny upper side of a clean leaf. Leave to dry on baking parchment, then peel the chocolate off the leaf, starting at the stem end. Rose and lily leaves work best.*

Making scrolls or caraque *Thinly spread melted chocolate as smoothly as possible on a clean flat surface and leave to set. Firmly push the edge of a pastry scraper away from you into the chocolate at a shallow angle and carefully scrape the chocolate off in long scrolls.*

Making shapes *Pour a 5mm (¼in) layer of melted chocolate on a baking sheet lined with baking parchment. Leave until set but still slightly soft. Carefully remove the chocolate slab and peel off the paper. Use biscuit cutters or a sharp-pointed knife to cut out a selection of shapes.*

MAKING A CHOCOLATE BOWL

This chocolate bowl began as an experiment but I now use it again and again as a container for fillings such as chilled soufflés, fruit mousses, fruit- or liqueur-flavoured ice creams or whipped cream incorporating soft fruits. I have even filled it with a fresh fruit jelly (page 225) – but wait for the jelly mixture to become cold before pouring it into the bowl.

Use either a bowl or a cake tin depending on the shape you want. To coat a fairly large deep bowl 200g (7oz) plain chocolate should be sufficient.

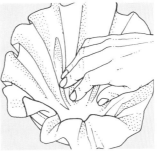

1 *Line a deep bowl with a large sheet of baking parchment, folding and pressing it down so it roughly fits the bowl. Bring the edges of the paper up above the bowl. Break the chocolate into a small bowl and add 1½ table-spoons water. Set over a pan of hot water until melted and stir in 25g (1oz) butter until smooth.*

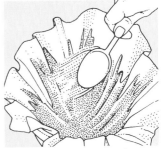

2 *Pour the chocolate into the lined bowl. Using the back of a spoon or spatula coat the base and sides thoroughly, drawing the chocolate around the top to give a jagged effect. Chill until firm. Holding the top of the paper lift out the chocolate bowl and gently unpeel the paper off the chocolate in strips.*

CHEESECAKES

I remember my mother telling me about the wonders of American cheesecake long before I ever tasted one. In those days the cheesecakes in England were the continental style, studded with raisins and cooked in an open pastry case. The dense, creamy richness of the cooked American cheesecake on its crunchy biscuit base is something quite different. Very different again is the uncooked cheesecake set with gelatine. This kind of cheesecake is lighter than a cooked cheesecake. It is served chilled and always on a biscuit base and, in my opinion, should be flavoured quite sharply with lemon, tasting best with a fruit topping.

What surprised me as a child was that cheesecakes do not really taste of cheese. Made with cream, curd, cottage or, indeed, any soft, bland white cheese which is then sweetened, mixed with eggs and often flavoured with lemon, the taste of cheesecake is more like a rich, eggy cream with a hint of sharpness. Cheesecakes are also much more like a tart than a cake: they do not rise like cakes, they are far more creamy and dense and they nearly always have either a base or a crust.

At one time cheesecakes were all the rage. Everyone made them, sometimes not terribly well, and they were an inevitable dinner party and buffet dish. As with quiches this may have resulted in a slight state of overkill. Now that there is such an enormous variety of soft white cheeses available, many far lighter and less rich than full-fat cream cheese, it is worth remembering how wonderful cheesecakes can be. For me, the best of all remains the cooked American type, chilled and served without a topping but with a bowl of soft fruit and perhaps a fruit coulis sauce (page 208).

CHEESECAKE BASES

Make cheesecake bases from either biscuit crumbs or pastry. The most important thing to remember with either is that they must never be thick and stodgy. I prefer the crunchiness of the biscuit base – it is also the easiest to make and can be varied according to the kind of biscuits you use: digestive, chocolate digestive or ginger biscuits, or a mixture of digestive biscuits and finely chopped walnuts are all good. Always use a loose-bottomed or springform tin (page 21).

For uncooked cheesecakes, bake biscuit bases blind (page 245) for 10 minutes at 180°C, 350°F, Gas Mark 4, then cool on a wire rack before filling. Otherwise, chill the biscuit base until firm before filling and baking.

Pastry is the traditional base for continental-style cheesecakes and can also be used with the cooked American-style cheesecake. Use either sweet shortcrust pastry (page 248) or sweet hot butter crust pastry (page 249) which is more biscuit-like than many pastries. Chill the pastry before using.

To make a biscuit base crush 175g (6oz) biscuit crumbs in a polythene bag. Mix with 50g (2oz) soft brown sugar and 75g (3oz) melted butter. Press over the base, and up the sides if you like, of a 23cm (9in) springform tin. Chill before filling.

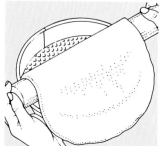

To make a pastry base roll out the pastry and use to line the base and sides of a buttered 23cm (9in) springform tin. Chill the pastry case for at least 20 minutes before filling with the cheesecake mixture and cooking.

FLAVOURING CHEESECAKES

• Although a cheesecake should taste rich and creamy you can, if you want, keep the fat content down by using one of the low-fat cheeses, the ultimate being virtually fat-free fromage frais. On the whole the creamier the cheese the smoother the texture will be.

• If you use egg yolks only in a cheesecake the texture will be richer and more creamy than if you use the yolks and whites.

• You can flavour cheesecakes with chocolate by adding cocoa to the cheese mixture for a cooked cheesecake or melted plain chocolate for an uncooked one. You can also ice the top with a layer of glossy melted chocolate mixed with a little soured cream.

• Incorporating a thick purée of fruit with the cheesecake mixture makes a fresh-flavoured cheesecake.

• Plain cheesecakes are greatly improved if you use vanilla sugar (page 235).

• Use soft muscovado sugar or honey to vary the taste of your cheesecakes.

• A wonderful cheesecake with the fragrance of muscatel and gooseberries can be made by folding about 2 tablespoons elderflowers into the mixture before cooking. Top with thick stewed gooseberries, also cooked with elderflowers.

• To give a chilled uncooked lemon cheesecake a more lemony flavour dissolve the gelatine in hot lemon juice instead of water. To top the cheesecake pour on a thin layer of strained lemon juice with added sugar and gelatine and leave to set.

• Ground spices such as cinnamon and nutmeg can be added to a biscuit or pastry base for extra flavour.

• One of my favourites for flavouring a cheesecake base, whether biscuit or pastry, is to add grated lemon or orange rind to the base mixture.

• Toppings can vary from the slightest whisper of icing sugar to an elaborate arrangement of glazed fruits. For glazing I used melted and strained apricot jam, redcurrant jelly or a jelly marmalade, according to the fruit I am using.

• Another way of topping cheesecakes is to arrange slices of uncooked fruit in a pattern on top of the mixture before chilling. You can also use apricots, blackcurrants or plums stewed to a thick jam-like consistency.

• Instead of fruit top a cheesecake with caramelized nuts (page 228), turning them straight from the pan on to the cheesecake so they stick together.

COOKED CHEESECAKE

There are two basic kinds of cooked cheesecake: the continental style and, my favourite, the American cooked type. To serve 6–8 use a 23cm (9in) springform cake tin with either a biscuit or pastry base which should be well chilled before filling.

You can use any kind of soft white cheese to make both kinds: the flavour will not be quite as rich and creamy with the low-fat cheeses but still very pleasant. Cottage cheese should be sieved before using. Quark, a low-fat skimmed mild soft cheese, also works well. Medium-fat Ricotta cheese is another traditional cheesecake ingredient. If you want to make a continental-style cheesecake, use the same amounts of curd cheese, sugar and eggs as below but omit the cream and fold in a handful of sultanas, then bake as below.

After baking, remove from the oven but leave the cake in the tin until completely cool, then using a knife to loosen the edges gently remove the base and sides (page 21). Dust the top with icing sugar just before serving. The higher you hold the sieve above the cheesecake the more delicate the layer of sugar.

UNCOOKED CHEESECAKE

This cheesecake is quite different in character from either of the cooked cheesecakes. It is set with gelatine and chilled so that it tastes more like a mousse. Use a 20cm (8in) springform tin with the bottom only lined with a biscuit base (opposite).

I think these cheesecakes are for summer eating and should be sharply flavoured with lemon and topped with fresh fruit which can be glazed or sprinkled with caster or icing sugar at the last moment. You can use cottage, curd or cream cheese. Fromage frais is also an excellent ingredient.

1 Beat together 375g (12oz) soft white cheese and 175g (6oz) caster sugar, then beat in the grated rind and juice of 1 lemon followed by 2 egg yolks. Fold in 1 sachet powdered gelatine dissolved in 4 tablespoons hot water or 4 tablespoons extra lemon juice, heated.

1 In a large bowl beat together 250g (8oz) each of cream cheese, curd cheese and caster sugar until soft and well combined, then whisk in 150ml (¼ pint) double cream and 4 beaten egg yolks thoroughly, a little at a time.

2 Whisk 2 egg whites with ½ teaspoon salt until they stand in soft peaks, then fold into the cheese and egg mixture gently but thoroughly. Pour the cheesecake mixture into the prepared tin, here a biscuit base.

2 In separate bowls whisk 150ml (¼ pint) double cream and 2 egg whites until they stand in soft peaks. Fold the cream into the cheese and yolk mixture, then fold in the egg whites.

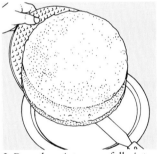

3 Pour the mixture carefully into the prepared tin over the biscuit base and chill for several hours or overnight. Remove from the tin carefully and transfer to a serving plate. Decorate with fresh fruit.

3 Bake in a preheated oven, 160°C, 325°F, Gas Mark 3 for about 1 hour until just firm, the top is golden and a skewer or tip of a knife inserted in the centre comes out clean. Turn off the heat and leave the cheesecake in the oven with the door slightly ajar for 30 minutes. Leave to cool completely on a wire rack, then carefully release the sides of the tin and transfer to a serving plate.

A rich and creamy baked American-style cheesecake with a crisp biscuit base.

SORBETS *and* ICE CREAMS

Homemade ice cream is well worth making – commercial ice creams can be excellent but they are never quite the same. In my experience ice creams and sorbets are also one of the most popular puddings of all, and they are not much trouble to make.

An ice cream maker, although creating the smoothest results, is not essential; the parfait-type ice creams (which is the method I use most) made with a base of Italian meringue (page 227) gives smooth results with no beating at all at mid-freezing point. Other ice creams and sorbets can be beaten very easily halfway through the freezing if you have a powerful electric beater or a food processor.

Sorbets and water ices are certainly the most refreshing of all puddings, which is why they are sometimes served in between courses at elaborate feasts. Sorbets consist of a sugar syrup and flavourings such as fruit juice or purée or a liqueur, sometimes with whisked egg white or an Italian meringue added halfway through to make them lighter and smoother. Savoury sorbets can also be served as a first course. A granita is a juice or alcohol-flavoured sorbet mixture which is mashed with a fork when it is almost frozen to give it the consistency of crystallized snow.

With both ice cream- and sorbet-making remember a few key facts. Flavours are subdued by freezing so your original unfrozen mixture should be extra-strong tasting. Sugar and alcohol both inhibit the freezing process so mixtures with a lot of sugar and alcohol in them will be far softer. On the other hand, ice cream and sorbet mixtures with liquid ingredients such as watery fruit purées freeze harder and tend to crystallize.

BASIC FRUIT SORBET

Blackcurrants make a delicious fruit sorbet because of their strength of flavour. Use this method here for other flavoured sorbets. Raspberries or strawberries won't need cooking, only mashing.

To make a blackcurrant sorbet for 6, you will need 250g (8oz) sugar, 300ml (½ pint) water, sieved purée made from 500g (1lb) blackcurrants and 2 egg whites. Stir the fruit in a pan over a gentle heat with just a little caster sugar until the juices run, then purée.

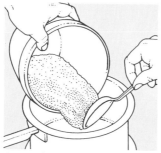

1 *Dissolve the sugar in the water in a small saucepan over a low heat, then increase the heat and boil rapidly for 3–4 minutes without stirring. Stir the fruit purée into the sugar syrup and then set aside to cool.*

2 *Spoon the cold syrup and fruit purée mixture into a shallow freezerproof container and freeze for 1–2 hours until the sorbet mixture is mushy. Then whisk the egg whites until they stand in soft peaks.*

3 *Turn the frozen mixture into a bowl and beat until softened, then fold in the egg whites. Return to the container and freeze. Transfer to the refrigerator for about 15 minutes before serving to soften the sorbet slightly.*

MAKING GRANITA

A granita or water ice is an Italian invention and makes a refreshing finish to a rich meal. Granitas are simple to make as they are only made from sugar, water and a flavouring. To serve 6 you will need 250g (8oz) granulated or caster sugar, 600ml (1 pint) water and 600ml (1 pint) freshly squeezed fruit juice.

To make, dissolve the sugar in the water over a low heat and then increase the heat and boil briskly for 5 minutes without stirring. Remove from the heat and set aside to cool.

Stir in the fruit juice, then transfer to a shallow freezerproof container and freeze until almost frozen. Stir through lightly with a fork and return to the freezer. When firm, granular and not too solid, spoon into tall glasses and serve.

Fruit sorbets make a refreshing pudding and because of their softness are usually served in individual glasses. From the top: mango, lemon and orange sorbets.

MY FAVOURITE ICE CREAM

This Italian meringue method makes a light and smooth parfait-type ice cream which needs no beating halfway through the freezing. Unless you have used a large quantity of fruit purée (thus adding a lot more water) the ice cream will be soft enough to spoon straight from the freezer. If the ice cream seems too hard to scoop, transfer it to the refrigerator for 15–30 minutes before serving.

To serve 6–8, you will need 2 egg whites (size 1–2), a pinch of salt, 175g (6oz) caster sugar, 6 tablespoons water and 300ml (½ pint) whipping cream and flavouring such as 125–175g (4–6oz) melted chocolate, 3–4 tablespoons well-sweetened thick fruit purée to taste or 2–5 tablespoons liqueur, again to taste. The exact amount depends on how liquid the flavouring is. For a toffee-like flavour use demerara instead of caster sugar.

Chocolate Peppermint Cream Ice (page 239) is flavoured with peppermint essence and pieces of chocolate peppermint creams.

1 *Make an Italian meringue with the egg whites, salt, sugar and water (page 227). Continue beating for about 2 minutes until the mixture is cool and thick. Fold the flavouring of your choice into the mixture.*

2 *Whip the cream until it is thick but not too stiff, then quickly fold it into the egg white mixture. Spoon the mixture into a freezerproof serving mould or bowl and freeze for several hours or overnight before turning out.*

IDEAS FOR ICE CREAMS AND SORBETS

• Ice creams and sorbets can be flavoured with almost any taste you can think of – just try to imagine your favourite flavours and combinations and then make them into something frozen.
• Try a tomato sorbet with strips of fresh basil leaves for an excellent first course or palette-refreshing savoury in the middle of a multi-course meal.
• Charentais or other aromatic melons with added sharpness of lemon can be used for both ice creams and sorbets.
• When adding ground spices to ice creams toast them first in a hot, dry pan for a minute to bring out their full aromas.
• If made with a really aromatic home-produced honey, a honey ice cream can be perfect, specially served with an apple tart. Or, you can make apple and Calvados sorbet, or a

simple Calvados ice cream to accompany a hot apple pie.
• Sauces are nearly always a welcome accompaniment to ice cream. They can be hot or cold: chocolate (see Hot Spiced Chocolate Sauce page 213), caramel, butterscotch or smooth fruit purées for vanilla and other creamy ice creams.
• Thin biscuits are nice as an accompaniment. Freezer biscuits (page 277) are particularly useful – keep a roll of biscuit dough in the freezer and then slice it very thinly and bake to make delicate fresh biscuits whenever you need them at short notice.
• To make vanilla sugar simply keep vanilla pods in a sealed jar of caster sugar. The sugar will absorb the flavour of the pods, and you can use it instead of plain sugar whenever you want a taste of vanilla.

TRADITIONAL VANILLA ICE CREAM

A true, smooth, old-fashioned vanilla ice cream is made with a rich egg yolk custard and a real vanilla pod for genuine flavour.

Long, thin, brown vanilla pods give the richest vanilla flavour, and the tiny dark seeds add slight speckles and more flavour to the creamy ice cream.

To serve 6, you will need 300ml (½ pint) single cream, 1 vanilla pod, 4 egg yolks, 125g (4oz) vanilla caster sugar (below) and 300ml (½ pint) whipping cream.

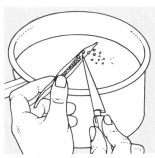

1 *Put the single cream in a saucepan. Split the vanilla pod lengthwise and add the seeds and pod to the pan. Bring the cream just up to the boil. Remove from the heat, cover and infuse for 30 minutes. Remove the vanilla pod.*

2 *Beat the egg yolks and caster sugar until pale and creamy. Reheat the vanilla-flavoured cream until nearly boiling, then pour gradually on to the egg yolk mixture, beating or stirring all the time. Put the bowl over a saucepan of gently simmering water and stir with a wooden spoon until the custard begins to thicken. Cool, stirring often.*

3 *Whip the whipping cream until thick but not stiff and fold into the custard mixture. Pour into a freezerproof dish and freeze for 3–4 hours. Remove the mixture and beat, preferably in a food processor, and then return to the freezer. Repeat at least once more at hourly intervals. To serve, soften the ice cream in the refrigerator for 10 minutes.*

FROZEN PUDDINGS

There is something about freezing puddings which makes them seem even more impressive, almost like something out of a fairy story. In fact, many chilled puddings can taste even better when frozen, and are particularly useful because, unlike sorbets and some ice cream recipes, they do not need beating halfway through the freezing and can usually be served straight from the freezer. All kinds of mousses and chilled soufflés fall into this category, as well as cakes layered with ice cream, meringue cakes and charlottes edged with sponge fingers.

Layered ice cream bombes, ice cream or sorbet spooned into containers such as scooped-out oranges, tangerines, and the ever-impressive baked Alaska are all ways of turning an ice cream mixture into a more elaborate and magnificent end to a special meal.

You can even make an iced Christmas pudding using an ice cream mixture combined with chestnut purée which has brandy- or rum-soaked fruit, nuts and spices incorporated into it. Make it in a pudding basin, then turn out and top with a holly sprig, of course.

Frozen soufflés can be made in the same way as chilled soufflés (page 229), using a foil or greaseproof paper collar which is then removed to reveal what looks like a dramatically risen pudding.

ICED CHOCOLATE MARQUISE

A chocolate marquise can either be chilled or frozen but I think this luxurious concoction is best as a glorious ice cream. As it is a pudding which can be made well ahead and is extremely impressive (though not difficult) it is ideal for a special dinner party. The frozen marquise is sliced across in thick slices to serve, and if you like accompany it with cream or soured cream to spoon either over or underneath the slices. To turn out the marquise for serving rub the outside of the tin with a hot cloth, then slip a warm palette knife carefully between the biscuits and the tin. Invert on to a serving dish, giving a good shake.

The quantity here serves 6. Use about 25–30 sponge fingers or boudoir biscuits, 75g (3oz) granulated sugar, 6 tablespoons brandy or rum, 2 tablespoons water, 125g (4oz) plain chocolate, 1 tablespoon top-of-the-milk, 1 sachet powdered gelatine, 3 large eggs (size 2), separated, 25g (1oz) caster sugar and 175ml (6fl oz) double cream plus extra chocolate for decoration.

Frozen chocolate marquise, a rich chocolate mixture encased in sponge fingers which have been steeped in a liqueur syrup, is decorated with grated chocolate.

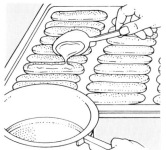

1 *Lay the sponge fingers in a shallow dish. Dissolve the sugar in the brandy or rum and water over a low heat, then bubble for a second or two before spooning over the sponge fingers. Leave for 30 minutes or more until the syrup is absorbed, carefully turning over each sponge finger once.*

2 *Line the base of a 1kg (2lb) loaf tin with a piece of baking parchment cut to fit. Line the base and sides of the tin with the soaked sponge fingers, cutting off neatly along the top of the tin with a sharp knife. Use the cut-off sponge finger tops to fill in any gaps.*

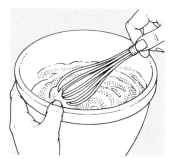

3 *Melt the chocolate and top-of-the-milk in a heatproof bowl set over a pan of gently simmering water. Dissolve the gelatine in about 3 tablespoons hot water, then stir it into the melted chocolate. Set the mixture aside to cool. Beat the egg yolks with the caster sugar until pale and thick, then beat in the slightly cooled chocolate.*

4 *Whip the cream until thick, and in a second bowl whisk the egg whites until soft peaks form. Fold the cream into the chocolate mixture, followed by the egg whites. Spoon into the biscuit-lined tin, smooth the top with a knife and freeze for several hours until firm. Unmould (above) on to a serving plate and top with grated chocolate, if you like.*

ICE CREAM BOMBE

Traditional bombes are made with contrasting layers of ice cream and sorbet. A thick fruit purée in the centre can replace some of the sorbet to make a pretty variation. Ice cream should always be used on the outer layer as it freezes the firmest.

Metal moulds with lids are best as they both freeze and unmould quickly. Most bombe moulds are dome-shaped but they can also be square or even rectangular. Freezerproof jelly moulds and pudding basins can be used also.

To serve 4–6, you will need a 1 litre (1¾ pint) mould, ½ quantity strawberry sorbet (page 234), and 200ml (7fl oz) blackcurrants stewed to a thick jam-like consistency (page 224).

To make the bombe ice cream mixture use 200g (7oz) caster sugar, 125ml (4fl oz) water, 4 egg yolks, finely grated rind and juice of 2 small oranges, 300ml (½ pint) double cream and 1 teaspoon vanilla essence. Dissolve the sugar in the water over a low heat, then increase the heat and boil rapidly for 1 minute. Remove from heat. Beat the egg yolks, then, still beating, pour on the hot but not boiling syrup. Add the orange rind and juice. Continue beating the mixture until cool. Chill. Lightly whip the cream and fold it into the mixture. Fold in the vanilla essence and any other flavouring such as liqueur. Freeze until solid, beating 2 or 3 times at hourly intervals.

Ice cream bombes can be constructed in many different ways, using various flavours and textures to create a dramatic effect when the bombe is turned out. The bombe here has a pale outer layer of homemade orange-flavoured ice cream with a second contrasting layer of strawberry sorbet and a centre of fresh blackcurrants which have been lightly cooked so that they are thick and jam-like.

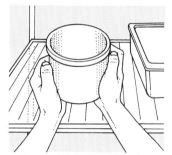

1 *Put the bombe mould in the freezer to chill for 2 hours. Soften the frozen bombe mixture for the outer layer until it spreads easily. Take care when you remove the chilled mould because it can 'burn' your fingers.*

2 *Using the back of a spoon line the mould with an even layer of bombe mixture 2.5cm (1in) thick. Cover the mould and return to the freezer for 2–3 hours until the bombe mixture is firm again.*

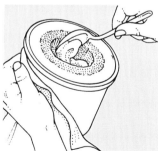

3 *Remove the mould from the freezer and quickly fill the centre with the strawberry sorbet, leaving a hollow in the centre. Freeze for 1 hour until firm. Fill the hollow with the thick blackcurrant purée, then cover and freeze for 8 hours.*

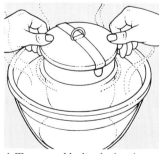

4 *To unmould, dip the bombe mould quickly in a bowl of hot water, then remove the top and invert on to a chilled serving plate, holding firmly with both hands. Soften the bombe for about 30 minutes in the refrigerator before serving.*

IDEAS FOR FROZEN PUDDINGS

• If you make a chocolate bombe you can have a centre of ice cream flavoured with peppermint so that the whole thing resembles a peppermint cream; thin peppermint creams can also be added to the bombe in layers.

• Successful bombe combinations include chocolate ice cream with lemon sorbet, apricot and gooseberry ice creams, Calvados ice cream and apple sorbet, strawberry ice cream and orange sorbet and raspberry ice cream with blackcurrant sorbet.

• Fruit incorporated into bombes should either be cooked with sugar until thick and jam-like, soaked in a liqueur or, if fresh, mixed with a light sugar syrup (page 208) to stop it solidifying to ice.

• If using dried fruit in a bombe soak it first in a little sherry, brandy or liqueur before using, unless it is already very soft.

• A wonderful pudding is a lemon sorbet frozen in a bombe mould, turned out on to a plate and frozen again before you pour a thick, hot chocolate sauce over it all just before putting on the table.

• If using sponge for an ice cream cake you can soak it in a liqueur or a fruit syrup before assembling it. Ice cream cakes can also be layered with meringue circles instead of sponge fingers.

• Meringue can also be used to add texture to smooth dishes. Bake a layer of crisp meringue, then crumble it and fold it into an ice cream mixture before freezing. Crushed biscuits, ratafias or macaroons can be used in the same way.

• A rich chocolate mousse made with gelatine is best of all when frozen and covered with strips of orange peel which have been boiled to soften and then boiled in an orange juice and sugar syrup (page 208) until it has reduced to coat the peel – this kind of candied peel is useful as a garnish or folded into all sorts of frozen puddings.

• When making Baked Alaska, try folding chopped nuts into the meringue or a little coarsely grated chocolate which will begin to melt into the meringue during the short time it is in the oven.

HOT LEMON AND PASSION FRUIT SOUFFLÉ *(228)*

Instead of a flour roux, this soufflé has a tangy lemon curd base. You can make the base in advance which will leave you only the whites to whisk and fold in shortly before you put the soufflé in the oven. Instead of one large soufflé, the mixture can also be divided between six 150ml (¼ pint) ramekin dishes, in which case cook for 12–15 minutes only. This pudding is delicious served with a fruit purée of damsons, raspberries, blackberries or blackcurrants as a sauce. *SERVES 6–8*

> 4 passion fruit
> 150ml (¼ pint) lemon juice
> 5 large eggs (size 1), separated
> 125g (4oz) caster sugar
> Finely grated rind of 2 lemons
> ½ teaspoon salt
> Icing sugar for dusting

Cut the passion fruit in half. Scoop out the flesh, juice and seeds from 2 passion fruit and put in a jug with the lemon juice. Sieve the juice from the remaining passion fruit into the jug. Discard the seeds. Mix the contents of the jug thoroughly with a fork.

Put the egg yolks in the top of a double boiler or in a heatproof bowl which will fit over a saucepan of water. Stir in the sugar, then add the lemon and passion fruit mixture a little at a time.

Set the double boiler or bowl over gently simmering water and stir with a wooden spoon until the mixture is thick enough to lightly coat the back of the spoon. Remove the bowl from the heat, stir in the grated lemon rind and leave on one side until cold.

Meanwhile, butter a 900ml (1½ pint) soufflé or other deep ovenproof dish. Put the egg whites in a large bowl with the salt and whisk until soft peaks form. Using a large metal spoon, lightly fold the egg whites into the cooled lemon and passion fruit mixture until well incorporated.

Spoon the mixture into the soufflé dish and cook just above the centre of a preheated oven, 150°C, 300°F, Gas Mark 2 for 50–60 minutes until the top of the soufflé is dark golden brown. Lightly dust the top of the soufflé with sifted icing sugar and serve at once while still puffed up.

CARAMELIZED ORANGE TART *(221)*

I first made this upside-down tart using the typically Moroccan flavourings of honey and cinnamon after a holiday in southern Morocco, where the scent of orange blossom and the taste of fresh orange juice had dominated our days. Serve the tart warm with cream, fromage frais or Greek yogurt. *SERVES 6–8*

FOR THE PASTRY
> 175g (6oz) plain flour
> 75g (3oz) caster sugar
> ½ teaspoon salt
> 75g (3oz) butter, just melted
> 1 egg, beaten

FOR THE FILLING
> 40g (1½ oz) butter
> 4 good tablespoons honey
> 2 teaspoons ground cinnamon
> 5–6 small seedless oranges

To make the pastry, sift the flour, caster sugar and salt into a bowl. Stir in the melted butter using a wooden spoon, then thoroughly mix in the beaten egg until the dough is smooth. Press the dough into a ball, cover with clingfilm and leave to chill in the refrigerator for at least 1 hour.

To prepare the orange filling, melt the butter and honey gently in a saucepan, then stir in the cinnamon. Pour the mixture over the bottom of a 25cm (10in) flan dish (the fluted ones turn out nicely). Slice the unpeeled oranges across as thinly as possible. First lay a pattern of orange slices on the base of the dish on top of the butter and honey mixture, then add the remaining slices on top in overlapping circles.

Roll out the pastry on a floured surface to a little larger than the size of the flan dish. Roll the pastry back over the rolling pin and lift it on to the dish. (If the pastry breaks, just press it together again – it won't show.) Press the edges firmly down within the flan dish and pierce 2 or 3 holes in the pastry.

Bake the tart in the centre of a preheated oven, 200°C, 400°F, Gas Mark 6 for 25 minutes, then reduce the oven temperature to 160°C, 325°F, Gas Mark 3 and cook for another 1¾–2 hours – the pastry will turn a rich dark brown. Remove the tart from the oven and leave to stand for 5–10 minutes before inverting on to a large serving plate.

SUMMER PUDDING *(214)*

Summer pudding is a simple but brilliant creation. Ideally you should turn out a dome entirely dark with absorbed juices but always keep some of the cooking juices in reserve for pouring over the pudding after turning it out in case some of the bread still shows. All kinds of juicy summer fruit can be used but a good proportion of blackcurrants and raspberries is important. Serve with more soft fruit and cream. *SERVES 6*

> 500g (1lb) blackcurrants
> 250g (8oz) redcurrants
> 150ml (¼ pint) fresh orange juice
> 4 tablespoons lemon juice
> 175g (6oz) caster sugar
> 500g (1lb) raspberries
> 1 small unsliced day-old white loaf
> Extra fresh fruit to decorate

Using a fork strip the blackcurrants and redcurrants off their stalks. Put the orange and lemon juices and the sugar in a saucepan and stir over a medium heat until the sugar has dissolved. Bring to the boil, then add the blackcurrants and redcurrants. Cover and cook over a low heat for 8–10 minutes until the juices have run and the fruit is soft. Stir in the raspberries and remove from the heat.

Cut the loaf of bread into thin slices and a circle to fit the base of a 1.2 litre (2 pint) pudding basin or mould. Cut off and discard the crusts. Line the base and then the sides with overlapping slices of bread, leaving no gaps. Fill the basin with the fruit mixture, reserving any remaining juices and then top with more layers of bread. Put a saucer or small plate on top and weight it down. Chill for several hours or overnight.

To serve, turn it out on to a serving plate, pour over the reserved fruit juices and arrange some fresh fruit on top.

PASSION FRUIT AND ORANGE PUDDINGS *(214)*

These light and moist little almond cakes are delectable. Remember that ripe passion fruit are those with very wrinkled skins. *SERVES 6*

FOR THE PUDDINGS
125g (4oz) butter, softened
150g (5oz) fine demerara sugar
Finely grated rind of 2 oranges
4 passion fruit
125g (4oz) ground almonds
3 large eggs (size 1), lightly whisked
Icing sugar for dusting
FOR THE SAUCE
6 passion fruit
Juice of 2 oranges
2 tablespoons caster sugar
150ml (¼ pint) double cream

To make the puddings, first butter 6 deep patty tins or individual dariole moulds and put a disc of baking parchment cut to fit in the bottom of each.

In a mixing bowl beat the butter and demerara sugar until soft and fluffy, then beat in the grated orange rind. Cut the 4 passion fruit in half and spoon the insides of 4 halves into the bowl with the whisked butter and sugar, then strain the juice from the remaining halves and add to the bowl; discard the seeds. Whisk in to break the flesh up and disperse the seeds, then alternately whisk in the ground almonds and the whisked eggs.

Spoon the pudding mixture into the individual tins or moulds and cook in the centre of a preheated oven, 190°C, 375°F, Gas Mark 5 for 25–35 minutes until a small sharp knife inserted in the centre of a pudding comes out clean. Leave the puddings in the tins for at least 10 minutes, then pass a knife round the edges to loosen them and turn out on to a cooling rack, removing the discs of baking parchment. Leave until cool.

To make the sauce, cut the 6 passion fruit in half and spoon the insides out into a nylon sieve set over a bowl. Rub with a wooden spoon until as much juice as possible has gone through the sieve. Discard the mass of seeds. Strain the orange juice through a fine sieve into the bowl and add the caster sugar, stirring thoroughly so that it dissolves. Finally stir in the double cream. Refrigerate the sauce until needed.

To serve, spoon the sauce equally on to 6 individual plates, place a pudding in the centre of each and sprinkle icing sugar on to the puddings through a fine sieve – I like enough to make them completely white on top.

CHOCOLATE PEPPERMINT CREAM ICE *(235)*

If you have a weakness for chocolate peppermint creams, this is the ice cream for you. *SERVES 6–8*

175g (6oz) caster sugar
½ teaspoon salt
4 large eggs (size 1), separated
300ml (½ pint) double cream
½ teaspoon peppermint essence
1 box (150g) wafer-thin chocolate after-dinner mints, cut into small pieces
Mint leaves to decorate

Put the caster sugar, salt and egg yolks in a bowl and gradually whisk in the cream until well mixed. Stir in the peppermint essence, set the bowl over a pan of simmering water, stirring with a wooden spoon for 10–15 minutes until the mixture has thickened slightly. Pour into a larger bowl and leave until cold.

Whisk the egg whites until soft peaks form, then fold them gently but thoroughly into the cold custard using a metal spoon. Stir in the pieces of chocolate after-dinner mints.

Pour the ice cream mixture into a freezerproof serving bowl and freeze for several hours. Thirty minutes before serving decorate the top with a few mint leaves and transfer to the refrigerator to soften slightly.

QUEEN OF PUDDINGS WITH FRESH POACHED APRICOTS *(214)*

Queen of puddings really does suit its name: for me it is an old-fashioned pudding of the highest order. I like to use fresh apricots when they are available instead of the usual jam. Later in the summer blackcurrants are excellent, too. Serve this pudding either hot or well chilled and with cream if preferred. *SERVES 6*

75g (3oz) fresh white breadcrumbs
300ml (½ pint) milk
300ml (½ pint) single cream
Finely grated rind of 1 lemon
50g (2oz) butter
3 large eggs (size 1), separated
150g (5oz) caster sugar
500g (1lb) fresh apricots, halved and stoned
75g (3oz) soft light brown sugar
4 tablespoons lemon juice
Pinch of salt

Butter a 1.5–1.8 litre (2½–3 pint) oven-proof baking dish and sprinkle the fresh white breadcrumbs evenly in the bottom. Put the milk and cream in a saucepan with the lemon rind and butter and heat until just warm. In a mixing bowl beat the egg yolks lightly with 75g (3oz) of the caster sugar, then gradually beat in the heated milk and cream. Pour this mixture into the baking dish over the breadcrumbs and bake in the centre of a preheated oven, 180°C, 350°F, Gas Mark 4 for about 25 minutes or until set to a light touch in the centre.

Meanwhile, put the apricot halves in a saucepan with the brown sugar and lemon juice and stir over a medium heat until the sugar has dissolved. Cover the pan and simmer gently for 10–15 minutes or until the fruit is mushy. If a lot of juice has emerged from the fruit remove the lid and bubble fiercely to reduce it to a thicker syrup. Remove from the heat and leave on one side.

When the custard and breadcrumb mixture is ready remove the dish from the oven and gently spoon the apricots evenly on top. Whisk the egg whites with the salt until stiff, then fold in the remaining 50g (2oz) of caster sugar. Pile the meringue on top of the apricots and return to the oven for another 15 minutes until the meringue is golden brown and crisp on top.

QUINCE PUDDING BRÛLÉE (214)

This light and creamy pudding is perfect for a large Sunday lunch. If your quinces feel very hard you can gently poach them for about 5 minutes before arranging them in layers in the dish. *SERVES 8*

750g–1kg (1½–2lb) ripe quinces or hard pears
Lemon juice or white wine vinegar
75g (3oz) soft dark brown sugar
375g (12oz) cream cheese
Finely grated rind of 1 large lemon
250g (8oz) caster sugar
300ml (½ pint) double cream
150ml (¼ pint) soured cream
6 large eggs (size 1), separated
1 teaspoon vanilla essence
½ teaspoon salt

Peel and core the quinces and slice very thinly, dropping the slices immediately into a bowl of water to which you have added a little lemon juice or white wine vinegar. Drain the quince slices and arrange them in the bottom of a deep 2.4–3 litre (4–5 pint) flameproof dish. Sprinkle all over with the brown sugar.

Beat the cream cheese with the grated lemon rind and 175g (6oz) of the caster sugar until soft. Gradually beat in the cream, soured cream, egg yolks and vanilla essence. Whisk the egg whites with the salt until soft peaks form, then fold into the creamy mixture. Pour on top of the fruit slices.

Bake in the centre of a preheated oven, 180°C, 350°F, Gas Mark 4 for 35–40 minutes until the pudding is a rich golden brown on top. Remove from the oven and leave for about 5 minutes.

Meanwhile, preheat the grill to a high heat. Sprinkle the remaining caster sugar evenly all over the top of the pudding and place it under the hot grill until the sugar has dissolved and become caramelized, brown and glossy, watching all the time to catch it at the right moment. Serve either warm or chilled.

RASPBERRY AND CHOCOLATE MERINGUE CAKE (226)

This meringue cake is one of the most useful summer party puddings as it can be assembled up to 3 hours before you eat. *SERVES 6–8*

FOR THE MERINGUE
4 large egg whites (size 1)
Pinch of salt
175g (6oz) caster sugar
1 teaspoon vanilla essence
1 teaspoon white wine vinegar
25g (1oz) cornflour
25g (1oz) toasted chopped hazelnuts
FOR THE FILLING
75g (3oz) plain chocolate, broken into pieces
1 tablespoon water
4 large egg yolks (size 1)
75ml (3fl oz) milk
2 tablespoons caster sugar
375g (12oz) raspberries
150ml (¼ pint) double cream
Cocoa powder
Extra caster sugar

Line the bottom of 2 ungreased 18cm (7in) sandwich tins with discs of baking parchment cut to fit. Whisk the egg whites with the salt until stiff, then whisk in half the sugar, a little at a time. Gently fold in the remaining sugar, the vanilla essence, vinegar, cornflour and chopped hazelnuts using a large metal spoon. Divide the mixture between the tins and bake just below the centre of a preheated oven, 140°C, 275°F, Gas Mark 1 for about 1½ hours until firm to a touch in the centre. Lay a tea towel on a wire rack and turn out the meringue cakes, removing the baking parchment.

While the meringues are baking make the filling. Put the chocolate in a small saucepan with the water and melt over a very gentle heat. Stir until smooth, then leave on one side. Put the egg yolks, milk and caster sugar in the top of a double boiler or a heatproof bowl set over a pan of gently simmering water. Stir until the mixture has thickened. Stir in the melted chocolate, then transfer the mixture to a bowl to cool.

When the filling and meringues are completely cold lay one meringue on a serving plate and spread with the chocolate mixture. Put a layer of raspberries on the chocolate, reserving a few for the top of the cake. Whisk the cream until stiff and spread it over the raspberries, then lay the second meringue on top. Chill until almost ready to serve. Sprinkle cocoa powder through a fine sieve all over the cake and gently arrange the reserved raspberries in a pattern on top. Sprinkle all over with a little caster sugar, again through a sieve.

CRÈME BRÛLÉE (214)

Crème brûlée, or 'burnt cream', is wicked but irresistible: a smooth creamy custard topped with a delicious crisp caramel glaze. It is usually made in individual little pots or ramekin dishes. *SERVES 6*

600ml (1 pint) double cream
1 vanilla pod
5 egg yolks
125g (4oz) caster sugar

Put the cream in a saucepan with the vanilla pod and heat gently until almost boiling. Remove from the heat, cover and leave to infuse for 10 minutes. Remove the vanilla pod.

Beat the egg yolks in a bowl with 50g (2oz) of the sugar until light in colour. Gradually add the hot cream, beating all the time until evenly mixed, then pour the mixture slowly and equally into 6 ramekin dishes. Put the ramekins into a roasting tin and pour in enough hot water to come halfway up the sides of the dishes. Bake the custards in the centre of a preheated oven, 150°C, 300°F, Gas Mark 2 for about 1 hour until just set – don't let the skin colour.

Meanwhile, preheat a very hot grill. Sprinkle the remaining caster sugar evenly over the top of the custards then put them under the grill for 2–3 minutes until an uneven caramel colour. Cool and chill before serving.

BANANA AND PECAN PIE WITH CRANBERRY AND ORANGE COULIS *(214)*

This easily made winter pudding is one of those which provoke ecstatic noises while being eaten. The chilled cranberry and orange coulis cuts perfectly into the warm richness of the pie. For convenience make the pie in advance and keep it in the refrigerator, then glaze and bake it shortly before your meal. *SERVES 6–8*

FOR THE COULIS
   175g (6oz) fresh cranberries
   300ml (½ pint) fresh orange juice
   4 tablespoons lemon juice
   125g (4oz) granulated sugar
FOR THE PIE
   250g (8oz) packet puff pastry, thawed if frozen
   250g (8oz) cream cheese
   75g (3oz) light brown sugar
   1 large egg (size 1), beaten lightly
   3–4 firm bananas (depending on size)
   Finely grated rind and juice of 1 lemon
   75g (3oz) shelled pecan nuts, halved
   Milk and caster sugar for glazing

Make the cranberry and orange coulis first. Put the cranberries in a saucepan with the orange and lemon juices and bring to the boil, then cover and simmer gently for 10–12 minutes until the cranberries are popped and mushy.

Add the granulated sugar and stir until dissolved. Whizz the mixture in a food processor until it is as smooth as possible – for perfect smoothness rub the purée through a sieve. Turn the coulis into a serving bowl and chill.

Generously butter a 20–23cm (8–9in) flan dish. Cut the pastry in half and shape it into 2 balls. On a lightly floured surface roll out 2 circles, one about the size of the flan dish and one slightly larger. Prick the circles lightly all over with a fork and line the dish with the larger circle.

Put the cream cheese and brown sugar in a bowl and whisk until fluffy. Thoroughly whisk in the beaten egg. Mash the bananas with the lemon juice and stir immediately into the cream cheese mixture with the halved pecan nuts and the lemon rind.

Spoon the mixture into the lined flan dish and lay the other circle of pastry on top. Cut off the excess pastry neatly, moisten the edges lightly with water and press round the edges to seal. Roll out the pastry trimmings. Cut out some decorations, moisten them on one side and arrange on top of the pie. Brush the top of the pie with milk and sprinkle evenly all over with caster sugar, then bake in the centre of a preheated oven, 200°C, 400°F, Gas Mark 6 for 30–35 minutes until the pastry is a rich, crispy brown. Serve hot or warm with the chilled coulis as a sauce.

CHOCOLATE RIPPLE HEART WITH RASPBERRIES *(214)*

Use a fairly shallow heart-shaped cake tin or jelly mould and this rather indulgent pudding of raspberries enclosed in a streaky mixture of fromage frais and dark chocolate will look especially effective. If you use a metal mould without a non-stick coating it is best to line it with clingfilm before adding the pudding ingredients. *SERVES 6*

   150g (5oz) plain chocolate, broken into pieces
   2 tablespoons water
   500g (1lb) 8% fat fromage frais
   50–75g (2–3oz) icing sugar, sifted
   1 sachet powdered gelatine
   3 tablespoons very hot water
   125g (4oz) raspberries
   Cocoa powder for dusting

Lightly oil a 900ml (1½ pint) heart-shaped cake tin or jelly mould. Put the chocolate and the 2 tablespoons water in the top of a double boiler or in a heatproof bowl set over a pan of barely simmering water and melt. Stir until smooth. Set aside to cool only slightly.

Put the fromage frais in a bowl and beat in the sifted icing sugar. Sprinkle the gelatine into the hot water and stir until completely dissolved, then whisk swiftly into the fromage frais. Roughly stir in the melted chocolate, leaving plenty of white streaks in the mixture.

Put the raspberries in the bottom of the mould and spoon the fromage frais and chocolate mixture on top, tapping the mould gently so the mixture settles round the raspberries. Refrigerate for at least 1 hour until set.

To turn out loosen the edges of the pudding with your fingers, then invert on to a serving plate and dust the top with cocoa powder.

COCONUT CREAM CUSTARD *(217)*

This is a good pudding to follow a spicy meal and can be accompanied by fresh exotic fruits. I like to serve the custard at room temperature rather than chilled. *SERVES 6*

   300ml (½ pint) double cream
   300ml (½ pint) milk
   50g (2oz) creamed coconut, chopped roughly
   1 teaspoon salt
   3 large eggs (size 2)
   2 egg yolks
   75g (3oz) caster sugar
   50g (2oz) shelled unsalted cashew nuts, chopped

Put a roasting tin three-quarters full of water on the centre shelf of the oven and preheat the oven to 160°C, 325°F, Gas Mark 3. Put the cream, milk and creamed coconut in a saucepan and stir over a medium heat until the coconut has dissolved completely. Stir in the salt and remove from the heat. Put the eggs, egg yolks and caster sugar in a bowl. Whisk together thoroughly, then whisk in the hot coconut cream a little at a time.

Sprinkle the chopped cashew nuts in the bottom of a 1.2 litre (2 pint) soufflé or other similar ovenproof dish. Pour the cream and egg mixture into the dish and stand it in the tin of water in the oven. Cook for 1–1¼ hours until the custard feels set to a very light touch in the centre but still wobbles slightly if you move the dish. Remove from the oven and leave to cool.

PASTRY

Perfect homemade pastry is a dream – rich and buttery, but at the same time light, with a crumbly or flaky texture. Yet many competent and even inspired cooks never attempt to make pastry. It may well seem that only the greatest skill could produce such a variety of textures from the same few basic ingredients – pastries which vary enough to suit quite different purposes, but many pastries are easily achieved and there is always something new to discover.

I love experimenting with pastry to try and create a texture and taste I haven't achieved before. Yet I used to be one of those who felt they couldn't make pastry – that was until the day I was told to add more fat and less water when making a simple shortcrust and to take as little time as possible crumbling the fat into the flour. The result was wonderful, and from then on I found pastry-making a real pleasure; once you realize how easy it is to produce a light and crumbly shortcrust, your cooking repertoire can be enormously extended.

There are three main types of pastry: shortcrust, puff or flaky pastry and choux pastry. Shortcrust can be plain or sweetened for making puddings. Puff or flaky pastry is made in a way which layers the flour and fat, creating a light, crisp flaky dough – it is exquisite but it does take time and some practice to achieve perfect results. Fillo or strudel pastry is a type of layered pastry, but it really does need practice and skill to make successfully, and it is far easier to buy the paper-thin sheets. Choux pastry is made in an entirely different way: cooking the flour into a paste and beating in whole eggs to make it rise and expand when baked – it is the most unbelievable pastry mix of all, and yet one of the easiest and most infallible. There are also special pastries for specific recipes, such as crisp, hot-water crust pastry for encasing pâtés and meat pies, and soft, open-textured suet crusts for sweet or savoury steamed puddings.

Successful pastry depends on using good ingredients in the exact proportions, although as you become more experienced, you can alter these to a degree. Flour, fat and eggs, the most important ingredients in pastry, can vary in flavour and quality, and care should be taken to choose the best. A soft wheat flour is said to be the best for pastry as it develops less gluten, but I have also had excellent results using strong, plain white bread flour. Wholemeal flour or ground nuts can be substituted for part of the flour in some pastry, depending on what fillings are to be used, but I have never yet tasted an all wholemeal flour pastry which was truly successful.

Sugar – caster or icing – is added to dessert pastry to give colour and sweetness. Vanilla, lemon or orange rind, as well as spices and herbs can also be used to flavour pastry. Pastry is such a versatile and useful ingredient that it is convenient to have it on hand. Ready-made fresh and frozen pastry is an acceptable alternative to homemade, particularly puff pastry, which is time-consuming to make, and certainly fillo or strudel pastry.

Sweet and savoury pastry dishes suitable for all occasions, clockwise from top left: Lime and Strawberry Tart (page 258) with a creamy, lime-flavoured filling; Fillo Pie with Caramelized Apples and Pine Kernels (page 258); an individual Sweet Onion, Garlic and Saffron Tart (page 259) served with a radish and mixed lettuce salad; a whole game pie (page 256) made with hot-water crust pastry and garnished with fresh herbs; and Special Steak and Kidney Pudding (page 259) made with a caraway-flavoured suet-crust pastry top and served here with brussels sprouts and carrots.

BASIC PASTRY TECHNIQUES

The most important thing to remember when making pastry is *to handle the dough as little as possible.* Work well with chilled ingredients as quickly as you can. If over-worked, the dough will shrink during baking and be tough after baking. Before refrigerating, flatten the dough to a disc of even thickness and wrap carefully for even chilling without drying the edges. Chilling the dough before baking allows it to 'relax' and firms the fat to prevent shrinkage. If the chilled dough is a little too firm for rolling, let it soften briefly at room temperature first.

Dough can be stored at this stage for two to three days, or it can be rolled out and shaped, then refrigerated and stored. It can be also baked, cooled, wrapped and stored for two to three days in an airtight container. Or, if not using immediately, it is best to freeze the dough, already rolled out into its tin. Do not freeze for longer than three months. You can then bake the dough from frozen when you are ready to use it.

After rolling out, use the dough to line or cover shallow or deep pie plates, flan or tart tins or tartlet tins. Pie edges can be finished with a simple fork or finger-pinched edge or a fancy border made from the trimmings (opposite). Any pastry trimmings can be used to decorate pie tops or to make shapes for use as decorations (opposite). I enjoy cutting out appropriate shapes such as a chicken to go on a chicken pie, or a short simple message or name.

MIXING PASTRY DOUGH

Most pastry for pie crusts is made by blending together chilled butter, flour and water. Mix the dry ingredients in a large bowl, rubbing in the butter with your fingertips, until the mixture resembles coarse crumbs. Alternatively, use a pastry blender or 2 knives scissor-fashion (page 246) to cut in the butter lightly. Stir in chilled water (or beaten egg yolk for a richer pastry) with a fork until the dough begins to hold together, then quickly form the dough into a ball and flatten slightly into a disc. Wrap well in clingfilm and chill for at least 30 minutes.

To rub in butter *or other chilled fat, pick up small amounts of diced butter and flour and quickly rub with your fingertips high above the bowl, letting the crumbs fall back into the bowl. Continue until all the fat is incorporated and the mixture resembles fine breadcrumbs, then add the water and mix together to a dough.*

ROLLING OUT PASTRY DOUGH

Before rolling out the chilled dough, allow it to soften until slightly pliable so the edges do not crack and break. Dust a dry work surface and rolling pin with flour. Use the pin to flatten the pastry disc into the correct shape before you begin rolling.

Roll out from the centre *to the edges, giving a quarter turn each time to make a round. Push the sides in with your hands to help the dough to keep its shape.*

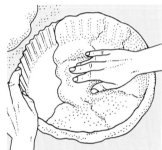

Very rich, sweet pastry *often sticks to the rolling pin. Instead, pat into position in the tin with your fingertips. The cracks won't show after baking.*

LINING PLATES, TINS OR DISHES

It is usually unnecessary to grease a tart tin, pie plate or dish, as the fat in the pastry prevents it sticking. The thickness of pastry depends on the type of container used and on the filling. For most fillings, 2.5mm (⅛in) is adequate but thicker pastry may be required for heavy pies or deep fillings.

The example here shows how to line a fluted loose-bottomed flan tin but the technique is the same for a plain plate or dish.

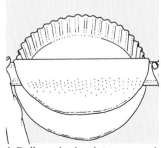

1 *Roll out the dough into a round about 5cm (2in) larger than the tin. Roll half the dough back on to the rolling pin and transfer to the centre of the tin. Unroll, being careful not to stretch.*

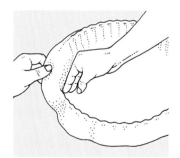

2 *Gently lift the edges of the dough with one hand while pressing into the base and sides of the tin. If using a pie dish, press the dough into the sides so pastry does not shrink during baking.*

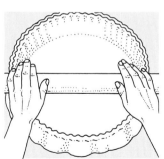

3 *Roll the rolling pin lightly over the top edge, cutting off any excess dough with a knife. If there is time chill in the refrigerator before baking either blind (opposite) or with a filling.*

DECORATIVE PIE EDGES

A simple fluted or crimped edge, fancy border or decorated pie top adds interest to plain tart fillings or a large top crust of pastry.

After making your pie, reroll the trimmings and use a biscuit cutter or knife to cut out enough leaves, hearts, or other shapes such as animals or people to decorate the pie, if you like. You can even cut out letters to spell names for special occasions.

To help the decorations stick, brush them with water before applying to the pie. Alternatively, glaze the surface of the pie with a beaten egg and add the cut-outs, then glaze again before putting it into the oven to bake.

Decorative pie edges give an impressive finishing touch to single crust and plate pies. Here, the easy fluted edge is used on a single crust pie as well as a plate pie with leaves cut from the pastry trimmings. Fork prongs make a simple crimped edge on the other pie.

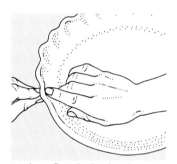

Make a fluted edge by placing your index finger on the inside rim of the pastry and with the index finger and thumb of your other hand pinching against the first finger to make a flute.

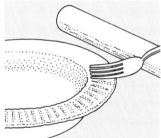

Make a simple crimped edge by pressing fork prongs all round the edge of the tin. Alternatively, press the tip of a pointed or round-bladed knife all round the pastry edge.

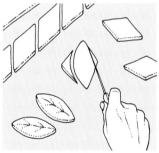

Use a sharp knife or small aspic or biscuit cutter to cut out leaves or other decorative shapes from the rerolled pastry trimmings. Use the back of a knife tip to mark the veins of leaves.

Brush the underside of the decorative shapes with a little water, twist slightly, then position them on the top crust or edge of the pie. Glaze the pie before putting it in the oven to bake.

GLAZES AND FINISHES

Glazing pastry dough adds shine and colour to baked pastry, and a glaze can also be used to seal a pastry shell if a moist filling is being used. The most common glaze to use on savoury pastry is a whole egg beaten with a pinch of salt and brushed on just before baking. Egg yolk beaten with 2 teaspoons water gives a slightly less shiny but even more golden colour to the baked pastry. Milk or single cream can also be used for a lighter glaze.

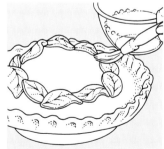

Apply the glaze before scoring or slashing the top crust so it does not soak into fillings or seal openings or edges. Egg glaze can also be used to secure pastry decorations in position.

BAKING BLIND

To bake blind is to partially or completely bake a pastry shell without its filling: if the filling needs no cooking at all, bake the shell completely; if it needs only quick cooking, bake the shell partially. Prepare as right. Bake at 220°C, 425°F, Gas Mark 7 for 10 minutes, then lower to 190°C, 375°F, Gas Mark 5 and bake for 5 more minutes. The times will vary depending on pastry thickness. Remove the paper and beans. If baking completely, bake for 8–10 more minutes.

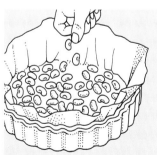

To bake blind prick pastry base all over, line the uncooked pie shell with greaseproof paper 5cm (2in) larger than the pie. Fill with dried beans or rice, making sure they are placed right to the edge.

BASIC SHORTCRUST PASTRY

Shortcrust pastry is the easiest to make and most frequently used pastry. It is the basis of most fruit pies, tarts and even versatile savoury flans, such as quiche lorraine. The pastry dough can also easily be flavoured, with herbs or spices for example, to complement the filling. The fat used can be butter, hard margarine, lard or vegetable oil depending on the baked flavour and texture you want. Increasing the amount of fat gives extra flavour and an even shorter pastry, though it will be more difficult to handle. If you have difficulty rolling out a rich pastry, press it into the container with your fingertips, pinching any cracks to seal so they will not show once baked.

The choices for filling shortcrust are almost endless.

Fruits and berries can fill open tarts or covered pies. Savoury meat, fish, vegetable or cheese fillings can be bound in an egg-based custard and baked like a quiche, and shortcrust pastry can be wrapped round pâtés and other fillings for baking *en croûte*.

Shortcrust pastry made with 250g (8oz) flour will make a 23cm (9in) open tart or pie or six 10cm (4in) tartlets. Pastry made with 300g (10oz) flour will make a 20cm (8in) plate or double crust pie, or cover a 1.2 litre (2 pint) pie dish. Once a container is lined with the dough, chill it again for 30 minutes before baking. Shortcrust pastry shells can be baked blind (page 245) before filling if the filling is very runny or to be left uncooked.

SHORTCRUST PASTRY

The basic shortcrust recipe can be varied to suit the size of the plate or tin. The usual proportion is half the amount of fat to the amount of flour but if you like a richer and more crumbly pastry, use a little more fat and decrease the amount of liquid. A mixture of butter and vegetable fat makes a very light pastry.

Remember to handle the dough as little as possible, work with well-chilled ingredients and mix them quickly. The dough does not need to be perfectly blended because if it is overworked the baked pastry will be tough and shrink during baking. It is important not to use too much water as it, too, can toughen the pastry. Pastries with a lot of fat need hardly any water and will be rich, short and crumbly after baking.

To make pastry for a 23cm (9in) tart tin, you will need 250g (8oz) plain flour, ½ teaspoon salt, 125g (4oz) diced chilled butter and 2–3 tablespoons well-chilled water. For an open tart it is best to use a loose-bottomed flan tin for easy removal but a ceramic quiche dish with an unglazed base to help conduct the heat works just as well.

SHORTCRUST VARIATIONS
If you make shortcrust pastry with soft margarine or vegetable oil, the technique is different from the traditional method (above). Put the fat, chilled water and one-third of the flour in a bowl and cream together with a fork, then stir in the remaining flour and lightly knead to make a soft dough.

You can make shortcrust pastry in a food processor, rather than by hand, but take care that it isn't overworked – never let the dough form into a ball in the machine. Instead, I sometimes just combine the chilled butter and flour in the food processor until it resembles fine breadcrumbs, then transfer to a bowl and mix in the water by hand.

To make a rich, crisp cream cheese pastry, put 75g (3oz) butter and 75g (3oz) cream cheese with 250g (8oz) flour and 2 tablespoons sugar in a food processor and blend until the dough just holds together. This dough will be difficult to roll out because it is so rich, so it will probably be easiest to pat it into the container or piece together as a top crust.

Using soured cream, rather than water in the basic shortened pastry recipe (above) results in a tender pastry, ideal for wrapping pâtés en croûte (page 99) or making tartlet shells.

1 *Before you begin place a small bowl of water in the refrigerator to chill. Mix the flour and salt together in a large bowl. Add the well-chilled, diced butter and cut in with 2 knives used scissor-fashion until the mixture resembles fine breadcrumbs. Alternatively, use your fingertips (page 244) or a pastry blender to rub in the fat lightly.*

2 *Make a well in the centre of the flour mixture and add 2 tablespoons well-chilled water, quickly and lightly mixing it in with a knife. The dough is moist enough if a little of the mixture squeezed between your fingertips sticks together; if it is too dry, add more well-chilled water little by little but be very careful not to add too much water which makes the pastry tough.*

3 *Press the crumbs together to form a more solid dough, picking up little flakes on the side of the bowl and gently kneading them together to form into a large ball. Only use 1 hand so you do not overwork the dough.*

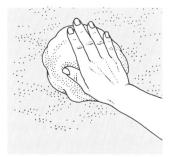

4 *Gently flatten the ball of dough on a lightly floured surface to a disc so it chills evenly. Wrap well in clingfilm and chill for at least 30 minutes before rolling out to the required shape. Allow to soften slightly before rolling.*

SAVOURY FLAN TECHNIQUE

A savoury flan, such as a quiche, made with shortcrust pastry is an ideal lunch dish or light supper when served with a crisp salad and some crusty French bread. Most flans use an egg custard as a base into which you set a selection of cooked and flaked fish, lightly sautéed or blanched vegetables, cheeses or any savoury ingredient.

Prepare shortcrust pastry (opposite), using 250g (8oz) plain flour and 125g (4oz) butter. Roll out and line a 23cm (9in) flan dish or loose-bottomed flan tin and bake blind (page 245) for 15 minutes until the shell is partially baked; remove the paper and dried beans. Prepare an egg custard by beating 4 eggs with 300ml (½ pint) milk and 300ml (½ pint) single cream. Serves 6.

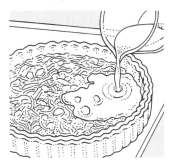

1 *Into the partially baked tart shell, scatter 125g (4oz) cooked diced ham and 125g (4oz) diced Brie or grated Cheddar cheese, or any other chosen filling. Place the flan dish on a baking sheet. Pour over the prepared egg custard.*

2 *Bake at 160°C, 325°F, Gas Mark 3 for about 45 minutes or until the mixture is set when tested with the tip of a knife. Serve the flan either straight from the oven, slightly cooled or at room temperature.*

FLAVOURING SHORTCRUST PASTRY

• One of the most usual variations is to make a delicious cheesy pastry by mixing finely grated strong-flavoured cheese, such as mature Cheddar or Parmesan into the flour before incorporating the fat.

• Red Leicester cheese will add a bright golden colour to pastry, and another alternative is to crumble strong blue cheese like Gorgonzola or Roquefort into the flour before adding the fat.

• Herb pastry is most successful with pungent dried herbs such as oregano, tarragon, thyme or dill. Very finely chopped fresh rosemary and tarragon and ground bay leaves also work well.

• You can make spiced pastries adding either one ground spice or a mixture of several. Turmeric gives a bright yellow colour and a little curry powder imparts an instant Indian touch.

• Cumin, either whole or ground, combined with dried mint, creates a Middle Eastern character and goes well in a pastry crust for lamb dishes.

• Make a luxurious saffron pastry by heating a little milk with a good pinch of saffron strands and leaving to cool. Use this as the binding liquid instead of chilled water.

• Whole spices such as caraway, dill or fennel seeds are effective in a pastry to be used for cheese, vegetable or fish fillings, as is a mixture of finely grated lemon peel and a pinch of ground cardamom.

• Tomato purée can be added to both cheese and herb pastries, and will bind, so you need little, if any, water.

• For garlic pastry, add very finely chopped garlic and mix it evenly into the flour – chopped fresh ginger is good with garlic.

• Finely chopped fresh red chilli adds an exciting bite to a spicy pie crust.

MAKING SAVOURY TARTLETS

Individual savoury tartlets can vary in size and shape, and are ideal for a first course or as bite-size canapés for a drinks party. Bake the shells blind (page 245) before adding a sweet or savoury filling. Cool on a wire rack.

The shortcrust pastry quantities (opposite) will make 18–20 small boat-shaped tartlets. If you bake the pastry shells in advance, store in an airtight container for 2–3 days or alternatively you can freeze them.

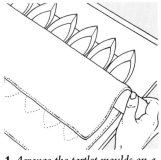

1 *Arrange the tartlet moulds on a baking sheet in neat rows. Roll out the pastry to 2.5mm (⅛in) thick (page 244), then use the rolling pin to place it gently over the moulds.*

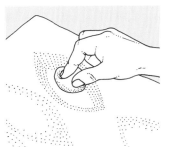

2 *Use a small piece of surplus dough to gently press the rolled-out dough into each mould, pushing it well into the sides and base and taking care not to stretch the dough. Using a dough ball avoids making unecessary fingermarks in the dough.*

3 *Roll the rolling pin over the tops of the moulds to cut off excess pastry. Prick the base of each one with a fork. Fill with greaseproof paper and beans and bake blind (page 245) for 8–10 minutes. Remove the paper and beans and bake for a further 6–8 minutes.*

Tartlet shells can be filled with many savoury fillings to make interesting first courses or snacks. Here, the shells contain fried onion slices with finely chopped parsley, red pepper purée and Greek yogurt combined with spring onions and walnuts.

RICH PASTRIES

These rich pastries are crisper than plain shortcrust pastry, making ideal containers for free-standing tarts with creamy or fruit fillings. Even traditional jam tartlets become special when you make them with a rich shortcrust pastry. The sweet hot butter crust pastry and chocolate crust pastry (both opposite) couldn't be easier to make, and the results are always wonderful.

You may find these rich pastries much more difficult to roll out than plain shortcrust pastry. I just use my fingertips to pat the dough into the tin or dish. When baked any small cracks will be gone, as if by magic.

If you are using sweet shortcrust pastry (below) for a fruit or custard tart, you can make the dough with ground nuts for a complementary flavour. Substitute up to half the amount of flour with ground blanched almonds, walnuts, pecans or hazelnuts and omit half the egg yolks. Because ground nuts do not contain the gluten found in wheat flour, this dough will be very difficult to handle. Don't even try to roll it out. Pat it out lightly instead with your fingertips. Sweet shortcrust pastry can also be flavoured with kirsch or other liqueurs, instead of the vanilla essence used in the recipe below.

SWEET SHORTCRUST PASTRY

This rich pastry, called *pâte sucrée* by the French, is crisp like a biscuit because of the sugar and egg yolks it contains. Unlike ordinary shortcrust pastry, the key to success here is using butter that is soft at room temperature, not well chilled. To make a rich nut pastry to complement a fruit filling substitute ground nuts for half the flour in this recipe and only use 2 egg yolks. Try ground almonds, walnuts, pecans or hazelnuts.

To fill a 23cm (9in) tart tin, use 200g (7oz) plain flour, ½ teaspoon salt (if using unsalted butter), 125g (4oz) diced, softened butter (preferably unsalted), 50g (2oz) caster sugar, 4 egg yolks and ½ teaspoon vanilla essence.

MAKING JAM TARTLETS

Little jam-filled tartlets make a rich pudding or teatime treat. Use sweet shortcrust pastry (left) and roll it out to about 2.5mm (⅛in) thick. These tartlets can't be patted into the tin because they are shaped with a biscuit cutter, but if it is too difficult to handle, roll the dough between 2 sheets of greaseproof paper. Knead pastry trimmings together and reroll, cutting out more rounds until all the pastry has been used. Cut out little hearts or leaves to put on top of the jam, if you like.

Jam tartlets do not need blind baking because the jam reaches a high enough temperature to cook the pastry base. Bake at 375°F, 190°C, Gas Mark 5 for about 10–12 minutes until the jam is bubbly and the pastry golden. Makes about 25 tartlets.

1 *Sift the flour and salt on to a work surface. Make a well in the centre, circling from the middle outwards with your fist.*

2 *Add butter, sugar, egg yolks and vanilla essence to the well. Use your fingertips in a quick 'pecking' motion to mix together.*

1 *After rolling out the pastry, dip a cutter in flour and cut as many rounds as bun cups, rerolling the dough as necessary.*

2 *Place pastry rounds into bun cups and press into the base and up the side of each. Chill for at least 30 minutes before baking.*

3 *As the mixture comes together use both hands to draw in the remaining flour and shape the dough into a ball.*

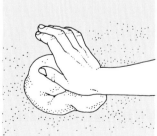

4 *Lightly knead the dough until smooth with the heel of your hand. Wrap the dough in clingfilm and chill for at least 30 minutes before using.*

3 *Add about 1 heaped teaspoon jam to each cup, taking care not to overfill as the jam bubbles up during cooking, and bake (above).*

4 *Leave to cool for about 5 minutes. Then use a palette knife to remove each tartlet, and place on a wire rack to cool further.*

SWEET HOT BUTTER CRUST PASTRY

This method is rather similar to hot–water crust pastry (page 256). I tried it out as an experiment years ago and have used it ever since. This pastry must be the easiest of all pastries to make, and produces a crisp, biscuit-like crust, ideal to hold a filling. It can be baked blind without being weighted down and doesn't shrink during baking although it is best to chill the uncooked crust first. If liked, you can use strained orange or lemon juice instead of water, and include the finely grated rind, too, for extra flavour.

1 *To make enough sweet hot butter crust pastry to line a 23cm (9in) loose-bottomed flan tin, sift 175g (6oz) plain flour, ½ teaspoon salt and 2 tablespoons icing sugar into a mixing bowl and stir together.*

2 *Gently melt 125g (4oz) butter and 1 tablespoon water in a saucepan, then gradually pour the warm liquid on to the flour mixture, mixing in with a wooden spoon until you have a soft dough.*

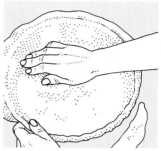

3 *Press the warm dough into the flan tin with your fingertips, lining the base and sides of the tin evenly. Press any cracks to seal together. Chill for at least 30 minutes before baking. If baking blind (page 245), prick the base lightly all over with a fork.*

FLAVOURING SWEET PASTRY

• You might not think of adding herbs to flavour sweet pastry but I think very finely chopped rosemary or mint leaves added to the flour can be lovely.
• Finely grated lemon, lime or orange rind is delicious for mince pie pastry.
• A mixture of grated orange rind and ground cardamom, cinnamon or nutmeg is splendid for apple pie pastry.
• Make a honey-flavoured pastry by sweetening the flour with honey instead of sugar; this works best if you melt 2 tablespoons honey with the butter as in the sweet hot butter crust pastry (above), omitting the water.
• Apart from the chocolate crust pastry method (right), flavour sweet shortcrust pastry with chocolate by adding 25g (1oz) cocoa powder to the flour, or by stirring coarsely grated chocolate into the flour. This results in an interesting dappled effect. These chocolate pastries are good with finely grated orange rind, too.
• For a mocha flavour, use a very strong mixture of cold coffee as the binding liquid, or, for a stronger taste, include some finely ground coffee in the flour.

CHOCOLATE CRUST PASTRY

This is another version of the sweet hot butter crust recipe (above) and is very simple to make. It produces a really dark and crisp chocolate case, which is delicious baked blind and then filled with fresh blueberries, raspberries or other soft or exotic fruits which you can glaze or dust with icing sugar or cover with flavoured fromage frais.

You can also use the baked case as a container for ice cream, spooning in balls just before serving.

1 *To make enough pastry to line a 23cm (9in) loose-bottomed flan tin, sift 125g (4oz) plain flour, 50g (2oz) cocoa powder, 75g (3oz) icing sugar and ½ teaspoon salt into a mixing bowl. Stir well.*

2 *Melt 75g (3oz) butter and 1 tablespoon water in a saucepan, then gradually pour on to the flour and cocoa mixture, stirring with a wooden spoon. Knead briefly to form a dough.*

3 *Press the warm dough into a flan tin with your fingertips, lining the base and sides evenly. Chill for at least 30 minutes before baking. If baking blind (page 245), lightly prick the base all over with a fork. This pastry can be baked blind without being weighted down with dried beans.*

This luscious Blueberry Tart with a Chocolate Crust (page 258) is simple to make. The pastry is baked blind and filled with cream and fresh berries. Melted bramble jelly is used for the glaze.

FLAKY PASTRY

Classic puff pastry is a light, flaky pastry which can be cut in a variety of shapes to make perfect containers for fillings of seafood, chicken, fish, ham or vegetables, or used to make sweet layered pastries. The flaky alternate layers of butter and dough rise as the oven heat melts the butter and turns the water to steam.

Although not as buttery as homemade puff pastry, which is very time-consuming to make, commercial puff pastry makes a perfectly acceptable and convenient alternative. However, the flaky pastry given here provides almost as good results as puff pastry with much less work.

Whatever method of flaky pastry you use, however, it needs baking at a high temperature. Unless the recipe or packet instructs differently, bake the pastry at 220°C, 425°F, Gas Mark 7 for 8–10 minutes, to help the pastry to start to rise during baking, then lower the temperature to 190°C, 375°F, Gas Mark 5 for the remaining time. A dampened baking sheet which creates steam also helps the pastry to rise during baking and so does a roasting pan full of hot water on the shelf below.

MAKING FLAKY PASTRY

Flaky pastry is quicker to make than traditional puff pastry. Begin by sifting 250g (8oz) plain flour into a bowl with 1 teaspoon salt. Add 50g (2oz) diced, chilled butter and rub or cut into the flour until the mixture resembles fine crumbs. Make a well in the centre and pour in 150ml (¼ pint) chilled water, mixing with a knife to form a soft, but not sticky dough. Form into a ball, wrap well in clingfilm and chill for 15 minutes. On a lightly floured surface, roll out the dough to a neat rectangle about 15 x 45cm (6 x 18in). Keeping the edges straight as you work distributes the fat evenly.

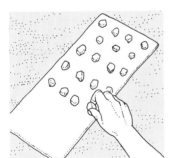

1 Cut 125g (4oz) more chilled butter into small pieces and dot evenly over the top two-thirds of the dough.

2 Fold up the unbuttered third of the dough, over half the buttered part of the rectangle. Fold the top third of the dough down on top.

3 Make sure the butter is completely encased. Press the edges of the dough down with a rolling pin to seal in the air. Wrap the dough and chill for 20 minutes. Place the dough on a lightly floured surface.

4 Turn it so the seam sides are top and bottom. Keeping the edges straight, roll into a rectangle and fold into thirds (steps 2 and 3) twice more, always turning in the same direction. Wrap and chill for 20 minutes before using.

MAKING PASTRY CASES

Flaky pastry, as well as homemade or commercial puff pastry, can be formed into a variety of shapes, most of which are baked blind (page 245) so they remain crisp when a sweet or savoury filling is added.

Vol-au-vents, deep pastry circles in a variety of sizes, are perhaps the best known pastry cases made from flaky or puff pastry. The quantity of flaky pastry (left) will make about eight 10cm (4in) lozenge-shaped cases.

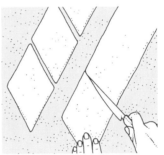

1 To make lozenge-shaped pastry cases, roll out pastry thinly to about 5mm (¼in) thick. Cut out 10cm (4in) wide strips, then cut into lozenge shapes.

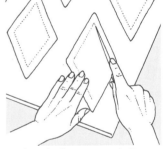

2 Place the lozenges on 1–2 dampened baking sheets. Score a line 2.5cm (1in) inside each lozenge, cutting halfway down; this will form the lid.

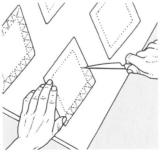

3 Glaze the top surface of each lozenge with an egg glaze (page 245) and cut to decorate the edges. This helps the pastry rise. Prick the lids so they don't rise too much. Bake at 200°C, 245°F, Gas Mark 7 for 10 minutes until golden and well risen.

4 After baking the centre of the lozenge will have risen to form a lid. Carefully cut out the scored pastry lid and peel off any uncooked dough underneath. Store in an airtight container and use within 24 hours. Fill with your chosen filling just before serving.

USING FLAKY PASTRY

- Add character to flaky pastry by sifting dry flavourings such as ground spices, dried herbs or even ground toasted hazelnut or almonds into the flour before adding the water.
- An extremely easy and featherlight cheese-flavoured pastry which is as effective as puff pastry for cheese straws can be made by mixing together 125g (4oz) plain or wholemeal flour, 2 teaspoons baking powder, ½ teaspoon cayenne pepper and 175g (6oz) grated cheese. Rub in 125g (4oz) diced well-chilled butter, then add 2 egg yolks and stir to make a dough. Press into a ball and chill. Roll out thickly and cut into straw shapes. Bake towards the top of the oven at 220°C, 425°F, Gas Mark 7 for about 10 minutes.
- Commercial puff pastry is excellent for wrapping up meat, fish or chicken to cook *en croûte*, as the flavours of the food seep in to the pastry, yet it holds together as a casing far better than homemade pastry. Use an egg yolk glaze (page 245) for savoury ingredients cooked *en croûte* in a puff pastry case.
- Sweet puff and flaky pastry pie tops and pastries can be given a caramel glaze by brushing lightly with a cold, heavy sugar syrup (page 208).

Use ready-made commercial puff pastry to make jalousie, filled here with jam and apple slices.

MAKING JALOUSIE

Use two 500g (1lb) packets of puff pastry and 500g (1lb) peeled dessert apples to make this jam and apple pudding with a semi-open top. You can replace the jam with mincemeat (page 306) or sweetened and flavoured cream or curd cheese. Instead of apples, you can also use pears or firm fresh apricots.

Defrost the pastry, if frozen, and roll out one packet to a 20 x 38cm (8 x 15in) rectangle. Place on a dampened baking sheet. Spread with enough jam to within 2.5cm (1in) from the edges. Top with thin peeled apple slices in neat rows, mounded up. Brush around the edges with water.

1 *Roll out the second packet of pastry to a 23 x 40cm (9 x 16in) rectangle. Lightly dust with flour and fold in half lengthwise. With a sharp knife, cut crosswise through the folded edge to within 2.5cm (1in) of the unfolded edge at 1cm (½in) intervals. Place the folded pastry over the filling with the fold in centre and unfold, cutting off any excess pastry.*

2 *Seal the outside edges of the jalousie by pressing down firmly with a bent index finger, then 'knock up' all around by cutting into the pastry edge with the back of a knife as you press. Glaze the pastry with an egg yolk glaze (page 245) and bake the jalousie at 200°C, 400°F, Gas Mark 6 for 30–35 minutes until the pastry is golden.*

SAUSAGE ROLLS

Good homemade sausage rolls are simple to make, especially if you use commercial puff pastry. The secret lies in using a good-quality sausagemeat to which you can add your own flavourings, such as wholegrain mustard, finely chopped fresh herbs, crushed garlic, chutney or even some crumbled blue cheese.

Allow 250g (8oz) each of sausagemeat and puff pastry. Makes 2 large sausage rolls or 12 bite-sized ones to serve with drinks.

1 *Roll out the pastry on a lightly floured surface to a 30 x 15cm (12 x 6in) rectangle. Spread with your chosen flavouring. Alternatively, add the flavouring by mixing it in with the sausagemeat.*

2 *Shape the sausagemeat, dusting lightly with flour, to the same length. Wrap it in the pastry, sealing the join with beaten egg and placing join-side down on a lightly greased baking sheet.*

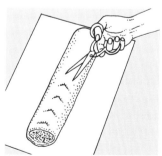

3 *Snip the top with scissors 6–8 times, or cut into individual rolls. Glaze well with beaten egg (page 245) and bake at 200°C, 400°F, Gas Mark 6 for about 20 minutes until golden.*

FILLO AND STRUDEL PASTRY

The word 'fillo' in Greek means leaf, which is what the sheets of this extra-thin dough are like. Commercially made fillo pastry is also suitable for making quick-and-easy strudel recipes. Fillo and strudel pastry made from flour, water, salt and oil is stretched to develop the gluten in the flour until the dough is so thin that you can actually read through it! It can be made at home but it takes skill and practice to achieve perfection and hardly seems worth the time or trouble when fresh or frozen fillo is so easily available. A packet of fresh fillo will last up to a month in the refrigerator and several months if frozen. Once you have defrosted fillo dough, however, do not re-freeze it.

Fillo pastry lends itself equally well to sweet or savoury fillings, and always provides a delicate crisp result.

WORKING WITH FILLO

Fillo is a versatile pastry which can be formed into many shapes or used to fill flan tins or other containers. It is very easy to use. The two important things to remember are to thaw frozen fillo in the refrigerator to avoid any excess condensation forming, which causes the sheets to stick together, and to keep any dough you are not using covered with a damp tea towel to prevent it drying out. It is best to use clarified butter (page 96) for brushing between the sheets, but depending on the filling, olive oil or melted goose or duck fat can also be used. A light brushing is all that is needed. Use a sharp knife to cut the pastry neatly to avoid compressing the edges. Bake to a deep golden colour to ensure it is cooked through. A brushing of oil or melted fat before and after baking helps moisten the pastry, but it often cracks anyway because the layers are so thin and crisp.

Versatile fillo pastry is used to make these spinach and Feta-filled fillo parcels and fillo cups filled with ratatouille (page 59).

SHAPING FILLO PASTRY

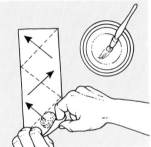 

To make fillo parcels: 1 *Cut 1 sheet fillo pastry into 7 x 23cm (3 x 9in) strips. Brush 1 strip with melted butter and keep the remainder covered with a damp tea towel. Place 1 large teaspoon filling, such as chopped spinach and crumbled Feta cheese in the bottom right-hand corner. Fold the bottom edge to meet the left side, forming a triangle and enclosing the filling.*

2 *Fold this triangle straight up, so the left sides are flush. Repeat these folds, working from left to right, until you reach the top. Tuck in any flap of leftover pastry. Brush with melted butter. Place on a lightly greased baking sheet and repeat with remaining strips to make more parcels. Bake at 190°C, 375°F, Gas Mark 5 for 12–15 minutes; brush again with melted butter.*

 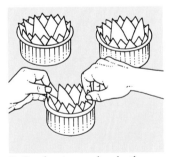

To make 4 fillo cups: 1 *You need 4 buttered ramekin dishes or shallow tartlet or patty tins and 2 fillo pastry sheets. Use 1 sheet at a time and cut each sheet in half; then each half into quarters. Working with 4 quarters at a time and keeping the remaining pastry covered, lightly butter the fillo. Place 1 piece in a ramekin dish. Place another quarter crosswise over the first 1 and continue with 2 more quarters.*

2 *Gently crimp and make the corners stand up. Repeat with the remaining fillo to make 3 more cups. Place the ramekins on a baking sheet and bake at 190°C, 375°F, Gas Mark 5 for 5 minutes until crisp. Remove the cups from the ramekin dishes and fill with hot or cold savoury ingredients, such as finely chopped ratatouille, soft white cheese mixed with herbs or spices, taramasalata or other fish pâtés.*

CLASSIC APPLE STRUDEL

This traditional pudding of light, flaky pastry layers enclosing spiced apple slices was originally Hungarian, but now it is usually associated with Austria. The strudel can be made ahead (it will keep in a freezer for a few weeks) but reheat before serving.

You can get a light, crisp, flaky result by using commercial fillo pastry. Unwrap the dough and keep it covered completely with a damp tea towel.

For this classic apple strudel, peel, core and thinly slice 3 large cooking apples. In a large bowl, toss the apple slices with 75g (3oz) caster sugar, 75g (3oz) raisins, 75g (3oz) chopped walnuts, 1 teaspoon ground cinnamon, ½ teaspoon grated nutmeg and 1 tablespoon lemon juice. Set the filling aside while preparing the dough.

You will need 4 sheets fillo pastry and about 75g (3oz) dry breadcrumbs to assemble the strudel. Melt 125g (4oz) butter for brushing the pastry as you go. Grease a large baking sheet with melted butter.

1 *Uncover the fillo pastry and place 1 sheet on the greased baking sheet; keep the remaining pastry covered. Brush with melted butter and sprinkle with about one third of the breadcrumbs.*

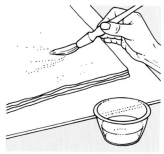

2 *Keeping the unused pastry covered, repeat the layering of fillo sheets, brushing each one with melted butter and sprinkling with breadcrumbs. Do not sprinkle crumbs on the top layer.*

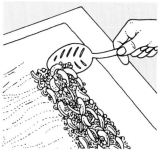

3 *Drain the juices from the prepared apple filling. Spoon the filling along one side of the fillo, placing it about 5cm (2in) in from the end to about 5cm (2in) from each of the long edges.*

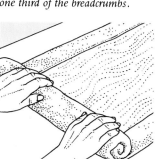

4 *Fold the long edges over the filling, then fold the end flap over to enclose the filling. Gently roll up the strudel like a Swiss roll (page 267), being careful to keep the long edges tucked in as you roll.*

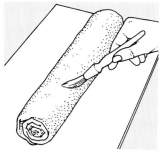

5 *Turn over so the seam side is underneath. Brush the strudel with melted butter. Bake at 190°C, 375°F, Gas Mark 5 for about 30 minutes until the pastry is golden and the apples are tender when pierced with a skewer.*

6 *Remove the strudel from the oven and brush with melted butter. To serve, cool slightly and transfer to a serving dish. Dust lightly with icing sugar. The strudel can be served warm or at room temperature.*

FILLING FILLO PASTRY

• Use fillo pastry for little stuffed appetizers. Prepare as for fillo cups (opposite) but add a filling before baking, then pinch the tops together to make ruffled tops, like money bags, and bake. The easiest fillings are curd, cream or crumbled Feta cheeses, seasoned and mixed with chopped herbs, spices, chopped anchovies, chopped spring onions, spinach, tuna, sliced mushrooms, sun-dried tomato paste, crumbled crisp bacon or diced ham, coarsely grated Parmesan, pesto sauce, curry paste or grated raw carrot.
• Precooked fillings for fillo cups can be various kinds of cooked or smoked fish and seafood (crab is wonderful) mixed with herbs and seasonings, or ratatouille-type mixtures of cooked vegetables.
• Make large fillo pies with layers of buttered fillo layered with a spicy mince mixture.
• Double crust fillo pies can also be made enclosing fillings of precooked meat, game, poultry, fish, vegetables, cheese and eggs – a good way of using leftover Christmas turkey.
• Make an impressive dome of rice encased entirely in crisp fillo pastry: line a pudding basin with several layers of fillo, well brushed with butter, and fill with a cold moist or buttery pilaff mixture with chicken, fish or other ingredients. Cover the top with the pastry and bake at 190°C, 375°F, Gas Mark 5 for 45 minutes, then turn out on to an ovenproof plate. Return to the oven for 10–15 minutes until golden.

A sweet use for fillo pastry is apple strudel, made by encasing spiced apple slices and raisins between delicate layers of pastry.

CHOUX PASTRY

This is truly a magical pastry, as a pasty thick sauce is transformed into incredibly light, puffy crisp pastry. Even though the results give the opposite impression, choux paste (the name in French means cabbage because that's what the little buns resemble) must be one of the easiest pastries to make as long as you follow a few simple rules.

It is also wonderfully versatile and after the first stovetop cooking stage will happily wait to be baked: the paste will keep for up to a day in the refrigerator. When ready to bake the paste needs no rolling – you simply pipe or spoon it on to a dampened baking sheet into all sorts of shapes from tiny little puffs to large gougère rings.

As canapés, bite-sized choux buns can be served hot and crisp with creamy and spicy chicken or fish fillings or cold with taramasalata or mayonnaise- or fromage frais-based mixtures. Baby walnut-sized buns can be flavoured with curry spices and cheese, then deep-fried as beignets and served warm, dusted with grated Parmesan cheese.

The classic thin, elegant chocolate éclair, which must be nearly everyone's favourite teatime treat, is surprisingly easy to make and can reappear in a different shape as the ever-popular dinner party pudding, round profiteroles. These are stuffed with cream and can be served with either a hot or cold chocolate or butterscotch sauce.

MAKING CHOUX PASTRY

There are two stages of making choux pastry, the mixing of the paste in a saucepan followed by baking in a hot oven when the thick paste puffs up miraculously into whatever shape is required. Because of this double cooking, it is important that the eggs, which give choux paste its delicate lightness, are not added too soon or they will set and cook in the heat instead of expanding dramatically in the oven.

It is also important when melting the butter in the water (in step 2) not to let it come to the boil before it has completely melted. When the flour is added all at once it looks quite alarming, but, press on with the beating, and smoothness will soon be restored. For a crisper choux pastry, use strong white flour usually used for ordinary bread-making, although plain flour can also be used. Do not, however, use self-raising flour.

Because choux pastry puffs up and out so much, leave lots of space for expansion when you pipe or spoon the paste on the baking sheet. As with flaky pastry, a little moisture on the baking sheet and a roasting pan of water on a lower shelf of the oven provides steam which again helps with the rising during the second stage of cooking.

1 Sift 100g (3½oz) strong plain flour with a pinch of salt into the centre of a sheet of greaseproof paper and place by the stove: this is so you can tip the flour into the saucepan all at once when the time comes. Put 75g (3oz) chopped butter into a medium-size saucepan with 200ml (7fl oz) cold water.

2 Melt the butter without stirring and bring slowly to the boil, still without stirring. When boiling immediately remove the pan from the heat and shoot all the flour into the pan in one go, slightly bending the greaseproof paper in the centre to form a funnel. Beat the flour and butter at once with a wooden spoon.

FLAVOURING CHOUX PASTRY

• Fillings for small choux bun canapés can be either mayonnaise or fromage frais mixed with fresh herbs, finely chopped smoked salmon, crumbled Roquefort cheese, sun-dried tomato paste with fresh basil leaves, chopped tuna with fresh garlic, and many other seasonings. Taramasalata makes a delicious filling, a thick red pepper purée with chopped fresh herbs is an exciting surprise, and the famous Italian combination of spinach with Ricotta cheese is always good.
• Profiteroles are best known with a chocolate covering, but are also delicious with caramel and butterscotch coatings, or with fresh fruit purées, sweetened to taste which serve as a thick sauce (page 208).
• Profiteroles can be filled with whipped cream or a mixture of cream and natural yogurt or fromage frais – you can also streak the whipped cream with a little cooled, melted chocolate, or you can fill the profiteroles with ice cream and then cover with hot chocolate fudge sauce (page 209).
• To make sweet fritters deep-fry spoonfuls of choux paste, then sprinkle with vanilla sugar (page 235) and serve with cream or ice cream.

3 The mixture will look awful at first, but keep beating with the wooden spoon and it will soon form a smooth glossy paste that comes cleanly away from the sides of the saucepan. Put to one side to cool for 10–15 minutes. Meanwhile, beat 3 eggs together in a measuring jug with a fork.

4 After the paste has cooled, gradually add the beaten eggs in stages, beating well after each addition with a wooden spoon until the egg is incorporated; you may not need all the egg. The mixture is ready to shape or pipe when it is of a stiff dropping consistency and still firm enough to hold a shape.

USING CHOUX PASTE

How you shape choux paste before baking is what determines what it becomes. Spoon the paste into a piping bag fitted with a small nozzle, about 1cm (½in) wide. The easiest way is to put the bag fitted with the tube into a tall jug (page 24) and fold the top of the bag over the top of the jug. Spoon in the paste, then remove the bag and twist the top closed ready for piping.

Choux pastry is nicest served crisp, so after baking it is best to pierce to let out the steam or cut open and scoop out any soft paste inside. Then return the choux to the turned-off oven for a few minutes to dry out.

After baking, choux buns can be filled with hot savoury fillings, or left to cool and then filled with sweet fillings. Éclairs are traditionally filled with whipped cream or pastry cream (page 211) and then coated with a smooth chocolate sauce (page 230) or simply melted chocolate softened with a little butter or cream. In the summer include a few fresh raspberries mixed in with the whipped or pastry cream.

Profiteroles are usually filled with whipped cream or pastry cream and drizzled with chocolate sauce. Chopped, toasted hazelnuts are also excellent mixed in with the cream.

Chocolate-covered éclairs and profiteroles, decorated here with a fresh raspberry sauce (page 208) and fresh raspberries, are two popular uses for choux pastry.

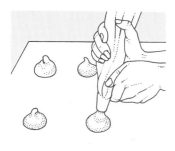

1 *To make profiteroles, lightly grease 1 or 2 baking sheets and splash with cold water. Fill a piping bag with the choux paste. Pipe 18–20 balls of paste, about the size of a walnut, on to the baking sheets, spacing them well apart to allow for expansion.*

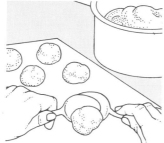

2 *If you do not have a piping bag and nozzle, simply spoon large teaspoonfuls on to the prepared greased and wet baking sheets, spacing them well apart. Bake at 200°C, 400°F, Gas Mark 6 until the profiteroles are golden brown and crisp on the outside.*

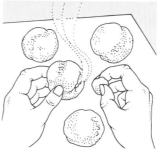

3 *Remove the baking sheets from the oven and cut open the profiteroles carefully. Scrape out any uncooked paste and return the shells to the turned-off oven to dry out for about 5 minutes. Transfer to a wire rack and cool until ready to fill.*

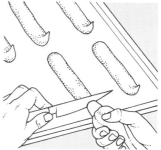

To make éclairs, *pipe about 18 7cm (3in) lengths on to a lightly greased and wet baking sheet as for profiteroles, cutting the paste from the nozzle with a wet knife. Bake as for profiteroles, then transfer to a wire rack and cool before filling and coating.*

GOUGÈRE

Choux paste is not always sweet. It can also be flavoured with strong grated cheese and baked and served with a delicious filling as in this classic French dish in which the paste rises up dramatically to produce a spectacular treat. The paste can either be spooned around a shallow ovenproof dish enclosing a filling, as here, or it can be spooned or piped into a large ring on a greased and wet baking sheet and baked. After baking split in half horizontally and spoon in your chosen filling.

Make up the choux paste (opposite), then stir in 75g (3oz) strong Cheddar or Gruyère cheese, cut into fine dice or grated coarsely. Season well. Make a filling of either 250g (8oz) smoked flaked haddock or diced mushrooms mixed with 300ml (½ pint) white sauce (page 196), flavoured with sautéed onions and carrots, 1 teaspoon of curry or tikka paste and finely chopped fresh parsley. You can also add leftover poultry, meat, finely chopped vegetables or crumbled, crispy fried bacon.

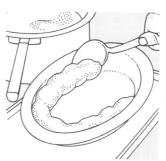

1 *Grease a very shallow pie or other ovenproof dish, about 23cm (9in) long. Place the dish on a baking sheet and spoon the cheesy paste around the sides, mounding it up well.*

2 *Spoon the filling into the centre, sprinkle with a little grated cheese, then bake at 200°C, 400°F, Gas Mark 6 for 35–40 minutes until the gougère is risen and golden brown. Serve at once.*

TRADITIONAL PASTRIES

Hot-water crust pastry and suet crust pastry are uniquely British pastries that have played an important part in the culinary traditions of meat pies and steamed puddings. Hot-water crust is only used for savoury pies, while suet crust pastry makes rich sweet or savoury baked, boiled or steamed puddings which can be delicious.

A raised meat or game pie (page 242), made with a hot-water crust, is well-worth preparing at home. Although time-consuming, it is not difficult. The tin or pie mould is lined with the warm dough to form a 'coffyn', as the old

recipes refer to it. This dense pastry forms a firm case which encloses the meat mixture. The thickness of the pastry allows the meat to cook slowly and retain all its juices while being 'protected' from the heat – the end results therefore remaining moist, tender and full of flavour.

Once baked, pies made with hot-water pastry can be stored in the refrigerator for about a week, but the pastry loses its crispness after a day or two. They freeze well, but you must allow a day for them to thaw at room temperature, if particularly large.

MAKING A GAME PIE

You need a 18–20cm (7–8in) deep round springform tin or use a 10 x 25cm (4 x 10in) traditional raised pie mould if you have one.

For the filling you will need about 750g (1½lb) pheasant, partridge, pigeon, venison or hare, or a combination of game. Remove the meat from the bones, discarding all skin. Keep the bones to make a game stock (page 29) which is then added to the cooked pie. Cut the breast meat into long strips and marinate for at least 6 hours in 125ml (4fl oz) port or brandy. Whizz the remaining chopped game flesh, 400g (13oz) diced pork, 50g (2oz) smoked streaky bacon, and 1 quartered onion, in a food processor. Add 1 teaspoon ground allspice, 1 teaspoon dried thyme, 1½ teaspoons salt and black pepper. Stir in 175g (6oz) unsmoked cooked, diced gammon and set aside. Adjust the seasoning and set aside.

To make the hot-water crust pastry, sift 500g (1lb) plain flour and 1½ teaspoons salt into a bowl and make a well in the centre. Melt 175g (6oz) lard in 250ml (8fl oz) water and bring to the boil. Pour into the well all at once and stir quickly to make a smooth dough, adding a little water if necessary. Cool only enough to handle, then knead just until smooth.

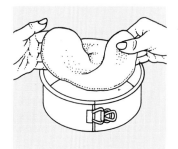

1 *While the dough is still warm, roll out three-quarters of it into a circle about 3 times the width of the tin or mould and about 1cm (½in) thick; keep the remaining dough warm under a tea towel. Fold the dough lightly in half and lower into the greased mould. Unfold and press smoothly and evenly into base and sides. Trim so there is a 1cm (½in) overhang.*

2 *Drain the port or brandy from the marinating breast meat and stir it into the filling. Spoon one-quarter of the filling into the pastry-lined tin or mould and lay one-third of the breast meat over the filling. Repeat the layers of meat and filling, pressing down lightly each time and mounding the final layer of filling slightly in the centre.*

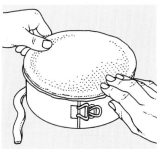

3 *Turn the overhanging dough edges back over the filling. Roll out the remaining dough about 5mm (¼in) thick to the shape of the tin or mould. Trim the overhang of the pastry lid to match the 1cm (½in) overhang of the sides to just fit. Lift the lid on to the filling and press the edges together to seal. Glaze the top with a beaten egg (page 245).*

4 *Make a small hole in the centre of the top to allow steam to escape during baking and insert a piece of rolled foil into the hole as a 'chimney' to prevent the hole from closing up. Reroll any pastry trimmings and cut leaves or flowers to decorate the pie top (page 245). Attach the decorations by lightly pressing them into the glaze.*

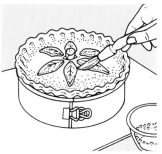

5 *Set on a baking sheet and glaze the top again with beaten egg. Bake at 200°C, 400°F, Gas Mark 6 for 15 minutes, then at 160°C, 325°F, Gas Mark 3 for a further 1¼ hours or until a skewer inserted into the centre feels hot to the touch. A meat thermometer in the centre should read 75°C, 170°F. Cover the top with foil if necessary.*

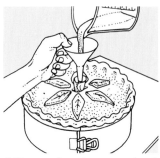

6 *Remove from the oven and cool completely. To make the aspic prepare 250ml (8fl oz) game stock dissolved with 1 sachet gelatine (page 33). Insert a funnel into the rolled foil and slowly pour in as much of the aspic as possible, about 125–175ml (4–6fl oz). Leave to chill for several hours; the stock will set to jelly around the meat.*

STEAMED SUET CRUST PASTRY

It seems amazing but this rich, flaky pastry is equally delicious made into the Special Steak and Kidney Pudding (page 259) as it is here in Sussex pond pudding, one of my favourite puddings. Make this soft pastry with all suet, or a suet-butter mixture, which I like for sweet puddings.

The classic suet crust pastry doesn't have breadcrumbs but I use them in this recipe because they give a much lighter finished texture. You can leave them out if you like, replacing their weight with extra flour.

Sussex pond pudding derives its name from the 'pond' of lemony, buttery juices which seeps out when the golden, flaky crust is cut. Do not be alarmed when the pudding sinks during cooking, this is simply because the filling isn't packed solid.

For the filling, use 175g (6oz) diced butter, 175g (6oz) demerara sugar and 1 large or 2 smaller lemons. Generously butter a 1.2 litre (2 pint) pudding basin, and line the base with buttered greaseproof paper cut to fit. Serves 4–6.

Hot, buttery, lemon-flavoured juices ooze out of Sussex pond pudding when the suet crust pastry is cut open.

1 *Sift 175g (6oz) self-raising flour, 1 teaspoon baking powder, and ½ teaspoon salt together into a large mixing bowl. Stir in 50g (2oz) fresh white breadcrumbs and 125g (4oz) shredded vegetable or beef suet. Make a well in the centre of the bowl and use a round-bladed knife to stir in 150ml (¼ pint) mixed cold water and milk, forming a soft, elastic dough.*

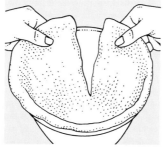

2 *Lightly dust with flour and form into a ball. Roll out the dough into a large circle about 5mm (¼in) thick. Cut out one-quarter of the dough in a triangle shape to use for the lid; set aside and keep covered. Shape the remaining three-quarters of dough into a cone and ease into the pudding basin, gently pressing on to the base and sides. Do not trim off the overhang.*

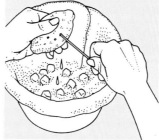

3 *Spoon half the butter and sugar into the lined basin. Pierce the lemon all over with a skewer and place in the centre. Cover with the remaining butter and sugar, adding extra if necessary to fill the basin but the filling will not be solid. Fold the pastry overhang back over the filling.*

4 *Reroll the remaining dough into a circle for the lid. Moisten the pastry edges and place the lid on top, pressing the edges together to seal. Top with 2 layers of greaseproof paper, the bottom sheet buttered, and pleated together across the middle to allow for expansion.*

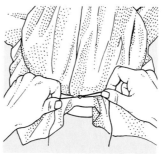

5 *Cover with a sheet of foil much larger than the top of the basin, moulding it round the basin and allowing room for expansion, and tie the paper and foil securely round the rim with string. Draw up the 4 corners of the foil and twist and scrunch together to make a handle for lifting the basin in and out of the saucepan (page 218).*

6 *Place a metal trivet in a large saucepan and fill with enough water to come halfway up the pudding basin. Bring to the boil and add the basin. Cover the saucepan and simmer for 3–4 hours, topping up with boiling water if necessary. Uncover the pudding and invert on to a large dish with a lip to contain the buttery sauces. Serve with cream.*

MODERN USES FOR TRADITIONAL PASTRIES

• Hot-water crust pastry can be flavoured like all other doughs by including spices and herbs in the flour. Alternatively, you can put crushed garlic with the water and lard when you heat them together.
• Sesame seeds included in the flour for hot-water crust pastry add flavour and more texture. Use milk instead of water to make a richer pastry and for an even richer effect, use butter instead of lard. You can also use a very good strong stock instead of the water to give the pastry real taste.

• If using self-raising wholemeal flour in a suet crust pastry, you should always include breadcrumbs and extra baking powder for added lightness.
• A savoury suet crust mixture can include grated cheese with or without chopped onion, and makes a lovely crust for a meat or vegetable pie which you can either steam or bake.
• A spicy chicken mixture cooked with lots of garlic and fresh ginger makes an unusual and delicious alternative to an ordinary steamed beef pudding.

FILLO PIE WITH CARAMELIZED APPLES AND PINE KERNELS (242)

Serve this spiced tart with cream, yogurt or crème fraîche. *SERVES 6–8*

> *125g (4oz) butter*
> *1kg (2lb) dessert apples, peeled, cored, halved and thickly sliced*
> *50–75g (2–3oz) pine kernels*
> *3 teaspoons ground cinnamon*
> *125g (4oz) light soft brown sugar*
> *Finely grated rind and juice of l lemon*
> *375g (12oz) fillo pastry, thawed if frozen*
> *Icing sugar*

Melt 50g (2oz) of the butter in a large frying pan over a medium heat. Fry the apples and toss them in the butter until soft, but not disintegrating. Add the pine kernels and stir around for a minute. Stir in the cinnamon, and after 1 minute add the sugar and lemon rind and juice. Stir the bubbling mixture until the juices have evaporated. Remove from the heat.

Melt the remaining butter and brush a large baking sheet, ideally a round pizza tin, with a little butter. Lay 2 sheets of fillo pastry overlapping on the baking sheet. Brush thinly with butter, then lay on another 2 sheets of fillo on top in the opposite direction. Continue for 3–4 more layers. Spoon the apple mixture on top in a circle. Fold the overlapping edges of the pastry over the mixture. Brush another 2 sheets with butter and lay them on top of the apples. Cover with another 2 buttered sheets in the opposite direction. Repeat with all the pastry, brushing the top sheets with butter. Press to seal in the apples and make a crinkly border, pinching with your fingers.

Bake at 200°C, 400°F, Gas Mark 6 for 35–45 minutes until the top is browned. Transfer to a serving dish. Just before serving dust with icing sugar.

LIME AND STRAWBERRY TART (242)

With this pretty tart – in which a mouthwatering mixture of fresh limes and strawberries top a creamy rich but thin filling encased in crisp sweet pastry – you will feel you have produced something extra special which might have come from a smart patisserie.   *SERVES 8*

> *3 fresh limes, sliced thinly*
> *250g (8oz) granulated sugar*
> *200–250g (7–8oz) medium or full fat soft white cheese*
> *4 tablespoons single cream*
> *75g (3oz) caster sugar*
> *Grated rind and juice of 1 lemon*
> *2 large eggs (size 1–2), beaten*
> *250g (8oz) fresh strawberries, hulled and halved*
> FOR THE PASTRY
> *125g (4oz) unsalted butter*
> *250g (8oz) plain flour*
> *½ teaspoon salt*
> *50g (2oz) caster sugar*
> *2 large egg yolks (size 1)*

To make the pastry, melt the butter, then set aside. Sift the flour, salt and caster sugar into a bowl. Add the egg yolks and mix well, then pour in the melted butter and mix until the dough sticks together and forms a ball. Chill for at least 1 hour before shaping. If it is too firm for rolling, let it soften at room temperature first. Roll out to a circle and line a 23cm (9in) loose-bottomed metal flan tin, using your fingertips to pat it into position. Chill until ready to add the filling.

Meanwhile, put the lime slices in a small saucepan and just cover with water. Simmer, covered, for 20 minutes. Strain off 150ml (¼ pint) water, and drain the slices. Put the measured water back into the pan with the granulated sugar. Dissolve the sugar, then simmer for 2 minutes until thickened. Add the limes and simmer, uncovered, for about 5 minutes. Set aside to cool.

Put the soft cheese into a bowl and mix in the cream and caster sugar. Gradually stir in the lemon juice, then the beaten eggs. Mix thoroughly and lightly stir in the lemon rind. Pour into the chilled pastry case.

Preheat a baking sheet in the oven at 180°C, 350°F, Gas Mark 4. To bake place the tart tin on the hot baking sheet and bake for 25–35 minutes until the pastry edge is well browned. Remove the tart from the oven and cool. Drain the lime slices from their syrup. Arrange the strawberries and lime slices on top of the tart, and then spoon the syrup all over. Remove the tart from the tin before serving. Do not refrigerate before serving.

BLUEBERRY TART WITH A CHOCOLATE CRUST (249)

This miraculous little tart can be adapted to any season by using any soft fruit which is available. Try it in particular with raspberries. *SERVES 6*

> *250ml (8fl oz) double cream*
> *1 rounded tablespoon Greek yogurt*
> *250–375g (8–12oz) fresh blueberries*
> *3 generous tablespoons bramble jelly*
> *1 tablespoon lemon juice*
> FOR THE CHOCOLATE CRUST
> *125g (4oz) plain flour*
> *25g (1oz) cocoa powder*
> *50g (2oz) icing sugar*
> *½ teaspoon salt*
> *75g (3oz) butter*

To make the crust, sift the flour, cocoa, icing sugar and salt into a bowl and mix. Melt the butter and pour into the flour mixture a little at a time, stirring in to make a dough. Press evenly over the base and about 4cm (1½in) up the sides of a buttered 15cm (6in) loose-bottomed cake tin, leaving an uneven edge. Chill for 20–30 minutes.

Put a large piece of greaseproof paper inside the tin, coming up well above the rim. Fill with dried beans and bake blind (page 245) in a preheated oven, 200°C, 400°F, Gas Mark 6 for 25 minutes. Remove the beans and greaseproof paper and put the crust back in the oven for another 5 minutes. Cool slightly then put the tin on to a jam jar and carefully push down the cake tin sides (page 20). Use a thin palette knife to transfer the crust on to a serving plate. Leave until cool.

Not more than 2 hours before serving, whip the cream until stiff, then fold in the yogurt. Spoon the mixture into the crust and level the surface. Arrange the blueberries on top. Melt the jelly with the lemon juice until smooth, then boil for 2–3 minutes. Remove from the heat, let the bubbles subside and then trickle over the blueberries. Leave at room temperature or in a cool place (but not the refrigerator) until ready to eat.

SWEET ONION, GARLIC AND SAFFRON TART *(242)*

Of all savoury tarts I think I like onion the best. In this recipe the sweet softness of boiled garlic and gently cooked onions are held in a rich eggy custard tinged with the subtle taste of saffron. Don't be alarmed by the quantity of garlic; when cooked in this way it is sweet and mild. To make six individual tarts instead of one larger tart, use 10cm (4in) tartlet tins.   *SERVES 4–6*

> *250ml (8fl oz) double cream*
> *Approximately 10 saffron strands*
> *8–10 cloves of garlic, unpeeled*
> *750g (1½lb) onions, sliced thinly*
> *2 tablespoons olive oil*
> *25g (1oz) butter*
> *1 generous teaspoon caster sugar*
> *1 large egg (size 2)*
> *2 egg yolks*
> *Salt and black pepper*
> *FOR THE PASTRY*
> *175g (6oz) plain flour*
> *1 teaspoon salt*
> *½ teaspoon cayenne pepper*
> *125g (4oz) butter*
> *1 tablespoon water*

To make the pastry, sift the flour, salt and cayenne pepper into a bowl. Melt the butter with the water, then pour into the flour gradually, mixing until you have a warm dough. Press the dough evenly over the base and sides of a 23cm (9in) fluted loose-bottomed flan tin. Chill for at least 30 minutes. Meanwhile, heat the cream and the saffron until just bubbling, then stir and set aside, stirring occasionally to infuse the cream with the saffron.

Place the garlic cloves in a small saucepan of water, bring to the boil, then simmer for 10–15 minutes until soft. Drain and set aside. Soften the onions in the olive oil and butter in a frying pan over a gentle heat, stirring, until soft but not browned. Transfer to a mixing bowl with any oil and butter from the pan. Pop the cloves of garlic out of their skins into the bowl, cut them in half lengthwise and add the sugar. Beat the cream and saffron with the whole egg and extra yolks. Add the onion and garlic mixture. Season with salt and pepper and stir.

Prick the base of the pastry case. Bake at 220°C, 425°F, Gas Mark 7 for 10 minutes, then turn the heat down to 180°C, 350°F, Gas Mark 4. Spoon the onion mixture into the pastry case, return to the oven and bake for 25–30 minutes, until the centre of the filling feels only just set to a light touch. Serve warm.

SPECIAL STEAK AND KIDNEY PUDDING *(242)*

A steamed steak and kidney pudding looks evocatively old fashioned, but it can be a leaden affair. However, with the following light crust, enriched with butter and spice, and a rich and tasty filling which has been precooked so that the crust doesn't have to steam for so long, it is a real treat. Use very tender lamb's kidneys unless you can find calves', the best kidneys of all. Start well in advance, the day before if you like.   *SERVES 6*

> *FOR THE FILLING*
> *25g (1oz) plain flour*
> *1kg (2lb) lean stewing steak, cut into*
>   *2.5cm (1in) pieces*
> *75g (3oz) butter*
> *1 very large onion, sliced*
> *250g (8oz) chestnut mushrooms, halved*
> *2 teaspoons juniper berries, crushed*
> *2 bay leaves*
> *4 or 5 whole cloves*
> *150ml (¼ pint) stout*
> *150ml (¼ pint) freshly squeezed orange*
>   *juice*
> *2 tablespoons tomato purée*
> *6 lamb's kidneys, skinned, halved or*
>   *quartered and cored or 3 calves' kidneys,*
>   *chopped*
> *Salt and black pepper*
> *FOR THE SUET CRUST*
> *175g (6oz) self-raising flour*
> *2 teaspoons ground mace*
> *½ whole nutmeg, grated*
> *1 teaspoon caraway seeds*
> *125g (4oz) fresh white breadcrumbs*
> *75g (3oz) shredded vegetable or beef suet*
> *75g (3oz) butter, frozen*
> *1 egg*

Season the plain flour with salt and pepper and use to coat the steak. Melt 50g (2oz) of the butter in a large, heavy frying pan, and fry the onion until golden. Transfer to an ovenproof casserole. Cook the mushrooms in the pan for a few minutes, then add to the casserole. Melt the remaining butter in the pan and brown the beef all over. Add the meat to the casserole with the juniper berries, bay leaves, cloves and any leftover flour. Stir in the stout, orange juice and tomato purée and season.

Cover and cook in a preheated oven, 240°C, 475°F, Gas Mark 9 for 15–20 minutes until beginning to bubble, then reduce the temperature to 150°C, 300°F, Gas Mark 2. Cook for about 1 hour, then add the kidneys and cook for a further 30 minutes until the meat is just tender. Check for seasoning and remove the bay leaves. Leave until cold.

Generously butter a 1.8 litre (3 pint) pudding basin. Mix together the self-raising flour, spices, seeds, breadcrumbs and suet. Holding the frozen butter in a cloth at one end, grate it coarsely into the mixture, mixing it in very lightly with your fingertips. Beat the egg in a measuring jug and bring it up to 175ml (6fl oz) with water. Gradually stir the liquid into the flour mixture, forming a soft, elastic dough. Form into a ball.

Roll out the dough fairly thinly on a lightly floured surface to a large round and cut out one-quarter of the dough in a triangle shape to use for a lid; set aside and keep covered with a tea towel. Shape the remaining three-quarters of dough into a cone and ease into the pudding basin, gently pressing on to the base and sides. Do not trim off the overhang. Add the filling and then fold the pastry overhang back over the filling. Reroll the remaining pastry into a circle for the lid. Moisten the pastry edges and place the lid on top, pressing the edges together to seal firmly.

Wrap the pudding basin in greaseproof paper and foil as for the Sussex pond pudding (page 257). Fill a large saucepan with enough water to come halfway up the pudding basin. Cover and simmer for about 2 hours, topping up with boiling water if necessary. Remove the basin from the saucepan. Serve the pudding straight from the basin with a white cloth tied round the lid.

CAKES and BISCUITS

I don't think anyone who decides to make a cake does it as a chore – to me it seems almost like a holiday. Both cake- and biscuit-making are not strictly necessary tasks and therefore should be pure pleasure; the pleasure of mixing the batter or dough, the pleasure of seeing how it becomes miraculously transformed in the oven, and finally, the intense pleasure, shared with family and friends, of eating what you have made. Many people feel they can't make cakes, either after suffering one disaster, or before having made a cake at all. But once anyone has made a successful cake and seen how it can be the centre of attraction, they are usually hooked.

Like pastry- and bread-making, cakes never seem to turn out exactly the same way twice. All sorts of things – the kind of flour, the type of oven and the temperature of your kitchen – seem to make a difference, but this should be part of the excitement. The cake will be your creation and you must use your judgement. If you remember a few rules, many cakes are foolproof, and the simplest homemade cake is always tremendously appreciated for its unique character and the real flavour of natural ingredients.

The most important thing to remember about cake-making is not on any account to open the oven door until the cake is at least three-quarters cooked. If you do, cold air will rush in and the cake may sink if it has not had time to set through to the centre.

Cakes vary tremendously in style according to the method used to make them. Victoria sandwich, the classic, which should be moist, springy and buttery, is made by creaming butter and sugar and beating in the eggs. On the whole, cakes containing a lot of butter are made by the creaming method, whereas with less rich mixtures, you can simply rub the butter into the flour. A whisked sponge seemed particularly magical to me when I first made one; this is a fatless cake in which the eggs and sugar are whisked to a creamy, billowing froth over hot water before folding in the flour. The mixture rises dramatically into the lightest cakes which are then sandwiched with cream and jam or fresh fruit, and eaten as soon as possible – though this is never a problem.

Fruit cakes can be made both by the creaming method for rich and buttery mixtures, or by rubbing the butter into the flour for plainer, lighter cakes. They can either be dotted sparsely with fruit as in a cherry sponge cake, or packed with different fruits as in rich fruit cakes. Some cakes can be so full of fruit that the result is simply fruit held together by a cake batter; this is expensive but very delicious. All kinds of dry fruit and nuts can be used: with fruit cakes it is always possible to be adventurous and vary combinations. Moist, sweet and squidgy cakes such as gingerbread are extremely easy to make as the butter is melted and simply stirred up with other ingredients.

Cakes do not necessarily need elaborate icing; a swift sprinkling of sieved icing sugar or caster sugar on top of the cake can look very effective, while a thin coating of glacé icing covered with little fresh flowers is often the prettiest decoration of all.

Homemade biscuits are as popular as cakes and can be made much more quickly – literally minutes – before you want to eat them. They are also a good thing to give children to do on an uneventful afternoon and they can be stored in a tin or frozen.

A selection for pudding, teatime or snack time, clockwise from top: crystallized primrose blossoms elegantly decorate Frosted Angel Cake with Lemon Curd and Blueberries (page 279); a coconut-flavoured sweetened cream cheese filling sandwiches together the layers of Exotic Chocolate Cake (page 279); toasted skinned hazelnuts add flavour and a crunchy texture to Chocolate and Hazelnut Thins (page 278); individual portions of old-fashioned, moist gingerbread (page 269) are topped with pieces of crystallized ginger; coated with icing sugar Snowballs (page 278) are round pecan biscuits with a rich taste like shortbread; fresh strawberries, shredded orange rind and a sprinkling of caster sugar decorate the light-textured Orange Velvet Cake with Strawberries (page 278).

BASIC BAKING TECHNIQUES

To be praised as a good cake baker is perhaps one of the great culinary accolades, and to achieve this goal you are best armed with basic cake chemistry.

Heat has a specific effect on liquids, flours, eggs, fats and sugars, which also react with each other during baking. Too low a heat and the cake will not cook thoroughly in the centre, producing a solid, cloying mass. Too high a temperature cooks the cake's outside quickly, causing a hard crisp exterior that forces any uncooked middle mixture to push up and erupt in a peaked and cracked appearance. Yet light, whisked sponges, for example, need quite a high heat to prevent them from becoming as flat as biscuits.

Ideally, ingredients should be at room temperature, particularly eggs which curdle more easily when cold, and butter, which mixes so much more easily when soft. Cakes should be made with soft white wheat flour. Except for some fruit or vegetable cakes, I think wholemeal flours are too dense to be used on their own but can be mixed with white. Raising agents are necessary for fat-enriched sponges, but fruit cakes and fatless whisked sponges have air mechanically introduced through beating.

Fine caster and soft brown sugars cream easily with butter, allowing lots of air to be beaten in. Granulated and demerara sugars will make acceptable cakes but give speckled top crusts. Fats not only add flavour and colour but also keeping qualities. Butter always gives the nicest flavour, but margarines make excellent cakes, too. This is why fatless whisked sponges have to be eaten very fresh, and richer cakes actually improve with keeping. Rich cakes also cut far better if left for a day or two in an airtight tin first.

PREPARING TINS

One of the keys to successful baking lies in preparing the tins before you start mixing the ingredients. Good quality non-stick tins need no preparation unless they are to be used for a rich fruit cake, which will need protection from the long baking with 1 or 2 sheets of greaseproof paper inside the tin, between the tin and cake mixture.

For really easy turning out, line the base of the tin with a disc of paper. Non-stick baking parchment needs no greasing but greaseproof paper does; secure it in the tin with a little oil or butter.

Tins for whisked sponges are best brushed with oil or melted fat, then the base lined with a disc of paper and greased again. Dust inside the tin with flour and tap upside down to remove any excess. Tins for creamed sponges just need brushing on the base and sides with oil or melted butter.

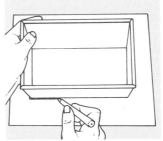

To line a loaf tin, trace around the base on greaseproof paper, then cut out. Grease the tin, fit the paper as the base and grease again. Most loaf tins are base-lined only. To line the sloping sides use a larger sheet of paper and cut into the corners as for a Swiss roll tin (below).

To line a deep square tin, cut out a base as for a loaf tin (left), then 2 paper strips, each just a bit longer than 2 sides and 2.5cm (1in) taller. Grease the tin, fit in the base paper, then the long strips in 2 sections, pressing each well into the corners to crease. Lightly grease the paper.

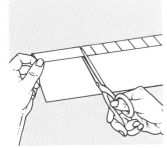

To line a deep round tin: 1 Cut out a strip of paper just longer than the circumference of the tin and 5cm (2in) taller. Fold in about 1.5cm (¾in) along 1 edge of the strip, then snip along the edge to the fold lines at 2.5cm (1in) intervals.

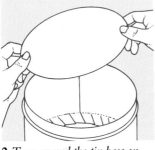

2 Trace around the tin base on greaseproof paper and cut out a disc. Grease the tin base and sides, fit in the long strip first, curving the snipped edge around on the base of the tin. Fit the disc on top and lightly grease the paper. Do not flour.

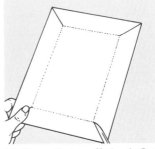

To line a Swiss roll tin: 1 Cut out a sheet of greaseproof paper large enough to cover the base of the tin comfortably and well up the sides. Trace out the tin base, then fold along the lines to crease. Cut diagonally into the 4 corners to the traced line.

2 Lightly grease the Swiss roll tin, fit in the prepared greaseproof paper, overlapping the corner diagonals for a snug fit. Secure these corner joins with metal paper clips, then lightly grease the paper.

PREPARING BAKING SHEETS

Baking sheets for biscuits should ideally be rigid and flat, and be rimless or with just 1 rim, so you can transfer the baked biscuits easily on to a wire rack to crisp as they cool. If the baking sheets are too thin and light the oven's heat will cause them to buckle. It is best to buy good-quality baking sheets with a dark surface, so they absorb heat to produce crisp biscuits (page 20).

It is a good idea to have several baking sheets, as homemade biscuits in particular spread during baking, taking up extra room.

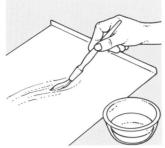

Lightly grease most baking sheets with a thin coating of flavourless oil before adding the dough to be baked. Doughs very high in fat, such as shortbread, however, are baked on ungreased baking sheets. After baking, just wipe the sheets with kitchen paper to keep them well seasoned.

To test fruit cakes such as Our Favourite Boiled Fruit and Nut Cake (page 278) for doneness, insert a metal skewer in the centre. If no uncooked mixture adheres to it, the cake is baked.

BAKING CAKES

A reliable oven is essential for successful cake and biscuit baking. Most are reliable, but no two ovens are quite the same, so recipe times should be taken only as guidelines, and you should test for doneness a few minutes before the time given in any recipe. Because temperature is so vital in baking, an oven thermometer is useful, and should be hung near the top part of the oven, unless the oven is fan-assisted. It is a good idea to read through your user's manual before baking.

Try not to peek into the oven until the cake has had time to set, especially for light cakes which might sink. And when you do check, do so very quickly and shut the door again gently. In general, position cakes on the shelf just above the centre of the oven and turn the cake if it is browning too quickly on one side.

After baking, test for doneness and then let cakes cool in their tins and biscuits cool on a baking sheet for a few minutes to settle and firm up before transferring to a wire rack to cool completely. Sponge cakes need 5–10 minutes cooling time in the tins; fruit cakes 30–60 minutes; biscuits 1–2 minutes.

Sponge cakes are baked if the top springs back when lightly pressed with a fingertip. Also, look at the cake sides, and if they have started to shrink back from the side of the tin, the cake is baked. If not baked, return to the oven for a few minutes, then retest.

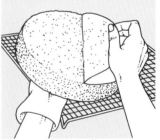

After a cake has rested in its tin (left), invert it on to your hand and peel off any lining paper immediately so the base of the cake does not become soggy. Turn base-side down on to a wire rack to cool completely. Leave until cool before icing or storing.

HINTS FOR SUCCESSFUL BAKING

• Always preheat ovens before baking and ideally use an oven thermometer to get an accurate temperature reading.
• Take care to weigh cake and biscuit ingredients accurately – the correct proportions are important for success.
• Use eggs at room temperature, so they incorporate air more easily. This results in lighter and crisper textures.
• Always use butter for a rich flavour but hard baking quality margarines can be used for simple everyday cakes as they

give better volume when beaten or creamed.
• Hard fats cream better and lighter if left out to soften at room temperature for a few hours before using. Otherwise soften on Defrost (30%) in a microwave for just a few seconds before using.
• To hold mixing bowls steady when beating place them on a folded damp tea towel.
• When adding eggs to creamed butter and sugar watch it doesn't curdle, as this can knock out air from the cake mixture. If the

mixture does curdle, add a tablespoon of flour to restore the smoothness and beat again.
• Sift flour, spices and raising agents on to a sheet of grease-proof paper when ingredients need to be added all at once, or into a bowl if added gradually.
• Always mix with wooden spoons, and fold in ingredients with large metal spoons so you knock out as little air as possible.
• 'Dropping consistency' is when the mixture drops easily off a wooden spoon when given a sharp shake. Stiff consistency

needs firmer shaking than dropping consistency.
• Brush tins and lining paper lightly but thoroughly with either oil, melted butter or pure lard or a flavourless oil. Wipe off excess oil with a crumpled piece of kitchen paper.
• Don't wash cake tins and baking sheets if possible. Often they just need a wipe with kitchen paper or a clean damp cloth. This helps keep them seasoned, so there is less chance of baked cakes and biscuits sticking during cooking.

CREAMED SPONGE CAKES

Creamed sponges have an unadulterated flavour of fresh, natural ingredients which is impossible to match in commercially made cakes. The best creamed sponge cakes contain all butter because it results in wonderfully moist, rich and springy cakes which are deservedly popular; a freshly made Victoria sandwich is the best cake of all. A true butter flavour is supremely important and it is worth spending extra. Sunflower margarine can be used but follow the all-in-one method (opposite).

Buttery sponge cakes are extremely versatile and suit anything from a children's birthday cake to a fruity upside-down pudding cake (page 221) for a family meal.

The key to a good sponge is lightness as well as rich flavour – every stage helps to achieve this. Begin by creaming the butter very thoroughly with the sugar using either an electric mixer or a wooden spoon. Caster sugar is best to use because it dissolves most easily into the butter – the cake mixture will become light, fluffy and smooth.

A sponge mixture should be soft enough to just drop from the mixing spoon – if it seems too stiff, you can fold in a little liquid, which like all the ingredients, should be at room temperature. This can be milk, fruit juice or a strongly flavoured liqueur such as rum or brandy but whichever you choose it should always be added gradually.

VICTORIA SANDWICH

The combination of fat, sugar, flour and eggs has served cooks well as the basis of simple cakes, buns and puddings. As you beat to cream the sugar and fat, air is incorporated in the mixture. Chefs sometimes do this initial creaming with a clean hand as hand warmth softens the fat and makes the sugar dissolve easier, but electric beaters or a wooden spoon will do as well. If you are using a wooden spoon, it helps to place the bowl on a folded tea towel or kitchen cloth to stop the bowl sliding on the surface.

After the eggs are beaten in, flour sifted with a raising agent is carefully folded in and the mixture moistened with a little liquid, usually water or milk. The mixture can then be baked as a single deep cake and sliced in half after baking or baked side by side in two shallow sandwich tins.

A classic Victoria sandwich cake is simply filled with jam and sprinkled with caster sugar but buttercream (page 274), whipped cream and soft cream cheese with crushed fruit are all memorable fillings. To make a chocolate sandwich cake, replace 25g (1oz) of the flour with cocoa powder. Makes one 18cm (7in) cake, enough to serve 4–6 people.

1 *Lightly grease two 18cm (7in) sandwich tins. Preheat the oven to 180°C, 350°F, Gas Mark 4. Beat together 125g (4oz) each softened butter and vanilla caster sugar (page 235) until pale, light and fluffy. Continue beating for about 5 minutes to make sure all the sugar has dissolved. It is easiest if you use an electric mixer.*

2 *When all the sugar has dissolved the mixture should no longer feel gritty. Lightly beat 2 eggs, and add half to the creamed butter and sugar. Beat thoroughly until well combined, then beat in the remaining egg, adding 1 tablespoon flour if the mixture looks as if it is beginning to curdle or separate.*

3 *Sift together 125g (4oz) self-raising flour and ½ teaspoon baking powder. Fold this in with a large metal spoon, then fold in 2 tablespoons water or flavoured liquid. Spoon into the prepared sandwich tins. Bake on the same shelf for 20–25 minutes, then test for doneness (page 263).*

4 *Cool for 5 minutes in the tins, then turn out and place base-side down on to a wire rack. When cold, spread 1 cake with 2–3 tablespoons jam, then top with the other cake and dust the top with sifted caster or icing sugar. Alternatively, use one of the filling suggestions (above).*

A homemade buttery sponge cake sandwiched together with raspberry jam is always a welcome teatime treat.

ALL-IN-ONE SANDWICH CAKE

It is possible to make an excellent sandwich cake by beating all the ingredients together at once, but the fat must be quite soft for it to be successful. Very soft butter gives the best flavour or you can use soft tub margarine, but not a low-fat spread which contains too much water. Because air is not beaten in during the initial creaming, extra baking powder is needed and the baked texture is slightly more holey.

This method is ideal for preparing in a food processor. Use this mixture as a quick sponge or upside-down pudding cake (page 221).

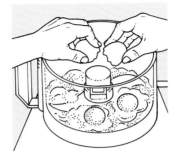

In a food processor combine 125g (4oz) each softened butter or soft tub margarine and caster sugar, self-raising flour sifted with 1 teaspoon baking powder, 2 eggs and 1–2 tablespoons water. Whizz for at least 1 minute, then spoon into 2 greased 18cm (7in) sandwich tins. Bake as for Victoria sponge (opposite).

A selection of butterfly and plain small cakes. Ice as you like, then decorate with sugared almonds and crystallized flowers.

FLAVOURING CREAMED SPONGE CAKES

• For a sponge cake with a true, traditional vanilla flavour, split a vanilla pod and extract some of the seeds with the tip of a knife. Add these to the butter and sugar as you cream them together. You can also use vanilla sugar (page 235).

• Use fine demerara or golden caster sugar instead of ordinary caster sugar for a more distinctive flavour.

• I sometimes add taste and texture to sponge cakes by stirring in whole caraway or cumin seeds, chopped toasted hazelnuts or chopped fresh rosemary or lavender leaves.

• If you are making small cakes, place a piece of chocolate in the middle of the mixture as a surprise centre. A blob of jam or a piece of fresh fruit, such as apricot or plum, are also good.

• There are many ways to fill a Victoria sandwich apart from jam and whipped cream. My favourites are lemon-flavoured buttercream (page 274), sweetened fromage frais with raspberries stirred in, curd or cream cheese sweetened with icing sugar with a little lemon juice and finely grated rind, jam with fresh soft fruits mixed into it, and fresh lemon or orange curd (page 302).

• Toppings for sponge cakes can be a smooth top of glacé icing (page 274) which you can decorate with fresh flowers, toasted nuts or sugar decorations – I always make glacé icing with lemon juice instead of water as I prefer the sharp taste.

• Caramelized nuts (page 228) are an ideal decoration for cakes.

• If you want to ice a cake's top and sides, buttercream icing (page 274) is the most suitable. This can be flavoured with finely grated lemon or orange rinds, melted chocolate, coffee, liqueurs or other flavourings.

• Sandwich cakes can either be filled or covered completely with whipped cream, especially if they contain fresh fruit in the centre. Softened cream cheese, sweetened with icing sugar, is another good quick icing.

• The most lemony sponge is made by piercing the hot cake with skewers and pouring a lemon-juice-flavoured sugar syrup (page 208) all over which the cake absorbs as it cools.

• You can also make an alcoholic cake in the same way by pouring over a rum- or brandy-flavoured syrup.

• Make sponge mixtures in loaf tins. Add some fresh cranberries, blueberries, fresh blackcurrants, glacé cherries, or other dried fruits or nuts to the mixture to make an interesting loaf cake for serving at teatime.

MAKING SMALL CAKES

Use the classic Victoria sponge recipe or the all-in-one variation for cupcakes and other individual cakes. These are just right for children's parties as you can make lots of delicious variations. Flavour them by adding 2 teaspoons finely grated orange or lemon rind, or 1 tablespoon orange flower water or rosewater to replace the water.

Cool the cakes in the paper cases on a wire rack. Top with buttercream (page 274), glacé icing (page 274) or sifted icing sugar and decorate.

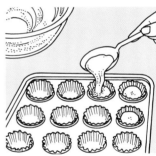

Put 18 paper cases into deep bun tins. Preheat the oven to 190°C, 375°F, Gas Mark 5. Divide the sponge mixture between the cases, filling each three-quarters full. Bake for 15–17 minutes, then decorate.

To make butterfly cakes, cut the tops off the small cakes. Spoon on 1 teaspoon buttercream and add a little jam. Cut the cake top in half and position as wings on top. Dust with icing sugar or a little cocoa powder if you like.

For madeleines, divide the sponge mixture between 8–10 dariole moulds. Bake on a baking sheet for 18–20 minutes. Cool in the moulds, then on wire racks. Brush with melted jam and roll in 75g (3oz) toasted coconut.

WHISKED SPONGE CAKES

Whisked cakes are the lightest cakes of all; certainly the fatless whisked sponge deserves its usual description of 'featherlight'. This soft-textured, delicately flavoured cake has no added raising agent, relying simply on the volume achieved by beating eggs over a pan of hot water. Because of this, it is vitally important that the eggs are fresh so that they whisk better, and that the flour is thoroughly sifted to make it as fine as possible so it can be folded very gently into the eggs without breaking down the air bubbles. Substitute 25g (1oz) of the flour for an equal amount of cornflour to make it even finer.

Whisked fatless sponges, although soft in texture, dry out quickly, so they should always be eaten on the day they are made, but this is not difficult as no other cakes disappear so fast! To make a richer, longer-lasting sponge, you can add some melted butter to the mixture but the fatless sponge here tends to be a more foolproof, and therefore, more 'miraculous' method.

Although whisked sponges seem so delicate and ethereal, the light texture is at the same time resilient and pliable, which is why it is such a successful mixture to use for making Swiss rolls and flan cases for holding fresh fruit.

WHISKED FATLESS SPONGE

A light, crisp fatless sponge is one of the easiest cakes to make, especially if you use a hand-held electric mixer.

Usually only plain flour is used for making this style of cake. If you use self-raising flour, the cake can rise too much and then collapse. For a more exotic flavour, fold in 1 tablespoon rosewater or orange flower water along with the flour.

Preheat the oven to 160°C, 325°F, Gas Mark 3. Brush a 20cm (8in) deep cake tin with oil or melted butter, then flour the base and sides well, shaking out the excess flour (page 262).

1 *Beat 3 eggs with 125g (4oz) vanilla caster sugar (page 235) in a heatproof bowl over simmering water using an electric mixer or rotary beater, until the mixture is voluminous, pale and thick and leaves a trail when the beaters are lifted. It is important to have a firm foam. Do not let the bottom of the bowl touch the water.*

2 *Remove the bowl from the heat and beat the mixture for 2 minutes more. Very gently, using a large metal spoon, fold in 125g (4oz) sifted plain flour. Pour the mixture into the prepared tin and bake for about 45 minutes until the top is a golden colour and springs back when lightly pressed with a fingertip.*

3 *Cool the sponge in the tin for 5 minutes, then turn out and place base-side down on to a wire rack to cool completely. Cut in half horizontally with a long serrated knife, then sandwich together with jam and whipped cream or crushed fresh fruit. Dust the top with finely sifted icing sugar, just before serving, if desired.*

The soft, delicate texture of a sponge flan case complements the textures of seasonal fruits. Add extra richness with a layer of pastry cream (page 211) or whipped cream under the fruit, if you like.

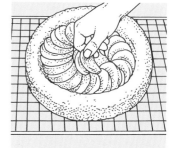

Use the whisked *sponge mixture to make a flan case for fruit. Grease and flour a 20cm (8in) sponge flan tin (page 20). Make up a reduced quantity mixture of 2 eggs with 75g (3oz) each of caster sugar and plain flour as in step 1. Bake for 25–30 minutes as in step 2, then cool as in step 3. Fill with fresh fruit and brush on a glaze with melted jelly.*

MAKING SWISS ROLL

To make a Swiss roll, simply use the basic whisked sponge mixture (opposite) but made with self-raising flour instead of plain to give a better volume. The thin flat cake is rolled and cooled around greaseproof paper so it keeps its characteristic shape. Preheat the oven to 220°C, 425°F, Gas Mark 7. Line a 30 x 23cm (12 x 9in) Swiss roll tin with greased greaseproof paper (page 262). Sift 125g (4oz) self-raising flour into a bowl.

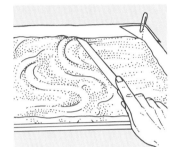

1 *Make the whisked sponge mixture (opposite) as in steps 1 and 2. Pour into the prepared tin and spread level with a palette knife. Bake for 8–10 minutes until just firm to touch.*

2 *Sprinkle a large sheet of greaseproof paper with caster sugar. Turn out the cake on to the sugary paper, peel off the lining paper and trim the edges. Roll up with the sugar paper inside. Cool.*

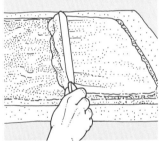

3 *Unroll, and spread with 2 tablespoons jam to about 2.5cm (1in) from the edge, then 125g (4oz) buttercream (page 274).*

4 *Reroll the cake and discard the sugar paper. Dust with icing sugar through a small, fine sieve, then serve cut into thick slices.*

This chocolate-flavoured Swiss roll is easily made from the basic whisked sponge recipe, substituting 25g (1oz) cocoa powder for an equal weight of flour. It is filled with whipped cream.

SPONGE FINGERS

These are like homemade boudoir biscuits and very useful for making superb trifles or charlottes or serving with sorbets and fruit compôtes. For a tea party sandwich two sponge fingers together with buttercream (page 274). A classic way to serve sponge fingers is with both ends dipped in melted chocolate, then leave to set on greaseproof paper after dipping.

The basic whisked sponge mixture (opposite) makes 18–20 fingers. If you don't need all the biscuits at once, freeze them in a plastic box so they don't get damaged, or store for several days in an airtight container. Preheat the oven to 200°C, 400°F, Gas Mark 6. Lightly grease and flour 2 baking sheets (page 263).

FLAVOURING WHISKED SPONGES

• Whisked sponges have a delicate, delicious taste which should not be masked by strong flavouring. I like adding a little orange flower water, rosewater or violet essence to the cake mixture and then simply filling the baked cake with whipped cream and topping it with sieved icing sugar. Crystallized rose or violet petals also make a pretty decoration.
• Finely grated lemon, orange or lime rinds are alternative flavourings for the whisked mixture, and with these a filling of fresh lemon or orange curd (page 302) with whipped cream is lovely.
• A whisked sponge is the perfect summer cake, as fresh soft fruit is an ideal filling. Raspberries and cream is one of the best mixtures of all, while strawberries taste wonderful mixed with fresh orange curd, or whipped cream containing a little orange juice and finely grated orange rind.
• Peaches or nectarines, peeled, sliced and smeared with lemon juice to stop them discolouring, are excellent with redcurrants and whipped cream, or with whipped cream with Greek yogurt folded into it.

1 *Make up the basic whisked sponge mixture. Fit a large piping bag with a plain 1.5cm (¾in) nozzle, stand it in a tall jug and fill with the mixture, refilling as necessary (page 24). Pipe out 7cm (3in) lengths on to the prepared baking sheet, using a wet knife to cut off the mixture.*

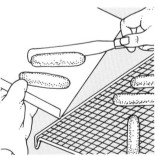

2 *Bake for 5–7 minutes until golden, changing the 2 baking sheets around halfway through baking for even cooking. Cool for 2 minutes on the baking sheets, then transfer the sponge fingers with a palette knife on to a wire rack to cool completely. Store in an airtight container.*

DRIED FRUIT *and* SPICED CAKES

After a day outside, on picnics or during the winter, there are few things more satisfying than a slice of fruit cake. Fruit and nut cakes can vary from dark, rich mixtures packed with fruit, nuts and alcohol, to much lighter, plainer cakes, dotted here and there with fruit or nuts – both are just as delicious in their different ways. Then there are sweet, gooey and often spicy cakes like gingerbread, made by melting butter and other ingredients together before mixing in the eggs and flour. In this style of extra moist cake, golden syrup, treacle or honey are often used instead of sugar, and I also find soft, dark molasses or muscovado sugar successful for flavouring.

Rich fruit cakes which contain a high proportion of butter and eggs are made by the creaming method, and as with creamed sponges, it is important to beat the butter and sugar vigorously until the sugar dissolves. During baking the cake mixture simply dries out, it does not rise. The richness and fruitiness of the cakes mean they actually improve and mature with keeping: keep wrapped in foil for at least several days before cutting.

For more everyday eating, the plainer fruit cakes also have great charm; these have far less butter which is rubbed lightly into the flour rather than creamed with the sugar. They contain fewer eggs but have a pleasing open texture. Plainer cakes can also be mixed and cooked far more quickly than rich fruit cakes, which need long and gentle cooking, gradually lowering the temperature because of the density and sweetness of the mixture.

PREPARING DRIED FRUITS

Most dried fruits now come ready washed and stoned to be used straight from the packet. If you have to wash the fruits, however, dry them thoroughly on kitchen paper and then toss in a little flour in a sieve. This distributes the fruits evenly and prevents them from sinking to the bottom of the mixture while the cake is baking.

I like to use larger dried fruits, too, such as chopped prunes, dates and apricots in my fruit cakes. Because these are sticky it is a good idea to toss them in flour, as well.

Glacé fruits, especially cherries, are best chopped first, then rinsed gently in warm water and thoroughly dried. Shake the cherries in a little plain flour in a sieve to coat lightly before adding to the cake mixture with other fruit and nuts.

A rubbed-in light fruit cake baked with a topping of chopped nuts for an extra special touch.

RUBBED-IN LIGHT FRUIT CAKE

This light cake is ideal for midweek eating. Unlike the creamed rich fruit cake (opposite), this version has lightness with added baking powder. Even though it is a homely cake, I still like to draw attention to its special nature by sprinkling the top with nuts or crushed cube sugar or even sparkling preserving sugar. The richness is provided by the butter.

Preheat the oven to 180°C, 350°F, Gas Mark 4. Grease and line a 20cm (8in) deep square cake tin or a 23cm (9in) deep round tin (page 262).

1 *Sift 500g (1lb) plain flour, 2 teaspoons baking powder and 2 teaspoons mixed spice into a bowl. Rub in 250g (8oz) butter with your fingertips until the mixture resembles fine bread-crumbs. Stir in 125g (4oz) each of brown sugar and caster sugar.*

2 *Beat 2 eggs with 6 tablespoons milk and the finely grated rind of 1 lemon. Beat into the cake mixture with a wooden spoon, until a smooth dropping consistency is achieved. If the mixture is too dry add a little extra milk and beat in. Carefully fold in 500g (1lb) dried mixed fruit with a large metal spoon.*

3 *Spoon into the tin, levelling the top. Sprinkle with chopped nuts and bake for 1 hour, then reduce the temperature to 160°C, 325°F, Gas Mark 3 and continue baking for about another hour. Test for doneness with a skewer (page 263). Cool in the tin for 1 hour, then turn out and invert on to a wire rack to cool.*

RICH FRUIT CAKE

What celebration is complete without a dark rich moist fruit cake presented with great pride? It takes time to make and cook and is expensive, but always worth the effort. When cool, wrap well in greaseproof paper and foil and store for up to 3 months.

Prepare a 23cm (9in) round or 20cm (8in) square deep cake tin (page 262) and preheat the oven to 140°C, 275°F, Gas Mark 1.

375g (12oz) softened butter
375g (12oz) soft dark brown sugar
6 eggs, beaten
500g (1lb) plain flour sifted with
*   1 teaspoon ground mixed spice*
2 tablespoons black treacle,
*   warmed*
5 tablespoons brown ale or milk
375g (12oz) currants
375g (12oz) sultanas
250g (8oz) seedless raisins
250g (8oz) pitted prunes,
*   chopped*
125g (4oz) glacé cherries,
*   quartered*
125g (4oz) candied peel,
*   chopped*
125g (4oz) blanched almonds or
*   walnuts, chopped*
Grated rind 1 lemon
3–5 tablespoons brandy or rum

FLAVOURING AND DECORATING IDEAS

• Dried apricots have a lovely sharp flavour and are delicious combined in a fruit cake with roughly chopped sweet almonds and crystallized ginger.
• Extra large raisins with dates and walnuts is a delicious combination, and so are glacé cherries with sultanas, candied peel and unsalted pistachio nuts.
• Make an American-style fruit cake by halving the quantities of flour, eggs, butter and sugar in the rich fruit cake (left) and omitting the milk and treacle. Double the amount of dried fruit, using a selection of chopped glacé fruits and cherries, pineapples and pears. Bake in a greased 23cm (9in) ring mould at 160°C, 325°F, Gas Mark 3 for about 1½ hours, then test for doneness (page 263).
• Fruit juices can be used in cake mixtures, instead of the milk.
• Spices are often used in cake mixtures; I like to use freshly ground individual spices instead of mixed spice – ground cloves, mace, nutmeg, cinnamon and cardamom are my favourites.
• Try the gingerbread recipe (below) using honey instead of treacle and adding a little finely chopped fresh lemon peel.
• Substituting ground almonds for some of the flour gives a fruit cake a lighter texture. It is very important to use really fresh nuts in cake mixtures as stale nuts have an unpleasant, rancid taste.
• Marzipan (page 275) and royal icing (page 275) are traditional in rich fruit cakes but if you don't like marzipan just brush the cake with a layer of melted jam and let it set before icing.
• To present a very different and striking fruit cake at a festive occasion, glaze the surface with melted redcurrant jelly, then scatter with silver balls, and decorate with a pattern of angelica leaves and berries made with bits of glacé cherry.
• Plainer cakes can be sprinkled with slivered or chopped nuts, or with coarse coffee sugar crystals or demerara sugar towards the end of the cooking.

1 *Cream together the butter and sugar well until pale and fluffy. Gradually beat in the beaten eggs, adding 1 tablespoon of the flour if the mixture looks like curdling. Fold in the spicy flour with a large metal spoon, stirring gently in a figure of eight.*

2 *Gently mix in the treacle and ale or milk, all the dried fruits, cherries, peel, nuts and lemon rind. The mixture should be stiff but not dry. Spoon into the prepared tin, and level the top making a slight hollow in the centre so the cake rises level.*

3 *Bake in the centre of the oven for 6–6½ hours. Test for doneness (page 263), then cool in the tin for 1 hour. Skewer the top and slowly pour in the brandy or rum. Turn out, peel off the paper and invert on to a wire rack to cool completely before wrapping.*

GINGERBREAD

As no air is beaten into this style of moist cake, its lightness comes from a raising agent, in this case, bicarbonate of soda. I like to make gingerbread extra spicy by adding chopped crystallized ginger but you can also add some sultanas, raisins or walnuts for extra gooeyness and texture. Gingerbread gets even stickier if wrapped and left for a few days in an airtight tin before cutting.

Prepare a 25 x 18cm (10 x 7in) shallow rectangular tin (page 262) and preheat the oven to 180°C, 350°F, Gas Mark 4.

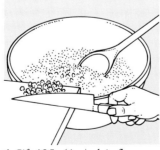

1 *Sift 125g (4oz) plain flour with 2 teaspoons bicarbonate of soda, 2 teaspoons ground ginger and 1 teaspoon mixed spice into a large mixing bowl. Stir in 75g (3oz) chopped crystallized or stem ginger. Stir in 125g (4oz) plain wholemeal flour.*

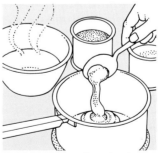

2 *Using a spoon dipped in hot water, measure out 4 tablespoons each of golden syrup and black treacle into a saucepan. Melt with 125g (4oz) butter over a low heat. Stir in 50g (2oz) soft brown sugar. Pour the mixture into the large mixing bowl and beat well.*

3 *Mix in 1 beaten egg and 150ml (¼ pint) milk. Pour into the tin and bake for about 45 minutes until a skewer comes out clean. Cool for 2–3 minutes, then turn out, peel off the paper and invert on to a wire rack. Cool completely and cut into squares.*

VEGETABLE, FRUIT *and* NUT CAKES

The idea of a cake made with vegetables does not conjure up something irresistible, yet that is exactly what carrot cake can be. Flour or ground nuts are needed to hold the eggs, but grated carrots add a very desirable texture as well as moisture, sweetness and colour. Grated courgettes and pumpkin also make delicious cakes – I particularly like pumpkin for its sweetness and brilliant colour.

Flour is by no means obligatory in cakes, but it must be substituted by something which will support the eggs and butter. Ground nuts give the most richness and taste. You can use ready-ground almonds, but grinding nuts freshly in a food processor gives a better flavour and texture. You can also experiment with different nuts which are difficult to buy ready-ground, such as walnuts, pecans and hazelnuts – and I like grinding sweet almonds which have not been blanched so that the ground nut cake is speckled with little bits of flavourful skin. The texture of the cake will vary depending on how finely you grind the nuts, so grind briefly if you want a really nutty, more crunchy cake. Fruits too, such as apples and pears, add moistness and body to cakes. If you use the sweet dessert varieties the sugar can be reduced.

CARROT CAKE

To me this cake is impossible to resist. Moist and gooey, it can very well be eaten with nothing except a fine sprinkling of icing sugar on the top, or you can sandwich it, top it or ice it completely with cream or curd cheese, softened and sweetened with icing sugar. Grated parsnips are an excellent alternative to carrots, using ground mace and whole caraway seeds as the spices instead of cinnamon.

Carrot cake keeps well in an airtight tin, or wrapped in foil, and can be made several days before eating. The addition of chopped nuts is optional, but I think it makes all the difference to the taste as well as the texture.

Preheat the oven to 180°C, 350°F, Gas Mark 4. Have ready a buttered 20cm (8in) deep round cake tin lined with a disc of greased greaseproof paper or baking parchment (page 262). If the top of the cake begins to look a little too brown before it is completely baked, lay a piece of foil lightly over the surface and continue baking. Serves 6–8.

1 *Beat 175g (6oz) caster sugar with 2 rounded tablespoons honey and 250ml (8fl oz) sunflower oil until well mixed. Beat in 3 large eggs (size 1), one at a time, beating well after each addition until pale and frothy.*

2 *Stir in 175g (6oz) self-raising wholemeal flour, a little at a time, then stir in 2 teaspoons ground cinnamon, ½ teaspoon salt, 300g (10oz) grated carrots, and 150g (5oz) chopped pecans or walnuts. Stir until well mixed.*

ADDING VARIETY TO VEGETABLE, FRUIT AND NUT CAKES

• Carrot cakes can be close and chewy like the one above or light and fluffy. For a lighter cake, fold 75–125g (3–4oz) finely grated carrot into a basic whisked sponge mixture (page 266) after you have added the flour and any spices.

• An unusual and glowing top for a carrot cake can be made by simmering coarsely grated carrots in a thick sugar and lemon juice syrup (page 208) and spreading the mixture on top of the cake when cold.

• Spices especially suitable for adding to vegetable cake recipes are ground cinnamon, mace, nutmeg, cardamom, coriander, cloves and allspice.

• Finely grated orange or lemon rind is always a good, flavourful addition to vegetable cakes, too.

• Walnuts or pecans, ground in a food processor, have a rich oil which gives a very distinctive flavour to nut-based cakes. They are delicious in the ground nut cake (opposite) or used instead of flour in a chocolate cake recipe made with dark chocolate. Use ready-ground almonds for a blander, finer taste.

• Try adding candied peel and finely grated orange rind to a ground nut cake. Alternatively, you can include a few sultanas, chopped dried apricots, halved glacé cherries or uncooked fresh cranberries or blueberries.

• For an excellent orange cake, boil 1 unpeeled orange until soft, then cut in half and remove the pips. Purée both the flesh and skin in the food processor, and mix this purée into the ground nut mixture (opposite) made with 40g (1½oz) plain flour as well as the 75g (3oz) ground almonds.

• Add 2 tablespoons marmalade to the basic ground nut mixture (opposite) for another style of orange-flavoured cake.

• For a delicious upside-down pear pudding cake with a ground nut mixture, spoon a layer of honey on to the bottom of a generously buttered 18cm (7in) deep cake tin. Arrange thin pear slices in overlapping circles, sprinkle with lemon juice and then spoon in the ground nut cake mixture (opposite). Bake in a preheated 180°C, 350°F, Gas Mark 4 oven for 45–50 minutes. Let it rest in the tin for 10 minutes, then turn out upside down on to a serving plate. Serve the pudding cake warm or at room temperature.

3 *Pour the mixture into the prepared cake tin and bake for 1½–1¾ hours until a thin skewer inserted in the centre of the cake comes out clean. Leave to cool in the tin for about 10 minutes, then remove the cake from the tin and peel off the base paper. Put the cake base-side down on a wire rack to cool completely. Dust the top with icing sugar or fine demerara sugar just before serving, if you like, or ice as suggested above.*

APPLE CAKE

There are countless apple cake recipes from all over the Western world, especially from apple-growing areas like France, the United States and New Zealand. The tang of the fruit balances well with a light toffee-like taste in this version. The fruit can be first peeled and chopped or cooked until fluffy and then mixed in.

This recipe has extra texture from the apple and crunchy streusel topping. It is moister than normal cakes and is nicest served warm with soured cream or crème fraîche. Try making it, too, with fresh, sweet pears or pitted and chopped fresh apricots or plums instead of apples. For extra flavouring add a little ground mixed spice with cinnamon or nutmeg.

Preheat the oven to 170°C, 325°F, Gas Mark 3. Grease and line the base of a 20cm (8in) springform tin with a disc of greaseproof paper to fit (page 262). Lightly grease the paper.

 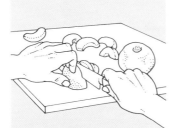

1 Beat 125g (4oz) softened butter with 150g (5oz) soft brown sugar until pale and fluffy, then beat in 2 eggs. Sift 250g (8oz) plain flour with 3 teaspoons baking powder and fold in with 2 tablespoons orange juice, 2 teaspoons grated orange rind and a few drops vanilla essence.

2 Peel 500g (1lb) Cox's or Granny Smith apples, then core and chop into medium-sized chunks. Stir the apple chunks into the cake mixture. Turn into the tin and level the surface with a palette knife. Tap the tin gently on the work surface so the mixture works its way down.

3 Rub 25g (1oz) butter into 50g (2oz) plain flour until the mixture resembles crumbs. Mix in 2 tablespoons demerara sugar, 1 pinch ground cinnamon and 1 tablespoon chopped hazelnuts. Sprinkle over the cake. Bake for 1–1¼ hours or until a fine skewer inserted in the centre comes out clean. Cool in the tin for 10 minutes, then turn out and peel off the paper. Place base-side down on a wire rack to cool.

GROUND NUT CAKE

Cakes made with ground nuts and no flour have a rich flavour and are very moist, but they also have a light and delicate texture. You can use ground nuts instead of some of the flour to improve the texture of fruit cakes, and chocolate cakes are excellent made with melted chocolate and ground nuts and no flour at all.

Vary the following simple recipe by using different kinds of ground nuts – hazelnuts are particularly good – and by adding chopped, toasted nuts, too, to the cake mixture. This cake has enough flavour and moisture to eat plain, but you can ice it, if you like or bake 2 cakes and sandwich them together with whipped cream, Greek yogurt or fresh fruit. Serves 6.

Preheat the oven to 180°C, 350°F, Gas Mark 4. Have ready a buttered and floured 18cm (7in) sandwich tin, the base lined with greaseproof paper or baking parchment (page 262).

1 Beat 125g (4oz) softened butter and 150g (5oz) golden caster sugar in a large mixing bowl until light and fluffy, then beat in the finely grated rind of 1 lemon and ½ teaspoon salt. Beat in 3 lightly beaten large eggs (size 1) and add alternately with 75g (3oz) ground almonds, beating well after each addition.

2 Pour the mixture into the prepared tin, smooth the top and sprinkle with demerara sugar. Bake for 45–50 minutes or until a fine skewer inserted in the centre of the cake comes out clean. Cool in the tin for 10 minutes before turning out, then peel off the paper and place base-side down on a wire rack to cool completely.

A trio of cakes suitable for teatime treats or a simple pudding: apple cake served with soured cream, ground nut cake with a demerara sugar topping and a carrot cake dusted with icing sugar.

CHOCOLATE CAKES

If I had to choose one kind of cake above all others, it would certainly be a chocolate one, and there are clearly many others who share my passion. Because chocolate has real body, it is possible to make a chocolate cake with no support from flour at all – the cake will be soft, delicate and moist, ideal for a pudding. But there are many other kinds of chocolate cake, from the lightest whisked sponge flavoured with cocoa to the irresistible dense Sachertorte. Good-quality melted chocolate with a cocoa solids content of not less than 50 per cent, combined with a little powdered cocoa, makes the most chocolaty cakes of all. You can also add a little strong coffee to intensify the taste, and dark brown muscavado sugar instead of white.

Chocolate cakes suit all occasions; my family always chooses one for birthday celebrations, and chocolate cake at an everyday tea cheers everyone up. They also make perfect puddings, served with whipped cream or as an accompaniment to soft fresh fruit and fruit compôtes. They are a delicious treat for mid-morning coffee – I must confess that I even like chocolate cake for breakfast!

SACHERTORTE

You can make this classic rich, chocolate cake from Vienna's Hotel Sacher easily at home. There are many different versions of the actual cake, but the crisp dark glossy icing with its sharp apricot layer underneath is always left relatively unadorned. I just decorate with chocolate leaves or you can add the name 'Sacher' drizzled in chocolate on top from a piping bag. After icing the cake can be stored for a day or two.

Preheat the oven to 160°C, 325°F, Gas Mark 3. Grease and line a 23cm (9in) springform tin.

1 *Melt 150g (5oz) plain chocolate (page 230) and cool. Cream 125g (4oz) softened butter with 125g (4oz) caster sugar, then beat in the chocolate and 4 egg yolks. Fold in 75g (3oz) self-raising flour, sifted with 2 tablespoons cocoa powder, stirring in a figure-of-eight motion.*

2 *Add 1 tablespoon rum, 1 teaspoon almond essence and 1 tablespoon water. Whisk 4 egg whites until stiff, then carefully fold into the chocolate mixture. Turn into the tin and bake for about 50 minutes, or until the cake springs back when lightly pressed with a fingertip.*

3 *Cool in the tin for 10 minutes, then turn out and peel off the paper. Place the cake base-side down on a wire rack to cool completely. When the cake is cool, melt and sieve 3 tablespoons apricot jam and brush on the top and sides of the cake with a clean pastry brush.*

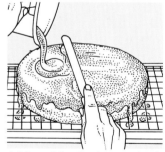

4 *Meanwhile, dissolve 75g (3oz) sugar in 5 tablespoons boiling water, then break in 125g (4oz) plain chocolate, stirring with a wooden spoon until the mixture is smooth. Boil for 1–2 minutes, then stir again and carefully pour over the cake top and sides, spreading with a palette knife. Allow the chocolate icing to cool and set. Make chocolate leaves (page 231) and arrange them decoratively on top.*

The ultimate in dark, rich chocolate cakes that few will be able to resist – chocolate fudge cake with walnuts, classic Sachertorte decorated with elegant chocolate leaves and gooey chocolate cake with whipped cream and chocolate curls.

GOOEY CHOCOLATE CAKE

Cake-eating is a most pleasurable indulgence, and the addictive qualities of chocolate make eating chocolate cake the most indulgent experience of all. The secret of a dark and gooey chocolate cake is that it should contain plenty of plain chocolate and little, if any, flour, but at the same time it should not be heavy. This is just such a cake.

Preheat the oven to 180°C, 350°F, Gas Mark 4. Have ready two 20cm (8in) greased deep sandwich tins, each lined with a disc of greased greaseproof paper or baking parchment (page 262).

After baking, leave the cakes in their tins to cool completely, then loosen the edges with a knife and turn out, removing the baking parchment. Sandwich the 2 cakes together with whipped cream or fromage frais and top with more cream or fromage frais and chocolate curls (page 231).

If you want to make this cake into a real orgy of chocolate, you can fill the middle with whipped cream or fromage frais, and then ice the whole cake with melted chocolate, into which you have stirred a little butter or cream. During the summer, fill the cake with fresh soft fruits such as raspberries, redcurrants, strawberries or peaches and whipped cream and cover with a simple sprinkling of icing sugar.

1 *Break up 250g (8oz) plain chocolate, put into a heatproof bowl set over a pan of barely simmering water and stir until the chocolate melts. Remove the bowl from the heat to cool slightly.*

2 *Put the yolks of 5 large eggs (size 1) into a large bowl, with 175g (6oz) soft, dark brown sugar and beat thoroughly with a wooden spoon or electric mixer until smooth and thick.*

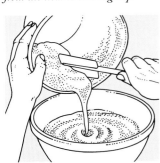

3 *Pour in the melted chocolate and beat thoroughly, then beat in 2 tablespoons hot water. Sift together 1 rounded tablespoon cocoa powder and 25g (1oz) plain flour and stir into the chocolate mixture. In another bowl, beat the egg whites with ½ teaspoon salt until they stand in soft peaks but are not too stiff.*

4 *Fold the egg whites gently but thoroughly into the chocolate mixture. Pour the cake mixture into the prepared cake tins and bake for 15–20 minutes until the cakes spring back when lightly pressed with a fingertip. Cool completely in the tin, then loosen the edges with a palette knife and turn out on to a serving plate.*

CHOCOLATE FUDGE CAKE

Americans often bake cakes with a batter mixture using oil instead of a solid fat, to produce a light texture.

Make the chocolate icing while the cake is cooling. Sift 300g (10oz) icing sugar and 25g (1oz) cocoa powder in a bowl. Melt 125g (4oz) butter with 4 tablespoons water, then beat into the icing sugar until just runny. The icing does crack once set, if moved, so ice the cake on the serving plate with pieces of greaseproof paper under the cake.

Preheat the oven to 160°C, 325°F, Gas Mark 3. Grease and line a 25cm (10in) square cake tin (page 262).

1 *Melt 125g (4oz) dark chocolate with 125g (4oz) soft brown sugar in 300ml (½ pint) milk, then stir in 150ml (¼ pint) sunflower oil and 1 teaspoon vanilla essence until well blended. Sift 350g (11oz) plain flour, 2 tablespoons cocoa powder, 1 teaspoon bicarbonate of soda and a pinch of salt into a large mixing bowl.*

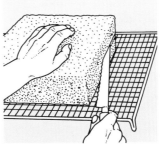

2 *Beat in the liquid ingredients, 250g (8oz) caster sugar and 4 eggs. Pour into the tin and bake for 1 hour or until a skewer comes out clean. Cool for 5 minutes, then turn out and remove the paper. Put on a wire rack and slice in half. Cool completely.*

3 *Meanwhile, make the icing (above). Use some icing to sandwich the cake halves together, then pour the rest immediately over the top and down the sides. Decorate with 12 walnut halves and allow to set. Cut into 12 pieces to serve.*

SIMPLE CAKE DECORATION

Simple cake decorations are so much prettier than formal, elaborate icing which, although it can still transform a cake into an exciting and impressive centrepiece for a special occasion, doesn't exactly make a cake look edible. Simple decoration such as sifted icing sugar on top is very effective, yet also reveals the mouthwatering aspects of the cake which make you want to eat it at once.

You don't need any skill to make attractive cake decorations, but it does require judgment. What must be learnt is that, like painting a picture, there is a point at which it is time to stop. This is when the appearance is perfect and further decoration will begin to look a muddle. Since cake decorating is the same as any decorating, your colour scheme is just as important. On the whole, one or two sympathetic colours are better than an unthought-out mixture. Certain combinations are especially effective: brilliant red, such as one perfect real red rose on dark brown chocolate, looks dramatic; silver looks lovely on white, and pale pink flowers with green leaves on the palest green icing look very summery.

BUTTERCREAM

This is a very versatile and easy icing which can be used as a filling, a coating and for simple piping. The only ingredients are softened unsalted butter and sifted icing sugar, with added flavourings (such as vanilla, almond, peppermint, lemon juice and rind, or flower water) and colourings. You can also mix the ingredients together in a food processor.

Makes enough to fill and cover one 20–23cm (8–9in) round cake or top 18–24 small cakes.

1 *Beat 125g (4oz) softened unsalted butter until light and fluffy. Sift 250g (8oz) icing sugar gradually on top, beating well with a wooden spoon. Scrape the sides of the bowl down with a rubber spatula.*

2 *Beat in a few drops of flavouring. Add colouring if desired, a drop at a time, from the tip of a cocktail stick. If the buttercream is too stiff, stir in 1 tablespoon milk, water or fruit juice to help lighten it.*

3 *Spread the buttercream with a palette knife first round the sides of the cake, then on top. Run the tip of the knife back and forth over the top for a simple but effective pattern. Or bring the icing up over the cake in little flicks.*

GLACÉ OR WATER ICING

This is one of the simplest icings – just sifted icing sugar and warm water. Because icing sugar is so sweet, glacé icing is often made with strained lemon juice, instead. The right consistency is reached when the icing flows thickly and finds its own level on a flat cake top.

Sift 175g (6oz) icing sugar into a large bowl standing on a damp cloth. Using a wooden spoon, beat in 1 tablespoon warm water or strained lemon juice. Add more water or juice in dribbles until you have a syrupy consistency.

Makes enough to ice the top and sides of a 20cm (8in) cake or 18 small cakes.

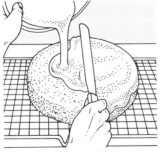

Pour the icing *steadily in an even stream on to the centre of the cooled cake placed on a wire rack over a piece of greaseproof paper. Carefully spread the icing with a palette knife, tapping the cake gently to discourage any air bubbles. Do not move the cake until the icing sets, which will be at least 4 hours, but fix any decorations on to the icing while it is still fairly liquid.*

IDEAS FOR SIMPLE CAKE DECORATION

• I sometimes ice cakes with delicate icings on the serving plate rather than a wire rack. This prevents their appearance from spoiling when the cake is moved. Keep the plate's surface neat by placing pieces of greaseproof paper under the cake to be removed before serving (page 273).

• Decorations such as a pattern of fresh leaves, coarse coffee sugar crystals or silver balls can be positioned on top of a sponge, loaf or fruit cake which has been brushed with a thick glaze of melted jelly to give a shiny glaze all over the cake.

• Natural coloured, halved angelica softened in warm water and then cut into holly leaves, makes a pretty Christmassy pattern on top of a jelly-glazed fruit cake.

• Glacé icing before it sets is an ideal base on which to arrange fresh flowers and leaves, silver balls or slivers of orange peel.

• Sifted caster sugar gives a frosty sparkle to the top of an uniced sponge cake.

• Chocolate curls (page 231) all over the top of a cake which has been iced with melted chocolate, look pretty dusted with lightly sifted icing sugar – like a slight snow fall.

• If you are icing a Christmas cake with royal icing, you can dip the edges of holly leaves into the icing and use them to decorate the cake – they look extremely effective, but if the cake has been iced long before (I don't like very hard royal icing so I only do it a day or two before) you should make a little more icing and add the holly later so that it is still a good green.

USING MARZIPAN

A paste of just ground almonds, sugar and egg white, marzipan is the traditional base for cakes iced with royal icing (below). Ready-to-roll white marzipan is of excellent quality, and it can be lightly kneaded then rolled into shape. Brush the cake top with melted, sieved apricot jam to help the marzipan stick. Marzipan can also be an effective decoration on its own, with pinched edges, an egg-white glaze and a sprinkling of sugar.

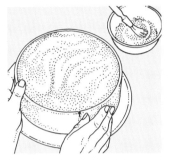

1 *For a 23cm (9in) round or 20cm (8in) square deep cake, brush the top and sides with about 4 tablespoons sieved melted apricot jam. Knead 500g (1lb) white marzipan. Roll two-thirds to a strip to fit round the cake sides, then press on and pinch together.*

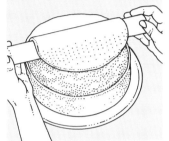

2 *Roll out the remaining marzipan to fit the cake top, using the cake tin as a template. Lift on with the rolling pin and gently press into place. Press the edges to seal. There is no need to let the marzipan dry before icing the cake (below).*

ROYAL ICING

This icing is used on rich fruit cakes and is best spread over a marzipan base. The icing holds peaks well and, depending on the consistency, can be piped attractively, swirled simply or, if made runnier, dribbled from a spoon or piped from a small bag for writing or making lacy patterns. Strained lemon juice adds flavour but will make the icing hard and brittle, so liquid glycerine is used as well. This makes enough to ice the top and sides of a 23cm (9in) round or 20cm (8in) square deep cake.

1 *Sift 500g (1lb) icing sugar into a bowl. Lightly beat 2 egg whites in a second large bowl, then gradually beat in the sugar, 1 tablespoon at a time. Add 2 tablespoons strained lemon juice and 2 teaspoons liquid glycerine, beating until glossy and fluffy, about 15 minutes. Cover with clingfilm until ready to use.*

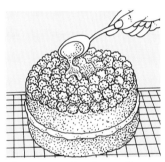

2 *Prepare a cake top and sides with marzipan (above). Spoon icing round the sides and spread evenly, swirling attractively with a palette knife. Spoon the remaining icing on top, and peak with the tip of the knife, dipping the knife quickly in hot water as necessary. Place decorations in the icing before it sets.*

A luscious rich fruit cake (page 269) with the traditional Christmas topping of marzipan and royal icing which is simply peaked all over the cake with the tip of a knife for an effective finish. No other decoration is necessary.

EASY DECORATING IDEAS

The simplest decorating touch to a cake can often be the most effective. Easiest of all is a delicate dusting of sieved icing sugar which totally transforms the appearance of a cake within seconds.

I like fresh flowers and pretty leaves as decoration best of all, and many flowers are edible, too. On cakes with roughly flicked buttercream or other icing, little silver balls dotted about on the flicks look very pretty, as do crystallized violets, primroses or mimosa balls.

Arrange raspberries, *seedless grapes or halved strawberries all over the top of a cake. To glaze melt 4 tablespoons redcurrant jelly with 1 tablespoon strained lemon juice, stirring until smooth, then spoon or trickle over the fruit.*

Use strips of paper *to make a striped pattern. Lay the strips on the cake, criss-crossing if liked, sprinkle over icing sugar through a fine sieve, then lift off the paper strips carefully one by one so as not to disturb the pattern.*

Crystallize small flowers *and petals for decorating by brushing them with whisked egg white and then dipping in caster sugar. Lay them on a baking sheet in an airing cupboard for 1–2 hours until dry, crisp and frosty looking.*

BISCUITS

Homemade biscuits are always eaten up. They can be made very quickly on a last minute whim and are nearly always eaten just as quickly. Biscuit-making is often something children can do, too.

Much of the delight of biscuits lies in their being so totally fresh, although the name biscuit is derived from the French *bis cuit*, meaning twice cooked, which was to preserve them. Biscuits are now hardly ever twice cooked, though many are very crisp and firm as if they have been. The American word 'cookie' comes from the Dutch *koekje*, meaning little cake, and cookies are usually drop-type biscuits which are made from a softer dough. They are chewier than cut-out pastry-like crisp biscuits.

Different types of oven will have varying effects on just how the biscuits cook, but as biscuits arranged on a large baking sheet are unlikely to cook completely evenly in any oven, you should watch and turn the sheet round once, probably about three-quarters of the way through the estimated cooking time. Biscuits can very suddenly become overcooked or burnt, so keep a keen eye on them for the last few minutes of cooking. It is always worth using real butter in biscuit-making.

SHORTBREAD

Homemade shortbread is rich, buttery and has a good crunchy bite if the flour is combined with some semolina or ground rice. The dough is patted out into a neat round using a cake tin base as a guide then baked slowly until very pale brown.

Preheat the oven to 160°C, 325°F, Gas Mark 3. Cream 250g (8oz) softened butter with 125g (4oz) caster sugar. Sift 250g (8oz) plain flour, then mix with 125g (4oz) semolina or ground rice. Work lightly into the buttery mixture until the dough is soft but not sticky but take care not to overknead.

Cut the dough *in half and pat out each piece on a baking sheet into a neat 20cm (8in) round, using a cake tin as a guide. Pinch the edges, then mark into 8 wedges. Prick with a fork. Bake for 30–40 minutes until golden. Cool for 5 minutes, then sprinkle with caster sugar and cut into the wedges. Cool on a wire rack.*

IDEAS FOR BISCUITS

• For children's parties, melting moments (above) can be rolled out and cut into different shapes with biscuit cutters, such as stars and hearts.
• These biscuits attract children more if you ice them with glacé icing (page 274); this can be coloured either in 1 colour or by mixing up 2 or 3 colours in separate bowls and making a pattern of colours on each biscuit or making a selection of differently coloured biscuits. A plate of red iced hearts and white iced stars looks lovely.
• Also for children sprinkle hundreds and thousands on top of iced biscuits.
• Before putting a baking sheet of uncooked biscuits into the oven, mark them with a fork or dot them all over with a skewer for a simple decoration.
• If you are making freezer biscuits (opposite), you can make 1 ball of lemon- or vanilla-flavoured dough and one of chocolate-flavoured dough. Roll each into a thin circle, put the circles on top of each other and roll up like a Swiss roll. Then wrap and freeze as instructed. When you come to slice and bake, you will produce very decorative biscuits with a dramatic swirl.
• Round biscuits dipped in icing sugar can be put back in the oven briefly to glaze.

MELTING MOMENTS

You will be popular if you make some quick biscuits when you have unexpected guests for tea. These easy biscuits really do seem to melt in your mouth. You can vary them by adding flavours to the flour such as finely grated lemon or orange rind, 25g (1oz) cocoa powder instead of 25g (1oz) of the flour and some chocolate drops too, chopped toasted nuts, vanilla essence, currants, finely chopped crystallized ginger and 1 teaspoon ground ginger.

These are best eaten the day they are made, but this isn't difficult! They are also a very good accompaniment to fruit fools and salads. Makes about 24 biscuits.

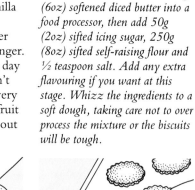

1 *Preheat the oven to 190°C, 375°F, Gas Mark 5. Put 175g (6oz) softened diced butter into a food processor, then add 50g (2oz) sifted icing sugar, 250g (8oz) sifted self-raising flour and ½ teaspoon salt. Add any extra flavouring if you want at this stage. Whizz the ingredients to a soft dough, taking care not to over process the mixture or the biscuits will be tough.*

2 *Using floured hands, gather the dough into a ball, then roll out on a lightly floured surface until it is about 5mm (¼in) thick. Cut out rounds of dough with a floured biscuit cutter or the rim of a glass, rerolling the dough as necessary, so that none is wasted.*

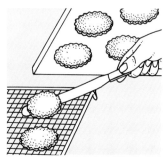

3 *Lay the rounds on a large ungreased baking sheet and bake for 8–10 minutes until pale brown. Cool on the baking sheet for 1–2 minutes, then transfer carefully to a wire rack with a palette knife to cool completely. Store the biscuits in an airtight container.*

FREEZER BISCUITS

DROP COOKIES

These biscuits are incredibly easy to make as well as being useful. Just form a rich biscuit dough into a roll and then wrap and keep in the freezer or ice-making compartment of the refrigerator. Then, at any time and within minutes, you can produce thin, light and crisp biscuits with a deliciously buttery flavour. These are perfect to serve with ice cream.

The richness of the dough makes the biscuit roll easy to slice, and you can achieve far thinner biscuits this way than by any other method I know. You can slice as many biscuits as you want from the frozen roll and then put it back in the freezer for another time.

Vary the biscuits by adding flavourings to the flour before mixing with the butter and egg. Try finely grated lemon or orange rind, finely chopped nuts, cocoa powder (for chocolate biscuits), finely chopped dried fruit or peel, desiccated coconut, and ground or whole spices. Makes about 60 biscuits.

Unlike most biscuit mixtures this does not need rolling out; you simply drop the mixture off a teaspoon on to a greased baking sheet and flatten with a fork. It is a rich mixture, ensuring a lovely short, crisp texture every time.

Flavour the basic dough with 50g (2oz) chopped nuts (especially honey-coated peanuts) or chocolate drops, currants, grated lemon or orange rind or chopped glacé cherries. Preheat the oven to 190°C, 375°F, Gas Mark 5. Lightly grease 2 baking sheets. Makes 25–30 cookies.

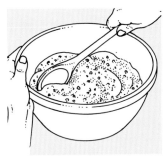

1 Cream 75g (3oz) softened butter or margarine with 75g (3oz) caster sugar, then mix in 1 egg yolk and 125g (4oz) plain flour, 1 teaspoon vanilla essence and 4 tablespoons milk or orange juice. Mix in chocolate drops or other flavouring, if liked (left).

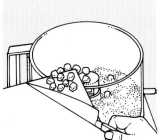

1 Sift 200g (7oz) plain flour with 2 teaspoons baking powder and a good pinch of salt. Put 150g (5oz) diced, chilled butter into a food processor with 200g (7oz) golden caster sugar, 1 beaten egg, 1 teaspoon vanilla essence and the sifted ingredients. Whizz to a soft, smooth dough.

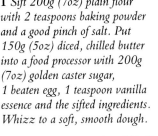

2 Scrape the dough on to a sheet of clingfilm or foil and shape into a roll 30–35cm (12–14in) long. Wrap the clingfilm or foil round the roll and continue to pat more neatly into an oblong or round. Freeze for at least 30 minutes. Preheat the oven to 200°C, 400°F, Gas Mark 6.

2 Spoon 25–30 teaspoons, spaced apart, on to the baking sheets. Flatten the mixture with a fork into rounds in a criss-cross pattern, dipping the fork occasionally into cold water to stop it sticking to the dough.

3 Bake for about 20 minutes, swapping the sheets halfway through, until the cookies are golden on the rims. Remove from the oven, leave for 2 minutes, then transfer to a wire rack to cool. Store in an airtight container.

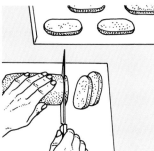

3 Unwrap the frozen dough and place on a board. Leave for a few minutes before slicing. Slice off as many biscuits as you want as thinly as possible with a serrated knife. Wrap the remaining dough again and put back in the freezer. Lay the biscuits 1.5cm (¾in) apart on a baking sheet and bake for 7–9 minutes, until golden. Leave for 1–2 minutes, then transfer to a wire rack to cool.

From left to right: chocolate-flavoured freezer biscuits, plain buttery melting moments, chocolate drop cookies and rich, crunchy shortbread.

OUR FAVOURITE BOILED FRUIT AND NUT CAKE (263)

This makes an extra rich, dark and squidgy fruit cake which lasts for months – except that it is always eaten up as soon as I make it! I make several of these cakes at the beginning of the summer holidays, as they are so useful on day-long picnics or boat trips.   SERVES 8–10

> *Coarsely grated rind and juice of 2 large oranges*
> *Dark rum or water*
> *175g (6oz) butter*
> *175g (6oz) muscovado sugar*
> *175g (6oz) ready-to-eat prunes, chopped*
> *50g (2oz) crystallized ginger, chopped*
> *50g (2oz) glacé cherries, chopped*
> *125g (4oz) sultanas*
> *125g (4oz) currants*
> *75g (3oz) walnut pieces*
> *250g (8oz) plain wholemeal flour, plus a little extra*
> *1 teaspoon bicarbonate of soda*
> *½ teaspoon ground cloves (optional)*
> *2 large eggs (size 1), beaten lightly*

Place the orange juice in a measuring jug, bring up to 300ml (½ pint) with rum or water and put it in a saucepan with the butter and sugar. Melt the butter and sugar in the liquid over a low heat, then stir in the orange rind, prunes, ginger, cherries, sultanas, currants and walnuts. Bring to the boil, cover, and simmer for 10–15 minutes, then remove from the heat and leave to cool.

Meanwhile, preheat the oven to 180°C, 350°F, Gas Mark 4. Grease a 18cm (7in) round deep cake tin or a 15cm (6in) deep square one, and line the base with a disc of baking parchment (page 262). Dust with flour.

When the fruit mixture is cool, stir together the flour, bicarbonate of soda and ground cloves. Stir in the mixture from the saucepan, then stir the eggs thoroughly into the fruit and flour mixture. Pour the mixture into the tin and bake for about 1¼ hours or until the tip of a fine skewer inserted in the centre comes out clean (page 263).

Leave in the tin for about 10 minutes, then loosen the sides with a palette knife. Turn out and peel off the paper, then place the cake base-side down on a wire rack to cool completely. If possible, store in an airtight tin and leave for a couple of days before eating.

ORANGE VELVET CAKE WITH STRAWBERRIES (260)

Cakes made with oil rather than butter are quick to mix and have particularly smooth and light textures. This cake can be eaten either for tea or as a pudding.   SERVES 8

> *150g (5oz) plain flour*
> *25g (1oz) cornflour*
> *2 teaspoons baking powder*
> *½ teaspoon salt*
> *150g (5oz) icing sugar*
> *75ml (3fl oz) sunflower oil*
> *90ml (3½fl oz) freshly squeezed orange juice*
> *2 large eggs (size 1), separated*
> *Finely grated rind of 1 orange, plus rind shreds for decoration*
> *4 tablespoons 8% fat fromage frais*
> *50g (2oz) caster sugar*
> *250–375g (8–12oz) small strawberries, halved and hulled*

Preheat the oven to 190°C, 375°F, Gas Mark 5. Grease two 18–19cm (7–7½in) deep sandwich cake tins and line the base of each with a disc of baking parchment (page 262). Sift the flour, cornflour, baking powder, salt and icing sugar into a large mixing bowl. Put the oil into another bowl, strain in the orange juice and add the egg yolks. Beat the oil mixture together lightly, then add to the sifted dry ingredients and beat to a smooth batter. Stir in the grated orange rind. Beat the egg whites until they hold soft peaks and fold gently into the cake mixture.

Pour the mixture into the sandwich tins. Bake for 25–30 minutes until well risen and the cake surface springs back when lightly pressed with a fingertip. Leave the cakes in the tins for about 5 minutes, then loosen the sides and turn out. Peel off the paper and place base-sides down on a wire rack to cool.

When cool and not too long before you want to eat, put 1 cake on a serving plate. Mix the fromage frais with the caster sugar. Stir the strawberries into the fromage frais, reserving some for decoration, and spread the mixture on to the cake on the plate. Top with the second cake. Decorate with reserved strawberries and orange rind, then sprinkle caster sugar through a sieve all over the top.

SNOWBALLS (260)

The other name for these delicious American cookies is pecan puffs, but with their coating of icing sugar, they look more like snowballs. In fact, they aren't puffy but more like a nutty shortbread.   MAKES 16–20

> *125g (4oz) butter, softened*
> *50g (2oz) caster sugar*
> *1 teaspoon vanilla essence*
> *150g (5oz) pecan halves, ground finely*
> *200g (7oz) plain flour*
> *½ teaspoon salt*
> *Icing sugar*

Preheat the oven to 140°C, 275°F, Gas Mark 1. Grease a baking sheet. Beat the butter until very soft, then beat in the caster sugar until fluffy. Beat in the vanilla essence. Stir in the pecans. Sift in the flour and salt and stir until mixed in.

Form the dough into balls the size of large marbles. Arrange on the baking sheet. Bake for 35–40 minutes. Remove from the oven and leave for 1–2 minutes. Sift icing sugar into a bowl and dip each ball into it to coat with sugar – handle delicately as they are crumbly while still warm. Cool on a wire rack.

CHOCOLATE AND HAZELNUT THINS (260)

These quickly made biscuits have the rich taste of brownies. They are good served with vanilla ice cream or a fruit fool – or simply eaten in a flash at teatime.   MAKES ABOUT 15

> *125g (4oz) butter*
> *25g (1oz) plain chocolate, broken up*
> *1 teaspoon instant coffee*
> *75g (3oz) soft dark brown sugar*
> *1 teaspoon vanilla essence*
> *1 egg, beaten lightly*
> *25g (1oz) plain flour*
> *½ teaspoon salt*
> *50g (2oz) skinned hazelnuts, toasted and chopped*

Preheat the oven to 190°C, 375°F, Gas Mark 5. Butter a 25 x 30cm (10 x 12in) Swiss roll tin. Melt the butter and chocolate together, over the lowest possible heat, stirring. Add the instant coffee and stir to dissolve. Remove from the heat and stir in the sugar and vanilla essence; then the egg. Sift in the flour and salt and mix until smooth.

Pour into the tin and spread evenly. Sprinkle all over with the chopped hazelnuts. Bake for 12–15 minutes, turning the tin round half way through. The biscuit mixture should firm up, but still seem soft – the biscuits will crisp up on top and round the edges as they cool.

Cut at once into squares or oblongs. Cool in the tin for 1–2 minutes, then transfer to a wire rack to cool completely.

EXOTIC CHOCOLATE CAKE (260)

I have called this exotic because the cream cheese filling is flavoured with coconut milk – a classic flavouring for sweets in the Far East. The combination of chocolate, cream cheese and coconut milk is truly superlative.   *SERVES 8*

FOR THE CAKE
> *175g (6oz) plain chocolate, broken up*
> *5 large eggs (sizes 1), separated*
> *175g (6oz) caster sugar*
> *2 rounded tablespoons cocoa powder*
> *2 rounded teaspoons ground cinnamon*
> *4 tablespoons warm water*
> *½ teaspoon salt*
> *Icing sugar*

FOR THE FILLING
> *50g (2oz) creamed coconut, crumbled*
> *125ml (4fl oz) milk*
> *¼ teaspoon salt*
> *75g (3oz) icing sugar, sifted*
> *250g (8oz) cream cheese*

Preheat the oven to 180°C, 350°F, Gas Mark 4. Grease two 19–20cm (7½–8in) deep sandwich tins, and line the base with a disc of baking parchment (page 262). Dust with flour. Melt the chocolate in a heatproof bowl set over a pan of simmering water, stirring occasionally. Remove the bowl from the heat.

Put the egg yolks into a large bowl, with the caster sugar and beat until pale and thick. Put the cocoa and cinnamon into a small bowl and gradually stir in the warm water until smooth. Stir into the melted chocolate, then beat the chocolate mixture into the egg yolks. Add the salt to the egg whites in another bowl and whisk until they stand in soft peaks. Fold the egg whites into the chocolate mixture.

Pour into the tins, and bake for 25–30 minutes until the cakes are firm to a light touch in the centres – the tops will probably be cracked, which is normal. Leave in the tins to cool – the cakes will sink slightly but this is also normal.

Meanwhile, make the filling. Melt the creamed coconut with the milk and salt, stirring until smooth. Do not boil. Remove from the heat. Beat the icing sugar into the cream cheese. Beat in the coconut milk and leave until cold but do not refrigerate.

When the cakes have cooled, loosen the edges, turn out and remove the paper. Put one cake base-side down on a serving plate and spread the cream cheese mixture on top. Top with the other cake, cracked top uppermost. Sift icing sugar over the top and keep in a cool place, but not the refrigerator, until ready to serve.

FROSTED ANGEL CAKE WITH LEMON CURD AND BLUEBERRIES (260)

This brilliant white cake makes a wonderful celebration cake – to make it look really festive, top with crystallized primroses or fresh flowers such as violets. Make a day ahead to allow the frosting to set.   *SERVES 8*

FOR THE CAKE
> *40g (1½oz) self-raising sponge flour*
> *15g (½oz) cornflour*
> *150g (5oz) vanilla caster sugar (page 235), or plain caster sugar*
> *4 large egg whites (size 1)*
> *1 tablespoon cold water*
> *½ teaspoon cream of tartar*
> *¼ teaspoon salt*

FOR THE LEMON CURD FILLING
> *5 large egg yolks (size 1) – those from the cake and icing eggs*
> *75g (3oz) caster sugar*
> *Finely grated rind of 2 lemons*
> *125ml (4fl oz) lemon juice*
> *250g (8oz) fresh blueberries or other berries*

FOR THE ICING
> *1 large egg white (size 1)*
> *2½ teaspoons lemon juice*
> *250–275g (8–9oz) icing sugar, sifted*

Preheat the oven to 140°C, 275°F, Gas Mark 1. Line the base of 2 ungreased 19–20cm (7½–8in) deep sandwich tins with discs of baking parchment (page 262).

Sift the flour and cornflour together several times to make them extra fine. Sift the vanilla sugar and add 1 heaped tablespoon of it to the sifted flours. Put the egg whites into a large bowl with the water, cream of tartar and salt and beat with an electric food mixer until they stand in soft peaks. With a large metal spoon, lightly fold in the remaining sugar, 1 tablespoon at a time. Fold in the sifted flours, a little at a time, sifting them directly on to the egg whites.

Pour the mixture into the tins and bake on the lowest shelf of the oven for about 1¼ hours until well risen and the cakes spring back when lightly pressed in the centre.

Meanwhile, prepare the lemon curd filling. Put the egg yolks into the top of a heatproof bowl set over a pan of simmering water. Stir in the sugar, lemon rind and lemon juice then cook over simmering water, stirring, until the mixture is thick enough to coat the back of a wooden spoon. Leave until cold.

Leave the baked cakes in their tins until cool, then loosen the sides with a palette knife. Turn out and peel off the paper, then place base-side down on a wire rack to cool completely.

Put 1 cake on to a large serving plate. Mix the blueberries into the cooled lemon curd mixture and then spread on to the cake. Top with the other cake.

To make the icing, beat the egg white until stiff, add 2 teaspoons lemon juice and beat in the icing sugar, a little at a time. Beat in the remaining lemon juice; the icing should have a thick, spreading consistency. If it is not thick enough to hold flicks, beat in a little more sifted icing sugar. Spread the icing all over the top and sides of the cake in rough flicks. Decorate and leave in a dry, fairly cool place for several hours or overnight for the icing to become softly set.

BREADS and YEAST COOKERY

Nothing whets the appetite as much as the smell of freshly baked bread filling the kitchen. There is something both soothing and rewarding about baking your own bread, and, once you have mastered the basic art and understood the principles of bread-making, you will realize how easy it is and will soon want to make it a regular part of your cooking life, and even to try more ambitious recipes.

The great advantage of making bread at home is the opportunity to vary and mix flours and add all sorts of flavourings, seeds, grains and enrichments. In any case, even with an identical dough mixture, homemade bread is unlikely to turn out exactly the same twice running. The atmosphere in your kitchen, the weather and the oven, quite apart from the brand of flour, all make small differences. The brown loaf which I make in the Calor gas stove of our holiday cottage looks, feels and tastes quite different to the one I make at home – I always think it is better, but it may be that appetites are keener and more appreciative as a result of outdoor life. The only disadvantage of homemade bread is that it does not contain improvers, so that it doesn't last as long as commercial bread, but brown bread with added oil or fat lasts fairly well.

With your own bread, you can shape loaves as you like. If you want to make your oven more like a traditional bread oven for hand-shaped, free-form loaves, you can carpet an oven shelf with unglazed tiles before you turn on the heat – the extra heat in the tiles will make the dough increase in volume before a crust forms to restrict it. Another easy way of making a lighter and crustier loaf (mainly with white breads or those with quite a large proportion of white flour) is to put a bowl of water on the bottom of the oven to increase the humidity, and you can also spray the bread a few times during baking with a fine spray of water.

No meal is really complete without some sort of bread to accompany it, and a few leftover ingredients can be made into a proper meal by adding a fresh loaf of good bread. Bread is not only full of flavour, but of nutritional value too; it is rich in complex carbohydrates, vitamins, particularly the B group, iron, calcium and fibre. Breads made from wholemeal flour have more fibre than white breads which are made from more refined flours.

When people think of bread, they think of a dough of flour and water, risen by yeast and then baked in an oven. Although this is true for the majority of breads, there is a surprising variety of breads that use either a chemical raising agent or no raising agent at all. Tea breads, scones and soda breads, for example, use baking powder or bicarbonate of soda to make them rise, and breads such as flat chapatis and parathas from India are unleavened breads that rely solely on heat to make them puff up.

Most countries have evolved their own version of bread, based on local crops. From Britain and North America come breads using wheat; from Asia and Africa flat breads of barley, millet, maize and buckwheat; from Latin America tortillas made of maize and from Germany, Scandinavia, central Europe and Russia breads made of rye.

Bread comes in all different types, shapes and sizes; plain or rich, savoury or sweet, or with added flavourings, breads range from the traditional British cottage loaf or hot cross buns to French brioches and croissants, Italian olive oil breads, German stollen and rye bread or Indian chapatis and parathas.

Clockwise from top right: Italian Hearth Bread with Black Olives and Rosemary (page 296) is quickly made with fast-action easy-blend dried yeast; Apricot and Currant Lardy Cake (page 296); Cheese and Tomato Swirl Loaf (page 297) combines the pronounced flavours of tomato purée and mature Cheddar cheese; Cheese and Spring Onion Soda Baps (page 296) are topped with grated Cheddar cheese before baking ; traditional brioche (page 290) makes for an elegant breakfast; Prune, Lemon and Honey Teabread (page 297) has a sharp lemon-juice syrup spooned over the hot loaf after baking; Seeded Brown Bread (page 297) combines sesame, pumpkin and caraway seeds as well as wholemeal and white flours.

BASIC BREAD TECHNIQUES

Most breads are made by adding yeast and liquid to flour to make a dough, which is then kneaded, left to rise, shaped, left to rise again and baked. Breads are easy to make but it is important to use the correct amounts of ingredients and you need time. Most yeasts do not like to be rushed!

Other important ingredients in bread-making are sugar, salt, fat and liquid. Sugar is the food yeast needs to make it grow. Fresh yeast can find enough natural sugar in the flour for fermentation but conventional dried yeast needs a little sugar added, when reconstituting, to activate it. Salt is an essential ingredient as it not only improves the bread's flavour but also strengthens wheat's gluten and prevents the yeast from rising too quickly. Fat, in the form of butter, margarine, lard or oil, is not essential but it produces a moister bread which keeps for longer. Too much sugar, salt and fat slows yeast down. Finally, the liquid used can be water or milk, or a mixture of both, and the amount used varies according to the flour's absorbency. The liquid should be added at a hand-hot temperature of 38°C (100°F). If it is too hot, the yeast will be killed.

USING YEAST

There are 3 types of yeast, and each is used in a different way. This chapter's recipes use only dried yeasts but here are the simple rules for using all yeasts. **Fresh yeast** is similar in colour and texture to putty, and should be firm and easy to break. It is measured by weight and is usually blended with a hand-hot liquid (38°C, 100°F) and then added to the flour, although it can also be rubbed directly into the flour. **Conventional dried yeast** is granular and comes in tins or sachets. It must first be reconstituted, and requires a little sugar to be activated. Stir into hand-hot water with a little sugar, then leave in a warm place for about 15 minutes until frothy. If the yeast does not froth, it is either too old to use or the water was too hot. **Easy-blend dried yeast** is wonderfully simple and quick to use. It comes in fine granular form in sachets and is added directly to the flour, not mixed with liquid first. The majority of easy-blend dried yeasts, called fast-action, contain an improver, usually vitamin C, and the dough only needs one rising. Check the sachet, however, because some brands of easy-blend require 2 risings.

One tablespoon or a 15g (½oz) sachet dried yeast equals 25g (1oz) fresh yeast.

BASIC BREAD

The ideal flours to use for yeast-risen breads are milled from hard wheat and are called strong flours. All wheat flour contains a sticky protein called gluten, which stretches like elastic and captures the carbon dioxide given off by the yeast. The gluten then hardens and forms the bread's structure. Several types of strong flour are available: white flour, where the bran and wheatgerm have been removed during milling; wholemeal flour which contains 100 per cent of the wheat; brown flour where some of the bran is removed during milling and malted wheat grain flour, such as Granary, which is a brown or wholemeal flour with added malted grains.

After mixing, the dough needs kneading to strengthen the gluten in flour. It is not as difficult as it may sound. Place the dough on a lightly floured surface. Fold it towards you, then push the dough down and away from you in a 'scrubbing' motion with the heel of your hand. Give a quarter turn and continue kneading for 10 minutes until the dough is smooth and elastic. The dough is ready when you press it and an impression remains.

To make a 1kg (2lb) loaf, you will need 750g (1½lb) strong flour, 2 teaspoons salt, a pinch of sugar, 15g (½oz) butter, 1 sachet easy-blend yeast and about 450ml (¾ pint) warm water.

1 *Put the flour, salt and sugar in a large bowl and rub in the butter. Add the easy-blend yeast. Make a well in the centre and pour in the warm water, mixing so all the flour is incorporated. Add a little extra water if necessary. Mix with a wooden spoon or your hands until the dough comes away clean from the side of the bowl. Place the dough on a lightly floured surface to knead.*

2 *Knead for 10 minutes until smooth and elastic, working in extra flour if necessary. Shape in a ball, put in a large bowl and place inside a plastic bag. Fold the bag under the bowl, trapping in plenty of air. Leave to rise in a warm place for 1–2 hours, until doubled. Knead again for 2–3 minutes to knock out all bubbles.*

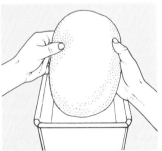

3 *Pat into an oblong the same length as a 1kg (2lb) loaf tin and 3 times as wide. Fold up in thirds, smooth the top by rolling it on the work surface, then place in the lightly greased tin, seam side down. Cover the tin and set aside to rise again in a warm place until the dough just rises to the top of the tin.*

4 *Bake at 230°C, 450°F, Gas Mark 8 for 30–40 minutes until well risen and brown. When baked, the loaf will sound hollow if you turn it out and knock the base with your knuckles. Cool on a wire rack. If not fully baked, return it to the oven without putting it back in the tin. After a couple of minutes test again.*

SODA BREAD

Soda bread is the most instant bread you can make and it is delicious as long as you eat it as fresh as possible, ideally the same day. It is made without yeast, relying instead on the chemical reaction of bicarbonate of soda and cream of tartar with buttermilk to make the dough rise. To make 1 large loaf, you will need 500g (1lb) plain white or wholemeal flour or a mixture of the two, 2 teaspoons bicarbonate of soda, 2 teaspoons cream of tartar, 1 teaspoon salt, 50g (2oz) butter, margarine or lard and about 300ml (½ pint) buttermilk.

A selection of wholemeal rolls, shaped as plaits, knots and mini bloomers, with a traditional cottage loaf (foreground) and plait, all made from the basic bread recipe.

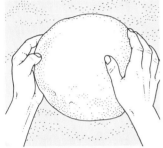

1 *Sift the dry ingredients together twice. Rub in the fat. Gradually add the buttermilk, mixing lightly to a soft but manageable dough. Without kneading shape into an 18cm (7in) round. Place on a greased and floured baking sheet.*

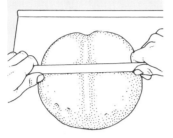

2 *Use the floured handle of a wooden spoon to press a deep cross on top. Immediately bake at 220°C, 425°F, Gas Mark 7 for about 30 minutes until the loaf sounds hollow when tested (opposite). Cool on a wire rack.*

FINISHING TOUCHES FOR BREADS

• One of the nice things about making bread is that you can add different finishes giving it an exciting, or even a very personal, appearance. For example, cut deeply into the dough to make what will become dramatic patterns; diamonds, stripes or even a half sun image with its rays spreading out. Sprinkle some sesame or poppy seeds or cracked grains into the cuts.

• Seeds and grains of all kinds can be mixed into the flour of a wholemeal or brown loaf, as well. I like to add green pumpkin seeds, sunflower seeds and whole grains of wheat soaked in water first to soften them slightly.

• Breads look beautifully shiny when they are glazed with either beaten egg, or egg beaten with milk or water at the second rise stage. You can also glaze a loaf just before you put it in the oven, but be very gentle when you brush on the glaze as a well-risen loaf can easily deflate.

• Give wholemeal bread a sheen too, by brushing with milk and water.

• Cracked wheat, sesame seeds and bran add texture and flavour to a loaf. Whole caraway seeds or cumin seeds give a definite taste which I like, especially with cheese.

• Bread need never be wasted – make fresh breadcrumbs in a food processor to use in stuffings, in suet pastry and cakes, or to coat foods before deep-frying. For toasted crumbs, toast thin slices of stale bread, put into a plastic bag and roll with a rolling pin, or whizz in a food processor.

• Slices of stale white bread can be used for bread and butter pudding (page 216) and summer pudding (page 238), or cut into cubes and deep-fried to make croûtons for soup (page 35).

• One of the most delicious teatime uses for stale bread is to soak slices in beaten egg and milk, then fry in butter and sprinkle with cinnamon and soft brown sugar.

SHAPING DOUGH

If baked on a baking sheet instead of in a tin bread dough can be made into many shapes, including rolls as well as loaves. Shape the dough before you leave it to rise a second time, unless you are using fast action easy-blend yeast, in which case shape it after the first kneading.

Grease the baking sheet before adding the dough so the baked loaves do not stick. Test that they are baked by knocking on the bases (opposite) and then leave to cool on a wire rack.

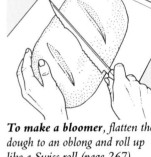

***To make a bloomer**, flatten the dough to an oblong and roll up like a Swiss roll (page 267), tucking the ends under. Place on a greased baking sheet. Cut 3 diagonal slashes across the top, then allow to rise.*

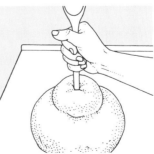

***To make a cottage loaf**, cut off one-third of the dough and shape both pieces into balls. Put the smaller ball on top of the larger one and place on a greased baking sheet. Push a floured wooden spoon handle through both balls.*

***To make a plait**, roll the dough into 3 pieces each 30cm (12in) long. Place side by side and plait from the centre to each end. Pinch the ends together and fold underneath. Place on a greased baking sheet, then allow to rise.*

SAVOURY BREADS

Savoury breads are great fun to make, extremely delicious and provide scope for inspiration. They can be made either by using a flour rich in flavour or by adding savoury ingredients to the dough. Rye flour is a popular flour to use for this purpose, examples including the traditional German and Dutch pumpernickels which are made entirely from rye flour. Because rye flour does not contain gluten, however, it makes a rather dense, heavy bread and is therefore best used with varying proportions of a strong wheat flour. Other flours to use in savoury breads include barley flour which also has a low gluten content and produces a bread with an earthy flavour; cornmeal, with its lovely golden colour, and malted wheat flour which has a sweet, nutty flavour and adds a certain gooeyness to the bread.

Many savoury ingredients can be added to a bread dough, from the more familiar cheese, garlic, nuts, seeds and herbs to the less usual shredded courgettes, puréed pumpkin, sun-dried tomatoes, pine kernels, anchovies and stoned olives. Most savoury breads should be baked a day before serving to allow their flavours to mature and make them easier for slicing. All are delicious served sliced and buttered, either on their own or as an accompaniment to soup, cheese, smoked fish or cold meats.

RYE BREAD

This recipe illustrates the use of rye flour which is stronger flavoured than wheat flour. This version has a lighter texture than many other rye breads, for example pumpernickel, as it includes some gluten-rich strong wheat flour. A variation can be made by adding seeds (below).

To make 2 cob loaves, you will need 250g (8oz) rye flour, 375g (12oz) strong white flour, 15g (½oz) salt, 1 sachet easy-blend yeast, 150ml (¼ pint) hand-hot water, 150ml (¼ pint) hand-hot milk and 1 tablespoon treacle.

1 *Mix together the flours, salt and easy-blend yeast in a large bowl. Mix together the water, milk and treacle. Add the liquid mixture to the flour and mix to a firm dough, adding extra flour if necessary. Knead the dough for about 10 minutes until it is smooth and elastic.*

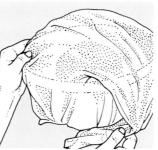

2 *Shape the dough into a ball, put back in the bowl and place inside a large plastic bag, folding the open end under the bowl. Leave to rise until doubled in size. Knead again for 2–3 minutes and shape into 2 smooth rounds or cobs. Place on a greased baking sheet, spaced well apart.*

3 *Cover and leave to rise again until doubled in size. Bake at 230°C, 450°F, Gas Mark 8 for 15 minutes. Brush the loaves with water, then reduce the oven temperature to 190°C, 375°F, Gas Mark 5 and bake for an additional 30–35 minutes. Cool on a wire rack.*

SEED BREAD

To vary the texture and flavour of rye bread, add whole seeds such as caraway, dill or cumin. Add 2–4 teaspoons of your chosen seeds to the flours in the basic recipe for rye bread (above).

Prepare as above but before the loaves rise the second time, lightly brush the surfaces with milk and then sprinkle with extra whole seeds, according to taste. Bake at 230°C, 450°F, Gas Mark 8 for 15 minutes, then at 190°C, 375°F, Gas Mark 5 for 30–35 minutes more. Cool on a wire rack.

IDEAS FOR SAVOURY BREADS

• One of my favourite savoury breads is cheese and onion bread; add grated cheese and finely chopped onion to the flour for bread dough before adding liquid. I use a mature Cheddar, Parmesan or Red Leicester cheese (to give extra colour) – and plenty of it, at least 175g (6oz) for 750g (1½lb) flour, with 1-2 onions – I like red ones for appearance. Frying the onion first to soften it and sweeten the taste is a good idea if there is time.
• Cheese bread is also excellent with added dried oregano or pieces of crisply fried bacon.
• Wholegrain mustard adds a good flavour to cheese and to many other savoury breads.
• Chopped anchovies, grated Parmesan cheese and crushed garlic is another mouthwatering combination for flavouring savoury bread.
• Many vegetables can be added to a basic bread dough; try adding grated carrots, parsnip, pumpkin, celeriac, turnip or swede. They all go well with spices such as ground coriander or cardamom and grated nutmeg.
• Grated, cooked beetroot makes an interesting scarlet loaf, and looks and tastes even better if you add some finely chopped, uncooked spinach to the dough.
• Finely chopped bulb fennel can be combined irresistibly with plenty of grated Parmesan cheese, and a few fennel seeds.
• Mashed pumpkin and grated nutmeg, or ground cinnamon, is excellent to add to breads, or you can use a yellow pepper or tomato purée with some finely chopped tomatoes, olive oil and strips of basil.
• Olive oil improves most savoury breads, and pesto sauce is an effective quick addition to dough when combined with extra olive oil. For extra flavour brush savoury loaves with olive oil and salt before baking.
• Stoned, chopped olives and walnuts go well with olive oil in a dough. Try them in the stuffed olive oil bread (opposite).

VEGETABLE AND CHEESE BREAD

Ideal for a picnic or for serving when you don't want anything too sweet, this bread is made using baking powder instead of yeast. It is very easy to mix, requiring no kneading. It is particularly good sliced and spread with cream cheese.

Before mixing the ingredients, grease a 1kg (2lb) loaf tin with sunflower oil. Cut a piece of greaseproof paper to fit the base and lightly oil the paper. Begin by sifting together 150g (5oz) wholemeal and 150g (5oz) plain white flours.

1 *Mix in 2½ teaspoons baking powder, 1 teaspoon salt and 1 teaspoon each ground cumin and coriander to the sifted flours. Coarsely grate about 125g (4oz) courgettes and 125g (4oz) carrots into the bowl.*

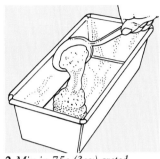

2 *Mix in 75g (3oz) grated mature Cheddar cheese, 1 teaspoon fennel seeds, 150ml (¼ pint) sunflower oil, 2 beaten eggs and about 4 tablespoons milk until just combined, then spoon into the prepared tin.*

3 *Bake at 180°C, 350°F, Gas Mark 4 for 40–45 minutes. After 25 minutes, sprinkle the top with some more grated cheese. Continue baking until a small skewer inserted in the centre comes out clean. Cool on a wire rack.*

STUFFED OLIVE OIL BREAD

The Italians make wonderful breads using olive oil for richness of flavour and texture, with delicious additions such as stoned, chopped olives or snipped sun-dried tomatoes, fresh or dried herbs, pieces of salami, or grated cheese.

This stuffed olive oil bread is sensational served fresh from the oven, but it will keep for 1-2 days.

To make 2 loaves, mix together 750g (1½lb) strong white flour, 1 teaspoon salt, 2 teaspoons dried oregano and 1 sachet easy-blend yeast in a large bowl.

A selection of savoury breads: vegetable and cheese bread (left), rye bread (centre) and stuffed olive bread with an Italian-style filling of stoned, chopped black olives and sun-dried tomatoes.

1 *Make a well in the centre of the flour mixture and pour in 5 tablespoons extra virgin olive oil and 450ml (¾ pint) warm water. Mix into a firm dough, adding extra water if needed. Place on a lightly floured surface and knead for 5 minutes or until smooth.*

2 *Shape the dough into a ball. Pour 3 more tablespoons olive oil into the bowl, then return the dough, turning to coat in the oil. Place in a large plastic bag, folding the ends under the bowl, trapping in plenty of air. Leave to rise until doubled in size.*

3 *Knead the dough for 2–3 minutes, then divide in half and knead again for 1 minute. Roll each half to a 30 x 20cm (12 x 8in) rectangle. Scatter with about 200g (7oz) of your chosen flavourings. Roll each piece up like a Swiss roll (page 267).*

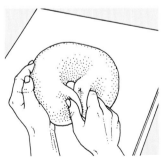

4 *Place on greased baking sheets. Curl into rounds or leave in long rolls, sealing the edges with water. Cover and leave to rise. Brush with more oil and bake at 200°C, 400°F, Gas Mark 6 for 35–40 minutes until golden. Cool the loaves on wire racks.*

SWEET YEAST BREADS

The addition of sweet ingredients in bread is popular all over the world. Many of them are regional or festive specialities, and breads of this kind include stollen from Germany, fruit breads from Britain, pear bread from Switzerland and walnut bread from France.

Many are popular at a specific time of the year, such as Christmas or Easter, or make ideal teatime treats. Fruity, spicy yeast breads make wonderful presents, too.

Some very rich, sweet doughs, such as for hot cross buns, start with a spongy flour and yeast mixture. This gives the yeast an extra boost so it develops a light texture even with all the rich ingredients. Dry ingredients can be mixed with the flour before the yeast is added but when a large quantity of dry, heavy ingredients are to be included, they should be kneaded into the dough after the first rising. Otherwise, they can hinder the rising of the yeast.

CURRANT LOAF

This is the basic recipe for an English currant loaf. You can vary the recipe by adding 2 teaspoons of ground mixed spice to the dry ingredients or use different dried fruits instead of the currants, such as snipped ready-to-eat dried apricots, if liked.

To make 1 loaf, you will need 500g (1lb) strong white flour, 50g (2oz) caster sugar, 1 teaspoon salt, 25g (1oz) butter, 125g (4oz) currants, 1 sachet easy-blend yeast, 300ml (½ pint) warm milk and water mixed, and a little beaten egg and milk to glaze.

1 *Mix the flour, sugar and salt in a bowl and rub in the butter. Add the currants, yeast and milk and mix to a soft dough. Knead until smooth, then put in a bowl, cover with a large plastic bag and leave until doubled in size. Knead again for 2–3 minutes.*

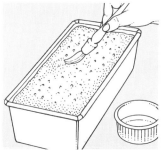

2 *Shape to fit a greased 1kg (2lb) loaf tin (page 282). Brush with egg and milk beaten together. Cover and leave to rise until the dough nearly reaches the top of the tin. Bake at 220°C, 425°F, Gas Mark 7 for 30 minutes. Turn out and cool on a wire rack.*

Slices of currant loaf and chocolate bread with hot cross buns and a German stollen loaf illustrate the varying styles of sweet yeast breads.

FLAVOURING IDEAS

• Chopped glacé apricots, peaches or mandarin oranges always add a touch of luxury to a currant loaf or stollen.

• Whole uncooked cranberries and coarsely grated orange rind, chopped soft, pitted prunes, candied citrus peel, grated lemon rind, chopped dried apricots and peaches, sultanas and raisins soaked overnight in brandy, roughly chopped walnuts, pecans, hazelnuts or almonds, dates, angelica, crystallized pineapple and ginger and fresh blueberries are all good in sweet breads.

• Spices I like in sweet breads are ground coriander, cardamom (which is so wonderful with sweet things), allspice, cinnamon, cumin, cloves, ginger, nutmeg and saffron. Infuse the spices in a warm liquid before adding it to the flour.

• I like using honey instead of sugar for the sweetener in these doughs, and if I want a strong flavour and dark colour, I use black treacle.

• Grated orange rind enhances chocolate bread (opposite), and so does ground cinnamon, the spice which goes unaccountably well with chocolate.

• Clear honey is an alternative glaze to milk and sugar or egg and milk. Use it to glaze hot bread or buns straight after baking.

• A sprinkling of coarsely ground coffee or preserving sugar on top of a glazed loaf adds sparkle and crunch.

• Sesame seeds can be sprinkled on top of a glazed loaf before baking.

STOLLEN

This German bread is traditionally eaten at Christmas. There are many variations, another one includes a thin marzipan layer.

To make 1 loaf you will need 1½ teaspoons dried yeast and a pinch of caster sugar, 6 tablespoons warm milk, 250g (8oz) strong white flour, ¼ teaspoon salt, 75g (3oz) butter, 25g (1oz) caster sugar, 150g (5oz) mixed dried fruit, 25g (1oz) quartered glacé cherries, 25g (1oz) chopped blanched almonds, ½ beaten egg and icing sugar.

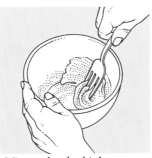

1 Mix together the dried yeast, a pinch of sugar, milk and 50g (2oz) flour. Leave in a warm place until frothy. Rub 50g (2oz) butter into the remaining flour and the salt. Stir in the sugar, fruit, cherries and nuts. Add the yeast liquid and egg.

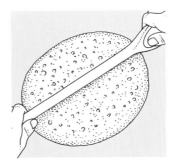

2 Mix well and knead for 10 minutes. Cover and leave until doubled in size. Knead again 2–3 minutes, then roll into a 25 x 20cm (10 x 8in) oval. Spread with remaining butter. Make an indentation along the centre.

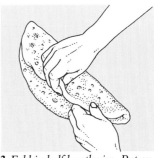

3 Fold in half lengthwise. Put on a greased baking sheet, cover and leave to rise again until doubled in size. Bake at 200°C, 400°F, Gas Mark 6 for 30 minutes. Cool on a wire rack, then dust the stollen with icing sugar.

HOT CROSS BUNS

Traditionally in Britain, bread baked on Good Friday was marked with a cross, in token of the Crucifixion.

To make 12 of these delicious spiced buns you will need 1 tablespoon dried yeast and 1 teaspoon caster sugar, 225ml (7½fl oz) warm milk, 500g (1lb) strong white flour, 1 teaspoon salt, 50g (2oz) butter, 50g (2oz) caster sugar, 3 teaspoons ground mixed spice, 125g (4oz) currants, 1 lightly beaten egg and some golden syrup or clear honey for glazing.

1 Combine the yeast, sugar, milk and 125g (4oz) of the flour. Leave in a warm place for 15 minutes until frothy. Sift remaining flour and salt and rub in butter. Stir in caster sugar, spice and currants. Add yeast liquid and egg and mix.

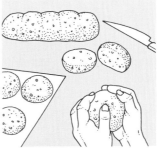

2 Knead until smooth. Return to bowl, cover and leave until dough doubles in size. Knead for 2–3 minutes, then divide into 12 pieces and shape into balls. Put on a greased baking sheet, cover and leave until doubled in size.

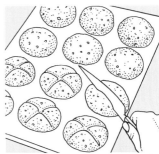

3 Using the back of a knife, make 2 indentations on each bun to form a cross. Bake at 190°C, 375°F, Gas Mark 5 for 15–20 minutes until golden. Brush a little warmed golden syrup over each bun. Cool on a wire rack.

CHOCOLATE BREAD

This is a wonderful breakfast or teatime bread. It is delicious spread thinly with butter and honey or homemade apricot or raspberry jam. The combination of melted chocolate and cocoa powder gives a lovely rich bread, which slices beautifully and toasts brilliantly. Try it spread with cream cheese.

Sift 625g (1¼lb) strong bread flour, 50g (2oz) cocoa powder, a pinch of salt and 3 tablespoons soft brown sugar into a large bowl then stir in 1 sachet plus 1 extra teaspoon easy-blend yeast. Melt 75g (3oz) plain chocolate in 50ml (2fl oz) milk, stir well and cool until warm.

Meanwhile, warm another 250ml (8fl oz) milk, soften 150g (5oz) butter until just runny but not liquid, and beat 2 eggs together. Set all aside while the chocolate cools. Lightly grease two 500g (1lb) loaf tins..

Make a well in the centre of the sifted flour mixture. Pour in the melted chocolate, the warm milk, softened butter and beaten eggs and mix together.

1 Add extra milk in dribbles, if necessary, and knead until smooth and elastic. Set the bowl aside in a large plastic bag to rise until the dough doubles in size. Knead again for 2–3 minutes and shape into 2 fat oblongs.

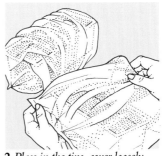

2 Place in the tins, cover loosely with plastic bags and leave until the dough just reaches the tops of the tins. Uncover, then brush with beaten egg white. Bake at 200°C, 400°F, Gas Mark 6 for 30–35 minutes. Cool on a wire rack.

CROISSANTS *and* DANISH PASTRIES

A yeast dough, spread with butter and repeatedly folded and rolled before being baked, produces a dough with flaky, puffy layers that can be used for a variety of delicious breads. The dough rises not only because of the yeast but also because of the moisture from the butter that turns to steam during baking and separates the layers into flakes.

Croissants conjure up breakfasts in France and are delicious served warm with steaming mugs of coffee or hot chocolate. Pull them apart to eat. They are usually made in the traditional crescent shape unless filled with chocolate and shaped into a small roll. Croissants are luscious eaten on their own but savoury fillings can include cheese and ham, and sweet fillings, jam and chocolate. Sweet croissants are usually given a dusting of icing sugar after baking.

There are many traditional shapes for Danish pastries, ranging from pinwheels, cushions and stars, and the filling for any shape can be savoury or sweet. This can be as simple as a little grated cheese or ham or a handful of sultanas, or can be a more moist filling such as almond paste, apple purée or cream cheese.

CROISSANTS

Although croissants are time-consuming to make, the results are worth the effort. Do not substitute any fat for butter when making them.

French croissants are characteristically light and flaky because of the flour used to make them. When made with British flour, croissants have a more bread-like texture, but they are still buttery tasting.

To make 12 croissants, you will need 1 tablespoon dried yeast and 1 teaspoon caster sugar, 250ml (8fl oz) warm water, 500g (1lb) strong white flour, 1 teaspoon salt, 25g (1oz) lard, 1 beaten egg, 250g (8oz) softened butter and a little extra beaten egg to glaze.

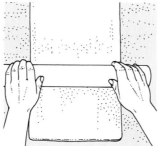

1 *Prepare the yeast and sugar with the warm water (page 282). Put the flour and salt in a bowl, and then rub in the lard. Add the yeast liquid and beaten egg and mix to form a smooth dough. Knead until smooth. Roll out to a 50 x 20cm (20 x 8in) rectangle, keeping the edges straight. Divide the softened butter into 3 equal portions.*

2 *Use 1 portion of butter to dot the top two-thirds of the dough, leaving a narrow border around the edges. Fold up the bottom third of the dough and fold down the top third of the dough. Seal the edges with a rolling pin, then give the dough a quarter turn. Press lightly at intervals, then roll the dough out to an oblong again.*

3 *Repeat step 2 again with the next portion of butter. Roll out the dough as in step 2. Dot with the last portion of butter and fold the dough in thirds again. Cover with a tea towel and chill for 30 minutes. Then repeat the rolling and folding 3 more times without adding any more butter. Cover the folded dough and chill again for 30 minutes.*

FILLINGS AND FLAVOURINGS

• Both Danish pastry and croissant dough can be spiced with a little ground cardamom, cinnamon or allspice, mixing it into the flour.
• All sorts of fillings can be made for Danish pastries. To make almond paste, the most traditional one, cream together 15g (½oz) butter and 40g (1½oz) caster sugar. Stir in 40g (1½oz) ground almonds and just enough beaten egg to bind the mixture.
• To make cinnamon butter, another delicious filling, cream together 50g (2oz) butter, 50g (2oz) sugar and 1 teaspoon ground cinnamon. Alternatively, try ground cardamom instead of cinnamon. A little finely grated orange rind can also be added for a refreshing tasting filling.
• I love the more intense taste of dried apricots soaked and then stewed with lemon juice and sugar until soft and thick. Fresh apricots cooked in a pan with caster sugar and no liquid are also delicious, and in spring you can add a head or two of elderflowers to the fruit – you can also do this with gooseberries, using lots of sugar and cooking them to an almost jam-like consistency.
• Soft, fresh white cheese, slightly sweetened and spiced is another good filling.

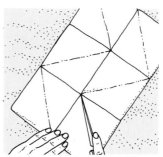

4 *Roll out the dough to a 50 x 30cm (20 x 12in) rectangle on a lightly floured surface, constantly patting in the edges to keep the shape. With a sharp knife, trim the edges neatly, then cut the dough in half lengthwise. Cut each strip of dough into 3 equal-sized squares and then cut each square in half diagonally to make 12 triangles.*

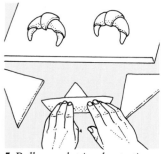

5 *Roll up each triangle, starting from the wide side and gently shape into a crescent. Any filling should be added before rolling each croissant. Put on ungreased baking sheets, cover and leave to rise for about 30 minutes until doubled in size. Brush with beaten egg. Bake at 220°C, 425°F, Gas Mark 7 for about 15 minutes. Cool on a wire rack.*

DANISH PASTRIES

Danish pastries are made in various traditional shapes. To make about 25 pastries, you will need 1 tablespoon dried yeast and a pinch of caster sugar, 150ml (¼ pint) warm milk, 500g (1lb) plain white flour, 1 teaspoon salt, 25g (1oz) lard, 25g (1oz) caster sugar, 2 beaten eggs plus 1 for glazing, 300g (10oz) softened butter, a selection of fillings (see box opposite), glacé icing (page 274), flaked almonds, redcurrant jelly or glacé cherries.

1 *Prepare the yeast and sugar with the warm milk (page 282). Put the flour and salt in a bowl and rub in the lard. Stir in the sugar. Add the yeast liquid and 2 beaten eggs, mix to a smooth dough and knead.*

2 *Put the dough in a bowl, cover and chill for 10 minutes. Shape the butter between 2 sheets of greaseproof paper into a 18 x 12cm (7 x 5in) rectangle. Roll out the dough to a 40 x 20cm (16 x 8in) rectangle.*

3 *Put the butter in the centre of the dough and fold the sides on top. Seal the edges. Give the dough a half turn, then roll into a 40 x 20cm (16 x 8in) rectangle. Fold the bottom third up and the top third down.*

4 *Cover the dough and leave for 10 minutes. Turn and repeat rolling, folding and resting twice more. Cover and leave for 30 minutes. Roll out to 5mm (¼in) thick, make a variety of shapes (right) and add the fillings.*

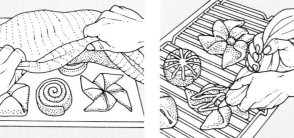

5 *Put shaped pastries on baking sheets, cover and leave for about 30 minutes. Brush with beaten egg. Bake at 220°C, 425°F, Gas Mark 7 for 15 minutes.*

6 *Place on a rack and pipe with glacé icing and sprinkle some with flaked almonds while slightly warm. Finish centres of stars with redcurrant jelly or a cherry. Cool.*

Butter-rich French-style croissants (above) and a selection of freshly baked Danish pastries, shaped as pinwheels, stars and cushions, contain a variety of flavourful fillings (see box opposite) and are decorated with glacé icing and almonds.

FINISHING DANISH PASTRIES

Almond paste is a traditional filling for Danish pastries but many other fillings can be used (see box opposite). I often make a hazelnut filling, exactly like the almond paste but made with ground hazelnuts instead of almonds. Fresh lemon curd (page 302) is another delicious filling.

Make the dough (steps 1–4) and shape into either cushions, stars or pinwheels. After shaping and filling bake and decorate as in steps 5–6 (left).

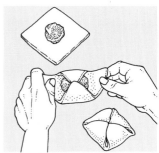

To make cushions, *cut 7cm (3in) squares. Add the filling to each square and fold in the corners towards the centre, securing the tips with beaten egg.*

To make pinwheels, *cut a 25 x 10cm (10 x 4in) rectangle. Spread with filling and roll up like a Swiss roll (page 267). Cut into 2.5cm (1in) slices and bake cut sides down on the baking sheets.*

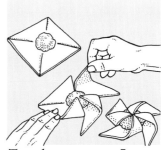

To make stars, *cut out 7cm (3in) squares. Cut from each corner to within 1cm (½in) of the centre. Add the filling to the centre and fold in the points to the centre, securing with beaten egg.*

BRIOCHES *and* SAVARINS

Butter and eggs can be added to a yeast dough to enrich it and produce a bread that is similar in many ways to a cake. The butter makes the dough soft while the eggs make it lighter and more moist, so that the finished bread almost melts in your mouth.

A brioche dough is the richest of all breads and can vary in shape and size from a small ball to a large crown shape. It can be served on its own or the dough can be filled with a sweet or savoury filling such as sausage. Other breads made from a brioche dough include a kugelhopf, which is a bread from Alsace in eastern France, layered with a sweet fruit and nut mixture or a savoury filling such as cream cheese and ham.

A savarin is also made from a brioche dough but has more liquid added to the dry ingredients. It is baked in a ring and then has syrup poured over it to give it a spongy texture. I sometimes replace the sugar syrup with melted honey simply mixed with lemon juice and jam or even whisky. Individual savarins are known as babas, and are an excellent pudding for serving on a buffet.

TRADITIONAL BRIOCHE

In France, brioche (page 280) is traditionally served warm for breakfast, with conserves and a large cup of milky coffee. At teatime, brioche also makes delicious light toast and is wonderful spread with thick cream and apricot jam. It should be baked in a brioche mould, which is a fluted tin with steeply sloping sides (page 20). The mould allows the dough to form a brioche's characteristic shape.

You will need 1½ teaspoons dried yeast and a pinch of caster sugar, 2 tablespoons hand-hot milk, 250g (8oz) strong white flour, 1 tablespoon caster sugar, a pinch of salt, 2 beaten eggs, 75g (3oz) softened butter and a little extra beaten egg to glaze. This recipe makes one large traditionally shaped brioche or 12 individual brioches, although the dough can also be baked in a loaf tin (see box opposite).

For a saffron-flavoured brioche, infuse a few strands of saffron with the milk, bringing both to the boil and then set aside until it is hand hot and can be combined with the yeast and sugar.

Another flavourful variation is to add a selection of dried fruit such as snipped soaked or ready-to-eat dried apricots, peaches or prunes to the brioche dough at the same time as you beat in the eggs and incorporate the butter in step 1.

1 *Prepare the yeast and sugar with the warm milk (page 282). Put the flour, sugar and salt in a bowl and add the yeast liquid. Gradually beat in the beaten eggs. Using your hands, incorporate the softened butter until well blended. Knead to a soft dough, adding extra flour only if really necessary. Knead for 5 minutes until smooth.*

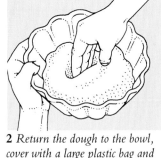

2 *Return the dough to the bowl, cover with a large plastic bag and leave to rise until the dough doubles in size. Knead again for 2–3 minutes. Cut off three-quarters of the dough and shape into a ball. Place in a greased 1.2 litre (2 pint) brioche mould. Using three fingers, press a hole in the centre of the dough down to the bottom of the mould.*

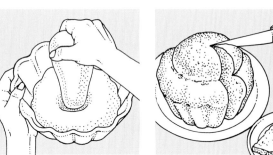

3 *Shape the remaining piece of dough into a cone. If necessary, slightly enlarge the hole in the main piece of dough with your fingers so that the pointed end of the cone will fit in neatly. Lower in the dough cone with the pointed end downwards. Gently pat the top of the dough cone to form the traditional well-rounded head on top of the brioche.*

4 *Cover the mould with a large plastic bag and leave to rise until the dough reaches the top of the mould. Lightly brush with beaten egg, avoiding the seam around the knob. Bake at 220°C, 425°F, Gas Mark 7 for 15–20 minutes, until golden. Turn out and serve warm, or cool completely on a wire rack. To serve, cut the brioche into vertical wedges.*

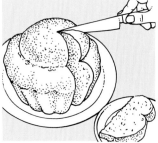

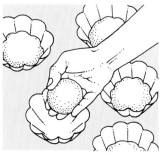

For individual brioches: 1 *complete step 1 (above). Put the kneaded dough back in the bowl, cover with a plastic bag and leave to rise until the dough doubles in size. Knead again for 2–3 minutes and divide into 12 pieces. Shape three-quarters of each piece into a small ball and put into 7cm (3in) diameter greased mini brioche moulds.*

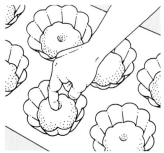

2 *Use your index finger to make a hole in the centre of each brioche bun. Shape the remaining pieces of dough into small knobs and place in the holes. Press down lightly. Complete step 4 but bake the individual brioches for only 10 minutes. Turn out the brioches and serve warm, or cool completely on a wire rack.*

SAVARIN

This rum-flavoured yeast cake is served as a cold pudding with fresh fruit in the centre. The mixture will also make 16 individual rum babas.

You will need 1 tablespoon dried yeast and 1 teaspoon caster sugar, 6 tablespoons warm milk, 250g (8oz) strong white flour, ½ teaspoon salt, 2 tablespoons caster sugar, 4 beaten eggs, 125g (4oz) softened butter, 125g (4oz) granulated sugar, 2 tablespoons each lemon juice and rum and 4 tablespoons apricot conserve.

Freshly baked rum babas and a large savarin filled with a selection of seasonal fruit. As the fruits vary with the time of year, the glaze can be flavoured with different liqueurs and juices that are appropriate to the season. Serve with pouring cream if you like.

1 *Blend together the dried yeast, sugar, hand-hot milk and 50g (2oz) flour in a large mixing bowl and leave in a warm place for 15 minutes until frothy. Stir in the remaining flour, salt, caster sugar, beaten eggs and butter. Beat well with a wooden spoon for 3–4 minutes until the mixture is well combined.*

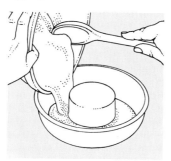

2 *Pour into a greased 1.5 litre (2½ pint) ring mould. Place a large plastic bag over the mould, folding under the ends, and leave to rise in a warm place until the dough has risen two-thirds up the sides of the mould. Bake at 200°C, 400°F, Gas Mark 6 for 30 minutes until the savarin is golden.*

3 *Cool for 5 minutes, then turn out of the mould to loosen. Return to the mould in order to add the syrup. Put the sugar, 300ml (½ pint) water and lemon juice in a pan, dissolve and boil until reduced by half. Remove from the heat and stir in the rum. Pour the syrup over the warm savarin and leave until well soaked in.*

4 *Unmould the savarin and leave it to cool completely on a wire rack. Meanwhile, gently melt the apricot conserve over a low heat in a small saucepan. Transfer the cooled savarin to a serving plate and brush with the melted conserve to glaze. Fill the centre with a selection of fresh fruit and serve with pouring cream.*

IDEAS FOR BRIOCHES AND SAVARINS

• Brioche dough can be baked in a loaf tin as well as in the traditional-shaped mould. This makes it possible to cut the baked brioche into slices which can be used to make excellent sandwiches; as it is a rich and also slightly sweet bread, fillings such as duck, pork, ham and pâté are successful. Season slivers of duck or pork with a little soy sauce and chopped spring onions.
• Brioche suits fillings of soft white cheese or fresh goat cheese mixed with fresh herbs, chopped walnuts, smoked fish or fresh prawns.
• Use brioche dough, with an added 25g (1oz) plain flour to make a stiffer dough, to wrap savoury fillings, such as a pâté or spicy minced beef mixture shaped into a loaf or sausage, any all-meat boiling sausage or a piece of skinless, filleted salmon – all of which should be lightly precooked. Roll out the dough and enclose the filling, sealing the seams with cold water. Mark the top into a diamond pattern with a knife and brush with beaten egg. Bake at 220°C, 425°F, Gas Mark 7 for 15–20 minutes until golden brown.
• I like to vary the syrup for savarins and rum babas by substituting the juice of ½ a large orange or 1 small orange for the lemon juice. You can also add kirsch instead of rum.
• The fresh fruits for the centre of savarins and babas can either have syrup spooned over them, or sit in a bowl with a mixture of kirsch and caster sugar for at least 1 hour before being spooned into the savarin.
• Instead of fruit, savarins can be filled with a thick vanilla custard (page 210) as well as with crème fraîche, sweetened fromage frais or simply with whipped cream.
• Glaze a savarin with melted apricot jam and make a pattern of glacé cherries, angelica and blanched almonds on top of the ring, glazing them as well.

For rum babas, *make the mixture as in step 1, and adding 125g (4oz) currants. Pour into 16 x 8cm (3½in) greased rum baba moulds and place on a baking sheet. Cover with a plastic bag, folding under the ends, and let rise in a warm place. Bake at 200°C, 400°F, Gas Mark 6 for 15–20 minutes. Complete steps 3 and 4.*

EXOTIC BREADS

Exotic breads include flat unleavened doughs, made without any yeast or other raising agent. The techniques here cover chapatis which are unleavened wholemeal breads and parathas which are made from a similar dough but are layered with ghee (Indian clarified butter) or melted butter to produce a much richer, flakier bread. They are also shallow-fried instead of dry fried.

Pitta bread, although containing yeast, is often thought of as a flat bread. The puffed-up 'pocket' produced in baking makes it an ideal container for all kinds of wonderful fillings. I sometimes add extra flavour to pitta bread by incorporating finely chopped fresh herbs or chopped black

olives into the dough while I am kneading it. It is the oven's intense heat that makes these soft, thinly rolled-out doughs rise. During baking, moisture in the dough is converted to steam and this creates a pocket which makes the bread puff up. Yeast relies on a flour with a high gluten content, so unleavened breads can be made with flours with little or no gluten, such as cornmeal, barley, oatmeal, rye and buckwheat flours.

All these exotic breads are quick to make and really delicious but should be eaten as soon as possible after being made as they do not have the keeping qualities of most yeast-leavened breads.

PITTA BREAD

Pitta breads are the ideal bread for light meals and snacks as you can open them up and fill them with almost anything. Unlike most bread doughs which are allowed to rise before shaping, pitta breads are shaped and then left to rise. When baked, they rise further to produce a bread with a pocket.

To make 12, you will need ½ teaspoon caster sugar, 2 teaspoons salt, 750–875g (1½–1¾lb) strong white flour, 1 sachet easy-blend yeast and 475ml (16fl oz) warm water. If you want a nuttier tasting bread use one third wholemeal flour to two-thirds strong white flour.

1 *In a large mixing bowl, combine the sugar, salt, 750g (1½lb) of the flour and the easy-blend yeast. Using a wooden spoon, stir in the water and mix to a smooth dough. Using your hands, slowly work in the remaining flour as necessary, kneading the dough along the sides of the bowl, until the dough is smooth and no longer sticky.*

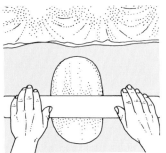

2 *Knead for at least 5 minutes on a lightly floured surface until the dough is smooth and elastic. Divide the dough into 12 equal pieces. Shape each into a smooth ball, then cover with a damp tea towel. Working with 1 ball at a time, roll out each one to an oval about 23cm (9in) long. Flip the ovals over and lightly roll out any creases on the second side.*

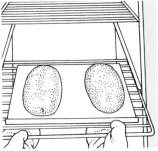

3 *As each pitta is rolled put it on a lightly floured surface and cover with the damp tea towel. Leave to rise in a warm place for 30–45 minutes. Place 2 pittas at a time on a preheated ungreased baking sheet and cook at 240°C, 475°F, Gas Mark 9 on the bottom shelf for about 3½ minutes until the pittas are puffed and browned on the base.*

FILLING AND FLAVOURING EXOTIC BREADS

• My favourite fillings for pitta bread are well-spiced and garlicked minced lamb fried over a high heat and stirred until the meat is well separated and all the liquid has evaporated. Also try mixed salad with chopped fresh mint and soft white cheese; cold chicken or lamb mixed with yogurt, ground cumin and chopped fresh mint; tuna mixed with a mild curry paste, yogurt and finely chopped spring onions; sliced fennel or peppers, halved garlic cloves or aubergine fried in olive oil until soft, and spiced with ground coriander.
• Brush pitta breads with olive

oil before baking and sprinkle with chopped blanched almonds, walnut halves or pistachios, or with tiny black onion seeds or sesame seeds.
• For a good hot snack, make a depression in the pitta dough, brush all over with olive oil mixed with 1 teaspoon paprika and break an egg over the depression. Sprinkle the egg and dough mixture with salt, pepper and dried oregano before putting into the oven to bake.
• In India, chapatis are normally used as the only implement for eating the meal and scooping up the juices, so they are almost

always a plain dough, though you may like to add some whole spices. Richer parathas, however, are eaten more as a bread on the side, and can contain delicious additions worked into the dough. Try fried onion or garlic slivers, chopped blanched almonds or pistachios, chopped fresh coriander and whole spices.
• Make a paratha into a snack meal in itself by adding not only onion, spices and fresh coriander, but also chopped hard-boiled egg and well-drained chopped, cooked spinach to the dough as well.

4 *When cooked, immediately wrap the pittas in a tea towel until cool enough to handle, then transfer to a wire rack. Bake the remaining pittas, two at a time. Serve warm or when cool, store in plastic bags, in the refrigerator for up to 1 week or in the freezer for up to 6 weeks.*

CHAPATIS

Chapatis are an unleavened bread and are the most common one served at an Indian meal. They are traditionally cooked on a *tava*, a flat Indian frying pan, but you can use a heavy frying pan or griddle. To make 8, you will need 250g (8oz) plain wholemeal flour, 150–200ml (5–7fl oz) water and a little ghee (Indian clarified butter) or melted clarified butter (page 96).

1 *Put the flour in a bowl. Slowly mix in the water to form a soft dough. Knead for at least 5 minutes until smooth. Return to the bowl, cover with a damp cloth and leave for 30 minutes.*

2 *Heat a dry, heavy frying pan or tava over a low heat until very hot. Meanwhile, divide the dough into 8 equal pieces and with floured hands, shape each one into a smooth ball.*

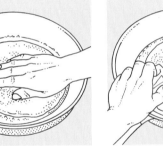

3 *Cook 1 chapati at a time. Put 1 ball on a lightly floured surface and coat in flour, then roll out to a circle about 12cm (5in) in diameter. Slap the chapati on to the hot pan.*

4 *Cook over a low heat and as soon as brown spots appear on the underneath, turn and cook the second side. Turn again and, using wads of kitchen paper, press on the edges so the chapati puffs up.*

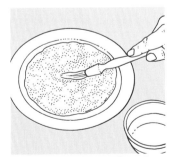

5 *Remove the chapatis from the frying pan or tava with a palette knife or fish slice and brush with melted ghee or butter. Serve the chapatis at once or keep warm wrapped in foil, while you cook the remaining dough as in steps 3 and 4 above.*

PARATHAS

Like chapatis, parathas are an unleavened bread often served with an Indian meal. They are similar to chapatis but the difference is that once the basic dough is made, it is then rolled and layered with ghee or melted clarified butter (page 96) and then rolled out into a variety of shapes, including rounds, squares and triangles (the shape used here). Instead of ghee or clarified butter you can also use concentrated butter for cooking. Follow steps 1 and 2 of the chapati recipe (left), then continue as here. Makes 8 parathas.

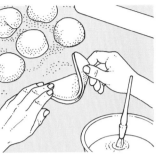

1 *On a floured surface, roll out 1 piece of dough to a circle about 10cm (4in) in diameter. Brush a little melted ghee or clarified butter on top. Fold the dough in half, brush more melted ghee or butter on top and fold in half again to form a triangle.*

2 *Roll out the triangle so that the sides measure about 15cm (6in). Cover with a damp tea towel while rolling out the remaining dough. Working with 1 triangle at a time, slap it in the hot frying pan or tava and, as soon as brown spots appear on the underneath, turn it over. Brush with melted ghee or butter and cook the second side.*

3 *Turn again and brush with more melted ghee or clarified butter. Using a fish slice, press on the edges of the paratha and move it around the pan to make sure that it cooks evenly and is lightly browned. Remove from the pan and brush again with ghee or butter. Serve at once or keep warm in foil. Cook the remaining parathas in the same way.*

Indian chapatis (left) and parathas served with traditional cucumber and yogurt raita and two spicy lentil dhals. These breads are ideal to serve with curry, as well.

SCONES *and* TEABREADS

Scones and teabreads are breads that are made without yeast. They are quick to make and are an irresistible alternative to plain bread. Teabreads are best when made the day before they are to be served so they can then be sliced without crumbling. Wrapped in foil, they can be kept for up to a week.

Scones, however, are best if eaten on the day they are made, as they go stale very quickly. The nicest thing of all is to eat them as soon as they come out of the oven and as they are so quickly made this is quite possible.

Both scones and teabreads are made with self-raising flour or plain flour and a chemical leavening agent. Bicarbonate of soda is one of the most widely used of all non-yeast leavenings. When added to liquid and heated, it gives off carbon dioxide which expands and raises the dough. Cream of tartar is often used with bicarbonate of soda as together they react to produce carbon dioxide. Cream of tartar also helps to neutralize the soapy taste which bicarbonate of soda gives.

Baking powder, a ready-made mixture of bicarbonate of soda and cream of tartar, can also be used as a leavening agent for baking. It also contains a little starch, usually cornflour, which helps keep it dry during storage.

If you like, you can sour milk for making a scone dough by stirring a little lemon juice into it. Use this to replace the milk, buttermilk or yogurt in the recipe below.

TRADITIONAL SCONES

This recipe uses self-raising flour and additional baking powder to make the scones rise but you can use other leavening agents; allow 1 teaspoon baking powder, or 1 teaspoon cream of tartar with ½ teaspoon bicarbonate of soda to 250g (8oz) flour. Make the dough quickly and handle it as little as possible to keep the scones light.

To make 10–12 scones, you will need 250g (8oz) self-raising flour, ½ teaspoon salt, 1 teaspoon baking powder, 40g (1½oz) caster sugar, 40g (1½oz) butter or margarine, and 150ml (¼ pint) buttermilk, milk or yogurt.

1 *Preheat the oven to 230°C, 450°F, Gas Mark 8 and put in a baking sheet. Sift the flour, salt, baking powder and sugar together into a bowl. Rub in the butter until the mixture resembles coarse breadcrumbs. Make a well in the centre, pour in the buttermilk, milk or yogurt and mix lightly to make a soft dough.*

2 *Turn the dough on to a lightly floured surface and knead only very lightly just to smooth the underside. Turn the dough smooth side up and roll or pat it out to a thickness of about 1.5cm (¾in). Using a 5cm (2in) floured round biscuit cutter, cut out 10–12 scones.*

3 *Place the scones on the preheated baking sheet and dust the tops with a little extra flour. Bake straightaway for 8–10 minutes until the scones are light brown and well risen. Cool on a wire rack for 15 minutes. Serve the scones split, with butter or clotted cream and a good-flavoured jam.*

For a traditional teatime treat serve scones with thick raspberry jam and clotted cream.

To make fruit scones, *stir 50g (2oz) currants, raisins or sultanas, and candied peel, if liked, into the flour and butter mixture in step 1 before adding the milk. Complete step 2 and bake as in step 3. These scones can be served plain or with clotted cream, jam, and butter.*

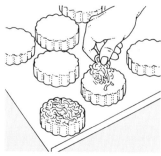

To make cheese scones, *add 175–250g (6–8oz) finely grated strong Cheddar cheese and 1–2 teaspoons wholegrain mustard to the mixture in step 1, but omit the sugar. Complete step 2 and bake the scones as above with extra grated cheese sprinkled on top before putting them in the oven.*

MALT BREAD

This recipe illustrates the use of self-raising flour as the only leavening in a bread. Like most teabreads, malt bread is at its best if, after cooling, it is wrapped in foil and stored for one or two days before eating, allowing the flavour to mature. Serve the bread sliced and buttered.

To make 1 large loaf, you will need 375g (12oz) self-raising flour, ½ teaspoon salt, 50g (2oz) butter or margarine, 250g (8oz) sultanas, currants or raisins, 200ml (7fl oz) milk, 5 tablespoons malt extract (available from chemists), 50g (2oz) soft brown sugar and 2 lightly beaten eggs.

Buttered slices of malt bread and a loaf of banana bread.

1 Put the flour and salt in a large bowl. Rub in the butter until the mixture resembles breadcrumbs. Stir in the dried fruit. Warm together the milk, malt extract and sugar, without boiling and stir into the dry ingredients with a wooden spoon. Add the beaten eggs and mix together well.

2 Turn the mixture into a greased and base-lined 1kg (2lb) loaf tin. Bake straight away at 180°C, 350°F, Gas Mark 4 for about 1 hour, until firm to the touch and a skewer inserted into the centre comes out clean. Leave in the tin for 5 minutes, then turn out and cool on a wire rack.

BANANA BREAD

This is a teabread that is loved by children and adults alike. It is also an excellent way of using up over-ripe bananas.

If you like, you can add some finely grated lemon rind or 1 teaspoon mixed spice for extra flavouring.

To make 1 large loaf you will need 500g (1lb) ripe bananas, 250g (8oz) self-raising flour, ½ teaspoon salt, 125g (4oz) butter or margarine, 125g (4oz) caster sugar, 2 lightly beaten eggs and 2 tablespoons honey.

1 Peel the bananas and mash the flesh with a fork, adding some lemon rind, if liked. Put the flour and salt in a bowl and rub in the butter until the mixture resembles breadcrumbs.

VARIATIONS ON TEABREADS AND SCONES

• I think plain scones made with white flour, served with clotted cream and homemade jam are best of all, but there are many variations . You can also make them with wholemeal flour or half wholemeal and half plain, which I prefer, and add some grated orange rind, 1 teaspoon ground mace and cinnamon, and ¼ teaspoon ground cloves.

• You can also leave out the sugar in a scone mixture so they are suitable to eat with savoury accompaniments, such as soft cheeses or fish pâtés.

• Add chopped fresh herbs to a plain scone dough.

• Cheese scones are also delicious with chopped walnuts and chopped fresh sage or dried oregano added to the mixture.

• Add some crispy fried onion slivers or chopped spring onions to a cheese scone mixture.

• Vary a malt loaf by using all honey instead of malt extract or for a dark, strong loaf, use black treacle.

• All sorts of dried fruit can be used for teabreads, including ready-to-eat dried apricots and peaches and chopped, soft, pitted prunes. Apricots and prunes are a good mixture, as are sultanas and lemon rind, and the classic combination of dates and walnuts.

• Roughly chopped toasted hazelnuts or pecans are a good addition to banana bread.

• Glaze teabreads by brushing with honey just as soon as they come out of the oven and sprinkle with toasted nuts or crushed sugar cubes.

• Grated lemon or orange rind or good candied peel usually enhances the flavour of a teabread mixture, and many breads are nice in winter with spices such as ground mace, cinnamon, cloves and cardamom or a few whole caraway seeds stirred in.

2 With a wooden spoon, stir in the sugar, eggs, honey and mashed bananas, beating together well. Turn the mixture into a greased and base-lined 1kg (2lb) loaf tin (page 262).

3 Bake at 180°C, 350°F, Gas Mark 4 for about 1¼ hours, covering if necessary. Leave in the tin for 5 minutes, then turn out and cool on a wire rack. Serve sliced and buttered.

ITALIAN HEARTH BREAD WITH BLACK OLIVES AND ROSEMARY *(280)*

Focaccia and *schiacciata* are both names for the flat, Italian hearth bread of which there are many varieties, but they all have one thing in common – the wonderful taste of fruity extra virgin olive oil and salt. It is best eaten warm.　*MAKES 1 LARGE LOAF*

> 375g (12oz) strong unbleached flour
> 1 sachet fast-action easy-blend dried yeast
> 4–5 teaspoons crushed sea salt
> Leaves from 1 large sprig fresh rosemary, chopped finely
> 175–250ml (6–8fl oz) water
> 5–6 tablespoons extra virgin olive oil
> 40–50g (1½–2oz) black olives, stoned and chopped roughly

Lightly grease a large pizza tin or baking sheet. Put the flour in a large bowl with the yeast, 2 teaspoons crushed sea salt and all but 1 teaspoon of the rosemary leaves. Stir with a wooden spoon, then pour in the water and 3 tablespoons olive oil, adding enough liquid to form a slightly sticky, soft dough. Knead on a very lightly floured surface for 8–10 minutes until smooth and elastic.

Form the dough into a ball, and then press out with your hand into a rough circle, about 25–28cm (10–11in) in diameter and 1cm (½in) thick – the surface should be slightly undulating.

Carefully transfer the circle of dough to the prepared tin or sheet. Using a wooden salad fork, prick the surface deeply all over. Put the tin inside a large plastic bag and fold the bag under the tin, trapping plenty of air, so that the bag is puffed up well above the bread. Leave at room temperature for 1–2 hours until the dough has doubled in thickness.

Using a finger, press the pieces of olive slightly down into the dough at intervals, then trickle the remaining 2–3 tablespoons olive oil over the bread,

spreading it very lightly with your fingers to cover the surface completely, but leaving it to sit in pools in the dips. Finally sprinkle with the reserved chopped rosemary and remaining crushed sea salt. Bake at 220°C, 425°F, Gas Mark 7 for about 20 minutes until golden brown.

CHEESE AND SPRING ONION SODA BAPS *(280)*

These are so quick to make and are delicious served as soon as they are baked for a light lunch or snack. Just slice in half and sandwich together with soft white cheese and tomatoes or other fillings.　*MAKES 6*

> 250g (8oz) strong wholemeal flour
> 250g (8oz) strong white flour
> 2 teaspoons bicarbonate of soda
> 2 teaspoons cream of tartar
> 1 teaspoon salt
> ½ teaspoon cayenne pepper
> 250g (8oz) strong Cheddar cheese, coarsely grated, plus a little extra for sprinkling over the tops
> 1 bunch spring onions, trimmed and chopped finely
> 1 tablespoon wholegrain mustard
> 300ml (½ pint) buttermilk or milk
> A little olive oil

Mix the wholemeal, strong white flour, bicarbonate of soda, cream of tartar, salt and cayenne pepper together in a bowl. Stir in 250g (8oz) of the cheese and the finely chopped spring onions. Mix the mustard with the buttermilk and add to the flour mixture, stirring until the dough leaves the sides of the bowl.

Knead the dough briefly on a lightly floured surface. Form into a roll about 10cm (4in) in diameter and then cut into 6 pieces. Lay the circles on a greased baking sheet, brush lightly with olive oil and sprinkle with the extra grated cheese. Bake at 200°C, 400°F, Gas Mark 6 for 20–25 minutes. Serve warm.

APRICOT AND CURRANT LARDY CAKE *(280)*

I find warm lardy cake one of the most irresistible teatime treats. Of course, a lardy cake should be made with lard, but adding butter improves the flavour.　*MAKES 1 LARGE LOAF*

> 500g (1lb) strong white flour
> 2 teaspoons salt
> 1 sachet fast-action easy-blend dried yeast
> 300ml (½ pint) warm water
> 1 tablespoon sunflower oil
> 75g (3oz) butter, cut into flakes
> 125g (4oz) fine light demerara sugar
> 2 teaspoons ground mixed spice
> 175g (6oz) ready-to-eat dried apricots, chopped
> 75g (3oz) currants
> 75g (3oz) lard, cut into flakes

Grease a 25 x 20cm (10 x 8in) roasting tin. Sift the flour and salt into a bowl and stir in the yeast. Add the water and oil, stirring with a wooden spoon to make a soft dough. Knead on a lightly floured surface for a few minutes until smooth. Put the dough in a lightly oiled bowl, cover with a tea towel and leave in a warm place until doubled in size.

Knead the dough on a lightly floured surface for about 5 minutes. Roll out into a rectangle about 5mm (¼in) thick. Dot the butter over the top two-thirds of the rectangle of dough, then sprinkle with 3 tablespoons sugar, 1 teaspoon mixed spice and half the chopped apricots and currants. Fold the uncovered bottom third of the rectangle up and the top third down, sealing the edges with a rolling pin. Roll out again to the same size rectangle and dot the top two-thirds of it with the lard, 3 more tablespoons sugar, the spice and the remaining apricots and currants. Fold and roll out the dough as before.

Put the pastry rectangle into the prepared roasting tin, pressing it to fill the corners and making a crisscross or diamond pattern with a sharp knife. Put the tin into a large plastic bag and fold the bag ends under the tin, trapping plenty of air so that the bag is well puffed up. Leave in a warm place until the dough has doubled in size.

Brush the lardy cake lightly with oil and sprinkle the remaining sugar all over the top. Bake at 220°C, 425°F, Gas Mark 7 for about 30 minutes until a rich brown. If possible, eat while still warm.

CHEESE AND TOMATO SWIRL LOAF *(280)*

The smell of this bread cooking is wonderful and the first cut into it causes impressed amazement as a perfect swirl of red tomato bread is revealed within the cheese dough. Your secret is that, using fast-action easy-blend dried yeast and with only one rising, it is extremely easy to make. *MAKES 1 LARGE LOAF*

> 750g (1½lb) strong white flour
> 1 rounded tablespoon crushed sea salt
> 1 sachet fast-action easy-blend dried yeast
> About 1 rounded tablespoon fresh chopped tarragon or 3 teaspoons dried oregano
> 375ml (13fl oz) warm water
> 2 rounded tablespoon tomato purée
> 2 teaspoons paprika
> 9 tablespoons olive oil, plus a little extra
> 150g (5oz) mature Cheddar cheese, grated
> ¼ teaspoon cayenne pepper
> 2 large cloves garlic, crushed

Put the flour into a large bowl with the sea salt and yeast and mix together. Measure out 300g (10oz) of this mixture and place into another large bowl. Stir in the chopped tarragon or dried oregano. Pour 150ml (¼ pint) of warm water into a measuring jug and stir in the tomato purée, paprika and 4 tablespoons olive oil. Using a wooden spoon, stir this mixture into the bowl containing the flour with herbs until it sticks together. Knead the dough on an unfloured surface for 2–3 minutes into a smooth ball.

Using either a wooden spoon or your hands mix all but 1 tablespoon of the grated cheese into the remaining flour, adding the cayenne pepper and the crushed garlic. Stir in the remaining warm water with 5 tablespoons olive oil. Knead the dough on a lightly floured surface for 2–3 minutes into a ball of fairly soft but just dry dough.

Roll out the cheese dough on an unfloured surface into a large circle about 5mm (¼in) thick. Roll out the tomato dough slightly thinner into a circle almost as big. Lay the tomato dough on top of the cheese dough and roll up both doughs together like a Swiss roll (page 267). Turn under at the ends.

Place the roll of dough on a large greased baking sheet, brush with olive oil and cut slanting slashes across the roll at 2.5–4cm (1–1½in) intervals. Sprinkle all over with the reserved grated cheese. Put the baking sheet into a large plastic bag and fold the bag ends under the baking sheet, trapping plenty of air. Leave at room temperature for 1½–2 hours, or until the dough has doubled in size.

Bake the loaf for 20 minutes at 230°C, 450°F, Gas Mark 8, then reduce to 200°C, 400°F, Gas Mark 6 for another 20–25 minutes. Cool the loaf on a rack and eat while warm, or slice and toast.

SEEDED BROWN BREAD *(280)*

If you are busy during the day, make up this dough within minutes in the morning, leave it all day in a cool place to rise, then put the risen dough into the oven when you get home. Or you can mix the dough before you go to bed and have freshly baked hot bread for breakfast. *MAKES THREE 1KG (2LB) LOAVES*

> Soft butter or margarine
> 1kg (2lb) strong wholemeal flour
> 500g (1lb) strong white flour
> 2 sachets fast-action easy-blend dried yeast
> 2 tablespoons crushed sea salt
> 4 tablespoons bran, plus a little extra
> 75–125g (3–4oz) sesame seeds
> 75g (3oz) pumpkin or sunflower seeds
> 2 teaspoons caraway seeds
> 125ml (4fl oz) sunflower oil
> 900ml–1 litre (1½–1¾ pints) warm water

Smear three 1kg (2lb) loaf tins very generously with soft butter. Combine the flours and yeast in a large bowl, then stir in the salt, 4 tablespoons bran and all the seeds, reserving some sesame and pumpkin seeds. Add the oil and water, stirring until the mixture sticks together. Knead on a lightly floured surface just for a few minutes until smooth. Cut it into 3 pieces, shape and put into the tins (page 282). Cut a pattern in deep gashes on the tops and sprinkle the reserved seeds into the gashes, scattering the extra bran all over. Put the tins into a large plastic bag which can be tucked under the tins to enclose them with plenty of air. Leave until the dough has doubled in size – in a warm kitchen this takes about 2 hours.

Bake at 230°C, 450°F, Gas Mark 8 for 20 minutes, then turn down the temperature to 200°C, 400°F, Gas Mark 6 for a further 20 minutes. Turn out and cool.

PRUNE, LEMON AND HONEY TEABREAD *(280)*

This teabread is glazed with a sharp lemon syrup, which is also absorbed by the loaf. *MAKES 1 LOAF*

> 175g (6oz) plain flour
> 1 teaspoon bicarbonate of soda
> ½ teaspoon cream of tartar
> 1 teaspoon ground mace
> ½ teaspoon salt
> Grated rind and juice of 2 small lemons
> 50g (2oz) butter
> 2 tablespoons honey
> 4 tablespoons milk
> 1 large egg, beaten
> 175g (6oz) soft, pitted prunes, roughly chopped
> 25g (1oz) caster sugar

Sift the flour, bicarbonate of soda, cream of tartar, mace and salt into a bowl. Stir in the lemon rind. Put the butter and honey into a saucepan and melt, stirring over a low heat and removing immediately they are liquid. Using a wooden spoon, stir the milk into the flour mixture, followed by the melted butter and honey, then the beaten egg. Mix thoroughly to make a smooth, soft dough. Fold in the chopped prunes. Spoon into a well-buttered 500g (1lb) loaf tin.

Bake at 160°C, 325°F, Gas Mark 3 for 40–50 minutes until well risen and firm to touch. Remove from the oven and pierce holes with a thin skewer right through the loaf at regular intervals all over. Strain the lemon juice into a saucepan, add the caster sugar, dissolve in the juice over a gentle heat and then boil rapidly for 2 minutes. Spoon the lemon syrup gradually all over the loaf, letting it seep in through the holes. Leave to cool in the tin. When almost cold, turn out, loosening the sides with a knife if necessary and cool completely on a wire rack.

PRESERVES

There is something very satisfying about seeing pantry shelves, or even a shelf in the kitchen cupboard, lined with homemade preserves. Making preserves used to be a traditional practice for keeping foods out of season but now, with the availability of fresh foods all the year around and the use of freezers, preserving has become a way of turning fresh foods into a delicious and lasting product. Making preserves is an enjoyable pastime and the finished products are extremely good in a quite different way from the fresh ingredients. Although commercial jams, jellies and marmalades can be excellent they never achieve the unique character of something homemade which also make lovely, very personal presents either to give or to be given.

The best time to make a preserve is when you have an abundance of produce growing in your garden such as gooseberries or apples, or have simply been blackberrying in the hedgerows.

Foods that are left in their natural state very quickly deteriorate, but if they are treated to extremes of temperature or to high concentrations of sugar, salt, vinegar or alcohol, their natural decaying process can be arrested. This is what preserving is all about — to take fresh foods in good condition and to keep them at this stage for a long period of time.

The original methods of preserving used were drying, smoking and salting which made use of the natural facilities available — sun, wind, smoke and salt. Using simple methods it is still possible to dry some foods at home, such as fruits, vegetables and herbs, but it is mostly done commercially. Nowadays smoking is rarely done at home, because few homes have a chimney especially designed. Small domestic home smokers are available but they are designed to give the food flavour and it is then eaten immediately rather than preserved. Salting, too, is limited now as it can be dangerous if not carried out correctly, but small fish, some vegetables and lemons can be preserved by this method without any problems although the products are best kept refrigerated.

Freezing (page 312) is the most modern method of preserving and certainly the easiest, though it rarely improves the texture or flavour in the way that some preserving methods do. It needs no extra salt and often very little extra sugar, so is healthier than other methods of preserving. Its success as a method of home preservation depends on a low temperature destroying some micro-organisms, in the form of bacteria, yeasts and moulds, and making others dormant.

Other methods of preserving include the use of sugar. A high concentration of sugar prevents the growth of micro-organisms and, combined with a high temperature, it preserves the fruits in jams, jellies, marmalades, cheeses and conserves. It is, therefore, important to follow a recipe accurately and never, for example, skimp the amount of sugar to be used, as this is the main preservative.

Preserving with high concentrations of vinegar and alcohol are also more modern methods of preserving. Like sugar, a high concentration of these prevents the growth of micro-organisms. Vinegar is used to preserve chutneys, relishes and pickles, and various kinds of alcohol are used to preserve fruits.

Preserves may look beautiful lined up on the pantry shelf and the intention may be to keep them for long periods — nevertheless, like all good food, the time comes when they must be eaten and enjoyed, so don't forget that that is what they are there for!

Preserves made throughout the year capture several seasonal flavours. Back row, left to right: Fresh Raspberry Jam (page 309) is made with small amounts of orange and lemon juices to accentuate the raspberry taste; Lemons Preserved in Salt (page 309) are made using a traditional Moroccan method and are ideal for adding extra flavour to meat stews: Orange, Lime and Sweet Pepper Chutney (page 308), flavoured with turmeric and cardamom pods. Front row, left to right: Elderflower and Hazelnut Honey (page 308) is an easy way to transform ordinary set honey into something extra special; (above) Mixed Pickled Mushrooms (page 309) can be made with any mushrooms in season; (below) Spiced Apricot and Tomato Relish (page 309), with ginger, cinnamon and cardamom, is ideal to serve with curries; (right) more jars of Mixed Pickled Mushrooms and Spiced Apricot and Tomato Relish.

JAMS *and* JELLIES

Jams and jellies are basically the same type of preserve, as both are made from cooked fruit to which sugar is added. It is the high concentration of sugar, combined with a high temperature, that enables the fruit to be preserved. The sugar also affects the fruits' setting quality, and the exact amount that is needed depends on the pectin strength of the fruit. These preserves will only set if there are sufficient quantities of sugar, acid and pectin present.

Fruits high in pectin include cooking apples, crab apples, red and blackcurrants, gooseberries, quinces and Seville oranges. Fruits containing a moderate amount of pectin include cranberries, eating apples, loganberries, apricots and raspberries. Fruits low in pectin include bananas, cherries, elderberries, figs, japonica, melons, nectarines, peaches, pineapple, rhubarb, medlars and strawberries. For low-pectin fruits a mixture of half pectin sugar and half granulated sugar gives good results. Soft fruits such as raspberries have a wonderfully fresh flavour if only boiled for a few minutes – using pectin sugar it is now possible to make successful jams this way which actually set.

The best type of sugar to use is granulated sugar. Although it is not necessary to use the more expensive preserving sugar, it does produce less scum. Caster and brown sugar produce a lot of scum.

CHOOSING FRUIT

The fruits used for jams and jellies should be firm and just ripe. Prepare according to the recipe, discarding any damaged parts. The fruit is then simmered to extract the pectin and acid it contains.

Only fruits with a high pectin content are suitable for jellies unless you use pectin sugar. They need little preparation, as any skin, core or pips will be extracted when the pulp is strained, though damaged parts should be removed before using.

ABOUT PECTIN

Some fruits contain a lot of pectin and acid, while others do not. Preserves made with fruits low in pectin must have pectin added to enable them to set. Lemon juice is usually used or, alternatively, commercially prepared liquid pectin or pectin sugar which is sugar with pectin added. Sometimes an acid only is added, such as citric or tartaric acid. These do not contain pectin but help to extract the natural pectin present in the fruit. Lemon juice often improves the flavour in any case.

TESTING FOR A SET

You can tell when a jam has been cooked enough by testing for a set. Remove the pan from the heat while you test as if the jam overcooks it will not set. If the test shows the jam mixture is still too liquid continue boiling and retesting every few minutes.

For a flake test, dip a wooden spoon into the pan and lift out a little jam. Cool slightly, then let the jam drop back into the pan. If the jam does not run off the spoon but drops off in flakes setting point has been reached.

For a saucer or wrinkle *test, put a little jam on a saucer into the freezer for a minute or so until just cooled. Push a finger gently through the jam. Setting point has been reached if the surface of the jam wrinkles.*

POTTING AND STORING

Once a setting point has been reached, it is time to pot the jam or jelly. Stop boiling and let the fruit mixture stand for 15 minutes (this will stop fruit rising to the top of the jars when you pot the jam), then remove any scum with a large slotted spoon. Stir to distribute the fruit.

Meanwhile, wash the jars well in hot water and rinse, then dry in a cool oven at 140°C, 275°F, Gas Mark 1. It is easiest to handle the hot jars if you place them in the oven on a baking sheet. Use the jars while still hot so they will not crack from the jam, and fill them right to the top. Wipe the rims and cover the surface of the still hot jam with a waxed paper disc, waxed-side down, making sure that it lies flat on top of the jam. Then brush one side of a cellophane disc with a wet pastry brush, stretch it on top of the jar, wet side up, and secure with a rubber band. Instead of waxed paper and cellophane discs, you can use ordinary metal screw tops provided they are rust-free and clean but cover the jars while the jam is still hot. Alternatively, leave the jam until quite cold before covering. Wipe the jars clean, label and store in a cool, dry, dark place. Most jams can be kept for up to a year.

Use a wide-mouthed *metal funnel with a short neck, and a ladle with a lip and a long handle to pot jams and jellies. These help protect your hands from the hot mixture, as well as making potting a neater operation. Take care not to overfill the jars, lifting the funnel to check underneath as you pour.*

To cover the jar *brush one side of a cellophane disc with a wet pastry brush to stretch the cellophane, creating an airtight seal when it dries and shrinks. Place the disc on top of the jar and secure with a rubber band, ideally from a pack of preserving or jam pot covers which contains wax paper discs and labels too.*

MAKING JELLY

Fruit for jelly is gently cooked to a pulp with any flavourings such as herbs or spices, and then left to drain through a jelly bag until all the juices have dripped out. If you haven't got a jelly bag (page 24), you can improvise by using a large double thickness of muslin. Whichever you use, scald the bag or muslin by pouring boiling water through it. Measure out the amount of extracted juice and return it to the cleaned preserving pan with the sugar, the quantity depending on the pectin content of the fruit. Pectin-rich extract needs 500g (1lb) sugar for each 600ml (1 pint), while extract from fruit with a medium pectin content will set with 375g (12oz) sugar for each 600ml (1 pint).

To make redcurrant jelly, a fruit with a naturally high pectin content, you will need 1.5kg (3lb) redcurrants, 600ml (1 pint) water and sugar (see method).

1 *Remove and discard any damaged fruit. Put the redcurrants and measured water in a preserving pan and simmer gently on a low heat, to extract as much juice as possible, for 30–45 minutes until the fruit is tender and thoroughly broken up. Stir occasionally with a large wooden spoon to prevent the fruit sticking to the bottom of the pan.*

2 *Meanwhile prepare your jelly bag and bowl. If you don't have a special plastic stand suspend the scalded bag from a broom handle placed between 2 chairs. Place a large bowl underneath the bag to catch the drips. Pour the cooked pulp into the bag and leave for at least 12 hours, until the dripping has stopped. Do not squeeze the bag at all or the jelly will cloud.*

3 *Discard the pulp in the jelly bag. Measure the extracted juice and return it to the pan. Add 500g (1lb) sugar to each 600ml (1 pint) juice. Heat gently until the sugar has dissolved, then bring to boiling point as quickly as possible and boil rapidly for about 10 minutes or until setting point is reached (opposite). Remove from the heat, skim, then pot and cover (opposite).*

MAKING JAM

When initially cooking the fruit for a jam it is important to simmer it gently until it is very tender before adding the sugar, as cooking afterwards will not soften the fruit. Those with tough skins, such as plums, will take about 30 minutes, while soft-skinned fruit, such as strawberries, will take about 20 minutes or less. It is this cooking that releases the pectin from the fruit.

To make about 5kg (10lb) plum jam you will need 3kg (6lb) plums, 900ml (1½ pints) water, 3kg (6lb) sugar and a knob of butter.

1 *Put the plums and water in a preserving pan and simmer gently, stirring occasionally, for about 30 minutes until the fruit is soft and the contents reduced. Remove the pan from the heat. Meanwhile warm the sugar slightly in a low oven so it dissolves more quickly.*

2 *Stir in the warmed sugar until dissolved, then add a knob of butter to reduce foaming. Return the pan to the heat, bring the jam to boiling point as quickly as possible and boil rapidly for about 10–15 minutes.*

3 *Remove from the heat and test for a set (opposite). Remove plum stones and carefully skim off any scum. It is not necessary to skim while the jam is boiling as too much clear jam would be lost. Pot and cover (opposite).*

Making your own jams and jellies lets you capture the fresh flavours of seasonal fruit. From left to right: Spiced Apple Jelly with Mint and Dill (page 308), ginger-flavoured pear jam and plum jam.

FRUIT CURDS *and* MARMALADES

Curds are usually made from citrus fruits and sugar which are thickened with eggs and butter. They have a thick, soft consistency and can be spread on bread or toast and used like jam or as a filling for a sponge cake or small tarts or other pastries (below). Because the addition of eggs diminishes a curd's keeping qualities these are not a true preserve, and should, therefore, be made in small quantities, kept in the refrigerator and eaten quickly – which is not difficult, as they are so delicious.

Marmalades are traditionally served with toast for breakfast but are also an effective ingredient in cakes and steamed pudding mixtures and for mixing with stewed apples and plums. Marmalades are a method of preserving similar to that used for jam but they are nearly always made from citrus fruits, including oranges, lemons, grapefruits and limes. Seville or bitter oranges make the best marmalade with a good flavour and clear appearance. Sweet oranges give marmalade a cloudy appearance and are usually only used in combination with other citrus fruits. Seville oranges are available in January and February, and this is, therefore, the best time to make a batch of marmalade. Alternatively, buy the fruit and freeze it. When making marmalade with frozen oranges add one-eighth extra weight of fruit to offset the loss of pectin caused by freezing and you can also use pectin sugar.

Marmalades need to be cooked for longer than jams in order to really soften the peel which is much tougher than that of most fruits used in jam, to extract the all-important pectin which is found in the pith, pips and membrane of citrus fruits, and to evaporate the larger quantity of water than is needed. If this is not done adequately the marmalade will not set properly.

LEMON CURD

I adore lemon curd and other fruit curds, and they really have to be homemade to taste authentic. As well as lemon juice, you can make fruit curds also with freshly squeezed lime or orange juice. Lemon and other citrus-flavoured curds are easy to make by the traditional method as here but they can be made in a microwave cooker in less than half the time (page 311).

This is the classic fruit curd recipe that you can use for cooking on top of the stove. To make 750g (1½lb) lemon curd you will need the finely grated rind and juice of 4 lemons, 4 lightly beaten eggs, 125g (4oz) unsalted butter and 375g (12oz) caster sugar.

1 *Put all the ingredients in the top of a double saucepan or in a heatproof bowl over a saucepan of simmering water, making sure the bottom of the bowl does not touch the water. Stir continuously with a wooden spoon until the butter has melted.*

2 *Cook very gently over a low heat, stirring frequently, for about 20 minutes until the sugar has dissolved and the mixture is creamy and thick enough to coat the back of a wooden spoon. The mixture should not be allowed to boil or it will curdle.*

Small pots of lemon and orange curds make lovely presents. As well as serving on toast, use curds to fill small pastry shells.

3 *Immediately strain the cooked mixture through a fine conical sieve, to remove any lumps of egg white, into small, clean, dry jars (page 300). Carefully fill the jars right to the top as the curd will thicken and shrink slightly as it cools and sets.*

4 *Cover the pots while still hot with waxed paper discs, then with dampened cellophane discs (page 300) and secure with rubber bands. Store in the refrigerator and eat within 2–3 weeks as curds are not true preserves and do not keep for long.*

SEVILLE ORANGE MARMALADE

The different ways of preparing and cooking the fruit each results in a different type of marmalade. Chunky marmalade, for example, is made by cooking the fruit whole and then chopping it. Coarse or thin-cut marmalade depends on how the peel is cut and fine-shred marmalade is made by adding shredded peel to strained citrus juices to produce a clear, jelly-like marmalade. You may find it easier to cut the peel after it has been cooked, scooping out the pips into a muslin bag for boiling up when the sugar is added.

This is the traditional recipe for Seville orange marmalade. Coarsely or finely chop the peel according to your preference. To make about 5kg (10lb) marmalade you will need 1.5kg (3lb) Seville oranges, 4 tablespoons lemon juice, 3.6 litres (6 pints) water and 3kg (6lb) granulated sugar or half granulated, half pectin sugar.

Sharp-tasting Seville orange marmalade, with its fresh colour, is always appreciated at breakfast time.

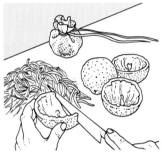

1 *Wash the oranges well, then halve them and squeeze the juice and pips into a nylon sieve set over a small bowl. Tie the pips and any extra pith and membrane that have come away during squeezing loosely in a piece of muslin as the pips and pith contain valuable pectin. Slice the orange peel thickly or thinly, depending on how you like it.*

2 *Put the sliced peel, orange juice, lemon juice, water and muslin bag in a preserving pan; tie the bag to the pan's handles for easy removal later on. Simmer gently, to extract the pectin, for 1–3 hours, depending on how quickly the contents evaporate. The contents should be reduced by about a half and the peel becomes really soft.*

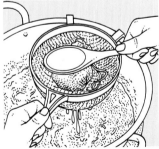

3 *Carefully remove the hot muslin bag from the side of the preserving pan and transfer it to a nylon sieve over the pan. Using the back of a wooden spoon, squeeze the bag well against the sides of the sieve, allowing the pulpy juice to run back into the preserving pan. Discard the remaining contents of the muslin bag. The muslin can be washed and reused.*

4 *Add the sugar, stirring until dissolved, then boil the mixture rapidly for about 15 minutes. Remove from the heat and test for a set (page 300), reboiling if not set. When the setting point is reached, skim any scum carefully from the surface. Cool for 10–15 minutes, then stir to distribute the peel. Pot and cover as for jams (page 300).*

EXCITING FLAVOURS FOR PRESERVES

• As well as using juice you can make fruit curds with smooth fruit purées which are not too thick (page 224). Purées made from stewed dried or fresh apricots, peaches or gooseberries, pears stewed with lemon juice, or a seedless purée of raspberries all work well – but the fruit should be sieved after puréeing to make it really smooth.

• Few marmalades can beat homemade Seville orange marmalade, but there are all sorts of other citrus fruits and combinations of fruits which produce an interesting change. Oranges can be combined with fresh pineapple or with lemons and sliced quinces, peaches or apricots.

• Grapefruit can be combined with oranges and lemons as in the traditional three-fruit marmalade.

• Kumquats make a good marmalade, either on their own or with blood oranges, and orange, lemon and rhubarb is a very good combination.

• Added flavour and interest can be infused into a marmalade mixture by including certain spices or herbs enclosed in a muslin bag in addition to the one which holds the oranges' pips and pulp. Slices of fresh ginger, 1 or 2 tablespoons whole cloves, star anise, coriander seeds, cardamom pods, sticks of cinnamon, rosemary, lavender, bay or mint leaves, are just some possibilities.

• My favourite homemade jam is gooseberry, and the inclusion of elderflowers raises this jam to a magical level. Amazingly, the musty-smelling elderflower imparts a scented flavour of muscatel grapes to gooseberries, and, I have discovered, to apricots and strawberries, too.

• Various liqueurs can be added to jams at the last moment before potting to make them more sophisticated and fragrant; brandy is excellent added to plum jam, and kirsch is a natural partner for cherry jam.

• Vegetables can be used in jams, jellies and marmalades. Marrow and pumpkin are traditional, tomato can be used on its own or combined with other fruits, and onion makes a wonderful jam to serve with pâtés and cold meats.

• My favourite jellies are made from quinces, medlars or crab apples – with their fragrant flavours and amber colours.

CHUTNEYS *and* PICKLES

I only began to enjoy chutneys after my first visit to India – the dark brown sticky mush which was called chutney at school had never captivated my taste buds. Away from India, chutney is less dry and sweeter, often more like a sweet and sour jam. Chutneys are made from a mixture of vegetables or fruits, or a combination of both, which is cooked with vinegar, sugar and spices that act as the preservatives. The ingredients are finely chopped or sliced and then cooked slowly to produce a smooth texture, whereas the ingredients in relishes are cut larger, the cooking time is shorter, and therefore the finished texture is chunkier. Use uneven or misshapen ingredients because their appearance is not important in the finished preserve.

Pickles are made from raw or lightly cooked vegetables or fruits which are preserved in clear, spiced vinegar. Only use crisp fresh ingredients. Vegetables are usually brined or salted to remove excess water which would otherwise dilute the vinegar and make it too weak to act as a preservative. Make sure you use a good-quality bottled vinegar with an acetic acid content of at least five per cent. The colour of vinegar is no indication of its strength, and malt vinegar, whether white distilled or brown, gives a good flavour and is economical. Use white distilled vinegar in light-coloured pickles for a better appearance, but I like the flavour of white wine and cider vinegar best of all. Do not use copper or brass pans for these preserves because the vinegar reacts adversely with them. It is important to use vinegar-proof tops such as plastic-coated ones. If metal caps are used take care not to let the vinegar come into contact with the metal. Glass preserving jars with clip tops are ideal.

FRESH GREEN APPLE CHUTNEY

Very dark, sweet, mushy chutneys are a great favourite with many people, but I personally prefer fresh chutneys with clear colours and separate flavours.

All sorts of ingredients which don't need cooking can be used for fresh chutneys, which are light and refreshing. Using a food processor this technique based on fresh green apple with mint and coriander only takes minutes to make, and will keep in a covered jar in the refrigerator for up to 1 week. Serve with cold or roast meat and poultry, spoon it into curries and casseroles, eat it with crusty bread and cheese or in sandwiches, or mix it with cottage cheese for a delicious baked potato filling.

Put 1 peeled, cored and chopped cooking apple, 4 tablespoons lemon juice, 1 deseeded green chilli cut in half (page 49), 1 generous handful fresh mint leaves, 2 tablespoons fresh coriander leaves and 1 teaspoon caster sugar into a food processor and whizz to a coarse paste. Add salt and cayenne pepper to taste. The mixture should be moist – if it seems too wet add some more mint leaves and whizz again.

TOMATO CHUTNEY

It is very easy to vary a basic chutney recipe and this means you can use more unusual combinations of different fruit and vegetables, as well as gluts from your own garden.

To make about 1kg (2lb) tomato chutney you will need 2 tablespoons mustard seeds, 1 tablespoon whole allspice, 1.5kg (3lb) skinned and quartered tomatoes (page 48), 500g (1lb) finely chopped onions, 1 teaspoon cayenne pepper, 250g (8oz) sultanas, 250g (8oz) granulated sugar, 2 teaspoons salt and 450ml (¾ pint) vinegar.

1 *Tie the mustard seeds and the allspice in a piece of muslin. Gather up the corners and tie the bag securely with a piece of string, then tie to the handle of the preserving pan. Add the tomatoes, onions and cayenne pepper to the pan.*

2 *Simmer on a low heat for about 45 minutes, breaking down the tomatoes until they are reduced to a pulp. Add the remaining ingredients and continue simmering, stirring occasionally, for about 1½ hours, until the mixture is thick.*

3 *Remove the muslin bag. Pour the hot chutney into clean, dry, preheated jars (page 300) and cover immediately with airtight, vinegar-proof tops. Store in a cool, dry, dark place for 2–3 months to allow the flavours to mature before use.*

IDEAS FOR CHUTNEYS AND PICKLES

• Chutney mixtures can be as varied as you wish, but almost all benefit from the inclusion of onions.
• Good chutney combinations include dried apricots and whole shallots and orange juice, rhubarb with thinly sliced whole orange, blackberry and apple with elderberries, seedless grapes with apples and green peppers, apples and prunes, quince and pear with thinly sliced whole lemons, grapefruit with pumpkin and sultanas, plums and apples with slices of fresh ginger, and tomato with apricots and pears.
• Small tomatoes, skinned and then put in a jar with strips of fresh basil leaves before being covered with sweetened wine vinegar and seasoned with salt and cayenne pepper, make an excellent pickle.
• Slightly bland exotic fruits such as kiwis, mangoes and papaya, pickle well and go well with game and pork.
• After packing ingredients into the jar and covering with spiced vinegar, pour a layer of extra virgin olive oil on top to seal and add flavour.

SPICED VINEGAR

Spices are added to vinegar to give it a good flavour and they also help as a preservative. The vinegar can be used at once but if you keep it for several months the flavours will mature.

Preparing your own vinegar means you can add a wider variety of flavours. Whole spices are best for spicing vinegar as ground ones will make the vinegar cloudy. The spices can be varied according to choice but the following is a typical combination for 1.2 litres (2 pints) vinegar: 3 x 5cm (2in) cinnamon sticks, 2 rounded teaspoons whole cloves, 10 blades mace, 2 heaped teaspoons whole allspice and 2 heaped teaspoons black peppercorns.

Place the whole spices in a saucepan and add 1.2 litres (2 pints) white distilled or white wine vinegar. Bring just to the boil (do not allow to bubble), then pour into a heatproof bowl and leave to cool and infuse for 2 hours. Store the vinegar with the spices in it in clean, dry bottles and seal well. Strain before use. If you keep it for 2–3 months before use the flavours will intensify and improve.

Pickles and chutneys are surprisingly easy to make. Here are (clockwise from top right) pickled onions, tomato chutney, fresh green apple chutney and pickled red cabbage.

PICKLED ONIONS

This recipe illustrates wet brining, in which the onions are covered with a brine solution to remove their surplus water. Use ordinary table salt and spiced vinegar (above) which has more flavour than plain vinegar. Cauliflower florets can also be pickled in this way. Store for 3–4 months before using.

You will need 2kg (4lb) pickling onions, 500g (1lb) salt, 4.8 litres (8 pints) water and 1.2 litres (2 pints) cold spiced vinegar.

1 Put the unskinned onions in a large bowl. Dissolve 250g (8oz) salt in 2.4 litres (4 pints) water to make a brine and pour on top of the onions. Leave to soak for 12 hours or a little longer.

PICKLED RED CABBAGE

This classic recipe is an example of dry brining, where the vegetable is layered with salt. As well as red cabbage, it is also suitable for cucumber, tomatoes and marrow. Slice cucumber and tomatoes and dice marrow. Peel or not as you prefer. This is the only pickle that should not be allowed to mature, as it loses its crispness after 2–3 months. You will need 5kg (3lb) finely shredded firm red cabbage (page 45), 2 sliced large onions, 4 tablespoons table salt, 2.4 litres (4 pints) spiced vinegar (above) and 1 tablespoon soft brown sugar.

2 Drain the onions, then skin and cover with fresh brine, made with the remaining salt and water. Leave to soak for 24–36 hours, then drain and rinse.

3 Pack the onions into clean, dry wide-necked jars, to within 2.5cm (1in) of the top. Pour over the spiced vinegar and seal with vinegar-proof tops.

1 Layer the cabbage and onions in a large bowl, sprinkling each layer with salt, then cover with a clean tea towel and set aside for 24 hours. The next day, drain the cabbage and onions well, rinse off the surplus salt thoroughly and drain again.

2 Pack loosely into clean, dry wide-necked jars to within 2.5cm (1in) of the top. Heat the spiced vinegar gently, add the sugar and stir until dissolved. Set aside to cool, then pour over the cabbage and onions and cover immediately with vinegar-proof tops.

SPECIAL PRESERVES

Special preserves include the less usual and more luxurious preserves. Some of them are an ideal method of preserving a small quantity of your favourite fruit or vegetable, while others are preserved in alcohol. All of them make very popular presents especially when you use attractive glass jars and labels.

Mincemeat, ever popular at Christmas, was originally a method of preserving meat without using the salting or smoking methods. Nowadays, however, it is a mixture of fruits, mostly dried, and spices, preserved in alcohol and sugar. Only the suet is a reminder of the past, although you can include a little lean minced beef, too, which adds a round mild flavour. I always make my own mincemeat but if you are short of time commercially made mincemeat can be improved enormously by stirring in fresh lemon juice, a little brandy, grated orange rind and peeled and chopped fresh cooking apples.

Fruits can be preserved in alcohol, in syrup alone and with spices in syrup and vinegar. The alcohol used in preserving fruits is usually brandy as it is the most compatible with the majority of fruits, including cherries, apricots, grapes, peaches, kumquats, pineapple and orange slices, but other spirits, such as kirsch, can be used. Kirsch goes well with cherries, pineapple and raspberries. Fruits in alcohol make delicious, quick and easy puddings and are also good mixed with soft fresh fruits. Fruits that are preserved with spices in syrup and vinegar can be served as accompaniments to meat and poultry.

It is possible to preserve some vegetables in oil and these include dried tomatoes, firm button mushrooms, olives, globe artichokes and grilled peppers. Lemons can also be preserved this way and also by salting, which is a method that goes back to Roman times and is now much used in North African cooking (page 309).

MINCEMEAT

Make up large quantities of this brandy-flavoured mincemeat, varying the ingredients to suit your family's favourite flavours. Give small pots as presents, or use to make individual mincemeat tarts with the sweet shortcrust pastry (page 248).

Although traditionally associated with the British Christmas, mincemeat can, of course, be used all the year round, and it is always useful to have a jar in the store cupboard. For mincemeat that will keep well, use a firm, hard variety of apple, such as Cox's Orange Pippin; a juicy apple may make the mixture too moist. Pot and store mincemeat in the same way as jam (page 300) but allow at least 2 weeks to mature before using. If it becomes dry, add a little extra of the original alcohol used.

To make 1.5kg (3lb) mincemeat, you will need 125g (4oz) raisins, 125g (4oz) sultanas, 75g (3oz) ready-to-eat dried apricots, 75g (3oz) glacé cherries, 75g (3oz) shelled pecans or walnut halves, 175–250g (6–8oz) cooking apples, the grated rind and juice of 2 lemons, 50g (2oz) cut mixed peel, 125g (4oz) currants, 125g (4oz) vegetable suet, 175g (6oz) demerara sugar, ½ teaspoon ground cloves, 1 teaspoon ground cinnamon and 75–150ml (3–5fl oz) brandy.

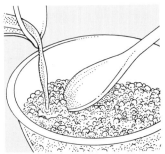

1 *Finely chop the raisins, sultanas, dried apricots, glacé cherries and nuts and put in a large bowl. Add the peeled, cored and chopped apple with the lemon rind and juice, mixed peel, currants, suet, sugar and spices. Stir in enough brandy to make a moist mixture.*

2 *Cover the bowl and leave for 2 days. Then stir again, adding a little more brandy. Spoon into clean, dry jars, packing down well with the back of a wooden spoon, cover and seal (page 300). Leave to mature for at least 2 weeks. If it becomes dry, add a little more brandy before using.*

BRANDIED CHERRIES

A wide variety of fruits can be preserved in alcohol but it is important that they are firm and fresh. The skins of stoned fruits must be pricked to allow the alcohol to permeate the flesh. Pot and cover the jars in the same way as pickles (page 305) and leave for at least 3 months before eating.

You will need 500g (1lb) cherries, 250g (8oz) granulated sugar, 300ml (½ pint) water, 1 cinnamon stick and 150ml (¼ pint) brandy, rum or kirsch.

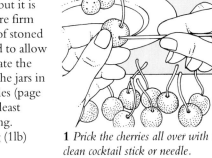

1 *Prick the cherries all over with a clean cocktail stick or needle. Dissolve half the sugar in the water, then add the cherries and cinnamon stick and poach gently for 4–5 minutes.*

2 *Lift the cherries from the syrup and arrange in small, clean, dry preserving jars. Dissolve the remaining sugar in the reserved syrup, then bring to the boil for 5–6 minutes.*

3 *Leave the syrup to cool, then measure the syrup and add an equal amount of brandy. Pour the brandy syrup over the cherries, cover with plastic-lined lids and leave to mature for 3 months.*

MORE IDEAS FOR SPECIAL PRESERVES

• I like changing my mincemeat recipe a little each year and adding different ingredients like chopped pineapple, angelica, dried apricots, peaches and pears.
• All kinds of fruits can be gently poached in a sugar syrup (page 208) and then arranged in jars. You can make alternate layers of different fruits, half cover with a liqueur and then fill to the top with the poaching syrup (reduced to thicken and then cooled before spooning into the jar). Jars should always be sterilized before using (page 300). Successful fruits to use are peeled peaches and apricots, quinces, stoned cherries, sliced mangoes, kiwi fruit and fresh figs – these last two need no cooking first. Dried apricots and prunes are also delicious.

• Halved clementines or pierced kumquats make an excellent accompaniment for roast game or pork: boil with spices in a mixture of water and wine vinegar until soft, then add sugar and after boiling again, pack the fruit into clean, dry jars. Reduce the syrup and pour over the fruit when cold.
• To preserve aubergines in oil, plunge thin slices into boiling white wine vinegar for 3–4 minutes, then drain and press thoroughly between kitchen paper to dry, pack in clean, dry jars, sprinkle with paprika, black pepper, salt, crushed garlic and dried oregano between the layers, and then cover completely with extra virgin olive oil before sealing.
• Flavour olive oil with fresh herbs, but there is no need to strain it before using.

Colourful jars of peppers in oil are ideal to have on hand to serve with sliced meats and salami or cheese. When making cherries in brandy leave the stems on or take them off as you prefer.

PEPPERS IN OIL

Vegetables preserved in oil can be used to liven up salads, in stews or as a pizza topping, and their oil can also be used in salad dressings. Peppers are always nicest grilled until blackened first and then skinned, as this gives them a wonderful mellow, smoky taste. To preserve peppers, you will need 2kg (4lb) red, green or yellow peppers – a mixture of all three looks very pretty. Sprigs of fresh herbs, peeled garlic cloves and olive oil or a mixture of olive and sunflower oil are also added.

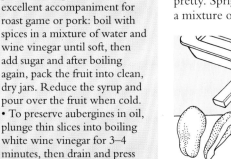

1 *Quarter the peppers lengthwise, then remove the stalks, cores and seeds. Arrange on a grill pan, skin-side uppermost. Grill until completely black. Wrap in a tea towel and leave to cool for 10 minutes. Strip off the skins (page 55), then cut the peppers into strips.*

2 *Pack the pepper strips into clean, dry jars, layering them with sprigs of fresh herbs and adding a peeled garlic clove to each layer. Pour over enough olive oil to cover the peppers completely. Seal the jars tightly. Store for about one month in a cool, dark place before using.*

SPICED APPLE JELLY WITH MINT AND DILL *(301)*

Apple jelly is a delicious and pretty-looking accompaniment to roast lamb. I use spices which are often used with lamb in the Middle East and the green colour is given by adding spinach juice.   *MAKES ABOUT 2KG (4LB)*

1.5kg (3lb) green cooking apples, unpeeled, chopped roughly
Good handful of fresh mint plus 2 tablespoons roughly chopped mint
2 cinnamon sticks, broken
900ml (1½ pints) water
125g (4oz) spinach, stems removed and chopped roughly
300ml (½ pint) cider vinegar
3 teaspoons cumin seeds
3 teaspoons coriander seeds, crushed
6–8 cardamom pods, crushed
Granulated or preserving sugar
Generous bunch of fresh dill, divided into small sprigs

Put the apples in a preserving pan with the handful of fresh mint and broken cinnamon sticks. Add the water, bring to the boil and simmer gently for about 45 minutes, stirring now and then. Add the spinach about halfway through the cooking. When the apples are very soft and mushy, add the cider vinegar and boil for another 5 minutes.

Spoon the apple and spinach mixture into a scalded jelly bag (page 301) over a large bowl and leave to strain for at least 12 hours, without pressing, until the dripping has stopped. Tie up the cumin seeds, coriander seeds and cardamom pods in a muslin bag, and wrap the 2 tablespoons of roughly chopped mint in a second muslin bag.

Measure the extracted juice from the apple and spinach mixture and put it in a preserving pan with 500g (1lb) of sugar for each 600ml (1 pint) of juice. Discard the pulp in the jelly bag. Put the pan over a medium heat and stir until the sugar has dissolved, then add the bags of spices and mint. Bring to the boil, boil rapidly for about 10 minutes, remove the pan from the heat and test for a set (page 300).

When the setting point has been reached, remove any scum with a large metal spoon. Add the dill sprigs to the jelly. Leave to cool for 8–10 minutes, then stir again and pour into clean, dry, hot jars (page 300), including some dill in each jar. Seal and store.

ELDERFLOWER AND HAZELNUT HONEY *(298)*

This is a wonderful way of making ordinary honey into something really special. The elderflowers, in season in May and June, infuse the honey with their magically scented flavour and the finely chopped, toasted hazelnuts give both taste and an exciting texture.   *MAKES 1KG (2LB)*

1kg (2lb) set honey
3–4 clean-looking elderflower heads
50g (2oz) toasted skinned hazelnuts, finely chopped

Spoon the honey into a saucepan. Shake the elderflower heads over the pan so the flowers drop in, pulling off the ones which don't drop off easily. Heat gently, stirring, until just beginning to bubble, then remove from the heat, cover and leave to infuse for at least 1 hour.

Reheat the honey until just bubbling, then pour through a strainer into clean, dry, hot jars (page 300), stirring some chopped hazelnuts into each jar. When cool, cover tightly and store for at least 2 weeks before using. The hazelnuts will rise to the top of the jar while the honey is cooling so when it begins to set again, stir to redistribute them.

ORANGE, LIME AND SWEET PEPPER CHUTNEY *(298)*

This is a translucent, beautifully coloured, mildly spiced chutney which goes specially well with duck, pork and venison dishes. It is also excellent with cold turkey and ham. It is more like a thick fruit compôte than a chutney though the onions and vinegar give it a definite savoury taste.   *MAKES ABOUT 1.5KG (3LB)*

3 large oranges
5 limes
2 large onions, cut into 1cm (½in) pieces
9–10 large cloves garlic, halved
2 red chillies, deseeded and chopped finely (page 49)
1 teaspoon turmeric
375g (12oz) granulated sugar
300ml (½ pint) white wine vinegar
300ml (½ pint) fresh, unsweetened apple juice
1 teaspoon salt
10–12 cardamom pods, lightly crushed
6–8 whole cloves
1 large red pepper, cored, deseeded and cut into 1cm (½in) pieces (page 49)
1 large yellow pepper, cored, deseeded, and cut into 1cm (½in) pieces (page 49)

Scrub the oranges and limes with soapy water, rinse thoroughly in clean water and dry. Squeeze the juice out of the oranges into a heavy stainless steel or enamelled saucepan, removing any pips. Scrape the pith out of the orange shells with a teaspoon and discard, then cut the peel into small pieces. Cut the limes into eighths, discarding any pips.

Add the orange peel, lime segments, onions, garlic and chillies to the saucepan and stir in the turmeric, granulated sugar, white wine vinegar, apple juice and salt. Tie up the crushed cardamom pods and the cloves in a muslin bag secured with a longish piece of string and tie to the saucepan handle. Bring to the boil then simmer gently, uncovered, stirring occasionally, for 1 hour. Add the prepared peppers and continue to simmer gently for another 30–45 minutes, stirring more often with a large wooden spoon as the mixture thickens.

Remove the muslin bag of spices and discard. Leave the chutney to cool in the saucepan. Then spoon into clean, dry jars (page 300), seal and keep in a cool place to mature for at least 2 weeks before using.

FRESH RASPBERRY JAM *(298)*

Soft fruit jams or ones made from non-pectin ingredients such as rose petals benefit enormously from pectin sugar because the mixture will set with only the briefest of boiling so the fruits retain their juicy freshness.   *MAKES 1.5–2KG (3–4LB)*

1kg (2lb) dry, fresh raspberries
Juice of 1 orange, strained
4 tablespoons lemon juice, strained
875g (1¾lb) pectin sugar

Put the raspberries in a preserving pan with the strained orange and lemon juices. Stir in the pectin sugar and bring gradually to the boil over a medium heat. Boil vigorously for 3–4 minutes and test for a set (page 300). When setting point has been reached, pour into clean, dry, hot jars (page 300) and seal.

LEMONS PRESERVED IN SALT *(298)*

After several holidays in Morocco, I have come to love these lemons which are used in many of their wonderful *tagines* (stews cooked in traditional earthenware pots). Slices of pickled lemons and their juice enhance chicken stew, and are good for a spicy lamb casserole which could also include dried fruits such as apricots or prunes. When matured, these lemons don't taste very salty, and the skin is soft and has lost all bitterness.   *MAKES ABOUT 1KG (2LB)*

About 1kg (2lb) fairly small lemons, plus
  about 6 lemons for extra juice
About 125g (4oz) sea salt

Scrub the lemons thoroughly with soapy water, then rinse well with cold running water and dry. Working over a bowl, cut the lemons lengthwise almost in quarters but stop before you cut right through at the stem end so the fruit still holds together. Remove any pips.

Sprinkle a heaped teaspoon of salt into each lemon then pack very tightly into clean, dry, wide-necked jars (page 300), pressing down firmly with a spoon. Pour any juice which escaped while you were cutting the lemons into the jars. The juice should completely cover the lemons: squeeze out more from the extra lemons and use more lemons if necessary.

Put a weight such as a well-washed, suitably shaped stone or small saucer in the top of each jar so that no bits of lemon rise above the juice, then cover the jars and leave at room temperature for 2–3 weeks. When the lemons are ready (the skins will be soft to cut) remove the weight. Once opened keep in the refrigerator and use as necessary.

SPICED APRICOT AND TOMATO RELISH *(298)*

This relish is rather like a chutney, only it is cooked for less time and has a fresher, sweet-and-sour flavour.
     MAKES ABOUT 2–2.5KG (4–5LB)

500g (1lb) fresh apricots, halved, stoned
  and chopped roughly (page 222)
750g (1½lb) tomatoes, skinned and
  chopped roughly (page 48)
250g (8oz) shallots, quartered lengthwise
2.5cm (1in) piece fresh root ginger, peeled
  and sliced thinly
4–5 cardamom pods, crushed roughly
1 cinnamon stick, broken into 2.5cm (1in)
  pieces
125g (4oz) light demerara sugar
1 tablespoon honey
150ml (¼ pint) cider vinegar
2 teaspoons green peppercorns

Put the prepared apricots, tomatoes, shallots, ginger, cardamom and cinnamon into a preserving pan, then stir in the sugar, honey, cider vinegar and green peppercorns. Bring to the boil and bubble, uncovered, for about 20 minutes until the shallots are soft and the mixture is thick. Spoon into clean, dry, hot jars (page 300), seal and cover. Store in a cool place for at least 3 weeks before opening.

MIXED PICKLED MUSHROOMS *(298)*

All over Eastern Europe and in Russia, pickled mushrooms are extremely popular, and rightly so. We had lunch once with an old lady in Prague who gave us four kinds of pickled mushrooms, some of which had an almost buttery consistency. Using a mixture of different mushrooms means there will be an interesting variation in textures and flavours. During a good autumn you could add some wild ones, too. Pickled mushrooms are delicious, eaten on their own, with cheese or fromage frais, or added to salads.
     MAKES ABOUT 750ML (1¼ PINTS)

250g (8oz) chestnut mushrooms
125g (4oz) shiitake mushrooms
125g (4oz) button mushrooms
125g (4oz) oyster mushrooms
3 tablespoons salt
300ml (½ pint) dry white wine
300ml (½ pint) white wine vinegar
2 teaspoons caster sugar
1 small red-skinned onion, sliced thinly
2 large cloves garlic, quartered lengthwise
2 teaspoons pink or green peppercorns,
  crushed roughly
1 teaspoon coriander seeds
2 sprigs fresh tarragon, separated into
  leaves
3–4 tablespoons extra virgin olive oil

If the mushrooms have any dirt on them, wipe with a damp cloth. Only cut off the bottom of the stalks, and cut any large mushrooms in half. Add the salt to a pan of water and bring to the boil, then add the mushrooms and boil for 4–5 minutes. Drain the mushrooms and leave to cool on one side.

Pour the dry white wine and white wine vinegar into a saucepan. Stir in the caster sugar then add the onion slices, garlic, crushed peppercorns, coriander seeds and tarragon leaves. Bring to the boil, cover and simmer for 5 minutes. Remove from the heat and leave to cool. Stir in the cooked mushrooms.

Pack the cooled mushrooms and vinegar mixture with the spices, garlic and tarragon in clean, dry jars (page 300). Make sure the mushrooms are well covered by the liquid. Spoon the olive oil over the tops. Cover tightly and leave to mature for at least 3 weeks before using. After opening, keep in the refrigerator.

MICROWAVING

Microwave ownership has increased dramatically in the last decade as more and more cooks realize its great potential. Although the microwave has the reputation for being a fast heating-up appliance, it can be a great kitchen aid for the keen conventional cook. Microwaving does take a little practice to master at first, however, if only because it is a different style of cooking. You have to get used to power coming in intense bursts of energy, which then have to be distributed through the dish either by a rotating turntable or by stirring. Microwave cooking is not always faster, but for many cooks it is more convenient, especially for some preparation steps in a recipe and for cooking simple everyday ingredients like vegetables.

Direct heat is not involved in microwave cooking. Instead, heat is generated within the food by the microwaves that vibrate the food's molecules, causing friction and heat. Food literally cooks itself and continues cooking even when the power is off.

The microwave oven has many advantages and a few disadvantages. For instance, it cannot brown food unless it is fitted with a special browning dish. In some cases it is easier and quicker to cook foods conventionally on the hob or in your ordinary oven. Microwave ovens do not fry well, nor do they give foods nice crisp coatings. You can only cook one dish at a time in most microwave ovens so if you are preparing a meal with a number of dishes the others will lose heat slightly, unless you are lucky enough to have more than one microwave. Some cooks do, as they find microwave cookers so indispensable, but this is not my idea of a real kitchen at all.

However, the great boon of a microwave is its convenience. The cooking can be controlled with a timer and food is often cooked in its serving dish. Washing up of pots and pans is considerably reduced. Small individual quantities are easier to handle and many single people find they eat fresher foods and cook more as a result of owning a microwave. Many foods do taste better cooked freshly in the microwave, especially those that benefit from quick light cooking such as delicate fish and crisp vegetables that need the minimum amount of water.

Special cooking techniques These are few, although you will find at first that you have to stir some foods more frequently than during conventional cooking and can't just leave some dishes to cook without attention. If there is no built-in turntable you will have to re-distribute foods by rotating, rearranging or stirring during cooking. This is vital to ensure the food is heated throughout to a high enough temperature to kill any bacteria that could cause food poisoning. Microwave ovens have hot and cold spots just like conventional ovens which also adds to the possibility of foods being heated unevenly. Your user's manual will give specific instructions but generally foods should be stirred from the outside inwards and thinner, more delicate sections of food positioned towards the centre.

You also have to allow for the fact that microwaved food continues to cook out of the oven, during what is known as standing time. Scrambled eggs, for example, should be removed while they are hot and runny, then 2 minutes or so later they firm up to the correct creamy consistency.

Power levels and wattage Microwaves work at varying power levels depending on the wattage of the oven. The most common wattage level is 650 watts, and instructions in this book are based on that level. But if your oven has a lower wattage, consult your user's manual, adjusting cooking times up or down accordingly. The different power settings on most microwaves – High (100%), Medium (50%), Defrost (30%) and Low (10%) – are the amount of energy produced in bursts in a given time. This means High is power coming on 100 per cent of the cooking time, Medium at about 50 per cent, Defrost at 30 per cent and Low at 10 per cent. You can actually hear the machine pulsing on and off, and between bursts the food is actually standing but still gently cooking. Different models have different settings and labels for the settings, so you must consult your manual before cooking.

Packaging Microwaves are deflected by metal but pass through other materials. Almost any heatproof dish or plate can be used in the microwave as long as it is not metal or has a metallic rim or pattern. Glass, glazed earthenware, china and rigid plastics that do not melt at low temperatures can all be used. Although dishes don't heat conventionally, they are heated by the hot food in them and can become very hot, so be sure to use oven gloves when taking dishes out of the microwave.

To cover a dish or bowl when cooking either use a special microwave plastic lid with adjustable vents, or microwave clingfilm. If you do use clingfilm, put food into a deep microwaveproof bowl. Many microwave experts now recommend that hot food, especially those with a high fat content, does not touch clingfilm so leave a head space when you cover the top. Either pierce it a few times or fold back a small section on the side to allow steam to escape. Alternatively, good old-fashioned greaseproof paper, wetted and crumpled, is ideal to cover flat foods which otherwise might come in contact with hot film.

Microwaving vegetables One of the big advantages of microwave ovens is the way they cook vegetables – quickly, cleanly and with the minimum of water and steam. Microwaves are excellent for producing a good texture and maintaining as many vitamins as possible. Anyone on a low-salt diet also benefits because maximum flavour is retained so seasoning can be reduced. Boiled vegetables, however, will take almost as long as if cooked on the hob, but the benefit is that they require less water and there's no danger of them boiling dry and burning. And, if you cook in a microwaveproof dish there's no pan to wash up. So, while a baked potato may take, say, 5 minutes, boiled new potatoes can take about 10 minutes, which is not much less than normal. Yet, with only a small amount of water they should taste better.

Prepare your vegetables as normal, pop into a deep bowl with just a few tablespoons of water, cover with pierced clingfilm, making sure it does not touch the food and cook on High (100%) for a few minutes. Your user's manual will give you timings. If you have a turntable there is no need to stir. Awkward-shaped vegetables such as broccoli, or those with thicker stalks than tips like asparagus should be positioned on a plate or dish with thick stalks to the outside. Larger vegetables like sweetcorn cobs will need to be rearranged halfway through cooking so they cook evenly.

The miracle microwave vegetable, however, has to be a baked potato. Instead of the hour or so it takes to cook conventionally, it takes a mere 5 minutes, although you won't get lovely crispy skins unless you have a combination oven.

Microwaving fish This really is when the microwave cooks to perfection. Because fish is best cooked lightly and quickly, microwave energy suits it well. Added to which, fishy smells in the kitchen are reduced because they are contained within the oven, and by placing fillets or steaks straight on a microwaveproof serving plate, you can save the delicious light juices as an instant sauce. Place fish fillets and steaks on a plate, dot with butter and season. Cover loosely with greaseproof paper and cook on High (100%) for 2–4 minutes, depending on thickness; consult your user's manual for specific times. Let stand for 2–3 minutes.

Microwaving meat and poultry A microwave oven does not brown meat unless it is a combination oven, so meat and

HELPFUL HINTS

Because heat levels are controlled and timed, there are lots of failsafe tasks a microwave does well, making preparation of foods much simpler. These are some of the most useful ones. Be sure to consult your user's manual for specific times.

• Simmer homemade meat stocks to concentrate flavours, uncovered, for up to 1 hour and fish and vegetable stocks up to 30 minutes: this avoids the pan boiling dry or the kitchen filling with steam and smells.

• Melt chocolate without it seizing, meaning that it turns stiff and lumpy. This is much safer in a microwave oven than conventionally in a heatproof bowl over hot water, which might overheat. Break the chocolate into a bowl and cook on High (100%) for about 2 minutes, stirring half way through. Check your user's manual for full instructions.

• Dissolve gelatine without any danger of it boiling and then losing its setting qualities. Mix with cold water, allow to sponge, then heat on Defrost (30%) for 2–3 minutes, stirring once, until clear.

• Honey and jam can be melted in the jar for easy measuring, but first remove metal tops. Melt apricot jam and redcurrant jelly in a bowl for glazing fruit tarts or pudding cakes this way, too.

• Make caramel more easily by dissolving caster sugar with water, according to the recipe (page 217), then cook on High (100%) for 6–8 minutes, until golden brown. Do not use a plastic container.

• Soften butter and hard baking margarine on Defrost (30%) for 1–3 minutes.

• To clarify butter, melt it on High (100%) for 1–3 minutes, then clarify (page 96).

• Warm milk and flavourings directly in a jug to infuse for béchamel sauce (page 196).

• Toast nuts and desiccated coconut on a flat plate on High (100%) for about 5 minutes, stirring occasionally, without any risk of burning and having to be discarded.

• Parcook marinated barbecue chicken, chops or thick sausages in the microwave until just cooked, then glaze with more marinade and finish over smoky charcoal. This way you can be sure the meat is thoroughly cooked.

• Soften homemade and dairy ice cream in the microwave on Defrost (30%) for 1–2 minutes until soft enough to scoop.

• Porridge is cooked in 2–3 minutes in the bowl, from 1 to 3 portions at a time (page 111). And there is no sticky pan to wash.

• Potatoes bake in minutes although without crispy skins. Score first and rub with a little olive oil (page 56). Cook on High (100%) for 5 minutes for 1 potato; 7–8 minutes for 2 potatoes; 10–12 minutes for 3 potatoes; 12–15 minutes for 4 potatoes.

• Cook the fruit to soften first for pies and crumbles in the pie dish, then transfer to a conventional oven to bake.

• Make homemade lemon curd in an instant. Melt 75g (3oz) butter on High (100%) then stir in 250g (8oz) caster sugar, the grated rind of 2 lemons, 4 tablespoons freshly squeezed lemon juice and 3 beaten eggs. Cook on High for 2–3 minutes, stirring occasionally, until the sugar has dissolved. Cook for 2-3 minutes more on High, stirring twice, until thickened. Cool and pot (page 300).

• If cooking boil-in-the bag foods, pierce the bag first to allow steam to escape during cooking and take care when cutting open.

• Take care when peeling back clingfilm after cooking; the build up of steam inside can burn your hand.

• It is a good idea always to keep a cup of water in the microwave when you are not using it. This way if the microwave is accidentally turned on the water will absorb the microwaves, otherwise they could bounce off the walls causing damage to the oven as there is no food to absorb the microwaves.

---

poultry are best brushed lightly with spices or sauces to give them an attractive colour. Many cooks, and I am certainly one of them, though, prefer to cook meat dishes conventionally. A roast or slowly cooked casserole is just as happy sitting without attention in an oven as being cooked faster but needing more stirring in a microwave.

Thinly sliced strips of quickly cooking meat such as chicken or pork are fine cooked in a microwave, as are small meatballs and meat loaves, although they may need a colourful accompanying sauce. If you do want to try roasting in a microwave, invest in a microwaveproof rapid-response thermometer; do not use a conventional metal meat thermometer. Combination ovens often have a built-in special temperature guide probe which is stuck into the joint telling you when the meat is cooked.

Microwaving rices, pasta and pulses Because these are cooked in water, they don't actually take less time to cook but many cooks find it more convenient as there is little risk of overcooking or boiling dry. To cook rice see page 108 and make sure that any clingfilm covering the bowl does not touch the rice.

To cook dried pasta, put it in a deep bowl with boiling water to cover, cover with pierced microwave clingfilm and cook for three-quarters the conventional time given on the packet, leave to stand for 2 minutes, then check. Drain if it doesn't need more cooking and toss with butter and nutmeg.

To cook pulses, first soak them conventionally (page 112), then drain. Place in a deep bowl, adding any flavouring herbs and vegetables but no salt and cover with boiling water. Cover with pierced microwave clingfilm, making sure it does not touch the pulses. Cook on High (100%) until boiling, then on Defrost (30%) for 35–50 minutes, until tender. Drain and toss with a little seasoning and oil.

Baking Unless you have a combination oven microwave cakes do not brown. But they do cook very fast and are a joy to watch rising as they cook. Children especially love to watch this and it is a good way to get them interested in learning to cook. Many cooks find the best microwave cakes are those that use dark coloured ingredients such as brown sugar, cocoa powder, treacle or spices like fruit malt loaves (page 295), chocolate cakes (page 272) and gingerbreads (page 269). You will, however, have to buy special microwaveproof cake 'tins' and dishes although heatproof glass dishes can be used.

Defrosting For busy cooks this is one of the greatest benefits of owning a microwave oven. Out of the freezer, into the microwave and on to the plate within, say, 30 minutes or so. And you don't have to think ahead in the morning about what to get out to thaw to eat that evening. Defrost power is about 30% output, fine for most foods, but certain thinly sliced meats and fish may need Low (10%) power so the edges do not to start cooking before the insides are fully thawed. Small chickens and joints thaw easily, but first place them on sheets of kitchen paper to absorb the juices, and check inside the bird to see it is free from ice before cooking. Many vegetables and fish fillets can be cooked straight from frozen, while sauces can be cooked from a frozen block until they are bubbling and very hot.

Hygiene and safety For cook-chill prepared meals and foods, always follow instructions and timings on the packet because it is vital that reheated food gets to the correct internal temperature to kill off potential food-poisoning bacteria and toxins. The same goes for home-cooked food that is being reheated, so follow the instructions for special cooking techniques (opposite).

Combination ovens One of the great improvements in modern cooking technology has been to combine the best of both worlds – the speed and cleanliness of microwave cooking with the browning and crisping ability of conventional ovens. And you can use either form of power separately or together. This can limit the type of dish you use so check your manual for suitable materials. Also as some combination ovens aren't very large it may limit the size of meat joint. But combination oven owners are very enthusiastic about roasted joints, cakes and pies although some feel they need a degree in maths to work out the controls.

FREEZING

Freezers in the home have now become almost indispensable for many of us. A freezer holds in a suspended state many creative home-cooked foods and elements of dishes that when thawed and combined, form the bases of wonderful meals. It has been said that a freezer saves time. In fact, it re-distributes time. You cook ahead and freeze when you have time, for when you need to produce a good home-cooked dish and time is short.

Freezing is a form of modern-day preservation. Traditional methods of salting, smoking and preserving in sugars and vinegars for jams, jellies and pickles slowed bacterial decomposition but altered the taste, texture and colour of the original foods. Freezing, when it is done correctly using good-quality ingredients is perhaps the nearest we can get to preserving foods in their most natural state. You only get out of a freezer the quality you put in. The freshest fruit and vegetables, the best meat, the firmest fish and home-baked goods, when frozen correctly, will thaw almost exactly to the same state they were in fresh. If freezing obtained a reputation for producing poor-quality food it was probably because that is what was used in the first place, or the food was not frozen properly.

All food contains water and during the freezing process it is frozen, the intense cold prevents bacterial growth and decay from developing further. The water forms crystals during freezing and their size is dependent on the rate at which freezing takes place. Food frozen very quickly forms a mass of tiny ice crystals, causing minimum disruption to the structure of the rest of the food. Freezing done slowly, however, means ice crystals take longer to form so they become bigger, causing more disruption to the structure. This affects the texture and overall eating quality of the thawed food. Added to which, foods with high-water contents suffer greater cell disruption. Think of a strawberry and a raspberry. Strawberries have a greater watery mass and go mushy when frozen and thawed. Raspberries fare better because their individual little berries clustered together have a smaller mass.

Uncovered food starts to dehydrate in the refrigerator or freezer, causing drying which diminishes the eating quality. This means proper wrapping is as important as fast freezing.

Practical freezing techniques When food with liquid freezes it expands, and packaging must allow for this. Such food needs head space, so only fill to within 2.5cm (1in) of the top of the container and seal after freezing. Many other foods can simply be wrapped in clingfilm or foil or bagged but many fragile or decorated foods benefit from being open frozen first, and then wrapped or boxed when solid. This way they do not become squashed or damaged.

For example, lay a cream-decorated gâteau or pretty fruit tart on a wire rack and freeze. When it is solid, pack it carefully in a freezerproof plastic box. To prevent certain fruits like raspberries or gooseberries from freezing together in a clump, lay out on trays and open freeze until solid, then bag, seal and label. They then take less thawing when needed and preserve their texture better.

Another useful technique, especially for casseroles, is to line a casserole dish with freezer-strength foil and cook the food in it, then cool and freeze. When solid lift out the casserole as a foil-lined block and place in a freezer bag. This way you don't have a useful casserole dish out of action for too long. Unwrap the frozen block and return it to the original container for reheating without initial thawing.

Packaging and wrapping If inadequately protected, food in the freezer dries out. This means wrapping and packing materials have to be thicker than normal and be strong enough not to tear easily. Intense cold leads to freezer burn (hard, dry greyish patches) which is not a health hazard but does affect the eating quality of food.

Freezer-quality materials prevent freezer burn but a double wrapping of normal quality is also suitable. The most useful packaging to have is clingfilm, if only because you can see into it and easily mould it around the food. Foil is useful, especially thick freezer foil, and freezer bags in a selection of sizes are a great boon, too: larger bags are ideal for joints and cakes and medium-sized ones for vegetables and fruit. To use, press the bag around the food leaving no pockets of air and tie securely.

For small items like sausages, pancakes, mince pies or tartlets, and chops, layering tissue or baking parchment is very useful because it allows you to separate the pieces easily for quick thawing.

Always, always label and date foods, even if you are sure you will remember what they are. The chances are that you will forget in a couple of weeks. A fish stock can look identical to chicken stock, and apple purée like jerusalem artichoke soup, for example.

Freezing meat, poultry and game If you put good-quality meat, poultry and game into the freezer, and thaw it correctly, you will get good quality meat out. Freeze meat, poultry and game as quickly as possible on the fast-freeze setting and wrap well, excluding all air, in freezer-quality wrap or foil to protect the meat or poultry from the effects of dehydration in the intense cold. Protruding bones should be wrapped first in foil so they do not puncture packaging.

Chops, sausages and slices of liver can be open frozen on wire racks and then bagged when solid, or interleaved with layering tissue or baking parchment. Hang and gut all game before freezing and wrap as for meat.

For best eating quality, use beef, poultry and venison within 8 months; lamb, veal, pork and other game in 6 months; offal in 3 months. Smoked bacon and ham can be kept for 2 months, unsmoked for 1 month. Cooked meat dishes with garlic, lots of spices or bacon should be used within 6 weeks, otherwise freeze for up to 3 months. Meat stock can be kept for 2–3 months.

Freezing fish Freeze only fish you are sure is absolutely fresh. Gut and remove the head, if liked (pages 118–121), then wrap whole fish individually in clingfilm and/or foil. Fillets and steaks can be interleaved with layering tissue or baking parchment, then wrapped well or bagged.

Frozen fish can be thawed, then cooked and used to make pies, fish cakes, quenelles and so on. These cooked dishes can then be frozen but should be used within 1 month and reheated thoroughly.

Use white fish within 3 months; oily fish such as mackerel and salmon within 2 months; and smoked fish within 6 weeks. Fish stock can be frozen for 2–3 months.

Freezing vegetables and fruit It's only worth freezing really fresh homegrown or pick-your-own produce in times of glut because of the work involved with blanching (below) or packing in syrups.

Watery produce like lettuce, cucumber, tomatoes and cress do not freeze well, unless made into purées or soups. A little loss of flavour can be noticeable, so sometimes I prefer to freeze away gluts in tasty vegetable mixtures like ratatouille (page 59).

Soft fruits can be open frozen or simply bagged without sugar. You can also sprinkle prepared fruits with sugar and pack dry in bags or plastic boxes. Fruits to be served cold without further cooking are best thawed slowly in the refrigerator to retain maximum flavour and texture. Use most vegetables and fruit within 1 year.

Blanching This is necessary before freezing vegetables and certain fruits. Enzymes in fresh produce continue to work even at freezing temperatures, albeit very slowly, leading eventually to deterioration.

A quick immersion in boiling water, followed by a dip in very cold water rapidly cuts this deterioration. Use a blanching basket that fits comfortably inside a deep pan. Time only from the moment the water returns to the boil after adding the vegetable and blanch in small quantities of about 500g (1lb) a time. Instantly plunge the vegetables straight from the pan into cold water for about the same time, then drain well, bag and freeze as soon as possible.

Freezing home-cooked dishes I always try to freeze in small manageable quantities, not great blocks. I think it is better to re-cook 2 or 3 portions at a time than to try and saw up one big frozen quantity.

Certain flavours intensify when frozen and shorten the time dishes containing them can be stored frozen. Spices, garlic and salty foods certainly should be used cautiously or dishes with them should be eaten within 6 weeks. Fatty foods like bacon can go rancid after about 6 weeks. Breads, pastry and cakes freeze very well as long as they are well wrapped. Sliced bread stays separate so if your family are light bread eaters, this is a good way of cutting down on wastage.

Freezing dairy products Freeze only clotted, double and whipping creams, lightly whipping them before putting into the freezer. So it doesn't separate, thaw cream slowly in the refrigerator.

Cheeses freeze well but mould-ripened ones such as Brie thaw softer. Cottage cheese does not freeze but cream cheese does because of the higher fat content. Divide big wedges of cheese into manageable chunks, then wrap well and freeze. Use hard cheeses such as Cheddar within 6 months; mould-ripened and cream cheeses within 6 weeks.

Overwrap butter tightly in foil or a bag, then freeze unsalted butter for 6 months and salted for 3 months.

Yogurts can be frozen but are thinner when thawed and need stirring well before using; use within 1 month.

Thawing and reheating All food will freeze, but it is the quality when it is thawed that determines how suitable it is for freezing. Fresh produce including meat, fish and fruit are best thawed slowly in the refrigerator to reduce 'drip', that is the liquids they exude.

Make sure you don't thaw meat or poultry above cooked dishes in case they drip into them, resulting in cross-contamination and possible food poisoning. Unwrap meat, poultry and game, put on a plate with a lip or in a shallow container, and cover loosely with foil or a food bag before putting in the refrigerator. Thawed food will deteriorate more quickly than fresh, so cook or eat as soon as possible.

Frozen cooked foods need to be either re-heated thoroughly until they are hot and bubbling, or consumed cold as soon after thawing as possible.

Large thick foods and dishes need thawing before cooking but it is surprising how many other foods or dishes don't. In general, foods that only need quick light cooking at room

USEFUL FREEZER STANDBYS

Here are some useful tips for making the most of your freezer. In addition, there are many things that are well-worth making to freeze down in bulk, ready to pull out when you are in a hurry.

• Stocks – homemade, of course – freeze beautifully with absolutely no effect on the flavour (page 26). To save space, boil the stocks right down to reduce them to an absolute minimum volume. I like to reduce stocks so much that I can freeze them in ice-cube trays and then transfer the frozen cubes to freezer bags. This is how I make my own stock cubes, ready to be either reconstituted with water for soups and casseroles, use 2 or 3 at a time to make delicious gravies or as the base of a cream or vegetable sauce.

• Another useful standby using ice-cube trays is fresh herb ice cubes. Chop fresh herbs finely, put teaspoonfuls in ice-cube trays and top with a little water. When frozen, pop out of the tray and bag according to the herb. Using these frozen herbs is much nicer than using dried. If you don't want to add any liquid to the dish, thaw the ice cubes in a fine sieve so the water drains away from the herbs.

• In high summer it's fun freezing edible flowers in clear mineral water to add to long, cool drinks. They look so pretty, too, especially borage flowers or violets.

• Blend softened unsalted butter with chopped herbs or lemon juice, curry paste, mustard or garlic. Freeze in small rolls or cut into pats ready to put on top of sizzling steaks. Use spicy and garlicky butters within 6 weeks.

• Fresh breadcrumbs are useful for bread sauce, stuffings, toppings and crispy fried coatings. Whenever you have a loaf spare or leftovers, grind it into crumbs, put into a bag and freeze. Rub to separate the crumbs and they will be easy to scoop out.

• Another use for stale sliced bread is to cut it into squares or shapes, fry in hot oil until golden, then cool and freeze as croûtons (page 35).

• Pastry cases are best frozen unbaked. They can then be baked from frozen and taste beautifully fresh and crisp. But they are more fragile frozen, so wrap well and tightly in foil once frozen.

• Small leftover pieces of pastry can be re-rolled and cut into attractive shapes to bake from frozen to use as garnishes.

• Watery strawberries and tomatoes freeze best as purées. Other fruits like apples, plums, raspberries, apricots and rhubarb also make good purées to be used later for fools (page 224), uncooked fruit purées (page 208) and sorbets (page 234).

• Save freezer space and containers by lining empty boxes with freezer bags, pouring in soups, stocks or sauces and freezing. Then remove the frozen block and bag and return to the freezer.

• One of the great freezer standbys is a selection of ragù-style mince sauces (page 213) to which you can add extra flavourings when thawed and re-cooked.

• Use layering tissue or baking parchment to keep pancakes and sausages separate when freezing. This way you can thaw the number you want at a time.

• If ice cubes are stuck together in a bag, drop from a little height. They will separate instantly.

• Freeze egg whites 2 at a time, as this is a useful quantity to whip up quickly for meringue toppings.

• Use yogurt pots for small quantities of purées, egg whites and baby foods. Sterilize the pots first in diluted baby bottle sterilizing solution.

• Foods which don't freeze well are hard-boiled eggs (they go leathery and watery) but they can be incorporated into a dish if finely chopped; mayonnaise and hollandaise sauce (they separate when thawed) but if mayonnaise is in a mousse it's fine; alcohol and strong sugar syrups (they never freeze); water-based icings such as royal icing (they dissolve); bananas and avocados (they go black); cream with less than 35 per cent butter fat but even those with higher are best whipped otherwise they go grainy when thawed; milk also separates unless it is homogenized or skimmed.

temperature can be cooked from frozen without thawing first. Vegetables that have been blanched and bagged in small quantities can be cooked from frozen by boiling for just a few minutes.

Sliced bread can be toasted frozen and thin chipolata sausages, pizzas, flat fillets of fish and flash fry steaks can also be cooked straight from the freezer. Heat frozen sauces and stocks gently until they melt, then bring to the boil and bubble for a few minutes.

Soft fruits also are best thawed gently in the refrigerator. Other foods can be thawed more quickly at room temperature but make

sure they are well covered first then use or cook them immediately.

All poultry must be thoroughly thawed before cooking so an internal cooking temperature high enough to destroy food-poisoning bacteria is reached before the outside of the bird is cooked. To check if whole birds are thawed, reach inside. If ice crystals remain in the cavity the bird needs longer to thaw.

Most everyday foods, except meat, take about 2 hours to thaw at room temperature; meat takes about 1½–2 hours per 500g (1lb) to thaw completely.

GLOSSARY

Acidulated water Water that has been made acid by a dash of lemon juice or vinegar. It is used to immerse peeled or cut fruit and vegetables to prevent discoloration.

Agar-agar A vegetarian alternative to gelatine, made from seaweed.

Al dente Meaning, in Italian, 'to the tooth', this is used to describe the point when a food is cooked but still has just a touch of bite to it. Most often applied to pasta and vegetables.

Aspic A clear savoury jelly made from clarified meat, fish or vegetable stock. It is used to glaze cold foods.

Bain-marie A water bath. Either a water-filled roasting tin (in the oven) or a double saucepan with water in the bottom half (on top of the stove), for cooking gently at low temperatures or for keeping food warm.

Bard To cover meat, poultry or game with thin sheets of bacon fat or pork fat to prevent the flesh from drying out during roasting.

Baste To spoon a food with fat or pan juices during cooking to prevent it from drying out.

Beurre manié Equal parts of butter and flour, kneaded together and used in small amounts to thicken and enrich soups and sauces.

Bind To add egg or other liquid to a mixture to hold the ingredients together.

Bisque A rich, creamy fish soup based on a thick purée.

Blanch To immerse briefly in boiling water.

Borsch A classic, brilliant red, Eastern European soup made with beetroot.

Bouquet garni A small parcel of herbs, usually including fresh thyme, parsley and bay leaves, used to flavour soups, stews and sauces.

Brandade A Provençal dish of puréed salt cod, flavoured with garlic.

Brown To sear the outside of meat and seal in its juices before stewing or braising.

Bruise To lightly crush an aromatic food such as garlic or ginger to release its flavour.

Bulgar Cracked wheat.

Caramelize To turn sugar into caramel by gentle heating so it dissolves and turns brown.

Chine To saw the backbone (also called the chine bone) from the ribs in a joint of meat for easier carving.

Clarify To remove impurities from stock. Also to remove the milk solids from butter by melting and straining.

Compôte Fresh or dried fruit stewed in a sugar syrup.

Coulis A thin purée of fruit or vegetables, served as a sauce.

Court bouillon A poaching stock for delicate foods such as fish, shellfish and chicken. Usually made from vegetables with water and wine, wine vinegar or lemon juice.

Cream To beat butter and sugar together until the sugar has dissolved and the mixture is light and smooth.

Crystallize To preserve fruit in sugar syrup.

Curdle Separation of a mixture into curds and liquids, due to overheating of egg and cream mixtures or beating together of cream or fat and sugar.

Cure To preserve meat or fish by drying, salting or smoking.

Deglaze To add liquid (usually wine) to a pan, scraping up the cooking juices from the bottom, to form the basis for a sauce.

Degorge To sprinkle a vegetable such as aubergine with salt so that any excess and bitter juices drain out and the flesh firms slightly.

Degrease To remove the surface fat from a sauce, stock or soup.

Dhal The general Hindi term for lentils, peas and other pulses; also used for spicy Indian lentil purées.

Dice To cut food such as vegetables into 5mm–1cm (¼–½in) cubes.

Dropping consistency The point at which a mixture will drop off a spoon which is given a sharp flick.

Emulsify To bind together ingredients that would otherwise separate, such as oil or butter with water, vinegar or lemon juice, using an emulsifier like egg yolk.

En croûte Baked in a pastry crust.

Essence A concentrated aromatic liquid used to flavour foods.

Fillet To take flesh off the bone.

Fillo Greek or Middle Eastern pastry made in paper thin sheets; also called strudel pastry.

Fold in To gently mix one ingredient with another whisked one using a cutting, lifting and turning-over movement of the spoon or spatula, so as not to knock out the air bubbles. It is best done with a large metal spoon.

Fumet A fish stock concentrated by reduction.

Galantine A dish of boned, stuffed and shaped white meat or poultry, cooked in aspic stock and glazed with aspic.

Garam masala An Indian mixture of roasted spices, such as coriander seed, cumin, cloves, cardamom and cinnamon.

Ghee Indian clarified butter.

Giblets The neck, liver, heart and gizzard (stomach) of a bird. They are useful to boil up in stock for gravy, for example, but care must be taken to remove any bitter, yellowish coating to the gizzard.

Glaze To give a glossy coating to both savoury and sweet foods. This can be done before cooking by brushing with milk or beaten egg, or after cooking by covering with aspic or sugar syrup, for example.

Gratin A golden breadcrumb or cheese crust on top of a dish, browned in the oven or under the grill.

Hull To remove the stalk and central core from soft fruit such as strawberries.

Infuse To steep ingredients such as herbs, spices or tea leaves in a hot liquid so that the flavours seep out into the liquid.

Julienne Matchstick strips of vegetables, or citrus rind, often used as a garnish.

Knead To work dough with a pushing, pressing motion of the heel of the hands to strengthen the gluten in the flour.

Lard To thread thin strips of fat (called lardons) into lean meat before roasting, to moisten the meat while it cooks. Usually done with a larding needle.

Macerate To steep fruit in syrup, spirits or liqueurs to soften and absorb the flavour of the liquid.

Marinate To soak raw food in a liquid. This not only tenderizes and adds flavour, but also helps preserve the food. A marinade is usually a blend of wine, oil, vinegar, herbs and spices.

Mirepoix A mixture of cut or finely diced vegetables.

Mousseline A purée of raw fish, poultry or pale meat into which unwhisked egg white, and often cream, are gradually beaten.

Oeufs mollets Medium-boiled eggs, with a just-firm white and semi-soft yolk.

Parcook To cook a food for a short time so that it is only partially cooked, to be finished by another method.

Parson's nose The fleshy bit on a plucked bird where the tail feathers would have been.

Pectin A natural gelling substance found in fruit and vegetables, needed in the setting of jams and jellies. Fruits high in pectin include cooking apples, gooseberries, quinces and Seville oranges.

Pith The bitter white part of the skin of a citrus fruit next to the zest.

Pot-roast To cook meat slowly in a tightly closed pan with some fat and a small amount of liquid.

Purée To mash, sieve or whizz food to a smooth consistency.

Reduce To concentrate a liquid by rapid boiling so that some of its water evaporates.

Refresh To immerse hot vegetables in cold water to stop the cooking process.

Roux Equal amounts of flour and butter (or oil), cooked together as the base for a sauce.

Rub in To mix butter and flour together, rubbing between the fingertips, so that the mixture reaches a breadcrumb consistency.

Sauté To cook in butter or fat until lightly browned.

Sear To brown the surface of meat very quickly over a high heat.

Shred To cut or tear into long fine strips.

Skim To remove any froth, scum or fat from the surface of a boiling liquid.

Steep To soak in liquid.

Stir-fry A traditional oriental cooking method in which equal-sized ingredients are cooked swiftly over a high heat.

Strain To remove any solids from a liquid by passing it through a sieve or muslin.

Suet A thin layer of hard fat found around an animal's kidneys.

Tempura A Japanese dish of batter-coated, deep-fried fish, shellfish or vegetables.

Truss To tie poultry and game into a neat shape before cooking, for even cooking and to hold shape.

Yeast Fungus cells that multiply rapidly in suitable conditions to cause bread dough to rise. Yeast can be fresh or dried. Brewer's yeast is used in wine- and beer-making.

Zest The coloured, oily outer part of the skin of citrus fruit. Used for flavouring or decoration.

INDEX

AUTHOR'S ACKNOWLEDGEMENTS

It is now nearly two years since I began the book and I am grateful to everyone who has encouraged and helped me during this time: to my husband and children, particularly my son Henry who has become my ally in the kitchen, to Gwen and Bert Grimmond whose help in the house and garden gave me time to work, to my friends John and Nicola Hilton, in whose house I cooked many of the recipes, and Christina Gascoigne, who listened patiently to my daily progress report. I am also grateful to Roz Denny, who independently checked everything in the book with her usual calm efficiency; to Sandy Carr, Fiona Holman and Beverly Le Blanc, my editors, who were unfailingly supportive however close the deadlines came, and to Susie Macdonald whose enthusiasm and swift typing of much of the manuscript was such a help.

Lastly I would like to thank my mother, who first introduced me to the pleasures of food.

CREDITS

The publishers would also like to thank the following individuals and institutions for the help, advice and information which they contributed towards the preparation of this book:

Judy Bastyra, Bodum, British Chicken Information Service, Elizabeth David Cookshop, Flour Advisory Bureau, Indigo, Leon Jaeggi & Sons Ltd, Norma MacMillan, Caroline Macy, Magimix UK Ltd, Stuart McClymont, David Mellor, Sea Fish Industry Authority, Petra Steenhamker, Susanna Tee, Villeroy and Boch Tableware Ltd, Josiah Wedgwood & Sons Ltd, Elizabeth Wolfe-Cohen.

Editorial Director Sandy Carr
Art Director Douglas Wilson
Editor Fiona Holman
Art Editors Sara Kidd, Michael Leaman
Deputy Editor Beverly Le Blanc
Deputy Art Editor Jane Haworth
Sub Editor Wendy Toole
Designer Sally Powell
Editorial Assistants Siobhan Bremner, Gemma Hancock
Photographers Clive Streeter, Struan Wallace,
Simon Wheeler (chapter openers)
Home Economists Mary Cadogan, Roz Denny,
Louise Pickford, Bridget Sargeson
Illustrations Diana Leadbetter (4-colour), Coral Mula (step-by-step)
Indexer Naomi Good
Stylists Rebecca Gillies, Jane Haworth